DIRECTORY OF BIBLE RESOURCES

A COMPREHENSIVE Guide to Tools for Bible Study

Compiled by Ronn Kerr
Program and Media Office
The National Committee for the Year of the Bible

THOMAS NELSON PUBLISHERS
Nashville • Camden • New York

Copyright © 1983 by Thomas Nelson Publishers

All rights reserved. Written permission must be secured from the publisher to use or reproduce any part of this book, except for brief quotations in critical reviews or articles.

Published in Nashville, Tennessee, by Thomas Nelson, Inc., Publishers and distributed in Canada by Lawson Falle, Ltd., Cambridge, Ontario.

Library of Congress Cataloging in Publication Data
Main entry under title:

Directory of Bible resources.

  1. Bible—Study and teaching—Bibliography.
I. Kerr, Ron. II. National Committee for the Year of the Bible (U.S.)
Z7770.D5 1983 [BS600.2]   016.22′007   83-13244
ISBN 0-8407-5876-6

1 2 3 4 5 6 7 8 9 10 11 12 13 14 15 — 85 84 83

CONTENTS

Introduction 5

Study, Annotated, and Reference Bibles 9

Concordances and Topical Bibles 25

Bible Dictionaries, Encyclopedias, Handbooks, and Atlases 37

Bible Surveys and Introductions 55

Bible Study/Reading Guides for Individuals 71

Bible Study/Reading Guides for Groups 105

Commentaries on the Hebrew Scriptures 125

Commentaries on New Testament Books 141

Commentaries on the Full Christian Bible 169

Resources on "How-to-Study" the Bible 177

Audio-Visual Bible Resources 193

Bible Resources for Children 221

List of Contributors 235

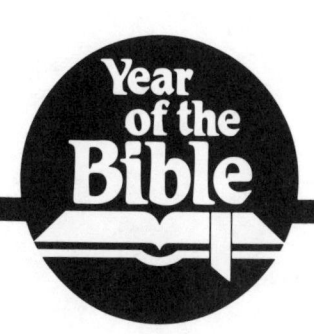

INTRODUCTION

In this *Directory of Bible Resources,* you will find more than 1,500 listings of Bible resources submitted and described by nearly 200 publishers, producers, and distributors. A serious attempt was made by the National Committee for the Year of the Bible to contact every producer, distributor, and publisher in the United States representing all of the different branches of the Jewish and Christian communities. The listings in this *Directory* are those supplied by these producers, publishers, and distributors and the thoroughness of the descriptions, the identification of slants, and the promotional or non-promotional nature of the definitions are products of the suppliers themselves. Approximately one-sixth of all entries were rejected because they did not fit the criteria for the *Directory* and only a handful of publishers, producers, and/or distributors failed to participate.

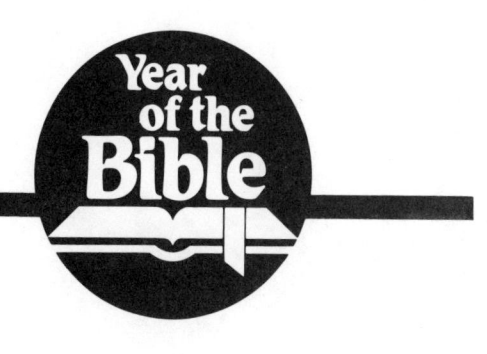

INTRODUCTION

President Ronald Reagan took the occasion of the National Prayer Breakfast in Washington, D.C. on February 3, 1983, to proclaim 1983 as "The Year of the Bible" in the United States.

The President's action implemented Public Law 97-280, a joint resolution of Congress which passed each of the two houses in 1982 and was signed into law by the President on October 4, 1982.

The resolution authorized and requested the President to "designate 1983 as a national 'Year of the Bible' in recognition of both the formative influence the Bible has been for our nation, and our national need to study and apply the teachings of the Holy Scriptures."

With the President as he signed the proclamation were Senator William L. Armstrong and Representative Carlos J. Moorhead, the primary sponsors of the joint resolution in the Senate and the House of Representatives respectively.

National Committee

Also with the President for the signing was Dr. William R. Bright, Chairman of the National Committee for the Year of the Bible, an interfaith, non-profit, non-governmental group of outstanding Christian and Jewish leaders formed independently to help focus attention on the year-long observance. The President also announced at the prayer breakfast that he agreed to serve as Honorary Chairman of the Committee. Senator Armstrong and Representative Moorhead serve as Honorary Co-Chairmen.

Broad Support

In addition to Dr. Bright, John Cardinal Krol, Senior Prelate of the Archdiocese of Philadelphia, is serving as Vice-chairman for the Roman Catholic community, Dr. Thomas F. Zimmerman, General Superintendent of the General Council of the Assemblies of God, is serving as Vice-chairman for the Protestant community, and Dr. Gerson D. Cohen, Chancellor of The Jewish Theological Seminary of America, is serving as Vice-chairman for the Jewish community.

More than sixty additional religious leaders serve on the National Committee for the Year of the Bible, including denominational officials such as Dr. Jimmy Draper, President of the Southern Baptist Convention; Bishop Edward L. Tullis, of The United Methodist Church; John F. Mandt, President of the American Baptist Churches in the U.S.A.; Bishop Nathaniel L. Linsey, of the Christian Methodist Episcopal Church; the Rev. Eugene L. Stowe, General Superintendent, Church of the Nazarene, and Presiding Bishop J.O. Patterson, of The Church of God in Christ.

In addition, a number of representatives of religious organizations also serve on the Committee, including Miss Alice E. Ball, General Secretary of the American Bible Society; Dr. Victor W. Eimicke, President of the Laymen's National Bible Committee; Father John Burke, Executive Director of the Word of God Institute; Dr. David Ng, Associate General Secretary for Education and Ministry, National Council of Churches; Rabbi Alexander M. Schindler, President of the Union of American Hebrew Congregations; Dr. Pat Robertson, President of the Christian Broadcasting Network; and Dr. Ted Engstrom, International President of World Vision.

The President's proclamation naming 1983 as the Year of the Bible pointed to the formative influence of the Bible in American history, its ongoing contribution to the development of both private and public benevolent institutions, and its impact on the development of the Declaration of Independence and the Constitution. It quotes President Andrew Jackson's description of the Bible as "the rock on which our Republic rests" and President Abraham Lincoln's identification of it as "the best gift God has ever given to man...But for it, we could not know right from wrong."

In response to the Congressional Resolution and Presidential Proclamation, the National Committee for the Year of the Bible planned a nationwide inter-faith program. This national thrust is aimed at giving the Year of the Bible nationwide attention and at providing resources and program concepts for city and state inter-faith committees and for local churches and synagogues.

The focus of the activities during the first half of 1983 was to give the movement nationwide attention—to make everyone aware that 1983 is the Year of the Bible. The distinct purpose of the activities in the second half of 1983 is to encourage every American to read, study, and apply the teachings of the Holy Scriptures.

This **Directory of Bible Resources** is one of the several resources being produced by the National Committee for the Year of the Bible to aid individuals and organizations in fulfilling the goal of the Year of the Bible movement.

Because of the unique inter-faith cooperative structure of the National Committee for the Year of the Bible, it has been able to do something never done before. It has collected and published this **Directory** of nearly all of the Bible study and Bible reading resources available in America. The **Directory** contains resources from Protestant, Roman Catholic, Orthodox, and Jewish organizations. It contains materials from extreme fundamentalists and from radical liberals in the same volume. It contains scholarly materials as well as resources for the beginning Bible reader and also a sprinkling of resources in languages other than English. The list of contributors and their addresses at the end of this book is one of the most comprehensive listings of its kind in existence.

Although the National Committee for the Year of the Bible is a short-term organization called together to give emphasis to 1983, it is the hope of everyone involved that the activities and programs of 1983 will have impact for many years. This **Directory** will hopefully continue to be a useful tool for several years and, in fact, it may well be updated and reissued regularly in future years.

Using The Directory

The primary reason for which this **Directory** was produced was to provide a handy reference work for churches, synagogues, schools, libraries, and individuals interested in Bible reading or Bible study activities. A religious school class looking for a study guide on Isaiah, a pastor searching for resources for a churchwide study or reading program, a teacher seeking a wide range of background resources on a particular biblical theme, or an individual looking for a daily Bible reading guide—all of these can now find resources in this one volume. And, in addition to titles, authors, and descriptions, the **Directory** provides prices and order information on each item as well as codes which identify the theological "slants" of the resources and the kinds of persons for which they were produced. Many entries are also accompanied by photographs.

All of the entries in this **Directory** were prepared by the publishers, producers, and distributors of the resources. There has been no objective evaluation of the items. The descriptions of the resources including the codes and classifications are in the language supplied by the producers and, in many cases, they are decidedly promotional. However, they still provide valuable information and most of the publishers and producers are very willing to provide you with further

INTRODUCTION

information about specific resources if you contact them.

The sections in this **Directory** overlap to some degree so that persons searching for specific items may have to check more than one section. For example, a commentary on Romans would most likely be found in the section, "Commentaries on New Testament Books." However, if the publisher believed it to be primarily a guidebook for either an individual or group study of Romans, it could be listed in either "Bible Reading and Study Resources for Individuals" or "Bible Reading and Study Resources for Groups."

Two sections in this **Directory** have been designed to overlap more than the others. "Audio Visual Bible Resources" and "Bible Resources for Children" both contain items which could also be listed in one or more other sections. However, the items are not cross-referenced. If a commentary is on video cassette, it will be found in "Audio Visual Bible Resources" rather than one of the sections on commentaries. If a Bible dictionary is primarily for children, it will be found in "Bible Resources for Children" rather than in the section on Bible dictionaries.

The entries are listed alphabetically by title in each section. At the beginning of each entry, immediately following the title, a group of code letters indicate persons for whom the resource has been produced and its particular theological or methodological "slants." The meanings of the code letters are:

For:

L	Laity
C	Clergy
S	College & Seminary Students
Y	Youth
Ch	Children
W	Women

Slant:

AW	Arminian/Wesleyan
C	Calvinist
RC	Roman Catholic
F	Fundamentalist
EP	Evangelical Protestant
MP	Mainline Protestant
LP	Liberal Protestant
RJ	Reformed Jewish
CJ	Conservative Jewish
OJ	Orthodox Jewish
L	Liturgical
D	Devotional
P	Practical
S	Scholarly
I	Inerrency
BC	Biblical Criticism
CP	Charismatic/Pentecostal
H	Holiness
M	Millennialist
PM	Premillennialist
LU	Lutheran
G	Greek Orthodox
DI	Dispensational

STUDY, ANNOTATED, AND REFERENCE BIBLES

Generally, this first section includes Bibles, New Testaments, and Hebrew Scriptures which include aids to reading and study. The primary differences between aids listed in this section and those listed as Dictionaries, Encyclopedias, or Handbooks is that Study Bibles contain Scripture as well as study helps. Because virtually all Bibles have a few study helps (suggested readings, small glossaries, a few maps, etc.) the compilers of this *Directory,* in many cases, had to decide arbitrarily whether or not a Bible or Testament contained enough "helps" to be listed as a study Bible. And, undoubtedly, some were included that should have been kept out and vice versa. The items included range from Bibles and Testaments with study helps for the average lay reader to scholarly materials in Greek and Hebrew. Study Bibles and Testaments in both English and Spanish are included. Some of the Bible study and Bible reading aids you can expect to find are alternate readings of complicated verses, cross reference systems to guide the reader to similar material, introductions to each book, selective concordances, outlines of books, interpretive notes about key passages, articles on archaeology and Bible texts, histories on the English Bible, tables of weights, measures, and money, glossaries of names and places, and topical indexes guiding readers to Scripture passages on specific subjects.

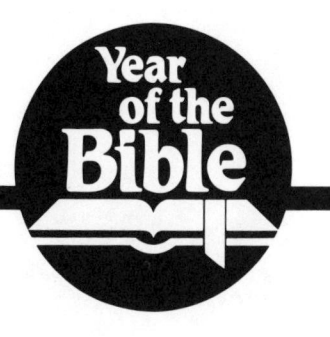

STUDY, ANNOTATED, AND REFERENCE BIBLES

THE AMG PUBLISHERS HEBREW-GREEK KEY BIBLE (AMG Publishers) For: L,C,S,Y. Slant: AW, C, F, EP, MP, LP, L, P, S, I.

Now, a King James Bible with key words in Hebrew and Greek transliterated and explained. Finally, you don't need to wonder what the Hebrew or the Greek really mean as you read the Bible. AMG Publishers has a Hebrew-Greek Key Bible that you will cherish. Knowledge replaces doubt and wonder! Features: giant red letter edition; King James Version; handy size; leather binding; soft cover. Highly recommended by Greek New Testament scholar Spiros Zodhiates, Editor-in-Chief, **Pulpit Helps. $49.00** (Add **$2.00** for postage and handling). From **Christian Media Supply, 524 Sycamore Circle, Ridgeland, MS 39157.**

THE AMPLIFIED BIBLE (Zondervan Bible Publishers) For: L,C,S. Slant: EP.

Hundreds of lost word meanings from the original biblical languages are revealed and difficult passages are explained through this Bible's system of punctuation, italics, references and synonyms that unlock subtle shades of meaning as found in those original languages. Hardcover edition, red. **$19.95.** Imitation leather edition, black. **$35.95.** Bonded leather edition, black, brown, or burgundy. **$49.95.** Bookstores or from **Zondervan Retail Marketing Service, 1420 Robinson Road, SE, Grand Rapids, MI 49506.**

THE ANNOTATED BIBLE (Loizeaux Brothers, Inc.) For: L,C,S. Slant: F,EP,D,P,I,M.

By **Arno C. Gaebelein.** A standard reference work for over half a century, **The Annotated Bible** is renowned for its helpful comments and concise annotations of the entire Bible. Published in four convenient volumes (3,136 pages). **Volume 1:** Genesis to 2 Chronicles; **Volume 2:** Ezra to Malachi; **Volume 3:** Matthew to Ephesians; **Volume 4:** Philippians to Revelation. Four volume set **$42.50**; single volumes **$11.95.** Bookstores or from **Loizeaux Brothers, Inc., P.O. Box 277, Neptune, NJ 07753.**

BAKER'S HARMONY OF THE GOSPELS (Baker Book House) For: L,C,S. Slant: EP,P.

By **Benjamin Davies.** King James Version. This is a vital tool for studying, preaching, and teaching the life of Christ and related events from the four Gospels. **$6.95.** Bookstores or from **Baker Book House, P.O. Box 6287, Grand Rapids, MI 49506.**

BIBLIA AMPLIADA DE ESTUDIO (AMPLIFIED STUDY BIBLE-SPANISH) (Vida Publishers) For: L,C,S. Slant: EP.

The features of this new Spanish Bible will give new inspiration, insight, and significance to your study of the Word of God. Dictionary; concordance; topical index; atlas; Messianic references in the Old Testament in red letters; how to study the Bible; general outline of the Bible; introduction to the Bible; how to interpret the Bible; outline, synthesis and facts about the author of each book; chronology of the Bible; chart of the lives of the kings and prophets of the O.T; history of Israel between the O.T. & N.T.; listing of all Messianic prophecies; a fascinating study of the tabernacle; a Jewish calendar and chart of feasts and sacrifices; a study of the parables; answered prayers from both Testaments; miracles in the O.T.; miracles of Jesus; other miracles of the N.T.; Herod's temple in the time of Jesus; Roman governors of Palestine; Harmony of the Gospels; through the Bible in a year reading guide; guide for the Christian worker; key verse of each book; how each book presents Jesus; the plan of God for man; map locator guide to all the places mentioned in the Bible; and 20 full-color maps. **$23.00-$80.00** depending on the cover material. Bookstores.

BIBLIA DE ESTUDIO LETRA GRANDE (LARGE PRINT STUDY BIBLE) (Vida Publishers) For: L,C. Slant: EP.

When letters this size help make the Bible more comfortable to read, you'll enjoy **Vida's Study Bible in Spanish,** features in large print. Get it with concordance and with or without thumb index added in the 1960 revision. Ref. #874, black with concordance. #875 black, with concordance and index. Price varies with features. Bookstores.

BIBLIA DE ESTUDIO PARA JOVENES

STUDY, ANNOTATED, AND REFERENCE BIBLES

(YOUTH STUDY BIBLE) (Vida Publishers) For: Y. Slant: EP.

Young as the youth of today—old as the Rock of Ages, that's the **New Vida Youth Bible** in Spanish, with washable embossed vinyl, two-color art cover. Add the special 371 questions youth ask, and it's something everyone should have. Ref. #1175. **$12.00**. Bookstores.

CHRISTIAN COUNSELOR'S NEW TESTAMENT (Baker Book House) For: L,C. Slant: P.

By Jay Adams. Christian counselors will find this the most convenient tool at their disposal. Featured in the text itself are a system of highlighting, marginal notations, and explanatory footnotes. **$24.95**. Bookstores or from **Baker Book House, P.O. Box 6287, Grand Rapids, MI 49506.**

THE CHRISTIAN COUNSELOR'S NEW TESTAMENT (Baker Publishing Company) For: L,C,S. Slant: C,EP,P,S,I.

By Jay E. Adams, Ph.D. The **Christian Counselor's New Testament** is an original translation from the Greek, containing footnotes, marginal keys and various helps for Christian counseling located in the back. It is designed to be used during counseling and contains the basic resources for biblical counseling. The translation is in modern, everyday English and brings out counseling emphases previously not emphasized. The **Christian Counselor's New Testament** has been purchased and used widely among pastors, counselors and active Christian laymen. It is practical and easy-to-use. **$20.00**. Bookstores or from **Baker Book House, P.O. Box 6287, Grand Rapids, MI 49506.**

COMPACT CENTER-COLUMN REFERENCE EDITION, NEW AMERICAN STANDARD (Holman Bible Publishers) For: C,S. Slant: EP.

A center-column reference Bible only 3/4 of an inch thin! The perfect size for those who want a small, easy-to-carry Bible with center-column references. The button-snap feature, in some styles, is useful for those who travel or carry their Bible with them wherever they go. The unique closure protects pages from abuse in pocket, purse, or luggage. Features words of Christ in red, concordance, presentation page, topical subheads, and Bible Atlas with index to maps. Size, 4 1/4 x 6 1/8 inches, 1,312 pages. Available in genuine leather or bonded leather in several colors. **$38.95** (semi-overlap) or **$41.95** (button-snap). Bookstores.

THE COMPACT VERSE REFERENCE BIBLE, King James Version (Holman Bible Publishers) For: L,C,S. Slant: EP.

A magnificently-produced compact black leather edition of the Bible with the exclusive Verse Reference Jewel feature for fast, easy comprehension of text and references. This is a fine-crafted Bible at a remarkably low price. Both the size and the unique button-snap feature, in some styles, make this Bible especially useful for people who travel or like to carry a Bible with them wherever they go. The button-snap closing offers protection for page edges in pocket, purse or luggage. Contains presentation page, Bible Atlas material (16 pages), pronouncing text, thin opaque India paper, concordance, Messianic prophecies starred, and in-verse references. Size, 4 1/8 x 5 7/8 inches, 1,426 pages. French Morocco leather binding in button-snap or semi-overlapping styles, in several colors. **$24.95** (semi-overlap) or **$28.95** (button-snap). Bookstores.

COUNSELOR'S NEW TESTAMENT (Jimmy Swaggart Ministries) For: L,C. Slant: CP.

This slender, pocket sized New Testament (with Psalms) is sure to become the "friend" of every counselor and soul winner. In the front is a quick reference counseling "library" with a guide to a host of problem areas counselors often confront such as alcoholism, backsliding, discouragement, financial problems, guidance, salvation, unsaved loved ones, plus many more. Following each area, there are suggestions and a list of Scriptures which give the counselor a total picture of ways to deal with the indivdual's problem. No counselor should be without this versatile and totally useable New Testament. It is designed to fit into a woman's purse or a man's inside coat pocket, comes with a genuine leather cover (burgundy color) and ribbon marker. It is printed on fine India paper in a red letter edition. **$15.00**. From **Jimmy Swaggart Ministries, P.O. Box 2550, Baton Rouge, LA 70821.**

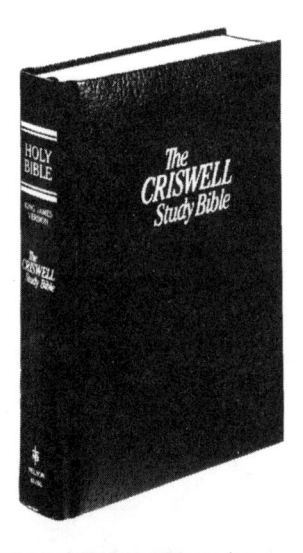

CRISWELL STUDY BIBLE (Thomas Nelson Publishers) For: L,C. Slant: EP,S,I.

This thoroughly researched study Bible represents over fifty years of pastoral scholarship. Acclaimed as one of the most helpful and meaningful resources available today, the **Criswell Study Bible** is endorsed by evangelist Billy Graham. **$21.95**. Bookstores.

THE DARBY BIBLE (Holman Bible Publishers) For: C,S. Slant: EP.

By John Nelson Darby. John Nelson Darby, early leader of the Plymouth Brethren, was a brilliant Bible scholar and linguist. Serious students of the Scriptures have long prized the **Darby Bible** for its explanatory notes and the literal character of the translation. Darby's writings influenced C.I. Scofield who worshipped with the Plymouth Brethren while working on the widely-known Schofield reference and notes. Black French Morocco binding, over-lapping covers, gold page edges. Size 3 1/2 x 5 1/2 inches. **$29.95**. Bookstores.

STUDY, ANNOTATED, AND REFERENCE BIBLES

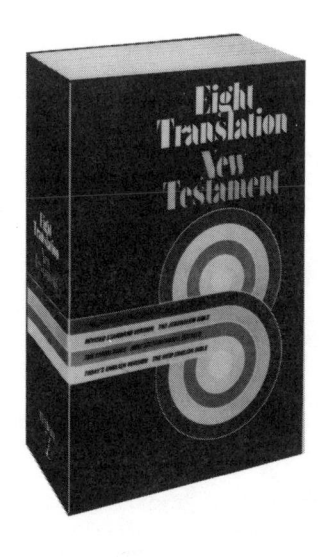

EIGHT TRANSLATION NEW TESTAMENT (Tyndale House Publishers) Slant: AW,C,F,EP,MP,LP,RJ,S,CP.

The only single-volume parallel New Testament with eight of the most popular translations for quick and easy comparison, reference and study. King James Version, Phillips Modern English, Revised Standard Version, The Jerusalem Bible, The Living Bible, New International Version, Today's English Version, and The New English Bible. Cloth. **$27.95.** Kivar. **$21.95.** Bookstores.

FAMILY BIBLE, REVISED STANDARD VERSION (Holman Bible Publishers) For: L. Slant: EP,MP.

Nothing is more precious to a family than its heritage, and here is a Bible especially designed to include the written record of all those special events in the history of any family. A cherished possession today...a priceless heirloom tomorrow. Includes presentation page, 16-page family record section, concordance, words of Christ in red, Verse Reference(R) feature, harmony of the life of Christ, 160-page encyclopedic index, pronouncing text, 64 pages of Old Masters reproductions, 16 pages of color photographs of the Holy Land, selected readings from the Bible, supplementary articles by leading Biblical authorities, and outline and survey of each Book. Size, 8 1/2 x 10 7/8 inches, 1,730 pages. In black or ivory imitation leather, padded cover. **$42.95.** Bookstores.

FROM 26 TRANSLATIONS (Zondervan Bible Publishers) For: L,C,S. Slant: EP.

Compare the King James Version with 25 other popular English versions. Each line or phrase from the KJV is in bold-face type and is followed by significant alternative readings from the other translations. Old Testament Books of Poetry contain Job, Psalms, Proverbs, Ecclesiastes, and Song of Solomon. Soft cover editions. Old Testament Books of Poetry. **$11.95.** New Testament. **$16.95.** Bookstores or from **Zondervan Retail Marketing Service, 1420 Robinson Road, SE, Grand Rapids, MI 49506.**

GIANT PRINT VERSE REFERENCE BIBLE, King James Version (Holman Bible Publishers) For: L,C,Ch. Slant: EP,MP.

The only Bible available with giant print text, giant print concordance, and giant print study helps. Easy-to-read 16-point type makes this the ideal choice for those who prefer or need a large type--the sight impaired, the elderly, children, and others. Features include: Giant Print Concordance, Giant Print Study Helps, Words of Christ in Red, Presentation Page/Family Record Section, Exclusive Verse Reference(R) Feature, Survey of Each Book, Harmony of the Life of Christ, Pronouncing Text, Full-Color Maps. Available in a variety of bindings, styles, and colors, including a children's edition with 42 full-color illustrations. **$18.50 - $49.95.** Bookstores.

GIANT PRINT REFERENCE BIBLE (SANTA BIBLIA LETRA GRANDE) (Holman Bible Publishers) For: L,Ch. Slant: EP.

Ideal for those who require a large print. Excellent for use in literacy programs with first-level readers. Orthography, punctuation, and words updated in 1979. Features include end-of-verse references, dictionary of Bible names, family record section, chronology of the Bible, chapter headings with dates of authorship, presentation page, and maps. Size, 7 x 10 inches. **$44.95** (black imitation leather) or **$64.95** (black deluxe bonded leather). Bookstores.

GOOD NEWS NEW TESTAMENT IN COLOR (American Bible Society) For: L,S,Y. Slant: S.

A special edition of the **Today's English Version** New Testament, illustrated with over 200 color photographs of Bible lands and nine color maps. Ideal Scripture for gifts and awards; also suitable for home, church or school library. Hardcover (7 7/8 x 10 5/8 inches). TEV Order No. 02871, **$6.00.** Paperbound (7 5/8 x 10 3/8 inches). TEV Order No. 02870, **$5.00.** From **American Bible Society, Box 5656 Grand Central Station, New York, NY 10163.**

GOSPEL PARALLELS, Fourth Edition (Thomas Nelson Publishers) For: C,S. Slant: S.

Gospel Parallels, now a classic in its field, provides a thorough study of the first three Gospels by allowing us to view corresponding passages in parallel columns. For instance, a reader consulting the book on Jesus' stilling of the storm told in Matthew 8, will also see on the same page that story as told in Mark 4 and in Luke 8. Pastors, students at Christian colleges and seminaries, and other dedicated readers of the Bible will find this unique treat-

STUDY, ANNOTATED, AND REFERENCE BIBLES

ment to be a revealing way of learning the Gospels. This fourth edition of **Gospel Parallels** updates the scripture text bringing it into conformity with the second edition of the Revised Standard Version of the Bible. The index of noncanonical parallels has also been supplemented. Hardcover. **$9.95.** Bookstores.

THE GREEK NEW TESTAMENT ACCORDING TO THE MAJORITY TEXT (Thomas Nelson Publishers) For: C. Slant: S.

This carefully edited text marks the first time in this century that the Greek New Testament has been produced using the vast bulk of extant manuscripts rather than the small body of Egyptian manuscripts that form the basis of current Greek texts. The Majority Text, similar to the text used for the King James Version, has never been printed before. And **The Greek New Testament According to the Majority Text** is the only traditional text which includes recent papyri discoveries with objective documentation to show which textual form they support. The editors have compiled a double apparatus (two sets of footnotes): the first tells the variations within the Majority Text tradition; the second shows the differences from other Greek New Testaments. **The Greek New Testament According to the Majority Text** features a modern format with a highly readable, non-italicized typeface. English paragraph titles are used throughout, and contemporary Western punctuation noticeably increases understanding. Hardcover. **$13.95.** Bookstores.

HARMONY OF SAMUEL, KINGS, AND CHRONICLES (Baker Book House) For: L,C,S. Slant: EP.

By William Crockett. In addition to harmonizing these Old Testament books, this book contains a complete listing of parallel passages from other books of the Bible. There is also a carefully constructed analytical outline. **$12.95.** Bookstores or from **Baker Book House, P.O. Box 6287, Grand Rapids, MI 49507.**

THE HEARTHSIDE FAMILY BIBLE, King James Version (Holman Bible Publishers) For: L. Slant: EP.

A Bible any family will treasure—an heirloom to be passed on from generation to generation. More than just the Bible text, this edition includes helpful study features and valuable information about Bible lands and people, how the Bible came to us, the inspiration and authority of the Scriptures, and more. Includes a 16-page family record section with presentation page and marriage certificate, 32 color reproductions of paintings by old masters, harmony of the life of Christ, index to favorite readings, glossary of Bible names and their meanings, 4,000 questions and answers on the Bible, encyclopedic subject index, a survey of each book of the Bible, supplementary articles by leading Bible authorities, concordance, center-column references, words of Christ in red, pronouncing text, large, easy-to-read print. Size 8 1/2 x 10 7/8 inches, 1,792 pages. Several styles and bindings in black and white. **$19.95-$124.95.** Bookstores.

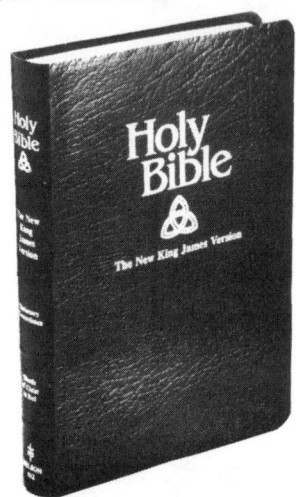

HOLY BIBLE, NEW KING JAMES VERSION, REFERENCE EDITION (Thomas Nelson Publishers) For: L,C,S. Slant: EP,MP.

This consistent favorite is sure to become even more popular in the **New King James Version.** Recognized for its fine quality and attractive price, the **Imperial Reference Edition** offers these exclusive features: easy-to-use center-column references; 115-page concordance; full-color family record; great Bible chapters and stories; life in Bible times; life and journeys of the Apostle Paul; eight pages of full-color maps; words of Christ in red; prophecies of the Messiah fulfilled in Jesus Christ; and parables and miracles of the Bible. **$14.95-$49.95.** Bookstores.

THE HOLY SCRIPTURES (The Jewish Publication Society of America) For: L,C,S. Slant: RJ, CJ, OJ.

The 1917 JPS English translation of the Holy Scriptures according to the Masoretic (traditional) text, used in English speaking countries for more than a half century. A presentation page is included in every volume. A family record is also included in the leatherette bindings. Blue cloth, stained edges 5 x 7 inches, **$9.95.** Black or white leatherette, gold edges, boxed, 5 x 7 inches, **$15.95.** White leatherette, gold edges, boxed, 3 3/4 x 5 1/8 inches, **$16.45.** Blue cloth, Hebrew and English in parallel columns, two volumes, 5 x 8 1/4 inches, **$25.00.** Bookstores or from **Jewish Publication Society, 1930 Chestnut Street, 21st Floor, Philadelphia, PA 19103.**

ILLUSTRATED NEW TESTAMENT (The Liturgical Press) For: L,C,S,Y. Slant: RC,P.

The entire New Testament, in the NAB translation, with more than 500 illustrations (photos, maps, drawings, diagrams, and reproductions of texts). Softbound, 260 pages. **$1.50.** Bookstores or from **The Liturgical Press, Collegeville, MN 56321.**

IN THE BEGINNING: A New English

STUDY, ANNOTATED, AND REFERENCE BIBLES

Rendition of the Book of Genesis (Schocken Books, Inc.) For: L,C,S. Slant: MP,LP,RJ,CJ,OJ,L,D,P,S,BC,H.

In The Beginning is the first volume of a new translation of the **Pentateuch** by Everett Fox. It presents a unique approach to the art of biblical translation that contributes to our understanding of the Bible. Unlike idiomatic or simply literal translations, this English rendition of Genesis seeks to restore the spoken character of the **Hebrew Bible**. What is lost in these literal translations is the repetition of key words and word-stems that form the echoes, allusions and powerful inner structures of sound that the text uses to develop its central themes. Based on principles developed by Buber and Rosenzweig when they translated the **Hebrew Bible** into German, **In The Beginning** reproduces in English the literary forms, linguistic features and, wherever possible, the rhythm of the original Hebrew. Fox's commentary, printed on pages facing the biblical text, alerts the reader to the ways the language of the text underscores its dominant motifs. **$14.95**, ($1.00 for postage when ordering by mail). Bookstores or from **Schocken Books, Inc., 200 Madison Ave., New York, NY 10016.**

INDIAN EDITION, GOOD NEWS BIBLE (American Bible Society) Slant: RC, EP, MP, LP.

This Bible relates to Native Americans. It is entitled, **The Creator Speaks**, because the name Native Americans use for God in most of the 1,200 tribes is Creator. **The Creator Speaks** says it is God's Word. The cover is a beautiful full-color paperback depicting animals, birds and corn in Indian seed beads sewn on smoked moosehide. Inside is a letter from Mohawk Evangelist Tom Claus, President of CHIEF, Inc., encouraging his people to read the Bible with a helpful guide to study the Bible using references that would effectively relate to the Indian culture. **The Creator Speaks** is a Good News Bible in the Today's English Version. **$2.00**. From **CHIEF, Inc., Box 37000, Phoenix, AZ 85069.**

INDIAN NEW TESTAMENT (Christian Literature International) Slant: RC, EP, MP, LP.

This CHIEF New Testament was especially translated for Native Americans and is unique because it has a controlled vocabulary of only 850 words. Anyone who uses English as a second language can really get a grasp on the Scriptures using this New Testament. It has a beautiful full-color paperback cover depicting the Good Shepherd holding the lamb in Indian seed beads sewn on buckskin. It has an easy-to-read type with paragraph titles. Single copy, **$5.00**; 2-5 copies, **20%** discount; 6-11 copies, **30%** discount; 12 or more **40%** discount. From **CHIEF, Inc., Box 37000, Phoenix, AZ 85069.**

THE INTERLINEAR BIBLE (Baker Book House) For: C,S. Slant: EP.

By Jay Green. Supplies a literal English translation for each Hebrew word in the Old Testament and for each Greek word in the New Testament. Allows the student to read the Hebrew and Greek texts without continually consulting a lexicon. Portable, one volume edition. **$44.95.** Bookstores or from **Baker Book House, P.O. Box 6287, Grand Rapids, MI 49506.**

INTERLINEAR GREEK-ENGLISH NEW TESTAMENT (Mott Media) For: L,C,S.

Numerically coded to **Strong's Exhaustive Concordance.** When George Ricker Berry issued this classic in 1897, it was a breakthrough. With this book, anyone could read a strictly literal translation of the Greek Scripture text, because Berry had placed the English between the lines of the Greek, word-for-word and phrase-by-phrase—and for added clarity, the King James in the margin. Now, Donald R. White gives us a new breakthrough. He adds a numerical code that refers every word to Strong's. This edition is part of the **Mott Media Bible Reference Library.** Bound in beautiful Lexitone, stamped in gold. **$24.95.** Bookstores or from **Mott Media, 1000 E. Huron Street, Milford, MI 48042.**

KING JAMES BIBLE (Star Bible Publications) For: L. Slant: F,EP.

Beautiful color paper cover. Old and New Testaments, plus 64 pages of helps. Weighs only 13 ounces for overseas. Over 130,000 in print. Used by World Bible School and many others for bus ministries, pews, gifts, jail ministries, etc. Catalog #1510H. **$3.50** each (carton of 42, **$125**). Bookstores or from **Star Bible Publications, Box 181220, Ft. Worth, TX 76118.**

KJV CHRISTIAN WORKERS NEW TESTAMENT AND PSALMS (Zondervan Bible Publishers) For: L,C,S. Slant: EP.

This New Testament will be a constant companion for the Christian who wants to effectively share the plan of salvation. Uses ingenious "instant reference" system which tells at a glance the subject matter of verses keyed. All marked passages are keyed to various aspects of the main theme of salvation. Index to all references. Flush cut edition, black imitation leather. **$3.95.** Deluxe edition, black skivertex. **$9.95.** Leather edition, black bonded leather. **$17.95.** Bookstores or from **Zondervan Retail Marketing Service, 1420 Robinson Road, SE, Grand Rapids, MI 49506.**

KJV COMPANION BIBLE (Zondervan Bible Publishers) For: L,C,S. Slant: EP.

The most complete and extensive one volume study Bible available in the King James Version. Notes within the text give insight into the original Greek and Hebrew, plus give alternate translations, explanations of figures of speech, cross-references and more. Each book and chapter is introduced with a detailed outline. Hardcover edition. **$46.95.** Leather edition. **$69.95.** Bookstores or from **Zondervan Retail Marketing Service, 1420 Robinson Road, SE, Grand Rapids, MI 49506.**

KJV LARGE PRINT REFERENCE BIBLE (Zondervan Bible Publishers) For: L,C,S. Slant: EP.

Large, easy-to-read Imperial Pica type in a very portable size for anyone who desires a clear, beautiful type for reading or study. Includes: center-

STUDY, ANNOTATED, AND REFERENCE BIBLES

column references; 16 pages of full-color maps; 96 pages of study helps; 106-page concordance. Hardcover edition. **$19.95.** Imitation leather editions in black, burgundy or brown. **$28.95.** Bonded leather editions in black, burgundy or brown. **$43.95.** Bookstores or from **Zondervan Retail Marketing Service, 1420 Robinson Road, SE, Grand Rapids, MI 49506.**

KJV NEW MARKED REFERENCE BIBLE (Zondervan Bible Publishers) For: L,C,S. Slant: EP.

One of the most unusual KJV study Bibles available. The New Marked Reference Bible combines a unique color-highlighting system with a complete chain-of-reference system to form a topical study Bible which can be easily used by any individual in following the main themes of Scripture step-by-step through the Bible. Hardcover, brown skivertex. **$29.95.** Limp edition, brown skivertex. **$37.95.** Limp edition, black or brown leather. **$47.95.** Top-grain cowhide, black, burgundy, or tan. **$56.95** each. Bookstores or from **Zondervan Retail Marketing Service, 1420 Robinson Road, SE, Grand Rapids, MI 49506.**

LADIES BIBLE (Jimmy Swaggart Ministries) For: L,W. Slant: CP.

Designed especially for ladies, this beautiful Bible contains an exclusive section on all of the women in the Bible. Each woman mentioned in the Bible is listed, along with what her name means, who she was, her contribution to Bible history, and her significance for women today. The smart compact size makes it easy to carry in a purse. Printed with easy-to-read type, this Bible also includes a full 64-page concordance, the words of Christ in red, and comes with a snap-over cover. Available in white (08-013) or burgundy (08-004) genuine leather, this Bible will stay new-looking for years and makes a handsome addition for any woman. **$30.00.** From **Jimmy Swaggart Ministries, P.O. Box 2550, Baton Rouge, LA 70821.**

LAYMAN'S PARALLEL NEW TESTAMENT (Zondervan Bible Publishers) For: L,C,S. Slant: EP.

This New Testament, featuring four translations of broad appeal, is ideal for studying and comparing the Scriptures. Contains the King James Version, Revised Standard Version, the Amplified, and the Living New Testament paraphrase. Has four texts, printed side-by-side on facing pages in parallel form. Hardcover. **$17.95.** Softcover. **$14.95.** Bookstores or from **Zondervan Retail Marketing Service, 1420 Robinson Road, SE, Grand Rapids, MI 49506.**

THE LINDSELL STUDY BIBLE (Tyndale House Publishers, Inc.) for: L,C. Slant: EP.

By Dr. Harold Lindsell. A study Bible using The Living Bible text. Features include: outline for every book; introductions to every book; the authorship and background of every book; extensive footnotes; index of persons and places; topical concordance; cross-references; wide margins; single column text. Cloth, 01-2185. **$24.95.** Bonded leather, black (01-2176) or brown (01-2175). **$36.95.** Bookstores or from **Christian Book Service, 336 Gundersen Drive, Carol Stream, IL 60187.**

THE LIVING BIBLE-PERSONAL GIFT EDITION (Tyndale House Publishers) For: L,C,S,Y. Slant: C,F,EP,MP,P.

The Living Bible text in an attractive personal gift edition. An outstanding value at the suggested retail price of just $10.95. Features include: words of Christ in red, presentation page, baptism page, marriage record page, history of the Bible, index of persons, index of places, topical concordance, full-color maps of the Holy Land, helpful diagrams, and a special gift package. Black, burgundy or brown imitation leather. **$10.95.** Bookstores.

THE LIVING BIBLE PERSONAL GIFT, CATHOLIC EDITION (Tyndale House Publishers) For: L,C,S,Y. Slant: RC.

The Living Bible text in an attractive personal gift edition. An outstanding value at the suggested retail price of $12.95. Features include: words of Christ in red, presentation page, baptism page, marriage record page, great Bible chapters (24), great Bible stories (75), index of persons, index of places, topical concordance, full-color maps of the Holy Land, helpful diagrams, and a special gift package. Now avail-

STUDY, ANNOTATED, AND REFERENCE BIBLES

able in a Catholic edition with Deuterocanonical Books. Imitation leather, black or burgundy. **$12.95**. Bookstores.

THE LIVING BIBLE: REFERENCE EDITION (Tyndale House Publishers) For: L,C,S,Y. Slant: C,F,EP,MP,D,P,S.

A study Bible with **The Living Bible** text. Each book of the Bible has introductory information. Center-column cross-references, footnotes, and concordance make it easy to trace events, topics and familiar words. Words of Christ in red. Color maps give added meaning to Bible locations. Padded cover. Brown hardback. **$19.95**. Bookstores.

THE LIVING BIBLE: SELF HELP EDITION (Tyndale House Publishers) For: L,C,S,Y. Slant: F,EP,MP,D,S.

The Living Bible in an attractive, lightweight edition. It has ten pages of helpful Bible references on many subjects as well as a list of the Bible's most often read stories and events. **$8.95**. Bookstores.

THE LIVING BIBLE: YOUNG READER'S GIFT EDITION (Tyndale House Publishers) For: Y. Slant: C, F, EP, MP, D, P, S.

The Living Bible for the junior age reader has 16 four-color illustrations by Richard and Frances Hook, topical concordance, maps, diagrams, history of the Bible, index of persons, presentation page, baptism page, words of Christ in red. Special gift packaging. Red and green imitation leather. **$10.95**. Bookstores.

THE LIVING/NEW INTERNATIONAL VERSION PARALLEL BIBLE (Tyndale House Publishers) For: L,C,S,Y. Slant: C,F,EP,MP,S.

The Living Bible and **The New International Version** both enjoy wide popularity. Many persons like to use **The Living Bible** for devotional reading and family reading and then use the **New International Version** when pursuing word study. Now for the first time, both of these popular Bible versions are available in a single volume! **The Living/New International Version Parallel Bible** features complete text of **The Living Bible**, complete text of the **New International Version**, side by side text for easy comparison, easy reading, clear type, quality hardback binding or deluxe bonded leather binding, and fine quality, long lasting Bible paper. Cloth. **$19.95**. Burgundy or Brown bonded leather. **$36.95**. Bookstores.

THE LIVING NEW TESTAMENT (Tyndale House Publishers) For: L,S,Y. Slant: AW,C,RC,F,EP,MP,LP,D,CP.

Includes marked references for steps toward salvation. Vest pocket paper, size 2 3/4 x 4 1/2 inches. **$3.50**. Bookstores.

THE LIVING SCRIPTURES-MESSIANIC BIBLE (Tyndale House Publishers) Slant: RJ,CJ,OJ,S.

The Living Scriptures is an excellent introduction to the Scriptures for Jewish people who have been afraid to read the Bible because they think of it as a "Gentile" book. At the same time, in this translation we have been mindful of first century conversational language which makes the Scriptures more meaningful to the present-day reader. **The Living Scriptures** stimulates new insights into God's Word for even the veteran Bible student because it includes the results of some of the latest Bible scholarship. In **The Living Scriptures**, the Hebrew names are maintained as they were heard during the days when the Messiah walked on the earth. Hellenistic phrases have been eliminated. Without altering the Word of God, **The Living Scriptures** brings back the Hebrew flavor of the Bible as it was understood and used by the first century Christians. **$16.95**. Bookstores.

LO MAS IMPORTANTE ES EL AMOR/SPANISH LIVING NEW TESTAMENT (Tyndale House Publishers) Slant: C,F,EP,MP,D.

Uses the paraphrase principle in the language and style of Latin America. Paper. **$4.95**. Bookstores.

LOOSE-LEAF AMERICAN STANDARD VERSION NEW TESTAMENT (Star Bible Publications) For: L. Slant: F,EP,P.

Beautiful, durable, gold stamped vinyl, three-ring binder. Has approximately two-thirds of each 8 1/2 x 11 page blank for notes and references. Plastic reinforced index tab included. 288 pages. Catalog #85LF, 1" binder with concordance, charts and New Testament, outline and text **$19.95**. Catalog #85L text, 1" binder and tabs, **$14.95**. Catalog #85Lp, text only with tabs, no binder **$9.95**. Bookstores or from **Star Bible Publications, Box 181220, Ft. Worth, TX 76118**.

STUDY, ANNOTATED, AND REFERENCE BIBLES

LOOSE-LEAF NOTE BIBLE (Holman Bible Publishers) For: C,S. Slant: EP, MP.

Available in King James Version or New American Standard. Both feature the complete Bible text, center-column references, wide margins on sides, book outlines and surveys, and topical subheads. Size 8 1/2 x 11 inches, printed on high quality opaque writing paper—accepts notes in pencil, ballpoint, or felt tip pen as well as Bible highlighter. Punched to fit any standard two- or three-ring binder. A flexible and inexpensive loose-leaf Bible for serious Bible study. Available Bible pages only (shrink-wrapped), or with binder. King James Version: 3800 shrink-wrapped sheets only **$21.95**; 3806 sheets with gold-stamped vinyl binder **$29.95**. New American Standard Version: 5800 shrink-wrapped sheets only **$21.95**; 5806 sheets with gold-stamped vinyl binder **$29.95**. Bookstores.

WALTER MARTIN'S CULTS REFERENCE BIBLE (Gospel Light Publications) For: L. Slant: F, EP, MP.

Edited by Professor Walter Martin, author of **The Kingdom of the Cults**. This work contains the entire King James Bible, with special notes and a topical index to help the reader identify what the major doctrines of the cults are, which Bible verses they misuse to support them, and how the Christian can respond to these cultic errors. In addition, the **Cult's Reference Bible** contains a detailed encyclopedia on the major cults, a glossary showing how the cults redefine important Christian terms, and a recommended reading list and extensive bibliography. Also included are a cults chart contrasting cult beliefs with the Bible, and several additional aids, including an article by Professor Martin on how to witness to the cults. In the process of learning about the cults, the reader will be thoroughly instructed in sound, biblical theology. **$24.95**. Bookstores or from **Christian Research Institute, P.O. Box 500, San Juan Capistrano, CA 92693**.

WALTER MARTIN'S CULTS REFERENCE BIBLE (Vision House, Inc.) For: L,C,S,Y. Slant: EP.

By Dr. Walter Martin. A complete King James Bible with notes explaining the key scriptures that cultists misuse to support their teachings. Focuses on doctrinal issues and compares the major cults with orthodox Christianity. Includes a thorough discussion of the beliefs of the major cults, an extensive topical index, a guide to witnessing to the cults and much more. Hardcover, 1248 pages, VH301. **$19.99**. Bookstores or from **Vision House, Division of GL Publications, 2300 Knoll Drive, Ventura, CA 93003**.

MASTER STUDY BIBLE, New American Standard/King James Version (Holman Bible Publishers) For: L,C,S. Slant: EP.

Choose the **Master Study Bible** in the popular King James Version or the literal, word-for-word New American Standard. Both have the same outstanding study helps; a variety of styles, colors, bindings, and prices; and the same fine quality craftsmanship. A FREE User's Guide comes with the **Master Study Bible**. Features include: A complete Bible Encyclopedia—over 500 pages; an extensive concordance; life and teachings of Jesus; the Gospels paralleled by A.T. Robertson, a tabular and detailed harmony of the Gospels; the teachings of Jesus arranged by subjects; parables, miracles, and discourses of Jesus; introductory outlines and surveys of all the books of the Bible; center-column references, notes and alternate readings—over 100,000; presentation page/family record section; words of Christ in red; full-color maps—eight pages plus index; and much more! Page size 6 1/4 x 9 1/4. **$27.95-$100.00**. Bookstores.

NAVE'S STUDY BIBLE (Baker Book House) For: L,C,S. Slant: EP.

By Orville J. Nave. Included in this study Bible are brief analyses at the beginning of each chapter; more than 80,000 annotated, marginal references to related passages; an index-concordance; a new glossary defining every word in the text that cannot be readily understood by reference to a standard desk dictionary; and many other features which have made **Nave's Study Bible** one of the favorites. **$24.95**. Bookstores or from **Baker Book House, P.O. Box 6287, Grand Rapids, MI 49506**.

NAVE'S STUDY BIBLE (Holman Bible Publishers) For: C,S. Slant: EP.

Revised and expanded edition. Nave's has long been respected as an excellent study edition of the King James Bible. Notes in the margins, immediately adjacent to the verses they help explain, provide alternate translations, supplementary information, and identify additional verses relating to the same subject. Includes summaries of each chapter, footnotes providing exhaustive analyses of important Bible subjects, pronunciation aids, concordance, cross-reference index, glossary of archaic words and phrases, geographical gazetteer, maps, and much more. Hardcover. **$24.95**. Bookstores.

THE NEW AMERICAN STANDARD REFERENCE BIBLE— THINLINE (Moody Press) For: L,C,S,Y.

New American Standard, red letter. The perfect Bible to carry in briefcase or purse, it's only three-quarters of an inch thick, yet contains all the features of much larger reference Bibles, like center-column cross-references, concordance, and maps. Clear, readable type on the finest India paper. Leather. **$29.95**; Cloth. **$17.95**. Bookstores or from **Moody Bookworld, 2101 West Howard Street, Chicago, IL 60645**.

THE NEW JPS TRANSLATION OF THE HOLY SCRIPTURES ACCORDING TO THE TRADITIONAL HEBREW TEXT: THE TORAH, THE PROPHETS, THE WRITINGS (The Jewish Publication Society of America) For: L,C,S. Slant: RJ, CJ, OJ.

The publication of the third and final volume of the new Jewish Publication Society translation of the Holy Scriptures, **The Writings—Kethubim**, marks the culmination of a 25-year effort of scholarship. Changes in language and new findings in biblical and archaeological research that occurred since the issuance in 1917 of the earlier JPS translation were accommodated in the new translation. **The Torah** appeared in 1962, **The Prophets** in 1978, and **The Writings** in 1982. The translations are the work of distinguished Jewish scholars who were assisted in their efforts by representatives of the three sections of organized Jewish life. **The Torah**, 393 pages, blue cloth, **$7.95**; black leather **$14.95**. **The Prophets**, 930 pages, blue cloth, **$9.00**; black leather **$15.95**. The Writings, 624 pages, blue cloth, **$10.95**; black leather **$17.50**. Bookstores or from **Jewish**

STUDY, ANNOTATED, AND REFERENCE BIBLES

Publication Society, 1930 Chestnut Street, 21st Floor, Philadelphia, PA 19103.

NEW LAYMAN'S PARALLEL BIBLE (Zondervan Bible Publishers) For: L,C,S. Slant: EP.

Comparison of translations has never been easier or more convenient than with this Bible. Each two-page spread contains a complete scripture portion from the New International Version, King James Version, Revised Standard Version, and Living Bible paraphrase. The four translations are printed in parallel form. Hardcover edition, brown imitation leather. **$36.95**. Bookstores or from **Zondervan Retail Marketing Service, 1420 Robinson Road, SE, Grand Rapids, MI 49506**.

NIV COUNSELORS NEW TESTAMENT AND PSALMS (Zondervan Bible Publishers) For: L,C,S. slant: EP.

Indexed to the 99 most needed and helpful topics referred to by counselors; Has: numerical chain-of-reference system; each passage on the key topics is color highlighted in the text; and step-by-step plan of salvation. Softcover, blue imitation leather. **$4.95**. Deluxe edition, "NIV Brown" Skivertex limp binding. **$11.95** Bookstores or from **Zondervan Retail Marketing Service, 1420 Robinson Road, SE, Grand Rapids, MI 49506**.

NIV INSIGHT NEW TESTAMENT (Zondervan Bible Publishers) For: L,C,S,Y. Slant: EP.

This New Testament uses photos by award-winning photographers and carefully constructed "word bridges" by Phillip Yancey, award-winning author and publisher of Campus Life Magazine, to explain concepts that are often overlooked or misunderstood because of the 2,000 year gap between the Bible and contemporary readers. Includes: 85 helpful insets of study notes; index to study notes; and 80 photographs. Softcover edition. **$7.95**. Bookstores or from **Zondervan Retail Marketing Service, 1420 Robinson Road, SE, Grand Rapids, MI 49506**.

NIV/LIVING PARALLEL BIBLE (Zondervan Bible Publishers) For: L,C,S. Slant: EP.

The perfect combination of Bible versions for both devotional reading and serious study. Has complete text of New International Version with translators' footnotes and exclusive subject headings; complete text of the Living Bible; side-by-side parallel columns of both versions—spaced accurately for "at a glance" comparison. Softcover edition, full-color Kivar. **$16.95**. Hardcover edition, imitation leather. **$19.95**. Bookstores or from **Zondervan Retail Marketing Service, 1420 Robinson Road, SE, Grand Rapids, MI 49506**.

NIV PICTORAL BIBLE (Zondervan Bible Publishers) For: L,C,S. Slant: EP.

The first Bible to place the study helps of a Bible handbook where they belong—right alongside the Bible text. Over 500 full-color photographs plus scores of charts, maps, diagrams, and illustrations bring the world of the Bible alive. Each book is introduced with helpful background information and outline. Includes: 24-page full-color section, "Introducing the Bible;" 100 drawings; 37 full-color maps; 8 double page full color charts; and color bars index the Bible's major divisions. Cloth edition. **$29.95**. Bookstores or from **Zondervan Retail Marketing Service, 1420 Robinson Road, SE, Grand Rapids, MI 49506**.

NIV TEXT CONCORDANCE BIBLE (Zondervan Bible Publishers) For: L,C,S. Slant: EP.

The first NIV Bible to include a concordance as well as optional red-letter editions. Features: double-column

STUDY, ANNOTATED, AND REFERENCE BIBLES

format; concordance has over 40,000 entries; 16 pages of exclusive four-color Zondervan maps; table of weights and measures. Hardcover, black-letter or red-letter. **$19.95.** Imitation leather editions: black-letter burgundy or black-letter brown; red-letter burgundy or red-letter brown. **$35.95.** Bonded leather editions, brown limp binding, red-letter or black-letter editions. **$49.95.** Bookstores or from **Zondervan Retail Marketing Service, 1420 Robinson Road, SE, Grand Rapids, MI 49506.**

THE OPEN BIBLE, EXPANDED EDITION, NEW KING JAMES VERSION (Thomas Nelson Publishers) For: L,C,S. Slant: EP.

Now, the most popular study Bible ever published with major improvements and available for the first time in the New King James Version! The **Open Bible**, expanded edition, contains over 500 pages of special helps for in-depth study of God's Word—including greatly expanded Reader's Guide Outlines that now cover both the Old and New Testaments. Plus: new cyclopedic Index exclusively for the New King James Version covering over 8000 subjects; all new, more comprehensive book introductions and a new system of subject heads; thousands of end-of-verse references and alternate translations, PLUS a new, easier-to-use system of textual footnotes; new 100 page concordance exclusively for the New King James Version; fourteen master outlines on major Bible doctrines; many more Messianic references; ALL NEW full color Bible maps; and prophecies, parables, and teachings of Jesus. **$24.95-$69.95.** Bookstores.

PEOPLE'S PARALLEL BIBLE: KING JAMES VERSION/THE LIVING BIBLE (Tyndale House Publishers) For: L,C,S,Y. Slant: C,F,EP,MP,D,P,S.

The two most popular Bibles of our time are now side-by-side in one volume, **The People's Parallel Bible.** It combines the eloquent King James Version and the easy-to-read and understand **Living Bible** in one convenient carry-to-church Bible. Features include: the words of Christ in red, and side-by-side column for easy text comparison. Imitation and bonded leathers in burgundy or black with gold edging. Leather. **$36.95.** Imitation leather. **$22.95.** Bookstores.

PERSONAL SIZE BIBLE WITH CENTER-COLUMN REFERENCES (SANTA BIBLIA MEDIANA CON REFERENCIAS CENTRALES), Reina-Valera, 1909 Revision (Holman Bible Publishers) For: L,C,S. Slant: EP.

A handy-size, easy-to-carry Bible—the perfect size for personal use. An excellent gift edition, too. Features include center-column references, maps, and presentation page. In this 1909 revision, words, archaic expressions, and punctuation were updated from the 1862 revision. Some 150,000 changes were made. This edition, sometimes called **de Valera Antigua,** continues to be widely used. In several bindings, styles, and colors. **$15.95-$28.95.** Bookstores.

THE PILGRIM STUDY BIBLE (Oxford University Press) For: L,S,Y. Slant: F,EP.

Edited by E. Schuyler English. Authorized King James Version, red-letter edition. Many Christians prefer the beauty of the original King James Version text, but it can be difficult to understand. **The Pilgrim Study Bible** is the easiest to use study Bible available today. It clarifies passages and phrases in very simple language—page-by-page as you read the text. Notes at the bottom of each page provide commentary that is understandable, simple, and direct. It's written in a layperson's words--to give fresh, new insights into Scripture. Within the text, words of Christ are printed in red. Pronunciation aids assist the reader with unfamiliar names and difficult words. A unique star reference system is the simplest offered in any study Bible today. Also included are a comprehensive concordance, 4,000 entry index, special articles on the Scriptures, historical data, and endpaper maps. Praised for its simplicity and readability, **The Pilgrim Study Bible** is the best way for Christians to begin an exciting adventure in faith. Size 5 1/2" x 8" x 1 3/8". 1,920 pages. Cloth, hardcover, printed jacket (120 RL) **$21.95.** Bonded leather, round corners, gold edges, one ribbon marker, black or burgundy (121 RL) **$39.95.** Bookstores.

POCKET INTERLINEAR NEW TESTAMENT (Baker Book House) For: C,S. Slant: EP.

By Jay Green. For the first time, a complete interlinear New Testament is available in a pocket sized paperback binding. **$5.95.** Bookstores or from **Baker Book House, P.O. Box 6287, Grand Rapids, MI 49506.**

THE REGAL REFERENCE BIBLE, King James Version (Holman Bible Publishers) For: C,S. Slant: EP.

Printed in the largest type available in a hand-size Bible <u>with</u> center-column references. Contains words of Christ in red, large, easy-to-read print, pronouncing text, Bible dictionary-concordance, harmony of the life of Christ, chronology of the Acts, color maps, biblical chronology, Paul's missionary journeys, presentation page, and family record section. Size 5 1/4 x 7 3/4 inches, one inch thick, 1,712 pages. A variety of fine leather bindings, semi-overlap style, in several colors. **$41.95-$69.95.** Bookstores.

THE RENAISSANCE NEW TESTAMENT SERIES (Pelican Publishing Company) For: L,C,S. Slant: EP, MP, P, S, I.

A Greek New Testament, a lexicon, a concordance, a word-by-word grammatical analysis of the scripture, and a translation from the original Greek, all are combined in **The Renaissance New Testament.** Widely acclaimed by scholars as one of the most important biblical works of the twentieth century, this monumental, multi-volume New Testament is the result of almost fifty years of meticulous research by Biblical scholar Dr. Randolph O. Yeager. It brings within reach of anyone in the English-speaking world an accurate understanding of the Greek New Testament. "The purpose of this work," Dr. Yeager says, "is to enable any student to understand exactly what the Bible says. The work enables a person to make his own translation, thus making his faith truly his own." **The Renaissance New Testament** series is a projected 18 volume set. Volumes 1-10 are now available. Volumes 11-14 will be published in July, 1983.

STUDY, ANNOTATED, AND REFERENCE BIBLES

$22.50 per volume. **25%** for Standing Order (of entire series). Bookstores or from **Pelican Publishing Company, Inc., 1101 Monroe Street, Gretna, LA 70053.**

RICE REFERENCE BIBLE (Thomas Nelson Publishers) For: L,C. Slant: F,P,I,M.

With notes and comments written in the language of lay people, this outstanding reference edition emphasizes soul winning and the filling of the Spirit of God in the conservative theological tradition of Scofield. Foreword by Jerry Falwell. **$24.95.** Bookstores.

RSV BREVIER REFERENCE BIBLE (Zondervan Bible Publishers) For: L,C,S. Slant: EP.

The finest reference Bible available in the Revised Standard Edition. Includes: complete text including footnotes and 1971 revisions; center-column references—clearly marked with chapter and verse number; 192-page concordance; 16 pages of full-color maps.

Bonded leather editions. Black-letter in black, brown or burgundy. **$36.95.** Red-letter in black, brown or burgundy. **$37.95.** Bookstores or from **Zondervan Retail Marketing Service, 1420 Robinson Road, SE, Grand Rapids, MI 49506.**

RSV HARPER STUDY BIBLE (Zondervan Bible Publishers) For: L,C,S. Slant: EP.

The most complete study Bible of the Revised Standard Version. Edited by renowned Bible scholar Harold Lindsell, D.D, Ph.D. The hundreds of annotations and helpful background information make this Bible popular with pastors, teachers, and adults active in Bible study. Hardcover edition **$24.95.** Bonded leather editions in black, brown, or burgundy **$53.95** each. Bookstores or from **Zondervan Retail Marketing Service, 1420 Robinson Road, SE, Grand Rapids, MI 49506.**

THE RYRIE STUDY BIBLE, New American Standard Bible and King James Version (Moody Press) For: L,C,S,Y. Slant: EP,S,I,M.

Still one of the best-selling study Bibles, it's deep enough for the scholar yet practical and understandable to the layman. Thousands of study notes explain difficult passages and Bible words. Also includes cross-references, maps, harmony of the gospel, summary of Bible doctrine, study of biblical interpretation how to study the Bible, time-line charts, notes on archaeology, an outline and introduction to each Bible book. Indispensible to your understanding of the Bible! **$25.95-$100.** Bookstores or from **Moody Bookworld, 2101 West Howard St., Chicago, IL 60645.**

SIDE-COLUMN REFERENCE EDITION, NEW AMERICAN STANDARD (Holman Bible Publishers) For: C,S. Slant: EP.

A popular side-column reference Bible with words of Christ in red letters. The Bible text is printed in a single column with references set in a wider, easier-to-read format than is possible in a hand-size Bible with center-column references. The type size is excellent for reading from the pulpit. An ideal Bible for pastors, teachers, anyone who wants large type in a convenient size Bible. Contains concordance, presentation/family record section (8 pages), full-color maps (8 pages), India paper. Size 6 x 9 inches, 1,882 pages. Available in a variety of fine bindings, styles, and colors. **$22.95-$64.95.** Bookstores.

SPANISH WORLD STUDY BIBLE (LA BIBLIA DE ESTUDIO, MUNDO HISPANO) Reina-Valera, 1960 Revision (Holman Bible Publishers) For: C,S. Slant: EP.

A Bible institute in one volume with a wealth of material for the Bible student. The best study Bible available in Spanish. Contains concordance—272 pages; center-column references; introduction and outline to each book of the Bible; footnotes explaining difficult words and Bible customs; full-color maps and photographs of Bible lands; background articles—**The Bible, the Book of Life** by Santiago Canclini, **Revelation and Inspiration of the Scriptures, How to Study the Bible** by Samuel Escobar, **The First Manuscripts of the Bible** by F.F. Bruce, **The Formation of the Canon** by David Allan Hubbard, **The Dead Sea Scrolls** by F.F. Bruce, **Current Approaches to Hermeneutics** by Moses Chávez, **Spanish Versions of the Bible, The Reina-Valera Version, The Bible in Spanish Literature, The Preacher and the Bible,** and more. Size 6 x 8 1/2 inches, 1,664 pages. **$27.95-$64.95.** Bookstores.

STUDY, ANNOTATED, AND REFERENCE BIBLES

JIMMY SWAGGART STUDY BIBLE (Jimmy Swaggart Ministries) For: L,C. Slant: CP.

Undoubtedly one of the finest Bibles you could buy, this Bible was two years in the making. The study helps, the commentaries, and the aids are all new. The only thing left unchanged is the beautiful King James Version. The features of this extraordinary Bible include: the finest goatskin available in the world; genuine India paper; complete concordance; one of the most beautiful and complete map systems ever assembled; large print; totally new center column reference which refers to other passages and explains many of the Greek and Hebrew words; many blank, lined pages for notations; words of Christ in red; hundreds of pages of study helps; and indepth commentary notes before each book, written by Jimmy Swaggart, exclusively copyrighted, and available only in this new Study Bible. Product Number 08-012. **$75.00.** From **Jimmy Swaggart Ministries, P.O. Box 2550, Baton Rouge, LA 70821.**

SYNOPSIS OF THE FOUR GOSPELS (American Bible Society) For: L,C,S. Slant: S, BC.

Edited by Burt Aland. English Edition, Revised Standard Version. An innovative system of presenting Matthew, Mark, and Luke enables the reader to follow the text of each of these three Gospels in its own order. Also contains the Gospel of John. Cloth bound, 361 pages. Order No. 08564. **$5.95.** From **American Bible Society, Box 5656, Grand Central Station, New York, NY 10163.**

TODAY'S ENGLISH VERSION, TEXT EDITION (Thomas Nelson Publishers) For: L,Y. Slant: EP,S.

The complete, modern language text, including informative introductions, study guides, and helpful aids to enhance the reader's understanding. Special features: chronology of the Bible; maps—10 pages; map index; subject index; and topical page headings. **$7.95.** Bookstores.

THE VERSE REFERENCE(R) JEWEL BIBLE, King James Version (Holman Bible Publishers) For: L,C,S. Slant: EP.

Old world standards of craftsmanship apply to this unique edition of the Bible. Verse Reference(R) is a registered trademark of Holman Bible Publishers. There are many imitations but only Holman Bibles may include the real Verse Reference(R) feature. References are set within the verse to which they refer and not in a center-column or at the end of a verse. The reader sees the references simultaneously with the verse. This format makes studying the Bible faster, easier, and more understandable. Features words of Christ in red (except one edition), presentation page, family record section with marriage certificate, 8 pages of full-color maps, dictionary/concordance, Old Testament references to Messiah marked with a star, thin, opaque India paper, and helpful in-verse reference. Size 5 1/4 x 7 3/4 inches, 1,488 pages. Available in one very fine black Pin Seal Grain Morocco leather binding, edge lined, and genuine leather lining; and other styles and colors in calfskin or French Morocco. **$38.95-$69.95.** Bookstores.

VERSE REFERENCE(R) STUDY BIBLE, REVISED STANDARD VERSION (Holman Bible Publishers) For: L,C,S. Slant: EP,MP.

The largest type available in a hand-size Revised Standard Version study Bible together with the exclusive Holman Verse Reference(R) feature—cross references set within the verses to which they apply. This provides for the immediate study advantages of speed, readability, and ease of comprehension. Contains concordance, presentation page, family record section with marriage certificate, 8 pages of full-color maps, thin opaque India paper, black letter, introductory outline-survey of each Bible book by 54 of the world's finest biblical authorities including: Geoffrey W. Bromiley, David A. Hubbard, Stephen W. Paine, Merrill C. Tenny. Size 5 1/4 x 7 3/4 inches, 1,448 pages. Available in a very fine black genuine calfskin with gold fillet line, bonded leather lined; a bonded leather edition in black, brown, burgundy, or white; and a cloth hardcover style. **$19.95-$59.95.** Bookstores.

THE WAY HOME (Johnson Publishing) For: S,Y,Ch. Slant: D,P.

New Testament which includes study aids on twenty-one subjects. Ready reference on these timely subjects. Inspiration and guidance material. Handy size measures 5 1/4 x 7 1/2 and only 3/8 inch thick. Beautiful heavy cover with attractive photography. **$1.00** per single copy which includes postage; bulk copies: 10-100 copies **$.80** each plus UPS charges; 100-1,000 copies **$.75** each plus freight; over 1,000 copies **special quotes.** From **Johnson Publishing, P.O. Box 100704, Nashville, TN 37210.**

WIDE MARGIN REFERENCE EDITION (Thomas Nelson Publishers) For: L,C. Slant: EP.

STUDY, ANNOTATED, AND REFERENCE BIBLES

Bible of choice for those who note personal observations as they study. Wide margins, study notes section, and thousands of center-column references—plus long lasting bindings—make this edition ideal for students, pastors, and lay workers. **$22.95.** Bookstores.

THE ZONDERVAN PARALLEL NEW TESTAMENT IN GREEK AND ENGLISH (Zondervan Publishing House) For: L,C,S. Slant: EP.

By Alfred Marshall. Uses Nestle's Greek text, the interlinear English text is Marshall's own literal translation. The English text consists of parallel versions of the King James and New International Version. **$19.95.** Bookstores or from **Zondervan Retail Marketing Service, 1420 Robinson Road, SE, Grand Rapids, MI 49506.**

CONCORDANCES AND TOPICAL BIBLES

With about 31,000 verses in a full Christian Bible, it takes a massive amount of time to search for all of the biblical passages dealing with a particular word or subject. And yet, discovering everything the Bible has to say on a specific subject is an important aspect of Bible study. Two kinds of aids—concordances and topical Bibles—greatly simplify this process. An "exhaustive" concordance lists every word in the Bible and tells the reader every verse which contains that word. Smaller "selective" concordances focus on the words and verses considered important by the compilers. A topical Bible does the same thing as a concordance except that it lists all of the verses which relate to a specific "topic" or theme rather than verses which contain a specific word. Of course, in many cases, a topical Bible ends up being a concordance because the "topic" appears as a word in the verse. However, a topical Bible can also guide the reader to important verses which explain or describe a subject even though the specific word is not mentioned. Many Bible teachers point to concordances and topical Bibles as the most important study aids beyond the Bible itself.

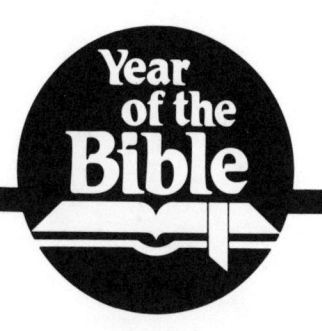

Year of the Bible

CONCORDANCES AND TOPICAL BIBLES

ALPHABETICAL CONCORDANCE OF THE BIBLE (CONCORDANCIA ALFABÉTICA DE LA BIBLIA) (Holman Bible Publishers) For: L,C,S. Slant: EP.

Based on the 1909 Reina-Valera Version. 1,024 pages. **$14.95**. Bookstores.

BAKER'S POCKET BIBLE CONCORDANCE (Baker Book House) For: L,Y. Slant: EP.

A compact but comprehensive tool to increase the effectiveness of Bible study, teaching, and preaching. **$5.95.** Bookstores or from **Baker Book House, P.O. Box 6287, Grand Rapids, MI 49506.**

THE BIBLE INDEX POCKETBOOK (Harold Shaw Publishers) For: L,C,S,Y.

The Bible Index Pocketbook is an easy to read index containing over 1,000 important subjects and their Bible references. Portable, affordable, it can be used with any Bible version. Paperback. **$1.95.** Bookstores or from **Harold Shaw Publishers, P.O. Box 567, 388 Gundersen Drive, Wheaton, IL 60189.**

COMPACT NAVE'S TOPICAL BIBLE, THE (Zondervan Publishing House) For: L,C,S. Slant: EP.

Formerly titled the **New Compact Topical Bible**, this is a compact but comprehensive reference tool for Bible students and teachers. Over 100,000 references included under almost 7,000 subject categories. A compact edition of **The New Nave's Topical Bible**. **$8.95.** Bookstores or from **Zondervan Retail Marketing Service, 1420 Robinson Road, SE, Grand Rapids, MI 49506.**

COMPLETE CONCORDANCE OF THE NEW AMERICAN BIBLE (The Liturgical Press) For: L,C,S. Slant: RC,S.

An alphabetical listing of all the words in the Bible, with references to the book, chapter, and verse where each is found. More than 300,000 entries, covering 18,000 key words, will lead you to the precise thought you wished to find. Cloth, 1,278 pages. **$39.95**. Bookstores or from **The Liturgical Press, Collegeville, MN 56321.**

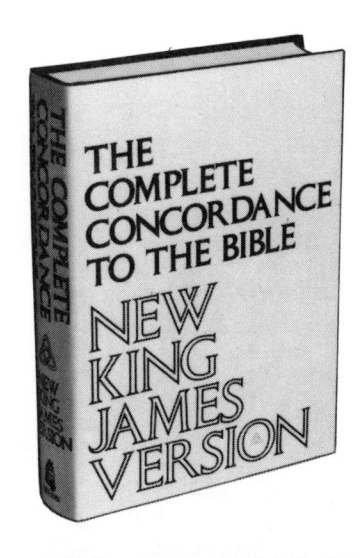

THE COMPLETE CONCORDANCE TO THE BIBLE, New King James Version (Thomas Nelson Publishers) For: L,C,S. Slant: P,S.

This book contains every reference (occurrence) in the NKJV Bible to 12,977 out of the 13,331 words of the NKJV vocabulary. Each of the remaining 354 words is referenced to the Preface. This preface will precede the concordance proper and will explain how the book was created, what kind of a concordance this is (and is not), how to use the concordance to its best advantage, and a list of the words that we have chosen not to index and the reasons for not including them in the concordance. Hardcover. **$19.95.** Bookstores.

CONCISE CONCORDANCE OF THE BIBLE (CONCORDANCIA BREVE DE LA BIBLIA) (Holman Bible Publishers) For: L,C,S. Slant: EP.

An abbreviated alphabetical list of important Bible words and their location in the Bible. **$3.50**. Bookstores.

A CONCORDANCE TO THE APOCRYPHA/DEUTEROCANONICAL BOOKS OF THE REVISED STANDARD VERSION (Wm. B. Eerdmans Publishing Co.) For: C,S. Slant: S.

"This **Concordance** is a welcome addition to the reference tools available for research into ancient Judaism. Such a work should contribute to more frequent and careful use of this literature so important to Jewish and Christian students, teachers, and scholars." David M. Scholer, Northern Baptist Theological Seminary. **$35.00**. Bookstores or from **Eerdmans Publishing Co., 255 Jefferson Ave., SE, Grand Rapids, MI 49503.**

CRUDEN'S COMPACT CONCORDANCE (Zondervan Publishing House) For: L,C,S. Slant: EP.

By Alexander Cruden. Cruden's famous concordance in a compact style. Slightly abridged from the complete concordance. **$8.95**. Bookstores or from **Zondervan Retail Marketing Service, 1420 Robinson Road, SE, Grand Rapids, MI 49506.**

27

CONCORDANCES AND TOPICAL BIBLES

CRUDEN'S COMPLETE CONCORDANCE (Zondervan Publishing House) For: L,C,S. Slant:EP.

By Alexander Cruden. Includes more than 200,000 references to both the King James Version and the Revised Version. Also included is an index to all the key words of the Bible. Cloth. **$13.95.** SC. **$6.95.** Bookstores or from **Zondervan Retail Marketing Service, 1420 Robinson Road, SE, Grand Rapids, MI 49506.**

CRUDEN'S CONCORDANCE: Handy Reference Edition (Baker Book House) For: L,S,Y. Slant: P.

A concordance free of the clutter of insignificant words. Persons looking for a handy listing of the key words in a specific Scripture verse will be picking up this edition time and again. **$6.95.** Bookstores or from **Baker Book House, P.O. Box 6287, Grand Rapids, MI 49506.**

CRUDEN'S CONCORDANCE: HANDY REFERENCE EDITION (Harvest House Publishers) For: L,C,S. Slant: EP,I.

Persons looking for a handy listing of the key words in a specific Scripture verse will be picking up this handy edition time and time again. Dr. Eadie has expertly selected the principal words in every Bible verse. The result is a concordance free of the clutter of insignificant and obscure words. Convenient and helpful for the general reader. Kivar. No. 3620. **$7.95.** Bookstores or from **Harvest House Publishers, 1075 Arrowsmith, Eugene, OR 97402.**

CRUDEN'S HANDY CONCORDANCE (Zondervan Publishing House) For: L,C,S. Slant: EP.

By Alexander Cruden. An abridged Cruden's Concordance which includes 64 pages indexing persons, places, and subjects. Softcover. **$2.95.** Bookstores or from **Zondervan Retail Marketing Service, 1420 Robinson Road, SE, Grand Rapids, MI 49506.**

CRUDEN'S UNABRIDGED CONCORDANCE (Baker Book House) For: L,C,S. Slant: P.

This edition is exactly as it came from the desk of its original author, featuring: (1) the author's original notes and comments, (2) an alphabetical listing of every word in the Bible, (3) a complete concordance to the proper names found in the Bible, (4) a complete list of the names and titles given to Jesus Christ, (5) a dictionary to the original meaning of the proper names used in Scripture, (6) a concordance to the apocryphal books, and (7) a biographical sketch of the author. **$17.95.** Bookstores or from **Baker Book House, P.O. Box 6287, Grand Rapids, MI 49506.**

THE ENGLISHMAN'S GREEK CONCORDANCE OF THE NEW TESTAMENT (Mott Media) For: L,C,S. Slant: AW, C, RC, F, EP, MP, LP, RJ, CJ, OJ, L, D, P, S, I, BC, CP, H, M.

Numerically coded to **Mott's Strong's Concordance.** This classic reference volume enables Bible students who know no Greek to unlock the word study treasures of a standard Greek concordance and a Greek-English lexicon, a skill formerly accessible only to those who mastered New Testament Greek. This edition is part of the beautiful and handy Mott Bible Reference Library. Lexitone bound, stamped in gold. **$29.95.** Bookstores or from **Mott Media, 1000 E. Huron St., Milford, MI 48042.**

THE ENGLISHMAN'S HEBREW AND CHALDEE CONCORDANCE OF THE OLD TESTAMENT (Mott Media) For: L,C,S. Slant: AW, C, RC, F, EP, MP, LP, RJ, CJ, OJ, L, D, P, S, I, BC, CP, H, M.

Numerically coded to **Strong's Concordance** (Mott edition). This helpful concordance presents in alphabetical order every word that appears in the Hebrew and Chaldee Old Testament, along with the English passages (King James Version) in which the word occurs. The English rendering of the Hebrew or Chaldee word is italicized for easy recognition. A Hebrew-English index and an English-Hebrew index add to the usefulness of this concordance. This edition is part of the handy **Mott Media Bible Reference Library.** Lexitone bound, stamped in gold. **$34.95.** Bookstores or from **Mott Media, 1000 E. Huron St., Milford, MI 48042.**

A GREEK-SPANISH LEXICON CONCORDANCE OF THE NEW TESTAMENT (LÉXICO-CONCORDANCIA DEL NUEVO TESTAMENTO EN GRIEGO Y ESPAÑOL) (Holman Bible Publishers) For: L,C,S. Slant: EP.

By George Parker. The only exhaustive Greek-Spanish concordance based on the Reina-Valera, Revision 1960. Lists significant textual variations found both in other modern Spanish translations and in leading critical Greek editions of the New Testament. Contains unique lexical value by listing all the important Greek words and their Spanish equivalents plus an index of Spanish terms and their transliterated Greek equivalents. Strong's numerical system is incorporated to facilitate identification of the Greek words. Highly useful reference even for the non-Greek reader. Size 5 1/2 x 8 1/2 inches. Hardcover. **$21.95.** Bookstores.

GREEK-SPANISH LEXICON OF THE NEW TESTAMENT (NUEVO LÉXICO GRIEGO-ESPAÑOL DEL NUEVO TESTAMENTO) (Holman Bible Publishers) For: L,C,S. Slant: EP.

By G.F. McKibben. A valuable contribution to the study of the New Testa-

CONCORDANCES AND TOPICAL BIBLES

ment in its original language. Contains an alphabetical listing of Greek words, their Spanish equivalents, and references to New Testament passages where each word appears. 306 pages. **$11.95.** Bookstores.

GUIDEPOSTS FAMILY TOPICAL CONCORDANCE TO THE BIBLE (Thomas Nelson Publishers) For: LC. Slant: P.

Guideposts Family Topical Concordance to the Bible combines in one volume the features of a concordance, a comprehensive biblical index, and a Bible dictionary in a practical way for everyday use by Bible readers everywhere. These three features are combined in one alphabetical listing of words to make the book easy to use. A concordance indexes biblical words as they appear in context and is useful for locating verses by specific words or for tracing the use of a word through Scripture. Many of the concepts of the Bible can best be described by words that may not even appear in Scripture. A comprehensive biblical index traces ideas—not just words—through the Bible. It also outlines topics specifically related to practical Christian living. A dictionary explains the ideas, people, places, objects, customs, and events of the Bible. Hardcover. **$14.95.** Bookstores.

HARPER'S PORTABLE BOOK OF BIBLE SELECTIONS—WITH THE COMPLETE PSALMS (Harper & Row Publishers, Inc.) For: L,C,S. Slant: D.

By Martin H. Manser. Available in September, 1983. Here is a convenient easy-to-use selection of key Bible passages that is at once an ideal, carry-anywhere devotional companion and an invaluable source of biblical quotations in the best and most familiar translations. This unique handbook offers help, comfort, and inspiration in a practical new format that remains faithful to the Bible itself. It is designed to help readers enjoy something of the riches of the Bible, while providing them the means to discover passages they may not have noted before. Over 5,000 key verses are listed under nearly 300 themes, arranged in alphabetical order; under each topic, the biblical texts are arranged in the order of the Bible itself. Here, at a glance, is what the Bible says on major topics—an ideal opportunity to study particular words and themes or simply discover where to find passages to meet a particular need. It includes the complete text of the Book of Psalms in the RSV translation. 240 pages; line drawings throughout; flexible sewn vinyl binding. RD 489. **$8.95.** Bookstores or from **Harper & Row Publishers, Inc., Mail Order Dept., 2350 Virginia Ave., Hagerstown, MD 21740.**

HOLMAN BIBLE CONCORDANCE (Holman Bible Publishers) For: L,C,S. Slant: EP.

Here is a valuable word concordance of the King James Version text. Each entry is listed in boldface type and is followed by brief explanations and a listing of principal references and key identifying phrases for quick and easy reference. Paper. **$3.50.** Bookstores.

HOLMAN TOPICAL CONCORDANCE (Holman Bible Publishers) For: C,S. Slant: EP.

This is a concordance of subjects rather than words. Each is listed alphabetically and contains all of the relating pertinent Scripture texts. It deals with persons, themes, and doctrines of the Bible, a most valuable tool for anyone interested in a study of the Bible. **$8.95.** Bookstores.

KING JAMES VERSION, HOLY BIBLE WITH CONCORDANCE (American Bible Society) For: L,C,S. Slant: P, S.

King James Version edition of the Bible with 70,000 entries to help readers locate important passages. Contains a listing of key words and names and one black and white map. Verse-style text. Black. Hardcover (5 1/2 x 8 inches). Order Number 00304. **$4.00.** From **American Bible Society, Box 5656, Grand Central Station, New York, NY 10163.**

THE LIFE AND WORDS OF JESUS (Harper & Row Publishers, Inc.) For: L. Slant: D.

Edited by Patricia Alexander. Available in September, 1983. This inspiring book, lavishly illustrated throughout with full-color photographs from the Holy Land, brings together the words of Jesus taken from the Gospels in a selection carefully chosen to present fully his life and his teachings. This book embodies the living heart of the gospel message— Jesus' own words—in a distinctive, reverent way; it invites readers to experience with new understanding and firsthand immediacy the course of the life and the unfolding of the message that changed the world for all times. The stunning photographs were taken in the Holy Land itself and vividly show the setting of Jesus' life and teaching. They remind us that Jesus lived at an actual time in a real place, as they bring a depth of meaning to his words, by capturing the atmosphere of the places where he lived, taught, and ministered. 96 pages; full color photographs throughout. Cloth. **$10.95.** Bookstores or from **Harper & Row Publishers, Inc., Mail Order Dept., 2350 Virginia Ave., Hagerstown, MD 21740.**

NAVE'S TOPICAL BIBLE (Baker Book House) For: C,S. Slant: EP.

By Orville Nave. Original edition with index. For the first time ever, perhaps the most practical study tool to be produced is available, complete and unabridged in kivar. Over 20,000 topics and subtopics. More than 100,000 Scriptures. An all time best seller for more than seventy-five years. **$14.95.** Bookstores or from **Baker Book House, P.O. Box 6287, Grand Rapids, MI 49506.**

NAVE'S TOPICAL BIBLE (Holman Bible Publishers) For: L,C,S. Slant: EP.

By Orville J. Nave. A complete analysis of the Bible by subject, this extraordinary volume offers the Bible student more than 20,000 topics and subtopics and 100,000 references to the Scriptures. It brings together in one volume all that the Bible says on specific subjects, conveniently arranged under familiar headings. Especially helpful is the elaborate system of cross references. Hardcover. **$17.95.** Bookstores.

CONCORDANCES AND TOPICAL BIBLES

NAVE'S TOPICAL BIBLE (Moody Press) For: L,C,S. Slant: EP,P,S,I,M.

By Orville J. Nave. A digest of the Scriptures with more than 20,000 topics and 100,000 references with the full Scripture. **$19.95.** Condensed edition, **$3.95.** Bookstores or from **Moody Bookworld, 2101 W. Howard Street, Chicago, IL 60645.**

NAVE'S TOPICAL BIBLE (Thomas Nelson Publishers) For: L,C. Slant: P.

For more than eighty years, **Nave's Topical Bible** has been recognized as the most authoritative and comprehensive Scriptural reference work ever published in America. One hundred thousand verses have been cross-referenced under 20,000 topics in this painstaking and methodical compilation of Scripture passages. **Nave's Topical Bible** is a complete collection of biblical thought, conveniently indexed in one volume. Scripture passages are quoted, a feature making Nave's the source book of first choice for preachers, Bible teachers, students, laymen, and anyone who enjoys personal Bible study. The unquestioned classic in its field, it is endorsed by virtually every major Christian leader. Hardcover. **$19.95.** Bookstores.

NAVE'S TOPICAL LIVING BIBLE (Tyndale House Publishers, Inc.) For: L,C,S. Slant: EP.

Easy-to-read-and-understand **Living Bible** text has been combined with the Nave's Topical organization! Now Bible readers involved in topical study can instantly know all that **The Living Bible** has to say on their topic of interest. This will be a tremendous aid to Bible scholars, students, pastors, Sunday school teachers, and virtually anyone who needs to understand better what the Bible says on a particular topic. The **Nave's Topical Living Bible** is the key to unlocking greater understanding in topical Bible study. Cloth, 01-4669. **$22.95.** Bookstores or from **Christian Book Service, 336 Gundersen Drive, Carol Stream, IL 60187.**

NELSON'S COMPLETE CONCORDANCE OF THE NEW AMERICAN BIBLE (Thomas Nelson Publishers) For: L,C. Slant: RC.

Nelson's Complete Concordance of the New American Bible, edited by Stephen J. Hartdegen, O.F.M., is the first Roman Catholic concordance produced from the modern language **New American Bible.** Contains over 300,000 entries. Hardcover. **$39.95.** Bookstores.

NELSON'S COMPLETE CONCORDANCE OF THE REVISED STANDARD VERSION, Second Edition (Thomas Nelson Publishers) For: L,C. Slant: P,S.

Bible readers will find every quotation from the Revised Standard Version, Second Edition, in this one volume. Over 2,000 pages. Hardcover. **$49.50.** Bookstores.

NEW AMERICAN STANDARD EXHAUSTIVE CONCORDANCE OF THE BIBLE (Holman Bible Publishers) For: L,C,S. Slant: EP.

The only exhaustive concordance based on the New American Standard Bible! Over 400,000 entries—lists every key word in the NAS Bible and every verse where it is found. There are three major sections—the concordance, a Hebrew-Aramaic dictionary, and a Greek dictionary. Through a complete system of references, any word listed in the concordance may be traced to either of the dictionaries to find its meaning and the ways it is translated

CONCORDANCES AND TOPICAL BIBLES

in the NAS Bible. Intensive word study is possible, even for those with no knowledge of Hebrew or Greek. The system of references is based on the same numbering system used in **Strong's**. Size 9 3/8 x 11 3/8 inches, 1,695 pages. **$29.95**. Bookstores.

NEW GREEK-SPANISH CONCORDANCE OF THE NEW TESTAMENT (LA NUEVA CONCORDANCIA GRECO-ESPAÑOLA DEL NUEVO TESTAMENTO) (Holman Bible Publishers) For: L,C,S. Slant: EP.

By H.M. Pelter. A basic reference work for studying the Spanish New Testament. Lists in alphabetical order important words from the Greek New Testament and gives every book, chapter, and verse where that word is found. Included is a Spanish-Greek index and a listing of Greek root words derived therefrom. 668 pages. **$14.95**. Bookstores.

NEW NAVE'S TOPICAL BIBLE, THE (Zondervan Publishing House) For: L,C,S. Slant: EP.

Formerly titled **The Zondervan Topical Bible** (1969), this is the most comprehensive revision and enlargement of the original Nave's. Presents the biblical text, in the King James Version, topically under nearly 21,000 subjects. Provides definitions of all persons, places, objects, and events in the Bible, supplies information on archaeological discoveries, suggests preaching themes and outlines, and offers a summary of Holy Scriptures.

$19.95. Bookstores or from **Zondervan Retail Marketing Service, 1420 Robinson Road, SE, Grand Rapids, MI 49506**.

THE NIV COMPLETE CONCORDANCE (Zondervan Publishing House) For: L,C,S. Slant: EP.

By Edward W. Goodrick and John R. Kohlenberger, III. A word index arranged alphabetically to which are added a brief context and location for every appearance of the key word. In this concordance every biblical reference to a particular word is included under the key entry word. 250,000 references are listed, covering every major word (and many minor words) of the NIV text. Over 12,800 words from the NIV text are indexed. **$19.95**. Bookstores or from **Zondervan Retail Marketing Service, 1420 Robinson Road, SE, Grand Rapids, MI 49506**.

THE NIV HANDY CONCORDANCE (Zondervan Publishing House) For: L,C,S. Slant: EP.

By Edward W. Goodrick and John R. Kohlenberger, III. A word index arranged alphabetically with over 35,000 Scripture reference entries with contexts for every occurrence of 1,239 key words in the NIV. Special entries for 260 Bible characters with descriptive phrases for references to key events in each character's life. **$4.95**. Bookstores or from **Zondervan Retail Marketing Service, 1420 Robinson Road, SE, Grand Rapids, MI 49506**.

POCKET BIBLE CONCORDANCE (Moody Press) For: L,C. Slant: EP,P.

An alphabetical index of 1,000 principal Bible words and 20,000 Scripture verses in which they appear. Mass paperback size for convenience. **$2.95**. Bookstores or from **Moody Bookworld, 2101 W. Howard, Chicago, IL 60645**.

POCKET TOPICAL INDEX OF THE BIBLE (Star Bible Publications) For: L,S. Slant: F,EP,P.

By Doyle Gilliam. A book of Bible facts in alphabetical arrangement. Ideal for the personal worker. Size 4 x 5 1/4. Now in eight languages. 183 pages. Catalog #1243, English. **$1.50**. Catalog #1243S, Spanish. **$1.50**. Bookstores or from **Star Bible Publications, Box 181220, Ft. Worth, TX 76118**.

PROMISES TO LIVE BY (Regal Books) For: L,C,S,Y. Slant: EP.

By David Wilkerson. Over 800 Bible promises arranged topically, including references and versions quoted. 96 pages. Paperback. **$1.95**. Bookstores or from **Regal Books, Division of GL Publications, 2300 Knoll Drive, Ventura, CA 93003**.

RSV BIBLE WITH CONCORDANCE (American Bible Society) For: L,C,S. Slant: P, S.

Includes a 224-page listing of entries and full-color maps. Black, hardcover, 5 3/8 x 8 inches. Order No. 00498. **$4.00**. From **American Bible Society, Box 5656, Grand Central Station, New York, NY 10163**.

CONCORDANCES AND TOPICAL BIBLES

RSV HANDY CONCORDANCE (Zondervan Publishing House) For: L,C,S. Slant: EP.

By Fritz Rienecker. Translated and revised by Cleon L. Rogers, Jr. A concise concordance that emphasizes key theological terms as well as favorite passages. **$4.95.** Bookstores or from **Zondervan Retail Marketing Service, 1420 Robinson Road, SE, Grand Rapids, MI 49506.**

SABBATARIAN CONCORDANCE AND COMMENTARY (Star Bible Publications) For: L,C,S. Slant: F,EP,P,S.

By Gerald Wright. Passages used by Sabbatarians from both Old and New Testaments in supporting present day Sabbath observance. Extensive Index of Scriptures and Bibliography. 167 pages. Paper, Catalog #1572. **$3.50.** Bookstores or from **Star Bible Publications, Box 181220, Ft. Worth, TX 76118.**

STRONG'S CONCORDANCE OF THE BIBLE, Popular Edition (Thomas Nelson Publishers) For: L,S,Y. Slant: P.

Strong's Exhaustive Concordance is one of the best known concordances available, but it is too bulky for many uses. This time-honored concordance is now available in the Popular Edition, a handy 864-page volume. This Popular Edition eliminates more than 100 words of minor importance, such as about, do, and who, and condenses more than 40 significant words, such as behold, know, and name. Thus all significant material is left intact. Key cross-references--the most important passages and passages that cannot be located using other words--have been retained. **Strong's Concordance of the Bible: Popular Edition** preserves the excellent scholarship of the Exhaustive edition. It will be prized by ministers, teachers, and others who need a complete concordance in a more convenient format. Hardcover. **$9.95.** Bookstores.

STRONG'S EXHAUSTIVE CONCORDANCE (Mott Media) For: L,C,S. Slant: AW, C, RC, F, EP, MP, LP, RJ, CJ, OJ, L, D, P, S, I, BC, CP, H, M.

Complete and unabridged, with dictionaries of the Hebrew and Greek words. Since its publication, **Strong's Concordance** has been widely considered the easiest to use analytical concordance of the English Bible. This edition is part of the beautiful **Mott Bible Study Reference Library.** Six massive volumes numerically coded to Strong's, oversized, Lexitone bound and stamped in gold. Ready for several lifetimes of heavy use. Cloth. **$17.95.** Bookstores or from **Mott Media, 1000 E. Huron, Milford, MI 48042.**

STRONG'S EXHAUSTIVE CONCORDANCE OF THE BIBLE (Abingdon Press) For: L,C,S. Slant: P,S.

Abingdon's Strong's Exhaustive Concordance of the Bible--the classic reference since 1894--continues to make understanding more accessible to modern Bible enthusiasts. Its exclusive **Key-Word Comparison** enables readers to compare words and phrases in the King James Version with five contemporary translations--New American Standard Bible, New English Bible, New International Version, Jerusalem Bible, and Revised Standard Version. Strong's irreplaceable main Concordance alphabetically lists every word in the Bible, along with the book chapter, and verse in which it appears. The useful dictionaries of Hebrew, Chaldee, and New Testament Greek include every significant word of the original scriptures with pronunciation. Available in two handsome editions--regular or helpful thumb-indexed edition--**Strong's Exhaustive Concordance** remains "...the best ever written." (Christian Herald). Regular edition. **$21.95.** Thumb indexed edition. **$26.95.** Bookstores or from **Abingdon Press, 201 Eighth Ave., South, P.O. Box 801, Nashville, TN 37202.**

STRONG'S EXHAUSTIVE CONCORDANCE OF THE BIBLE (Holman Bible Publishers) For: L,C,S. Slant: EP.

By James Strong. S.T.D., L.L.D. A complete index to the Scriptures listing every word in the King James Version and every passage where each word is found. Also includes Hebrew and Greek dictionaries for intensive word study. A standard Bible reference work. **$19.95.** Bookstores.

STRONG'S EXHAUSTIVE CONCORDANCE OF THE BIBLE (Thomas Nelson Publishers) For: L,C. Slant: P,S.

By James Strong. Strong's Exhaustive Concordance of the Bible lists every word in the King James Version of the Bible except prepositions and articles. Includes dictionary of the Hebrew Bible and Greek New Testament. Favorite for over a century. Hardcover. **$19.95.** Hardcover, indexed. **$22.95.** Bookstores.

THE TOPICAL CHAIN STUDY BIBLE (Thomas Nelson Publishers) For: L,C,S. Slant: EP,MP,D,P.

Thousands of references, hundreds of

CONCORDANCES AND TOPICAL BIBLES

commentaries, and color-coded great Bible themes make this new concept in study Bibles ideal for laypeople. Every two-page spread is complete in itself, with no flipping to the front or back for needed information. Designed for everyday devotional use as well as for more in-depth study, Nelson's NAS **Topical Chain Study Bible** is easy-to-use, clearly written, and practical for Bible lovers of all ages. **$29.95.** Bookstores.

TOPICAL DICTIONARY OF BIBLE TEXTS (Baker Book House) For: C,S. Slant: EP.

By James Inglis. Includes every subject that has a place in the Bible. Alphabetically arranged and supplemented by an extensive index of cross-references. **$3.95.** Bookstores or from **Baker Book House, P.O. Box 6287, Grand Rapids, MI 49506.**

WALKER'S COMPREHENSIVE BIBLE CONCORDANCE (Kregel Publications) For: L,C,S. Slant: P.

A complete alphabetical listing of the words of Scripture. All references are given in order so you can find that elusive verse quickly. Based on the KJV, this concordance contains over 50,000 more references than Cruden's. **$10.95.** Bookstores or from **Kregel Publications, P.O. Box 2607, Grand Rapids, MI 49501.**

WISDOM FOR TODAY'S ISSUES: A TOPICAL ARRANGEMENT OF PROVERBS (Presbyterian and Reformed Publishing Co.) For: L,C,S,Y. Slant: P.

By Stephen Voorwinde. This book is designed to make the Proverbs readily accessible to the reader who needs to know at once all that the Proverbs have to say on a particular subject. Every verse in Proverbs is categorized here and printed in full for quick reference. Anger, Counsel, Education, Food, Greed, the Home, Justice, Self-Control, Woman, and Work are just a few of the more than 50 categories included in this handy Bible-study companion. Stephen Voorwinde is a graduate of Westminster Theological Seminary and is a pastor in New Zealand. 186 pages. **$3.75.**

Bookstores or from **Presbyterian and Reformed Publishing Company, P.O. Box 817, Phillipsburg, NJ 08865.**

THE WORD STUDY NEW TESTAMENT AND CONCORDANCE (Tyndale House Publishers, Inc.) For: L,C,S. Slant: EP.

This reference work provides instant cross references of key New Testament words with the four most widely used New Testament study aids, including: Kittel-Frederick **Theological Dictionary of the New Testament;** Moulton and Geden's **Concordance to the Greek New Testament;** Arndt and Gingrich's **Greek Lexicon;** and Strong's **Exhaustive Concordance.** The Word Study Concordance prints every reference to each key word in one location. Cloth. No. 018390. **$36.95.** Bookstores or from **Christian Book Service, 336 Gundersen Drive, Carol Stream, IL 60187.**

THE WORD TOPICAL BIBLE OF ISSUES AND ANSWERS (Word Books) For: L,C,S,Y. Slant: EP.

By William M. Pinson. This practical guide to biblical teaching treats more than 300 subjects of concern to today's Bible student. The themes range from everyday areas such as family life, work, money, and sexuality, to difficult and controversial issues such as drugs, abortion, labor relations, and war. And hundreds of other topics are cross-referenced under the main subjects. Unlike a concordance, the **Word Topical Bible** presents Scriptural passages in full, with two lists of related references—one of biblical examples of the issues and answers in question, and another of additonal Scripture references on the subject you're looking for. No other topical Bible is this fresh and contemporary. The practicing layman can use it to look up topics like friendship, faithfulness, humility, peace, righteousness, self-control, truth, or the will of God. The minister or preacher can use it to compare passages in the Old and New Testaments and let Scripture interpret Scripture. Paperback, catalog number 2934-2. **$7.95.** Bookstores.

YOUNG'S ANALYTICAL CONCORDANCE TO THE BIBLE (Wm. B. Eerdmans Publishing Co.) For: L,C,S. Slant: S.

By Robert S. Young. The most complete and accurate Bible concordance available. Its 311,000 references outnumber other comparable volumes by more than 118,000. Includes separate index-lexicons to both the Old and New Testaments, and a complete list of Scripture proper names, indicating modern pronunciation and the exact form of the original Hebrew or Greek. "Of the various available concordances to the English Bible, the one most helpful to the general student is **Young's**" - **Christianity Today. $19.95.** Bookstores or from **Eerdmans Publishing Co., 255 Jefferson Ave., SE, Grand Rapids, MI 49503.**

CONCORDANCES AND TOPICAL BIBLES

YOUNG'S ANALYTICAL CONCORDANCE TO THE BIBLE (Thomas Nelson Publishers) For: L,C,S. Slant: S.

Young's Concordance—a valued reference book since 1879—has been revised to make it even more helpful than ever. This new, enlarged edition contains the exclusive Universal Subject Guide to the Bible, a massive topical reference section which enables Bible readers to use Young's with any contemporary translation—including the NKJV, NAS, TEV, NIV, or RSV—as well as the King James Version. To make it even more useful, the revised edition of Young's has the same easy-to-use numerical system as **Strong's Exhaustive Concordance**. Containing almost 311,000 references and nearly 5,000,000 words, the concordance is an effective guide to the full historical context of Bible times—the ideas, the people, the places. Dr. Donald Gutherie's introduction explains how the new edition is organized and how to use it profitably. **Young's Concordance** is one of the most helpful tools for Bible study available today. Hardcover. **$22.95.** Hardcover, indexed. **$26.95.** Bookstores.

The last word in Bible resources is America's first name in religious publishing.

Strong's Exhaustive Concordance of the Bible with the exclusive Key-Word Comparison
". . . the best ever written . . ."   —Christian Herald
Regular Edition, $21.95. No. 400309.
Thumb-Indexed Edition, $26.95. No. 400317.

The Interpreter's Bible
". . . the Scriptures have seldom been so fully revealed . . ."
                                            —The New York Times
Twelve-Volume Set, $210.00. No 192064.
Single Volumes, $18.95.

The Interpreter's Dictionary of the Bible
". . . an essential purchase for every library."   —Library Journal
Five-Volume Set, $99.50. No. 192684.
Supplementary Volume, $20.00. No. 192692.

JUST PUBLISHED!

The Interpreter's Concise Commentary
   An easy-to-use, affordable new resource for Bible enthusiasts. The work of over forty scholars, it contains commentary on the entire Bible, including Apocrypha.
Eight-Volume Set in Slipcase, $34.95. No. 192315.

Order from your local bookstore or

Abingdon Press

201 Eighth Ave., So., Box 801 Nashville, TN 37202

Now is the time to start planning your Year of the Bible activities—

President Reagan has proclaimed 1983 to be The Year of the Bible. The proclamation offers many opportunities for churches to proclaim the Word, and especially to encourage regular Bible reading among their members and among the members of the communities they serve.

The Year of the Bible Manual
3036; $1.95; by Orrin Root, Dr. Lewis Foster, June Crabtree, and numerous other writers.

The Year of the Bible Manual has been prepared by Standard to assist church leaders in planning Year of the Bible observances and activities. Among the many helps the 96-page manual offers are
- An introduction to The Year of the Bible and the many opportunities it offers the church
- Ten sermon outlines on the subject of the Bible
- 52 tips for promoting Bible reading and study (practical ways to keep excitement high all year long)
- Complete scripts for church drama and Bible readings (with permission to copy)
- Quotations about the Bible for use in sermons, newsletters, worship bulletins, etc.
- Clip art for illustrating newsletters, bulletins and posters.
- Descriptions of the many products available from Standard that will be useful for a Year of the Bible program

"I Believe the Bible" Stickers
1757; $10.00 per roll.

Use on correspondence, newsletters, and bulletins to promote The Year of the Bible, or wear as a lapel tag. Colorful open Bible and flame design, 1½" diameter. Stickers are self-adhesive. 500 stickers per roll.

"I Believe the Bible" Bulletin
73126; $5.50 per 100, 500 for $20.00, $37.00 per 1000

For use in church services to promote and observe The Year of the Bible. Colorful design. Shipped flat (8½"x11") to facilitate printing. High quality paper assures good reproduction.

"I Believe the Bible" Button
7816; $5.95 pkg. of 50

Wear to proclaim your faith and to promote The Year of the Bible. Metal, 1½" diameter, pin-style back. Colorful open Bible flame design.

"I Believe the Bible" Poster
2606; 40c each, 3 for $1.00

Brightly colored, 12½"x19" poster for church bulletin boards. Can also be placed in prominent locations in the community. Excellent way to promote The Year of the Bible. Open Bible and flame design.

Available in July . . .

Basic Bible Survey
3210; $2.95; by Elsie E. Howard

This enjoyable, easy-to-read book will help many persons gain a better basic knowledge of God's Word, especially those who are discouraged by more formal Bible surveys.

How to Use Your Bible
3200; $2.50; 12 or more, $2.25; by Wanda Milner

A fun-to-use workbook for would-be Bible readers from age 9 through adult. Step-by-step exercises help the reader master the location skills essential to enjoyable reading and study of God's Word.

A Through-the-Bible Reading Program
3076; $3.95; T. Thurman, R. McKinney, and G. Hall

A chronological outline for reading the Bible through in one year, the program including a method to check reading progress, notes on each reading to provide background and motivate reading, plus maps and charts for visual reference. Only five readings a week are required.

Selecting a Translation of the Bible
39975; $3.95; by Dr. Lewis Foster

Many Bible translations are available to today's Bible reader. Which is the best one for your personal needs? This book will help you decide.

A History of the English Bible
39974; $3.50; by Jonathan Underwood

How do we know that the Bible we have today is really THE Bible, THE Word of God as it claims to be? *A History of the English Bible* provides the assurance you need that the Bible we have today is beyond all doubt the Word of God for all ages.

Bible Programs and Dramas
$1.95 each

Bible verses for recitation, monlogues, imagination-capturing dramas, and scripts for attention-getting puppet plays.
Bible Programs and Dramas for Children, 3350
Bible Programs and Dramas for Youth and Adults, 3351

At your dealer, or

STANDARD PUBLISHING

8121 Hamilton Ave. Cincinnati, OH 45231

BIBLE DICTIONARIES, ENCYCLOPEDIAS, HANDBOOKS, AND ATLASES

A wide variety of Bible "handbooks" are available in many different forms. Many list subjects alphabetically and are therefore called dictionaries or encyclopedias. These usually list all of the Bible persons, Bible places, theological subjects, Bible-related topics, and background information about the Biblical world. Some dictionaries and encyclopedias deal only with words which appear in the Bible but most also cover extra-biblical terms of interest to Bible students. Most Bible dictionaries and encyclopedias also feature a variety of helpful photographs, illustrations and maps which further clarify words and concepts. Many Bible dictionaries and encyclopedias are written by large groups of authors so that each entry can be described by a scholarly specialist in that particular area. Bible handbooks usually contain the same kind of information as dictionaries and encyclopedias but they collect it in some other logical order such as by books of the Bible, in historical chronological order, or by broad subject headings such as "the Roman Empire," "Jewish Religion," or "Family Life in Bible Times." Bible atlases are usually much more than collections of maps. In fact, most Bible atlases are actually handbooks organized around a series of maps.

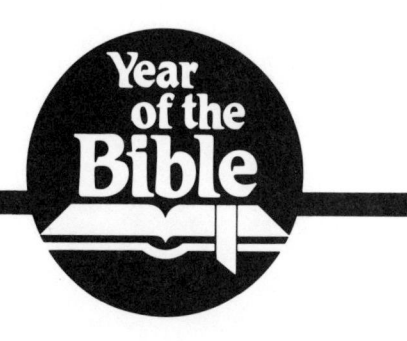

BIBLE DICTIONARIES, ENCYCLOPEDIAS, HANDBOOKS, AND ATLASES

ALL THE PEOPLE AND PLACES OF THE BIBLE (Thomas Nelson Publishers) For: L,C,S. Slant: P,S.

This new series of easy-to-digest handbooks provides insights into the people and cultures of Bible times. Maps, tables, diagrams and photos pull together little-known and tantalizing facts. The latest discoveries of archaeologists, historians and language specialists have been assembled in a colorful account of the biblical world. Flexibind. **$5.95.** Bookstores.

ARCHAEOLOGY IN BIBLE LANDS (Moody Press) For: L,C,S. Slant: EP, S,I,M.

By Howard Vos. An extensive presentation of every major biblical country and archaeological site with sixteen pages of full-color maps. **$11.95.** Bookstores or from **Moody Bookworld, 2101 W. Howard St., Chicago, IL 60645.**

ARCHAEOLOGY OF THE BIBLE: BOOK BY BOOK (Harper & Row Publishers, Inc.) For: L,C,S. Slant: P,S,BC.

By Gaalyah Cornfeld and David Noel Freedman. First paperback edition of the only book-by-book archaeological commentary on the Bible, including the intertestamental period. A wealth of photographs, line drawings, and maps illustrates the historical and cultural setting of each book. The authors blend archaeology, history, and sound critical scholarship to bring events into sharpened focus and to clarify frequently misunderstood passages. This is a compact, comprehensive, balanced reference work designed to give readers the clearest possible picture of the biblical world in order to increase appreciation of the Bible's message and its role in Western culture and thought. 344 pages; 200 black-and-white photographs; maps; index. RD 389. Paperback. **$12.95.** Bookstores or from **Harper & Row, Publishers, Inc. Mail Order Dept., 2350 Virginia Ave., Hagerstown, MD 21740.**

BACKGROUND TO THE BIBLE (Servant Publications) For: L. Slant: P.

By Richard T.A. Murphy. Many Christians who want to read Scripture and understand its message simply do not know where to start. Scripture studies are often too technical for the general reader or too simple to provide real help. **Background to the Bible** provides readable, non-technical background information to help all who are interested in studying Scripture. **$4.95.** Bookstores.

BAKER'S BIBLE ATLAS (Baker Book House) For: L,C,S. Slant: EP.

By C.F. Pfeiffer. A Bible geography containing 26 colored maps, 75 photographs to illustrate, numerous black-and-white maps. Emphasis on geography follows the Scriptural narrative from Genesis through Revelation. A brief review of Biblical archaeology containing the highest evangelical authorship. **$15.95.** Bookstores or from **Baker Book House, P.O. Box 6287, Grand Rapids, MI 49506.**

BAKER'S HANDBOOK OF BIBLE LISTS (Baker Book House) For: L,C,S. Slant: EP.

By Andrew Hill. Meaningfully supplements standard Bible reference tools and offers speedy access to basic Bible information. **$6.95.** Bookstores or from **Baker Book House, P.O. Box 6287, Grand Rapids, MI 49506.**

BAKER'S POCKET DICTIONARY OF RELIGIOUS TERMS (Baker Book House) For: L,S. Slant: EP.

By Donald Kauffman. The entries range from major world faiths to the smallest religious groups. Contains much other information too. **$5.95.** Bookstores or from **Baker Book House, P.O. Box 6287, Grand Rapids, MI 49506.**

BENNETT'S GUIDE TO THE BIBLE: Graphic Aids and Outlines (The Seabury Press) For: C,S. Slant: P,S.

By Boyce M. Bennett. Provides learning and memory aids for all students of the Bible. In Part I, each book is outlined chapter by chapter, showing its structure, characters, and incidents. In Part II, a time-line of history from Abraham to the beginnings of the Church includes relevant extra-biblical history in graphic form. Part III gives a brief explanation of the formation of the Bible's text and of how archaeology improves our understanding of it. Paperback. **$9.95.** Bookstores or from **Seabury Service Center, Somers, CT 06071.**

THE BIBLE ALMANAC (Thomas Nelson Publishers) For: L,C,S. Slant: P,S.

A comprehensive Bible handbook, **The Bible Almanac** is a layman's guide to the people and cultures of Bible times. It presents detailed information about the Bible in a clear, interesting and logical fashion. New maps, tables, and

39

BIBLE DICTIONARIES, ENCYCLOPEDIAS, HANDBOOKS, AND ATLASES

diagrams put obscure facts about the Bible within the grasp of every reader. **The Bible Almanac** draws upon the latest discoveries of archaeologists, historians and language specialists to assemble a reliable, colorful account of the biblical world. **The Bible Almanac** first describes the ancient world in which God revealed himself to Abraham and his descendants. Then a comprehensive article traces the history of God's revelation through the Old and New Testaments. This serves as a springboard to a discussion of a variety of topics associated with Bible times, such as law, trade, transportation, and family life. Altogether 46 major articles cover the many aspects of biblical culture. It contains dozens of new full-color photographs from the land of the Bible with nearly 500 black-and-white photographs. A thorough index guides the reader to points of interest throughout the text. Hardcover. **$16.95.** Bookstores.

THE BIBLE, FAMILY HANDBOOK OF CHRISTIAN KNOWLEDGE (Here's Life Publishers) For: L. Slant: EP,S.

A full-color, illustrated book on how the Bible was written, what books were selected for inclusion, the translation process and what makes the Bible trustworthy today. Product # 403089. **$15.95.** Bookstores or from **Here's Life Publishers, P.O. Box 1576, San Bernardino, CA 92402.**

BIBLE TREASURE BOOK (Baker Book House) For: L,Y. Slant: EP.

By **William E. Cameron.** More than two thousand questions and answers covering Bible facts, people, and events are organized under meaningful topics. **$1.45.** Bookstores or from **Baker Book House, P.O. Box 6287, Grand Rapids, MI 49506.**

BIBLE VOCABULARY BUILDER (Mott Media) For: L,S,Y. Slant: AW,C,RC,F,EP,MP,LP,L,D,P,CP,H,M.

By **Terry R. Reiff.** Build your Bible word bank--broaden your Bible horizons! This unique book brings improved understanding and reading pleasure plus an easier grasp of abstruse biblical terms. It includes more than 2,000 of the best loved verses in the New Testament, word studies and quizzes to help you check your vocabulary development. Also a Scripture index and a pronunciation guide. 259 pages. Paper. **$5.95.** Bookstores or

from **Mott Media, 1000 E. Huron St., Milford, MI 48042.**

BOYD'S BIBLE DICTIONARY (Holman Bible Publishers) For: L,C,S.

This Bible dictionary is accepted as the standard edition by scholars everywhere. It is a concise, compact dictionary with thousands of biblical references. It lists and identifies all proper names, gives data on places and events of the Scriptures, pronunciations, definitions and textual references. Paper. **$3.50.** Bookstores.

BOYD'S BIBLE HANDBOOK (Harvest House Publishers) For: L,C,S. Slant: EP,P,S,I,M.

This colossal volume of biblical research is a terrific reference for pastors, students, and lay people who seek a better understanding of God's Word. It contains over 100 helpful maps and illustrations to make your Bible study more realistic and applicable. Plus over 200 archaeological tidbits relating to Scripture, 140 fulfilled prophecies listed, 100 scientific facts explained, a condensed survey of the Bible, its divisions, and what each book is about. Top quality composition makes this handbook a lifetime resource. Cloth, No. 3523. **$24.95.** Bookstores or from **Harvest House Publishers, 1075 Arrowsmith, Eugene, OR 97402.**

CHRISTIAN WORDS (Thomas Nelson Publishers) For: L,C. Slant: C,MP,S.

Early Christians developed a revolutionary form of writing, singular in both style and syntax. To understand the message of the New Testament, it is necessary to understand the sacred vocabulary of the first century when new terminology was devised and old terminology was charged with new meaning. **Christian Words** is a dictionary of more than 300 New Testament words that goes beyond other such dictionaries which usually only reflect the Koine Greek meaning of words. Rather, **Christian Words** shows how early Christians gave new meaning to many words such as double-minded, evangelist, and hypocrite. **Christian Words** analyzes the similarities and differences of Jewish, secular, and Christian writings of the Hellenistic and Roman periods. It reflects the latest and most thorough scholarship on New Testament Greek, yet its writing is warm and personal. Hardcover. **$14.95.** Bookstores.

COMPACT BIBLE ATLAS WITH GAZETTEER (Baker Book House) For: L,C,S,Y. Slant: EP.

Nineteen full color Hammond maps and a comprehensive gazetteer with 1,300 entries make this compact atlas a convenient guide for students of the Bible. **$3.95.** Bookstores or from **Baker Book House, P.O. Box 6287, Grand Rapids, MI 49506.**

CONCORDIA BIBLE DICTIONARY (Concordia Publishing House) For: L. Slant: EP.

By **Erwin L. Lueker.** More than 6,300 entries giving concise up-to-date definitions of biblical terms in the Old and New Testament, plus materials from the Apocrypha. 152 pages. Paper, Item No. 12-2213. **$4.75.** Bookstores or from **Concordia Publishing House, 3558 South Jefferson, St. Louis, MO 63118.**

CRUDEN'S CONCORDANCE/SMITH'S BIBLE DICTIONARY (Jimmy Swaggart Ministries) For: L,C. Slant: CP.

BIBLE DICTIONARIES, ENCYCLOPEDIAS, HANDBOOKS, AND ATLASES

These two time-tested study volumes have aided Bible students for years. **Smith's Bible Dictionary** is a total reference tool. It contains every word in the Bible, giving extensive definitions, backgrounds, and Scripture references where each word is found. **Cruden's Concordance** is an exhaustive resource to help you locate every Scripture imaginable. Simply pinpoint the word you desire to research and **Cruden's** gives you every Scripture where it is located. These two are essential additions to your Bible study library! Product Number 99-515. **$15.00.** From **Jimmy Swaggart Ministries, P.O. Box 2550, Baton Rouge, LA 70821.**

CRUDEN'S POCKET DICTIONARY OF BIBLE TERMS (Baker Book House) For: L,C,S. Slant: EP.

A concise presentation of the important meaning of scriptural terms whether doctrinal, historical, geographical, or common objects of the natural and cultural world of Bible lands and times. **$5.95.** Bookstores or from **Baker Book House, P.O. Box 6287, Grand Rapids, MI 49506.**

DAILY LIFE IN BIBLE TIMES (Thomas Nelson Publishers) For: L,C,S. Slant: P,S.

This new series of easy-to-digest handbooks provides insights into the people and cultures of Bible times. Maps, tables, diagrams and photos pull together little-known and tantalizing facts. The latest discoveries of archaeologists, historians and language specialists have been assembled in a colorful account of the biblical world. What would it be like to have grown up in Bible times? This is an intriguing book about family relationships, womanhood, marriage and divorce, childhood, adolescence, food, clothing, cosmetics, architecture, furniture, music, worship, medicine, and more. Flexibind. **$5.95.** Bookstores.

DAILY LIFE IN THE TIME OF JESUS (Servant Publications) For: L.

By Henri Daniel-Rops. One of the most popular and comprehensive surveys of daily life as it was in the time of our Lord. Written in a clear, attractive, and informative style. A masterful synthesis of the complex array of economic, political, and cultural currents of the pivotal era of human history. Creates an accurate and lasting image of the world in which Jesus lived. An invaluable aid for understanding the gospels. **$7.95.** Bookstores.

DICCIONARIO BÍBLICO (BIBLE DICTIONARY) (Vida Publishers) For: L,C,S. Slant: EP.

Bible Dictionary in Spanish combines an easily understood style with profound understanding of major Bible themes. Documentation with photographs and maps makes truth easily understood by all who use this tool. Ref. #534, Paper, **$2.75.** Ref. #540, Hardback. **$4.00.** Bookstores.

DICTIONARY OF THE BIBLE (Baker Book House) For: L,C,S,Y. Slant: EP.

By John Davis. This revised edition is one of the most important reference books for the Christian home and the Bible student's library. It has approximately five thousand entries, on over eight hundred pages. **$18.95.** Bookstores or from **Baker Book House, P.O. Box 6287, Grand Rapids, MI 49506.**

DICTIONARY OF THE NEW TESTAMENT (Harper & Row, Publishers, Inc.) For: L,C,S. Slant: RC, P, S, BC.

By Xavier Léon-Dufour. Available in September, 1983. Here is the most comprehensive, up-to-date dictionary of important words, names, and concepts of the New Testament, by one of the world's foremost biblical scholars. Although designed to provide basic, accurate answers to questions arising from reading the New Testament, the impressive scholarship will appeal to serious students and teachers as well. Over 1,000 key words requiring historical, geographical, archaeological, literary, or theological explanation are clearly and concisely defined. Each entry ends with biblical references and cross references to other entries and to a detailed, fifty-page introduction to the land, people, culture, and morality of New Testament times. The author takes fully into account the most recent contributions to New Testament scholarship and presents a wealth of material in a clear and eminently readable manner. 464 pages; maps; index. RD 486. Paperback. **$12.95.** Bookstores or from **Harper & Row, Publishers, Inc. Mail Order Dept., 2350 Virginia Ave., Hagerstown, MD 21740.**

DISCOVERING THE WORLD OF THE BIBLE (Thomas Nelson Publishers) For: L,C. Slant: P.

For most people, the "world of the Bible" means Israel and a few other Middle Eastern areas. Travelers call Palestine the "Holy Land." Yet, biblical history covers virtually all of the

BIBLE DICTIONARIES, ENCYCLOPEDIAS, HANDBOOKS, AND ATLASES

Mediterranean world, from ancient Babylon to the forum at Rome. **Discovering the World of the Bible** is an "armchair tour" of these lands. It will take you on a country-by-country, city-by-city, site-by-site journey through the ten countries in which the events of the Bible occurred: Cyprus, Egypt, Greece, Iraq, Israel, Italy, Jordan, Lebanon, Syria, and Turkey. Less familiar ancient civilizations assume clear identities through the generous use of more than 200 maps, diagrams, black-and-white and full-color photos. Significant Scripture references are cited. **Discovering the World of the Bible** provides a historical, contemporary, biblical picture of the ten countries that make up our "Holy Land." For travelers as well as Bible students, this is the book. Hardcover. **$14.95.** Bookstores.

EERDMANS ATLAS OF THE BIBLE (Wm. B. Eerdmans Publishing Company) For: L,C,S,Y. Slant: P.

Edited by Pat Alexander. This compact guide to the world of the Bible includes full-color maps, charts, and photographs, as well as an easy-to-read text, to help Bible readers better understand the historical and geographical context of significant events in both the Old and New Testaments. **$7.95.** Bookstores or from **Eerdmans Publishing, 255 Jefferson Ave., SE, Grand Rapids, MI 49503.**

EERDMANS' CONCISE BIBLE ENCYCLOPEDIA (Wm. B. Eerdmans Publishing Co.) For: L,C,S,Y. Slant: EP,P.

An A-Z fact-finder for the entire family covering people, places, events, daily life, and key teachings of the Bible. Based on the popular **Eerdmans' Family Encyclopedia of the Bible**, this concise edition includes historical, geographical, and cultural information as well as scriptural cross-references. Illustrated. **$8.95.** Bookstores or from **Eerdmans Publishing Co., 255 Jefferson Ave., SE, Grand Rapids, MI 49503.**

EERDMANS' CONCISE BIBLE HANDBOOK (Wm. B. Eerdmans Publishing Co.) For: L,C,S,Y. Slant: EP,P.

An informative, compact, book-by-book guide to the Bible. Based on the million-copy bestseller, **Eerdmans' Handbook to the Bible**, this volume also features separate articles by experts on biblical history, archaeology, and interpretation. Line drawings, maps, and charts complement the text. **$9.95.** Bookstores or from **Eerdmans Publishing Co., 255 Jefferson Ave., SE, Grand Rapids, MI 49503.**

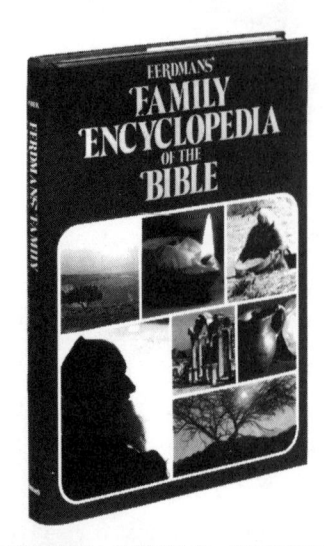

EERDMANS' FAMILY ENCYCLOPEDIA OF THE BIBLE (Wm. B. Eerdmans Publishing Co.) For: L, C, S, Y. Slant: EP, P.

Edited by Pat Alexander. "...won't collect dust on any family's bookshelf. Well-illustrated and easy-to-use..." —**Christian Herald**. "...a stunningly beautiful picture encyclopedia which ought to answer every question one might have about biblical life."— —**Christian Ministry**. Here's a Bible reference book for use by the whole family. Its 10 easily read major sections answer questions that frequently arise through devoted Bible study. Alphabetical listing of people, places and Bible words make finding them easy for even the youngest reader. The other sections, grouped by theme with a comprehensive index, thoroughly explore such topics as archaeology, religion and worship, and work and society. Completely reliable and scripturally faithful, **Eerdmans' Family Encyclopedia** will open up the Bible in a new way, making its meaning and message clear for every family member. **$18.95.** Bookstores or from **Eerdmans Publishing Co., 255 Jefferson Ave., SE, Grand Rapids, MI 49503.**

EERDMANS' HANDBOOK TO THE BIBLE (Wm. B. Eerdmans Publishing Co.) For: L,C,S,Y. Slant: EP,P.

Edited by David and Pat Alexander. A comprehensive, fully illustrated reference book in which the reader can see and understand the Bible in its historical context, and will find answers to almost every imaginable question about biblical times and places. "Surpassing all currently available Bible handbooks in form, content, and accuracy...One of the few books of which it can truly be said that every family should have one."—**Christianity Today**. "...one of the finest single-volume reference books we know."—**Eternity**. **$24.95.** Bookstores or from **Eerdmans Publishing, 255 Jefferson Ave., SE, Grand Rapids, MI 49503.**

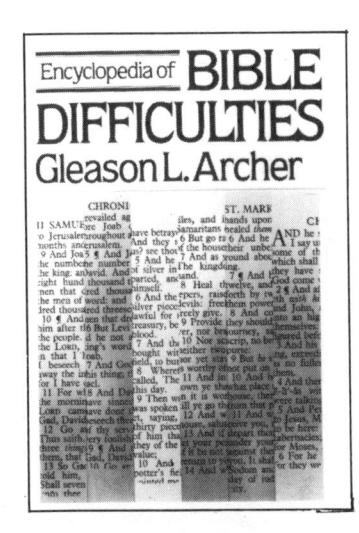

BIBLE DICTIONARIES, ENCYCLOPEDIAS, HANDBOOKS, AND ATLASES

AN ENCYCLOPEDIA OF BIBLE DIFFICULTIES (Zondervan Publishing House) For: L,C,S. Slant: EP.

By Gleason L. Archer. Addresses the problems and questions in the biblical text which are raised against the doctrine of inerrancy. Addresses these issues in the order they appear in the Scripture. Fully indexed. **$16.95.** Bookstores or from **Zondervan Retail Marketing Service, 1420 Robinson Road, SE, Grand Rapids, MI 49506.**

ENCYCLOPEDIA OF BIBLICAL PROPHECY (Baker Book House) For: L,C,S. Slant: EP.

By J.B. Payne. A complete guide to scriptural predictions and their fulfillment. Provides a systematic analysis of biblical prophecy and a discussion of every predictive prophecy in each biblical book. **$15.95.** Bookstores or from **Baker Book House, P.O. Box 6287, Grand Rapids, MI 49506.**

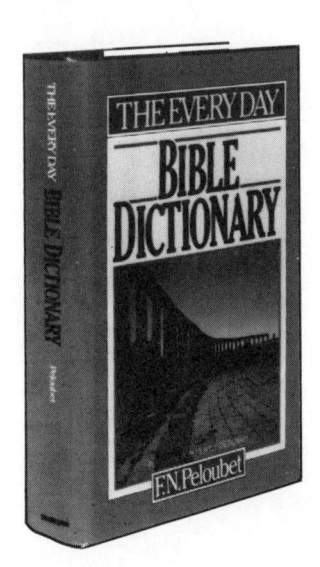

THE EVERYDAY BIBLE DICTIONARY (Zondervan Publishing House) For: L,C,S. Slant: EP.

By F.N. Peloubet. Formerly titled **Peloubet's Bible Dictionary**, gives explanation of subjects and characters in the Bible for understanding and Bible study. One volume edition includes up-to-date maps. Established reference work based on earlier **Smith's Bible Dictionary**. **$14.95.** Bookstores or from **Zondervan Retail Marketing Service, 1420 Robinson Road, SE, Grand Rapids, MI 49506.**

AN EXPOSITORY DICTIONARY OF NEW TESTAMENT WORDS (Thomas Nelson Publishers) For: L,C. Slant: P.

By W.E. Vine. A dictionary, concordance, and commentary all in one volume. It shows which Greek words are represented by one English word. Wealth of scriptural insight. Hardcover. **$14.95.** Bookstores.

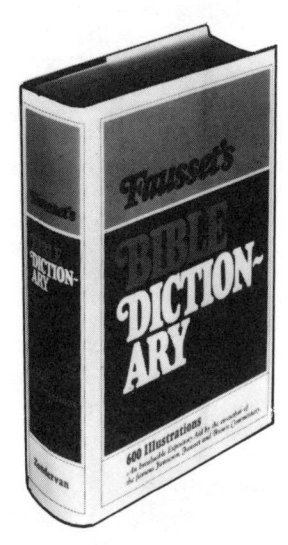

FAUSSET'S BIBLE DICTIONARY (Zondervan Publishing House) For: L,C,S. Slant: EP.

By A.R. Fausset. An encyclopedia dictionary, arranged alphabetically, 600 illustrations. A major work by a renowned Bible scholar of the late nineteenth century. Scripture index. **$15.95.** Bookstores or from **Zondervan Retail Marketing Service, 1420 Robinson Road, SE, Grand Rapids, MI 49506.**

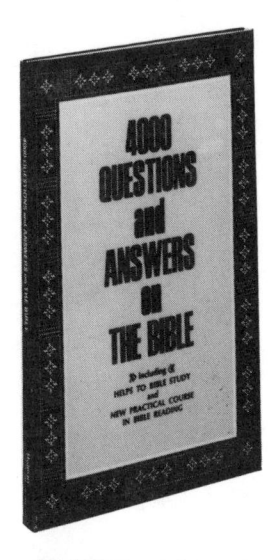

4,000 QUESTIONS AND ANSWERS ON THE BIBLE (Broadman Press) For: L,C,S. Slant: MP.

Edited by A. Dana Adams. Exactly what the name implies—4,000 questions and answers from Genesis to Revelation. An excellent resource for those studying and teaching the Bible. Also included are the sections "Helps to Bible Study" and "New Practical Course in Bible Reading." Hardback. **$3.95.** Paperback. **$1.95.** Bookstores.

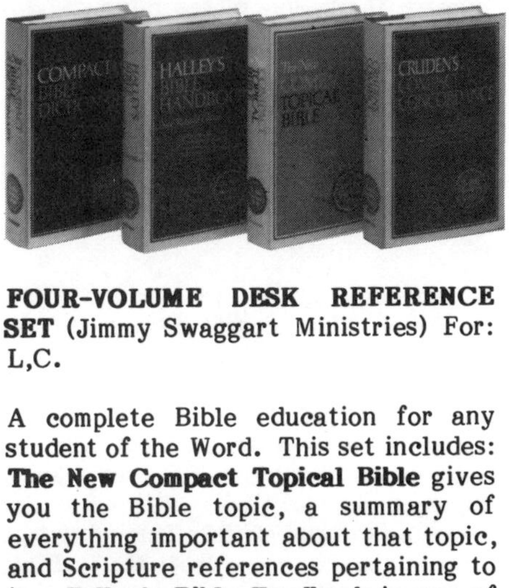

FOUR-VOLUME DESK REFERENCE SET (Jimmy Swaggart Ministries) For: L,C.

A complete Bible education for any student of the Word. This set includes: **The New Compact Topical Bible** gives you the Bible topic, a summary of everything important about that topic, and Scripture references pertaining to it. **Halley's Bible Handbook** is one of the most widely accepted and used Bible handbooks in existence today. **The Compact Bible Dictionary** includes

BIBLE DICTIONARIES, ENCYCLOPEDIAS, HANDBOOKS, AND ATLASES

picture and explanations of every single entry in the Bible. **Cruden's Compact Concordance** gives the reference for every word found in the Bible. Product Number 99-598. **$30.00**. From **Jimmy Swaggart Ministries, P.O. Box 2550, Baton Rouge, LA 70821**.

GEOGRAFIA HISTÓRICA DE LA BIBLIA (HISTORICAL BIBLE GEOGRAPHY) (Vida Publishers) For: L,C,S. Slant: EP.

By Netta Kemp de Money. New, Spanish, revised edition with full-color illustrated covers. This book will be a valuable supplement to your study of the life of Christ in particular and of the geography of the biblical world in general. It offers a systematic study of the setting in which the divine revelation took place and the influence of the environment and geography in the lives of the people of the Bible. **$2.95**. Bookstores.

GESENIUS' HEBREW-CHALDEE LEXICON TO THE OLD TESTAMENT (Mott Media) For: L,C,S. Slant: S.

Numerically coded to **Strong's Concordance**. The classic dictionary that formed the bases for the exhaustive lexicon of Brown, Driver and Briggs. Helpful introduction explains how to use this easily with Strong's huge 35 page index for those who don't know Hebrew; comparative table: 14 ancient and modern alphabets. This edition is part of the extensive **Mott Media Bible Reference Library**. Bound in Lexitone, stamped in gold. **$24.95**. Bookstores or from **Mott Media, 1000 E. Huron St., Milford, MI 48042**.

HALLEY'S BIBLE HANDBOOK (Zondervan Publishing House) For: L,C,S. Slant: EP.

By H.H. Halley. A Bible handbook including a concise Bible commentary, important discoveries in archaeology, related historical data, church history, maps, and more. Indexed. Paper. Large print. **$8.95**. Cloth. Large print. **$17.95**. Kivar. **$12.95**. Bookstores or from **Zondervan Retail Marketing Service, 1420 Robinson Road, SE, Grand Rapids, MI 49506**.

HANDBOOK TO THE GOSPELS (Servant Publications) For: L. Slant: RC.

By John Wijngaards, M.H.M. More detailed than a general introduction, wider-ranging and more broadly usable than a verse-by-verse commentary, The **Handbook to the Gospels** provides all the background information necessary for understanding the gospel texts—including political movements, religious and political leaders, historical data, and patterns of daily life. Illustrated with dozens of line drawings and photos, the **Handbook** includes chapters on: the purpose, structure and themes of each gospel; daily life in first-century Palestine; the Jewish calendar and feasts; temple and synagogue; religious life of the times; politics in Palestine; language and speech; miracles and parables. John Wijngaards, M.H.M., holds the licentiate in Sacred Scripture from the Pontifical Institute and the doctorate in Dogmatic Theology from the Gregorian University. 302 pages, size $5\frac{1}{4}$ x 8 inches, paperback, illustrated. **$8.95**. Bookstores.

THE HANDY BIBLE DICTIONARY AND CONCORDANCE (Zondervan Publishing House) For: L,C,S. Slant: EP.

By Merrill C. Tenney and Alexander Cruden. A one-volume edition of both the **Handy Bible Dictionary** (1965) and **Cruden's Handy Concordance** (1737 abridged 1963). Makes resource information available and enables one to find Scripture references when a key word is known. Concise yet with a remarkable fullness. Convenient, easy-to-read type. **$3.95**. Bookstores or from **Zondervan Retail Marketing Service, 1420 Robinson Road, SE, Grand Rapids, MI 49506**.

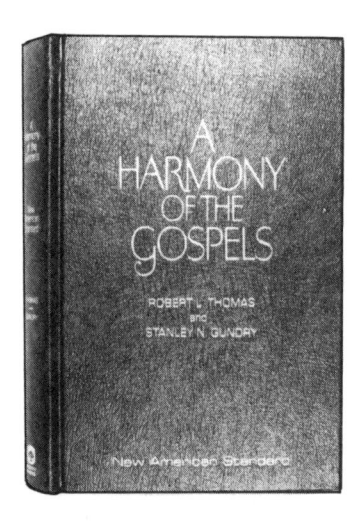

A HARMONY OF THE GOSPELS (Moody Press) For: L,C,S. Slant: EP, S,I,M.

By Stanley Gundry and Robert Thomas. A resource harmonizing the chronology of events in the four gospels—will encourage a deeper understanding of Jesus Christ, His life, and His ministry. **$13.95**. Bookstores or from **Moody Bookworld, 2101 W. Howard St., Chicago, IL 60645**.

HARPER'S BIBLE DICTIONARY (Harper & Row, Publishers, Inc.) For: L,C,S. Slant: MP,P.

By Madeleine S. and J. Lane Miller. This latest edition of the standard reference work explains all the important topics of the Bible, from "Aaron" to "The Book of Zephaniah." The latest in scholarship, archaeological findings, and biblical theology is blended with over 400 photographs, more than 100 line drawings and diagrams, and 16 full-color maps. Interestingly written and conveniently arranged, this is an indispensable tool for all Bible readers and students. Authoritative, responsible, useful, and illuminating, this is the ideal one-volume reference for achieving a more complete and rewarding understanding

BIBLE DICTIONARIES, ENCYCLOPEDIAS, HANDBOOKS, AND ATLASES

of the Bible. 864 pages; 424 photographs; over 100 line drawings, tables, diagrams; 16 maps; index. Cloth. **$18.95.** Bookstores or from **Harper & Row Publishers, Inc. Mail Order Dept., 2350 Virginia Ave., Hagerstown, MD 21740.**

HARPER'S ENCYCLOPEDIA OF BIBLE LIFE (Harper & Row, Publishers, Inc.) For: L,C. Slant: MP.

By Madeleine S. and J. Lane Miller. A completely revised edition of the indispensable reference for understanding the background of the people in the Old and New Testaments. In light of the latest findings and information, this book serves as a guide on the day-to-day life of priests, sailors, musicians, mourners, scribes, craftsmen—everyone who inhabits the pages of the Bible. An essential resource, it contains 150 illustrations, 74 subjects arranged in 14 convenient sections, and an up-to-date bibliography. This remarkable compendium "offers all the crucial background information on daily life in biblical times we need in order to better interpret what is happening in the Old and New Testaments. How the people at the time lived and worked, the 'little details' of their world, are authoritatively researched and gracefully offered." —Paul L. Maier. 424 pages; 150 illustrations; charts; maps; diagrams; bibliography; scriptural index; general index. RD 436. Paperback. **$10.95.** Bookstores or from **Harper & Row, Publishers, Inc. Mail Order Dept., 2350 Virginia Ave., Hagerstown, MD 21740.**

HARPER'S WORLD OF THE NEW TESTAMENT (Harper & Row, Publishers, Inc.) For: L,C,S. Slant: EP.

By Edwin Yamauchi. This informative, illustrated guide offers a detailed description of the first century and the cultural context of early Christianity. The book immerses us in the many forces that shaped the early Church: Roman politics, Eastern mystery religions, Greek philosophy, Gnosticism, and Jewish religion. Yamauchi provides us with an unparalleled understanding of the world of the conquerors and priests, architects and scholars, warriors and merchants who formed the background for—and were sometimes directly affected by—the coming of Jesus and the establishment of Christianity. Maps, illustrations, and striking color and black-and-white photographs further illuminate the New Testament world. The book sheds light on the Gospels and Epistles, while providing a remarkably clear glimpse into the first century. This book forcefully demonstrates that the events of the New Testament took place in a real world, at an actual time in history, and in places that can be seen, photographed, and appreciated today. 128 pages; 100 color and black-and-white photographs; 20 maps; 23 line drawings. RD 349. Paperback. **$9.95.** Bookstores or from **Harper & Row, Publishers, Inc. Mail Order Dept., 2350 Virginia Ave., Hagerstown, MD 21740.**

THE HEART OF HEBREW HISTORY (Broadman Press) For: L,S. Slant: MP.

By H.I. Hester. In its fortieth printing, this is a practical and comprehensive textbook for Old Testament studies. It presents the leading facts in history of the Hebrew people and contains maps and the latest updated biblical archaeological discoveries. See the companion book, **The Heart of the New Testament. $10.95.** Bookstores.

THE HOLMAN BIBLE ATLAS (Holman Bible Publishers) For: L,C,S. Slant: EP.

Here is a single-volume Bible atlas so expansive and so complete that it is comparable only to the most expensive multi-volume works. It includes 88 full-color maps and illustrations plus extensive indexes to the maps, sites, illustrations, and Scripture. For example, the "Land and People" section is a summary of the major geographical areas, the history, geology, topography, climate, vegetation, animals, minerals, and people who helped to develop this land. Illustrations of the actual sites mentioned in the article are included. Softcover. **$6.95.** Bookstores.

HOLMAN CONCISE BIBLE ATLAS (Holman Bible Publishers) For: L,C,S. Slant: EP.

Church school teacher and lay Bible student will appreciate this handy go-anywhere atlas with its complete range of 33 full-color maps. Five study areas include The Ancient Near East, The Old Testament, The Hellenistic World, The New Testament, and Key Maps (Palestine in Old and New Testament times and the Holy Land Today). Also contains a chronological table and an index of maps. Size 6 7/16 x 9 3/8 inches, 48 pages. Softcover. **$3.50.** Bookstores.

ILLUSTRATED BIBLE DICTIONARY (Baker Book House) For: L,C. Slant: EP.

By M.G. Easton. This convenient Bible dictionary makes such subjects as doctrine, history, biography and archaeology readily understandable to the layman and student. **$12.95.** Bookstores or from **Baker Book House, P.O. Box 6287, Grand Rapids, MI 49506.**

ILLUSTRATED BIBLE DICTIONARY (Harvest House Publishers) For: L,C,S. Slant: EP,P,I,M.

This convenient Bible dictionary makes a wide range of biblical subjects readily understandable to the layman and student. The easy-to-read text is enhanced by more than 400 photos, drawings, and maps, and is supplemented by an excellent appendix which charts Old and New Testament history. A volume that will make any Bible study a fascinating journey. Paper, No. 3841. **$12.95.** Bookstores or from **Harvest House Publishers, 1075 Arrowsmith, Eugene, OR 97402.**

BIBLE DICTIONARIES, ENCYCLOPEDIAS, HANDBOOKS, AND ATLASES

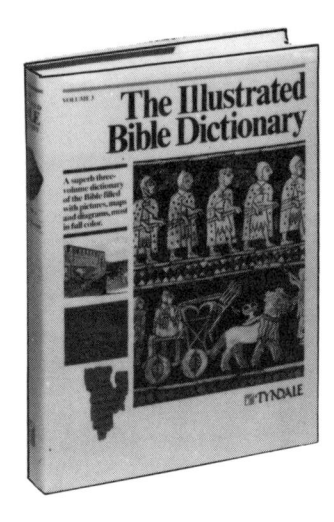

THE ILLUSTRATED BIBLE DICTIONARY (Tyndale House Publishers) For: L,C,S,Y. Slant: AW,C,RC,F,EP, MP,LP,P,CP.

An authoritative, up-to-date dictionary of biblical information for teachers, pastors, Sunday school leaders, group leaders, students, parents, and even children. Features 1¼ million words of reliable information; 2,150 entries with subjects ranging from notes on place names to comprehensive articles on the books of the Bible, from studies of words to studies of doctrines. It contains nearly 1,800 carefully researched photographs, full color relief maps, charts, diagrams, with helpful background information on the history, geography, customs, and culture of Bible people. A three-volume, up-to-date, illustrated edition of the classic single-volume **New Bible Dictionary**. Cloth. **$99.95**. Bookstores.

INDEX TO BROWN, DRIVER, AND BRIGGS HEBREW LEXICON (Einspahr) (Moody Press) For: C. Slant: EP,P,S.

A sequential listing of every significant Hebrew word in the Old Testament that will save hours of searching through the BDB. **$23.95**. Bookstores or from **Moody Bookworld, 2101 W. Howard St., Chicago, IL 60645**.

THE INTERNATIONAL CRITICAL COMMENTARY (T & T Clark of Edinburgh, Scotland, distributed in the U.S. by The Seabury Press) For: C,S. Slant: P,S.

"The most important British commentary series on the Bible." **Currents**. "...that landmark in English-speaking biblical erudition, **The International Critical Commentary...**"—The Catholic Biblical Quarterly. "The ICC still remains an indispensable tool for the contemporary theological student or pastor"—**Christianity Today**. "For almost a century T & T Clark's **International Critical Commentary** has stood supreme among English language commentaries on the Bible."—**The Clergy Review**. The **International Critical Commentary** is now being extended and renewed. Under the editorship of Professor J.A. Emerton of Cambridge and Professor C.E.B. Cranfield of Durham it is intended to produce commentaries on books of the Bible which have never appeared in the **ICC** and to replace some of the older volumes. The first of the contributions to the commentaries on the Old Testament is a volume by Professor William McKane on Jeremiah 1-25, to be published early next year. Jeremiah XXV. **$46.95**. Romans Vol. 1 and Romans Vol. 2. **$28.95** per volume. Genesis; Numbers; Judges; Kings I and II; Chronicles I and II; Job; Proverbs; Ezekiel; Daniel; Micah, Zephaniah, Nahum, Habakkuk, Obadiah, and Joel (one volume); Haggai, Zechariah, Malachi, and Jonah (one volume); Isaiah, Vol. I; St. Luke; Romans; I Corinthians; II Corinthians; Galatians. **$22.25** per volume. Psalms Vol. 1; Psalms Vol. 2; St. John Vol. I; St. John Vol. II; Revelation Vol. 1; Revelation Vol. II. **$20.95** per volume. Deuteronomy; Samuel I and II (one volume); Ezra and Nehemiah (one volume); Esther; Amos and Hosea (one volume); Ephesians and Colossians (one volume); The Johannine Epistles. **$19.95**. Ecclesiastes; St. Matthew; St. Mark; Philippians and Philemon; Thessalonians; Pastoral Epistles; Hebrews; St. James; St. Peter and St. Jude. **$17.50**. Bookstores or from **Seabury Service Center, Somers, CT 06071**.

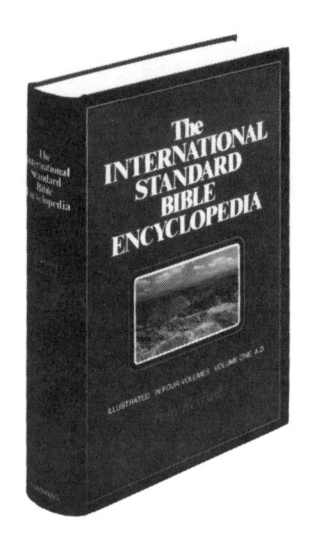

INTERNATIONAL STANDARD BIBLE ENCYCLOPEDIA (Revised) (Wm. B. Eerdmans Publishing Company) For: C,S. Slant: EP, MP, S.

Edited by G. W. Bromiley. First published in 1915, the **International Standard Bible Encyclopedia** has long been considered a standard among biblical reference works. And now, after years of careful editing and rewriting, the first revision of this classic work since 1929 is available. Combining the defining function of a dictionary with the encyclopedia's presentation of comprehensive information, the revised ISBE summarizes the state of knowledge about each of its topics and leads the reader to further sources of information and insight. "Promises to be without a doubt the best comprehensive Bible encyclopedia available." —Walter Elwell, Book Review Editor, **Christianity Today**. Volume 1 (A-D). **$32.50**. Volume 2 (E-J). **$35.00**. Bookstores or from **Eerdmans Publishing, 255 Jefferson Ave., SE, Grand Rapids, MI 49503**.

THE INTERPRETER'S DICTIONARY OF THE BIBLE (Abingdon Press) For: L,C,S,Y. Slant: AW,EP,MP,LP,P,S, BC.

The Interpreter's Dictionary of the Bible (five-volume set, including Supplementary Volume) is a complete treasury of biblical knowledge for serious students. It explains and defines every biblical person, town, region, hill, stream, plant, animal, mineral, daily household object, and doctrine. General articles on each Bible book, the Apocrypha, the Dead Sea Scrolls, and other extra canonical books are also included. The Supplementary Volume updates the original four with informa-

BIBLE DICTIONARIES, ENCYCLOPEDIAS, HANDBOOKS, AND ATLASES

tion on recent archaeological findings and contemporary Bible studies. Features include full-color photos and maps, pronunciations, and full-length articles on major subjects with bibliographies. Each volume is arranged for easy use--first and last words are listed in dictionary style at the top of each page. "The most comprehensive and authoritative Bible dictionary to appear in English in over half a century...an essential purchase for every library." **Library Journal.** Five Volume Set. **$99.50.** Supplementary Volume. **$20.00.** Bookstores or from **Abingdon Press, 201 Eighth Ave., South, P.O. Box 801, Nashville, TN 37202.**

JOSEPHUS, THE COMPLETE WORKS (Kregel Publications) For: L,C,S. Slant: S.

Complete, accurate documentation of Jewish history. Used by various individuals as a historical background of Scripture. It contains the first known reference to Jesus Christ by a secular historian. Ideal for understanding Jewish culture and thinking. Hardback. **$16.95.** Kivar. **$12.95.** Bookstores or from **Kregel Publications, P.O. Box 2607, Grand Rapids, MI 49501.**

MANNERS AND CUSTOMS OF BIBLE LANDS (Moody Press) For: L,C,S. Slant: EP,S,I,M.

By Fred Wight. Gives the Bible student a thorough background of Scripture so he can interpret and appreciate its meaning more fully. Hardback. **$10.95.** Paperback. **$4.95.** Bookstores or from **Moody Bookworld, 2101 W. Howard St., Chicago, IL 60645.**

NELSON'S BIBLE ENCYCLOPEDIA FOR THE FAMILY (Thomas Nelson Publishers) For: L,Y,Ch. Slant: P.

How did the people of Bible days live? What did they wear? How were they governed? Now the entire family can find the answers to these and other important questions about the cultures and people in the Bible. **Nelson's Bible Encyclopedia for the Family** combines careful scholarship with a clear, readable style and hundreds of full color illustrations so that it will meet the Bible study needs of the entire family. The major sections of this book are: The Story of the Bible; The Contents of the Bible; Translating the Bible; The Archaeology of the Bible; The Home; The Family; Clothes, Jewelry and Cosmetics; Geography of the Bible Lands; Plant Life; Animal Life; Government and Administration; Warfare; Travel and Communication; Business and Trade; Farming and Fishing; Sport and Leisure; Education and Training; Religion; Health and Sanitation; and The World of the Bible. Unlike most biblical reference works, **Nelson's Bible Encyclopedia for the Family** was designed to be understandable and appealing to young people. But its accuracy and format will make it an important book for all students of the Bible. Hardcover. **$19.95.** Bookstores.

NELSON'S EXPOSITORY DICTIONARY OF THE OLD TESTAMENT (Thomas Nelson Publishers) For: L,C. Slant: P,S.

This comprehensive study tool will help the student without Hebrew training trace the root and development of biblical words from the original tongue. **Nelson's Expository Dictionary of the Old Testament** describes over 500 of the most important Hebrew terms arranged by their English equivalents. It gives the root of each word, its use in various contexts, and its impact upon Old Testament theology. Drs. Unger and White have provided scholarly introductory material about the basic mechanics of the Hebrew language and a panel of outstanding evangelical scholars, including Gleason Archer and R.K. Harrison, have written the text. This essential reference work will open up a "treasure house of truth contained in the Hebrew Bible." Hardcover. **$16.95.** Bookstores.

NELSON'S NEW COMPACT ILLUS-

47

BIBLE DICTIONARIES, ENCYCLOPEDIAS, HANDBOOKS, AND ATLASES

TRATED BIBLE DICTIONARY (Thomas Nelson Publishers) For: L,Y,Ch. Slant: P.

Descriptions of biblical places, names, events, and books of the Bible. Convenient size is practical for students and pastors. Well illustrated. Leatherflex. **$1.95**. Bookstores.

THE NEW BIBLE DICTIONARY, Second Edition (Tyndale House Publishers) For: L,C,S. Slant: AW,C,RC,F,EP,MP, LP,P,CP.

Edited by J.D. Douglas. First published twenty years ago, has now been completely revised and updated. **The New Bible Dictionary**, Second Edition, features: over 2,000 complete, concise, readable entries totaling over 1,340 pages; entries on all the books, people, and major doctrines of the Bible and studies of key Bible words; background information on the history, geography, customs, and cultures of Israel and her Near Eastern neighbors; new evidence resulting from recent advances in biblical research, particularly in the field of archaeology. Durable cloth binding with attractive four-color dust jacket. 1,344 pages. Cloth. **$24.95**. Bookstores.

NEW COMBINED BIBLE DICTIONARY AND CONCORDANCE (Baker Book House) For: L. Slant: P.

More than ten thousand entries, all in convenient alphabetical order. **$3.95**. Bookstores or from **Baker Book House, P.O. Box 6287, Grand Rapids, MI 49506**.

THE NEW COMPACT BIBLE DICTIONARY (Zondervan Publishing House) For: L,C,S. Slant: EP.

Edited by T. Alton Bryant. Concise definitions of people, places, objects and events in the Bible, providing a reference tool for lay readers, students, teachers and ministers. Cloth. **$8.95**. Mass market paper. **$4.95**. Bookstores or from **Zondervan Retail Marketing Service, 1420 Robinson Road, SE, Grand Rapids, MI 49506**.

THE NEW INTERNATIONAL DICTIONARY OF BIBLICAL ARCHAEOLOGY (Zondervan Publishing House) For: L,C,S. Slant: EP.

Edited by E.M. Blaiklock and R.K. Harrison. Fascinating presentations of archaeological findings in various parts of the Middle East. Copious black-and-white photographs. An eight-page section of color photographs. Chronological chart. Maps. **$24.95**. Bookstores or from **Zondervan Retail Marketing Service, 1420 Robinson Road, SE, Grand Rapids, MI 49506**.

OLD TESTAMENT WORD STUDIES (Kregel Publications) For: L,C,S. Slant: P,S.

A valuable tool for those who do not know Hebrew, but want to know the meaning of Old Testament words. Wilson gives the precise meaning of Hebrew words in the Bible. It clarifies Scripture and fully discusses the Hebrew language. Various meanings, constructions, and references are discussed. **$16.95**. Bookstores or from **Kregel Publications, P.O. Box 2607, Grand Rapids, MI 49501**.

PRONOUNCING BIBLE NAMES (Holman Bible Publishers) For: L,C,S. Slant: EP.

By W. Murray Severance. All the proper names in the Bible are here marked for pronunciation with a system of diacritical marks together with a phonetic respelling. Includes proper names as they appear in five translations: King James Version, New American Standard, Revised Standard Version, New International Version, and TEV (Good News Bible). A valuable resource for ministers; church school teachers; college, Bible school and seminary students and faculty; anyone who speaks publicly or needs help in pronouncing Bible proper names. Hardcover. **$5.95**. Bookstores.

SMITH'S BIBLE DICTIONARY (Holman Bible Publishers) For: L,C,S. Slant: EP.

This is the acknowledged and best-known standard Bible reference work. It is a one-volume reference to answer questions about people, places, customs, history, geography, and textual content of the Bible. It also features a complete analytical and comparative concordance to the Old and New Testaments and 4,000 questions and answers on the Bible, history of the books of the Bible, chronological index, and missionary journeys of Paul. Paper. **$6.95**. Cloth. **$9.95**. Bookstores.

SMITH'S BIBLE DICTIONARY (Thomas Nelson Publishers) For: L,C. Slant: D,P.

A new revision of the classic Bible dictionary. Completely revised and updated, William Smith's monumental

BIBLE DICTIONARIES, ENCYCLOPEDIAS, HANDBOOKS, AND ATLASES

volume has been made even more useful and understandable. For Sunday school teachers, Bible students, and preachers, **Smith's Bible Dictionary** is one of the most valuable Bible reference books available. It includes articles on Bible antiquities, chronological tables, geography, natural history, a harmony of the Gospels, over 400 illustrations, and 18 full color maps. Hardcover. **$8.95.** Paperback. **$5.95.** Bookstores.

SMITH'S BIBLE DICTIONARY (Zondervan Publishing House) For: L,C,S. Slant: EP.

By William Smith, revised by F.N. and M.A. Peloubet. Compendium of Bible subjects, with more than 400 illustrations that set the tone for later reference works. Includes section of 5,500 questions and answers of Bible information. **$9.95.** Bookstores or from **Zondervan Retail Marketing Service, 1420 Robinson Road, SE, Grand Rapids, MI 49506.**

SMITH'S DICTIONARY OF THE BIBLE (Baker Book House) For: C. Slant: EP.

By William Smith. No Bible dictionary today rivals the prodigious efforts of this unabridged, four-volume edition. **$95.00.** Bookstores or from **Baker Book House, P.O. Box 6287, Grand Rapids, MI 49506.**

STANDARD BIBLE ATLAS (Standard Publishing) For: L. Slant: P.

Survey of Bible history, Holy Land photographs, 17 full-color maps. 32 pages. 6 x 9¼ inches. Code 3169. **$3.50.** Bookstores or from **Standard Publishing, 8121 Hamilton Ave., Cincinnati, OH 45231.**

A STUDENT'S DICTIONARY FOR BIBLICAL AND THEOLOGICAL STUDIES (Zondervan Publishing House) For: L,C,S. Slant: EP.

By Bruce Corley and F.B. Huey, Jr. Nearly 1,300 entries ranging from grammatical terms to theological jargon. Succinct, cross references. Covers entire field of Old and New Testament studies. Helpful to students of theology. **$6.95.** Bookstores or from **Zondervan Retail Marketing Service, 1420 Robinson Road, SE, Grand Rapids, MI 49506.**

THAYER'S GREEK-ENGLISH LEXICON OF THE NEW TESTAMENT (Mott Media) For: L,C,S. Slant: S.

A classic for nearly a century. Wilbur M. Smith called Thayer's "the one indispensable book for the study of the words of the Greek text in the New Testament." Includes words peculiar to the New Testament and to each New Testament writer. This edition is part of the **Mott Bible Reference Library.** Bound in Lexitone, stamped in gold. **$22.95.** Bookstores or from **Mott Media, 1000 E. Huron St., Milford, MI 48042.**

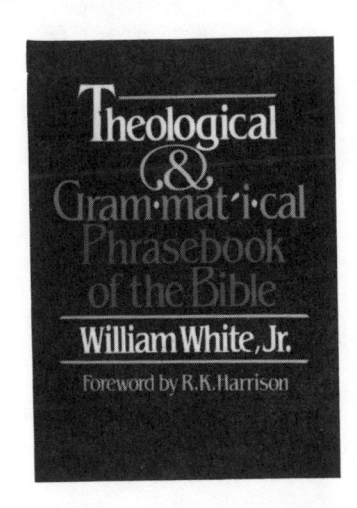

THEOLOGICAL AND GRAMMATICAL PHRASEBOOK OF THE BIBLE (Moody Press) For: L,C,S. Slant: EP,S.

By William White, Jr. Unique reference work that explores the phrases found in the Bible—phrases important to your understanding of theology, doctrine, and biblical meaning. More than one hundred phrases from the Old and New Testaments are examined for linguistical composition, historical significance, and importance today. All Hebrew and Greek is transliterated. **$11.95.** Bookstores or from **Moody Bookworld, 2101 W. Howard St., Chicago, IL 60645.**

THEOLOGICAL WORDBOOK OF THE OLD TESTAMENT (2 Volumes) (Moody Press) For: C,S. Slant: EP,S,I,M.

Extensive discussion of every Hebrew word of theological significance in the Old Testament. Keyed to **Strong's Concordance.** **$39.95.** Bookstores or from **Moody Bookworld, 2101 W. Howard St., Chicago, IL 60645.**

THEOLOGY OF THE NEW TESTAMENT (The Liturgical Press) For: L,C. Slant: RC,S.

This four-volume set studies the theology of the New Testament through an examination of the more weighty words, concepts, and themes that emerge. The Old Testament roots for each study are traced and unravel and reveal new heights and depths in the meaning of the New Testament. Volume 1 presents the theme of Creation and views of the world as the prime product of God's creative act. Other aspects of time and history flow from this and are treated in Volume 2, SALVATION HISTORY—REVELATION where Jesus' miracles, passion, atonement, resurrection and exaltation are examined. Volume 3, Morality, deals with the theme through the instruction and challenge of Jesus, sin and grace, reward and punishment. Volume 4 closes with the motif of the RULE OF GOD: CHURCH—ESCHATOLOGY where special communities—Pharisees, Qumran, Jesus' disciples, the Church—and final things are covered. Cloth. Volume I, 175 pages. **$6.50.** Volume 2, 353 pages. **$9.50.** Volume 3, 374 pages. **$7.95.** Volume 4, 382 pages. **$10.00.** All four volumes. **$25.00.** Bookstores or from **The Liturgical Press, Collegeville, MN 56321.**

BIBLE DICTIONARIES, ENCYCLOPEDIAS, HANDBOOKS, AND ATLASES

A TREASURY OF BIBLICAL QUOTATIONS (Thomas Nelson Publishers) For: L,C. Slant: D,P.

This topical anthology of the best-known and most interesting scripture quotations is like a biblical version of **Bartlett's Familiar Quotations**. Over 4,300 scripture quotations for 1,200 different topics arranged alphabetically. In minutes, students and public speakers can locate what the Bible has to say about an event, a person, a doctrine, or an aspect of Christian life. Quotations are drawn from the King James Version and are arranged in the same order as their appearance in the Bible. Many topics include cross references. Hardcover. **$9.95**. Bookstores.

UNGER'S BIBLE DICTIONARY (Moody Press) For: L,C,S. Slant: EP,P,S,I,M.

By Merrill F. Unger. One of the most complete, comprehensive Bible dictionaries available to expand and illustrate Bible background and history. A must for quality Bible study. Hardback. **$22.95**. Affordable paperback. **$12.95**. Bookstores or from **Moody Bookworld, 2101 W. Howard St., Chicago, IL 60645**.

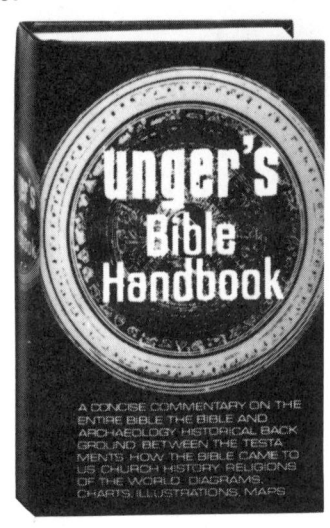

UNGER'S BIBLE HANDBOOK (Moody Press) For: L,C,S. Slant: EP,P,S,I,M.

By Merrill F. Unger. A treasury of biblical truth, a companion to Bible study, an encyclopedia of biblical information. Indispensable to teachers, students, clergy, and laymen. Hardback. **$9.95**. Paperback. **$5.95**. Bookstores or from **Moody Bookworld, 2101 W. Howard St., Chicago, IL 60645**.

UNGER'S CONCISE BIBLE DICTIONARY (Baker Book House) For: L. Slant: EP.

Conciseness and clarity mark this handy, authoritative dictionary of the Bible. **$4.95**. Bookstores or from **Baker Book House, P.O. Box 6287, Grand Rapids, MI 49506**.

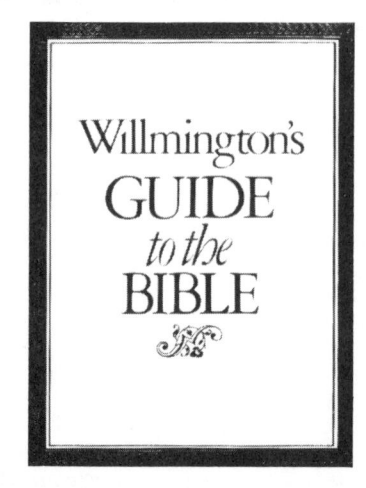

WILLMINGTON'S GUIDE TO THE BIBLE (Tyndale House Publishers, Inc.) For: L,C,S. Slant: EP.

A treasury of Bible knowledge written in layman's language so it is easy to understand. Eight Bible reference volumes in one: Bible commentary, topical dictionary, archaeological handbook, Old Testament/New Testament cross-reference guide, theological manual, illustrated Bible encyclopedia, prayer fact-finder, and history of Israel textbook. 60-8804. Cloth. **$29.95**. Bookstores or from **Christian Book Service, 336 Gundersen Drive, Carol Stream, IL 60187**.

THE WORD BIBLE HANDBOOK (Word Books) For: L,C,S. Slant: EP.

By Lawrence O. Richards. Here is just what a Bible handbook should be for today. Compact, easy-to-use, yet loaded with authoritative, current information selected with the busy Bible student in mind. Every book in the Bible receives a survey and outline. Scores of important themes are covered. Carefully illustrated, this handbook abounds with photographs, maps, and charts. The latest archaeological discoveries, historical research, and translations receive clear, balanced, and fair treatment. Most important, **The Word Bible Handbook** regards Scripture not as mere history but as "God's communication in written language," encouraging the reader to approach the Bible with excitement and expectation. Hardcover, catalog #0279-7. **$10.95**. Bookstores.

THE WORLD OF THE NEW TESTAMENT (Thomas Nelson Publishers) For: L,C,S. Slant: P,S.

This new series of easy-to-digest handbooks provides insights into the people

BIBLE DICTIONARIES, ENCYCLOPEDIAS, HANDBOOKS, AND ATLASES

and cultures of Bible times. Maps, tables, diagrams and photos pull together little-known and tantalizing facts. The latest discoveries of archaeologists, historians, and language specialists have been assembled in a colorful account of the biblical world. Meet the people who surrounded the world in which Jesus lived and delivered his message. Includes the history of the Greeks and Hellenists, Romans, Jews in New Testament times, Jesus, the Apostles, the early church and Paul. Flexibind. **$5.95.** Bookstores.

WYCLIFFE BIBLE ENCYCLOPEDIA (2 Volumes) (Moody Press) For: L,C,S. Slant: EP,S,I,M.

Includes discussion on every proper name and place in the Bible as well as on theology and Bible background. Hardback. **$49.95.** Paperback. **$24.95.** Bookstores or from **Moody Bookworld, 2101 W. Howard St., Chicago, IL 60645.**

THE ZONDERVAN PICTORIAL BIBLE ATLAS (Zondervan Publishing House) For: L,C,S. Slant: EP.

By **E.M. Blaiklock.** Describes the biblical narrative, with special emphasis on geography. The 512 pages of text are complemented by 220 pictures and more than 80 maps. Indexes include: Scripture references, persons, places, and subjects; color map index. **$19.95.** Bookstores or from **Zondervan Retail Marketing Service, 1420 Robinson Road, SE, Grand Rapids, MI 49506.**

THE WORLD OF THE OLD TESTAMENT (Thomas Nelson Publishers) For: L,C,S. Slant: P,S.

This new series of easy-to-digest handbooks provides insights into the people and cultures of Bible times. Maps, tables, diagrams, and photos pull together little-known and tantalizing facts. The latest discoveries of archaeologists, historians and language specialists have been assembled in a colorful account of the biblical world. The people and kingdoms of the ancient world provide the stage upon which the grand drama of Bible history has been enacted. Includes pagan religions, cultures of the Egyptians, Babylonians, Assyrians, Persians, and Cannaanites, as well as other historical data. Flexibind. **$5.95.** Bookstores.

WYCLIFFE HISTORICAL GEOGRAPHY OF BIBLE LANDS (Moody Press) For: L,C,S. Slant: EP,S,I,M.

Examines and evaluates available biblical, historical, and archaeological evidence about ten Bible lands. An invaluable aid to Bible study as it provides needed historical and geographical background for serious study. **$19.95.** Bookstores or from **Moody Bookworld, 2101 W. Howard St., Chicago, IL 60645.**

THE ZONDERVAN PICTORIAL BIBLE DICTIONARY (Zondervan Publishing House) For: L,C,S. Slant: EP.

Edited by **Merrill C. Tenney.** A one-volume reference work. Includes more than 5,000 entries with important monographs on biblical and theological topics. Includes more than 700 pictures and maps. **$21.95.** Bookstores or from **Zondervan Retail Marketing Service, 1420 Robinson Road, SE, Grand Rapids, MI 49506.**

BIBLE DICTIONARIES, ENCYCLOPEDIAS, HANDBOOKS, AND ATLASES

ZONDERVAN PICTORIAL ENCYCLOPEDIA OF THE BIBLE (Zondervan Publishing House) For: L,C,S. Slant: EP.

Edited by Merrill C. Tenney. An extended reference work, with 242 contributors. Includes over 1500 photographs and illustrations and nearly 300 maps. Cross-referenced bibliographies and references to significant Greek and Hebrew words. Five volumes. **$119.95.** Bookstores or from **Zondervan Retail Marketing Service, 1420 Robinson Road, SE, Grand Rapids, MI 49506.**

Vida celebrates Year of the Bible 1983 with drastically reduced prices on most Bible models.

RESOURCES

FOR THOSE REACHING OUT TO THE FASTEST GROWING SEGMENT OF THE AMERICAN POPULATION, THE "FOREIGN LANGUAGE" COMMUNITY.

Bibles, Christian Education Curriculum, Books, Tracts, Music

SPANISH □ FRENCH □ PORTUGUESE □ ITALIAN

At a bookstore near you or call (800) 327-7488

Editorial Vida
3360 N.W. 110th Street
Miami, Florida 33167

BIBLE SURVEYS AND INTRODUCTIONS

The sweep of biblical history, the great themes and doctrines of the Scripture, and the relationship of books, authors, and themes from one part of Scripture to another are the special focus of *Bible Surveys and Introductions.* And, while most biblical reference tools tend to deal with the entire Christian Bible as a single unit, Surveys and Introductions tend to deal with just the New Testament as a whole or just the Hebrew Scriptures as a whole. Generally, "surveys" are summaries of the content of Scripture and "introductions" provide analysis of the authorship, background, themes, and critical examination. However, these distinctions are rarely precise. In fact, any works which appear to be general overviews of the New Testament, the Hebrew Scriptures, or the full Christian Bible have been included in this section.

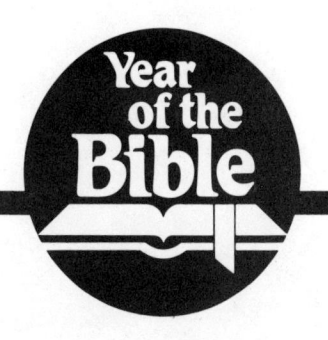

BIBLE SURVEYS AND INTRODUCTIONS

ABOUT JESUS CHRIST (Channing L. Bete Co., Inc.) For: L, Y, Ch. Slant: RC, MP.

Highlights important events in Christ's life, outlines some major teachings and tells how the foundation for Christianity was laid. This is a Scriptographic Booklet ideal for New Testament study programs. **$.39** each. Minimum order, 100 copies (titles may be mixed). Quantity discounts offered. Can be personalized on the front and back cover at buyer's request. From **Channing L. Bete Company, Inc., 200 State Road, South Deerfield, MA 01373.**

ABOUT THE APOSTLES AND PAUL (Channing L. Bete Company, Inc.) For: L,Y,Ch. Slant: RC, MP.

Presents biographical sketches of Paul and each of the Apostles. Explains, through the use of Scriptography, how 13 ordinary men helped shape Christianity. **$.39** each. Minimum order of 100 copies is required (titles may be mixed). Quantity discounts offered. Booklets can be personalized on the front and back covers at the buyer's request. From **Channing L. Bete Company, Inc., 200 State Road, South Deerfield, MA 01373.**

APOSTLE TO THE NATIONS (The Life and Letters of St. Paul) (Daughters of St. Paul) For: L,C,S. Slant: RC, EP, MP, S.

The historical background of the letters as well as reference to the cultural milieu - Greek, Roman, and Jewish - are shown as vital for understanding the heart of Paul's message. Major Pauline themes such as the justification of sinful man, the second coming, the theology of the cross and the supremacy of Christ are discussed and explored. A scholarly work, yet written in a style that can be absorbed by the general reader. The glossary and discussion questions at the end of each chapter make it possible for the book to also be used as a college text. Cloth. **$15.00.** Paper. **$14.00.** (Add .75 for mail orders). Bookstores or from **Daughters of St. Paul, 50 St. Paul's Ave., Jamaica Plain, Boston, MA 02130.**

ARCHAEOLOGICAL BACKGROUNDS TO BIBLE PEOPLE (Baker Book House) For: C. Slant: EP.

By Jack P. Lewis. Presents archaeological investigations directly related to specific Bible characters and cultures. **$4.95.** Bookstores or from **Baker Book House, P.O. Box 6287, Grand Rapids, MI 49506.**

BASIC BIBLE SURVEY (Standard Publishing) For: L,Y. Slant: EP,P.

This enjoyable, easy to read book will help many persons gain a better basic knowledge of God's Word, especially those who are discouraged by more formal Bible surveys. It is comprehensive in that it provides a look into all 66 Bible books. For each book there is a hidden word puzzle and memory verses to help the reader learn key Scripture truths in an especially pleasant way. Also included are a number of useful user helps. Code 3210. **$2.95.** Bookstores or from **Standard Publishing, 8121 Hamilton Ave., Cincinnati, OH 45231.**

BASIC INTRODUCTION TO THE NEW TESTAMENT (Wm. B. Eerdmans Publishing Co.) For: L,C,S. Slant: EP,P.

By John R.W. Stott. A clear and concise introduction to the New Testament which provides a precise examination of the distinctive contribution of each writer and in the case of the apostolic writers, to introduce the men as well as to expound their message. **$2.95.** Bookstores or from **Eerdmans Publishing Co., 255 Jefferson Ave., SE, Grand Rapids, MI 49503.**

BETWEEN THE TESTAMENTS (Baker Book House) For: L,C,S. Slant: EP.

By C.H. Pfeiffer. A good study book of the historical background of the Biblical period. Interest in this period has been quickened by the discovery of the Dead Sea Scrolls. **$4.95.** Bookstores or from **Baker Book House, P.O. Box 6287, Grand Rapids, MI 49506.**

THE BIBLE AND YOU (Channing L. Bete Co., Inc.) For: L,Y,Ch. Slant: RC MP.

An excellent introduction to the Bible written in Scriptography. Presents synopses of all books of the Bible. It tells who wrote the Bible, when and why it was written, and offers some helpful hints for getting the most out of reading the Bible. Also available in Spanish. **$.39** each. Minimum order of 100 copies is required (titles may be mixed). Quantity discounts are offered. Booklets can be personalized on the front and back covers, as space allows, at the buyers request. From **Channing L. Bete Company, Inc., 200 State Road, South Deerfield, MA 01373.**

THE BIBLE BOOK BY BOOK (Wm. B. Eerdmans Publishing Co.) For: L,C,S. Slant: F, EP, D, P.

By J. B. Tidwell. As a concise, sound guide to a first hand study of the background, messages and writers of the Bible, this book is ranked at the top by reviewers and Bible teachers. It is used as a textbook in many secondary schools, colleges and Bible classes; it is also well adapted for individual study and reference work. **$6.95.** Bookstores or from **Eerdmans Publishing Co., 255 Jefferson Ave., SE, Grand Rapids, MI 49503.**

THE BIBLE BOOK-BY-BOOK (Moody Press) For: L,S. Slant: EP,P,I,M.

By G. Coleman Luck. A survey of the Bible as a whole with a summary

BIBLE SURVEYS AND INTRODUCTIONS

of each book's context, outline and content. **$3.95.** Bookstores or from **Moody Bookworld, 2101 W. Howard, Chicago, IL 60645.**

THE BIBLE CAME TO ME (Channing L. Bete Company, Inc.) For: L,Y,Ch. Slant: RC,MP.

A Scriptographic Booklet which studies the historical development of the Bible: how the books that make up the Bible were chosen and accepted as authoritative; and covers the many versions that have appeared through the centuries. **$.39** each. Minimum order of 100 copies required (titles may be mixed). Quantity discounts offered. Booklets can be personalized on the front and back covers at the buyer's request. From **Channing L. Bete Company, Inc., 200 State Road, South Deerfield, MA 01373.**

BOOKS OF THE NEW TESTAMENT (Concordia Publishing House) For: L. Slant: EP.

By Herbert T. Mayer. This book introduces the reader to the fascinating drama of how the New Testament was written and how it continues to have meaning for us today. Contains helpful, reliable information on the author, historical background, central message and its application for each book. 133 pages, Item No. 12-2310. Paper. **$3.95.** Bookstores or from **Concordia Publishing House, 3558 S. Jefferson, St. Louis, MO 63118.**

BOOKS OF THE OLD TESTAMENT (Concordia Publishing House) For: L. Slant: EP.

By Walter W. Stuenkel. All 39 books of the Old Testament are reviewed in chronological order and placed in their proper historical context. Background material on each book and its writer is given, as well as an outline of the contents of the book. Special passages and features of all books are included. All material is presented in non-technical language. 136 pages, Item No. 12-2653. Paper. **$3.95.** Bookstores or from **Concordia Publishing House, 3558 S. Jefferson, St. Louis, MO 63118.**

BRIEF INTRODUCTION TO THE NEW TESTAMENT (Warner Press, Inc.) For: L,C,S. Slant: AW.

By Adam W. Miller. Surveys the New Testament books with emphasis on purpose and content of each. Scripture references are given, along with suggested topics for study. Although intended for group study, the book will provide interesting reading for anyone who wants greater appreciation and understanding of the New Testament. Paperback, order number D2403. **$1.50.** Bookstores or from **Warner Press, Inc. P.O. Box 2499, Anderson, IN 46018.**

DOCTRINAS BÍBLICAS (BIBLE DOCTRINES) (Vida Publishers) For: C,S. Slant: EP.

By P.C. Nelson. In Spanish, this work treats fundamental Bible truths in commentary form. Recommended for new converts and for all believers who want to grow in the knowledge of their faith. Ref. #539. **$2.75.** Bookstores.

EXPLORE THE BOOK (Zondervan Publishing House) For: L,C,S. Slant: EP.

By J. Sidlow Baxter. Six volumes condensed into one. A complete Bible survey course, designed to give a thorough and workable grounding and foundation in the Word of God. **$29.95.** Bookstores or from **Zondervan Retail Marketing Service, 1420 Robinson Road, SE, Grand Rapids, MI 49506.**

EXPLORING THE NEW TESTAMENT (Beacon Hill Press of Kansas City) For: L,S. Slant: AW,EP,H.

Edited by Ralph Earle. A survey of the New Testament. Book by book outlines and expositional material that includes dating, authorship, contents, background setting, historical influences, and so on. This is a unified study that is readable and highly usable for all laymen, as well as teachers. Cloth, 476 pages. **$9.95.** From **Beacon Hill Press of Kansas City, Box 527, Dept. B, Kansas City, MO 64141.**

BIBLE SURVEYS AND INTRODUCTIONS

EXPLORING THE OLD TESTAMENT (Beacon Hill Press of Kansas City) For: L,S. Slant: AW,EP,H.

Edited by W.T. Purkiser. This volume traces the literature and history of the Hebrew nation in an easy to follow outline form. At the end of each chapter are recommended readings, with questions for further study. Based on KJV and conservative in point of view. Used as a college text by numerous institutions. Cloth, 472 pages. **$9.95.** From **Beacon Hill Press of Kansas City, Box 527, Dept. B., Kansas City, MO 64141.**

THE EXPOSITOR'S BIBLE COMMENTARY, VOLUME 1 (Zondervan Publishing Co.) For: L,C,S. Slant: EP.

Edited by Frank E. Gaebelein. This volume contains 35 articles of an introductory nature. These articles, written by leading evangelical scholars, deal with a variety of subjects, from the authority and inspiration of the Bible to biblical theology, criticism, and chronology. **$22.95.** Bookstores or from **Zondervan Retail Marketing Service, 1420 Robinson Road, SE, Grand Rapids, MI 49506.**

FROM GOD TO US (Moody Press) For: L,S,Y. Slant: EP,P,I,M.

By Geisler and Nix. The basic facts of how we got our Bible in a simple, clear style, including discussion on inspiration, textual criticism, and translations. **$8.95.** Bookstores or from **Moody Bookworld, 2101 W. Howard, Chicago, IL 60645.**

GENERAL INTRODUCTION TO THE BIBLE (Moody Press) For: L,S. Slant: EP,S,I,M.

By Norman Geisler and William Nix. A resource book dealing with subjects like canonicity, the apocrypha, and Bible translations. Deluxe hardback. **$17.95.** Affordable paperback. **$8.95.** Bookstores or from **Moody Bookworld, 2101 W. Howard St., Chicago, IL 60645.**

GOD'S WORD A.D. (Standard Publishing) For: L. Slant: EP,P..

Similar to **God's Word B.C.**, this is a survey of the whole New Testament by a practical preacher. Designed to help the reader put Bible principles to work in everyday life. Leaders guide also available. Code 41022. **$2.50.** Leaders guide. Code 41023. **$2.95.** Bookstores or from **Standard Publishing Co., 8121 Hamilton Ave., Cincinnati, OH 45231.**

GOD'S WORD B.C. (Standard Publishing) For: L. Slant: EP,P.

In thirteen brief chapters, the author brings the reader to a new and deeper appreciation of the teachings of the Old Testament. Wade's view is one that many Bible readers never get; it's also the most comprehensive survey of the Old Testament available in such a short book. Helps place the well-known in the larger scope of ancient history. Accompanying leaders guide available. Code 41020. **$2.95.** Leaders guide, code 41021. **$2.95.** Bookstores or from **Standard Publishing, 8121 Hamilton Ave., Cincinnati, OH 45231.**

THE GREAT SUPERBOOK TRIAL (St. Croix, Inc) For: L,C,S. Slant: RC, F, EP, MP, LP, RJ, CJ, OJ, S, BC.

By Katherine Yurica. Is the history of the Jewish civilization as written in the Bible true, or is it, as many reference books imply, a fraudulent misrepresentation perpetrated by a corrupt Orwellian society? Juxtaposing the Old Testament history against popular reference book histories, the book asks and answers, which version is the fraud? This brilliant book is an exposé of a pseudo-scientific critical method; it destroys

BIBLE SURVEYS AND INTRODUCTIONS

our old nineteenth century paradigms. It provides the general reader with valid rules of criticism for judging the Bible as a literary work. This fascinating introduction to the Old Testament unfolds like a mystery story. A New York editor called it, "an important and monumental work." Another said, "It may be the most important defense of the Bible ever written." A former seminary president said, "It takes a completely fresh point of view. It grabs you. There are things in there that I didn't know. It's fascinating!" Hardcover. **$24.95**. Paperback. **$10.95**. Add **$2.00** for postage and handling. Bookstores or from **St. Croix, Inc., 14918 E. Dunton Dr., Whittier, CA 90604**.

THE GROWTH OF THE GOSPELS (The Paulist Press) For: L,C,S. Slant: RC.

By Neil J. McEleney, C.S.P. A small book designed to give the non-specialist, general public a brief explanation of the process by which the Gospels came to their present form. Separate chapters set forth the theology and characteristics of each of the Gospels. **$3.95**. Bookstores or from **The Paulist Press, 545 Island Road, Ramsey, NJ 07446**.

A GUIDE TO THE PROPHETS (John Knox Press) For: L,C.S. Slant: C, RC, EP, MP, LP, S.

By Stephen Winward. Popular account of the Old Testament prophets in chronological order. Looks at Israel's history and the lives, writings, and teachings of the prophets. Each book is introduced and outlined; authorship, date and composition are discussed briefly. Paperback. **$6.50**. Add **$1.00** for postage; Georgia and Virginia residents add sales tax. Bookstores or from **John Knox Press, 341 Ponce de Leon Ave., Atlanta, GA 30365**.

A HARMONY OF THE GOSPELS (Presbyterian and Reformed Publishing Co.) For: L,C,S. Slant: F,P,I.

The purpose of this book is to weave together the material in Matthew, Mark, Luke, and John, into one continuous account that includes everything, but does not repeat anything, and, so far as possible, to put it in chronological order giving places and dates. In instances where two or more of the writers have recorded the same event of teaching, the account that gives it most fully is printed in full, while the additional material is inserted in parentheses. It has been divided into 136 chapters, with appropriate headings. It is thus systematically arranged, and all that the four writers have to say about any particular event or teaching appears in one compact statement. Full scripture references are given, usually by means of a footnote. 130 pages. **$3.95**. Bookstores or from **Presbyterian and Reformed Publishing Co., P.O. Box 817, Phillipsburg, NJ 08865**.

HARPER'S INTRODUCTION TO THE BIBLE (Harper & Row Publishers, Inc.) For: L,C,S. Slant: EP.

By Gerald Hughes and Stephen Travis. This comprehensive, colorful, fully illustrated introduction charts the background of all the books of the Bible and sets major biblical events in their historical, cultural, and geographical context. The authors clarify images used by biblical writers to describe their beliefs and insights about God--concepts rooted in customs and a culture far removed from our own. Illustrated with maps, charts, drawings, and color and black and white photographs, this book recaptures the lifestyles and attitudes of the times, bringing us closer to an understanding of the biblical message. The excellent running commentary is accompanied by full chronological data, chapter/verse references, and expanded discussions of key ideas, personalities, and historical considerations. Incorporating the best recent scholarship and major archaeological findings, this guide brings the biblical world to life, from the pilgrimage of Abram to the journeys of St. Paul. 128 pages. Photographs throughout; maps; and line drawings. RD 350. Paperback. **$10.95**. Bookstores or from **Harper & Row, Publishers, Inc., Mail Order Department, 2350 Virginia Ave., Hagerstown, MD 21740**.

THE HERITAGE OF BIBLICAL FAITH (Bethany Press) For: L,C,S,Y. Slant: MP,P,BC.

By J. Philip Hyatt. A classic among simple introductions to the Christian canon. The writer explains and defends the critical approach to scripture but also emphasizes the faith which pervades it. This is an excellent textbook for college students and for all those wishing to know more about how the Bible came to be. **$7.95**. From **Bethany Press, P.O. Box 179, St. Louis, MO 63166**.

HERMENÉUTICA INTRODUCCÍON BÍBLICA (HERM.–INTRODUCTION TO THE BIBLE) (Vida Publishers) For: C,S. Slant: EP.

Por E. Lund y Alicia C. Luce. Se presentan en un solo volumen estas dos prestigiosas obras que llenan una sentida necesidad entre el pueblo evangélico de habla hispana. No solamente sera utílisima para el pastor, el evangelista y el obrero cristiano, sino para todo creyente amante de los estudios Biblicos. No debe faltar en su biblioteca. **$2.25**. Bookstores.

HIGHLIGHTS OF THE BIBLE: GENESIS —NEHEMIAH (Regal Books) For: L,C,S,Y. Slant: EP.

By Ray C. Stedman. Here's a bird's eye view of 16 books in the Old Testament that will give laymen an understanding of Genesis-Nehemiah in capsule form. This Bible study is unique in helping the reader to digest the vastness of the material covered. The author makes the contents easy to grasp by showing that there is but one message in the Bible, one story to learn and one Person magnified—the Lord Jesus Christ. This book is a real motivator to Bible study and whets the appetite for the next two books in this series. This is the first book in a three volume series that will provide a systematic overview of the entire Bible. This first volume traces the events, themes and people of the Old Testament. The author leads readers in understanding the significance of the centuries of preparation by which God made His people ready for the coming of Christ. The reader can survey the Old Testament record of man's preparation, trace the nature of God,

BIBLE SURVEYS AND INTRODUCTIONS

identify man's sinfulness, study God's attitude toward sin and finally understand God's plan for man's salvation. 256 pages. S333147. Paperback. $3.50. Bible Commentary for Laymen Series. Teaching materials available. Bookstores or from **Regal Books, Division of GL Publications, 2300 Knoll Drive, Ventura, CA 93003.**

HIGHLIGHTS OF THE BIBLE: NEW TESTAMENT (Regal Books) For: L,C,S,Y. Slant: EP.

By William L. Lane. In writing **Highlights of the Bible: New Testament**, William Lane sketches the life situation that accounts for the writing of each Gospel, letter or sermon. He shows the distinctive emphases of each book and, at the same time, brings a cohesiveness to the New Testament which makes for greater appreciation and comprehension on the part of the reader. **Highlights of the Bible: New Testament** begins with the Gospel of Mark as the first of the New Testament books to be written. Dr. Lane gives the comprehensive historical background of each book, disputes a few commonly held opinions and beliefs, and emphasizes the primary reason for the writing of each document. He spotlights significant events and reveals specific problems that New Testament Christians encountered every day, and he shows how the New Testament guided them, as it can us, to victorious, abundant, Spirit-filled Christianity. 160 pages. S343118. Paperback. $2.50. Bible Commentary for Laymen Series. Teaching materials available. Bookstores or from **Regal Books, Division of GL Publications, 2300 Knoll Drive, Ventura, CA 93003.**

HIGHLIGHTS OF THE BIBLE: POETS AND PROPHETS (Regal Books) For: L,C,S,Y. Slant: EP.

By Ray C. Stedman. Dr. Stedman divides this new commentary into two parts. The first discusses "the Makeup of Man" as found in the books of poetry: Job, Psalms, Proverbs, Ecclesiastes and the Song of Solomon. The second part of the commentary discusses "the Character of God" as revealed in the 17 books of the prophets. The first part of the commentary reflects both the rejoicings and the protests of man in response to life. There we find the sighs and the exaltations, the anger, contentment, tears and laughter of life written in the language which the Hebrews employed, a special kind of poetry. The second part of the commentary—the Major and Minor Prophets—records the prophetic messages of various men over the course of several centuries. Each book is built around a theme revealing an attribute or character of God. The author points out that man discovers himself only when he begins to understand the self-disclosure of God. 224 pages. S352108. Paperback. $3.50. Bible Commentry for the Laymen Series. Teaching materials available. Bookstores or from **Regal Books, Division of GL Publications, 2300 Knoll Drive, Ventura, CA 93003.**

HISTORICAL SURVEY OF THE OLD TESTAMENT (Baker Book House) For: L,S. Slant: EP.

By E.H. Merrill. Contains excellent historical background material for any student of the Bible. $7.95. Bookstores or from **Baker Book House, P.O. Box 6287, Grand Rapids, MI 49506.**

HISTORY OF ISRAEL (Baker Book House) For: L,C. Slant: EP.

By Davis and Whitcomb. From conquest to exile. This volume spans the Old Testament era of Israel's nationhood combining three previously published works: **Conquest and Crisis, The Birth of a Kingdom** and **Solomon to the Exile.** $15.95. Bookstores or from **Baker Book House, P.O. Box 6287, Grand Rapids, MI 49506.**

INTERPRETING BIBLICAL TEXTS (Abingdon Press) For: L,C,S. Slant: AW, C, RC, EP, MP, LP, P, S, BC.

Designed with both clergy and laity in mind, Abingdon's **Interpreting Biblical Texts** offers simple, solid study of modern Bible scholarship. This bestselling series demonstrates how proper orientation to the Bible and basic interpretive techniques can help you determine, as much as possible, the original meanings of specific texts and their relevance today. Written by widely recognized Bible scholars, each soft cover volume includes an introduction to the selected Bible writings; an exposition of representative texts; an annotation to the exposition that clearly explains how the author has applied historical, theological, and hermeneutical considerations to this interpretation; and a helpful "Aids to the Interpreter" section that suggests additional references. Filling an obvious gap in Christian resources, the **Interpreting Biblical Texts** series will help every individual who seeks a deeper understanding of the Bible through improved interpretative techniques. **The Gospels,** Fred B. Craddock, $6.95. **New Testament Apocalyptic,** Paul S. Minear, $6.95. **The Pentateuch,** Lloyd R. Bailey, $6.95. **The Prophets,** James M. Ward, $6.95. **Wisdom Literature and Psalms,** Roland E. Murphy, $6.95. **Deuteronomic History,** Terence E. Fretheim, $7.95. Bookstores or from **Abingdon Press, 201 Eighth Ave., South, Nashville, TN 37202.**

INTRODUCING OLD TESTAMENT BOOKS (Baker Book House) For: L,S. Slant: EP.

By S.S. Urberg. With an emphasis on their chronological relationship. Christians using this handbook will learn in a short time the chronological relationships, content, setting, and literature type of all the Old Testament Books. $5.95. Bookstores or from **Baker Book House, P.O. Box 6287, Grand Rapids, MI 49506.**

INTRODUCTION TO THE BOOKS OF THE BIBLE (Concordia Publishing House) For: L. Slant: EP.

By Christopher F. Drewes. From Genesis to Revelation the author sketches the historical setting in which the apostles and evangelists wrote their books and describes the Biblical figures' lives. The outline, purpose and contents summary of each book of the Bible is given. Also included are genealogical tables and geographical lists and maps. The origin of the Bible and the relation of the books to each other are explained. 244 pages. Paper, Item Number 12-2110. $4.95. Bookstores or from **Concordia Publishing House, 3558 South Jefferson, St. Louis, MO 63118.**

BIBLE SURVEYS AND INTRODUCTIONS

INTRODUCTION TO THE NEW TESTAMENT (Wm. B. Eerdmans Publishing Co.) For: C,S. Slant: EP,S.

By Everett F. Harrison. This eminently readable and well organized work on New Testament introduction is ideally suited to the needs of seminaries as well as colleges offering a major in Bible, and to preachers who wish to refresh themselves on past and current scholarship regarding authorship, date, audience, and purpose of each book of the New Testament. **$15.95.** Bookstores or from **Eerdmans Publishing Co., 255 Jefferson Ave., SE, Grand Rapids, MI 49503.**

INTRODUCTION TO THE NEW TESTAMENT (Three Volumes) (Moody Press) For: C. Slant: EP,S,I,M.

By Hiebert. Scholarly and comprehensive studies covering basic introductory and historical material. Three volumes. **$11.95** per volume. Bookstores or from **Moody Bookworld, 2101 W. Howard, Chicago, IL 60645.**

INTRODUCTION TO THE OLD TESTAMENT (Warner Press, Inc) For: L,C,S. Slant: AW.

By Adam W. Miller. An illuminating and provocative study of the Old Testament religion and how it shaped the basis for Christianity. The author deals with such questions as, "Who wrote these books? When? Under what circumstances? For whom? Why?" A must for every minister, teacher, and Bible student. Order number D2401. **$1.75.** Bookstores or from **Warner Press, Inc., P.O. Box 2499, Anderson, IN 46018.**

INTRODUCTION TO THE NEW TESTAMENT (Wm. B. Eerdmans Publishing Co.) For: C,S. Slant: EP,S.

By H. C. Thiessen. An up to date, critical study of the New Testament from the conservative point of view, based on classroom lectures at Dallas Seminary and at Wheaton College. **$10.95.** Bookstores or from **Eerdmans Publishing Co., 255 Jefferson Ave., SE, Grand Rapids, MI 49503.**

AN INTRODUCTION TO THE OLD TESTAMENT (Wm. B. Eerdmans Publishing Co.) For: C,S. Slant: EP,S.

By R.K. Harrison. This book will serve as a comprehensive introduction to the history of Old Testament criticism for the beginner, while the full documentation of sources in the various areas of study will prove of value for the more advanced student. 1,344 pages. **$20.95.** Bookstores or from **Eerdmans Publishing Co., 255 Jefferson Ave., SE, Grand Rapids, MI 49503.**

INTRODUCTION TO THE OLD TESTAMENT POETIC BOOKS (Moody Press) For: L,C,S. Slant: EP, S, I, M.

By C. Hassell Bullock. Covers introductory matter for the Old Testament poetic books while sharing much of the motivation and compulsion of the wisdom teachers. **$14.95.** Bookstores or from **Moody Bookworld, 2101 Howard St., Chicago, IL 60645.**

BIBLE SURVEYS AND INTRODUCTIONS

INTRODUCTIONS TO THE BOOKS OF THE NEW TESTAMENT (Daughters of St. Paul) For: L,C,S. Slant: RC, EP, MP, P.

Based on the most recent studies in Scriptural exegesis, these introductions offer information on the author, the socio-historical and cultural background of his times, his purpose, and the theme of his work. Thus the reader of the New Testament will gain a deeper spiritual insight into each of the sacred books and be induced to make frequent even daily use of God's holy word as a means of growth in supernatural wisdom and divine grace. 76 pages, #SC0080. Paper. **$1.00** (include .75 postage). Bookstores or from **Daughters of St. Paul, 50 St. Paul's Ave., Jamaica Plain, Boston, MA 02130.**

JENSEN'S SURVEY OF THE NEW TESTAMENT (Moody Press) For: L,C,S. Slant: EP,S,I,M.

By Irving L. Jensen. Leads the reader to study and personal reflection, considering the practical implications of the New Testament themes. Includes review questions, outlines, reading lists, and charts. **$18.95.** Bookstores or from **Moody Bookworld, 2101 Howard St., Chicago, IL 60645.**

INTRODUCTORY GUIDE TO THE OLD TESTAMENT (Zondervan Publishing House) For: L,C,S. Slant: EP.

By Merrill F. Unger. Intended as a "guidebook to conduct the Christian student through the labyrinth past the pitfalls of modern destructive criticism." More of a handbook than an Old Testament introduction. Bibliography and index. **$13.95.** Bookstores or from **Zondervan Retail Marketing Service, 1420 Robinson Road, SE, Grand Rapids, MI 49506.**

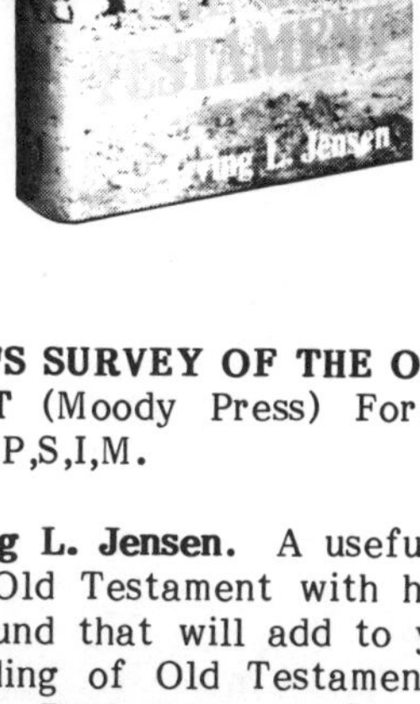

JENSEN'S SURVEY OF THE OLD TESTAMENT (Moody Press) For: L,C,S. Slant: EP,S,I,M.

By Irving L. Jensen. A useful survey of the Old Testament with historical background that will add to your understanding of Old Testament times. **$18.95.** Bookstores or from **Moody Bookworld, 2101 W. Howard St., Chicago, IL 60645.**

JESUS ACCORDING TO LUKE (The Seabury Press) For: L,C,Y. Slant: MP,P.

By William Sydnor. A presentation of Jesus' ministry as Luke understood it, providing a guide to each passage. More than three-fourths of the Gospel is reproduced in the Revised Standard Version. The results of modern scholarship are presented, but are never allowed to hide the good news. Paperback. **$7.95.** Bookstores or from **Seabury Service Center, Somers, CT 06071.**

LAYMAN'S GUIDE TO THE NEW TESTAMENT (John Knox Press) For: L,S. Slant: C, RC, F, EP, MP, LP, S, BC.

By William R. Ramsay. Features an honest, objective approach to all the books of the New Testament. Emphasizes the relationship of the Bible to history. Demonstrates the role of history in the New Testament. Designed for students, interested lay readers, and ministers. Includes maps. **$10.95.** Add 10% for shipping and handling. Georgia and Virginia residents please add appropriate sales tax. All orders shipped UPS unless otherwise indicated. Bookstores or from **John Knox Press, 341 Ponce de Leon Ave., Atlanta, GA 30365.**

A LOOK AT THE BIBLE (Here's Life Publishers) For: L,S. Slant: EP, P, S.

A fast moving, informative tour of Bible highlights. Product #950626. **$7.95.** Bookstores or from **Here's Life Publishers, P.O. Box 1576, San Bernardino, CA 92402.**

BIBLE SURVEYS AND INTRODUCTIONS

LO QUE NOS DICE LA BIBLIA (WHAT THE BIBLE IS ALL ABOUT) (Vida Publishers) Slant: EP.

By Henrietta Mears. **What the Bible is All About** in Spanish, by Henrietta Mears has sold over 1,700,000 copies world wide. It explains how the Bible was written and why. Answers and helps for meaningful Bible study. Ref. # 485. **$7.50.** Bookstores.

NEW TESTAMENT COMMENTARY (Baker Book House) For: C,S. Slant: C, EP.

By William Hendriksen. Offers the student an introduction, new translation, commentary, summary, critical notes, and bibliograpy. Eight volumes. Bookstores or from **Baker Book House, P.O. Box 6287, Grand Rapids, MI 49506.**

NEW TESTAMENT INTRODUCTION (InterVarsity Press) For: L,C,S. Slant: EP,P,S.

By Donald Guthrie. Gives the Bible student a comprehensive library of source materials for each book of the New Testament, carefully arranged to get at the heart of evidence currently available. Donald Guthrie, Ph.D., lecturer in New Testament language and literature reveals an untiring zest for research into every meaningful alternative to accurate biblical understanding. For each New Testament book he marshals all available resources answering questions such as: To whom was this document written? When was it written? From what place? For what purpose? What does this book tell us about the recipients? What can we learn from the structure and language of this book? How does this book relate to others customarily associated with it? His general bibliography lists about 600 titles, and classifies them for the New Testament books. **$24.95.** Bookstores.

THE NEW TESTAMENT, ITS BACKGROUND, GROWTH, AND CONTENT (Abingdon Press) For: L,S,Y. Slant: EP,MP.

Written in non-technical language, Dr. Metzger presents basic information concerning both the content and the historical background of the New Testament, and shows the critical processes by which scholars have sought to solve some of the chief literary problems of the Gospels. Second edition contains Appendix on the Transmission and Translation of the Bible. **$7.95.** Bookstores or from **Abingdon Press, P.O. Box 801, Nashville, TN 37202.**

NEW TESTAMENT SURVEY (Baker Book House) For: C,S. Slant: EP.

By Robert G. Gromacki. A new textbook designed to provide Christian students with a working understanding of the New Testament books. Illustrated. **$15.95.** Bookstores or from **Baker Book House, P.O. Box 6287, Grand Rapids, MI 49506.**

NEW TESTAMENT SURVEY (Wm. B. Eerdmans Publishing Company) For: C,S. Slant: EP,S.

By Merrill Tenney. This historical and analytical survey is a beautifully illustrated work that considers the literary, social, economic, political, and religious backgrounds and clearly sets forth the full import of the New Testament message. Foremost among New Testament surveys, this new volume contains four color endsheet maps, and more than 70 instructive illustrations, together with outlines, charts, appendices, indices, and extensive bibliography. **$14.95.** Bookstores or from **Eerdmans Publishing Co., 255 Jefferson Ave., SE, Grand Rapids, MI 49503.**

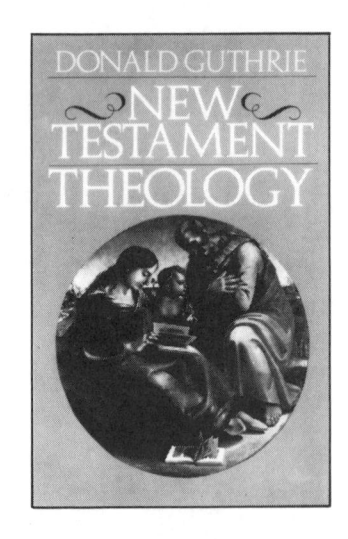

NEW TESTAMENT THEOLOGY (InterVarsity Press) For: L,C,S. Slant: EP,P,S.

By Donald Guthrie. The culmination of a life time of study, this comprehensive thematic work brings out the rich

64

variety of New Testament thought while demonstrating its inner unity. New Testament theology, Guthrie maintains, centers on Jesus Christ—his person, work and mission—and is unified by repeated emphasis on the fulfillment of Old Testament promise, community, the Spirit and the future hope. An extended introduction surveys the history, nature and method of New Testament theology and sets forth the distinctives of Guthrie's synthetic approach. In developing individual themes Guthrie examines the distinctive contributions of the synoptic Gospels, the Johannine literature, Acts, Paul, Hebrews, the remaining Epistles and Revelation. Marked by scholarly rigor and thoroughness, this volume will serve as a standard reference and text, reflecting mature conservative scholarship at its best. Cloth. **$24.95.** Bookstores.

OLD TESTAMENT SURVEY: THE MESSAGE, FORM AND BACKGROUND OF THE OLD TESTAMENT (Wm. B. Eerdmans Publishing Co.) For: C,S. Slant: EP,S.

By W.S. LaSor, D.A. Hubbard, and F.W. Bush. Understanding the Old Testament as "the indispensable foundation on which the New Testament is built," the authors examine comprehensively the nature and contents of the thirty-nine books of the Old Testament. They combine critical concern for the historical and cultural setting of the writings and their literary and linguistic character with an evangelical interpretation of the Old Testament author's purposes and meaning for both their original audience and the modern Christian. **$24.95.** Bookstores or from **Eerdmans Publishing Co., 255 Jefferson Ave., SE, Grand Rapids, MI 49503.**

THE NEW TESTAMENT WRITINGS (John Knox Press) For: L,C,S. Slant: C, RC, EP, MP, LP, S, BC.

By James M. Efird. This introduction to the New Testament is for everyone. Concise and direct, **The New Testament Writings** does not use technical language. The literature, history and critical problems of the New Testament are discussed with an emphasis on faith development. In addition to the Gospels, the Pauline Letters and John are emphasized. Paperback. **$5.95.** Georgia and Virginia residents add appropriate sales tax. Bookstores or from **John Knox Press, 341 Ponce de Leon Ave., Atlanta, GA 30365.**

THE OLD TESTAMENT WRITINGS: HISTORY, LITERATURE, INTERPRE-

BIBLE SURVEYS AND INTRODUCTIONS

TATION (John Knox Press) For: L,C,S. Slant: C, RC, EP, MP, LP, S, BC.

By James M. Efird. A simple and direct introduction to the Old Testament. The background and context of the development of the Old Testament is discussed to provide help in understanding the faith of the Bible. Paperback. **$11.95.** Add 10% for shipping and handling. Georgia and Virginia residents please add appropriate sales tax. Bookstores or from **John Knox Press, 341 Ponce de Leon Ave., Atlanta, GA 30365.**

OPENING THE OLD TESTAMENT (Christian Publications, Inc.) For: L,S. Slant: MP.

By H. Robert Cowles. In an easy to read, fast moving style, Cowles presents the rich spiritual heritage found in the first thirty-nine books of the Bible. He takes the reader on a journey through the Old Testament that makes it come alive. A leader's guide is also available. **$4.50.** Leader's Guide, **$4.25.** From **Christian Publications, Inc. 3825 Hartzdale Drive, P.O. Box 8070, Camp Hill, PA 17011.**

OUTLINE OF THE NEW TESTAMENT (Star Bible Publications) For: L,C,S. Slant: F,EP,P,S.

By Dexter Sammons. Mr. Sammons, a college Bible instructor, has given us this survey for high school, college and adult ages. 64 pages. Available three hole punched, inserted into "file folder" binder. Catalog # 85LS. **$1.75.** Bookstores or from **Star Bible Publications, Box 181220, Ft. Worth, TX 76118.**

BIBLE SURVEYS AND INTRODUCTIONS

OUTLINE OF NEW TESTAMENT SURVEY (Moody Press) For: L,S. Slant: EP,P,S,I,M.

By Walter Dunnett. Examines the authorship, date, destination, purpose, and content of each New Testament book simply and concisely. **$4.95.** Bookstores or from **Moody Bookworld, 2101 Howard, Chicago, IL 60645.**

POPULAR SURVEY OF THE OLD TESTAMENT (Baker Book House) For: L,C,S. Slant: EP.

By N.L. Geisler. Well illustrated with photos, charts, and maps, and written in an easy, informal style, this survey will be enjoyed by all Christians who want to enrich their understanding of Old Testament people and events. **$8.95.** Bookstores or from **Baker Book House, P.O. Box 6287, Grand Rapids, MI 49506.**

READING THE BIBLE WITH UNDERSTANDING: A GUIDE FOR BEGINNERS (Bethany Press) For: L,C,S,Y. Slant: MP,P.

By John D. Trefzger. This guide includes a brief introduction to every book in the Christian canon. The time and circumstances under which each part was written are explained. Helpful information about the nature of the Bible is provided. A scheme for organizing a reading program makes this a valuable tool and a handy reference. **$1.95.** From **Bethany Press, P.O. Box 179, St. Louis, MO 63166.**

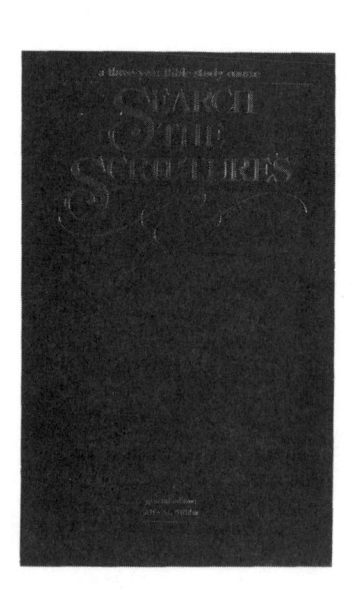

is led into the Scripture with brief notes explaining passages of particular difficulty. Introductions to each biblical book are provided, including authorship, outline, critical problems and overall message. A successful course for busy people who want to discover what God has to say through his Word. Paper. **$8.95.** Bookstores.

SURVEY OF THE BIBLE (Baker Book House) For: L,C,S. Slant: C,EP.

By William Hendriksen. Fourth Revised Edition-Illustrated. Packed with Bible information, well organized, and presented for easy study and ready reference, for individual study or ministerial use. Also includes a study manual. **$16.95.** Bookstores or from **Baker Book House, P.O. Box 6287, Grand Rapids, MI 49506.**

OUTLINE OF OLD TESTAMENT HISTORY (Moody Press) For: L,C,S. Slant: EP,S,I,M.

By Charles Pfeiffer. Background material on the entire Old Testament, with maps, charts, index, and extensive bibliography. **$5.95.** Bookstores or from **Moody Bookworld, 2101 W. Howard, Chicago, IL 60645.**

SEARCH THE SCRIPTURES (Inter-Varsity Press) For: L,S. Slant: EP,D,P.

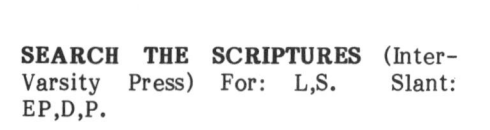

Edited by Alan M. Stibbs. A one volume study guide to the whole Bible. Through pointed questions the reader

A SURVEY OF THE NEW TESTAMENT (Zondervan Publishing House) For: L,C,S. Slant: EP.

By Robert H. Gundry. Attempts to acquaint the reader with biblical text by a continual dialogue. The dialogue takes the form of comments on and references to the Scriptural section assigned for reading. Leading questions introduce chapters and summary questions for further discussion assist in utilizing and applying the information learned. Updated and enlarged. Many new pictures and improved maps. **$16.95.** Bookstores or from **Zondervan Retail Marketing Service, 1420 Robinson Road, SE, Grand Rapids, MI 49506.**

A SURVEY OF OLD TESTAMENT INTRODUCTION (Moody Press) For: L,C,S. Slant: EP,S,I,M.

By **Gleason Archer, Jr.** An examination of various problems relating to authorship, historicity, inspiration, canonicity, textual issues, and higher criticism of the Old Testament. **$17.95.** Bookstores or from **Moody Bookworld, 2101 W. Howard, Chicago, IL 60645.**

THE SYNOPTIC GOSPELS: CONFLICT AND CONSENSUS (John Knox Press) For: L,C,S. Slant: C, RC, EP, MP, LP, S, BC.

By **Keith F. Nickle.** Explores the major faith issues that influenced these evangelists. Uses widely accepted insights from form criticism, literary criticism, tradition criticism, and redaction criticism to uncover the meaning in Gospel stories. Paperback. **$7.95.** Add **$1.00** for postage; Georgia and Virginia residents add sales tax. Bookstores or from **John Knox Press, 341 Ponce de Leon Ave., Atlanta, GA 30365.**

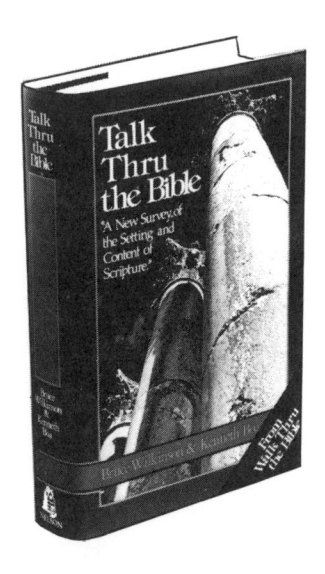

TALK THRU THE BIBLE (Thomas Nelson Publishers) For: L,C. Slant: D,P.

By **Bruce Wilkinson and Kenneth Boa.** Who came first: Hezekiah or Samuel? What is the purpose of the book of Hebrews? Why is the Song of Solomon in the Bible? How does Jude contribute to overall understanding of God's program for his people? Bruce Wilkinson and Kenneth Boa answer these questions and more in their guided tour through both Old and New Testaments. This basic book is especially helpful for pastors, students, and anyone needing a quick refresher course in the major people, events, teachings, and helps of the Bible. **Talk Thru the Bible,** adapted from the popular **Walk Thru the Bible** seminars, traces Messianic themes and presents often overlooked information in a clear, easy to follow format. Includes charts, illustrations, and extensive outlines of all books of the Bible. Hardcover. **$14.95.** Bookstores.

THE THOMPSON CHAIN-REFERENCE BIBLE SURVEY (Word Books) For: L,C,S. Slant: EP.

By **Howard A. Hanke.** The **Thompson Chain-Reference Bible Survey** comes in the same chain reference format used in the **Thompson Chain-Reference Bible** which has sold more than one million copies in the last ten years. Thousands of helps are packed in the **Survey,** from introductions to every book in the Bible to articles on worship, personalities of the Bible, the process of inspiration, the plan of redemption, and hundreds of other vital topics. Unsurpassed in versatility, this combination encyclopedia, dictionary, atlas, and study guide will serve the Bible buying public for years to come.

BIBLE SURVEYS AND INTRODUCTIONS

Hardcover, catalog number 0272-X. **$17.95.** Bookstores.

THROUGH THE BIBLE IN 55 MINUTES (Pacific Press Publishing Association) For: L. Slant: EP.

This 32-page booklet provides the historical backgound for each of the 39 books of the Old Testament and the 27 books of the New Testament, plus a brief resume of the subject matter of each book. **$1.00** each; or **$.75** if 20 or more. From **Voice of Prophecy, P.O. Box 55, Dept. YOB, Los Angeles, CA 90053.**

A TRAVÉS DE LA BIBLIA (THROUGH THE BIBLE) (Vida Publishers) For: L,C,S. Slant: EP.

A one volume commentary in Spanish, that beginning students from all walks of life will find helpful for basic Bible knowledge and inspiration. Available in two cover styles. Paper, #500. **$3.75.** Hard back #501. **$4.75.** Bookstores.

UNDERSTANDING THE BIBLE (William C. Brown Company Publishers) For: L,Y. Slant: RC.

The objective of this introductory source book is to help students explore the Bible as a work of literature and, more importantly, as God's revelation to people. Students not only develop a working knowledge of the Bible, but also a clearer understanding of what the Bible is, what it says, and what it means. School Edition: Student #1786, **$4.60**; Teacher #1787, **$3.75.** Parish Edition: Student #1659, **$3.60**; Teacher #1665, **$4.25.** Bookstores or from **Wm. C. Brown Company Publishers, 2460 Kerper Blvd., P.O. Box 539, Dubuque, IA 52001.**

BIBLE SURVEYS AND INTRODUCTIONS

UNDERSTANDING THE BOOKS OF THE NEW TESTAMENT (John Knox Press) For: L,C,S,Y. Slant: C, RC, EP, MP, LP.

Edited By Patrick H. Carmichael. Explains the message, background, and formation of the New Testament books of the Bible. Complete survey which treats each book in a brief and clear manner. Summaries and outlines throughout. Paperback. **$5.95.** Add $1.00 for postage; Georgia and Virginia residents add sales tax. Bookstores or from **John Knox Press, 341 Ponce de Leon Ave., Atlanta, GA 30365.**

UNGER'S SURVEY OF THE BIBLE (Harvest House Publishers) For: L,C,S. Slant: C,EP,P,I,M.

From the well-known author of **Unger's Bible Dictionary** and **Unger's Bible Handbook** comes this handy tool that will add meaning and interest to Bible study. This book features an easy to grasp view of the purpose and most prominent teachings of each book of the Bible. Included in this well-written survey are introductory insights about the Bible as a whole, background studies, and an intensive book by book survey. Truly a lifetime reference. No. 2985. Paper. **$10.95.** Bookstores or from **Harvest House Publishers, 1075 Arrowsmith, Eugene, OR 97402.**

WHAT THE NEW TESTAMENT IS ALL ABOUT (Regal Books) For: L,C,S,Y. Slant: EP.

By Henrietta Mears. A panorama of each New Testament book. 288 pages. 5015618. Paperback. **$3.95.** Bookstores or from **Regal Books, Division of GL Publications, 2300 Knoll Drive, Ventura, CA 93003.**

WHAT THE BIBLE IS ALL ABOUT REVISED (Regal Books) For: L,C,S,Y. Slant: EP.

By Henrietta Mears. Since it was first copyrighted in 1953, **What the Bible is All About** has become a classic for those desiring to grow in their understanding of God's Word. The book is not a commentary. Instead, it gives an overview of the whole Bible, with chapters on each book of the Old and New Testaments. This type of survey enables the reader to see the themes running through all of Scripture, to put each biblical book into perspective, and to see how each part of the Bible fits into the whole. It also underscores the main themes of the Bible, gives valuable background information, and highlights principle characters. Renowned biblical scholars, Dr. Ronald Youngblood, from Bethel Seminary West, and Dr. Merrill C. Tenney, from Wheaton College, Illinois, have updated and clarified Miss SMears' material while retaining her style. The book contains many study helps including aids for remembering content, a time line of the Old Testament, maps and daily Bible readings. New artwork and design make the book more appealing from a visual standpoint as well. Over two million copies of the book are already in print. Trade Paper. 658 pages. 5417202. **$9.95.** Bookstores or from **Regal Books, Division of GL Publications, 2300 Knoll Drive, Ventura, CA 93003.**

WHAT THE OLD TESTAMENT IS ALL ABOUT (Regal Books) For: L,C,S,Y. Slant: EP.

By Henrietta Mears. A brief, easy to understand overview that helps you grasp the sequence, major events, names and themes of the Old Testament. 192 pages. S111128. Paperback. **$2.25.** Teaching materials available. Bookstores or from **Regal Books, Division of GL Publications, 2300 Knoll Drive, Ventura, CA 93003.**

WOMEN OF THE BIBLE (Channing L. Bete Company, Inc.) For: L,Y,Ch,W. Slant: RC, MP.

Examines the roles of key women in the Old and New Testaments and shows how their lives influenced Biblical history. Included are Eve, Sarah, Ruth, Deborah and many others. Presented in Scriptography. **$.39** each. Minimum order 100 copies (titles may be mixed). Quantity discounts are offered. Booklets can be personalized on the front and back covers at the buyer's request. From **Channing L. Bete Company, Inc., 200 State Road, South Deerfield, MA 01373.**

AGAIN!

After 500 years a translation of the New Testament in the **REAL** language of the people. Bring a Reformation to your Bible reading; The *Easy-To-Read* New Testament.®

Today, Martin Luther could read it this way:

... God's way of making people right begins and ends with faith. Like the Scripture says, "The person who is right with God by faith will live forever." (Romans 1:17)

The Easy-to-Read NEW TESTAMENT

Ask For It At Your Local Bookstore.

LIFE PUBLISHERS INTERNATIONAL
3360 N.W. 110th St., Miami, Fl 33167 (800) 327-7488

BIBLE STUDY/READING GUIDES FOR INDIVIDUALS

This section is undoubtedly the most complicated and confusing of all sections in this *Directory.* Even though most of the entries in this section are specifically designed as aids to individual reading and study of the Bible—such as daily reading guides—others are "general books about the Bible" which do not fit cleanly into any of the other sections. Many of these trace specific themes in the Scripture or are commentaries on Biblical doctrines. This was a difficult section for the compilers of the *Directory* because a fine line often had to be drawn between merely "religious books" and "religious books which are aids to Bible reading and/or study." And, unquestionably, some items have been omitted and vice versa. However, even though this section is something of a "catch all" for items which are not easily classified, it may also be the most valuable section for the average reader seeking all of the richness and variety available from the study of Holy Scripture. There is also considerable overlap between this section and the one on aids to group study and the commentary sections because most individual study aids and commentaries are also valuable as group study guides.

BIBLE STUDY/READING GUIDES FOR INDIVIDUALS

ABOUT JESUS CHRIST (Channing L. Bete Co., Inc.) For: L,Y,Ch. Slant: RC,MP.

Highlights important events in Christ's life, outlines some major teachings and tells how the foundation for Christianity was laid. This is a Scriptographic Booklet ideal for New Testament study program. **$.39** each. Minimum order, 100 copies (titles may be mixed). Quantity discounts offered. Can be personalized on the front and back cover at buyer's request. From **Channing L. Bete Company, Inc., 200 State Road, South Deerfield, MA 01373**.

ABOUT THE APOSTLES AND PAUL (Channing L. Bete Company, Inc.) For: L,Y,Ch. Slant: RC, MP.

Presents biographical sketches of Paul and each of the Apostles. Explains thoroughly the use of Scriptography, how 13 ordinary men helped shape Christianity. **$.39** each. Minimum order of 100 copies is required (titles may be mixed). Quantity discounts offered. Booklets can be personalized on the front and back covers at the buyer's request. From **Channing L. Bete Company, Inc., 200 State Road, South Deerfield, MA 01373**.

ABRAHAM: TRIALS AND TRIUMPHS (Regal Books) For: L,C,S,Y. Slant: EP.

By Gene A. Getz. Welcome to an exciting story! This book introduces the reader to an unusual personality—Abraham! It looks at his strengths and weaknesses, his successes and failures—his trials and triumphs. It uncovers profound principles that will guide the reader in discovering and doing God's will. Abraham stands out as one of the greatest Old Testament examples for New Testament Christians. Abraham was also a normal human being. He made mistakes, but his direction was always "one way." His eyes were on God--and Jesus Christ. Though he lived thousands of years ago, Abraham still speaks authoritatively to every 20th century child of God. Dr. Getz makes Abraham come alive. The chapters of this book are graphic, and full of the historical and social settings of Abraham's day. Each chapter also contains "Life Response" and "Family or Group Response" sections. 160 pages. 5404509. Quality paper. **$4.95**. Bookstores or from **Regal Books, Division of GL Publications, 2300 Knoll Drive, Ventura, CA 93003**.

ACTS: AN INDUCTIVE STUDY (Moody Press) For: L,S. Slant: EP,P,I,M.

By Irving Jensen. A manual for personal, analytical study of the book of Acts. **$7.95**. Bookstores or from **Moody Bookworld, 2101 W. Howard St., Chicago, IL 60645**.

THE ACTS STORY (Gospel Publishing House) For: L,C,S. Slant: EP,P,CP.

An excellent companion to the Bible, this book provides a fascinating background for the Acts narrative and sheds light on especially difficult passages. Catalog number 02-0913. 127 pages. Paper. **$2.50**. Add 15% for postage and handling. Bookstores or from **Gospel Publishing House, 1445 Boonville Ave., Springfield, MO 65802**.

AFTER DEATH, WHAT? (Herald Press) For: L. Slant: EP.

By Gerald C. Studer. Provides a careful examination of the Scriptures revealing what God has chosen to tell us about life after death. Written for people in search of answers to questions on an existence between death and resurrection. 1976. 183 pages. Paper. 1792-1. **$1.95**. Bookstores.

AN INQUIRY INTO SOTERIOLOGY (Warner Press) For: L,C,S. Slant: AW.

Edited by John E. Hartley and R. Larry Shelton. The first book in a new series of Wesleyan theological writings. A contemporary restatement of salvation from the Old Testament through the Book of Revelation. The focus is that of John Wesley that deliverance is not only from the consequences of sin, but from sin itself. Prepared by nine leading Wesleyan scholars, the entire volume is solidly based on the Bible. It is practical in emphasis and scholarly in method. Colthback Hardbound. Number 4850. **$14.95**. Bookstores or from **Warner Press, Inc., P.O. Box 2499, Anderson, IN 46018**.

AND THEN COMES THE END (Herald Press) For: L,C,S. Slant: MP.

By David Ewert. The author believes at the heart of the Christian's hope is the expectation that Christ will return in great glory to usher in the age to come. He presents a non-technical understanding of the major themes of New Testament eschatology. A properly understood Christian hope leads to holy living and faithfulness in missions, to a spiritual alertness and committed discipleship to Jesus Christ. 1980. 216 pages. Paper. 1921-5. **$6.95**. Bookstores.

BIBLE STUDY/READING GUIDES FOR INDIVIDUALS

APPOINTMENT WITH GOD (NavPress) For: L,C,S,Y. Slant: EP,D.

This two-book set introduces a person to several approaches to the quiet time Bible discipline. The first book states, "The most important and exciting relationship you will ever experience is with Jesus Christ." This book explores this unique relationship and how it can be matured or stunted depending on our attitudes and actions. The first book also presents reasons for having a quiet time and effective methods that can be used. The second is a workbook which puts these approaches into a practical thirty-day program. **$2.95.** Bookstores or from **NavPress, P.O. Box 6000, Colorado Springs, CO 80934.**

AWAKE TO THE WORD (Bible Reading Fellowship) For: L,C,S. Slant: MP,D,P.

The **Awake to the Word** daily Bible study notes are a simple, practical way of studying the Bible. The Bible is covered every five years by just a few minutes of study each day. Awake consists of approximately 10-15 verses of Scripture to be read each day and a page of commentary. Each year begins with one of the Gospels or Acts and the rest of the year is spent in Bible themes or books of the Bible, switching back and forth between the Old Testament and the New Testament for variety. For each Sunday there is a page of devotional thoughts. Prepared by Anglican Bible scholars, the material is carefully screened through an editorial staff to insure the quality and clarity of the commentary and that the language is understandable by laypeople. There are three Awake booklets per year (Jan.-April, May-Aug. and Sept.-Dec.) From **The Bible Reading Fellowship, P.O. Box M, Winter Park, FL 32790.**

BASIC BIBLE STUDIES (Tyndale House Publishers) For: L,S. Slant: AW,C, RC,F,EP,MP,LP,P,CP.

By Francis A. Schaeffer. Introductory Bible study of Christian doctrine. Useful for individual or group study. 86 pages. Paper. **$2.95.** Bookstores.

BE CHALLENGED! (Moody Press) For: Y. Slant: EP,D,I,M.

Teenaged heroes, Joseph, Daniel, Mary, Timothy, David, and Jesus challenge today's teens to learn and apply principles that guided the Bible teens to success. **$3.95.** Bookstores or from **Moody Bookworld, 2101 W. Howard St., Chicago, IL 60645.**

BEFORE YOU MARRY (Tyndale House Publishers) For: L,S. Slant: AW,C, RC,F,EP,MP,LP,P.

By Allan Petersen with Elven and Joyce Smith. A unique Bible study book for singles and engaged couples, giving biblical insights on preparing for marriage. 96 pages. Trade paper. **$2.95.** Bookstores.

BETRAYED! (Chosen Books) For: L,C,S,Y. Slant: EP,P.

By Stan Telchin. Betrayed. That's how Stan Telchin, a successful businessman, felt when his daughter told him she believed in Jesus. Hoping to prove her wrong and save his family from a heartbreaking split, Telchin launched a personal search through the Bible. There, in the pages of history, he found crucial answers to his questions: How did a work begun by a Jew for Jews become a non-Jewish world religion? Where did the split between the Jews and Christians begin? Why do Jews reject Jesus? More than a suspenseful family story, **Betrayed!** is a fascinating historical overview. Paperback. Number 13084p. **$4.95.** Bookstores or from **Zondervan, 1415 Lake Drive, SE, Grand Rapids, MI 49506.**

THE BIBLE AND THE LITURGY (Servant Publications) For: L. Slant: RC, L.

By Jean Danielou, S.J. Presents a biblical view of the sacraments through his synthesis of the early fathers' teaching on baptism, confirmation, the Eucharist, the Lord's Day, and the feasts of the church. Provides valuable insights for all Christians who seek a deeper liturgical life and greater experience of the Lord in the sacraments. 0638. **$5.95.** Bookstores.

BIBLE CROSSWORD PUZZLES - 8 (Star Bible Publications) For: L,S,Y. Slant: F,EP,P.

These Bible crossword puzzles are often used as Bible correspondence course material, quarterly class study and personal home courses. 8 puzzles in all. Numbers 126, 517, 825, 880, 952, 965, 990, 1834. **$2.50** for 8. Bookstores or from **Star Bible Publications, Box 181220, Ft. Worth, TX 76118.**

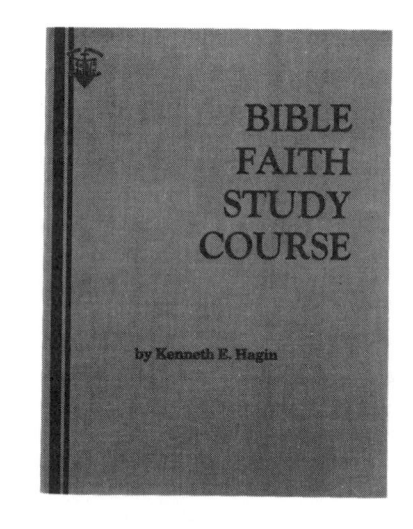

BIBLE FAITH STUDY COURSE (Kenneth Hagin Ministries) For: L,C,S,Y. Slant: P,CP.

By Kenneth E. Hagin. A 128-page concentrated study guide on the Bible subject of faith—what faith is, how it comes, and how the believer can turn his faith loose to receive all of God's promises and to live a victorious Christian life. Writing with the wisdom gleaned from almost 50 years of experience in the ministry, Kenneth E. Hagin teaches the subject with practical simplicity in lessons such as: What It Means to Believe with the Heart; Six Big Hindrances to Faith; Seven Steps to the Highest Kind of Faith; and How To Train the Human Spirit. **$5.00.** (Send payment with

BIBLE STUDY/READING GUIDES FOR INDIVIDUALS

order when ordering from the publisher). Bookstores or from **Kenneth Hagin Ministries, P.O. Box 50126, Tulsa, OK 74150.**

THE BIBLE HAS THE ANSWER (Creation-Life Publishers, Inc.) For: L,C,S,Y. Slant: F,EP,P,S,I.

By **Henry M. Morris, Ph.D. and Martin Clark, D.Ed.** Comprehensive answers to 150 of the most frequently asked questions about God and the Christian life. Both new and mature Christians will profit from answers to such questions as: How can God be three persons? What did Jesus look like? What was God doing before "the beginning?" Chances are that you'll find the answer to that question that has always troubled you. (Orientation is nondenominational, with the exception of a few questions on doctrinal issues which are pre-millenial and Baptistic). Book Number 023. **$7.95** (add **$1.00** shipping on mail orders; California residents add 6% sales tax). Bookstores or from **Creation-Life Publishers, P.O. Box 15908, San Diego, CA 92115.**

BIBLE HELPS INSERT (Star Bible Publications) For: L. Slant: F,EP,P.

This 64 page section of valuable Bible helps can be inserted in any Bible size 4" x 7" or larger. Number 1510BH. **$1.00.** Bookstores or from **Star Bible Publications, Box 181220, Ft. Worth, TX 76118.**

THE BIBLE IN FUTURE EVENTS (Zondervan Publishing House) For: L,C,S. Slant: EP,PM.

By **Leon Wood.** A compact survey to the future events of the world. Examines the rapture, the tribulation, the Antichrist, the millennium, and other topics. Holds to a pretribulation, premillennial view. Bibliography and index. **$5.95.** Bookstores or from **Zondervan Retail Marketing Service, 1420 Robinson Road, SE, Grand Rapids, MI 49506.**

BIBLE OVERVIEW CORRESPONDENCE LESSONS (Bible Questions Ministries) For: L,C,S. Slant: C,F,EP,I.

A 38-lesson outline which covers highlights from the creation to the eternal state. The lessons are designed to give a general overview of the flow of the scriptural story. First lesson Free with a SASE. Other lessons. **$2.00** each. A certificate of completion is available. From **Bible Questions, Box 736, Galesburg, IL 61401.**

BIBLE OVERVIEW JOURNAL (Institute for Biblical Literacy, Inc.) For: L,S. Slant: MP,LP,P.

A time saving kit for the serious Bible student. Makes up a 92-page loose leaf notebook for storage, retrieval, review, of biblical material. A cross reference system saving 50% study time, the kit provides easy familiarity with basic themes of each book of the Bible as setting for research findings. Easy to use—adapts to material at any level, start-up to graduate. User need never say, "I know it's in there, but I don't know where to find it!"—if any word of topic or idea is recalled. **$4.50** each, postpaid. From **Institute for Biblical Literacy, Inc., 337 S. Milledge Ave., Athens, GA 30605.**

BIBLE PATHWAY (Bible Pathway Ministries) For: L,C,S,Y,Ch.

A daily devotional guide, published monthly. It is designed to take the reader through the Bible, chapter by chapter, reading 15 minutes a day. Readers may begin anytime and finish one year later. This enjoyable Bible-reading guide is a perfect companion to carry in your Bible at all times--ideal for personal, family or group devotions. Featured are word studies, an introduction to each book of the Bible, maps and charts, a weekly memory verse, cross references to Christ in the Old and New Testaments, and important prayers in the Bible. Also included are world prayer needs and the religious status of all countries in the world as well as a book mark Bible-reading checklist. At the end of the year, the reader has an invaluable commentary of all 66 books of the Bible and receives a certificate of accomplishment from Bible Pathway Ministries. **$12.00** per year (Canadian and overseas orders add **$2.00**; pastors write for brochure on the cost for churches). From **Bible Pathway Ministries, P.O. Box 1515, Murfreesboro, TN 37133.**

THE BIBLE PRAYER BOOK (Ave Maria Press) For: L,C. Slant: RC,MP, D,P.

A collection of all the prayers, songs, hymns, canticles, psalms, and blessings of the Bible, gathered into a convenient pocket sized volume. A treasury

BIBLE STUDY/READING GUIDES FOR INDIVIDUALS

of scriptural prayer for all Christians; the praying heritage of the people of God from the Old and New Testaments. For those just beginning to pray; for those who pray daily; for those who are searching for the inexhaustible prayerbook; and for those who are looking for a prayer to suit a particular occasion. 528 pages. Paper. **$4.95**. Bookstores or from **Ave Maria Press, Notre Dame, IN 46556**.

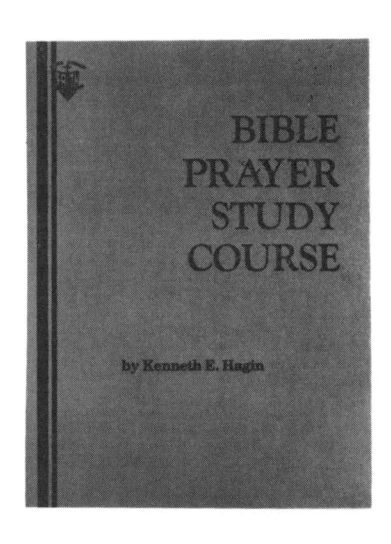

BIBLE PRAYER STUDY COURSE (Kenneth Hagin Ministries) For: L,C,S,Y. Slant: P,CP.

Since prayer is joining forces with God to carry out His will upon the earth, it is crucial that Christians know how to pray. A comprehensive study guide on the Bible subject of prayer, this course contains 24 chapters of detailed instruction, explaining the biblical rules for the different kinds of prayer, and the means by which the believer can insure that his prayers are answered. Sample chapters are: Seven Steps To Answered Prayer; Seven Most Important Things in Prayer; The Prayer of Faith; and The Will of God in Prayer. **$5.00**. Send payment with order when ordering from the publisher. Bookstores or from **Kenneth Hagin Ministries, P.O. Box 50126, Tulsa, OK 74150**.

BIBLE PROMISES FOR SUPERNATURAL LIVING (Here's Life Publishers) For: L. Slant: EP,D.

A collection of uplifting promises topically arranged for dealing with every-day problems. **Bible Promises** offers peace to the fearful, comfort to the lonely, relief to the frustrated, healing to the wounded and hope to the depressed. Number 400481. **$2.25**. Bookstores or from **Here's Life Publishers, P.O. Box 1576, San Bernardino, CA 92402**.

BIBLE PROPHECY: QUESTIONS AND ANSWERS (Herald Press) For: L,C,S,Y. Slant: EP.

By Paul Erb. Guide through the myriad of words and phrases used to discuss biblical prophecy. It raises ninety questions and provides insight and understanding regardless of one's particular prophetic persuasion. The easy-to-use Table of Contents enables the reader to look up specific questions. 1978. 216 pages. Paper. Number 1841-3. **$4.95**. Bookstores.

BIBLE SELF-STUDY GUIDES (Moody Press) For: L,S. Slant: EP,P,I,M.

By Irving Jensen. Exploring the Bible's message is easy and exciting with these complete do-it-yourself Bible study guides. Includes helpful outlines, charts, maps, diagrams, and explanations. For personal, group or classroom use. Covering every book of the Bible. **$2.95** each. Bookstores or from **Moody Bookworld, 2101 W. Howard St., Chicago, IL 60645**.

BIBLE STUDIES FOR A FIRM FOUNDATION (Maranatha Publications) For: L,S,Y. Slant: CP.

A fill-in-the-blank Bible study designed for young people to discover the foundations of their lives under the Lordship of Jesus Christ. Excellent for new believers and those just coming into the things of the Spirit; stresses total commitment to Christ and how to walk in holiness and love. Used by pastors to teach new believers' classes in churches around the nation. Includes a powerful study on deliverance from demonic oppression. Also features a study called "God's Perfect Choice" concerning a Christian alternative to the dating system. Teaching how a young person can trust God for his marriage partner and not be involved in the "lust of the eyes, lust of the flesh, and the boastful pride of life." A series on Baptism of the Holy Spirit, the gifts of the Spirit and fruits of the Spirit is also included in this thorough compendium of charismatic theology published in simple, Bible study format. Commitment to a New Testament church is emphasized with studies dealing with the Christian's place in the Body of Christ, particularly a local body, is included. There is also a study on praise and worship and the place that music has in ministering for the Lord Jesus Christ. **$5.95** per copy. Bookstores or from **Maranatha Publications, P.O. Box 1799, Gainesville, FL 32602**.

BIBLE STUDIES MAGAZINE (The Bible Study Hour) For: L. Slant: EP,D,P.

Features the in-depth verse-by-verse Bible study of Bible Study Hour teacher Dr. James Montgomery Boice. Each monthly issue features the entire month's messages. The month's study is complete within itself, yet fits into the larger ongoing study by Dr. Boice. The current study is in the book of Genesis. In addition, each summer features a shorter, interesting study such as on the minor prophets. Study questions and footnotes are added for your personal or group Bible study and are printed in an attractive journal format. The Bible Study Hour was founded by Bible teacher, Dr. Donald Grey Barnhouse, in 1949 to "help people understand God's Word better." One year subscription. **$10.00**. From **The Bible Study Hour, 1716 Spruce Street, Philadelphia, PA 19103**.

BIBLE STUDY/READING GUIDES FOR INDIVIDUALS

BIBLE WORKBOOKS (Moody Press) For: L,S,Y. Slant: EP,P,I,M.

By Catherine Walker. Designed for use as a Bible study guide. Pre-punched for inserting in two and three ring notebooks. Old Testament. **$3.95.** New Testament. **$3.95.** Bookstores or from **Moody Bookworld, 2101 W. Howard St., Chicago, IL 60645.**

THE BIBLE'S ANSWER (Faith For Today) For: L,C,S,Y. Slant: P.

A home seminar series ideal for today's busy person. Focusing on such felt-need topics as marriage, the happiness/freedom equation, God's ways of answering prayer, security, stress, and others, **The Bible's Answer** blends in a practical measure of health-filled living ideas with exploration into overweight and exercise, meatless menus, achieving perfect protein balance and so much more. If you're searching for a truly practical guide for happy, healthy Christian living—look no further. Join the nearly 25,000 folks who have learned so much from **Bible's Answer.** Free to individuals. **$1.75** per set in quantities of 10 sets of 17 lessons. From **The Bible's Answer, Box 1000, Thousand Oaks, CA 91359.**

BIBLICAL GUIDELINES FOR DISCOVERING GOD'S KINGDOM (Liguori Publications) For: L. Slant: RC,P.

This book is a guide for individuals or study groups. It traces the biblical idea of kingship and kingdom—beginning with the Old Testament and continuing in the New Testament. Each of 28 lessons is followed by an activity page for discussion and reflections—to help you welcome the idea of kingdom into your daily life. **$4.25.** Quantity discounts available. Bookstores or from **Liguori Publications, One Liguori Drive, Liguori, MO 63057.**

BIBLICAL NUMEROLOGY (Baker Book House) For: L,C,S. Slant: EP.

By John J. Davis. A basic study of the use of numbers in the Bible. **$4.50.** Bookstores or from **Baker Book House, P.O. Box 6287, Grand Rapids, MI 49506.**

BIBLICAL PREDESTINATION (Presbyterian and Reformed Publishing Co.) For: L,C,S. Slant: C,F,S,I.

By Gordon H. Clark. A study of the Bible will show that predestination is not an obscure doctrine, or one infrequently mentioned. It permeates the Bible and turns out to be very fundamental. The author explores how the doctrine of predestination is so fundamental to the message of Scripture, and documents that predestination is indeed a biblical doctrine. 159 pages. **$3.50.** Bookstores or from **Presbyterian and Reformed Publishing Co., P.O. Box 817, Phillipsburg, NJ 08865.**

BIRTH OF THE KING (Regal Books) For: Y,Ch. Slant: EP.

By Alice Schrage. In her unique "you'll want to read on" style, Alice Schrage relates the early life and ministry of Jesus in twelve captivating stores. Adventures in Jesus' life include his journey to Jerusalem at age 12, his birth (as told by his mother), his baptism by John, his temptation in the wilderness, and the calling of his disciples. Mrs. Schrage also tells stories of Jesus' miracles, how he showed love to a ruler and to a sinful woman, how he helped some fishermen, and how he provided a picnic lunch for thousands. But as the book closes...we see danger ahead! **Birth of the King** includes a map showing where the events in Jesus' life took place and a Bible dictionary section to clarify words for young readers. Illustrations also enhance its appeal. Illustrated. 128 pages. Paperback. Number 5810507. Bookstores or from **Regal Books, Division of GL Publications, 2300 Knoll Drive, Ventura, CA 93003.**

BOOK OF ACTS (Baker Book House) For: L,C. Slant: EP.

By Walter M. Dunnett. A no-nonsense study aid for individuals or groups studying Acts. Bookstores or from **Baker Book House, P.O. Box 6287, Grand Rapids, MI 49506.**

THE BOOK OF ACTS (Gospel Publishing House) For: L,C,S. Slant: EP,S,CP.

By Dr. Stanley M. Horton. A 28-chapter book suitable for ministers, Sunday school teachers, and Bible students. From the Ascension, to the Day of Pentecost, to the ministries of the apostles, and the development and persecution of the Early Church, Dr. Horton carefully explains difficult passages. Dr. Horton who is known for his exegetical scholarship, is professor in Biblical Studies at the Assemblies of God Graduate School. Catalog number 02-0317. 312 pages. Cloth. **$10.95.** Add 10% for postage and handling. Bookstores or from **Gospel Publishing House, 1445 Boonville Ave., Springfield, MO 65802.**

THE BOOK OF FIRST CORINTHIANS (Gospel Publishing House) For: L,C,S. Slant: EP,S,CP.

By Paul A. Hamar. A commentary dealing with difficult problems in the church: disunity, incestuous relationships, unconcern for weaker members, misuse of spiritual gifts, and more. Catalog number 02-0316. 192 pages. Cloth. **$6.95.** Add 15% for postage and handling. Bookstores or from **Gospel Publishing House, 1445 Boonville Ave., Springfield, MO 65802.**

THE BOOK THAT WOULD NOT GO AWAY (It Is Written Telecast) For: L. Slant: MP,P,I.

The incredible story of the Book that would not go away. Through these pages you visit the land of the Pharaohs and learn how the Royal Papyrus was made for the early preservation of the Sacred Word. You travel to Qumran near the Dead Sea where earnest Essene scribes copied the manuscripts and hid them in caves to prevent their destruction. The evangelistic zeal of John Wycliffe and the Lollards is brought to mind as you stand in the world-famous Bodleian Library in Oxford, England. These pages will help to renew your faith in the certainty of God's Word and its

BIBLE STUDY/READING GUIDES FOR INDIVIDUALS

urgent message for men and women in this troubled age. **$2.00** per copy. Three Copies. **$5.00**. From **It Is Written, Box 0, Thousand Oaks, CA 91360**.

BREAD FOR LIFE (Greek Orthodox Archdiocese) For: L,C,S,Y. Slant: G.

By Theodore Stylianopoulos. A small book dedicated to introducing the Bible to the reader as a life giving source. "I am firmly convinced," states the author in his introduction, "that whenever the Bible is prayerfully read and Christ is proclaimed, lives change." Based on reading the Bible from the Orthodox Christian tradition and the Fathers of the Church, **Bread For Life** offers the reader a spiritually rewarding experience that has proven popular with young and old alike. **$3.50**. From **Greek Orthodox Archdiocese, Department of Christian Education, 50 Goddard Ave., Brookline, MA 02146**.

THE BREAD OF LIFE: SCRIPTURE READINGS AND REFLECTIONS TO PREPARE FOR THE EUCHARIST (Servant Publications) For: L. Slant: RC, L,D.

By David E. Rosage. A series of Scripture-based meditations designed to lead Christians to a deeper prayer life and fuller experience of the Lord in the Eucharist. Each meditation centers on a Scripture reading and is developed into a reflective, prayerful essay, and concludes with suggestions for further reading. Number 0670. **$1.75**. Bookstores.

BRIEF NOTES (Bible Reading Fellowship) For: L,C,S,Y. Slant: MP,D,P.

A simple, practical method of daily Bible study especially for beginners in Bible study, but useful to anyone who wants a convenient daily discipline. **Brief Notes** consists of a printed passage of Scripture and commentary upon the passage, with one page of the booklet set aside for each day of study. Each year begins with one of the Gospels or Acts and the rest of the year is spent in Bible themes or books of the Bible, switching back and forth between Old Testament and New Testament for variety. For each Sunday there is a page of devotional thoughts. Prepared by Anglican Bible scholars, the material is carefully screened through an editorial staff to insure the quality and clarity of the commentary and to insure that the language is understandable by lay people. There are three **Brief Notes** booklets per year (Jan.-April, May-August, and September-December). Annual subscription of three mailings. **$5.00**. From **Bible Reading Fellowship, Winter Park, FL 32790**.

CARING ENOUGH TO CORRECT (Star Bible Publications) For: L,S. Slant: F, EP,P.

By Jimmy Jividen. A refined and practical study on a much neglected biblical doctrine: Church Fellowship and Discipline. This beautiful paperback is arranged in 13 lessons with questions. Suitable for adult and senior high classes. 96 pages. Number 1938. **$1.50** each. Bookstores or from **Star Bible Publications, Box 181220, Ft. Worth, TX 76118**.

CHOSEN FAMILIES OF THE BIBLE (Moody Press) For: L. Slant: EP,P,I, M.

By Ethel Herr. A Bible study guide that helps readers discover biblical principles for family living, with suggested activities to apply those principles. **$3.95**. Bookstores or from **Moody Bookworld, 2101 W. Howard St., Chicago, IL 60645**.

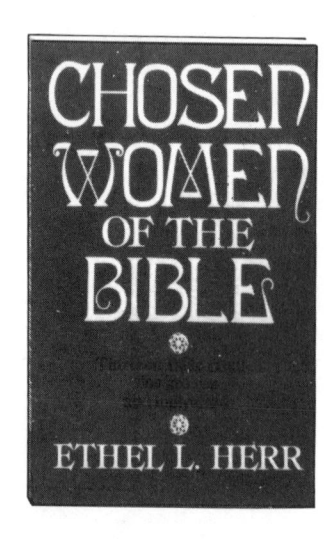

CHOSEN WOMEN OF THE BIBLE (Moody Press) For: L,W. Slant: EP,P, I,M.

By Ethel Herr. Individual Bible studies that stimulate thinking about women of the Bible and draw principles of living from their stories. **$3.95**. Bookstores or from **Moody Bookworld, 2101 W. Howard St., Chicago, IL 60645**.

CHRIST AND THE KINGDOM (Servant Publications) For: L. Slant: P.

By A.M. Hunter. When Christ told his disciples to "seek first the kingdom of God", he was inviting them to share his wholehearted dedication to the coming kingdom. A.M. Hunter looks at selected passages to help modern Christians discover new and deeper meaning in living each day fully for the kingdom of God. Number 0921. **$3.95**. Bookstores.

CHRISTIAN HISTORY MAGAZINE (Christian History Institute) For: L,C,S,Y. Slant: EP,MP.

Christian History Magazine is publishing a special commemorative issue, October, 1983, celebrating the 600th anniversary of the translation of the Bible into English by John Wycliffe. This special issue treats in-depth the history and development of the Bible in English. **$2.50**. Quantity discount available. When ordering by mail, specify "Special Bible Issue." Bookstores, film rental libraries, or from **Christian History Magazine, Box 540, Worcester, PA 19440**.

CHRIST'S CABINET (The Salvation Army) For: L,C,S,Y. Slant: AW.

By McIntyre. These individual character studies of the twelve Apostles endeavor to show something of their human side—their weaknesses, their faults, and the things in their make-up that required attention and remolding after the fashion of the Master. **$3.25**. Bookstores.

COME ALIVE! (Faith for Today) For: L,C,S,Y. Slant: P.

A practical personal seminar designed to introduce you to the basics of Christianity: answered prayer, being born again, spiritual growth, Bible reading, fellowship, and more. Nine stimulating, postpaid, Bible-centered guides for personal growth. Free to individuals. **$.75** per set in quantities of 10 complete sets. From **Come Alive, Box 1000, Thousand Oaks, CA 91359**.

BIBLE STUDY/READING GUIDES FOR INDIVIDUALS

COME RECEIVE THE LIGHT—BIBLE STUDIES PARTS 1 AND 2 (Greek Orthodox Archdiocese) For: L,C,S,Y. Slant: G.

16 Bible studies provide young people with an honest, direct approach to the basic challenges confronting all Christians. Questions, discussion topics, and liturgical prayers at the end of each lesson complete and round out each study. Part 1, **$3.25**; Part 2, **$3.50**. From **Greek Orthodox Archdiocese, Department of Religious Education, 50 Goddard Ave., Brookline, MA 02146.**

COMPASS PROGRAM (Bible Reading Fellowship) For: L,C,S. Slant: MP,D,P.

A "four point" program for Christian growth, incorporating the Awake to the Word daily Bible study program (see explanation elsewhere in the Directory) with other features. Designed to provide well-rounded spiritual nurture to the Christian disciple, the primary focus of **Compass** is toward a regimen of daily Bible study. However, the subscriber also receives in each of three mailings per year (Jan-April, May-Aug., Sept.-Dec.) a paperback book on some aspect of Christian growth, a teaching booklet (**Salt**) on a subject vital to Christian discipleship, and a resource newsletter (**Pepper**). **$12.00** per year. From **The Bible Reading Fellowship, P.O. Box M, Winter Park, FL 32790.**

THE CORINTHIAN CORRESPONDENCE (Gospel Publishing House) For: L,C,S. Slant: EP,P,CP.

Abuses of spiritual gifts, immorality, and other problems Paul dealt with in his letters to the Corinthians still plague the church today. This interpretive analysis of Corinthians confronts the problems and issues of today. Catalog number 02-0892. 125 pages. Paper. **$2.50**. Add 15% for postage and handling. Bookstores or from **Gospel Publishing House, 1445 Boonville Ave., Springfield, MO 65802.**

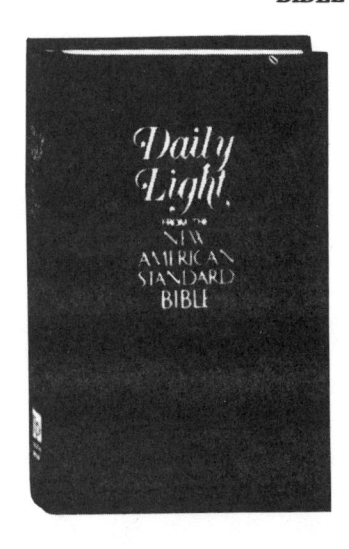

DAILY LIGHT FROM THE NASB (Moody Press) For: L,S,Y. Slant: EP, D,I.

Selected Scripture readings for each day—taken from the New American Standard Bible. **$8.95**. Bookstores or from **Moody Bookworld, 2101 W. Howard St., Chicago, IL 60645.**

DAILY MANNA (Moody Press) For: L,S. Slant: EP,D,I,M.

By William L. Banks. Scripture readings that offer a year's worth of wisdom and encouragement to enhance the time you spend with God. **$9.95**. Bookstores or from **Moody Bookworld, 2101 W. Howard St., Chicago, IL 60645.**

THE DAILY WALK (Walk Thru the Bible) For: L,C,S,Y. Slant: F,EP,MP, LP,D,P.

A monthly devotional guide that provides a delightful path through the Bible in one year. What better "habit" can a person develop than that of reading and responding to the Bible's imperatives on a daily basis. Each monthly issue of **The Daily Walk** brings the reader 40 pages of: informative introductions to each book of the Bible; overview paragraphs and helpful charts; how-to-put-it-to-work-in-your-life suggestions; weekly memory verses; and insights into related portions of Scripture. You can "grow in grace and in the knowledge of our Lord and Savior Jesus Christ" (2 Peter 3:18) each day as you develop **The Daily Walk** Bible reading habit. One year subscription. **$15.00**. Bulk quantities of 25 or more per month at **$.60** per copy per month (church order). From **Walk Thru the Bible, 61 Perimeter Pk., NE, Atlanta, GA 30341.**

DANIEL (Regal Books) For: Y, Ch. Slant: EP.

By Ethel Barrett. The "I can't believe it's true" story of a young man who had experiences beyond his wildest dreams because he obeyed God. Paperback. Illustrated. 128 pages. Number 5607906. **$1.95**. Bookstores or from **Regal Books, Division of GL Publications, 2300 Knoll Drive, Ventura, CA 93003.**

THE DANIEL STUDY GUIDE (Jimmy Swaggart Ministries) For: L,C. Slant: CP.

This 248-page study guide examines the Book of Daniel verse-by-verse with special emphasis on both the prophecies fulfilled and those that remain to be. This text features a loose-leaf format, large, easy-to-read type, wide margins for personal notes and a series of review questions at the end of each chapter. Number 06-013. **$20.00**. From **Jimmy Swaggart Ministries, P.O. Box 2550, Baton Rouge, LA 70821.**

BIBLE STUDY/READING GUIDES FOR INDIVIDUALS

DAVID (Regal Books) For: Y,Ch. Slant: EP.

By Ethel Barrett. Ethel Barrett gives children a David who is as amazed at his own accomplishments as anyone, yet who learns confidence through his very special relationship with the Lord. They will see David as a lonely young shepherd boy who is one day anointed as the future king. David learns that God is with him always and this gives him the courage to do surprising things. When he finally becomes king, David gives all the glory back to God. As described by Ethel Barrett, the great King David is a young man that all kids will be able to relate to. He gets lonesome, afraid, and sometimes envious and wistful. Each chapter is loaded with action and adventure that will keep any child reading. Paperback. 4 1/4" x 7". 128 pages. Number 5811007. **$2.50.** Bookstores or from **Regal Books, Division of GL Publications, 2300 Knoll Drive, Ventura, CA 93003.**

THE DEITY OF CHRIST (Star Bible Publications) For: L,C,S. Slant: F,EP, P,S.

By Leon Crouch. Leon Crouch, professor of Bible and Greek at Lubbock Christian College, is the author of this text for excellent study by serious students from high school level through adult. Paper. 111 pages. Number 1875. **$1.95.** Bookstores or from **Star Bible Publications, Box 181220, Ft. Worth, TX 76118.**

DEVOTION FOR EVERY DAY (Standard Publishing) For: L,C. Slant: D.

Popular 12-month daily guide to meditation for families and individuals. A page for each day presents a devotion based on scriptural passages and significant life applications, with prayer thoughts and a suggested hymn. Emphasis on making the Scriptures meaningful and practical for everyday living. Regular and large print editions. Regular, Number 3084, **$3.95.** Large print, Number 4084, **$5.95.** Bookstores or from **Standard Publishing, 8121 Hamilton Ave., Cincinnati, OH 45231.**

DEVOTIONAL DIARY (NavPress) For: L,C,S,Y. Slant: EP,D.

This workbook is a one-year plan for recording quiet time thoughts from selected passages in both testaments. Each day of the week has a space to record a "wondrous thing" found in the Bible passsage, the "wondrous thing in context" and the "wondrous thing applied to my life." This introduction includes suggestions to help a Christian develop his walk with God as he feeds on His Word. **$3.50.** Bookstores or from **NavPress, P.O. Box 6000, Colorado Springs, CO 80934.**

DEVOTIONS ON BIBLE PRAYERS (Baker Book House) For: L. Slant: D.

By Ron Hembree. Based on actual prayers within the Bible which comprise dynamic prayer models for today. An expert guide from examples of prayer into a vital practice of prayer. **$2.45.** Bookstores or from **Baker Book House, P.O. Box 6287, Grand Rapids, MI 49506.**

DISCOVERING GOD (Zondervan Publishing House) For: L,C,S. Slant: EP.

By D. Stuart Briscoe. This study is designed to encourage you to dig into the Word of God for yourself. **$1.25.** Bookstores or from **Zondervan Retail Marketing Service, 1420 Robinson Road, SE, Grand Rapids, MI 49506.**

DISCOVERING THE BIBLE, BOOK ONE (Spanish Edition Also Available) (Liguori Publications) For: L. Slant: RC,P.

This book unfolds the core message of both the Old Testament and New Testament, offering eight simple keys to help you discover the book that is centuries old, yet ever new. Helpful for the Bible beginner or the long-time Bible student. Each chapter includes: background information, Scripture references, discussion questions, and prayer service. **$3.95.** (Spanish edition, **$2.95.**) Quantity discounts available. Bookstores or from **Liguori Publications, One Liguori Drive, Liguori, MO 63057.**

DISCOVERING THE BIBLE, BOOK TWO (Spanish Edition Also Available) For: L. Slant: RC,P.

This book explores eight new themes and compares them as they appear first in the Old Testament and then in the New Testament. Each chapter includes: background information, Scripture references, discussion questions and prayer service. **$3.95.** (Spanish edition, **$2.95.**) Quantity discounts apply. Bookstores or from **Liguori Publications, One Liguori Drive, Liguori, MO 63057.**

DISCOVERY (Scripture Union) For: L,S. Slant: EP,MP,D.

Daily Bible-reading guide for the Christian who wants to know more about God's Word and who wishes to begin a daily conversation with God. **Discovery** is the Basic Series Bible Reading and Prayer Guide and is Scripture Union's most popular publication. The **Discovery** user finds that he is spiritually enriched through a discipline of daily prayer, Bible reading and meditation. And he is challenged with thoughtful study questions, cross references, prayer suggestions, and Christ-centered textual comment. Scripture readings average 11 verses daily, an appropriate length for

BIBLE STUDY/READING GUIDES FOR INDIVIDUALS

thoughtful, prayerful study. Most of the New Testament is covered twice and much of the Old Testament once in a four year reading plan. Supplemental readings of **Through the Bible in One Year** are suggested as well. Try **Discovery** for an effective and enjoyable means to a daily walk with God. Basic annual membership contribution, **$10.00**. From **Scripture Union, 1716 Spruce Street, Philadelphia, PA 19103**.

DO-IT-YOURSELF IN DEVOTIONS (Christian Outreach) For: L,S,Y,Ch. Slant: EP,P,I.

By Lyman Coleman. A practical workbook introducing inductive Bible study in the devotional life. Slanted toward young people. Foreword by Billy Graham. **$1.50**. From **Christian Outreach, 200 Asbury Drive, Wilmore, KY 40390**.

THE EARLY CHRISTIANS (Harper & Row, Publishers, Inc.) For: L,C,S. Slant: EP.

By John Drane. This richly illustrated documentary account unfolds the vibrant, illuminating story of the First Christians. Drane investigates historical and cultural contexts, conflicts following Jesus' death, the spread of the Gospel, and emerging organizational structures. He examines the growth of the church beginning with the teachings of Jesus himself and the implementation and observance of these teachings by the early church fathers. The author explores both the problems and conflicts that were prevalent following Jesus' ascension and the consequences of these conflicts in the formal spreading of the Gospel. The author enhances his insightful text with the inclusion of beautiful photographs, maps, and charts to present the initial growth of the church in a fresh and exciting way. He offers first-rate scholarship that is always accessible and appealingly presented as he sheds crucial new light on the vigorous, diverse character of the early church. 144 pages; black-and-white illustrations; bibliography; and index. Paperback. Number RD 378. **$9.95**. Bookstores or from **Harper & Row, Publishers, Inc., Mail Order Department, 2350 Virginia Avenue, Hagerstown, MD 21740**.

ELIJAH & ELISHA (Regal Books) For: Y,Ch. Slant: EP.

By Ethel Barrett. With her unique storytelling ability, Ethel Barrett will fascinate children with the exciting stories of these two invincible prophets. Paperback, illustrated, 128 pages. Number 5606802. **$1.95**. Bookstores or from **Regal Books, Division of GL Publications, 2300 Knoll Drive, Ventura, CA 93003**.

ENCOUNTER WITH GOD (Scripture Union) For: L,C. Slant: EP,MP,D.

Scripture Union's advanced Bible Reading and Prayer Guide and is designed for the knowledgeable Christian who wants to make his quiet time fresher and more dynamic. A four-step personal worship method of Prayer, Reading, Meditation, Prayer, provides the reader with a solid structure for his regular Bible reading and prayer. Scripture readings take a reader through the New Testament twice and most of the Old Testament once in five years. Inductive study questions, cross references, prayer suggestions, keynote reflections and supplemental readings encourage the reader to take an active, thoughtful part in his study. In addition, **Encounter with God** offers Christ-centered comments on Scripture, introductions to major books of the Bible and excerpts from significant Christian literature to further revitalize his study. Basic annual membership contribution, **$10.00**. From **Scripture Union, 1716 Spruce St., Philadelphia, PA 19103**.

ESTABLISHED BY THE WORD OF GOD (Christian Outreach) For: L,C,S,Y,Ch. Slant: EP,P,I.

By Robert E. Coleman. Bible lessons for new Christians. Following the question-and-answer approach, you are helped to find the truth for yourself in the Scripture, and to apply it to your life. Used around the world in 50 languages. **$1.50**. Bookstores or from **Christian Outreach, 200 Asbury Drive, Wilmore, KY 40390**.

EVIDENCE GROWTH GUIDE PART II: UNIQUENESS OF THE BIBLE (Here's Life Publishers) For: L,S. Slant: EP, P,I.

By Josh McDowell. The second in Josh McDowell's Truth Alive Series, this growth guide covers the topic of the uniqueness of the Bible. Number 402677. **$3.50**. Bookstores or from **Here's Life Publishers, P.O. Box 1576, San Bernardino, CA 92402**.

EXPLORING SERIES (Moody Press) For: L,C,S. Slant: EP,P,I,M.

By John Phillips. A Bible study series with clear, concise commentaries, parallel subjects, outlines, and capable explanations that will add new depth and meaning to your study times. Available on the books of Genesis, Hebrews, Revelation, Romans, the Bible as a whole, and the world of the ancient Jew. **$10.95–$11.95**. Bookstores or from **Moody Bookworld, 2101 W. Howard St., Chicago, IL 60645**.

A FAITH TO LIVE BY (Gospel Publishing House) For: L,C,S. Slant: EP,P,CP.

A systematic, chapter-by-chapter examination of Ephesians, illuminating God's powerful promises. An in-depth study, establishing solid principles for Christian living in the home, community, and business. Catalog number 02-0899. 125 pages. Paper. **$2.50**. Add 15% for postage and handling. Bookstores or from **Gospel Publishing House, 1445 Boonville Ave., Springfield, MO 65802**.

FAITH'S CHECKBOOK (Moody Press) For: L,C,S. Slant: EP,D,I,M.

BIBLE STUDY/READING GUIDES FOR INDIVIDUALS

By Spurgeon. 365 promises of God to be claimed every day of the year. **$3.95.** Bookstores or from **Moody Bookworld, 2101 W. Howard St., Chicago, IL 60645.**

FAMILY WALK (Walk Thru the Bible) For: L,C,S,Y,Ch. Slant: F,EP,MP,LP,D,P.

The family—the foundation unit of society—is in trouble. Bombarded on every side by secular values and conflicting voices, families struggle to cope with the growing pressures that seek to destroy them. The need for answers has never been greater. And God's Word, the Bible, has never been more relevant. **Family Walk** provides a blueprint for brief but significant family times around God's Word on a daily basis. Each monthly issue of **Family Walk** brings the reader 40 pages of: weekly themes that are biblical, practical, and timely; informative introductions to each week of reading; special feature articles by family experts, packed with proven tips for building strong families God's way. **Family Walk**—a blueprint for meaningful family devotions. Individual subscriptions. **$15.00.** Bulk quantities of 25 or more per month at **$.60** per copy per month (church order). From **Walk Thru the Bible Ministries, 61 Perimeter Park, NE, Atlanta, GA 30341.**

THE FESTIVAL REPRODUCIBLE NOTEBOOKS (American Festival of Evangelism) For: L,C,S,Y,W. Slant: F,EP,MP,LP,D,P,S,CP.

Four loose-leaf notebooks filled with approximately 200 manuscripts, giving the essence of Bible studies, and topical studies presented at the historic American Festival of Evangelism. Each manuscript is available in a special format that can be photocopied or reprinted for classroom use without infringement of copyright. The set of four books is like a library on the subjects of evangelizing, discipling, and equipping. **$79.80** per set. From **American Festival of Evangelism, P.O. Box 17093, Washington, DC 20041.**

FIGURES OF SPEECH USED IN THE BIBLE (Baker Book House) For: C,S. Slant: EP.

By E.W. Bullinger. The author regards figures of speech to be the key to the interpretation and elucidation of the Scriptures. A classic study which stands by itself. **$24.95.** Bookstores or from **Baker Book House, P.O. Box 6287, Grand Rapids, MI 49506.**

FIRSTHAND JOY (NavPress) For: L,C,S. Slant: EP,P.

By Dr. Rick Yohn. "One of the greatest experiences of life is the exciting firsthand study of the Scriptures...I am convinced that firsthand Bible study is not the privilege of a few, but the responsibility of all," says Rick Yohn, author of **Firsthand Joy.** The premise behind **Firsthand Joy** is that all Christians have the ability to grasp biblical truth on their own. This is a step-by-step guide for doing personal Bible study. **Firsthand Joy** guides the reader through the "big three" questions: "What do I see?" "What does it mean?" and "What does it mean to me?" But it is more than a guide to Bible study...it is also a workbook. The disciple actually does a study as he reads the book, thus unlocking key principles of Bible study. Dr. Yohn is pastor of the Evangelical Free Church of Fresno, California and has authored eight other books on practical Christian growth. **$3.50.** Bookstores or from **NavPress, P.O. Box 6000, Colorado Springs, CO 80934.**

FIVE WOMEN: BIBLE STUDY GUIDE (Tyndale House Publishers) For: L,S,W. Slant: AW,C,RC,F,EP,MP,LP,D,CP.

By Denise Rinker Adler. Modern women, though separated by time and circumstances from Bible women, can learn much through the defeats and victories of these Bible characters. A Tyndale Bible Study. 48 pages. **$2.50.** Bookstores.

FOCUS ON LIVING BIBLE GUIDES (Voice of Prophecy) For: L. Slant: EP.

Inspirational series of 11 full-color leaflets prepared by international Christian radiobroadcaster H.M.S. Richards. Practical answers to questions about family, peace, faith, and the future. Especially designed for beginners in Bible study, but enjoyed even by mature Christians as a fresh look at basic themes of the Christian faith. **$2.00** per set; **$1.50** if 20 or more are ordered. From **Voice of Prophecy, P.O. Box 55, Dept. YOB, Los Angeles, CA 90053.**

FOLLOW ME (Servant Publications) For: L. Slant: RC,D.

By David Roasge. If finding time to pray is a problem, **Follow Me** could be the beginning of personal renewal in anyone's prayer life. In this book David Rosage develops themes for each month that use Jesus' own words to form a daily program of scriptural prayer and reflection. Every day each month, **Follow Me** presents Jesus' words on a particular theme like holiness, being poor in spirit, or growing in love. The passages are short enough for easy memorization, and Roasge's brief but insightful comments provide food for further meditation and prayer throughout the day. The handy pocket size and simple format of **Follow Me** make it an ideal gift for the person on the go. Msgr. David E. Roasge is the founder and director of Immaculate Heart Retreat House in Spokane, Washington. His other books include **Speak Lord, Your Servant Is Listening; Listen to Him; A Lenten Pilgrimage;** and **The Bread of Life.** 3 1/4 x 5 3/8 inches. 244 pages. **$3.95.** Bookstores.

FREEDOM: A GUARANTEE FOR EVERYBODY (Gospel Publishing House) For: L,C,S. Slant: EP,P,CP.

This study of Romans examines the epistle's "freedom and truth" theme. Paul examined great doctrines such as justification by faith and offered advice on applying those doctrines to everyday living. This book examines Paul's teachings, making the Book of

BIBLE STUDY/READING GUIDES FOR INDIVIDUALS

Romans understandable and applicable. Catalog number 02-0891. 126 pages. Paper. **$2.50**. Add 15% for postage and handling. Bookstores or from **Gospel Publishing House, 1445 Boonville Ave., Springfield, MO 65802**.

FRUIT OF THE SPIRIT (InterVarsity Press) For: L,S. Slant: EP,D,P.

By Hazel Offner. Love, joy, peace, patience, kindness, goodness, faithfulness, gentleness, and self-control. Not only a description of Christ, but of our goal to be like him. To be spiritually mature is to show the fruit of the Spirit of Christ in our lives. It is, indeed, to be like Christ. Paul summarizes the fruit of the Spirit in Galatians 5:22-23, but many passages throughout the Old and New Testaments highlight them. Hazel Offner has chosen nine such passages for study by individuals or groups, all aiming to help us walk by the Spirit. Paper. **$2.50**. Bookstores.

FRUITS OF THE SPIRIT (Baker Book House) For: L. Slant: D.

By Ron Hembree. Inspirational thoughts that will change your life. A careful and prayerful study of Galatians 5:22,23. **$2.95**. Bookstores or from **Baker Book House, P.O. Box 6287, Grand Rapids, MI 49506**.

THE GARIMUS FILE (Here's Life Publishers) For: L,S. Slant: EP,D,P.

A look at persons and events behind New Testament letters. Insightful enriched with extensive footnotes for exciting follow-up study. Product Number 403113. **$7.95**. Bookstores or from **Here's Life Publishers, P.O. Box 1576, San Bernardino, CA 92402**.

GENESIS: LESSONS ABOUT GOD AND MAN (Tyndale House Publishers) For: L,S. Slant: AW,C,RC,F,EP,MP,LP,P,CP.

By T.M. Moore. The book of God's revelation to us about the universe, about Himself, about man, about sin, and redemption. For individual or group Bible studies. A Tyndale Bible Study. Number 0-8423-0993-4. 78 pages. **$2.50**. Bookstores.

GLEANINGS SERIES (Moody Press) For: L,C. Slant: EP,P,S,I,M.

By A. W. Pink. Exhaustive studies that bring out deep theological and spiritual truths from the Bible. Excellent resource books. Available on Elisha, Paul, Exodus, Genesis, Joshua, the Bible as a whole, and the Godhead. **$10.95**. Bookstores or from **Moody Bookworld, 2101 W. Howard, Chicago, IL 60645**.

GOD OF THE BIBLE (Baker Book House) For: C,S. Slant: EP.

By Robert Lightner. Though there is much talk about God in our day, there is too little study of and knowledge about the only true God—the God of Holy Scripture. Who is He? What is His plan for the world? Does He exist? These issues and others are encompassed in a way that Bible students, whether beginning or advanced, can understand. **$4.95**. Bookstores or from **Baker Book House, P.O. Box 6287, Grand Rapids, MI 49506**.

GOD'S ANSWERS TO FINANCIAL PROBLEMS (Harvest House Publishers) For: L,C,S. Slant: EP,P,I,M.

By Rick Yohn. By utilizing the realistic and practical principles for money management given in the Scriptures, we can be assured that we are acting in God's will. Here are the answers to the questions we have about money, such as, "Can a Christian enjoy money and nice things?" Rick Yohn's inductive format encourages direct Bible study. Paper. Number 1296. **$3.95**. Bookstores or from **Harvest House Publishers, 1075 Arrowsmith, Eugene, OR 97402**.

GOD'S ANSWERS TO LIFE'S PROBLEMS (Harvest House Publishers) For: L,C,S. Slant: EP,P,I,M.

By Rick Yohn. This manual allows the reader, individual or group Bible study, to see himself and his problems in the light of God's plan. Learn how to handle the pressures of being a Christian in this highly secular world. Paper. Number 0508. **$3.95**. Bookstores or from **Harvest House Publishers, 1075 Arrowsmith, Eugene, OR 97402**.

GOD'S WORD TODAY (God's Word Today) For: L,C,S. Slant: RC,D,P.

BIBLE STUDY/READING GUIDES FOR INDIVIDUALS

A monthly magazine which provides a daily Scripture reading guide for Roman Catholics, leading its readers through the books and major themes of the Bible. **God's Word Today** is published to increase both the faith and the knowledge of its readers. Its goal is to help its readers understand the words of Scripture and apply them to their lives. **God's Word Today** is intended for ordinary Catholics, not Scripture scholars. It does, however, aim at helping its readers understand the Bible and their faith in greater depth. Although published primarily for individuals, it is used by many groups as the basis of Scripture sharing. One year subscription. USA. **$10.00**. Outside USA. **$12.00**. Discounts for bulk subscriptions available. From **God's Word Today, P.O. Box 7705, Ann Arbor, MI 48107.**

GOOD WORKS IN THE NEW TESTAMENT (Bible Questions) For: L. Slant: C,F,EP,P.

A short study, geared toward salvation, of the subject of works. **$1.50**. From **Bible Questions, Box 736, Galesburg, IL 61401.**

GOSPEL AND KINGDOM: A CHRISTIAN'S GUIDE TO THE OLD TESTAMENT (Winston Press) For: L,C,S. Slant: MP.

By Graeme Goldsworthy. A highly readable, nontechnical, do-it-yourself manual that shows readers how to find Jesus Christ in the Old Testament even though it is a collection of pre-Christian writings. Helps answer the question, "Why read the Old Testament?" **$6.95**. Bookstores or from **Winston Press, 430 Oak Grove, Minneapolis, MN 55403.**

GOSPEL JOURNEY: FORTY MEDITATIONS DRAWN FROM THE LIFE OF CHRIST (Winston Press) For: L,C,S. Slant: RC,EP,MP,D.

By Ernest Ferlita. Forty open-ended meditations that follow Jesus from the river Jordan, Cana, and Jericho to familiar Jerusalem landmarks: the Temple and the Upper Room, the Mount of Olives and Golgotha. Quoting a gospel passage at each "stop," Ferlita turns the journey into a spiritual excursion and supports his comments on what Jesus said and did with contemporary references. Includes maps of the Holy Land. Paperback. **$5.95**. Bookstores or from **Winston Press, 430 Oak Grove, Minneapolis, MN 55403.**

THE GOSPEL OF JOHN (Tyndale House Publishers) For: L,S,Y. Slant: C,F,EP,MP,D.

Emphasis on the deity of Christ. Sold in packs of 25 only. Vest pocket paper. **$11.95** per pack. Bookstores.

THE GOSPEL OF THOMAS AND CHRISTIAN WISDOM (The Seabury Press) For: L,C. Slant: MP.

By Stevan L. Davies. Investigates the historical significance of the Gospel of Thomas—a set of at least 114 sayings attributed to Jesus, found buried in the Egyptian desert in 1945. Scholars now believe that the sayings found in Thomas' gospel are unique and were passed down in a line of tradition independent from that of the New Testament. This study shows that the sayings are not the product of a late and heretical Gnostic Christianity, but are derived in part from the Jewish Wisdom tradition in combination with Jewish apocalyptic ideas. Paperback. **$9.95**. Bookstores or from **Seabury Service Center, Somers, CT 06071.**

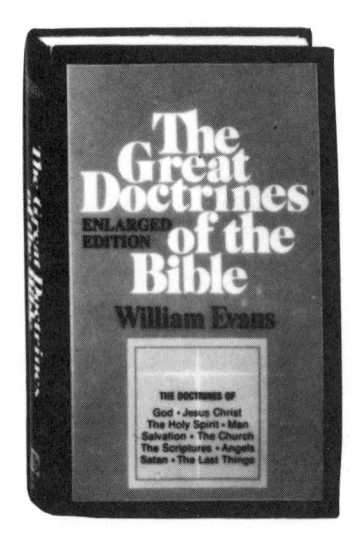

GREAT DOCTRINES OF THE BIBLE (Moody Press) For: L,S. Slant: EP,I,M.

By William Evans. Designed to supplement personal Bible study, this is a well-organized examination of ten major Bible doctrines, including eighty subjects by topical listing. **$9.95**. Bookstores or from **Moody Bookworld, 2101 W. Howard, Chicago, IL 60645.**

GREAT WOMEN OF THE BIBLE (Baker Book House) For: C. Slant: EP,MP.

By Clarence E. MaCartney. These feminine portraits from the Bible "offer the preacher to press home upon people the claims of Christ as friend and redeemer." **$5.95**. Bookstores or from **Baker Book House, P.O. Box 6287, Grand Rapids, MI 49506.**

GROWING IN THE WORD (Fleming H. Revell) For: L,C,S,Y,Ch. Slant: EP, P,I.

By Robert E. Coleman. Bible lessons for growing Christians. Includes the

BIBLE STUDY/READING GUIDES FOR INDIVIDUALS

essential content of **Established By the Word, Life in the Living Word,** and **The Spirit and The Word.** Carries a student through a weekly study for six months. One of the most complete question-and-answer Bible studies available. **$2.95.** Bookstores or from **Christian Outreach, 200 Asbury Drive, Wilmore, KY 40390.**

HAMMERS IN THE FIRE (It Is Written Telecast) For: L. Slant: MP,D,P,I.

This unusual book is the story of hammers. Hammers in the fire of a long and still-unfinished controversy. It is the story of the Holy Bible that through the centuries, quietly but persistently, has been wearing the hammers out one by one. Wearing them out with the help of spades and rocks, and water, honeybees and stars. And fuzzy wuzzy angels. Your faith will be strengthened in the sure Word of God. **$2.00** each, or three for **$5.00** (postage paid). From **It Is Written Telecast, Box 0, Thousand Oaks, CA 91360.**

HANDBOOK OF BIBLICAL PROPHECY (Baker Book House) For: L,C,S. Slant: EP.

By Armerding and Ward. This book sorts out the mass of conflicting claims concerning "biblical prophecy" and gives basic principles for interpreting it correctly. The chapter topics include astrology, the return of Christ, the Last Judgement, and many others. **$3.45.** Bookstores or from **Baker Book House, P.O. Box 6287, Grand Rapids, MI 49506.**

HERALD BIBLICAL BOOKLETS (Franciscan Herald Press) For: L. Slant: RC,P,CP.

Covers the important books of the Old Testament and all the books of the New Testament. Each booklet succinctly explains the text or a biblical problem, e.g., God's Words into Human Words. **$1.75.** Bookstores or from **Franciscan Herald Press, 1434 West 51st Street, Chicago, IL 60609.**

THE HOLY SPIRIT AND HIS GIFTS STUDY COURSE (Kenneth Hagin Ministries) For: L,C,S,Y. Slant: P,CP.

An in-depth study on the person of the Holy Spirit, with 24 chapters detailing aspects of His personality and His work within and through individual believers and the Body of Christ as a whole. Comprehensive explanation is given to vital questions in the church today in chapters such as: The Holy Spirit in the Denominational Church; Seven Steps to Receiving the Holy Spirit; and Ten Reasons Why Every Believer Should Speak in Tongues. Also featured are separate lessons on each of the nine gifts of the Spirit. **$5.00.** (Send payment when ordering from the publisher). Bookstores or from **Kenneth Hagin Ministries, P.O. Box 50126, Tulsa, OK 74150.**

HOME CORRESPONDENCE STUDY (Washington Bible College) For: L. Slant: F,P,I,M.

Study of the Word of God has been a great blessing to multiplied thousands of earnest Christians. **WBC Correspondence Courses** bring the classroom into the home within reach of all who desire a knowledge of the Bible. You are encouraged to join the multitudes enjoying systematic Bible study at home. Our primary purpose is to encourage as many Christians as we can to study the Bible and related subjects. We seek to provide you with excellent materials clearly and logically presented. There is no satisfaction or blessing equal to the personal reward derived from a study of the Word. Anyone may enroll in the WBC Correspondence School. An earnest determination to study the Word is essential. One year from the date of registration is allowed for the completion of each course. When the student faithfully sets aside a certain period of time for systematic study, rapid progress will be the reward. A certificate is awarded by the College upon satisfactory completion of each subject. In addition, the student may earn a Preliminary Teachers Certificate issued by The Evangelical Teacher Training Association, Wheaton, Illinois, upon satisfactory completion of the six courses numbered C1, C2, C3, C70, C71, and C80. The cost of the E.T.T.A. certificate is **$5.50.** Correspondence course. **$10.00-$12.00.** From **Correspondence School, Washington Bible College, Lanham, MD 20706.**

HOW RELEVANT IS THE BIBLE (Thomas More Press) For: L,C,S. Slant: RC.

By John L. McKenzie. To long-time McKenzie fans and readers who may be turning seriously to the Bible for the first time, these thoughtful and insightful studies will be equally rewarding. Father McKenzie is one of the world's foremost Scripture scholars, but his writings (including **The Two-Edged Sword, Authority in the Church, Dictionary of the Bible** and, most recently, **The New Testament Without Illusion**) have also been appreciated by the general reader because his style is superbly clear, concise, and free of jargon. Here he focuses on, "the real Jesus," "the real Mary," "war and peace in the New Testament," "myths in the Bible," and other fascinating aspects of biblical studies, sharing with his readers his original and outspoken thoughts on serious issues. **$12.95.** Bookstores or from **Thomas More Association, 225 W. Huron St., Chicago, IL 60610.**

HOW TO BE A CHRISTIAN IN AN UNCHRISTIAN WORLD (Regal Books) For: L,C,S,Y. Slant: EP.

By Fritz Ridenour. Expresses real empathy for what the author calls the "typical Christian" and does not attempt to provide "pat" answers to bewildering, baffling, vexing problems faced in today's pluralistic society. Instead, this study confronts these unsettling questions with the person of Jesus Christ, who claimed to be final Truth. **How to be a Christian in an Unchristian World** could properly be described as "popular apologetics"—in other words, what the Christian defends because he believes it to be right, based on Colossians. This book seeks to help readers: Understand how secular man thinks—why he says there is no absolute truth...anywhere; determine how today's Christian thinks, if he is willing to take his Bible seriously; design a practical achievable Christian life-style in the midst of a secular society influenced by atheistic existential views. 192 pages. Number S123150. Paperback. **$2.25.** Teaching materials available. Bookstores or from **Regal Books, Div. GL Publications, 2300 Knoll Drive, Ventura, CA 93003.**

HOW TO GROW IN CHRIST (Presbyterian and Reformed Publishing Co.) Slant: C,F,P,I.

By Jack Kinneer. Here is a clear and practical workbook designed to help the average Christian cultivate genuine, fruitful, spiritual growth in his or her life. Each chapter zeroes in on key biblical passages and how-

BIBLE STUDY/READING GUIDES FOR INDIVIDUALS

to information for growth in a specific area such as prayer, living by the Holy Spirit, profiting from the Bible, overcoming sin, loving others, building a Christian marriage, and witnessing to others. Basic questions about each passage of Scripture enable the reader to discover clear implications for daily living. For the person who wants to know how to grow in Christ, this workbook will prove a valuable aid in individual use or group study. Jack Kinneer is an ordained minister in the Orthodox Presbyterian Church and serves as pastor of New Life Presbyterian Church, Easton, Pennsylvania. 87 pages. **$2.75**. From **Presbyterian and Reformed Publishing Co., P.O. Box 817, Phillipsburg, NJ 08865**.

HUSBAND AND WIFE: THE SEXES IN SCRIPTURE AND SOCIETY (Zondervan Publishing House) For: L,C,S. Slant: EP.

By **Peter DeJong** and **Donald R. Wilson**. Examines male and female roles biologically, sociologically, and biblically. Integrates these areas to present a Christian perspective emphasizing family responsibilities. **$6.95**. Bookstores or from **Zondervan Retail Marketing Service, 1420 Robinson Road, SE, Grand Rapids, MI 49506**.

"HUSTLE" WON'T BRING THE KINGDOM OF GOD: JESUS' PARABLES INTERPRETED FOR TODAY (Bethany Press) For: L,C,S. Slant: MP,P.

By **Brian A. Nelson**. This series of meditations on the parables sparkles with witty comments. The essential message of each parable is identified. Contemporary situations are held up for examination in the light of the parables. Ministers and lay persons will find here a mine of information and insight. **$1.80**. From **Bethany Press, P.O. Box 179, St. Louis, MO 63166**.

HYPOCRITICAL SEPARATION VS. BIBLE SEPARATION (CBC Publications: For: L,C,S. Slant: F.

By **Dr. Cecil Johnson**. Confusion reigns in the area of biblical separation. The present trend by a handful of militant isolationists to excommunicate or exclude hundreds of sound brethren is contrary to scriptural teaching and historical precedent. Dr. Cecil Johnson has strengthened the cause of fundamentalism by masterfully presenting a logically balanced and biblically oriented exposition of this topic. His work will help restore the sorely needed unity and love among all true believers. **$2.95**. Bookstores or from **Christian Bible College Publications (CBC), P.O. Box 262, Enfield, NC 27823**.

IN THE LIGHT OF THE BIBLE (VOLS. I AND II) (Daughters of St. Paul) For: L,C,S,Y. Slant: RC,P.

These two volumes present basic teaching for Christian living in Christ and present them in the clear light of the written Word. Anyone interested in studying or teaching the Christ-life will find these books helpful and authoritative because their authority rests on God's inspired Scripture. Paperback. Vol. I, 141 pages, Number SC0060. **$2.00**. Vol. II, 117 pages, Number SC0061. **$2.00**. May be purchased separately. Mail orders please add **$.75** for one set; **$.20** for each additional set. Bookstores or from **Daughters of St. Paul, 50 St. Paul's Ave., Jamacia Plain, Boston, MA 02130**.

THE INCOMPARABLE STORY (Gospel Publishing House) For: L,C,S. Slant: EP,P,CP.

A panoramic overview of the entire Bible serving as an introduction for further Bible study. Students and teachers alike will appreciate the clarity and simplicity of this book. Catalog number 02-0907. 125 pages. Paper. **$1.50**. Add 15% for postage and handling. Bookstores or from **Gospel Publishing House, 1445 Boonville Ave., Springfield, MO 65802**.

THE INSPIRED SCRIPTURES (Gospel Publishing House) For: L,C,S. Slant: EP,P,CP.

A comprehensive study for laymen and clergy alike, this book discusses the authority, infallibility, and inspiration of the Scriptures. This treatise on Bible authenticity is written in nontechnical, easy-to-read terminology. Catalog number 02-0914. 127 pages. Paper. **$1.50**. Add 15% for postage and handling. Bookstores or from **Gospel Publishing House, 1445 Boonville Ave., Springfield, MO 65802**.

INTRODUCTION TO PRAISE (Aglow Publications) For: L,W. Slant: CP.

Christians searching for answers to questions about how to praise the Lord, can take a joyful step forward in their walk with God as they study Aglow's workbook, **Introduction to Praise**. God has placed a high priority on praise—so high that He talks about it approximately 500 times in the Bible. God wants and deserves our praise, and this workbook shows how to enter into His presence, step-by-step. Each chapter begins with review questions, self-evaluation, getting acquainted ideas (for groups) and discussion questions. **$4.95**. Add **15%** of total order for postage plus **$1.00** handling for each order. Washington State residents add 7.3% sales tax. Ask for free catalog. Bookstores or from **Aglow Publications, P.O. Box I, Lynwood, WA 98036**.

ISRAEL'S FINAL HOLOCAUST (Thomas Nelson Publishers) For: L,C,S,Y. Slant: F.

Israel is the key to prophecy. The Bible clearly describes the past, present and future of the Jewish nation.

BIBLE STUDY/READING GUIDES FOR INDIVIDUALS

Israel's Final Holocaust illuminates passages of Bible prophecy and explains their implications for the entire world, carefully tracing the history of the Jewish people from their dispersion at the fall of Jerusalem to their present partial return to a Jewish homeland. Such terminologies as the Rapture of the church, the Tribulation period, the Antichrist, the Mark of the Beast, Armageddon and the Millennium, are discussed thoroughly and made easy to understand. 14 chapters, 172 pages, with notes and index. **$7.00**. From **Jack Van Impe Ministries, P.O. Box J, Royal Oak, MI 48068**.

IRVING JENSEN'S DO-IT-YOURSELF BIBLE STUDY, MARK (Here's Life Publishers) For: L,S. Slant: EP,P.

An inductive Bible study in a large format, with complete study on facing pages. A do-it-yourself commentary. Product Number 950410. **$3.95**. Bookstores or from **Here's Life Publishers, P.O. Box 1576, San Bernardino, CA 92402**.

IT BEGAN IN AN UPPER ROOM (Gospel Publishing House) For: L,C,S. Slant: EP,P,CP.

The story of the early church presented in a topical study of the Book of Acts. The author provides insight into the lives of Peter, Paul, James, and others as he examines the doctrines they believed and preached. Catalog number 02-0528. 128 pages. Paper. **$1.50**. Add 15% for postage and handling. Bookstores or from **Gospel Publishing House, 1445 Boonville Ave., Springfield, MO 65802**.

JESUS CHRIST THE SON OF GOD (Star Bible Publications) For: L. Slant: F, EP,MP,P,S.

By O. Kelly Lawson. A 268-page paperback that contains every event in the life of Jesus Christ as told in the four gospel records; all told in one chronological narrative. Based upon the ASV Bible, arranged uniquely. Catalog Number 1995. **$2.95** each; ten for **$25.00**. Bookstores or from **Star Bible Publications, Box 181220, Ft. Worth, TX 76118**.

JESUS PERSON POCKET PROMISE BOOK (Regal Books) For: L,C,S,Y. Slant: EP.

By David Wilkerson. The format is truly "pocket" size (3 1/2" x 5 1/2") with a four-color cover, making this treasure of promises easy to carry and use. Wilkerson has compiled over 800 of God's Promises and organized them for quick, easy access into three classifications: Spiritual Needs (doctrinal teachings); Personal Needs (questions and answers to daily problems); and Future Needs (biblical teachings), with descriptive subheadings for easy reference aids. **$1.95**. Gift Edition, Burgundy Number 5007953. **$3.95**. Gift Edition, Tan, Number 5007938. **$3.95**. Bookstores or from **Regal Books, Div. of GL Publications, 2300 Knoll Drive, Ventura, CA 93003**.

JESUS THE LIBERATOR, BIBLE STUDY GUIDE (Tyndale House Publishers) For: L,S. Slant: AW,C,RC,F,EP, MP,LP,P,CP.

By John C. Souter. Presenting an honest, realistic view of the God-man Leader, Souter gives strength to the Christian and hope to a seemingly leaderless world. 96 pages. **$1.95**. Bookstores.

JESUS, THE NEW ELIJAH (Servant Publications) For: L. Slant: P.

By Paul Hinnebusch. Offers fresh insights into the Lord and our mission as Christians. Shows how the Gospel of Luke portrays Jesus in a way that recalls the Old Testament stories of Elijah. Concentrates on what the parallels between Jesus and Elijah teach Christians about following and serving the Lord today. Number 062X. **$2.95**. Bookstores.

JONAH, BIBLE STUDY GUIDE (Tyndale House Publishers) For: L,S. Slant: AW, C,RC,F,EP,MP,LP,P,CP.

By Denise Rinker Adler. The book of Jonah is a study of God's love for one wayward man. More like that disobedient prophet than we want to be, we can learn much from his experiences. A Tyndale Bible Study. 32 pages. Study Guide Paper. **$1.95**. Bookstores.

KEYNOTES (Scripture Union) For: Y. Slant: EP,MP,D.

Keynotes is a Bible reading and prayer guide aimed directly at today's 11 to 14-year-old. Young people must have a foundation in Scripture if they are to find the answers to the questions and problems they face in these distinctive years. **Keynotes** first directs the reader to a daily Bible passage and then provides interest-catching comments. Instructive comics and diagrams help to highlight important themes and enliven the text. Additional features of real significance are the projects, puzzles, questions, and prayer suggestions. These help to completely absorb a young person's attention and to encourage active involvement and personal discovery. Young teens need God's guidance, and **Keynotes** may be a means to help them remember to turn to Him for strength. From **Scripture Union, 1716 Spruce St., Philadelphia, PA 19103**.

KING AND THE KINGDOM (Baker Book House) For: C,S. Slant: EP.

By William Barclay. Traces the theme of "Kingship" through the Old and New Testaments. **$3.95**. Bookstores or from **Baker Book House, P.O. Box 6287, Grand Rapids, MI 49506**.

BIBLE STUDY/READING GUIDES FOR INDIVIDUALS

THE LAST WORD ON THE MIDDLE EAST (Chosen Books) For: L,C,S. Slant: EP,P.

By Derek Prince. Why is Israel—a nation the size of New Jersey—the most explosive center of world influence? A renowned author and teacher, Derek Prince, examines history and the Bible for "the last word on the Middle East." This book offers a comprehensive look at Israel's historical and spiritual development. With the clarity always associated with his writing, Prince exposes the newest threat to Israel, and the latest developments that are drawing the world toward an inevitable climax. Hardcover. Number 13105. **$9.95.** Bookstores or from **Zondervan, 1415 Lake Drive, SE, Grand Rapids, MI 49506.**

THE LATE GREAT PLANET EARTH (Zondervan Publishing House) For: L,C,S. Slant: EP.

By Hal Lindsey with C.C. Carlson. Through study of the Scriptures, the author illustrates prophecy as foretold in the Bible. **$4.95.** Bookstores or from **Zondervan Retail Marketing Service, 1420 Robinson Road, SE, Grand Rapids, MI 49506.**

A LENTEN PILGRIMAGE: SCRIPTURE MEDITATIONS IN THE HOLY LAND (Servant Publications) For: L. Slant: RC,D.

By David E. Rosage. A fresh and inspiring approach to Lenten prayer. Contains a series of meditations for each day in Lent, based on Scripture and the author's travels in the Holy Land. Each meditation contains a passage from the gospels and is tied to a particular location in the Holy Land. These meditations lead the reader to a deeper appreciation of Christ's immense love for his people. Number 0816. **$2.50.** Bookstores.

THE LETTERS OF PAUL (Gospel Publishing House) For: L,C,S. Slant: EP,P,CP.

Ideal for use in sermon preparation or Bible studies, this book provides an excellent overview of Paul's writings. Each of his epistles is outlined and special notes are added to explain difficult passages. Catalog number 02-0546. 144 pages. Paper. **$2.00.** Add 15% for postage and handling. Bookstores or from **Gospel Publishing House, 1445 Boonville Ave., Springfield, MO 65802.**

LETTERS TO TIMOTHY (Gospel Publishing House) For: L,C,S. Slant: EP,P,CP.

Written in a flowing commentary style, this study covers such practical topics as how to act in church, how to deal with false doctrine, how to treat others, the rewards of faithfulness, and more. Teacher's guides available. Catalog number 02-0877. 125 pages. Paper. **$1.95.** Add 15% for postage and handling. Bookstores or from **Gospel Publishing House, 1445 Boonville Ave., Springfield, MO 65802.**

LIFE IN THE LIVING WORD (Christian Outreach) For: L,C,S,Y,Ch. Slant: EP,P,I.

By Robert E. Coleman. A sequel to **Established by the Word.** Helps you see more of what is yours in Christ. Also gives instruction in maintaining Bible discipline. Used around the world. **$1.50.** Bookstores or from **Christian Outreach, 200 Asbury Drive, Wilmore, KY 40390.**

LIFE OF CHRIST (Baker Book House) For: C,S. Slant: EP.

By Robert D. Culver. An essential study for all Christians but specifically designed to help students in Bible institutes and colleges and first year seminarians. A well-organized work divided into four parts following Jesus' own summary of His career. **$9.95.** Bookstores or from **Baker Book House, P.O. Box 6287, Grand Rapids, MI 49506.**

LIFE OF CHRIST ACCORDING TO THE BOOK OF ST. MARK (Jimmy Swaggart Ministries) For: L,C. Slant: CP.

This study guide gives a complete portrait of the Life of Christ. A verse-by-verse interpretation of the gospel according to St. Mark was taken directly from the Greek Scriptures. A set of review questions follows each chapter to help you study this exciting series. Read about the personality of Christ: His conduct, attitude, and actions while here on this earth. Study the themes of salvation and forgiveness as Christ first related them according to Mark. Other unique features include a loose-leaf format with large, easy-to-read type and, wide margins for personal notes. Number 06-017. **$20.00.** From **Jimmy Swaggart Ministries, P.O. Box 2550, Baton Rouge, LA 70821.**

BIBLE STUDY/READING GUIDES FOR INDIVIDUALS

LIFE OF JESUS (Thomas More Press) For: L,C,S. Slant: RC.

By Francois Mauriac. Long out-of-print this classic, widely acclaimed life of Christ by the French Nobel Prize-winner is now available again in an unusually beautiful paper edition. "Rich in detail and in spiritual insight, told by a modern master. There have always been lives of Jesus and there always will be; Mauriac's is likely to remain one of the best"--**Christian Review.** Paper. **$7.95.** Bookstores or from **Thomas More Association, 225 W. Huron St., Chicago, IL 60610.**

THE LIFE WORTH LIVING (Gospel Publishing House) For: L,C,S. Slant: EP,P,CP.

A devotional commentary on the Gospel of John. Examining the claims of Jesus and how they relate to individuals today, this volume points the way to a satisfying and meaningful life through Jesus Christ. Catalog number 02-0876. 128 pages. Paper. **$1.95.** Add 15% for postage and handling. Bookstores or from **Gospel Publishing House, 1445 Boonville Ave., Springfield, MO 65802.**

LIGHT ON THE EPISTLES: A READERS GUIDE (Thomas More Press) For: L,C,S. Slant: RC.

By John L. McKenzie. This unique reader's guide is ideally suited to close that gap between the contemporary Christian and the Epistles. Written by the most distinguished Catholic Scripture scholar of our day and designed to be read in conjunction with the New Testament, it provides lucid and expert commentary and explanation. With a guide like John L. McKenzie and the option of setting your own pace — the difficult suddenly becomes not only possible, but pleasurable. Paper. **$8.95.** Bookstores or from **Thomas More Association, 225 W. Huron St., Chicago, IL 60610.**

LIGHT ON THE GOSPELS: A READER'S GUIDE (Thomas More Press) For: L,C,S. Slant: RC.

By John L. McKenzie. This unique reader's guide is ideally suited to close the gap between the contemporary Christian and the New Testament. Written by the most distinguished Catholic scripture scholar of our day, it provides lucid and expert commentary and explanation. "Could be the best book of its kind available." New Book Review. Paper. **$8.95.** Bookstores or from **Thomas More Association, 225 W. Huron St., Chicago, IL 60610.**

LISTEN TO HIM: A DAILY GUIDE TO SCRIPTURAL PRAYER (Servant Publications) For: L. Slant: D.

By David E. Rosage. An easy-to-use program of Scripture reading and meditation to help Christians enter into communion with God every day. Provides a Scripture passage and meditation for each day of the year, arranged around weekly themes. Number 1081. **$2.50.** Bookstores.

LIVING BY FAITH (Gospel Publishing House) For: L,C,S. Slant: EP,P,CP.

The author examines Hebrews 11, the most complete treatise of faith in the Bible. Old friends rediscovered present some remarkable surprises—all serving as examples of faith. A devotional Bible study. Catalog number 02-0552. 127 pages. Paper. **$1.50.** Add 15% for postage and handling. Bookstores or from **Gospel Publishing House, 1445 Boonville Ave., Springfield, MO 65802.**

LIVING FAITH (Faith for Today) For: L,C,S. Slant: P.

A Home Seminar series for the searching Bible student, the **Living Faith** program helps you discover biblical truths in every area of practical Christian living, and answers those inner questions with which we so often struggle; facts about life and death; the truth about faith healing; the real purpose behind Satan's attack on God's character; and how to find God. Thirty easy-to-read, postpaid, personal seminar guides designed to bring you in close touch with God's Word and His loving character. Nearly 60,000 lives have already been enriched by this thoughtful seminar. Individuals. **Free.** Quantities of 10 or more. **$2.75** per set. From **Faith for Today, Box 1000, Thousand Oaks, CA 91359.**

LIVING LIGHT BIBLE GUIDES (Voice of Prophecy) For: L,S,Y. Slant: EP.

A glowing relationship with Jesus, the Living Light, is offered teens and young adults as they relive episodes from His life in 26 guides. More than 50 illustrations, created especially for this series, highlight the narrative. A question sheet for each guide reinforces the major points. Guides are sent, a few at at time, to match each person's own pace, and a diploma is awarded upon completion of the series. **No charge** for individual enrollment. From **Voice of Prophecy, P.O. Box 55, Dept YOB, Los Angeles, CA 90053.**

LIVING THE LORD'S PRAYER (Chosen Books) For: L,C,S,Y. Slant: EP,D.

By Rev. Everett L. Fullam. Central to the Lord's Prayer is the most crucial truth for mortal man. God has a specific plan for every person on earth. Terry Fullam, renowned speaker and teacher, explains that the key to finding this purpose is hidden in words millions repeat each day: The Lord's Prayer. This "pattern" of prayer given to Jesus' followers helps you enter into an intimate relationship with God, and be satisfied to let God reign in your life. An excellent book for study groups or personal devotions. Paperback. Number 13108p. **$4.95.** Bookstores or from **Zondervan, 1415 Lake Drive, SE, Grand Rapids, MI 49506.**

LIVING THE WORD: How To Apply Scripture To Your Life (Servant Publications) For: L. Slant: P.

By Jim Durkin. Outlines the principles of applied faith to show that when Christians believe, confess, and act upon God's word, all the promises of scripture will be fulfilled in their lives. Number 0697. **$1.95.** Bookstores.

BIBLE STUDY/READING GUIDES FOR INDIVIDUALS

LIVING WORD BOOKLETS (Institute for Christian Renewal) For: L,C,S. Slant: RC,EP,MP,D,P,CP.

A series of teaching booklets designed to help people to grasp basic points of the Bible's teaching. Many people use the booklets to gain a concise but comprehensive overview of a given point of doctrine before plunging into the matter in-depth. Their concise format also makes them useful for people to give or send to their friends. Over 100,000 have been distributed in five years. Distinctive denominational viewpoints are avoided for basic teaching common to all biblical Christians. Line drawings enhance the beauty and readability. **$.25 - $.40**. From **Institute for Christian Renewal, 26 Washington St., Malden, MA 02148**.

LORD, WHEN? (Creation House) For: L,C,S. Slant: EP.

What does the Bible say about Christ's return for His people? How should the church prepare for endtime events? What tasks has God given to Christians to prepare the way for His coming Kingdom? How can one be sure of his own personal destiny in view of God's endtime plans? These questions and others are probed in this Bible study guide on the return of Christ. Utilizing the inductive study method, this guide does not provide the student or group with didactic answers. Instead it enables those using it to find the Bible's answers to their own questions. **$1.50**. Add **$.75** for postage. Bookstores or from **Creation House, 396 E. St. Charles Road, Wheaton, IL 60188**.

THE LORD'S PRAYER (Gospel Publishing House) For: L,C,S. Slant: EP,D,P,CP.

This is a perceptive devotional treatment of the familiar Lord's Prayer which is often quoted with little thought given to its meaning. Perfect as a gift or remembrance. Catalog number 02-0566. 45 pages. Paper. **$.95**. Add 15% for postage and handling. Bookstores or from **Gospel Publishing House, 1445 Boonville Ave., Springfield, MO 65802**.

MANY INFALLIBLE PROOFS! (Creation-Life Publishers, Inc.) For: L,C,S,Y. Slant: F,EP,D,P,S,I.

By Henry M. Morris, Ph.D. One of the best in its field. As it scripturally supports each basic tenet of the Christian faith, it strengthens new Christians as well as convincing the unblieever of the integrity of God's Word. This is a real help to personal growth and effective witnessing in today's skeptical society. This volume has been adopted as a complete textbook for college courses in apologetics and Christian evidences. Book Number 102. Paper. **$7.95**. Book Number 103. Cloth . **$9.95**. Add **$1.00** for shipping, California residents add 6 percent sales tax. Bookstores or from **Creation-Life Publishers, P.O. Box 15908, San Diego, CA 92115**.

MANY WITNESSES, ONE LORD (Baker Book House) For: C,S. Slant: EP.

By William Barclay. The author paints the varied backgrounds of the New Testament books and marks the distinctive viewpoints from which several writers see and interpret the significance of the Gospel. **$3.95**. Bookstores or from **Baker Book House, P.O. Box 6287, Grand Rapids, MI 49506**.

MASTER THEME OF THE BIBLE (Tyndale House Publishers) For: L,S. Slant: AW,C,RC,F,EP,MP,LP,P,CP.

By J. Sidlow Baxter. The concept of the Lamb and its significance in redemption. 336 pages. Paper. **$5.95**. Bookstores.

MEMOIRS OF PETER (The Salvation Army) For: L,C,S,Y. Slant: AW.

By Pitcher. The response with which **Memoirs of Peter** has been received proves beyond doubt that Peter was speaking directly to hearts that throb with the same fluctuant emotions as those which plagued the fisherman disciple. **$2.95**. Bookstores.

THE MINISTRY GIFTS STUDY GUIDE (Kenneth Hagin Ministries) For: L,C,S. Slant: P,CP.

A definitive study guide on the Bible subject of ministry gifts in the Church. The 15 chapters outline the biblical characteristics of the ministries mentioned in the Bible, such as apostle, prophet, evangelist, pastor, teacher, and helps, and give explanation concerning their role in the Body of Christ. Other important chapters include: The Divine Call; Whom God Calls, He Equips; and Faithfulness to the Call. **$10.00**. Please send payment with order. Bookstores or from **Kenneth Hagin Ministries, P.O. Box 50126, Tulsa, OK 74150**.

MORALITY TODAY - THE BIBLE IN MY LIFE (Daughters of St. Paul) For: L,C,S. Slant: RC,EP,MP,P.

Presents the biblical approach to God's precepts in a personal style, which inclines the reader to vital dialogue with Him. Each commandment is explained in all its aspects. We are invited to ponder...adore...and speak to God so that through instruction, reflection, and prayer we may understand and love His holy law. Number SC 0088. Cloth. **$3.25**. Paper. **$2.25**. Bookstores or from **Daughters of St. Paul, 50 St. Paul's Ave., Jamaica Plain, Boston, MA 02130**.

BIBLE STUDY/READING GUIDES FOR INDIVIDUALS

MOSES: MOMENTS OF GLORY...FEET OF CLAY (Regal Books) For: L,C,S,Y. Slant: EP.

By Gene A. Getz. Moses was a great man in many ways. He was a natural leader—a military commander, a nation-builder, a prophet! A legend in his own time, Moses was a man whom God used mightily. But Moses was also a very ordinary human being. Like most of us, he had his own share of hang-ups. His weaknesses were as great as his strengths. He had faults, and he knew failure. Christians living in today's pressurized society have a lot in common with Moses. We can all identify with him and learn from his experiences. Blending careful biblical exposition with practical psychological insights, the author covers 12 areas that are concerns for everyone. Included are: making difficult choices; living with mistakes; coping with inferior feelings; building a good self-image; learning to mature; developing personal discipline; handling depression; and facing unjust criticism. Each chapter has a "life response" section to help you apply biblical principles to your own life. There are also personal or family projects that give you specific ideas for taking steps of spiritual growth. Get to know Moses. You will know yourself better and learn how to be the kind of person God uses. Quality paper. 160 pages. Number 5403200. **$4.95.** Bookstores or from **Regal Books, Div. of GL Publica- tions, 2300 Knoll Drive, Ventura, CA 93003.**

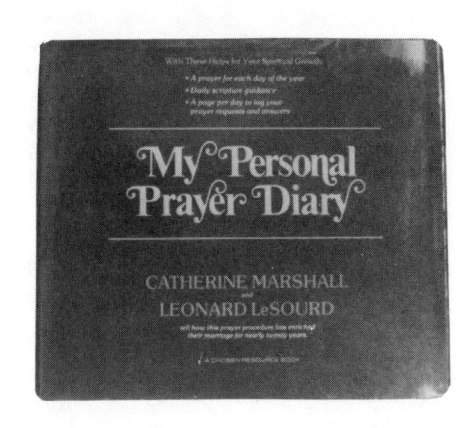

MY PERSONAL PRAYER DIARY (Chosen Books) For: L,C,S,Y. Slant: D,P.

By Catherine Marshall and Leonard LeSourd. A daily devotional designed by a couple who has shared a morning hour of prayer and Bible study for more than twenty years. Each page contains a Scripture for study and a thought for prayer-meditation with space where each individual may log prayer requests and God's exciting answers. This volume is an outgrowth of Leonard and Catherine's own prayer time which started shortly after their marriage when they were faced with a multitude of problems involving four children, a new home, and two busy careers. A tool to be used for a richer devotional time by individuals, couples, and families. Hardcover. Number 13003. **$11.95.** Bookstores or from **Zondervan, 1415 Lake Drive, SE, Grand Rapids, MI 49506.**

NEHEMIAH: A MAN OF PRAYER AND PERSISTENCE (Regal Books) For: L,C,S,Y. Slant: EP.

By Gene A. Getz. Identify with Nehemiah's problems, learn from his approach to solutions and his leadership skills, be challenged by his prayer and persistence in spiritual and emotional struggles that lead you to become a more effective follower of Christ. Quality paper. 176 pages. Number 5414500. **$4.95.** Bookstores or from **Regal Books, Div. of GL Publications, 2300 Knoll Drive, Ventura, CA 93003.**

NEW TESTAMENT EXPERIENCE OF FAITH (Bethany Press) Slant: MP,P.

By Leander Keck. This book provides a unique perspective on early Christianity by describing its nature in five great cities: Jerusalem, Antioch, Corinth, Ephesus, and Rome. We see how the faith developed and the kinds of issues with which early Christians were forced to deal. **$4.95.** Bookstores or from **Bethany Press, P.O. Box 179, St. Louis, MO 63166.**

THE NEW TESTAMENT WITHOUT ILLUSION (Thomas More Press) For: L,C,S. Slant: RC.

By John L. McKenzie. "An enlightening, scholarly, and refreshing book on N.T. themes... There are twenty-one chapters. The contents range from the world in which Jesus was born to where we go from here... I heartily recommend this book to every serious-minded intellectual and disciplined person who wishes to do both creative and critical thinking about the business of the Church." Leonard Badia, **Theological Studies.** **$13.95.** Bookstores or from **Thomas More Association, 225 W. Huron St., Chicago, IL 60610.**

THE NEW WAY OF JESUS (Faith and Life Press) For: L,S. Slant: S.

The ten biblical studies in this volume were contributed by colleagues of Howard Charles in his honor. The essays deal with topics from both the Old and New Testament as well as the Apocryphal and Rabbinic writings. Together they represent an attempt to illuminate the new way of Jesus spoken of in Isaiah 43:19. **$7.95.** From **Faith and Life Press, Box 347, Newton, KS 67114.**

NOTES ON THE MIRACLES OF OUR LORD (Baker Book House) For: C,S. Slant: EP.

By R.C. Trench. No student of the Scripture should study the miracles without consulting Trench. **$5.95.** Bookstores or from **Baker Book House, P.O. Box 6287, Grand Rapids, MI 49506.**

NOTES ON THE PARABLES OF OUR LORD (Baker Book House) For: C,S. Slant: EP.

By R.C. Trench. This book retains first place among the works on the parables. Unsurpassed in its depth and spiritual insight. **$5.95.** Bookstores or from **Baker Book House, P.O. Box 6287, Grand Rapids, MI 49506.**

NOW THAT I'M A DISCIPLE (Harvest House Publishers) For: L,C,S. Slant: EP,P,I,M.

BIBLE STUDY/READING GUIDES FOR INDIVIDUALS

By Rick Yohn. Discover what the Bible says about being a disciple, and how we can grow in our faith as disciples. Rick Yohn outlines the topic with thought-provoking questions, and then space is provided for the reader to answer by referring to Scripture provided. Great for Bible studies! Paper. **$3.95.** Bookstores or from **Harvest House Publishers, 1075 Arrowsmith, Eugene, OR 97402.**

100 DAYS BIBLE STUDY (Officers' Christian Fellowship of the USA) For: L,S. Slant: EP.

By Lt. Gen. Sir Arthur Smith. A topical guide for personal or group Bible study designed to be accomplished in 100 days. 73 pages. This is especially designed for new Christians. **$1.00** per copy. From **OCF, P.O. Box 36200, Denver, CO 80236.**

ONE PLUS ONE EQUALS ONE (InterVarsity Press) For: L. Slant: EP,D,P.

By Andrew T. and Phyllis J. LePeau. We all long for intimacy. And many of us seek it in marriage. But when a minister pronounces two people husband and wife, that doesn't instantly make them one. Intimacy takes work. For Christian couples there is the added desire to know what God has to say about marriage. Through 16 Bible-oriented discussions, Andrew and Phyllis LePeau help couples or small groups of couples to work at their marriages. Topics covered include expectations, self-image, sex, family-life, submission, communication, forgiveness, divorce, children, possessions, and priorities. In an appendix, the LePeaus, who are also the authors of **Faith That Works** (a study guide to James) and, with John D. Stewart, **Just Living By Faith** (a study guide to Habakkuk), give practical suggestions for planning in marriage. A guide to help couples really make one plus one equal one. Paper. **$3.95.** Bookstores.

OPENING THE BIBLE (The Liturgical Press) For: L,C. Slant: RC,D.

By Thomas Merton. With a master's technique interest, the author presents the demands and purposes of God's Word to the reader, and few will be able to resist taking further steps toward the pearl of revealed truth. The Bible is opened to the believer, the skeptic, and to anyone just looking. 84 pages. Softbound. **$2.95.** Bookstores or from **The Liturgical Press, Collegeville, MN 56321.**

THE PAMPHLET BIBLE SERIES (The Paulist Press) For: L,C,S. Slant RC.

A series of 48 pamphlets (booklet size) which presents portions of the Old Testament together with sufficient explanation to help the general reader to a fuller appreciation of the biblical text. The commentaries are written by experts in non-technical language. Self-quizzes in the pamphlets help the reader grasp the meaning of the books studied. Over a million copies have been sold of this popular work. **$1.00.** Bookstores or from **Paulist Press, 545 Island Road, Ramsey, NJ 07446.**

PARABLES OF JESUS (Baker Book House) For: C. Slant: C,EP.

By Simon Kistemaker. A contemporary analysis of the parables by an acknowledged New Testament scholar. **$10.95.** Bookstores or from **Baker Book House, P.O. Box 6287, Grand Rapids, MI 49506.**

PARENTING WITH LOVE AND LIMITS (Zondervan Publishing House) For: L,C,S. Slant: EP.

By Bruce Narramore. Challenges Christian parents to develop a comprehensive biblical view of parenting. **$4.95.** Bookstores or from **Zondervan Retail Marketing Service, 1420 Robinson Road, SE, Grand Rapids, MI 49506.**

THE PASSION AND DEATH OF OUR LORD JESUS CHRIST (Daughters of St. Paul) For: L,C,S. Slant: RC,D.

By Goodier. The author has guided his writing by the fundamental questions: "How does the passion reveal Christ to us? What manner of Man does He show Himself during that ordeal? What were his thoughts and feelings? And hence...what is the meaning of Jesus' crucifixion to me here and now?" Cloth. Number SC0423. **$7.50.** Please include **$.75** for mail orders. Bookstores or from **Daughters of St. Paul, 50 St. Paul's Avenue, Jamaica Plain, Boston, MA 02130.**

PAUL: APOSTLE FOR TODAY (Tyndale House Publishers) For: L,S. Slant: AW,C,RC,F,EP,MP,LP,P,CP.

By George Allen Turner. See Paul in his historical and geographical milieu, the ancient Greco-Roman sphere of trade, travel, and influence. The result of Turner's own research and travel through the Apostle Paul's world, this book combines a scholar's eye for detail with attention to the human values. Trade paper. **$7.95.** Bookstores.

BIBLE STUDY/READING GUIDES FOR INDIVIDUALS

PERSONAL BIBLE STUDY NOTEBOOK (Tyndale House Publishers) For: L,S. Slant: AW,C,RC,F,EP,MP,LP,P,CP.

By John C. Souter. A book for those who have difficulty studying the Bible regularly and meaningfully. Includes a daily log, various Bible study methods and many secrets for success. 176 pages. Trade paper. **$4.95.** Bookstores.

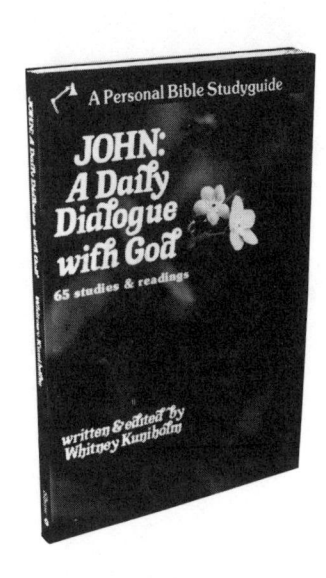

PERSONAL BIBLE STUDYGUIDES (Harold Shaw Publishers) For: L,C,S. Slant: EP.

If you're a busy person who wants to strengthen and deepen your daily time with God, **Personal Bible Studyguides** may be just what you are searching for. These studyguides let you discover (or rediscover) the excitement of hearing God speak directly to you through his Word, and the value of dialogue with him. In 20 to 40 minutes each day you will pray, read Scripture, discover meaning through inductive questions, read commentary notes by Scripture Union authors, respond to God, and work on memorizing a key verse. These daily studies provide just the right balance between discovering truth for yourself and learning from trusted Bible scholars. Studyguides include: John: A Daily Dialogue with God; Galatians, Ephesians, Philippians & Colossians: A Daily Dialogue with God; and Hebrews, James, I and II Peter: A Daily Dialogue with God. **$4.95.** Bookstores or from **Harold Shaw Publishers, P.O. Box 567, 388 Gundersen Drive, Wheaton, IL 60189.**

PHILIPPIANS—THE JOYFUL LIFE (Gospel Publishing House) For: L,C,S. Slant: EP,P,CP.

A practical study based on Paul's personal experiences—God turns apparent disasters to glorious triumphs. This study will help readers find hope and the key to a joyful life. Teacher's guide available. Catalog number 02-0880. 123 pages. Paper. **$2.50.** Add 15% for postage and handling. Bookstores or from **Gospel Publishing House, 1445 Boonville Ave., Springfield, MO 65802.**

PHILISTINES AND THE OLD TESTAMENT (Baker Book House) For: C. Slant: EP.

By Andrew Hindson. The purpose of this book is to demonstrate from history and archaeology the significant place the Philistines occupy in the early history of Israel in the Old Testament. **$5.95.** Bookstores or from **Baker Book House, P.O. Box 6287, Grand Rapids, MI 49506.**

A PLACE TO START: THE BIBLE AS A GUIDE FOR TODAY (Winston Press) For: L,C,S. Slant: MP.

By Brooks. Over 30 short commentaries on today's issues sketch the broad outlines of what the Bible says about things like values, self-respect, disarmament, jealousy, cruelty in nature, and much more. One man's impression of the way lines of thought developed throughout the Bible can place current issues on a kind of map— a map of values and of an understanding of human life. First broadcast on BBC radio, the author's Bible-based comments on contemporary issues drew an overwhelming response. **$4.95.** Bookstores or from **Winston Press, 430 Oak Grove, Minneapolis, MN 55403.**

POCKET PROVERBS (Regal Books) For: L,C,S,Y. Slant: EP.

By David Wilkerson. Gives the Christian practical scriptural advice on some of the most perplexing problems and concerns in our world today. Its topical format provides quick, easy reference to answers on a variety of contemporaey issues—such as the Christian's responsibility to the poor; overcoming fear, jealousy, a bad temper; handling prosperity; financial planning and management. The answers are straight from God's Word— and over 450 verses from the book of Proverbs and from other books of the Bible are organized into 69 categories that reveal the mind of God. The pocket-sized format (3 1/2" x 5 1/2") makes **Pocket Proverbs** a handy resource which is easy to carry and use. It's perfect as a companion to **The Jesus Person Pocket Promise Book**, David Wilkerson's phenomenal bestseller. Wilkerson stresses the importance of knowing and applying these proverbs: "Every promise and proverb is yours," he says. "Every jot and tittle." Mass paperback. 112 pages. Number 5018103. **$2.50.** Bookstores or from **Regal Books, Div. of GL Publications, 2300 Knoll Drive, Ventura, CA 93003.**

POINTERS TO JESUS: HERE IS JESUS (Scripture Union) For: Y. Slant: EP, MP,D.

Young people must discover that Jesus is the answer to their questions. Here are two intelligent, well-written, and boldly illustrated Bible commentaries which present the life of Jesus to young people in a manner designed specifically for them. **Pointers to Jesus** based on the Psalms, Isaiah, and Mark, and **Here is Jesus**, based on Luke, are divided into a variety of sections with emphasis on direct Bible reading. Each section begins with an informative introduction and overview of the historical setting. After the Scripture reading there is a verse-by-verse commentary geared to today's young person. Then an Extension Work section presents questions for reflection and encourages creative projects. Finally there is a helpful section with suggestions for those who may lead a youth group study. These are excellent, lively commentaries which young people will really want to use! **$2.95** each. From **Scripture Union, 1716 Spruce St., Philadelphia, PA 19103.**

BIBLE STUDY/READING GUIDES FOR INDIVIDUALS

PRIESTHOOD OLD AND NEW (The Salvation Army) For: L,C,S,Y. Slant: AW.

Good Bible teaching material. A comparative study, relevant to the needs of God's people today! **$1.95.** Bookstores.

PROPHECY FOR TODAY (Zondervan Publishing House) For: L,C,S. Slant: EP.

By J. Dwight Pentecost. Uncomplicated, fascinating and complete ... this book is a simple digest of world events relating to biblical prophecy. **$3.95.** Bookstores or from **Zondervan Retail Marketing Service, 1420 Robinson Road, SE, Grand Rapids, MI 49506.**

READ AND PRAY BIBLICAL BOOKLETS (Franciscan Herald Press) For: L. Slant: RC,P,CP.

Covers all the books of the New Testament with individual booklets. It is designed to assist the ordinary lay Bible reader to get first rate scholars' interpretation of the passage (indicated at the top of each page); to reflect on the passage; and, to offer a prayer related to the passage. **$1.25** per booklet. Bookstores or from **Franciscan Herald Press, 1434 West 51st Street, Chicago, IL 60609.**

READING THE ACTS, EPISTLES AND REVELATION (Daughters of St. Paul) For: L,C,S. Slant: RC,P,S.

This volume is designed for individual readers, students, teachers and study groups alike. A brief synopsis of each book is given, as well as the different themes presented in the text. Points for reflection and discussion on each passage help the reader understand and apply its message to daily life. Charts, maps and quizzes interspersed throughout the text are handy aids to learning; a topical index provides quick reference on individual subjects. Number SC0431. Cloth. **$6.95.** Paper. **$5.95.** Bookstores or from **Daughters of St. Paul, 50 St. Paul's Avenue, Jamaica Plain, Boston, MA 02130.**

READY ANSWERS TO RELIGIOUS ERRORS (Star Bible Publications) For: L. Slant: F,EP,P,S.

By A.C. Williams and J. Harvey Dikes. The perfect guide for every personal worker—the ideal faith-builder for every Christian. Offers you over 200 pages of religious errors and biblical answers—yet fits compactly in the palm of your hand or in your pocket. Over 100,000 copies already in use. No Christian should be without it. Number 2056. **$1.95.** Bookstores or from **Star Bible Publications, Box 181220, Ft. Worth, TX 76118.**

REVELATION REVEALED BOOK (Jack Van Impe Ministries) For: L,C,S,Y. Slant: F.

By Dr. Jack Van Impe. Want to understand the Book of Revelation? Verse-by-verse! Then you'll want to request a copy of Dr. Van Impe's newest and most exciting work on prophecy... **Revelation Revealed...** available at last as a 300-page paperback book! Featuring: concise easy-to-understand wording; a detailed, individual analysis of all 404 verses; and Dr. Van Impe's own "Revelation Reviewed" question and answer section. **$10.00.** From **Jack Van Impe Ministries, P.O. Box J, Royal Oak, MI 48068.**

THE REVELATION STUDY GUIDE (Jimmy Swaggart Ministries) For: L,C. Slant: CP.

Bible students and laymen everywhere are becoming increasingly interested in the book of Revelation. What does Revelation say about the present world events? What plans does God have for His people? The world? In this day and age, what more important study could there be? This 248-page study guide will lead you unerringly through the fascinating events of Revelation. With special emphasis on symbols, signs, types, and timetables, it features a loose-leaf format with large, easy-to-read type. Number 06-001. **$20.00.** From **Jimmy Swaggart Ministries, P.O. Box 2550, Baton Rouge, LA 70821.**

RUTH (C.B.C. Publications) For: L,C,S. Slant: F.

By Dr. Cecil Johnson. After an in-depth study and preaching a series on the book of Ruth, Dr. Johnson felt compelled by the Holy Spirit to write this book. Ruth paints a beautiful tapestry of Christ and His Gentile bride (the church). It is literally filled with the imagery of God's matchless grace. After you have read this inspiring account your spiritual life will never be the same again. **$2.95.** Bookstores or from **Christian Bible College Publications (C.B.C.), P.O. Box 262, Enfield, NC 27823.**

SCRIPTURAL LIGHT ON SPEAKING IN TONGUES (The Salvation Army) For: L,C,S,Y. Slant: AW.

By Bouterse. " It is not the Blessing we seek, but the Blesser." Examine the extensive explanation in all the Bible on spiritual gifts in general and the gift of tongues in particular. **$.85.** Bookstores.

BIBLE STUDY/READING GUIDES FOR INDIVIDUALS

SCRIPTURE AND THE CHARISMATIC RENEWAL (Servant Publications) For: L. Slant: CP.

Within the charismatic renewal, Scripture holds a place of central importance for preaching, teaching, and evangelizing. In order to examine the theological and pastoral issues regarding the use of Scripture in the renewal, a symposium was held in Milwaukee, December 1-3, 1978, and was attended by theologians, exegetes, pastoral leaders, and diocesan liaisons to the charismatic renewal. **Scripture and the Charismatic Renewal** contains the proceedings from that symposium. **$4.00**. Bookstores.

SCRIPTURE OF TRUTH (Mott Media) For: L,C,S.

By George and Charlotte Symes. In this comprehensive, easy-to-read book, the Bible teaching team of George and Charlotte Symes answers the unnerving questions arising in the minds of today's Christian on the controversial issue of the authority of the Scripture. Normally complex issues such as inspiration, canonicity, transmission, preservation and textual criticism are treated in an accurate, understandable fashion. The book lends itself well to group or individual study. It offers centuries of accumulated knowledge about the Bible and its trustworthiness, without bogging down in scholastic details. It is meat without the bones, to nourish the hungry believer. Paperback. **$5.95**. Bookstores or from **Mott Media, 1000 E. Huron, Milford, MI 48042**.

SCRIPTURE UNION'S 1983 BIBLE STUDY JOURNAL (Scripture Union) For: L,C,S. Slant: EP,MP,D.

A unique, new tool which can transform your daily devotions into a time of deeper, more meaningful reflection on God's Word--in just a few weeks! Each day of the year you are provided with space for writing your understanding and application of a Scripture passage. As you use the **Journal**, you'll quickly discover that writing down your insights is the secret to in-depth meditation on the Scriptures. The **Journal** is usable with any Bible reading schedule (and even includes a choice of two reading schedules if you don't have one). Also, the **Journal** gives you space to keep notes on your prayer life. So, at the end of the year you will have created a written record of your adventures with God in his Word and in prayer—a valuable record you will refer back to year after year. **$3.95**. From **Scripture Union, 1716 Spruce St., Philadelphia, PA 19103**.

SEEING THE STORY OF THE BIBLE (Gospel Publishing House) For: L,C,S. Slant: EP,P,CP.

Readers can see the unity of the entire Bible--both Old and New testaments with this detailed study. Using charts, diagrams, outlines, and a story-text, the author depicts the impressive size, construction, and beauty of the Word. Catalog number 02-0581. 128 pages. Paper. **$2.50**. Add 15% for postage and handling. Bookstores or from **Gospel Publishing House, 1445 Boonville Ave., Springfield, MO 65802**.

SERMON ON THE MOUNT (Baker Book House) For: L,C. Slant: EP,P.

By Clovis G. Chappell. Chappell's human insights and spiritual applications add greatly to the messages of Matthew 5-7. **$3.95**. Bookstores or from **Baker Book House, P.O. Box 6287, Grand Rapids, MI 49506**.

SHEPHERD'S PSALM (Baker Book House) For: L. Slant: D.

By Ron Hembree. Here is a phrase-by-phrase journey through the majestic "great hymn of faith," the Twenty-Third Psalm. **$1.75**. Bookstores or from **Baker Book House, P.O. Box 6287, Grand Rapids, MI 49506**.

SIGNS AND WONDERS TODAY (Christian Life Missions) For: L,C,S. Slant: EP,CP.

Overwhelming!... That was the response to the October 1982 issue of **Christian Life** magazine. The entire issue was devoted to reporting on various aspects of a course being taught for the first time at Fuller Theological Seminary... The study included the theological basis of the biblical phrase, "Signs and Wonders." It traced the history of signs and wonders through Old Testament, New Testament and early church history. Reports included evidence of signs and wonders today on mission fields as well as in churches throughout the U.S. Faculty member reaction, as well as student response, also was detailed. So enthusiastic has been the reception of this issue that the editors of **Christian Life** have now produced an enlarged and expanded edition of the study, which includes a 13-session study of the subject, "Signs and Wonders," with questions and answers prepared under the direction of Dr. Peter Wagner, professor at Fuller. 1-10 copies. **$4.95** each. 11 or more. **$3.95** each. Add for postage and handling: 1 book **$1.00**. 2-10 books **$1.50**. 11-20 books **$3.00**. Bookstores or from **Christian Life Missions, 396 E. St. Charles Road, Wheaton, IL 60188**.

SIMPLE MESSAGES ON ROMANS (The Brethren Press) For: L,C,S. Slant: EP.

By Harold S. Martin. This book examines the Book of Romans. It is written in everyday language and contains illustrations which relate directly to life experiences. This thought-provoking guide begins with a description of our sinfulness, explores the three stages of God's salvation, and concludes with a practical discussion of common duties in the Christian life. Number 8-7938. **$3.95**. From **The Brethren Press, 1451 Dundee Ave., Elgin, IL 60120**.

SIMPLE STUDIES IN ROMANS (Baker Book House) For: L,C. Slant: EP,P.

By Charles Cunningham. The author holds that the practical lessons in the Book of Romans are absolutely essential for the Christian life. **$1.45**. Bookstores or from **Baker Book House, P.O. Box 6287, Grand Rapids, MI 49506**.

SPEAK, LORD, YOUR SERVANT IS LISTENING (Servant Publications) For: L. Slant: D.

BIBLE STUDY/READING GUIDES FOR INDIVIDUALS

By David E. Rosage. A daily guide to scriptural prayer. Thousands of people looking for a more meaningful prayer life have found valuable help in this popular best-seller. A Scripture passage and reflection to inspire prayer for each day of an entire year, as well as weekly insights. Practical help for growing closer to the Lord through a life of faithful prayer. Number 0468. **$2.45**. Bookstores.

THE SPIRIT AND THE WORD (Christian Outreach) For: L,C,S,Y,Ch. Slant: EP,P,I.

By Robert E. Coleman. Insightful study of the Holy Spirit's ministry in the believer's life. A sequel to **Established by the Word** and **Life in the Living Word**, though it may be used separately. **$1.50**. Bookstores or from **Christian Outreach, 200 Asbury Drive, Wilmore, KY 40390**.

THE SPIRIT BIBLE (Ave Maria Press) For: L,C. Slant: RC,MP,D,P,CP.

A compilation of all the passages in Holy Scripture—both Old and New Testaments—that refer to the spirit, providing the reader with a unique type of meditation book on the Holy Spirit. Its completeness and special concordance-index make it a handy reference tool. An appendix on the Holy Spirit in the Church contains various prayers to the Holy Spirit, selections from the documents of Vatican II, as well as statements by Pope Paul VI. Paper. 272 pages. **$2.25**. Bookstores or from **Ave Maria Press, Notre Dame, IN 46556**.

SPIRITUAL LIFE IN THE BIBLE (Daughters of St. Paul) For: L,C,S. Slant: RC,D,P.

This book sets forth a biblical approach to the spiritual life. Written in a warm, prayerful, dialogue form, the author continually draws from the Bible as such subjects as family and social life, sin, Jesus, miracles, Mary, the Church, the purpose of life, the way to peace, eternity and many more topics are discussed. Item number SCO445. Paperback. **$4.00**. (Add **$.75** for postage.) Bookstores or from **Daughters of St. Paul, 50 St. Paul's Avenue, Jamaica Plain, Boston, MA 02130**.

STILL IN THE IMAGE (Faith and Life Press) For: L. Slant: S.

Subtitled, "Essays on Biblical Theology and Anthropology," this volume offers several groupings of essays that attempt to respond biblically to the questions: "What does it mean to live as a human being under God?" The general areas covered are: divine-human communication; human existence and limitations; our orientation in God's world; and, the problem of human destructiveness. **$10.95**. From **Faith and Life Press, Box 347, Newton, KS 67114**.

STORIES OF FAITH (Thomas More Press) For: L,C,S. Slant: RC.

By John Shea. Faith in Jesus, Father Shea explains, "is a process of relating our lives to his life story." In retelling the Jesus stories, the life of the teller is interwoven with the tale. **Stories of Faith** continues the brilliantly original examination of mankind's confrontation with the mystery of existence and faith which this rising young theologian began in his highly praised **Stories of God**. Father Shea combines the art of the storyteller with the scholarship of the theologian in this remarkable synthesis of theology and spirituality. Paper. $7.95. Bookstores or from **Thomas More Association, 225 W. Huron St., Chicago, IL 60610**.

STORIES OF GOD: AN UNAUTHORIZED BIOGRAPHY (Thomas More Press) For: L,C,S. Slant: RC.

By John Shea. Revelation is where we start, but faithful people have been reading and telling stories of God and their relationship to him for centuries. In this brilliant but highly readable successor to his extremely popular, **The Challenge of Jesus**, Father Shea reexamines these classic stories of God to show that we are, in fact, God's story. "Brilliant, evocative, profound and above all, original."—Andrew Greeley. Paper. **$7.95**. Bookstores or from **Thomas More Association, 225 W. Huron St., Chicago, IL 60610**.

SURVEYING THE SCRIPTURES (The Salvation Army) For: L,C,S,Y. Slant: AW.

By Huggard. Capture the Divine Perspective of God's Word in viewing it as a whole-mystery and miracle, poetry and parable, history and biography—the most amazing drama ever presented to the mind of man. **$2.25**. Bookstores.

SYSTEMATIC BIBLE STUDY COURSE (The Restitution Herald) For: L,C,S. Slant: D,M.

Consists of 29 lessons arranged in a systematic way to provide a thorough, basic understanding of the Bible. The only textbook necessary is the Bible, used with the attractively printed, interestingly written lessons. Here is a helpful way to study the Bible in your own home and at your own convenience without obligation. Loose-leaf edition. **$1.75**. Bound edition. **$2.35**. From **The Restitutional Herald, Box 100, Oregon, IL 61061**.

TEACH YOURSELF THE BIBLE SERIES (Moody Press) For: L,S. Slant: EP,P,I,M.

Designed to help you discover important basic Bible truths for yourself, this series takes you carefully through each book of the New Testament and six other subjects crucial to the understanding of all growing Christians. **$2.25**. Bookstores or from **Moody Bookworld, 2101 W. Howard, Chicago, IL 60645**.

THE TEN COMMANDMENTS FOR TODAY (Harper & Row, Publishers, Inc.) For: L,C. Slant: EP.

By William Barclay. Available in September, 1983. For the first time in Harper paperback, here is the noted evangelical scholar's presentation of the timeless meaning of the Ten Commandments, and their relevance to

BIBLE STUDY/READING GUIDES FOR INDIVIDUALS

today's moral and ethical dilemmas. William Barclay stresses their positive inner principles of self-limitation and self-discipline that make it possible for people to live together. He devotes a chapter to each commandment, blending traditional wisdom and fresh insights. This is a welcome reminder of our moral beginnings and a timely challenge to rediscover both the necessity and the opportunities of the responsible, ethical life. "Scholarly, brilliant, and lucid." Malcolm Muggeridge 206 pages. Paperback. Number RD 476. **$5.95.** Bookstores or from **Harper & Row, Publishers, Inc., Mail Order Department, 2350 Virginia Ave., Hagerstown, MD 21740.**

THESSALONIANS: A STUDY FROM THE LIVING BIBLE (Tyndale House Publishers) For: L,S. Slant: AW,C, RC,F,EP,MP,LP,P,CP.

By John C. Souter. A Bible study designed to help you discover on your own what the Word of God is saying. For personal or group Bible study. 80 pages. Paper. **$1.95.** Bookstores.

THINGS WHICH BECOME SOUND DOCTRINE (Zondervan Publishing House) For: L,C,S. Slant: EP.

By J. Dwight Pentecost. The doctrinal studies in this book are based on fourteen tremendous words of faith: Grace, Redemption, Sanctification, Regeneration, Reconciliation, Security, Imputation, Propitiation, Predestination, Substitution, Depravity, Resurrection, Repentance, Justification. **$4.95.** Bookstores or from **Zondervan Retail Marketing Service, 1420 Robinson Road, SE, Grand Rapids, MI 49506.**

THIS MORNING WITH GOD (Inter-Varsity Press) For: L,S. Slant: EP,D, P.

A unique daily devotional guide. It leads readers to study the Bible itself. The method is simple: Each day a few well-worded questions direct attention to a selected passage of Scripture. Readers are not spoonfed. They are allowed to come to their own conclusions. And before they've gone through the Bible (in four years) they will have mastered an approach that will last a lifetime. Paper. **$8.95.** Bookstores.

THIS WE BELIEVE (Baptist Publishing House) For: L,S. Slant: F,EP,P.

By Mrs. Z.W. Swafford. Basic Bible studies set forth with Scriptures given for reference and further study. Five chapters: The Essence of God (God, Jesus, Holy Spirit); From Depravity to Security (Depravity, Justification, Sanctification, Eternal Security); New Testament Church (Nature, Institution, Commission, and Perpetuity of it); Jesus Will Come (Coming to Call His Children, to Reward, to Execute Wrath, To Reign, to Punish the Wicked, and To give Rest). **$2.50.** From **Baptist Publishing House, 712 Main, Little Rock, AR 72201.**

THOUGHTS FOR GROWING CHRISTIANS (Moody Press) For: L,S,Y. Slant: EP,D,P,I,M.

By David R. Reid. Devotionals that are each mini-Bible studies geared to high school and college students and arranged to complement the school year. **$3.95.** Bookstores or from **Moody Bookworld, 2101 W. Howard St., Chicago, IL 60645.**

THOUGHTS FOR THE QUIET HOUR (Moody Press) For: L. Slant: EP,D,I, M.

By D.L. Moody. From Genesis to Revelation, a meditation for every day of the year. **$2.95.** Bookstores or from **Moody Bookworld, 2101 W. Howard St., Chicago, IL 60645.**

THROUGH THE BIBLE BOOK BY BOOK, BOOK 1 (Genesis to Esther) (Gospel Publishing House) For: C,S. Slant: EP,S,CP.

BIBLE STUDY/READING GUIDES FOR INDIVIDUALS

A systematic Bible study covering the general contents of Genesis to Esther. The author records the original recipients of each book as well as a concise study of the actual Bible text. Catalog number 02-0660. 99 pages. Paper. **$2.50.** Add 15% for postage and handling. Bookstores or from **Gospel Publishing House, 1445 Boonville Ave., Springfield, MO 65802.**

THROUGH THE BIBLE BOOK BY BOOK, BOOK 2 (Job to Malachi) (Gospel Publishing House) For: C,S. Slant: EP,S,CP.

A systematic Bible study covering the general contents of Job to Malachi. The author records the original recipients of each book as well as a concise study of the actual Bible text. Catalog number 02-0661. 112 pages. Paper. **$2.50.** Add 15% for postage and handling. Bookstores or from **Gospel Publishing House, 1445 Boonville Ave., Springfield, MO 65802.**

THROUGH THE BIBLE BOOK BY BOOK, BOOK 3 (Gospels to Acts) (Gospel Publishing House) For: C,S. Slant: EP,S,CP.

A systematic Bible study covering the general contents of the Gospels to Acts. The author records the original recipients of each book as well as a concise study of the actual Bible text. Catalog number 02-0662. 96 pages. Paper. **$2.50.** Add 15% for postage and handling. Bookstores or from **Gospel Publishing House, 1445 Boonville Ave., Springfield, MO 65802.**

THROUGH THE BIBLE BOOK BY BOOK, BOOK 4 (Epistles to Revelation) (Gospel Publishing House) For: C,S. Slant: EP,S,CP.

A systematic Bible study covering the general contents of the Epistles to Revelation. The author records the original recipients of each book as well as a concise study of the actual Bible text. Catalog number 02-0663. 128 pages. Paper. **$2.50.** Add 15% for postage and handling. Bookstores or from **Gospel Publishing House, 1445 Boonville Ave., Springfield, MO 65802.**

A THROUGH THE BIBLE READING PROGRAM (Standard Publishing) For: L,C,S,Y,Ch. Slant: P.

A chronological outline for reading the Bible through in one year, the program includes a method to check reading progress, notes on each reading to provide background and motivate reading, plus maps and charts for visual reference. Only five readings are required, providing two "make up" days to avoid discouragement should the reader miss a reading—or to use for review of the week's readings. The most comprehensive and easy-to-use Bible reading program available in one volume. Number 30760. **$3.95.** From Bookstores or from **Standard Publishing, 8121 Hamilton Ave., Cincinnati, OH 45231.**

TOPICAL MEMORY SYSTEM (NavPress) For: L,C,S,Y. Slant: EP,P.

Contains 60 key verses on the life of discipleship. This revised Scripture memory system, developed and refined in the Navigator disciplemaking ministry, results from more than 30 years of experience in teaching Scripture memory. The **TMS** teaches memory skills and encourages review, application, and life-long Scripture memory. Verses relate to basic discipleship topics, so the student can always be prepared with Scripture to answer questions others have about Christianity, to fight off temptations, and to meditate on scriptural principles. Materials for this system include a course booklet, a vinyl verse pack, and 60 verse cards. The King James Version and New International Version are printed back-to-back on one set of verse cards and the New American Standard Bible and the Revised Standard Version are printed back-to-back on the second set. **$6.95.** Bookstores or from **NavPress, P.O. Box 6000, Colorado Springs, CO 80934.**

TWO BECOME ONE (Tyndale House Publishers) For: L,S. Slant: AW,C, RC,F,EP,MP,LP,P,CP.

By J. Allan Petersen with Elven and Joyce Smith. A guide to help individuals, couples, and small groups learn what the Bible teaches about marriage and the family. 127 pages. Trade paper. **$3.95.** Bookstores.

UNDERSTANDING BIBLE TRUTHS, THE BIBLE (Here's Life Publishers) For: L,S. Slant: EP,P.

A study of the essential facts that the Bible teaches about the Bible. Product Number 950279. Package of five. **$7.50.** Bookstores or from **Here's Life Publishers, P.O. Box 1576, San Bernardino, CA 92402.**

UNDERSTANDING THE TIMES OF CHRIST (Gospel Publishing House) For: L,C,S. Slant: EP,P,CP.

Understanding the historical setting of the Scriptures is crucial to understanding the Scriptures. Every Christian teacher, minister, and Bible student will benefit from the archaeological discoveries and cultural insights discussed in this book. Catalog number 02-0622. 128 pages. Cloth. **$1.50.** Add 15% for postage and handling. Bookstores or from **Gospel Publishing House, 1445 Boonville Ave., Springfield, MO 65802.**

UNLOCKING HEAVEN'S STOREHOUSE (It Is Written Telecast) For: L. Slant: MP,D,P.

The Holy Bible is the revelation of God to the human race. It is a storehouse filled with promises of justice and mercy, love and forgiveness, and the power for victorious living. Prayer is heaven's appointed key to unlocking the storehouse and putting a sincere soul in touch with Omnipotence. This 64-page book is designed to help you understand the relationship of prayer in finding a vibrant, personal relationship with God through meaningful Bible study. Individual copies. **$2.00.** Three copies. **$5.00.** From **It Is Written Telecast, Box 0, Thousand Oaks, CA 91360.**

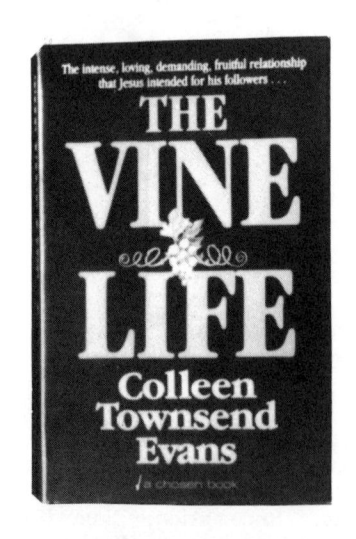

THE VINE LIFE (Chosen Books) For: L,C,S,Y. Slant: EP,D.

BIBLE STUDY/READING GUIDES FOR INDIVIDUALS

By Colleen Townsend Evans. Jesus promised us a harvest of joy, fulfillment, and good healthy fruit if we would depend on Him the way a branch depends on a vine. "Apart from Me," he said, "you can do nothing." These words from John 15 beckoned to Colleen Townsend Evans, and her search began: to discover what it means to rely on Jesus. In **The Vine Life** she describes that search and what it has meant to her and her family. Beyond the personal experiences this book is an eleven-part study of John 15. Even greater relevance is captured as the author describes botanical aspects of growing grapes in the Holy Land at the time of Jesus. Paperback. Catalog number 13034p. **$4.95.** Catalog number 13034. Hard-cover. **$6.95.** Bookstores or from **Zondervan, 1415 Lake Drive, SE, Grand Rapids, MI 49506.**

THE WAY HOME (Johnson Publishing) For: S,Y.

A systematic study of the Bible (Bible correspondence study). Designed for diligent study of the Bible, for mature students who are challenged by an in-depth study of the Scriptures. This series only offered in a set of twenty-six lessons. Each lesson with questions to answer, which require serious study. Each lesson produced as 4 pages in 5 1/2 x 8 1/2 inch format. Printed on easy-to-read white paper. Ideal lessons for churches to use for members or in personal evangelism in their community, or even foreign countries. Only sold in complete sets of 26 lessons along with grading key. One set (26 lessons and grading key). **$3.00.** Plus postage. Ten sets (26 lessons along with grading key). **$2.75** each. Plus UPS charge. More than ten sets, special quotes available by mail. From **Johnson Publishing, P.O. Box 100704, Nashville, TN 37210.**

A WAY THROUGH THE WILDERNESS (Chosen Books) For: L,C,S. Slant: EP,D.

By Jamie Buckingham. The Sinai desert, with its scorching sands and craggy mountains, is a place of purification, of preparation—as Moses and the children of Israel discovered. For forty years they wandered the barren ridges and valleys, learning about God's care and provision. Jamie Buckingham, facing a desolate time in his own life, felt compelled to travel the Sinai in the footsteps of Moses. The trip was torturous. Often, he doubted that he would even survive. Yet he became totally fascinated with the rugged land and its cleansing effect on his own spirit. He returned again and again with new groups of pilgrims who wanted to retreat from the world's clamor into the stillness of God's presence. What they discovered, you can discover, too—the love, comfort, encouragement, and provision that God offers anyone who faces a "wilderness" experience. Buckingham has captured the essence of spectacular lessons from God: the Burning Bush, the Rod, the Staff, silence, and Mount Sinai itself. Catalog number 13022. Hardcover. **$10.95.** Bookstores or **Zondervan, 1415 Lake Drive, SE, Grand Rapids, MI 49506.**

WHAT DOES IT MEAN TO BELIEVE IN JESUS (Aglow Publications) For: L,W. Slant: CP.

Written with the new Christian in mind. Based on the Gospel of John, this attractive mini-book clearly explains who Jesus is, what He can be to you and your part in establishing a relationship with Him. Catalog number 533004. **$2.00** Add **15%** of total order for postage plus **$1.00** handling for each order. Washington state residents add 7.3% sales tax. Ask for free catalog. Bookstores or from **Aglow Publications, P.O. Box I, Lynnwood, WA 98036.**

WHAT EVERY CHRISTIAN SHOULD KNOW ABOUT GOD (Harvest House Publications) For: L,C,S. Slant: EP, P,I,M.

By Rick Yohn. Provides a solid outline for Bible students and laypersons who want to know more about God. Based solidly on Scripture, this manual encourages us to turn to the Word for answers to our questions. An exciting resource for group or individual Bible study. Paper. **$3.95.** Bookstores or from **Harvest House Publishers, 1075 Arrowsmith, Eugene, OR 97402.**

WHAT THE BIBLE TEACHES (Warner Press, Inc.) For: L,C,S. Slant: AW.

By F.G. Smith, condensed by Kenneth Jones. A valuable book based on the doctrines of the Church of God as taught in the Bible. This long-popular work has passed through 20 editions in various forms since its original publication and is still up-to-date. Discusses such topics as redemption, divine healing, footwashing, and the second coming of Christ. Paper. Order number D8850. **$4.95.** Bookstores or from **Warner Press, Inc., P.O. Box 2499, Anderson, IN 46018.**

WHAT THE BIBLE TEACHES ABOUT CHRISTIAN LIVING (Tyndale House Publishers) For: L,S. Slant: AW,C, RC,F,EP,MP,LP,P,CP.

By Gilbert Kirby. The author shares his discoveries from the Bible about how to develop Christian character and put it to work in the world. A "Layman Series" book. 110 pages. Trade paper. **$3.95.** Bookstores.

WHAT THE BIBLE TEACHES ABOUT THE CHURCH (Tyndale House Publishers) For: L,S. Slant: AW,C,RC,F,EP, MP,LP,P,CP.

By John F. Balchin. Deals with the historical church, the present-day

BIBLE STUDY/READING GUIDES FOR INDIVIDUALS

church and its role in the world, and the future of the church. A "Layman Series" book. 141 pages. Trade paper. **$3.95**. Bookstores.

WHAT THE BIBLE TEACHES ABOUT DEATH (Tyndale House Publishers) For: L,S. Slant: AW,C,RC,F,EP,MP,LP,P,CP.

By Peter Cotterell. The Bible is the authority the author uses to help us understand and cope with the reality of death. A "Layman Series" book. 118 pages. Trade paper. **$3.95**. Bookstores.

WHAT THE BIBLE TEACHES ABOUT THE END OF THE WORLD (Tyndale House Publishers) For: L,S. Slant: AW,C,RC,F,EP,MP,LP,P,CP.

By Bruce Milne. Is the world coming to an end? How should we interpret signs? It's time for us to look carefully at the source of information, the Bible itself. A "Layman Series" book. 159 pages. Trade Paper. **$3.95**. Bookstores.

WHAT THE BIBLE TEACHES ABOUT THE HOLY SPIRIT (Tyndale House Publishers) For: L,S. Slant: AW,C,RC,F,EP,MP,LP,P,CP.

By John Peck. The Holy Spirit is the personage of God at work in the world today. This scriptural study will help reveal his person and his work. A "Layman Series" book. 144 pages. Trade paper. **$3.95**. Bookstores.

WHAT THE BIBLE TEACHES ABOUT JESUS (Tyndale House Publishers) For: L,S. Slant: AW,C,RC,F,EP,MP,LP,P,CP.

By Geoffrey W. Grogan. What does the Bible say about the person of Jesus Christ, historically and prophetically, his return, and eternal state? A "Layman Series" book. 136 pages. Trade paper. **$3.95**. Bookstores.

WHAT THE BIBLE TEACHES ABOUT WHAT JESUS DID (Tyndale House Publishers) For: L,S. Slant: AW,C,RC,F,EP,MP,LP,P,CP.

By F.F. Bruce. Christ is God's revelation of himself to the world. It is important to know Him, and understand Him, so that we may love and serve Him better. A "Layman Series" book. 144 pages. Trade paper. **$3.95**. Bookstores.

WHAT TO DO TILL THE LORD COMES: STUDIES IN 1 and 2 THESSALONIANS (Tyndale House Publishers) For: L,S. Slant: AW,C,RC,F,EP,MP,LP,P,CP.

The author parallels Thessalonian believers with 20th-century Christians—both serving God in an ungodly world, awaiting the second coming of Christ. 13-week study. Book. **$6.95**. Leader's Guide. **$2.95**. Bookstores.

WHO IS THIS MAN JESUS? (Regal Books) For: L,C,S,Y. Slant: EP.

Paraphrased by Kenneth N. Taylor. A chronological presentation of the life of Jesus from The Living Bible. 288 pages. Paperback. Number S4107. **$2.25**. Bookstores or from **Regal Books, Div. of GL Publications, 2300 Knoll Drive, Ventura, CA 93003**.

WHO'S WHO AMONG BIBLE WOMEN (Gospel Publishing House) For: L,C,S,W. Slant: EP,P,CP.

By looking at women of the Bible such as Esther, Miriam, Sarah, and Mary, this book draws parallels that speak to women today. It shows the biblical message that women are persons of value to God, to their families, and to their neighbors. Catalog number 02-0883. 128 pages. Paper. **$2.50**. Add 15% for postage and handling. Bookstores or from **Gospel Publishing House, 1445 Boonville Ave., Springfield, MO 65802**.

WILL MAN SURVIVE? (Zondervan Publishing House) For: L,C,S. Slant: EP.

By J. Dwight Pentecost. An understandable book that will dispel the darkness of uncertainty and show who is really in control of humanity's destiny. **$5.95**. Bookstores or from **Zondervan Retail Marketing Service, 1420 Robinson Road, SE, Grand Rapids, MI 49506**.

WOMEN OF THE BIBLE (OLD TESTAMENT) (Daughter's of St. Paul) For: L,S, Y, W. Slant: RC,EP,MP,RJ,D.

Meet the women who influenced the patriarchs, prophets, judges and kings of the Old Testament. Penetrate their hopes and dreams, struggles and sorrows. 144 pages. Beautiful full-color illustrations. Cloth. SC0460. **$5.95**. Please include **$.75** postage. Bookstores or from **Daughters of St. Paul, 50 St. Paul's Avenue, Jamaica Plain, Boston, MA 02130**.

WOMEN OF THE GOSPEL (NEW TESTAMENT) (Daughters of St. Paul) For: L,S,Y,W. Slant: RC,EP,MP,RJ,D.

Profile of twenty women found in the New Testament. 138 pages. Beautiful full-color illustrations. Cloth. Number SC0470. **$5.95**. Please include **$.75** for postage. Bookstores or from **Daughters of St. Paul, 50 St. Paul's Avenue, Jamaica Plain, Boston, MA 02130**.

WORD KEYS WHICH UNLOCK SCRIPTURE (Word of Grace) For: L,C,S,Y. Slant: C,P,S.

In-depth studies of single words... Bound ('75 publication includes TULIP). Not bound...single word studies covering Doctrines of Grace and other subjects...Semitic Symbols...Last Things... Second Coming...Wedding and Divorce... Doctrine of God...Doctrine of Christ and Salvation...Doctrine of Man... Doctrine of Angels and Demons. '75 issue bound. **$10.00**. Not-bound single issues. Four for **$1.00**. From **Word of Grace, P.O. Box 7, San Antonio, TX 78291**.

WORDS OF WISDOM: A PROVERB FOR EVERY DAY (Daughters of St. Paul) For: L,C,S,Y. Slant: RC,EP,MP,RJ,D.

A proverb for every day of the year interspersed with over 100 full-color pictures. Cloth. Number SC0478. **$9.50**. Bookstores or from **Daughters of St. Paul, 50 St. Paul's Ave., Jamaica Plain, Boston, MA 02130**.

BIBLE STUDY/READING GUIDES FOR INDIVIDUALS

WRITTEN IN BLOOD (Christian Outreach) For: L,C,S,Y,Ch. Slant: EP,P,I.

By Robert E. Coleman. A thorough study of references to blood in the Bible. Each chapter contains suggested readings and questions, all pointing to the truth that what the blood of Christ has accomplished for us, the spirit of Christ effects in us. Foreword by John R.W. Stott. Seventh Printing. "For the last half of the 20th-century, this book stands out. The studies never lack depth of treatment, scholarship, or dependability"—**Bibliothecasacra.** Cloth. **$7.95.** Quality Paper. **$4.95.** Mass market compact. **$1.95.** Bookstores or from **Christian Outreach, 200 Asbury Drive, Wilmore, KY 40390.**

YEAR OF THE LORD, PARTS 1 AND 2 (Greek Orthodox Archdiocese) For: L,S,Y. Slant: G.

By Theodore Stylianopoulos. Follows the sequence of Sundays and feasts of the Orthodox liturgical year. Together with many passages from the Old and New Testaments, the reader will find in the series numerous feasts, hymns, and relevant explanations unified in a coherent whole. (Parts 3, 4, and 5 to be added). Part 1, **$5.25**; Part 2, **$5.00**. From **Greek Orthodox Archdiocese, Department of Religious Education, 50 Goddard Ave., Brookline, MA 02146.**

YOU CAN'T BEAT THE BEATITUDES (Gospel Publishing House) For: L,C,S. Slant: EP,P,CP.

In concise language, this book analyzes each of the Beatitudes, offering interesting and helpful conclusions to help readers live the way God wants them to live. Catalog number 02-0719. 96 pages. Paper. **$1.25.** Add 15% for postage and handling. Bookstores or from **Gospel Publishing House, 1445 Boonville Ave., Springfield, MO 65802.**

YOU TAKE THE WHEEL (Faith for Today) For: L,C,S,Y. Slant: P.

A delightful Home Seminar series for young people (and oldsters, too!). **You Take the Wheel** shares biblical insights into such topics as personal responsibility, love, creationism/evolutionism, freedom vs. license, honesty, life's limits, and much more. Designed to lead the youthful mind into a personal friendship with Jesus, **You Take the Wheel** has already brightened the lives of more than 15,000 satisfied people. Individuals. Free. **$1.75** per set in quantities of 10 complete sets. From **You Take the Wheel, Box 1000, Thousand Oaks, CA 91359.**

YOUR ADVERSARY THE DEVIL (Zondervan Publishing House) For: L,C,S. Slant: EP.

By J. Dwight Pentecost. This book will teach from the Scriptures the true nature of our adversary, the devil—so that we may know and be able to detect his movements, in our daily experience. **$5.95.** Bookstores or from **Zondervan Retail Marketing Service, 1420 Robinson Road, SE, Grand Rapids, MI 49506.**

YOUR WORD (Scripture Meditations) (Servant Publications) For: L. Slant: D.

By George Martin. Profound, perceptive, and inspiring. Contains 44 of Dr. Martin's best meditations—perhaps the best selection of writing about Scripture available in any one publication. 144 pages. 4 3/16 x 6 7/8 inches. **$2.25.** Bookstores.

YOUTH BIBLE STUDY NOTEBOOK (Tyndale House Publishers) For: Y. Slant: AW,C,RC,F,EP,MP,LP,P,CP.

By John and Susan Souter. Various study methods that help young people grow strong in faith. Used a few minutes each day, this write-in book helps them dig nuggets of truth from God's Word. Logs their journey so they can see their progress. 192 pages. Trade paper. **$4.95.** Bookstores.

A YEAR OF THE BIBLE
"SPECIAL"
* Special Prices
* Special Designs

GOOD NEWS BIBLE.
Today's English Version.
Paperbound – only $2.00

**GOOD NEWS
NEW TESTAMENT.**
Today's English Version.
Paperbound – only $.65

**HOLY BIBLE.
KING JAMES VERSION.**
Flexible cover – only $2.00

**NEW TESTAMENT.
KING JAMES VERSION.**
Paperbound – only $.65

SHARE IN THE CELEBRATION...

Make this a year for reaching out in new ways – to friends and neighbors, to your community, to the whole nation – with these handsome, low-priced Bibles and New Testaments. Their sturdy, richly-colored bindings and extra-low cost make them ideal Scriptures for sharing widely in your special Year of the Bible programs and activities.

The Good News Bible and Good News New Testament feature the easy-to-read-and-understand language of Today's English Version. Both are paperbound, and the Good News Bible is a special, non-illustrated, newsprint edition. The King James Version Holy Bible and New Testament are in the classic translation, beloved by generations, and both are printed in an easy-to-read typeface.

EASY ORDER FORM

ORDER NO.	QUANTITY	ITEM	PRICE	TOTAL
00671		Good News Bible. Today's English Version. Paperbound (5¼ x 8 in.)	$2.00	
02917		Good News New Testament. Today's English Version. Paperbound (4½ x 7 in.)	$ .65	
00215		Holy Bible. King James Version. Flexible cover. (5¼ x 8 in.)	$2.00	
02129		New Testament. King James Version. Paperbound. (4½ x 7 in.)	$ .65	

SHIP TO: _____
(please print)
ADDRESS: _____
CITY: _____ STATE: _____ ZIP: _____

SUB TOTAL
GIFT FOR WORLD OUTREACH
GRAND TOTAL

California residents please add applicable sales tax.
Payment must accompany order
Enclosed ☐ CHECK ☐ MONEY ORDER
Amount Enclosed $ _____

AMERICAN BIBLE SOCIETY, BOX 5656, Grand Central Station, New York, N.Y. 10163

1XG

BIBLE STUDY/READING GUIDES FOR GROUPS

Bible study aids for groups are primarily those books and other resources aimed specifically at group study in Sunday School classes, prayer and praise groups, living room study groups, and more formal classroom settings. Many have leader/teacher materials and discussion guidelines as well as general texts and most (but not all) are organized around a weekly gathering of a student group. Persons seeking resources for group study should also check the section on guides to individual study and the three sections on commentaries because many of these items could justifiably be listed in more than one place. Also, those group study programs which are primarily organized around an audio-visual such as a film, audio cassette, or video cassette, are listed in the section on audio-visuals. In fact, it is safe to assume that most of the items in the audio-visual section are actually aids for group Bible study.

BIBLE STUDY/READING GUIDES FOR GROUPS

ADULT BIBLICAL INTERDEPENDENT LEARNING (Biblical Andragogy Clinic) For: L,C. Slant: C,RC,MP,LP,S,BC.

Adult Biblical Interdependent Learning (ABIL) is the effective and successful adult Bible study program, designed for the local church, that incorporates: current biblical scholarship; adult learning theory; leadership training; and skills in the building of Christian community. ABIL's 40 sequenced learning units are carefully written syntheses of scholarly insights that are continuously updated under the auspices of internationally established biblical specialists. The comprehension level is that of a Master of Divinity program taught at seminary or university. Ordinary adults, learning in the setting of their local church, are highly successful in comprehending and articulating the content of the **ABIL** program because the learning methodology is truly adult, supportive and enabling. High priority is given to the careful training of facilitators to lead **ABIL** groups in the local congregation. Two-week Facilitator Clinics are conducted in the U.S. and Canada. Training of a leader at an **ABIL** Facilitators Clinic is a prerequisite to a congregation's enrolling in the **ABIL** program. Training schedules available from **Dr. Eugene F. Trester, Biblical Andragogy Clinic, 1253 Woodland Ave., Mississauga, Ontario, Canada L5G 2X8.**

AFTER DEATH, WHAT? STUDENT ACTIVITY BOOK (Herald Press) For: L. Slant: EP.

By Gerald Studer and Laurence Martin. Ten-session student activity book based on **After Death, What?** Written for youth and adults. 1978. 40 pages. Paper. 1866-9. **$1.25**. Bookstores.

ALDERSGATE BIBLE STUDIES (Light and Life Press) Slant: AW.

The Aldersgate Bible Study is an indepth inductive book by book Bible study of the entire Bible. It may be used in Sunday school classes, small group Bible studies or individual study. Leader's Guide is included for use in group studies. Each book. **$2.25**. From **Light and Life Press, 999 College Ave., Winona Lake, IN 46590.**

ALPHA TEENS (Christian Ed. Publishers) For: Y. Slant: EP.

Junior high program where implementation is the keynote. This Bible-based, Christ-centered program leads junior high youth toward spiritual maturity. The teens are challenged to go into action and to live the Christian life in a personal and practical way. The junior high youth are encouraged to help in the planning and preparing of each youth meeting. This program features weekly lessons as well as student Bible study worksheets and daily devotions. Annual subscription. **$88.00**. From **Christian Ed. Publishers, 7348 Trade Street, San Diego, CA 92121.**

BAKER'S BIBLE STUDY GUIDE (Baker Book House) For: L,S. Slant: EP.

By Derek Prime. For individual Bible study, youth groups, and discussion groups of all ages, this book makes use of an easily understood question and answer method, followed by relevant Scripture passages, to provide the most comprehensive statement of what evangelicals believe. **$8.95**. Bookstores or from **Baker Book House, P.O. Box 6287, Grand Rapids, MI 49506.**

BEACON SMALL-GROUP BIBLE STUDY WORKBOOKS (Beacon Hill Press of Kansas City) For: L,C,S,Y. Slant: AW,EP,H.

A series of Bible study workbooks which can be used for individual study, but written for group use. Includes discussion questions, fill in the blanks, informative introductions and outlines. For leader and students. Books now available: Matthew (Part 1); Mark; Luke (Parts 1 and 2); John (Parts 1 and 2); Acts (Part 1); 1 Corinthians; Ephesians; Philippians/Colossians; Thessalonians; 1 and 2 Timothy and Titus; Hebrews; James; 1 and 2 Peter; 1,2, and 3 John; and The Revelation. The Old Testament series is just getting started with a study of selected Psalms. 64 to 80 pages. Paper with full color covers. 6 x 9 inches. **$2.25** each. Bookstores or from **Beacon Hill Press of Kansas City, Box 527, Dept. B, Kansas City, MO 64141.**

BEHOLD YOUR GOD: A WOMAN'S WORKSHOP ON THE ATTRIBUTES OF GOD (Zondervan Publishing House) For: L,W. Slant: EP.

By Myrna Alexander. The workshop study guide format is easy to follow, with questions at the end of each study session. **$2.95**. Bookstores or from **Zondervan Retail Marketing Service, 1420 Robinson Road, SE, Grand Rapids, MI 49506.**

BIBLE COMPREHENSION WORKBOOK (Aletheia Community Church) For: L,S. Slant: EP,D,P.

A workbook for personal or group use which takes you through the basic steps of understanding what the Scripture is saying to believers by providing them the tools required for understanding the diction and language used in the English translations closest to the original. It includes worksheets, a bibliography and is kept to self-teaching exercises which can be used by anyone who can comprehend English. Included is a checklist to use in enhancing your techniques for biblical understanding. **$3.95**. From **Aletheia Community Church, 1432 E. Elizabeth Street, Pasadena, CA 91104.**

THE BIBLE CREATIVE: THE EXPERIENTIAL COMMENTARY FOR CREATIVE BIBLE STUDY, SPEAKING AND PREACHING (Group Books) For: L,C,S,Y. Slant: EP,MP,P.

BIBLE STUDY/READING GUIDES FOR GROUPS

By Dennis C. Benson. Combination of commentary and scores of creative ideas for group study, speaking, and preaching. Benson goes through John chapter by chapter, offering workable ideas for helping youth and adults experience the message of the gospel. Benson, who enlisted the ideas of hundreds of local Christian workers, encourages readers to let the Bible itself offer clues for not only what to communicate, but also how to communicate it. Most of all, this series engenders a certain creative spirit in Bible teachers, speakers and peachers. Volumes completed to date: The Gospel of John; The Acts of the Apostles. Each volume is hardcover, completely indexed and contains bibliographies. **$19.95** per volume. Bookstores or from **Group Books, Box 481, Loveland, CO 80539.**

BIBLE SHARING: HOW TO GROW IN THE MYSTERY OF CHRIST (Alba House) For: L,C,S. Slant: RC,EP,LP,P.

The purpose of this book is to motivate and instruct Christians to study the Bible and share the fruits of their reflections with others. In this book, Fr. Burke helps make the challenging task of Bible sharing easier and more rewarding by providing certain perspectives and proven methods for arriving at the total meaning of Scripture. He also shows how to form and conduct successful Bible sharing groups and provides a list of some of the best study resources available today. **$5.95**, plus postage. Bookstores or from **Alba House, 2187 Victory Blvd., Staten Island, NY 10314.**

THE BIBLE SPEAKS TO YOUTH (Michael Glazier, Inc.) For: L,S,Y. Slant: RC,P.

A four-year program designed to teach students how to read the Bible, talk about it and apply its teachings to their own lives. Each year of the program is conducted through thirty meetings that are scheduled to run between one to one-and-a-half hours. A catechist's manual is provided and each student receives his own workbook in which he can make personal notes regarding the fruits of the discussions of the biblical texts which constitute the heart of the program. Adult groups looking for discussion guidance also find the program helpful. Student's Workbook. **$3.95**. Catechist's Manual. **$3.95**. From **Michael Glazier, Inc., 1732 Delaware Ave., Wilmington, DE 19806.**

BIBLE STUDY FOR BUSY PEOPLE (Roper Press) For: L,S. Slant: EP,D.

A simple 13 lesson study of basic Bible truths designed to help "busy adults" know and understand the Scriptures. It covers topics such as: what Christ is like; how to know our Bible; how God exists in three persons; how God made man; what Christ has done for man; and how God saves man. Each lesson is presented in a simple format but provides an in-depth foundation for further Bible study. It is ideal for individual or group Bible study. **$1.75**. Bookstores or from **Roper Press, 915 Dragon St., Dallas, TX 75207.**

A BIBLE STUDY ON THE PURSUIT OF HOLINESS (NavPress) For: L,C,S,Y. Slant: EP,P.

By Jerry Bridges. God commands us to live holy lives, but why do we so rarely experience holy living? The central issue confronting us, says Jerry Bridges in the bestseller, **The Pursuit of Holiness**, is that Christians fail to understand their own responsibility for holiness. "If we sin," he writes, "it is because we choose to sin—not because we lack the ability to say no to temptation. We are not defeated, we are simply disobedient." Fortunately, the Bible gives us practical principles which build character and help us rely on the power of our sinless Lord. Bridges, longtime Navigator staff member in both field ministries and administration, describes how to use these principles in the day to day practice of holiness. In his foreword, Dr. Herbert Lockyer, Sr. describes Bridges' book as "incisive" and "conscience-stirring." **Christianity Today** calls it "profitable reading" in every way. **The Pursuit of Holiness** has a twelve-chapter companion Bible study. **$2.95**. Bible study. **$2.25**. Bookstores or from **NavPress, P.O. Box 6000, Colorado Springs, CO 80934.**

BIBLE STUDY SERIES (Tyndale House Publishers) For: L,S. Slant: AW,C, RC,F,EP,MP,LP,P,CP.

By Marilyn Kunz and Catherine Schell. Acts; Amos; Choose Life; The Coming of the Lord; 1 Corinthians; 2 Corinthians and Galatians; Ephesians and Philemon; Four men of God; Genesis; Hebrews; John, Book 1; John, Book 2; 1 John and James; Luke; Mark; Matthew, Book 1; Matthew, Book 2; 1 and 2 Peter; Philippians and Colossians; Psalms and Proverbs; and Romans. **$2.50** per book. Bookstores.

BIBLE STUDY STARTERS (Servant Publications) For: L. Slant: P.

By Peter and Vita Toon. This concise, easy to use program of Scripture study faithfully upholds the Bible as God's revealed word and combines serious study of the Bible with a challenge to live according to what it teaches. Each booklet contains an introduction and ten studies with explanatory notes and background information. Each chapter concludes with a set of questions carefully designed to stimulate discussion about the meaning of the text and the way it can be applied to our lives today. Now available: Exodus; Psalms; Isaiah 1-39; Mark; John 1-11; Romans 1-8; Acts 1-12; Joshua; Letters of John; Matthew 1-12; Nehemiah; and Philippians. **$1.50** per booklet. Package of ten booklets. **$12.50**. Bookstores.

BIBLICAL FOUNDATIONS (Faith and Fellowship Press) For: L. Slant: EP, LU.

By David Rinder. A thirteen lesson study guide on the basic teachings of the Bible. Bible references are used extensively to help the student discover what the Bible says about each subject. **$2.50**. Postage paid on cash orders. From **Faith & Fellowship Press, Box 655, Fergus Falls, MN 56537.**

BUILDING BELIEVERS (The Wesleyan Church) For: L,C,S,Y. Slant: AW,P,H.

A creative training manual dealing with 21 major issues of faith and prac-

BIBLE STUDY/READING GUIDES FOR GROUPS

tice. Built-in process techniques help the learner become a group leader of Bible study. Study methods and group dynamics suggestions are provided in a resource section. Designed primarily for small groups, it may be adapted for individual and larger group use. 1-9 copies. **$12.95** each. 10 or more copies. **$9.95** each. From **The Wesleyan Church, Local Church Education, Box 2000, Marion, IN 46952.**

THE CALL OF JESUS (Aglow Publications) For: L,W. Slant: CP.

The call Jesus makes on the life of the believer is the same as that he made when he walked on earth, seeking disciples. In this Bible study we learn how to make his call applicable to our lives today. 521009. **$2.95.** Add 15% postage plus **$1.00** for handling per each order. Washington State residents add 7.3% sales tax. Ask for free catalog. Bookstores or from **Aglow Publications, P.O. Box I, Lynnwood, WA 98036.**

CALLED TO BE SAINTS (Baker Book House) For: L,C,S. Slant: EP.

By Robert G. Gromacki. This study of I Corinthians is extremely informative and readily understandable. Each of the thirteen chapters is followed by challenging discussion questions. **$5.95.** Bookstores or from **Baker Book House, P.O. Box 6287, Grand Rapids, MI 49506.**

CARPENTER STUDYGUIDES (Harold Shaw Publishers) For: L,C,S,Y. Slant: EP.

A series designed specifically for living room sized groups within the church that want to study God's Word, build strong relationships, deepen their prayer and worship together, and reach out to each other. Inductive Bible study forms the core of the program, but the leader's handbook is full of helpful, group tested ideas for structuring small group meetings with creativity, variety, and balance. The member's handbook includes material for group meetings, along with a prayer notebook and suggested home assignments. A total program for small groups! Studies include: James: Hear It, Live It!; Mark: Good News for Today; and Ruth & Jonah: People in Process. Member's handbook. **$1.95.** Leader's handbook. **$2.95.** Bookstores or from **Harold Shaw Publishers, P.O. Box 567, 388 Gundersen Drive, Wheaton, IL 60189.**

CHOOSE LIFE (Trinity Bible Studies) For: S,Y. Slant: P.

A weekly Bible study resource for youth and young adults. Offered by Trinity Bible Studies, **Choose Life** comes in thirteen week segments (quarters) for church school or evening classes. Each student has a notebook, reading guides and response sheets. Teacher's notebooks include live cassette of each lesson, teaching outline, maps and more. Designed for Bible basics taught by laity. Old and New Testament surveys available. Intro kit sampler with two notebooks. **$15.00.** Notebook binders. **$2.50.** Each course (quarter) **$2.50.** From **Trinity Bible Studies, Box 25101, Dallas, TX 75225.**

CHRIST IN YOU (Aglow Publications) For: L,W. Slant: CP.

One of the mysteries of our faith is the fact that we actually have Christ living within us. This Bible study on the Book of Colossians helps us gain a deeper appreciation of what his indwelling really means. Number 521010. **$2.95.** Postage 15% of total order, plus **$1.00** handling per each order. Washington State residents add 7.3% sales tax. Ask for free catalog. Bookstores or from **Aglow Publications, P.O. Box I, Lynnwood, WA 98036.**

COLOSSIANS: A PORTRAIT OF CHRIST (Tyndale House Publishers) For: L,S. Slant: AW,C,RC,F,EP,MP, LP,P,CP.

By Dr. James T. Draper. This thirteen week study elective on the book of Colossians lends valuable insight into the person of Christ. A Living Studies book. Trade paper. **$3.95.** Leader's Guide available. Bookstores.

CONTEMPORARY NEW TESTAMENT SERIES - 22 BOOKLETS PLUS INDEXES (Daughters of St. Paul) For: L,C,S. Slant: RC,EP,MP,S.

Each booklet of the **Contemporary New Testament Series** is in an 8½ x 11 inch magazine format with photographs of biblical sites and scenes, color masterpiece paintings and sculptures. The text is the New American Bible with footnotes and cross references. The clear, up to date commentaries are by noted biblical scholars. The issues are available in the following sets: Matthew, #1 (SC0161), #2 (SC0162), #3 (SC0163); Mark, #4 (SC0164), #5 (SC0165); Luke, #6 (SC0166), #7 (SC0167), #8 (SC0168); John, #9 (SC0169), #10 (SC0170), #11 (SC0171); Acts, #12 (SC0172), #13 (SC0173), #14 (SC0174); Letters of St. Paul, #15 (SC0175), #16 (SC0176), #17 (SC0177), #18 (SC0178), #19 (SC0179), #20 (SC0180); Revelation, #21 (SC0181), #22 (SC0182); Index for Gospel issues (SC0183); Index for Acts, Letters, and Revelation (SC0184). **$1.20** per issue. Must be purchased in sets as listed. Indexes, **$.50** each. Bookstores or from **Daughters of St. Paul, 50 St. Paul's Ave., Jamaica Plain, Boston, MA 02130.**

CONVERSATIONAL BIBLE STUDIES: NEW TESTAMENT (Baker Book House) For: L. Slant: EP.

BIBLE STUDY/READING GUIDES FOR GROUPS

By James Schacher. All types of sharing groups will find this book to be unusually helpful in discovering truths contained in God's Word. **$1.65.** Bookstores or from **Baker Book House, P.O. Box 6287, Grand Rapids, MI 49506.**

DESIGN FOR DISCIPLESHIP (NavPress) For: L,C,S,Y. Slant: EP,P.

This is the most popular Navigator Bible study. It aims to lead the student into a deep commitment to God through a personal, scriptural examination of what discipleship involves. The first six books in the series offer a challenging study of the authority of the Bible, servanthood, purity of life, the lordship of Christ and world vision. Book seven teaches how to do the chapter analysis Bible study method with I Thessalonians. The Leader's Guide explains how to get a Design for Discipleship group started, how to pray for the group, how to prepare for the studies, how to lead a discussion group and how to evaluate one's own leadership. Those who are leading a group or individual through the **Design for Discipleship** series will find it an invaluable aid. All seven books, **$9.00.** Individual books, **$1.50.** Leader's Guide, **$2.95.** Bookstores or from **NavPress, P.O. Box 6000, Colorado Springs, CO 80934.**

DISCIPLING RESOURCE SERIES (Zondervan Publishing House) For: L,C,S. Slant: EP.

By Larry Richards and Norm Wakefield. Discipling. An old concept that's sweeping today's church. And now there's a series of books that can form the basis of any discipling group. Includes: **Fruit of the Spirit; First Steps for New and Used Christians; Basic Christian Values;** and **The Good Life: A Study of Romans 12-16. $4.95.** Bookstores or from **Zondervan Retail Marketing Service, 1420 Robinson Road, SE, Grand Rapids, MI 49506.**

DISCOVER JOY: STUDIES IN PHILIPPIANS (Tyndale House Publishers) For: L,S. Slant: AW,C,RC,F,EP,MP,LP,D,CP.

Believers can face any circumstance of life or death without despair, but with joy! These studies lend themselves to group discussion. (13 week study). **$4.95.** Leader's Guide. **$2.95.** Bookstores.

DRAWING CLOSER TO GOD (Aglow Publications) For: L,W. Slant: CP.

The book of Ruth contains all the elements of an old fashioned drama: pathos, loyalty, romance, suspense, even ending on a "they lived happily ever after" note. However, this charming little book is so much more. Containing one of the clearest patterns of the Christian's growing relationship with the Lord, it will teach you in a way that will bring joy to your spirit for a long time to come. Number 521014. **$2.95.** Postage 15% of total order, plus **$1.00** handling per each order. Washington State residents add 7.3% sales tax. Ask for free catalog. Bookstores or from **Aglow Publications, P.O. Box I, Lynnwood, WA 98036.**

THE EQUIPPING MINISTRY (National Church Growth Research Center) For: L,C. Slant: EP,P.

Makes a bold plea for equipping every Christian to be a servant of Jesus Christ. The ministry of the church is seen as a shared responsibility of the whole body as church members work with their leaders in carrying out the great commission. Not only does the author deal with biblical mandates found in Ephesians and I Peter, but also he brings them to practical application in the reader's life and in his church. **$3.95** per single copy. Study Guide. **$1.50.** From **National Church Growth Research Center, P.O. Box 17575, Washington, DC 20041.**

1983-84 EVANGELICAL SUNDAY SCHOOL LESSON COMMENTARY (Pathway Press) For: L. Slant: EP.

An annual Sunday school commentary that is based on the Evangelical Curriculum Commission Bible Lesson Series Outlines. Includes verse by verse exposition, lesson outlines, illustrations, dictionary of difficult terms, sentence sermons, practical applications, discussion and review questions, golden text homilies and daily reading guide. **$7.95.** Bookstores or from **Pathway Press, 1080 Montgomery Avenue, Cleveland, TN 37311.**

EXPERIENCING GOD'S ATTRIBUTES (NavPress) For: L,C,S. Slant: EP,P.

By Warren and Ruth Myers. This study helps Christians grow in their understanding of God and His character and helps them apply scriptural insights to experience Him more intimately. Students discover who God reveals Himself to be as they examine twelve attributes of God by studying, meditating, and praying on selected Scripture passages. Each chapter allows for a deeper study of God's attributes: beauty, holiness, goodness, power, knowability, love, total forgiveness, sovereignty, grace, faithfulness, and worthiness. Individuals who feel God to be aloof, critical, or impersonal can gain a more accurate, biblical understanding of the Father. **$4.50.** Bookstores or from **NavPress, P.O. Box 6000, Colorado Springs, CO 80934.**

EXPERIENCING GOD'S PRESENCE (NavPress) For: L,C,S. Slant: EP, P.

By Warren and Ruth Myers. This study of selected Scripture passages leads Christians to a discovery of the thrilling aspects of God's desired relationship with His children. Depending on Him, serving Him, confiding in Him,

BIBLE STUDY/READING GUIDES FOR GROUPS

enjoying His support and delighting in Him are some of the topics studied. Individuals become much more involved with the God who longs to relate personally with them and meet their needs. **$4.50**. Bookstores or from **NavPress, P.O. Box 6000, Colorado Springs, CO 80934.**

FACING YOURSELF IN THE BIBLE (Baker Book House) For: L. Slant: EP.

By William Krutza. Studies in human personalities from the Bible. This treatment of Bible personalities reinforces the great fact that the Word of God is the best mirror of human nature. **$1.25**. Bookstores or from **Baker Book House, P.O. Box 6287, Grand Rapids, MI 49506.**

FAITH THAT WORKS: STUDIES IN JAMES (Tyndale House Publishers) For: L,S. Slant: AW,C,RC,F,EP,MP,LP,D,CP.

A challenge to action! This book encourages us to be doers of the Word and not hearers only. (13 week study). Book. **$5.95**. Leader's Guide. **$2.95**. Bookstores.

FAMOUS COUPLES OF THE BIBLE (Tyndale House Publishers) For: L,S. Slant: AW,C,RC,F,EP,MP,LP,P,CP.

By Dr. Richard Strauss. A thirteen week study elective which uses the examples of Bible marriages to point to ways Christians can strengthen their marriage today. A Living Studies book. Trade paper. Book. **$3.95**. Leader's Guide. **$2.95**. Bookstores.

FIRST STEPS/HOW TO FOLLOW-THRU (Christian Business Men's Committee of USA) For: L,S,Y.

A four lesson introductory Bible study for those with little or no knowledge of the Bible or the life of Jesus Christ as recorded in the New Testament. It can be used by individuals or in a group setting in a home, office, or church. **First Steps** covers these basic questions of the Christian faith: "Is the Bible Credible?", "Who is Jesus Christ?", and "Eternal Life in Christ." The Scripture passages used for each lesson are included within the booklet for those looking for the answers to the questions. **How To Follow-Thru** is a leader's guide, not only for **First Steps**, but also for evangelistic and follow-thru activities in your home.

How To... offers step-by-step instructions and outlines for leading a **First Steps** study, plus guidelines for having home dinner parties and film showings to help new believers grow. A special section with hints for planning and preparation is also included. **First Steps. $1.25** each; ten or more, **$1.00** each. **How To Follow-Thru. $2.00** each, plus 10% postage. From **Christian Business Men's Committee of USA, 1800 McCallie Ave., Chattanooga, TN 37404.**

FISHERMAN BIBLE STUDYGUIDES (Harold Shaw Publishers) For: L,C,S. Slant: EP.

These inductive Bible studies provide a way for people in neighborhood, student and church groups to discover together what God is saying through His Word. **Fisherman Bible Studyguides** are arranged in a sequence to allow the groups flexibility while providing a structure that assures study of the major areas of Christian life and belief in a systematic and balanced plan. By moving in the general sequence outlined in the back of each studyguide, groups will grow in maturity and learn how to study God's Word in depth. Thirty-three studies to choose from, including New and Old Testament book studies and topical studies. The ten most popular **Fisherman Studyguides** are: David: Man After God's Own Heart; Psalms: A Guide to Prayer and Praise; Proverbs & Parables; The God Who Understands Me: The Sermon on the Mount; Mark: God in Action; John: Eyewitness; Romans: Made Righteous by Faith; James: Faith in Action; Guidance and God's Will; Higher Ground; and Women Who Believed in God. **$2.50** each. Bookstores or from **Harold Shaw Publishers, P.O. Box 567, 388 Gundersen Drive, Wheaton, IL 60189.**

THE FRUIT OF THE SPIRIT (Aglow Publications) For: L,W. Slant: CP.

What is this spiritual fruit the Bible speaks of? How does it grow in our lives? This Bible study answers these questions and helps us to grow and recognize what might be hindering this growth in us. The study is based on Galatians 5:22-23. Number 521003. **$2.95**. Postage 15% of total order, plus **$1.00** handling per each order. Washington State residents add 7.3% sales tax. Ask for free catalog. Bookstores or from **Aglow Publications, P.O. Box I, Lynnwood, WA 98036.**

GETTING INTO GOD (Zondervan Publishing House) For: L,C,S. Slant: EP.

By D. Stuart Briscoe. This study provides the basic guidance every Christian needs to become grounded in Bible study, meaningfully involved in prayer, and knowledgeable enough to become an effective witness for Christ. **$2.95**. Bookstores or from **Zondervan Retail Marketing Service, 1420 Robinson Road, SE, Grand Rapids, MI 49506.**

GOD, MAN AND JESUS CHRIST (NavPress) For: L,C,S. Slant: EP,P.

Here's a valuable tool for leading evangelistic discussion groups. Church members on campus, in business groups, in women's evangelistic coffees, and in church evangelism programs can learn how to invite people to join a study, how to lead the discussion, how to share the Gospel, and how to follow-up new Christians. The studies ask probing questions frequently posed by non-Christians and direct participants into the Bible for answers. They do not require any advance

BIBLE STUDY/READING GUIDES FOR GROUPS

preparation except by the leader and can be easily duplicated for distribution in a group. **$2.95.** Bookstores or from **NavPress, P.O. Box 6000, Colorado Springs, CO 80934.**

GOD'S DAUGHTER (Aglow Publications) For: L,W. Slant: CP.

Today's woman is adrift in a sea of conflicting ideas about her "place" in God's scheme. This Bible study shares our Creator's very practical truths for women in relation to their husbands, families and in all areas of home life. Number 521002. **$2.95.** Postage 15% of total order, plus **$1.00** handling per each order. Washington State residents add 7.3% sales tax. Ask for free catalog. Bookstores or from **Aglow Publications, P.O. Box I, Lynnwood, WA 98036.**

GOD'S DESIGN FOR THE FAMILY (NavPress) For: L,C. Slant: EP,P.

This four book question-and-answer series examines four relationships in the family structure: husband and wife, parents and children, the family and God, and the family and society. By doing this study, couples examine what the Scriptures say about such topics as healthy self-image, love, conflicts, the sexual relationship, children a vital relationship with God, the unique responsibilities of husbands and wives, and a family's relationship to the church and non-Christians. **God's Design for the Family** will guide couples into God's Word to discover biblical truths which can serve as a foundation for their family's well-being. All four books. **$9.50.** Individual books. **$2.50.** Bookstores or from **NavPress, P.O. Box 6000, Colorado Springs, CO 80934.**

GOD'S LETTERS TO US (WELS Board for Parish Education) For: L,Y. Slant: LU.

This publication consists of 178 devotions for use in Christian junior high schools. Nine entire New Testament epistles (1 and 2 Peter, Philippians, Galatians, Colossians, Romans, 1 John, 1 and 2 Thessalonians) are read by the students. The format of each devotion is as follows: The Setting (read by instructor); the Reading (by a student); a series of questions on the reading (asked by instructor); and a Summary (read by instructor). This series of devotions is based on the NIV Bible. Experience has shown that **God's Letters to Us** can be readily adapted for home family devotions. It can also be used by individuals. Number 06-2183. **$9.95.** From **Northwestern Publishing House, 3624 W. North Avenue, Milwaukee, WI 53208.**

GOD'S PLAN IN ALL THE AGES (Zondervan Publishing House) For: L,C,S. Slant: EP.

By Herbert VanderLugt. The two themes of personal salvation and the kingdom of God run concurrently in the Bible. This book traces them from Genesis through Revelation. **$4.95.** Bookstores or from **Zondervan Retail Marketing Service, 1420 Robinson Road, SE, Grand Rapids, MI 49506.**

THE GOOD NEWS ABOUT JESUS CHRIST ACCORDING TO MARK (Faith and Life Press) For: L,Y. Slant: EP.

This study guide of Mark is prepared for a variety of study settings but was originally intended for students in grades 9 and 10. **$1.50.** From **Faith and Life Press, Box 347, Newton, KS 67114.**

GOSPEL LIGHT LIVING WORD CURRICULUM (Gospel Light Publications) For: L,Y,Ch. Slant: EP, P, I.

Bible study materials for all ages, providing five overviews of Scripture from early childhood through adult. All materials are designed to involve students in direct study of the Bible, then apply its truths to life situations. Lessons are intended for use in once-a-week sessions. Materials include Teacher's Guides, Student Guides, and a variety of visual resources appropriate to each age level. Write for catalog. Prices vary with different pieces. Most materials are available for quarterly use. Bookstores or from **Gospel Light Publications, 2300 Knoll Drive, Ventura, CA 93003.**

GROWING IN CHRIST (NavPress) For: L,C,S,Y. Slant: EP,P.

Introduces new and young Christians to some of the important promises God makes to those who trust in Him. Part one of the study concentrates on five assurances God has promised to all believers. This part directs a person into the Bible for answers to questions about the assurances, and helps him claim and apply them in daily circumstances. Part two studies eight biblical principles which help the new believer ward off temptation and grow in the Christian life. To complete each of the thirteen chapters an individual must memorize a verse, think over its meaning and answer questions about it, study related passages, write out the verse from memory, and write an application to his everyday life. The **Leader's Guide** includes practical tips for helping a growing Christian, preparing as the group leader, conducting the discussion sessions, and stimulating good discussion. **$3.95. Leader's Guide. $2.50.** Bookstores or from **NavPress, P.O. Box 6000, Colorado Springs, CO 80934.**

HELP STAMP OUT BIBLICAL ILLITERACY (Institute for Biblical Literacy, Inc.) For: L,S,Y. Slant: MP,LP,P.

This work manual is a collation of basic biblical information every Christian ought to know. This study guide operates under the philosophy that biblical literacy starts with content. Divided into four self-contained stages of five sessions each, the manual can be fit easily into the church year for a start-up "Year of the Bible." Non-threatening. Highlights great texts, personalities of Old and New Testament, reviewed by multiple choice, matching drills, keyed to answer list. Manual includes suggestions for group use. Leaders work groups 5-15 in shared information reports. Field developed through several printings, the manual stimulates discussion, questions, fellowship and trust. Excellent preparation for study in depth. Optional studies include work on basic Bible geography, definitions of key terms, suggestions for congregational enrichment of current Bible study in various activities. Information ori-

BIBLE STUDY/READING GUIDES FOR GROUPS

ented, the manual enables people of various theological views and denominations to work side by side. Suitable for seventh grade and up. Contest version available. **$6.00** each; **$5.50** each for 50-99; **$5.00** each for 100 or more, postpaid. From **Institute for Biblical Literacy, Inc., 337 S. Milledge Avenue, Athens, GA 30605.**

HER NAME IS WOMAN, BOOKS 1 AND 2 (NavPress) For: L,C,S,W. Slant: EP, P.

By Gien Karssen. The stories of the women of the Bible and the lives they influenced come vividly alive in **Her Name is Woman** Books 1 and 2. Dutch author and Navigator staff woman Gien Karssen captures the spirit of the times and settings which surrounded these women. She places them in their geographical and cultural contexts and cuts through surface appearances to reveal women whose lives hold a message for us today. Women's groups will find this an ideal Bible study guide. Both books are supplemented by scriptural accounts and footnoted cross references throughout the book. Mrs. Karssen encourages readers, through her observations on other Scripture verses, to decide for themselves the secret of each biblical woman's success or failure in life. Questions are included to stimulate further Bible study. Book 1 and Book 2. **$3.95** each. Bookstores or from **NavPress, P.O. Box 6000, Colorado Springs, CO 80934.**

THE HOLY SPIRIT (Aglow Publications) For: L,W. Slant: CP.

Who is this mysterious Person/Force/Power, whatever it is we call the Holy Spirit? This study is an understandable approach to the "Mr. X" of the Trinity. Through a directed search of the Scriptures, both Old and New Testament, we learn of His role throughout the ages, from Creation to the present; we are led to a proper appreciation of the Holy Spirit; and we are given intensely practical suggestions on how to appropriate His work in our lives today. Number 522003. **$2.95.** Postage 15% of total order, plus **$1.00** handling per each order. Washington State residents add 7.3% sales tax. Ask for free catalog. Bookstores or from **Aglow Publications, P.O. Box I, Lynnwood, WA 98036.**

HOMEMAKING (NavPress) for: L,W. Slant: EP,P.

By Baukje Doornenbal and Tjitske Lemstra. "A happy homemaker, convinced of her importance as an individual and as a contributor to the lives of those around her, forms the backbone of the family," say the Dutch authors of **Homemaking—A Bible Study for Women at Home.** "And in turn, good families constitute the building blocks of society. Women in the home, therefore, can exert crucial influence on their society. This Bible study is intended for women who want to be motivated and led by God's Word in their responsibilities at home. **Homemaking** is an extremely practical question and answer study designed exclusively for the homemaker. Each of the twelve chapters has three parts: a brief introduction of the topic to be studied, the study questions, and a short concluding section entitled "To Think About" which summarizes the importance of that particular topic for the Christian homemaker. **$2.95.** Bookstores or from **NavPress, P.O. Box 6000, Colorado Springs, CO 80934.**

JERUSALEM TO ROME (Baker Book House) For: L,S. Slant: EP.

By Homer Kent, Jr. Studies in Acts. For use by study groups, class use, or personal study. Numerous charts, maps, and photographs help to illuminate the text. **$4.95.** Bookstores or from **Baker Book House, P.O. Box 6287, Grand Rapids, MI 49506.**

JOHN AND 1 JOHN (Tyndale House Publishers) For: L,S. Slant: AW,C,RC, F,EP,MP,LP,P,CP.

By Chip Ricks. A Tyndale Bible Study. This stimulating parallel study of John's Gospel and 1 John brings into focus the truths John teaches through his symbols and themes, offering a wonderfully fresh understanding of Jesus Christ. The Discussion Leader's Guide at the back of the book complements this weekly Bible Study Guide with background information and other helps. **$2.50.** Bookstores.

THE KERYGMA STUDY OF THE BIBLE (The Kerygma Program) For: L. Slant: EP,MP,LP,P,S.

Kerygma is a program of adult Bible study for local congregations. In addition to curriculum resource Kerygma provides a total program design for a complete study of the whole Bible. Kerygma's approach to the Bible is thematic. The thirty-three lesson units are developed around an introduction to the Bible and ten themes. The thematic study provides more than an overview and enables students to focus in depth on the message as well as the stories and events of Scripture. The study relates the various parts of Scripture to the whole. Kerygma is appropriately described as a study in depth of the people of God. The goal of Kerygma is to enrich the life of the congregation through a challenging program of effective Bible study. Kerygma is flexible. It can be taught as one course of study in 33 sessions or presented in shorter study units. While it is usually offered during the week, it can be adapted for Sunday morning use. The Kerygma class may be led by a pastor, Christian educator or qualified lay person. Enrollment fee. **$150 to $350.00.** Books. **$17.50.** From **The Kerygma Program, 300 Mt. Lebanon Blvd., Suite 2217, Pittsburgh, PA 15234.**

KEYS TO CONTENTMENT (Aglow Publications) for: L,W. Slant: CP.

The apostle Paul said, "I have learned to be content in whatever circumstances I am." In prison for the cause of the Gospel at the time, Paul did not know what his future held. How could this man, who had been hungry, in need, in desperate circumstances of all kinds, say such a thing? What was the secret of his contentment? This Bible study, based on Philippians, shares this secret with all who will learn it. As we apply to our lives the principles espoused by Paul, we, too, will experience that abundant, joy-filled life that Jesus promised. Number 521013. **$2.95.** Postage 15% of total order, plus **$1.00** handling per

BIBLE STUDY/READING GUIDES FOR GROUPS

each order. Washington State residents add 7.3% sales tax. Ask for free catalog. Bookstores or from **Aglow Publications, P.O. Box I, Lynnwood, WA 98036.**

THE KINGDOM OF GOD (CSI Publications) For: Y. Slant: C,EP,P.

By Francis Breisch. The Kingdom of God: A Guide for Old Testament Study shows historical development of God's work of redemption. Treats Old Testament books in estimated order of their writing. Forty-eight chapters with introduction, outline, analysis, and exercises for Grades 9-10. 1958. 244 pages. Softcover. **$5.00.** School discounts available. From **CSI Publications, 3350 East Paris Ave., P.O. Box 8709, Grand Rapids, MI 49508.**

KNOW YOUR BIBLE CONTEST MANUAL (Institute for Biblical Literacy, Inc.) For: L,S. Slant: MP,LP,P.

A manual reworking **Help Stamp Out Biblical Illiteracy** for contest purposes. Complete with instructions on how to run a "Bible Bowl"—adult/youth, adult/adult, youth/youth, intercongregational. Includes suggestions for original skit on relating Scripture to life, with suggestions on evaluation for contest purposes. This contest system has the advantage of dealing with basic biblical material throughout the whole of Scripture rather than intense, detailed work on one or two books. Thus, participants do not memorize material of little value. **$5.00** each postpaid. From **Institute for Biblical Literacy, Inc., 337 S. Milledge Avenue, Athens, GA 30605.**

LABORATORY MANUAL IN DOCTRINE (CSI Publications) For: Y. Slant: C,EP,P.

By John S. Brondsema. Workbook format for Grade 12 uses Bible as the prime source to develop student's analytical thinking and study skills about relevant topics: religion, theology, revelation, Scripture, God, union with Christ, grace, and eschatology. Correlated with Berkhof's **Manual of Christian Doctrine.** Teacher Guide gives ideas and answers. Paper/74, 101 pages, 1967. Laboratory Manual in Doctrine. **$2.80.** Teacher Guide. **$6.00.** School discounts available. From **CSI Publications, 3350 East Paris Avenue, P.O. Box 8709, Grand Rapids, MI 49508.**

THE LATE GREAT PLANET EARTH Study Guide (Zondervan Publishing House) For: L,C,S. Slant: EP.

By Hal Lindsey with C.C. Carlson. Through study of the Scriptures, the author illustrates prophecy as foretold in the Bible. **$.75.** Bookstores or from **Zondervan Retail Marketing Service, 1420 Robinson Road, SE, Grand Rapids, MI 49506.**

LAYMAN'S BIBLE STUDY NOTEBOOK (Harvest House Publishers) For: L,C,S. Slant: EP,P,I,M.

Here is a practical New Testament Bible study, with workable units of material arranged alongside the familiar King James Version (for in-depth study) and the New International Version (for modern day application). Every pair of pages represents a complete study, with inductive questions and space for answers. For personal or group study. Now you can have working knowledge of the New Testament in one year! Kivar. Number 1164. **$24.95.** Bookstores or from **Harvest House Publishers, 1075 Arrowsmith, Eugene, OR 97402.**

LAYMEN'S SCHOOL OF MINISTRY (Grace World Outreach Center) For: L. Slant: CP.

Two volumes designed for group Bible study and discussion, these twenty-four lessons set out the basic doctrines of the Christian faith in clearly defined terms. They examine the necessary ingredients for maturing in that faith and accomplishing God's will in your life. **Foundations for Christian Growth** (Volume 1) includes: The Bible, The Nature of God, Righteousness, The New Birth, Baptism in the Holy Spirit, The Renewed Mind, Freedom from Sin, Faith, Faith's Confession, Faith and Patience, Healing, Divine Health. (272 pages of text; 48 pages of questions; 6 complementary teaching cassettes). **God's Plan for Christian Service** (Volume 2) includes: Spiritual Maturity, The Love Nature, The Love Life, Guidance, The Prayer Life, Prayer Warfare, The Abundant Life, Spiritual Gifts I and II, Christian Service, Priorities, Evangelism. (370 pages of text; 48 pages of questions; 6 complementary teaching cassettes). Excellent for self-study. **$43.00** per manual. From **Grace Outreach Ministries, P.O. Box 2158, Maryland Heights, MO 63043.**

LET THE BIBLE BE YOUR GUIDE (Laity of Central Christian Church) For: L,S,Y. Slant: MP,D,P.

New light and fresh applications from the Scriptures break forth in open dialogue when every participant has an opportunity to share. New explorers and long-time Christians grow in discovering the great texts of the Bible related to 146 basic questions of faith and life issues under a broad spectrum of classical Christian beliefs and ministry concerns of the church. The

BIBLE STUDY/READING GUIDES FOR GROUPS

Bible Guide is an attractive quality-printed 30 page booklet prepared as a nonprofit project by an adventuresome congregation which has tested and distributed over 110,000 copies to over 1,200 congregations, interdenominational military chapels, and prison groups. Excellent for beginning new classes and groups or for short-term catch up on biblical basics and foundations; groups begin where needs are felt; vital questions and balanced biblical answers serve as catalyst for a good spirit of searching, sharing, growth in confidence in awareness of the message of the whole Bible. **$1.50** per copy. **$1.00** each for ten or more copies. Postage paid. From **Bible Guide, Central Christian Church, P.O. Box 876, Arkansas City, KS 67005.**

THE LIFE AND MINISTRY OF JESUS CHRIST With Leader's Guide (NavPress) For: L,C,S. Slant: EP,P.

This three book series will influence individuals to become more like Jesus Christ by helping them learn what His life was like on earth and apply what they learn to their own lives. Probing questions direct students through the biblical record of Christ's life and are supplemented with background narratives, maps, charts, and excerpts from important historical, geographical, and cultural sources. A harmony of the Gospels in chart form is included as well as a continuous column for note taking. The **Leader's Guide** not only gives an overview of the life and ministry of Jesus Christ, but it also helps the leader decide who should be in the group and how he should prepare for and lead the discussion. For each chapter, the guide provides objectives for the session, questions on every area to stimulate discussion and assignments for the next week's session. All three books. **$11.95.** Individual books. **$4.50.** Leader's Guide. **$4.95.** Bookstores or from **NavPress, P.O. Box 6000, Colorado Springs, CO 80934.**

LIGHT IN THE DARKNESS (Baker Book House) For: L,S. Slant: EP.

By Homer Kent, Jr. Studies in the Gospel of John. This study is a happy balance between the detailed verse by verse commentary and the sketchy outline study. Bible study groups will welcome the discussion questions that accompany each chapter. **$5.95.** Bookstores or from **Baker Book House, P.O. Box 6287, Grand Rapids, MI 49506.**

LIVE LIKE A KING (Moody Press) For: L,S. Slant: EP,P,I,M.

By Warren Wiersbe. Study course designed for the adult Sunday school class or group Bible study. A practical study of the Beatitudes that teaches Christians how to live victoriously here on earth. **$2.95.** Free leader's guide with ten books (Leader's guide is normally **$1.50**). Bookstores or from **Moody Bookworld, 2101 W. Howard St., Chicago, IL 60645.**

LIVE UP TO YOUR FAITH: STUDIES IN TITUS (Tyndale House Publishers) For: L,S. Slant: AW,C,RC,F,EP,MP, LP,P,CP.

By James Draper, Jr. Paul's epistle to Titus stresses both right believing and right living. In this book James Draper examines Paul's important letter and encourages us to follow the example set by Titus. (13 week study). Book. **$3.95.** Leader's Guide. **$2.95.** Bookstores.

LORD, WHO ARE YOU? (Argus Communications) For: L,C,S,Y. Slant: RC, EP, P,LP,L,D,P.

By Mark Link. Focuses on the story of Christianity's remarkable growth during the thirty years after Jesus' crucifixion, as described in Acts, Letters, and Revelation. The Christian community emerges, reaches out, and embraces the world. **Lord, Who Are You?** retraces the footsteps of Jesus: preaching, healing, loving, praying, suffering. The book is richly illustrated, and features excerpts from modern biblical analysis and modern parallels to the experiences of the Apostles. Comprehensive program including teacher guide and reproducibles. Student book. **$7.95.** From **Argus Communications, Dept. 50, One DLM Park, Allen, TX 75002.**

MASTERING NEW TESTAMENT FACTS (VOLS. I-IV) (John Knox Press) For: L,S,Y. Slant: C,EP,MP,LP.

By Madeline Beck and Lamar Williamson, Jr. Very popular series of workbooks for high school students, seminary students and adults. Easy stages to a thorough understanding of the Bible's basic content and structure. Uses highly acclaimed programmed learning techniques of reading, art (including maps, charts, diagrams, and line drawings), activities, and quizzes with answers in the back of each book. Paperback. **$5.95** per volume. Add 10% or **$1.00** minimum for shipping and handling. Georgia and Virginia residents please add appropriate sales tax. Bookstores or from **John Knox Press, 341 Ponce de Leon Ave., Atlanta, GA 30365.**

MASTERING OLD TESTAMENT FACTS

115

BIBLE STUDY/READING GUIDES FOR GROUPS

(VOLS. I-IV) (John Knox Press) For: L, C,S,Y. Slant: EP,MP,LP.

By Madeline Beck and Lamar Williamson, Jr. Popular series of workbooks for high school students, seminary students and adults. Easy stages to a thorough understanding of the Bible's basic content and structure. Uses highly acclaimed programmed learning techniques of reading, art, activities, and quizzes with answers in the back of each book. Paperback. **$5.95** each volume. Add 10% for shipping and handling. Georgia and Virginia residents please add appropriate sales tax. Bookstores or from **John Knox Press, 341 Ponce de Leon Ave., Atlanta, GA 30365.**

DAWSON McALLISTER YOUTH MANUALS (Roper Press) For: Y. Slant: EP,P.

By Dawson McAllister. These student discussion manuals, authored by Dawson McAllister, a nationally known youth communicator, speak in-depth to the life-related, gut-level issues facing junior high and high school students. The series consists of three studies dealing with relationships, discipleship, and the person of Jesus Christ and are packed with superb art illustrations, challenging questions, scriptural answers and practical applications to student needs. **Relationship Manuals** (3 volumes): accurately handle the tough relationship issues such as sex, self-image, dating, cliques, habits, guilt and loneliness. **Discipleship Manuals** (2 volumes): equip the student for a growing walk with Christ. Manuals deal with the new life, trials, quiet time, prayer, love, endurance and more. **A Walk with Christ Manuals** (2 volumes): take the student on a journey that deals with the important doctrines of the faith—the Cross of Jesus Christ and his resurrection. Students will find the books fun and exciting. Youth leaders will find the teacher's manual and transparencies valuable tools in creating student interest and involvement. Manuals are designed for use in small groups, one on one discipleship, Sunday school classroom, retreats, camps and personal Bible study. Student Manuals. **$7.95.** Teacher Manuals. **$5.95.** Bookstores or from **Roper Press, 915 Dragon St., Dallas, TX 75207.**

THE MINISTRY OF CHRIST (CSI Publications) For: Y. Slant: C,EP,P.

By Francis Breisch. A study of Christ and his apostles in three parts, for Grades 9-11. "Throughout Palestine," "In Jerusalem," and "To the Ends of the Earth." Thirty-six lessons each, grouped by themes. Study and check-up questions and explanatory readings. 1963. 448 pages. **$12.50.** School discounts available. From **CSI Publications, 3350 East Paris Ave., P.O. Box 8709, Grand Rapids, MI 49508.**

MINOR PROPHETS (Baker Book House) For: L,C,S. Slant: EP.

By Jack P. Lewis. A study guide working through each of the minor prophets. Each lesson is followed by relevant questions. **$3.95.** Bookstores or from **Baker Book House, P.O. Box 6287, Grand Rapids, MI 49506.**

MORE THAN CONQUERORS (Aglow Publications) For: L,W. Slant: CP.

Not only Christians, but the world, too, is sorely in need of seeing God's power working in and through each child of God. If you aren't experiencing increasing victory over the forces of evil, perhaps you do not understand your authority in the Lord. In this potent new Bible study, the author shows the reader exactly what authority is, why we have it, and finally, how to use it. This is a study that could change a student's life. Number 522005. **$2.95.** Postage 15% of total order, plus **$1.00** for handling per each order. Washington State residents add 7.3% sales tax. Ask for free catalog. Bookstores or from **Aglow Publications P.O. Box I, Lynnwood, WA 98036.**

NEW HORIZONS BIBLE STUDIES (Light and Life Press) For: L. Slant: AW.

A popular inductive Bible study of selected books of the Bible. It may be used for Sunday school classes, small group Bible studies or individual study. Leader's Guide is available for group study. Student Books. **$2.50.** Leader's Guide. **$1.95.** From **Light and Life Press, 999 College Ave., Winona Lake, IN 46590.**

A NEW TESTAMENT ODYSSEY (Kerr Associates) For: L,S,Y. Slant: AW, C,RC,EP,MP,LP,P,BC.

By Leonard Walcott and Ronn Kerr. A 13-to 26-week overview of the New Testament designed specifically for weekly classroom use with either a multi-colored flipchart for groups of up to 12 persons, or a full-color filmstrip for larger groups, plus a leader's guide and student's book. The flipchart or filmstrip (each with identical material) are weekly "Teaching Outlines" backed up with enough instruction in the leader's guide to allow non-technically trained teachers to lead without the need of additional resources. The course is divided into a general background of New Testament literature followed by overviews of the authorship, style, and themes of the Gospels, Acts, Paul's letters, general letters, and the Revelation. Introductory packet contains one flipchart, one filmstrip, one leader's guide and one student's book. Number 794. **$43.95.** From **Kerr Associates, 460 Woodycrest Avenue, Nashville, TN 37210.**

OLD TESTAMENT STUDIES, BOOK ONE (CSI Publications) For: Y. Slant: C,EP,P.

By Edward Bossenbroek. A plan for a half year of study for Grades 7-8. From Creation to Canaan. Workbook format helps students gather biblical data and understand implications. Designed for teacher selection. Teacher Guide contains guidelines, aids, and answers. 1958/1965. 93, 96 pages. Paper. **$4.80.** Teacher Guide. **$7.50.** School discounts available. From **CSI Publications, 3350 East Paris Ave., P.O. Box 8709, Grand Rapids, MI 49508.**

BIBLE STUDY/READING GUIDES FOR GROUPS

OLD TESTAMENT STUDIES, BOOK TWO (CSI Publications) For: Y. Slant: C,EP,P.

By Edward Bossenbroek. A plan for a half year of study for Grades 7-8. From Canaan to Solomon. Workbook format helps students gather biblical data and understand implications. Designed for teacher selection. Teacher Guide contains guidelines, aids, answers. 1959/1966. 69, 66 pages. Paper. **$4.80.** Teacher's Guide. **$7.50.** School discounts available. From **CSI Publications, 3350 East Paris Ave., P.O. Box 8709, Grand Rapids, MI 49508.**

OLD TESTAMENT STUDIES, BOOK THREE (CSI Publications). For: Y. Slant: C,EP,P.

By Edward Bossenbroek. A semester study from Solomon to Malachi for Grades 7-8. Workbook format features questions to answer and reviews. Allows teacher choice of activities. Teacher Guide suggests efficient strategies. 1959/1966. 89, 137 pages. Paper. (Student text also available in softcover combined edition.) **$4.80.** Teacher Guide. **$7.50.** School discounts available. From **CSI Publications, 3350 East Paris Ave., P.O. Box 8709, Grand Rapids, MI 49508.**

OMEGA TEENS (Christian Ed. Publishers) For: Y. Slant: EP.

Senior high youth program. This program encourages the senior high youth to become all God intends them to be. This Bible based Christ honoring program invites the youth to take an active part in the planning and preparing of each weekly meeting. This program has student books that go hand in hand with each weekly program. Annual subscription. **$88.00.** From **Christian Ed. Publishers, 7348 Trade Street, San Diego, CA 92121.**

OPERATION TIMOTHY (Christian Business Men's Committee of USA) For: L,S,Y. Slant: P.

A one-to-one Bible study patterned after Paul's relationship to Timothy in the New Testament. Its purpose is for one person to help another grow in his faith so that he in turn can help someone else grow. Each set includes student workbooks, verse cards for Bible memorization, and a step-by-step Leader's Guide to direct the lessons in an easy to understand manner. Subjects covered in the 12 lesson course include: Eternal Life, the Work of Christ, Forgiveness, the Holy Spirit, Prayer, God's Will, Giving, Witnessing, and Having A Ministry in another person's life. **Operation Timothy** is a discipleship program designed by laymen for businessmen, housewives, students and anyone interested in the biblical basics for the Christian life. Although created for one-to-one application, **Operation Timothy** is easily adapted for group situations. Each person in study needs a separate set. **$5.95** per set. **$5.50** each for 10 or more sets. (Mail orders include 10% for postage, **$1.00** minimum.) Bookstores or from **Christian Business Men's Committee, 1800 McCallie Ave., Chattanooga, TN 37404.**

PARABLES IN PROFILE (Star Bible Publications) For: L,C,S. Slant: F,EP, P.

By Wayne Jackson. Gives the New Testament student some valuable material on the parables of Christ. Enough material for a six month study course. 85 pages. Paper. Number 1802. **$1.95.** Bookstores or from **Star Bible Publications, Box 181220, Ft. Worth, TX 76118.**

A PLACE FOR GOD TO LIVE (Aglow Publications) For: L,W. Slant: CP.

The Tabernacle was not just a place of sacrifice, cleansing, prayer and worship, but a detailed blueprint for Christian living. This Bible study reveals the significance of the Tabernacle to the Twentieth Century Christian. Number 521011. **$2.95.** Postage 15% of total order, plus **$1.00** for handling per each order. Washington State residents add 7.3% sales tax. Ask for free catalog. Bookstores or from **Aglow Publications, P.O. Box I, Lynnwood, WA 98036.**

PROVERBS: GOD'S POWERHOUSE OF WISDOM (Tyndale House Publishers) For: L,S. Slant: AW,C,RC,F,EP,MP, LP,RJ,CJ,OJ,P,CP.

By Chuck Colclasure. A comprehensive study of the book of Proverbs, suitable for individual or group Bible study. An excellent choice for an elective adult Bible class in Sunday school. A Tyndale Bible Study book. Paper. **$2.50.** Bookstores.

THE PUBLIC LIFE OF OUR LORD JESUS CHRIST (TWO VOLUMES) (Daughters of St. Paul) For: L,C,S. Slant: RC,D.

By Goodier. This biography is a synthesis and elaboration of the four Gospels, composed as the author himself wrote, "in search of the living Christ, as He was yesterday, as He is today, and as He will be forever." Cloth. Two volume set. **$15.95.** Please include **$.75** for postage. Bookstores or from **Daughters of St. Paul, 50 St. Paul's Avenue, Jamaica Plain, Boston, MA 02130.**

READING THE NEW TESTAMENT (Wm. C. Brown Company Publishers) For: L, Y. Slant: RC.

A widely-used source book that guides high school students in a study of not only the content and development of the New Testament, but also the message of the Gospels and the revelation of Jesus. School edition: Student (#1810) **$4.00**; Teacher (#1811) **$3.00**. Parish edition: Student (#1673) **$3.30**; Teacher (#1680) **$3.75**. Insights (Spirit Masters) (#1674) **$12.95**. Bookstores or from **Wm. C. Brown Company Publishers, 2460 Kerper Blvd., P.O. Box 539, Dubuque, IA 52001.**

SCRIPTURE SERVICES (The Liturgical Press) For: L,C,S,Y. Slant: RC,L.

Bible themes, eighteen of them, arranged for immediate group use in biblical prayer. Themes include: God's plan, sin, penance, God with us, the Spirit of renewal, etc. 127 pages. Softbound. **$1.50.** Bookstores or from **The Liturgical Press, Collegeville, MN 56321.**

SEARCH THE SCRIPTURES (36 VOLUMES) (Beacon Hill Press of Kansas City) For: L. Slant: AW,EP,H.

BIBLE STUDY/READING GUIDES FOR GROUPS

A general book by book study of both the O.T. and N.T., especially good for new Christians. Provides a general introduction to each book (authorship, date, purpose, outline, and analysis). Thorough outlines are expanded by explanatory comments. Fill in the blanks study questions test user's comprehension. Excellent for a quick overview or for more leisurely study. The entire set will give a comprehensive understanding to the whole Bible. The books are colorfully bound and are printed on excellent weight paper. Old Testament has twenty volumes, the New Testament, 16 volumes. Each is written by a Bible student/communicator. Average number pages, 56. Complete set (36 volumes) U-5003: a **$54.00** value for **$43.65**. Each volume **$1.50**. From **Beacon Hill Press of Kansas City, Box 527, Kansas City, MO 64141**.

THE SEVENTH TRUMPET (Argus Communiations) For: L,C,S,Y. Slant: RC, EP,MP,LP,L,D,P.

By Mark Link. The early Christian community grew from the vision of a living and present Lord. In **The Seventh Trumpet**, Mark Link captures this vision in a portrait study of the people, settings, and events of the four Gospels. For a deeper understanding of the Gospels, the book offers critical commentary, many illustrations, modern parallels to Gospel events, and Mark Link's vivid narrative style. **$7.95**. (Comprehensive program including teacher guide and reproducibles.) From **Argus Communications, Dept. 50, One DLM Park, Allen, TX 75002**.

SHARE THE WORD (The Paulist Fathers) For: L,C. Slant: RC.

A Catholic program of regular home Bible study, enriched with a daily reading guide and teaching section. It is centered on the Scripture readings for each Sunday's Mass and follows the church's liturgical calendar. The publication was created to help Catholic men and women share Christ with others by reaching out in love and friendship. Through small neighborhood prayer groups, these men and women can share their knowledge with those in need of a spiritual family to call their own. Individual subscriptions are offered free of charge to all who request a subscription, so that everyone, including the poor, elderly and those on fixed incomes can enjoy the benefits of **Share the Word**. The publication is, in turn, supported by the free-will offerings of its generous readers. All gifts are tax deductible, deeply appreciated and very necessary to insure the success of the Catholic Bible Ministry. Bulk subscription rate information is available from **Paulist National Catholic Evangelization Association, 3031 Fourth St., NE, Washington, DC 20017**.

SMALL GROUP BIBLE STUDIES (Church Bible Studies, Inc.) For: L,S. Slant: EP,D,P,S,I,M.

An interdenominational, not for profit corporation established in 1970 for the purpose of providing local churches with printed lessons and an exciting and unique method of Bible study involving small groups. It has been used effectively for week night classes, day classes, Sunday School and in homes. One-day seminars for explaining the materials, methods, and manpower of a class are held periodically in cities across North America. The curriculum offered by **Church Bible Studies** covers books of the Bible as well as topical subjects. Twenty-three different studies have been published thus far and others are added annually. For a sample lesson and other information, write to us. **Church Bible Studies** requests a contribution of **$1.00** for each lesson used, but no church is refused merely on the basis of cost. From **Church Bible Studies, Inc., 191 Mayhew Way, Walnut Creek, CA 94596**.

STAR BIBLE SURVEY COURSE (Star Publications) For: L,S,Y. Slant: F, EP.

By Alvin Jennings, Editor. Surveys Genesis to Revelation in 14 lessons by various authors. Over 20,000 sets in print. (Also eleven other Bible Correspondence Courses available, one in Spanish, one with cassettes.) Catalog #BCC-1 to #BCC-7 *Spanish Course, **$.75** each. Also #BCC15, **$.75** #BCC8 to #BCC13, **$.40** each. #BCC-14, **$2.50** with cassettes. Bookstores or from **Star Bible Publications, Box 181220, Ft. Worth, TX 76118**.

STUDIES IN CHRISTIAN LIVING (NavPress) For: L,C,S,Y. Slant: EP, P.

This Bible study series is ideal for anyone, from senior high age and above, who wants to study the Bible, but doesn't know where to begin. This series is similar to NavPress **Design for Discipleship**, but is in a simpler form, requiring less intensive preparation. Books one through six in this question and answer series teach basic character development, practical principles of discipleship, how to apply the Scriptures to daily living and how to know God better. Books seven through nine introduce chapter analysis Bible study methods. The Leader's Guide gives an overview of each book of the series and each chapter in the books, a detailed format for each session, with practical suggestions for session objectives, applications, discussion questions, prayer times, assignments and Scripture memory. All nine books. **$10.00**. Individual books. **$1.25**. Leader's Guide. **$3.50**. Bookstores or from **NavPress, P.O. Box 6000, Colorado Springs, CO 80934**.

TEACH US TO PRAY (Aglow Publications) For: L,W. Slant: CP.

This study is one that makes its readers look at what the Bible actually says about prayer, what it will and won't do, what we can and what we shouldn't expect—in other words, it is what its sub-title says it is, a study of the scriptural principles of prayer. Number 522002. **$2.95**. Postage 15% of total order, plus **$1.00** for handling per each order. Washington State residents add 7.3% sales tax. Ask for free catalog. Bookstores or from **Aglow Publications, P.O. Box I, Lynnwood, WA 98036**.

BIBLE STUDY/READING GUIDES FOR GROUPS

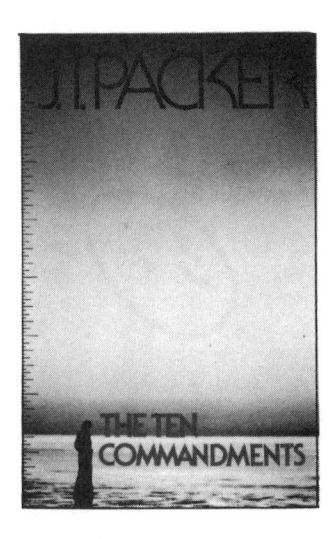

THE TEN COMMANDMENTS (Tyndale House Publishers) For: L,C,S. Slant: AW, C, RC, F, EP, MP, LP, RJ, CJ, P, CP.

By **J.I. Packer.** Examination of the ten commandments. Leader's Guide available. Book. **$3.95.** Leader's Guide. **$2.95.** Bookstores.

THESE STONES WILL SHOUT (Argus Communications) For: L,C,S,Y. Slant: RC,EP,MP,LP,L,D,P.

By **Mark Link.** Presents the Jewish Scriptures in a way that not only remains faithful to them, but also relates them to what people today are doing and thinking. More importantly, **These Stones Will Shout** tries to present the Jewish Scriptures in a way that leads to a prayerful reflection of them. The method and approach of the book grew out of the author's nine years of classroom teaching experience. Student book. **$7.95.** (Comprehensive program including teacher guide and reproducibles.) From **Argus Communications, Dept. 50, One DLM Park, Allen, TX 75002.**

THROUGH THE BIBLE IN ONE YEAR (Virgil W. Hensley, Inc., Publisher) For: L,C,S,Y. Slant: EP,MP.

A three-volume study of God's Word. Each volume is an independent year-long workbook of 52 lessons, with space for making notes, writing answers to questions, jotting down key verses, penciling in your own thoughts. Volume 1, Basic Study, provides an overview of all 66 books, covering the major themes, central purpose and chief verses of each book. Volume 2, Bible Characters, deals with 61 of the Scriptures' most fascinating characters, 39 from the Old Testament, 22 from the New, and shows how God used them—real men and women—to bring about His sovereign will. Volume 3, Great Truths of the Bible, teaches the fundamental principles of the Christian faith and covers all the cardinal truths every mature Christian should know. Churches nationwide of most denominations are now participating in one or more of these studies. 1-10 copies **$16.95**; 11-24 copies **$14.45**; 25-99 copies **$12.45**; 100 or more copies **$11.45**. Add shipping charges to all prices. From **Virgil W. Hensley, Inc., Publisher, 6116 E. 32nd St., Tulsa, OK 74135.**

THROUGH THE BIBLE STUDY (Roper Press) For: L,S,Y,Ch. Slant: EP,P.

Designed to bring individuals into personal involvement with the Word of God. **Through the Bible Study** is published for all ages—preschool through adult—in a quarterly format and offers complete coverage of all 66 Bible books. The format varies by age level, but the fundamental concept that the Bible is the textbook does not change. We want every student to experience the joy of personal discovery of scriptural truth. Within each age level—Beginner, Primary, Junior, Junior High, High School and Adult—there is a series of non-dated books covering Genesis-Revelation. All books are available at any given time. For beginner and primary, the course is organized by main character and event. For junior through adult, a comprehensive, chapter by chapter inductive approach is followed. **Through the Bible Study** provides a rich experience for home Bible studies, Sunday school classes, Sunday/Wednesday evening classes and personal/family devotions. A unique feature of **Through the Bible Study** is its unified lessons, whereby every member of the family (junior through adult) may study the same passage at the same time. A Church Sampler Kit is available for a Free 60 day review. Contact Roper Press for details. Bookstores or from **Roper Press, 915 Dragon, Dallas, TX 75207.**

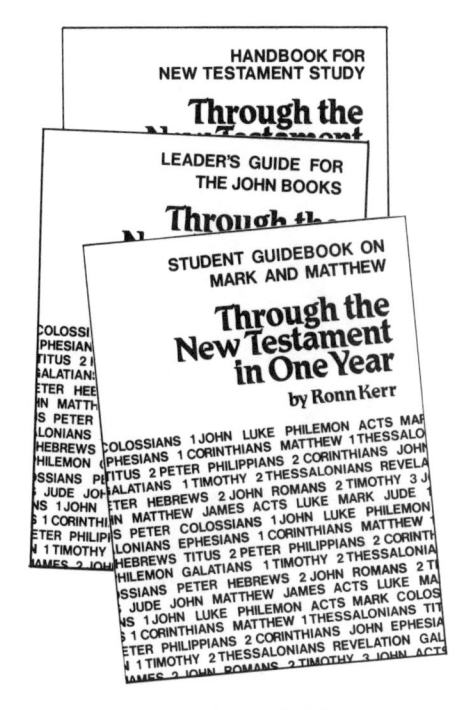

THROUGH THE NEW TESTAMENT IN ONE YEAR (Kerr Associates) For: L,S,Y. Slant: AW,C,RC,EP,MP,LP, P,BC.

By **Ronn Kerr.** A one-year word-by-word, day-by-day, week-by-week, intensive study of the New Testament designed specifically for use in adult or youth Sunday School classes or other weekly settings. The study involves a specific daily reading from the New Testament plus a short "background reading" for every day of the year. It also includes weekly worksheets for "homework assignments" which require the class members to search out related themes, events, and characters; to investigate irregularities; and to examine what the Scripture means to them personally. In addition to six Initial Daily Reading Guides and Weekly Worksheets (each covering two months), the basic study includes an extensive New Testament dictionary in lay language with ample charts, maps, and illustrations, and six Teaching Packets filled with background materials, charts, and wall maps to guide the weekly sessions. The introductory packet includes the Daily Reading Guide, Weekly Worksheets, and a Teaching Packet for Mark-Matthew (sample material for first 60-days, plus one copy of the New Testament Dictionary). **$19.95.** From **Kerr Associates, 460 Woodycrest Avenue, Nashville, TN 37210.**

BIBLE STUDY/READING GUIDES FOR GROUPS

TIME FOR THE FAMILY (2 VOLUMES) (Scripture Union) For: L,Y,Ch. Slant: EP,MP,D.

A devotional activity magazine series which brings the entire family together for daily worship. This is Scripture Union's special contribution to meet the need of concerned parents. Each magazine is undated with material for six months of family Bible reading and prayer; these can be begun at any time. Special material is included in each issue for Easter and Christmas weeks. **Time for the Family** gives a specially chosen Bible passage for each day, built around weekly themes. Plus there is a daily prayer suggestion and a weekly "Family Focus" section. And the material is lively, well illustrated, and contemporary. The children especially will be drawn in by the questions, work puzzles, and projects to make. This is an ideal workbook for parents and children to enjoy together. **$2.95** per issue. From **Scripture Union, 1716 Spruce Street, Philadelphia, PA 19103.**

TRINITY BIBLE STUDIES (Trinity Bible Studies) For: L,C,Y. Slant: P.

A Bible academy for the local church. Consists of ten courses of ten weeks each based on research into best learning times and church seasons. Allows local pastor/teacher to lead Old Testament Survey, then New Testament, followed by eight other indepth courses. Each student has detailed notebook, reading guides, illustrations and review tests. Enrolled churches receive seminar training, posters, promotional brochures, overhead slides and more. Also available on VHS video. In Spanish, Korean, and soon in French. Intro kit includes complete notebook, Old and New Testament Surveys and cassette tape. **$15.00**. Notebook binders. **$3.00**. Each course **$5.00** (Spanish or Korean, **$4.00**). From **Trinity Bible Studies, Box 25101, Dallas, TX 75225.**

TRIUMPH THROUGH TEMPTATION (Aglow Publications) For: L,W. Slant: CP.

Although we are loath to admit it, temptation is a fact of the Christian walk. This Bible study teaches us, through Jesus' example, how to walk through those times of temptation victoriously. Number 521012. **$2.95**. Postage 15% of total order, plus **$1.00** for handling per each order. Washington State residents add 7.3% sales tax. Ask for free catalog. Bookstores or from **Aglow Publications, P.O. Box I, Lynnwood, WA 98036.**

26 NEW TESTAMENT LESSONS (Baptist Publishing House) For: L,C,S. Slant: F,EP,P.

By G.E. Jones. There is a renewed interest in Bible study. Study groups meet in homes, churches and places of business. Books which supply helps are in great demand. Many are little more than workbooks. **26 New Testament Lessons** is a tried and tested series of studies. The author was a Bible teacher. His knowledge of the Bible is manifested in the presentation of the lessons. **$2.00**. From **Baptist Publishing House, 712 Main, Little Rock, AR 72201.**

UNDERSTANDING BIBLE DOCTRINE (Moody Press) For: L,S. Slant: EP,P,I,M.

By Charles C. Ryrie. Basic survey of Bible doctrine designed for the adult Sunday school class or group Bible study. **$2.95**. One free leader's guide with every ten books (normally **$1.50**). Bookstores or from **Moody Bookworld, 2101 W. Howard St., Chicago, IL 60645.**

VISIONS OF GLORY (The Brethren Press) For: L,C,S. Slant: MP.

By David J. Wieand. An exciting way for a group to study the book of Revelation. Using his own translation of the Scripture, Dr. Wieand, Professor at Bethany Theological Seminary, retells the visions in a simple, yet dramatic way. The result is a Bible study which appeals first not to the academic intellectual nor to the speculative prophet of the end, but directly to the imagination and the emotions of wonder and awe. Number 8-9051. Paper. **$4.95**. Bookstores or from **The Brethern Press, 1451 Dundee Ave., Elgin, IL 60120.**

WHAT EVERY CHRISTIAN SHOULD KNOW ABOUT BIBLE PROPHECY (Harvest House Publishers) For: L,C,S. Slant: EP,P,I,M.

By Rick Yohn. This sixth and most recent of Rick Yohn's study manuals is a fresh approach to the widely-studied topic of Bible prophecy. Highly scriptural questions are posed and then expertly answered. Space for notes and personal answers is provided, making this manual handy for individual or group study. Lively illustrations add flare to the informative study manual. Paper. Number 3116. **$3.95**. Bookstores or from **Harvest House Publishers, 1075 Arrowsmith, Eugene, OR 97402.**

WHAT MAKES YOU SO SPECIAL? (Baker Book House) For: L,S. Slant: EP.

By Stanley Baldwin. A study of the book of Ephesians. This study of Ephesians has a fresh beat, one that will

BIBLE STUDY/READING GUIDES FOR GROUPS

encourage Christians to step out with new power—God's power—and live triumphant, exciting lives. **$2.45.** Bookstores or from **Baker Book House, P.O. Box 6287, Grand Rapids, MI 49506.**

WHOLENESS FROM GOD (Aglow Publications) For: L,W. Slant: CP.

In her thought-provoking study, the author works from the premise that "Christianity is very real and workable." The key to health and healing is a daily, dynamic walk with Jesus, the Great Healer. Through thorough study of the Scriptures, she guides her readers toward understanding and incorporating into their hearts and lives the biblical principles upon which healing and wholeness are based. Number 522001. **$2.95.** Postage 15% of total order, plus **$1.00** for handling per each order. Washington State residents add 7.3% sales tax. Ask for free catalog. Bookstores or from **Aglow Publications, P.O. Box I, Lynnwood, WA 98036.**

A WOMAN'S WORKSHOP ON THE BEATITUDES—Leader's Manual (Zondervan Publishing House) For: L,W. Slant: EP.

By Diane Brummel Bloem. Approaches the Beatitudes in an interesting and easy to follow method. **$3.95.** Bookstores or from **Zondervan Retail Marketing Service, 1420 Robinson Road, SE, Grand Rapids, MI 49506.**

A WOMAN'S WORKSHOP ON THE BEATITUDES—Student's Manual (Zondervan Publishing House) For: L,W. Slant: EP.

By Diane Brummel Bloem. Approaches the Beatitudes in an interesting and easy to follow method. **$2.95.** Bookstores or from **Zondervan Retail Marketing Service, 1420 Robinson Road, SE, Grand Rapids, MI 49506.**

A WOMAN'S WORKSHOP ON BIBLE MARRIAGES—Leader's Manual (Zondervan Publishing House) For: L,W. Slant: EP.

By Robert and Diane Bloem. Reveals the personal dynamics of the marriage relationship by looking at such Bible characters as Mr. and Mrs. Simon Peter, Abraham and Sarah, Zechariah and Elizabeth, Ananias and Sapphira and others. **$3.95.** Bookstores or from **Zondervan Retail Marketing Service, 1420 Robinson Road, SE, Grand Rapids, MI 49506.**

A WOMAN'S WORKSHOP ON BIBLE MARRIAGES—Student's Manual (Zondervan Publishing House) For: L,W. Slant: EP.

By Robert and Diane Bloem. Reveals the personal dynamics of marriage relationship by looking at such Bible characters as Mr. and Mrs. Simon Peter, Abraham and Sarah, Zechariah and Elizabeth, Ananias and Sapphira and others. **$1.95.** Bookstores or from **Zondervan Retail Marketing Service, 1420 Robinson Road, SE, Grand Rapids, MI 49506.**

A WOMAN'S WORKSHOP ON FAITH—Leader's Manual (Zondervan Publishing House) For: L,W. Slant: EP.

By Martha Hook. Through twelve Bible studies, this small-group oriented study can help a woman cope with the conflicts in her life, mix with her new role, reflect the past and emerge as an inwardly beautiful, whole, free, rational person. **$3.95.** Bookstores or from **Zondervan Retail Marketing Service, 1420 Robinson Road, SE, Grand Rapids, MI 49506.**

A WOMEN'S WORKSHOP ON FAITH—Student's Manual (Zondervan Publishing House) For: L,W. Slant: EP.

By Martha Hook. Through twelve Bible studies, this small group oriented study can help a woman cope with the conflicts in her life, mix with her new role, reflect the past and emerge as an inwardly beautiful, whole, free, rational person. **$1.95.** Bookstores or from **Zondervan Retail Marketing Service, 1420 Robinson Road, SE, Grand Rapids, MI 49506.**

A WOMAN'S WORKSHOP ON JAMES (Zondervan Publishing House) For: L,W. Slant: EP.

By Carolyn Nystrom and Margaret Fromer. The twelve Bible studies in this workshop provide interesting, thought-provoking questions that illuminate this letter from the brother of Jesus. **$2.50.** Bookstores or from

BIBLE STUDY/READING GUIDES FOR GROUPS

Zondervan Retail Marketing Service, 1420 Robinson Road, SE, Grand Rapids, MI 49506.

A WOMAN'S WORKSHOP ON MASTERING MOTHERHOOD (Zondervan Publishing House) For: L,W. Slant: EP.

By Barbara Bush. Filled with verses from the Bible that pertain to mothering and parenting. **$3.95.** Bookstores or from **Zondervan Retail Marketing Service, 1420 Robinson Road, SE, Grand Rapids, MI 49506.**

A WOMAN'S WORKSHOP ON PROVERBS: Leader's Manual (Zondervan Publishing House) For: L,W. Slant: EP.

By Diane Bloem. Proverbs ... one of the more confusing books of the Bible has been demysticized and made more understandable by the author. **$2.95.** Bookstores or from **Zondervan Retail Marketing Service, 1420 Robinson Road, SE, Grand Rapids, MI 49506.**

A WOMAN'S WORKSHOP ON PROVERBS: **Student's Manual** (Zondervan Publishing House) For: L,W. Slant: EP.

By Diane Bloem. Proverbs ... one of the more confusing books of the Bible has been demysticized and made more understandable by the author. **$2.50.** Bookstores or from **Zondervan Retail Marketing Service, 1420 Robinson Road, SE, Grand Rapids, MI 49506.**

A WOMAN'S WORKSHOP ON ROMANS: Leader's Manual (Zondervan Publishing House) For: L,W. Slant: EP.

By Carolyn Nystrom. In this interesting format with penetrating questions, Bible students will come step by step to a better understanding of God's Word and gain new insights into doctrinal issues. **$2.50.** Bookstores or from **Zondervan Retail Marketing Service, 1420 Robinson Road, SE, Grand Rapids, MI 49506.**

A WOMAN'S WORKSHOP ON ROMANS: Student's Manual (Zondervan Publishing House) For: L,W. Slant: EP.

By Carolyn Nystrom. In this interesting format with penetrating questions, Bible students will come step by step to a better understanding of God's Word and gain new insights into doctrinal issues. **$2.95.** Bookstores or from **Zondervan Retail Marketing Service, 1420 Robinson Road, SE, Grand Rapids, MI 49506.**

WOMEN OF THE NEW TESTAMENT (Zondervan Publishing House) For: L,W. Slant: EP.

By Abraham Kuyper. This collection of 30 devotional messages for women's groups follows significant characters of the New Testament. **$3.95.** Bookstores or from **Zondervan Retail Marketing Service, 1420 Robinson Road, SE, Grand Rapids, MI 49506.**

WOMEN OF THE OLD TESTAMENT (Zondervan Publishing House) For: L,W. Slant: EP.

By Abraham Kuyper. This book contains 50 devotional messages that have been gathered for the benefit of women's study groups or people wishing to study the Old Testament individually. **$4.95.** Bookstores or from **Zondervan Retail Marketing Service, 1420 Robinson Road, SE, Grand Rapids, MI 49506.**

WORKBOOK ON THE BOOK OF ACTS (Standard Publishing) For: L. Slant: EP,P.

Practical study of the Book of Acts. Includes problems and projects. Code 3349. **$1.50.** Bookstores or from **Standard Publishing, 8121 Hamilton Ave., Cincinnati, OH 45231.**

WORKBOOK ON THE FOUR GOSPELS (Standard Publishing) For: L. Slant: EP,P.

Practical study of the life and teachings of Jesus. For individual or group study. Code 3347. **$3.50.** Bookstores or from **Standard Publishing Co., 8121 Hamilton Ave., Cincinnati, OH 45231.**

YOUNG FISHERMAN BIBLE STUDY-GUIDES (Harold Shaw Publishers) For: Y.

Uses the inductive method—thought provoking questions in each study motivate even the most passive teens to read the Bible text, analyze its meaning, apply it to their lives and discuss their discoveries with each other. Whether the group studies an Old Testament or New Testament book or selected Scriptures in a topical study, every **Young Fisherman Studyguide** challenges students to develop a genuinely biblical approach to life as they discover for themselves what the Bible teaches. Features: illustrated workbook with exam. Teacher edition has reduced student page, background material, and teacher's aids. **Young Fisherman Studyguides** are designed for use in Christian day schools, youth groups, Sunday school classes, summer camps, and CCD programs. The study courses to choose from include Old

BIBLE STUDY LEADERS: IMPROVE YOUR SKILLS

How to Lead Small Group Bible Studies contains everything you need to know to start and continue a group successfully—how to •invite prospective members •conduct your first meeting •prepare practical lesson plans with stimulating questions •introduce conversational prayer •handle conflict •turn problems into opportunities—and more. $2.95

These leader's guides will help give you the quiet confidence of knowing your direction during each discussion. NavPress has guides for—

Studies in Christian Living, a nine-book series for those just starting out in Bible study. Leader's guide, $3.50

The Life and Ministry of Jesus Christ, an intensive, three-book series on Jesus' life while on earth. This guide also contains a special section on the biblical principles of a spiritual leader. Leader's guide, $4.95

Design for Discipleship, a seven-book series, for a deeper study of discipleship. Leader's guide, $2.95

Growing in Christ, a 13-week course booklet for new Christians. Leader's guide, $2.50

Ask for these products at your Christian bookstore, or write NavPress Bible Study Coordinator, P.O. Box 6000, Colorado Springs, CO 80934. For orders totaling $20 or more, phone toll free 800-525-7151.

NAVPRESS, HELPING CHRISTIANS GROW

BIBLE STUDY/READING GUIDES FOR GROUPS

and New Testament and selected topical studies. The five most popular studyguides are: Mark: God on the Move; James: Roadmap for Down-to-Earth Christians; Romans: Christianity on Trial; Joshua: Promises to Keep; and Choices: Picking Your Way Through the Ethical Jungle. Student edition. **$2.95.** Teacher edition. **$4.95.** Bookstores or from **Harold Shaw Publishers, P.O. Box 567, 388 Gundersen Drive, Wheaton, IL 60189.**

Weekly Bible study series for youth and young adults for morning or evening. Builds solid faith by Bible knowledge. Introductory Kit/Cassette and Teacher's Manual: $15.00 Box 25101, Dallas, TX 75225

YOUR FAMILY (Moody Press) For: L. Slant: EP,P.

By John MacArthur, Jr. Study of the biblical principles governing the family. Very practical in creating a quality Christian home. Designed for use in the adult Sunday school or Bible study group. **$2.95.** One free leader's guide with every ten books (normally **$1.50**). Bookstores or from **Moody Bookworld, 2101 W. Howard St., Chicago, IL 60645.**

— complete in two volumes —

Foundations For Christian Growth
12 lessons — 6 complementary cassettes — 322 pages

God's Plan For Christian Service
12 lessons — 6 complementary cassettes — 418 pages

For more information call (314)291-6647 or write to:

Grace Outreach Ministries
P. O. Box 2158
Maryland Heights, MO 63043

THE LAYMEN'S SCHOOL OF MINISTRY

An excellent Bible study designed for group discussion or personal use

$43.00 each postpaid

(Quantity discounts available on request.)

COMMENTARIES ON THE HEBREW SCRIPTURES

In general, books listed as commentaries are those which contain verse-by-verse exposition of a portion of Scripture by one or more authors. This section includes works with verse-by-verse interpretations of the entire Hebrew Testament as well as elaborate interpretations of individual books and even of short biblical passages such as the Ten Commandments. Biblical commentaries have a rich historical tradition. In fact, some parts of the Hebrew Scriptures themselves are actually commentaries on other parts and the earliest extra-biblical writings in both Hebrew and Christian circles were commentaries on the Scriptures. However, because commentaries are usually one person's interpretation of Scripture, knowledge of the author's theological "slant" is more important than for other biblical reference works. Included in this section are commentaries on those canonical Hebrew Scriptures (called the Old Testament by Christians) accepted by all Jews and Christians as well as the books identified as Apocrypha by most Protestants and as Deuterocanonicals by Roman Catholics.

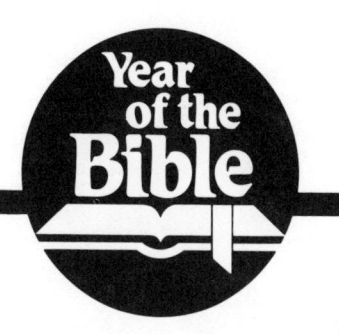

Year of the Bible

COMMENTARIES ON THE HEBREW SCRIPTURES

ALWAYS A WINNER (Regal Books) For: L,C,S,Y. Slant: EP.

By Cyril Barber and John D. Carter. Everyone wants to be successful, respected, fulfilled—a winner in life. But not everyone is. Why not? What makes a winner is illustrated by three men in Old Testament times. They were leaders and wanted to be winners. But...Samuel encountered frustrating obstacles...Saul consulted with a witch...David was an adulterer and murderer. What happened? Were they winners? Cyril J. Barber and John D. Carter answer these questions in their study of First Samuel. They show how God worked through these men in spite of their failures. They point out that God will do the same with us today. He will bless and use us—including our weaknesses and mistakes—if we permit Him to do so. Then, even when we lose we can be **Always a Winner**. Each chapter concludes with thought-provoking discussion questions for individual or group study. Bible Commentary for Laymen Series. Teaching materials available. 160 pages. Paperback. **$2.50**. Bookstores or from **Regal Books, Div. GL Publications, 2300 Knoll Drive, Ventura, CA 93003**.

AMOS: BIBLE STUDY COMMENTARY (Zondervan Publishing House) For: L,C,S. Slant: EP.

By D. David Garland. A lay-oriented commentary with no Hebrew used in its text. Deals with each biblical book section-by-section with discussion questions at the end of each chapter. No bibliography, although occasional reference to other works occurs in the text. **$4.95**. Bookstores or from **Zondervan Retail Marketing Service, 1420 Robinson Road, SE, Grand Rapids, MI 49506**.

AMOS AND JONAH (Faith and Life Press) For: L,C. Slant: EP.

By LaVernae Dick. This thirteen lesson booklet is primarily a leader's guide for the study of the prophets Amos and Jonah, and elicits inductive study of the two biblical books. It is based on Today's English Version by the American Bible Society. **$2.00**. From **Faith and Life Press, P.O. Box 347, Newton, KS 67114**.

ARGUING WITH GOD: THE ANGRY PRAYERS OF JOB (Bethany Press) Slant: MP,P,S,BC.

By Dale Patrick. This includes a fresh translation of Job with critical notes. Patrick has several incisive essays on the nature of this book and the issues it raises. He sees Job as an angry man who refuses to accept his sufferings without complaint. While Job's questions are not answered, he at last meets the God of power and justice. **$1.80**. From **Bethany Press, P.O. Box 179, St. Louis, MO 63166**.

BIBLE HISTORY COMMENTARY-OLD TESTAMENT (Board for Parish Education) For: L,C,S. Slant: LU.

By Werner H. Franzmann. The conscientious Christian teacher will find this commentary especially suited to his needs. The author expounds the historical accounts of the Old Testament. In a simple, easy-to-read style, Pastor Franzmann explains difficult passages, offers essential background information, and voices needed warnings where the teacher may be tempted to misapply the biblical narrative. Above all, the reader is constantly reminded of the golden thread of the Gospel that is woven throughout the Old Testament. The book contains twelve maps especially designed for the book, five full-color maps illustrated charts and tables of weights and measures, a Hebrew calendar of months and seasons, indexes of proper names and scripture references and explanation of biblical chronology. 616 pages. Cloth, Number 15-2780. **$15.95**. From **Northwestern Publishing House, 3624 West North Avenue, Milwaukee, WI 53208**.

A BIBLICAL APPROACH TO PERSONAL SUFFERING (Moody Press) For: L,C,S. Slant: EP,P,S,I,M.

By Walter C. Kaiser. A commentary on the Book of Lamentations that studies the Old Testament view of suffering. An excellent help for those who hurt today. **$5.95**. Bookstores or from **Moody Bookworld, 2101 W. Howard St., Chicago, IL 60645**.

BOOK OF JEREMIAH (Baker Book House) For: L,S. Slant: EP.

By Owen White. In this brief commentary, Dr. White captures the spirit and struggles of Jeremiah the man and his message. **$3.45**. Bookstores or from **Baker Book House, P.O. Box 6287, Grand Rapids, MI 49506**.

THE BOOK OF JOB (Baker Book House) For: L,C,S. Slant: EP.

By Gleason Archer, Jr. God's answer to the problem of undeserved suffering. Speaks to the heart as well as to the mind. **$5.95**. Bookstores or from **Baker Book House, P.O. Box 6287, Grand Rapids, MI 49506**.

THE BOOK OF JOB (Baker Book House) For: L,C,S. Slant: EP.

By Andrew MacBeath. This volume guides the reader through the maze of eloquent passages found in Job and clarifies the major themes found in this Old Testament book. **$2.95**. Bookstores or from **Baker Book House, P.O. Box 6287, Grand Rapids, MI 49506**.

COMMENTARIES ON THE HEBREW SCRIPTURES

THE BOOK OF JOB (The Jewish Publication Society of America) For: L,C,S. Slant: RJ,CJ,OJ.

The Book of Job, concerned with the nature of God's justice, is at once one of the most sublime creations of ancient Hebrew literature and a supreme achievement of the human spirit. It is here presented in a new translation, the work of a distinguished committee of Jewish biblical scholars. Introductions by Moshe Greenberg, Jonas C. Greenfield, and Nahum M. Sarna. Facing Hebrew and English texts. 88 pages. **$7.50.** Bookstores or from **Jewish Publication Society, 1930 Chestnut Street, 21st Floor, Philadelphia, PA 19103.**

BOOK OF NAHUM (Baker Book House) For: C. Slant: EP.

By Walter A. Maier. A thorough, evangelical commentary that assumes the essential authenticity of the masoretic text. **$6.95.** Bookstores or from **Baker Book House, P.O. Box 6287, Grand Rapids, MI 49506.**

THE BOOK OF PSALMS (The Liturgical Press) For: L,C,S. Slant: RC, D.

An interpretative version of the Psalms in measured rhythm designed to make praying easier. The larger type also makes reading easier. 418 pages. Cloth. **$2.00.** Bookstores or from **The Liturgical Press, Collegeville, MN 56321.**

THE BOOK OF WISDOM (The Liturgical Press) For: L,C,S. Slant: RC, D.

In order to make the **Book of Wisdom** clearer to the ordinary reader, this version is presented in measured rhythm, adding ease and delight to the reading. Softbound. **$.50.** Bookstores or from **The Liturgical Press, Collegeville, MN 56321.**

BREAD IN THE WILDERNESS (The Liturgical Press) For: L,C,S. Slant: RC,D.

By Thomas Merton. Thomas Merton's interest in the Psalms carries over into this book, and he calls them "the most significant collection of religious poems ever written." Here he explores such themes as "Psalms and Contemplation," "From Praise to Ecstasy," and "The Silence of the Psalms." 126 pages. Softbound. **$3.00.** Bookstores or from **The Liturgical Press, Collegeville, MN 56321.**

THE COMING RUSSIAN INVASION (Moody Press) For: L,S. Slant: EP,P,I,M.

By McCall and Levitt. A new outlook on the text of Ezekiel and the meaning of his prophecies. **$4.95.** Bookstores or from **Moody Bookworld, 2101 W. Howard St., Chicago, IL 60645.**

A COMMENTARY ON THE MINOR PROPHETS (Baker Book House) For: L,C,S. Slant: EP.

By Homer Hailey. A clear and lucid commentary, useful and satisfying for pastor and layman alike. **$11.95.** Bookstores or from **Baker Book House, P.O. Box 6287, Grand Rapids, MI 49506.**

COMMENTARY ON THE OLD TESTAMENT (Wm. B. Eerdmans Publishing Co.) For: C,S. Slant: F,EP,S.

By Keil and Delitzsch. First published in 1861-1875, this commentary has become a classic of conservative biblical scholarship, a rich source of information for evangelical pastors and Bible scholars. The expansive, exegetical material of this ten-volume series is without parallel. Beginning with a discussion of the nature and format of the Old Testament, the commentary includes extensive discussions of the historical and literary aspects of the text, as well as grammatical and philological analyses. Each book is given a thorough introduction covering historical character, title, contexts, and plan. The authors' conscientious and thorough attention to detail, as well as to the overall scope of the Old Testament, places the work among the best theological commentaries produced in Germany. Ten-volume set. **$169.50.** Bookstores or from **Eerdmans Publishing Co., 255 Jefferson Ave., SE, Grand Rapids, MI 49503.**

COURAGE AND SUBMISSION (Regal Books) For: L,C,S,Y. Slant: EP.

By Stanley Collins. A Bible commentary which focuses on Ruth and Esther--two women who uniquely combined courage and submission, thus fulfilling two God-ordained destinies. 96 pages. Bible Commentary for Laymen Series, No. S292122. Paper. **$2.25.** Bookstores or from **Regal Books, Division GL Publications, 2300 Knoll Drive, Ventura, CA 93003.**

DANIEL: BIBLE STUDY COMMENTARY (Zondervan Publishing Co.) For: L,C,S. Slant: EP.

A lay-oriented commentary with no Hebrew employed within its text. The commentary deals with each biblical book section-by-section, with discussion questions at the end of each chapter. Brief bibliography. **$4.95.** Bookstores or from **Zondervan Retail Marketing Service, 1420 Robinson Road, SE, Grand Rapids, MI 49506.**

DANIEL: THE KEY TO PROPHETIC REVELATION (Moody Press) For: L,C,S. Slant: EP,S,I,M.

By John F. Walvoord. A detailed, systematic analysis of the Book of

COMMENTARIES ON THE HEBREW SCRIPTURES

Daniel with emphasis on studying and refuting nonbiblical views. **$13.95.** Bookstores or from **Moody Bookworld, 2101 W. Howard Street, Chicago, IL 60645.**

DAVID (Baker Book House) For: C,S. Slant: EP.

By F.W. Krummacher. The King of Israel. Translated by M.G. Easton. The stimulating, fast pace of the author's style reflects the tone of his powerful preaching. **$6.95.** Bookstores or from **Baker Book House, P.O. Box 6287, Grand Rapids, MI 49506.**

DAVID: GOD'S MAN IN FAITH AND FAILURE (Regal Books) For: L,C,S. Slant: EP.

By Gene A. Getz. Psalmist. King. Warrior. Fugitive. Shepherd. Friend. Adulterer. Murderer. Who was this man God designated as "a man after His own heart?" These events epitomize David's life. Because of his strong commitment and faith, he often stood head and shoulders above his peers in doing great exploits for God. But because of some inherent weakness in his personality he at times found himself entangled in a web of sinful behavior that is difficult for the average twentieth-century Christian to comprehend. Through careful biblical exposition and practical insights into his life, Gene Getz helps us really know this man David. And what we can learn from David will help us live more devoted lives for Jesus Christ. 160 pages. Quality paper, no. 5409608. **$3.95.** Bookstores or from **Regal Books, Div. GL Publications, 2300 Knoll Drive, Ventura, CA 93003.**

THE DISCOVERY OF GENESIS (Concordia Publishing House) For: L. Slant: EP.

By E. Nelson and C. Kang. Astounding parallels are revealed between the Genesis account of Creation and the ages-old Chinese alphabet. The authors have isolated key Chinese symbols from the Chinese pictograph alphabet and carefully defined the various components of each symbol. The results: some of the most exciting linguistic discoveries of our age! 120 pages. Paper. Item no. 12-1755. **$4.95.** Bookstores or from **Concordia Publishing House, 3558 So. Jefferson, St. Louis, MO 63118.**

ECCLESIASTES: BIBLE STUDY COMMENTARY (Zondervan Publishing House) For: L,C,S. Slant: EP.

By Louis Goldberg. A lay-oriented commentary with no Hebrew used within the text. Deals with Ecclesiastes section-by-section, with discussion questions at the end of each chapter. Brief bibliography. **$4.95.** Bookstores or from **Zondervan Retail Marketing Service, 1420 Robinson Road, SE, Grand Rapids, MI 49506.**

ERDMAN COMMENTARIES ON THE OLD TESTAMENT (Baker Book House) For: L,S,Y. Slant: EP.

By Charles R. Erdman. These brief but insightful expositions of Old Testament books of the Bible have been an appreciated resource for generations of Bible students who have sought succinct, understandable explanations of the biblical message. Seven volumes. **$28.95.** Bookstores or from **Baker Book House, P.O. Box 6287, Grand Rapids, MI 49506.**

ESTHER: THE ROMANCE OF REDEMPTION (Thomas Nelson Publishers) For: L. Slant: F,EP,D.

Was it luck that Esther was in a royal position to avert a large scale Semitic slaughter instigated by Haman, the ruthless, jealous enemy of Esther's cousin Mordecai? Or was it providence? This informal analysis reveals an appealing new dimension of the Book of Esther as it becomes apparent that God in His providence is guiding our lives today just as He did then. Paperback. **$4.95.** Bookstores.

EXODUS: BIBLE STUDENT'S COMMENTARY (Zondervan Publishing House) For: L,C,S. Slant: EP.

By W. H. Gispen. A commentary for lay readers which is highly regarded by scholars for its exegetical insights. Includes introduction to Exodus and a verse-by-verse explanation of the text. Part of the series translating the Dutch Korte Verklaring. **$15.95.** Bookstores or from **Zondervan Retail Marketing Service, 1420 Robinson Road, SE, Grand Rapids, MI 49506.**

EXODUS: BIBLE STUDY COMMENTARY (Zondervan Publishing House) For: L,C,S. Slant: EP.

By F.B. Huey, Jr. A lay-oriented

COMMENTARIES ON THE HEBREW SCRIPTURES

commentary with no Hebrew used within its text. Deals with each biblical book section-by-section with discussion questions at the end of each chapter. Brief bibliography. **$4.95** Bookstores or from **Zondervan Retail Marketing Service, 1420 Robinson Road, SE, Grand Rapids, MI 49506.**

EXPLORING GENESIS (Moody Press) For: L,C. Slant: EP,S,I,M.

A commentary on the Book of Genesis with outlines, parallel subjects, and capable explanations of difficult passages that will add new depth and meaning to your study times. Extremely clear and concise. **$14.95.** Bookstores or from **Moody Bookworld, 2101 W. Howard Street, Chicago, IL 60645.**

FAITH OF OUR FATHERS (Regal Books) For: L,C,S,Y. Slant, EP.

By Ronald Youngblood. A commentary on Genesis 12-50. The centuries of the patriarchs flow with drama and excitement as they reveal the historical beginnings of Christianity. 160 pages, No. S302101. Paperback. Commentary for Laymen Series. Teaching materials available. **$2.25.** Bookstores or from **Regal Books, Div. GL Publications, 2300 Knoll Drive, Ventura, CA 93003.**

FROM FEAR TO FAITH (Baker Book House) For: L,C,S. Slant: C,EP.

By D. Martyn Lloyd Jones. Studies in the Book of Habakkuk. With his rare expository powers, the author amplifies the wealth of the passages which grapple with the fundamental problem of the existence of evil. **$2.75.** Bookstores or from **Baker Book House, P.O. Box 6287, Grand Rapids, MI 49506.**

GENESIS (Baker Book House) For: L,S. Slant: EP.

By C.F. Pfeiffer. A study manual and commentary. **$2.95.** Bookstores or from **Baker Book House, P.O. Box 6287, Grand Rapids, MI 49506.**

GENESIS: ANALYZED BIBLE (Baker Book House) For: L,C,S. Slant: EP.

By G. Campbell Morgan. Offers a dependable guidance for personal Bible study, rich resources for sustained expository preaching, and practical insights for Bible study groups, it stands as a tribute to Dr. Morgan's lifetime of Bible study and exposition. **$6.95.** Bookstores or from **Baker Book House, P.O. Box 6287, Grand Rapids, MI 49506.**

GENESIS: BIBLE STUDENT'S COMMENTARY (Zondervan Publishing House) For: L,C,S. Slant: EP.

By G. Ch. Aalders. A commentary for the lay reader which is highly regarded by scholars for its exegetical insights. Includes introduction to the Pentateuch and Genesis followed by verse-by-verse explanation of the text. This is the first of a series translating the Dutch Korte Verklaring. Two-volume set. **$27.95.** Bookstores or from **Zondervan Retail Marketing Service, 1420 Robinson Road, SE, Grand Rapids, MI 49506.**

GENESIS: BIBLE STUDY COMMENTARY (Zondervan Publishing House) For: L,C,S. Slant: EP

By Leon Wood. A lay-oriented commentary with no Hebrew employed within its text. The commentary deals with each biblical book section-by-section, with discussion questions at the end of each chapter. Brief bibliography. **$4.95.** Bookstores or from **Zondervan Retail Marketing Service, 1420 Robinson Road, SE, Grand Rapids, MI 49506.**

GENESIS INTERPRETATION: A BIBLE COMMENTARY FOR TEACHING AND PREACHING (John Knox Press) For: L,C,S. Slant: C, RC, EP, MP, LP, P, S, BC.

By Walter Brueggemann. The **Interpretation** series is a pioneering concept in Bible commentaries. It combines the qualities of scholarship and devotion as has not been done before in a commentary. Written specifically for the teaching and preaching tasks of the church, it draws out and describes the significance of the biblical text for Christian faith and life. Designed for use by both clergy and laity, the language has been kept clear and nontechnical. Author Walter Brueggemann is one of the most respected biblical writers of our time. **Genesis** was voted Book of the Year by the Academy of Parish Clergy (1982). Cloth. **$23.95** (add 10% for shipping and handling, Georgia and Virginia add appropriate sales tax). Bookstores or from **John Knox Press, 341 Ponce de Leon Ave., Atlanta, GA 30365.**

GOD REMEMBERS (Multnomah Press) For: C,S. Slant: EP,S,M.

By Charles L. Feinberg. A study of Zechariah. A major work on this important and too often neglected pro-

COMMENTARIES ON THE HEBREW SCRIPTURES

phetic book. Includes an introduction, subject and Scripture indexes and an annotated bibliography. Hardback. **$8.95.** Bookstores or from **Multnomah Press, 10209 S.E. Division Street, Portland, OR 97266.**

GOD SPAKE BY MOSES: AN EXPOSITION OF THE PENTATEUCH (Presbyterian and Reformed Publishing Co.) For: L,C. Slant: C,F,P,I.

By O.T. Allis. A brief exposition of the Pentateuch, based upon its Mosaic authorship. O.T. Allis was a leading Reformed scholar in the early 20th century, and is still a major authority on the books of the Pentateuch. 159 pages. **$2.95.** Bookstores or from **Presbyterian and Reformed Publishing Co., P.O. Box 817, Phillipsburg, NJ 08865.**

HALF HOURS WITH ISAIAH (Baker Book House) For: L. Slant: D.

By J.P. Wiles. Wiles applies the messianic passages in Isaiah to the redemptive work of Jesus Christ in this superb devotional commentary. **$3.45.** Bookstores or from **Baker Book House, P.O. Box 6287, Grand Rapids, MI 49506.**

HANDBOOK ON THE PENTATEUCH (Baker Book House) For: C,S. Slant: EP.

By Victor Hamilton. This handbook features the interpretation of the biblical text—not in a verse-by-verse style, but with each chapter dealing with a major thematic unit within one of the Pentateuch books. **$15.95.** Bookstores or from **Baker Book House, P.O. Box 6287, Grand Rapids, MI 49506.**

HANDBOOK TO THE GOSPELS (Servant Publications) For: L. Slant: RC.

By John Wijngaards, M.H.M. More detailed than a general introduction, wider-ranging and more broadly usable than a verse-by-verse commentary, The **Handbook to the Gospels** provides all the background information necessary for understanding the gospel texts—including political movements, religious and political leaders, historical data, and patterns of daily life. Illustrated with dozens of line drawings and photos, the **Handbook** includes chapters on: the purpose, structure and themes of each gospel; daily life in first-century Palestine; the Jewish calendar and feasts; temple and synagogue; religious life of the times; politics in Palestine; language and speech; miracles and parables. John Wijngaards, M.H.M., holds the licentiate in Sacred Scripture from the Pontifical Institute and the doctorate in Dogmatic Theology from the Gregorian University. 302 pages, size 5¼ x 8 inches, paperback, illustrated. **$8.95.** Bookstores.

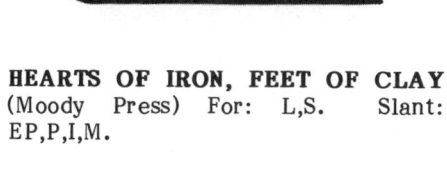

THE HANDY BIBLE DICTIONARY AND CONCORDANCE (Zondervan Publishing House) For: L,C,S. Slant: EP.

By Merrill C. Tenney and Alexander Cruden. A one-volume edition of both the **Handy Bible Dictionary** (1965) and **Cruden's Handy Concordance** (1737 abridged 1963). Makes resource information available and enables one to find Scripture references when a key word is known. Concise yet with a remarkable fullness. Convenient, easy-to-read type. **$3.95.** Bookstores or from **Zondervan Retail Marketing Service, 1420 Robinson Road, SE, Grand Rapids, MI 49506.**

A HARMONY OF THE GOSPELS (Moody Press) For: L,C,S. Slant: EP, S,I,M.

By Stanley Gundry and Robert Thomas. A resource harmonizing the chronology of events in the four gospels—will encourage a deeper understanding of Jesus Christ, His life, and His ministry. **$13.95.** Bookstores or from **Moody Bookworld, 2101 W. Howard St., Chicago, IL 60645.**

HEARTS OF IRON, FEET OF CLAY (Moody Press) For: L,S. Slant: EP,P,I,M.

By Gary Inrig. A study of the Book of Judges that will reveal the great principles of God's work in people like ourselves. **$6.95.** Bookstores or from **Moody Bookworld, 2101 W. Howard Street, Chicago, IL 60645.**

HOSEA: BIBLE STUDY COMMENTARY (Zondervan Publishing House) For: L,C,S. Slant: EP.

By D. David Garland. A lay-oriented commentary with no Hebrew used in its text. Deals with each biblical book section-by-section with discussion questions at the end of each chapter. No bibliography, although occasional reference to other works occurs in the text. **$4.95.** Bookstores or from **Zondervan Retail Marketing Service, 1420 Robinson Road, SE, Grand Rapids, MI 49506.**

COMMENTARIES ON THE HEBREW SCRIPTURES

HOW IT ALL BEGAN (Regal Books) For: L,C,S,Y. Slant: EP.

By Ronald Youngblood. Genesis 1-11, often called the "primeval history" because of its clear theme, tells us about the beginning of the universe, of the heavenly bodies, of the earth with its seas and lakes and rivers and streams and mountains and hills, of inanimate plant life, of animate life including water creatures and air creatures and land creatures. Most important of all, these chapters tell us about the beginning of human life and love, of marriage and family, of work and play, of food and drink, of pleasure and delight. And unfortunately, on the darker side, we also learn about the beginning of sin and its consequences: fractured human relationships, alienation from God, divine judgment and death. Dr. Youngblood's significant contribution teaches what the Bible says about Creation, the Fall, the Flood and the Dispersion of the nations. He makes the Bible truths come alive. Though Genesis was written thousands of years ago, the lessons it teaches are still relevant for those of us living in the twentieth century. Bible Commentary for Laymen Series. 160 pages, number S342103. Paperback. **$2.50.** Bookstores or from **Regal Books, Div. GL Publications, 2300 Knoll Drive, Ventura, CA 93003.**

HOW TO READ AND PRAY THE PROPHETS (Liguori Publications) For: L,Y. Slant: RC,D,P.

This book gives new meaning to the familiar readings of the prophets. It should be especially popular with young people who seek justice and deeper relationships with others and God, just as the prophets did. **$1.50.** Quantity discounts available. Bookstores or from **Liguori Publications, One Liguori Drive, Liguori, MO 63057.**

IN THE BEGINNING GOD (Baker Book House) For: L. Slant: D.

By William Hartley. Jottings from Genesis. Each "jotting" takes as its starting point the first verse of a chapter in Genesis. To read Genesis again with these prompters will make the ancient Scripture more real and significant. **$1.45.** Bookstores or from **Baker Book House, P.O. Box 6287, Grand Rapids, MI 49506.**

ISAIAH (Baker Book House) For: C,S. Slant: EP.

By George L. Robinson. A compact and lucid exposition of this well-known prophecy designed as a guide in the systematic study of this book. **$3.95.** Bookstores or from **Baker Book House, P.O. Box 6287, Grand Rapids, MI 49506.**

ISAIAH: A NEW TRANSLATION (The Jewish Publication Society of America) For: L,C,S. Slant: RJ,CJ,OJ.

Of the prophetic books of the Bible, none has been held in such high esteem as the Book of Isaiah. The popularity is well deserved, for the prophecies connected with Isaiah, especially his message of comfort and his vision of the future, contain some of the most eloquent poetry in Scripture, unsurpassed in loftiness of conception and felicity of expression. This new translation captures all the passion and beauty of the original. Accompanying the text is a series of powerful drawings, specially commissioned for this volume. Illustrated by Chaim Gross. 192 pages. 10 3/8 x 13 1/4 inches. **$12.50.** Bookstores or from **Jewish Publication Society, 1930 Chestnut Street, 21st Floor, Philadelphia, PA 19103.**

ISAIAH: BIBLE STUDY COMMENTARY (Zondervan Publishing House) For: L,C,S. Slant: EP.

By D. David Garland. A lay-oriented commentary with no Hebrew used in its text. Deals with each biblical book section-by-section with discussion questions at the end of each chapter. No bibliography, although occasional reference to other work occurs in the text. **$4.95.** Bookstores or from **Zondervan Retail Marketing Service, 1420 Robinson Road, SE, Grand Rapids, MI 49506.**

ISAIAH: THE GLORY OF THE MESSIAH (Moody Press) For: C. Slant: EP, S, I, M.

By Alfred and John A. Martin. Section-by-section commentary on the Book of Isaiah for the serious layman or Bible student who wishes to master the factual content of Isaiah's prophecy. Highlights the messianic character and predictions of the book. Selective bibliography and listing of New Testament quotations from Isaiah. **$9.95.** Bookstores or from **Moody Bookworld, 2101 W. Howard Street, Chicago, IL 60645.**

ISAIAH'S IMMANUEL (Baker Book House) For: C. Slant: EP.

By Edward E. Hindson. A sign of his times or the sign of the ages? A concise historical and exegetical study of Isaiah 7:14, affirming that it is an exclusive prediction of the virgin birth of Christ. **$3.50.** Bookstores or from **Baker Book House, P.O. Box 6287, Grand Rapids, MI 49506.**

JEREMIAH (Zondervan Publishing House) For: L,C,S. Slant: EP.

By Charles L. Feinberg. Includes an introduction to the Book of Jeremiah that explains the book's historical background, the life of Jeremiah, the theology of his prophecies, an outline of the book, and a bibliography. The commentary is a detailed verse-by-verse discussion of the text with footnotes that deal with technical matters. **$13.95.** Bookstores or from **Zondervan Retail Marketing Service, 1420 Robinson Road, SE, Grand Rapids, MI 49506.**

JEREMIAH: A NEW TRANSLATION (The Jewish Publication Society of America) For: L,C,S. Slant: RJ, CJ, OJ.

The prophet Jeremiah emerges as the most tragic of all the biblical seers. Of an essentially tender and lyrical nature, his soul was torn between love

COMMENTARIES ON THE HEBREW SCRIPTURES

for his people and the dire compulsion of his prophetic mission to announce doom and destruction. Extraordinary woodcuts enhance this splended volume. Illustrated by Nikos Stavroulakis. 92 pages. 10 1/2 x 11 3/4 inches. $12.50. Bookstores or from **Jewish Publication Society, 1930 Chestnut Street, 21st Floor, Philadelphia, PA 19103.**

JEREMIAH: BIBLE STUDY COMMENTARY (Zondervan Publishing House) For: L,C,S. Slant: EP.

By F.B. Huey, Jr. A lay-oriented commentary with no Hebrew used within its text. Deals with each biblical book section-by-section with discussion questions at the end of each chapter. Brief bibliography. $4.95. Bookstores or from **Zondervan Retail Marketing Service, 1420 Robinson Road, SE, Grand Rapids, MI 49506.**

JOB: BIBLE STUDY COMMENTARY (Zondervan Publishing House) For: L,C,S. Slant: EP.

By D. David Garland. A lay-oriented commentary with no Hebrew used in its text. Deals with each biblical book section-by-section with discussion questions at the end of each chapter. No bibliography, although occasional reference to other works occurs in the text. $4.95. Bookstores or from **Zondervan Retail Marketing Service, 1420 Robinson Road, SE, Grand Rapids, MI 49506.**

JOEL (Baker Book House) For: L,C. Slant: EP.

By Mariano Digangi. A study guide and commentary. $1.95. Bookstores or from **Baker Book House, P.O. Box 6287, Grand Rapids, MI 49506.**

JONAH (Baker Book House) For: C. Slant: EP.

By Patrick Fairbairn. An exposition of the life, character, and mission of Jonah. $3.95. Bookstores or from **Baker Book House, P.O. Box 6287, Grand Rapids, MI 49506.**

JONAH: BIBLE STUDY COMMENTARY (Zondervan Publishing House) For: L,C,S. Slant: EP.

By John W. Walton. A lay-oriented commentary with no Hebrew used within the text. Deals with the book section-by-section, with discussion questions at the end of each chapter. Brief bibliography. $3.95. Bookstores or from **Zondervan Retail Marketing Service, 1420 Robinson Road, SE, Grand Rapids, MI 49506.**

JOSEPH: FROM PRISON TO PALACE (Regal Books) For: L,C,S,Y. Slant: EP.

By Gene A. Getz. Explores the life of an incredible man. His oldest brother saved seventeen-year-old Joseph from brutal murder by his jealous brothers. But rather than being returned to the "favorite son" position in his father's household, Joseph was sold into slavery in Egypt. When it seemed things could get no worse, they did. Joseph was unjustly accused by his master's wife. Without so much as a hearing he was thrown into prison. And there he stayed for over a decade, a forgotten Hebrew slave far from his family and home. By all human standards, Joseph's life should have ended in broken-hearted bitterness. Rather, he rose above the jealousy, hatred, false accusations and imprisonment to become prime minister of Egypt. Gene Getz, in this sixth of his Old Testament personality studies, explores the life of Joseph in the light of his culture and time. Yet, in his own perceptive way, Getz gleans important lessons about accepting disappointments, giving and accepting forgiveness and the sovereignty of God from Joseph's life and finds many present-day parallels. Through thought-provoking questions and challenges at the conclusion of each chapter, Getz helps his readers ponder the lessons Joseph learned and make personal applications of the truths in their own lives. 5 1/8 x 8 inches. 168 pages. Quality paper. $4.95. Bookstores or from **Regal Books, Div. GL Publications, 2300 Knoll Drive, Ventura, CA 93003.**

JOSHUA: BIBLE STUDY COMMENTARY (Zondervan Publishing House) For: L,C,S. Slant: EP.

By Paul P. Enns. A lay-oriented commentary, with no Hebrew employed within its text. Deals with each biblical book section-by-section with discussion questions at the end of each chapter. Brief bibliography. $4.95. Bookstores or from **Zondervan Retail Marketing Service, 1420 Robinson Road, SE, Grand Rapids, MI 49506.**

JOSHUA: DEFEAT TO VICTORY (Regal Books) For: L,C,S,Y. Slant: EP.

By Gene A. Getz. In this very biblical yet psychologically relevant study of the man Joshua, Dr. Gene A. Getz helps you see: how God can turn your mistakes into pluses; how to turn feelings of inadequacy into confidence;

COMMENTARIES ON THE HEBREW SCRIPTURES

why God doesn't expect you to operate on blind faith; the real reasons why obedience always pays; when trusting God is most important; why spiritual degeneration is only one generation away; why customs and traditions are worth keeping; and how to know God's will for your life...today. 176 pages. Trade Paper, No. 5410509. **$3.25.** Bookstores or from **Regal Books, Div. GL Publications, 2300 Knoll Drive, Ventura, CA 93003.**

JUDGES: BIBLE STUDY COMMENTARY (Zondervan Publishing House) For: L,C,S. Slant: EP.

By Paul P. Enns. A lay-oriented commentary, with no Hebrew employed within its text. Deals with each biblical book section-by-section with discussion questions at the end of each chapter. Brief bibliography. **$4.95.** Bookstores or from **Zondervan Retail Marketing Service, 1420 Robinson Road, SE, Grand Rapids, MI 49506.**

LAST DAYS OF ELISHA (Baker Book House) For: C,S. Slant: EP.

By F. W. Krummacher. A vivid portrait of Elisha and other Bible figures by one of the best Bible biographers. **$4.45.** Bookstores or from **Baker Book House, P.O. Box 6287, Grand Rapids, MI 49506.**

LEVITICUS (Baker Book House) For: L,S. Slant: EP.

By C.F. Pfeiffer. A study manual and commentary. **$2.95.** Bookstores or from **Baker Book House, P.O. Box 6287, Grand Rapids, MI 49506.**

LEVITICUS: THE BIBLE STUDENT'S COMMENTARY (Zondervan Publishing House) For: L,C,S. Slant: EP.

By A. Noordtzij. A commentary for lay readers which is highly regarded by scholars for its exegetical insights. Includes introduction to Leviticus and a verse-by-verse explanation of the text. The fourth volume in a series translating the Dutch Korte Verklaring. **$16.95.** Bookstores or from **Zondervan Retail Marketing Service, 1420 Robinson Road, SE, Grand Rapids, MI 49506.**

LEVITICUS: BIBLE STUDY COMMENTARY (Zondervan Publishing House) For: L,C,S. Slant: EP.

By Louis Goldberg. A lay-oriented commentary with no Hebrew employed within its text. Deals with Leviticus section-by-section with discussion questions at the end of each chapter. Brief bibliography. **$4.95.** Bookstores or from **Zondervan Retail Marketing Service, 1420 Robinson Road, SE, Grand Rapids, MI 49506.**

LOVE AND THUNDER: A SPIRITUALITY OF THE OLD TESTAMENT (The Liturgical Press) For: L,C. Slant: RC, D, H.

By John Craghan, C.SS.R. To help this generation in its encounter with the Old Testament, Scripture teacher and author John Craghan, C.SS.R., presents these reflections on texts and topics from Genesis to the Song of Songs. The chapters are a series of invitations: to biblical spirituality, to image God, to be human, to covenant, to communal concern, and to newness.

This is a clearly written answer to the ever growing need among Christians to be nourished by the Word of God in their daily lives. Softbound. 250 pages. **$11.00.** Bookstores or from **Liturgical Press, Collegeville, MN 56321.**

LOVE CARVED IN STONE (Regal Books) For: L,C,S,Y. Slant: EP.

By Daniel R. Seagren. The Ten Laws God carved in stone on Mount Sinai have always occupied an important place in the life of God's people. These laws have formed a part of the bedrock of faith, describing the God of Christianity and His will for His followers. However, many in our day now see the Ten Commandments as a threat to their well-being. Making absolute statements of right and wrong is unthinkable. Daniel Seagren helps today's Christians face the unprecedented challenges to the Decalogue they encounter both inside and outside the church. His practical interpretations and timely illustrations will help Christians better understand each commandment. Through this understanding they will come to realize that the commandments are designed to foster well-being for individuals and families who keep them. Most importantly, Seagren emphasizes that we cannot divorce God's law from a belief in God Himself. Paperback. 4 1/2 x 7 inches. 160 pages, no. S371101. Bookstores or from **Regal Books, Div. GL Publications, 2300 Knoll Drive, Ventura, CA 93003.**

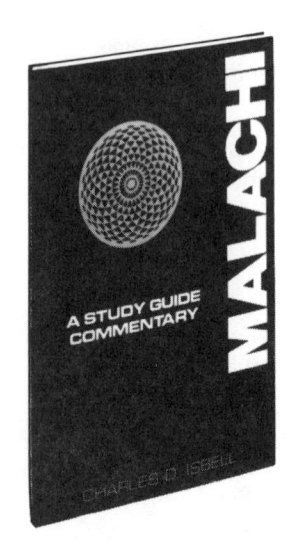

MALACHI: BIBLE STUDY COMMENTARY (Zondervan Publishing House) For: L,C,S. Slant: EP.

By Charles D. Isbell. A lay-oriented commentary with no Hebrew used with-

COMMENTARIES ON THE HEBREW SCRIPTURES

in its text. Deals with each biblical book section-by-section with discussion questions at the end of each chapter. Brief bibliography. **$3.50.** Bookstores or from **Zondervan Retail Marketing Service, 1420 Robinson Road, SE, Grand Rapids, MI 49506.**

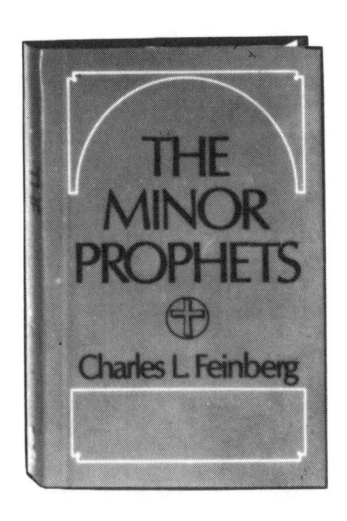

MINOR PROPHETS (Moody Press) For: C. Slant: EP,P,S,I,M.

By Charles L. Feinberg. Comprehensive commentary on all twelve of the minor prophets—deep insight into difficult passages. **$13.95.** Bookstores or from **Moody Bookworld, 2101 W. Howard Street, Chicago, IL 60645.**

A MODERN STUDY IN THE BOOK OF PROVERBS (Mott Media) For: L,C,S.

By Charles Bridges, updated by George Santas. Charles Bridges' magnificent exposition of Proverbs, for more than a century regarded as the classic Proverbs commentary, is now revised for today's reader. The language has been carefully updated to increase its particular usefulness, but neither Bridges' own meanings nor his intent have been changed. A study guide is also available for use with the Mott Media edition. Cloth. 752 pages. **$17.95.** Bookstores or from **Mott Media, 1000 E. Huron St., Milford, MI 48042.**

MOSES AND THE GODS OF EGYPT (Baker Book House) For: L,C. Slant: EP.

By John J. Davis. Studies in the Book of Exodus in the light of recent archaeological and historical studies. **$7.95.** Bookstores or from **Baker Book House, P.O. Box 6287, Grand Rapids, MI 49506.**

MY SERVANT JOB (Baker Book House) For: L,C,S. Slant: EP, D.

By Morris A. Inch. A Discussion Guide on the Wisdom of Job. Focuses not on the sufferings of the patriarch, but on his wisdom. **$2.95.** Bookstores or from **Baker Book House, P.O. Box 6287, Grand Rapids, MI 49506.**

THE NEW INTERNATIONAL COMMENTARY ON THE OLD TESTAMENT (Wm. B. Eerdmans Publishing Co.) For: C,S. Slant: EP, MP, S.

General Editor, R.K. Harrison. Conceived with the needs of pastors, scholars, and students in mind. Like its companion series, the **New International Commentary on the New Testament**, it devotes considerable care toward achieving information helpful for appreciating in depth the biblical writer's meaning and the homiletical and devotional suggestions which enable the writer's words to speak clearly today. Essential to **NICOT'S** orientation are the complementary convictions that the Old Testament represents the Word of God as spoken to His people Israel and that these thirty-nine books contain His inspired and authoritative message. Six volumes available. **$12.95 - $22.50.** Bookstores or from **Eerdmans Publishing Company, 255 Jefferson Ave., SE, Grand Rapids, MI 49503.**

NUMBERS: BIBLE STUDENT'S COMMENTARY (Zondervan Publishing House) For: L,C,S. Slant: EP.

By A. Noordtzij. A commentary for lay leaders that is highly regarded for its exegetical insights. Includes introduction to Numbers and verse-by-verse explanation of the text. The fourth volume in a series translating the Dutch Korte Verklaring. **$16.95.** Bookstores or from **Zondervan Retail Marketing Service, 1420 Robinson Road, SE, Grand Rapids, MI 49506.**

NUMBERS: BIBLE STUDY COMMENTARY (Zondervan Publishing House) For: L,C,S. Slant: EP.

By F.B. Huey, Jr. A lay-oriented commentary with no Hebrew used within its text. Deals with each biblical book section-by-section with discussion questions at the end of each chapter. Brief bibliography. **$4.95.** Bookstores or from **Zondervan Retail Marketing Service, 1420 Robinson Road, SE, Grand Rapids, MI 49506.**

OLD TESTAMENT WISDOM: AN INTRODUCTION (John Knox Press) For: C,S. Slant: C, RC, EP, MP, LP, S, BC.

By James L. Crenshaw. Comprehensive, scholarly and innovative examina-

COMMENTARIES ON THE HEBREW SCRIPTURES

tion of the wisdom literature of the Old Testament. Offers insights into the history of wisdom research and presents the latest critical debate. Crenshaw presents wisdom as an alternative to traditional prophetic and priestly religion. Paperback. **$10.95.** Cloth. **$16.95.** Add 10% for shipping and handling; Georgia and Virginia please add appropriate sales tax. Bookstores or from **John Knox Press, 341 Ponce de Leon Ave., Atlanta, GA 30365.**

ON FOOLISHNESS (Bible Questions) For: L,C,S. Slant: C, F, EP, S, I, BC.

A study of the date of Daniel. The conclusion reached is that the prophet wrote the book which bears his name during the time of Babylonian captivity and shortly thereafter. **$2.00.** From **Bible Questions, Box 736, Galesburg, IL 61401.**

PARADISE TO PRISON (Baker Book House) For: L,C,S. Slant: EP.

By John J. Davis. Studies in Genesis. A superior textbook and complete study guide on the Book of Genesis interwoven with maps, photos, and vivid text. **$14.95.** Bookstores or from **Baker Book House, P.O. Box 6287, Grand Rapids, MI 49506.**

EL PENTATEUCO (PENTATEUCH) (Vida Publishers) For: C,S. Slant: EP.

By Pablo Hoff. El Pentateuco abarca la quinta parte del Antiguo Testamento y ocupa un espacio igual a las dos terceras partes del Nuevo Testamento. Esta obra sobre el Pentateuco la preparó su autor para el aprovechamiento individual, y para enseñar en institutos nocturnos y cursos de extensión. El autor espera que este libro sea de gran bendición para todos los lectores, estimulándolos a buscar un conocimiento más profundo de las Sagradas Escrituras y proveyéndoles de un rico alimento espiritual para sus vidas. **$4.00.** Bookstores.

POETRY OF THE OLD TESTAMENT (Herald Press) For: L,S. Slant: EP.

By S.C. Yoder. Acquaints the student with the great truths of the Bible which are expressed in the form of poetry. Each section is opened with an introductory chapter giving the historical background of the time out of which it grew. Currently used as a textbook in colleges, seminaries, and universities. 1948. 426 pages. Paper. No. 1709-3. **$7.95.** Bookstores.

PRAISE? A MATTER OF LIFE AND BREATH (Thomas Nelson Publishers) For: L,C. Slant: EP,D,P.

By Ronald Barclay Allen. The Psalms comprise the longest book in the Bible, and these lyric hymns of Israel are the sourcebook of praise. These hymns are music without notation, the poetry of the Hebrew people. The current excitement about praise inspires a new awareness of God's use of the Psalms, and Allen approaches the subject in a warm, scholarly manner. The excitement is contagious, and everyone who delights in the experience of language will be caught up in the drama and majesty of biblical Hebrew poetry. This study of the Psalms is in two parts: the first enables the reader to get to know the Psalms better, and the second delves into the richness of seven specific Psalms. Paper. **$5.95.** Bookstores.

PRAYING THE PSALMS (The Liturgical Press) For: L,C. Slant: RC, D.

By Thomas Merton. Early in his religious life, Thomas Merton discovered what he calls the perfect book of prayer, the Psalms. In this slim but solid book, he guides readers through the more representative psalms and offers an explanation of why the Roman Catholic Church also considers the Psalms the best way to praise God. 32 pages. Paper. **$.75.** Bookstores or from **The Liturgical Press, Collegeville, MN 56321.**

THE PROMISED LAND (Servant Publications) For: L. Slant: P.

By Matthew E. Clancy. The saga of God's Chosen People from Abraham to David. A clear picture of the first thousand years of salvation history. Unravels the knot of recorded facts found in Scripture and tells the story of salvation, beginning with the call of Abraham and ending with the building of the temple at Jerusalem. A continuous narrative that simplifies the complex history of salvation and uncovers the richness of our Old Testament heritage. 0581. **$3.95.** Bookstores.

COMMENTARIES ON THE HEBREW SCRIPTURES

THE PROPHECY OF EZEKIEL (Moody Press) For: C. Slant: EP, S, I, M.

By Charles L. Feinberg. An excellent commentary on the prophet Ezekiel with outlines and extensive background information. **$14.95.** Bookstores or from **Moody Bookworld, 2101 W. Howard Street, Chicago, IL 60645.**

sales tax). Bookstores or from **John Knox Press, 341 Ponce de Leon Ave., Atlanta, GA 30365.**

PSALMS FOR GOD'S PEOPLE (Regal Books) For: L,C,S,Y. Slant: EP.

By Robert K. Johnston. The Book of Psalms presents responses from believers to God as they encountered a variety of life's experiences. The Psalms are models for our responses to God as well...Today! In this Bible study the author deals with questions that everyone can relate to: Should we complain to God in public? Is confession really necessary? Should the church bear its suffering patiently? How should we respond when we are wronged? Can we ask God to avenge us? Do we really believe God is our "shepherd"? What is justice? How are we to feel when wrongdoers prosper? How do we cope with suffering? This book is designed to encourage readers to fill their hearts and minds with these inspired prayers of God's people and learn the joy of responding similarly. S362105. Mass paper. 160 pages. **$2.50.** Bookstores or from **Regal Books, Division GL Publications, 2300 Knoll Drive, Ventura, CA 93003.**

RAHAB: THE HARLOT AND THE SPIES (Bible Questions) For: L,Y. Slant: C,F,EP,D.

A study of the picture of salvation given in this Old Testament event. **$1.50.** From **Bible Questions, Box 736, Galesburg, IL 61401.**

RUTH: AN EXPOSITIONAL COMMENTARY (Moody Press) For: L,S. Slant: EP,D,P,I,M.

By Cyril J. Barber. Careful exposition of the Book of Ruth, with life-related material drawn from the text—making this commentary devotional, and very relevant to your life today. Excellent commentary for a wide range of readers. **$6.95.** Bookstores or from **Moody Bookworld, 2101 W. Howard Street, Chicago, IL 60645.**

RUTH: BIBLE STUDY COMMENTARY (Zondervan Publishing House) For: L,C,S. Slant: EP.

By Paul P. Enns. A lay-oriented commentary, with no Hebrew employed within its text. Deals with each biblical book section-by-section with discussion questions at the end of each chapter. Brief bibliography. **$3.95.** Bookstores or from **Zondervan Retail Marketing Service, 1420 Robinson Road, SE, Grand Rapids, MI 49506.**

RUTH: THE ROMANCE OF REDEMPTION (Thomas Nelson Publishers) For: L,C. Slant: F, EP, P.

By J. Vernon McGee. The story of Ruth, the gentile maid from Moab, is a powerful and passionate portrayal of pure love—the devoted love of Ruth for her Hebrew mother-in-law, Naomi, the romantic love between Ruth and Boaz, and the redemptive love of God. J. Vernon McGee's examination of the Book of Ruth provides insight into redemption and love as they were codified by law, then perfected by grace. Paperback. **$5.95.** Bookstores.

PROPHETS AND THE POWERLESS (John Knox Press) For: L,C,S. Slant: C, RC, EP, MP, LP, S, BC.

By James Limburg. Enables students and laypersons to understand what prophecy really is. Also explains the relevance of the Old Testament prophets to social justice today. Paper. **$5.95** (add **$1.00** for postage; Georgia and Virginia residents add appropriate

COMMENTARIES ON THE HEBREW SCRIPTURES

SACRIFICIAL WORSHIP OF THE OLD TESTAMENT (Baker Book House) For: C. Slant: EP.

By J. H. Kurtz. Translated by James Martin. A thorough, scholarly, and orthodox study of Old Testament sacrifices. **$8.95.** Bookstores or from **Baker Book House, P.O. Box 6287, Grand Rapids, MI 49506.**

1, 2 SAMUEL: BIBLE STUDY COMMENTARY (Zondervan Publishing House) For: L,C,S. Slant: EP.

By Howard F. Vos. A lay-oriented commentary with no Hebrew used within the text. Provides much in the study of Israel's history, doctrines about the nature of God, and spiritual and practical wisdom. Discussion questions at the end of each chapter. Brief bibliography. **$5.95.** Bookstores or from **Zondervan Retail Marketing Service, 1420 Robinson Road, SE, Grand Rapids, MI 49506.**

SEEK YE FIRST (Baptist Publishing House) For: L,S. Slant: F, EP, P.

By Maggie Chandler. The Song of Solomon is a love song which can fruitfully be viewed as typifying the Savior's love for His people and theirs for Him. **Seek Ye First** is a verse-by-verse commentary in which Maggie Chandler develops that analogy in detail. The benefits which come from a study of this volume include a better comprehension of the Song of Solomon, a new appreciation for the beauty of inspired Scripture, a fresh awareness of Christ's love as a Savior, and a rekindled affection for the Lord. Individual readers and study groups will find this book stimulating in their quest for an understanding of the Scriptures. **$2.50.** From **Baptist Publishing House, 712 Main, Little Rock, AR 72201.**

SERMONS FROM JOB (Baker Book House) For: C,S. Slant: C.

By John Calvin. These twenty sermons deal with God's majesty, inscrutability, and all-inclusive providence. This series on Job is probably the most famous of all Calvin's published sermons. **$5.95.** Bookstores or from **Baker Book House, P.O. Box 6287, Grand Rapids, MI 49506.**

A STUDY OF THE BOOK OF GENESIS (Christian Publications, Inc.) For: L,S. Slant: MP.

By Gordon Talbot. In simple non-technical language, Dr. Talbot guides the reader through the high points of the origin of the universe, the planet Earth, and the human race. From the Fall of man, he unfolds the history of Redemption as revealed in the families of Adam, Noah, and Abraham. A leader's guide is also available. **$6.95.** Leaders Guide, **$2.95.** From **Christian Publications, Inc., 3825 Hartzdale Drive, P.O. Box 8070, Camp Hill, PA 17011.**

THEMES FROM THE MINOR PROPHETS (Regal Books) For: L,C,S,Y. Slant: EP.

By David Allan Hubbard. While modern man thinks he has "come of age" and is far ahead of those who lived in Bible times, he has yet to catch up with the truth of Scripture, according to David Hubbard in this commentary which was formerly published under the title, **Will We Ever Catch Up with the Bible?** The author plumbs the theological, philosophical and psychological depths of each minor prophet (each is given a separate chapter) to speak to basic problems and issues that have plagued and puzzled man since the dawn of history. This study sounds like it comes out of today's headlines. Examples of chapter titles are: Worship Idols? Who, Me? (Hosea); Why Can't I Do My Own Thing? (Amos); Where Can I Find an Honest Politician? (Micah); Is Democracy the Way to God's Will? (Nahum); My Priorities? They're Straight...I Think (Haggai); Me? Rob God? (Malachi). 144 pages. S323109. Bible Commentary for Laymen Series. **$2.25.** Teaching materials available. Bookstores or from **Regal Books, Division GL Publications, 2300 Knoll Drive, Ventura, CA 93003.**

THIS LAND IS YOUR LAND (Regal Books) For: L,C,S,Y. Slant: EP.

By Paul E. Toms. This historical account of the conquest of Canaan becomes a springboard into the concepts of victorious Christian living today. A commentary on Joshua. 160 pages. S312107. Bible Commentary Series. **$2.50.** Teaching materials available. Bookstores or from **Regal Books, Division GL Publications, 2300 Knoll Drive, Ventura, CA 93003.**

THRU THE BIBLE WITH J. VERNON McGEE, VOLUME I (GENESIS THROUGH DEUTERONOMY) (Thomas Nelson Publishers) For: L,C. Slant: F, EP,P,S,DI.

By J. Vernon McGee. An informal commentary on the books of Genesis through Deuteronomy, the first volume of a series of five which will cover the entire Bible. These popular messages, the outgrowth of the **Thru the Bible** radio program, are geared to meet the needs of the average person, and as such, the writing deliberately avoids confusing academic rhetoric. The simplicity of McGee's approach

COMMENTARIES ON THE HEBREW SCRIPTURES

and the scope of this series is unique in this generation. Readers will feel comfortable with McGee's relaxed sincerity, and biblical truth will come alive through his comments, anecdotes, and observations. This commentary is meant to be read and enjoyed, and readers won't want to tuck this volume among the dusty shelves of unused books. Highly recommended for lay people. Hardcover. **$19.95**. Bookstores.

THRU THE BIBLE WITH J. VERNON MCGEE, VOLUME II (JOSHUA THROUGH PSALMS) (Thomas Nelson Publishers) For: L,C. Slant: F, EP, P, S, DI.

By J. Vernon McGee. This second volume of J. Vernon McGee's five-part series covers fourteen books of the Old Testament, Joshua through Psalms. Followers of Dr. McGee's popular radio broadcast, **Thru the Bible**, will welcome his informal, enthusiastic approach to Bible study. The simplicity of Dr. McGee's style and the scope of this series is unique in this generation. Readers feel comfortable with his relaxed sincerity, and biblical truth comes alive through his lively comments and pointed anecdotes. "Behind these messages," says Dr. McGee, "is a great deal of research and study in order to interpret the Bible from a popular rather than from a scholarly (and too-often boring) viewpoint." Hardcover. **$19.95**. Bookstores.

THRU THE BIBLE WITH J. VERNON McGEE, VOLUME III (PROVERBS THROUGH MALACHI) (Thomas Nelson Publishers) For: L,C. Slant: F,EP,P, S,DI.

By J. Vernon McGee. Proverbs through Malachi, the last twenty books of the Old Testament, are included in Volume III of this five-part series based on Dr. McGee's popular radio broadcast, **Thru the Bible**. Dr. McGee brings to this volume a tremendous amount of research and study, yet he interprets biblical truths in a popular, informal style. His enthusiasm for the Bible and its messages for today come alive through his lively comments and pointed anecdotes. Hardcover. **$19.95**. Bookstores.

THE TORAH: A MODERN COMMENTARY (Union of American Hebrew Congregations) For: L,C,S. Slant: RJ.

By Rabbis W. Gunther Plaut and Bernard J. Bamberger. This historic volume includes the Five Books of Moses and liberal contemporary interpretations that offer valuable insights into the Torah. In addition to the enlightening commentaries, this work includes an array of features that enhance our understanding of the Torah both as a literary document subject to critical examination and as the bearer of a sacred message: Clearly written essays; Gleanings; Footnotes; Maps. The original Hebrew and the 1967 JPS translation are followed by notes that give the plain meaning of the text, explanations of terms, names and references to other biblical books and all the traditional haftarot. **$30.00** (plus postage). Specify type of opening desired: English or Hebrew style. Bookstores or from **Union of American Hebrew Congregations, Book Order Dept., 838 Fifth Ave., New York, NY 10012**.

THE TRIUMPH OF TRUST (Baptist Publishing House) For: L,C,S. Slant: F, EP, P.

By Dr. E. Harold Henderson. "The just shall live by his faith" is more than a pretty slogan; it is a statement of divinely revealed truth. It is true when applied in the area of private life or the arena of international affairs. This commentary was written against a background of personal experience which enabled the author to identify with Habakkuk's heart. Internationally, I have asked as he asked, "How can God let sin go unchecked in my nation?" I have seen as he saw how God is actively using international crises to discipline an erring people. I have feared as he feared what would happen to the just if the judgment of God fell in my generation. I have found as he found peace in the assurance that God is faithful to provide for His own, whatever the circumstances. Personally, being involved in a ministry where we must depend upon God to provide for our needs day by day, I have found that Habakkuk is right. Circumstances do not govern God's provision for His people. He who does right and depends on God will experience **The Triumph of Trust**. **$2.00**. From **Baptist Publishing House, 712 Main, Little Rock, AR 72201**.

TWELVE MINOR PROPHETS (Baker Book House) For: L,C,S. Slant: EP.

By G.L. Robinson. Intended to be a textbook for use in seminaries and Bible schools. A classic on the subject. **$4.95**. Bookstores or from **Baker Book House, P.O. Box 6287, Grand Rapids, MI 49506**.

TYNDALE OLD TESTAMENT COMMENTARIES (InterVarsity Press) For: L,C,S. Slant: EP, P, S.

Edited by D.J. Wiseman. Up-to-date

COMMENTARIES ON THE HEBREW SCRIPTURES

commentaries on the Old Testament books with primary emphasis on a passage-by-passage exegesis. While undue technicalities are avoided, major critical questions are discussed in the introductions and, where necessary, in additional notes along with issues of date, authorship, style, structure and historical background. The TOTC includes commentaries in the following order: Genesis by Derek Kidner; Exodus by R. Alan Cole; Leviticus by R.K. Harrison; Numbers by Gordon J. Wenham; Deuteronomy by J.A. Thompson; Judges and Ruth by Arthur E. Cundall and Leon Morris; Ezra and Nehemiah by Derek Kidner; Job by Francis I. Andersen; Psalms 1-72 by Derek Kidner; Psalms 73-150 by Derek Kidner; Proverbs by Derek Kidner; Ecclesiastes by Michael Eaton; Jeremiah and Lamentations by R.K. Harrison; Ezekiel by John B. Taylor; Daniel by Joyce G. Baldwin; and Haggai, Zechariah, Malachi by Joyce Baldwin. Paper. **$6.95**, per commentary. Cloth. **$10.95**, per commentary. Set of sixteen volumes. Cloth. **$159.95**. Paper. **$94.95**. Bookstores.

UNGER'S COMMENTARY ON THE OLD TESTAMENT (Moody Press) For: L,C,S. Slant: EP, S, I, M.

By Merrill F. Unger. An excellent book-by-book, secton-by-section commentary on the entire Old Testament. Volume 1, Genesis through Song of Solomon; Volume 2, Isaiah through Malachi. **$23.95** per volume. Two volume set. **$43.05**. Bookstores or from **Moody Bookworld, 2101 W. Howard St., Chicago, IL 60645.**

WISDOM IN THE OLD TESTAMENT TRADITIONS (John Knox Press) For: C,S. Slant: C, RC, EP, MP, LP, S, BC.

By Donn F. Morgan. Morgan's new methodology presents the academic community with a workable alternative for biblical studies. Shows the various ways in which wisdom literature has been analyzed in recent years. Paper. **$8.95**. Cloth. **$17.50**. Add 10% for shipping; Georgia and Virginia residents please add appropriate sales tax. Bookstores or from **John Knox Press, 341 Ponce de Leon Ave., Atlanta, GA 30365.**

WISE UP AND LIVE (Regal Books) For: L,C,S,Y. Slant: EP.

By Paul E. Larsen. A book of wisdom from Proverbs that meets us where we are and begins to move us to where God wants us to be. **Wise Up and Live** has down-to-earth applications of the brief, terse, pungent sayings of this Old Testament book. It deals not with vapid theory, not with idle speculation, not with vague generalizations, but with Christian discipleship as it is to be lived, taught, felt. Here is reading not only for the study but for the kitchen, the living room, the bedroom, the shop, the store, the office. The selections from Proverbs made by Mr. Larsen are discussed topically in three categories: Relationships with God; Relationships with self; and Relationships with others. **Wise Up And Live** emphasizes that Proverbs is one of the most comprehensive statements of divine wisdom in all literature. These capsules of wisdom are more than clever hints about how to run your life. They convey a deep spiritual insight that points to the Person of all wisdom, Jesus Christ. Knowing Him, rather than memorizing a list of rules and catchy phrases, is the secret of "wising up and living." 256 pages. S274124. Bible Commentary for Laymen Series. Paperback. **$3.50**. Teaching materials available. Bookstores or from **Regal Books, Division GL Publications, 2300 Knoll Drive, Ventura, CA 93003.**

WOMAN IN ANCIENT ISRAEL UNDER THE TORAH AND TALMUD WITH A CRITICAL COMMENTARY ON GENESIS 1-3 (Ide House, Inc.) For: L,C,S,W. Slant: S,BC.

Discussion of the role of women to the time of the Maccabees, based on Genesis 1-3 and how it was interpreted with the evolution of ancient Israeli civilization; includes complete Genesis 1-3 text in parallel translation: Greek, Hebrew, and English. Cloth. **$15.95**. Paperback. **$10.95**. Bookstores or from **Ide House, Inc., 4631 Harvey Drive, Mesquite, TX 75150.**

WOMEN IN THE ANCIENT NEAR EAST (Ide House, Inc.) For: L,C,S. Slant: S, BC.

Includes a commentary on the evolution of woman and her contributions to civilization through the Minoan Age; it includes the complete text of the Book of Esther in parallel (Greek, Hebrew, English) translation with critical discussion. Review in **Mauscripta** states, "a detailed account of how women had greater personal freedom and social involvement in society prior to the Roman Age." Buckram/library binding only. **$15.95**. Bookstores or from **IDE House, Inc., 4631 Harvey Drive, Mesquite, TX 75150.**

PSALMS 1-50: THE WORD BIBLICAL COMMENTARY (Word Books) For: C,S. Slant: EP.

By Peter C. Craigie. Ancient poetry like the Psalms expresses "the most profound of human feelings and insights—prayer, praise, liturgy, wisdom, and lament." Thus does Dr. Peter Craigie indicate his respect for his subject matter in this important entry in the Word Biblical Commentary Series. Dr. Craigie sets a high standard for future volumes in this scholarly yet usable series. The author is a careful analyst of language and form. He is also concerned to communicate the emotional and theological impact of the Psalms as originally experienced by the people of Israel at public worship and in private devotions. 0218-5. Hardcover. **$18.95**. Bookstores.

COMMENTARIES ON NEW TESTAMENT BOOKS

In general, books listed as commentaries are those which contain verse-by-verse exposition of a portion of Scripture by one or more authors. This section includes works with verse-by-verse interpretation of the entire New Testament as well as elaborate interpretations of individual New Testament books and even of short biblical passages such as the Lord's Prayer or the Sermon on the Mount. Biblical commentaries have a rich historical tradition. In fact, some parts of the New Testament itself are actually commentaries on the Hebrew Scriptures and most of the earliest extra-biblical writings of the Christian church were commentaries on either the Hebrew Scriptures, the Gospels, or the letters of Paul. However, because commentaries are usually one person's interpretation of Scripture, knowledge of the author's theological "slant" is more important than for other biblical reference works. Included in this section are commentaries on the New Testament books—and portions of those books—accepted as canonical by virtually all of Christendom.

COMMENTARIES ON NEW TESTAMENT BOOKS

ACTS: BIBLE STUDY COMMENTARY (Zondervan Publishing House) For: L,C,S. Slant: EP.

By **Curtis Vaughan**. A lay-oriented commentary, with no Greek used within its text. The commentary deals with each biblical book section-by-section, with discussion questions at the end of each chapter. Brief bibliography. **$4.95**. Bookstores or from **Zondervan Retail Marketing Service, 1420 Robinson Road, SE, Grand Rapids, MI 49506**.

ALL ABOUT WITNESSING (Baker Book House) For: L,S. Slant: EP.

By **Robert J. Martin**. The Book of Acts. Biblically based discussions that will rekindle in the Christian today the excitement, enthusiasm, and boldness exemplified first by the Early Church. There are brief, practical suggestions for successful group discussions. **$1.65**. Bookstores or from **Baker Book House, P.O. Box 6287, Grand Rapids, MI 49506**.

THE APOSTLE PAUL AND WOMEN IN THE CHURCH (Regal Books) For: L,C,S,Y,W. Slant: EP.

By **Don Williams**. Should women be silent in the church? Where do women fit in God's hierarchy? Should women be veiled? Should women teach men? Should women be ordained? What about male headship? Facing these issues squarely, author Don Williams deals definitely with key questions for the church and Christians everywhere concerning true women's liberation in Christ. **The Apostle Paul and Women in the Church** reviews current popular literature that shapes the thinking about women today, then presents a verse-by-verse study of all Paul says about women. A scholarly and highly readable study of the biblical role of women in the church today. Carefully annotated. Quality paper. 160 pages. Number 5411505. **$3.95**. Bookstores or from **Regal Books, Division of GL Publications, 2300 Knoll Drive, Ventura, CA 93003**.

AS I HAVE LOVED YOU: THE GOSPEL OF JOHN (Dove Publications) For: L,C,S. Slant: RC,P.

By **Fr. Jim Wolff**. A contemporary but pastoral exegesis of John's Gospel that highlights its saving message: Jesus is the revelation of the Father's love for each of us. Fr. Wolff is an experienced counselor and retreat master. **$5.95**. Add **$.85** postage. Bookstores or from **Dove Publications, Pecos, NM 87552**.

AUTOBIOGRAPHY OF GOD (Regal Books) For: L,C,S,Y. Slant: EP.

By **Lloyd John Ogilvie**. Scriptural insight, intriguing anecdotes and practical illustrations all combine in this contemporary commentary on the parables, giving us a fresh look at the nature of God. 324 pages. Quality paper. Number 5415106. **$5.95**. Bookstores or from **Regal Books, Division of GL Publications, 2300 Knoll Drive, Ventura, CA 93003**.

BARNES' NOTES ON THE NEW TESTAMENT (Kregel Publications) For: L,C,S. Slant: P,S.

A verse-by-verse exposition of the entire New Testament. All difficult passages are intelligently discussed; all book introductions are properly established. This is one of the greatest single-volume, complete New Testament commentaries ever produced. **$34.95**. Bookstores or from **Kregel Publications, P.O. Box 2607, Grand Rapids, MI 49501**.

BEACON BIBLE EXPOSITIONS (Baker Book House) For: L,C,S. Slant: AW.

This expanding set of expositions is a systematic, devotional Bible study program for laymen and a fresh, homiletical resource for preachers. The best biblical scholarship is combined with nontechnical language in this valuable tool. **$6.95**. Bookstores or from **Baker Book House, P.O. Box 6287, Grand Rapids, MI 49506**.

BEACON BIBLE EXPOSITIONS (12 VOLUMES) (Beacon Hill Press of Kansas City) For: L,C. Slant: AW, EP, H.

A set of twelve volumes covering the New Testament. In-depth look at selected passages in each book (although, outline covers the total book). It is a systematic, devotional Bible study for lay persons, and a fresh, homiletical resource for preachers. All the benefits of excellent Bible scholarship are found in each book, but communicated in nontechnical language. Volumes include: Volume 1, Matthew; Volume 2, Mark; Volume 3, Luke; Volume 4, John; Volume 5, Acts; Volume 6, Romans; Volume 7, Corinthians; Volume 8, Galatians/Ephesians; Volume 9, Philippians/Colossians/Philemon; Volume 10, Thessalonians/Timothy/Titus; Volume 11, Hebrews/James/Peter; Volume 12, John/Jude/Revelation. Based on KJV. Cloth bound. 230-298 pages. 5 1/2 x 7 3/4. **$6.95** per volume. From **Beacon Hill Press of Kansas City, Box 527, Dept. B, Kansas City, MO 64141**.

BEATITUDES AND THE LORD'S PRAYER (Baker Book House) For: L,S. Slant: EP.

By **A.W. Pink**. Those familiar with Pink's typically rich and reverent treatment of God's Word will welcome this book centered on two key passages of the New Testament. **$4.95**. Bookstores or from **Baker Book House, P.O. Box 6287, Grand Rapids, MI 49506**.

BEHOLD THE KING (Multnomah Press) For: C,S. Slant: EP, S, M.

By **Stanley D. Toussaint**. A study of Matthew. The Gospel of Matthew is unique among the gospel accounts as a distinctly Jewish writing that clearly and powerfully portrays Jesus as the Messiah. Matthew, as well as the other gospel writers wrote with the intention of setting forth an argument, of proving a point. In this new com-

COMMENTARIES ON NEW TESTAMENT BOOKS

mentary, Toussaint argues that the significance of Matthew's gospel can only be appreciated when the purpose for which it was written is properly understood. Hardback. **$16.95.** Bookstores or from **Multnomah Press, 10209 S.E. Division Street, Portland, OR 97266.**

BEHOLD YOUR KING (Moody Press) For: L,S. Slant: EP,P,I,M.

By J.C. McCauley. A study of the gospel of Matthew geared to fit the needs of Christian laymen at various stages of spiritual development. **$9.95.** Bookstores or from **Moody Bookworld, 2101 W. Howard, Chicago, IL 60645.**

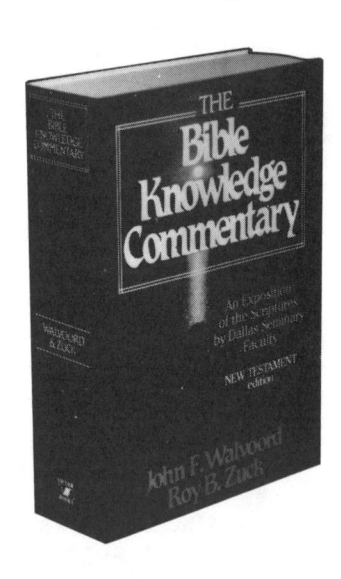

THE BIBLE KNOWLEDGE COMMENTARY (NEW TESTAMENT EDITION) (Victor Books) For: L,C,S. Slant: EP,P,I,PM.

An exposition of the New Testament by Dallas Theological Seminary faculty members, based on the New International Version of the Bible, commenting on the New Testament verse-by-verse. Explains problem passages, alleged discrepancies, key Greek and Aramaic words. Contains maps, charts, and diagrams. Incorporates numerous cross references to parallel passages. Based on thorough scholarship, but written in a popular, readable style. **$19.95.** Bookstores or from **Scripture Press, 1825 College Avenue, Wheaton, IL 60187.**

BIBLICAL THEOLOGY OF THE NEW TESTAMENT (Moody Press) For: C,S. Slant: EP,S,I,M.

By Charles C. Ryrie. Discusses the truths of God's Word as they were revealed--progressively. **$9.95.** Bookstores or from **Moody Bookworld, 2101 W. Howard, Chicago, IL 60645.**

BIRTH OF THE BODY (Vision House, Inc.) For: L,C,S,Y. Slant: EP.

By Ray Stedman. The first book in this three-volume series on the book of Acts looks at the lives of the early Christians and reveals how to yield fully to Christ and experience joyous living today. Covers Acts 1-12. 208 pages. Number A424491. Quality paper. **$4.95.** Packaged set also available. **The Acts Trilogy.** Bookstores or from **Vision House, Division of GL Publications, 2300 Knoll Drive, Ventura, CA 93003.**

BOUND FOR JOY (Regal Books) For: L,C,S,Y. Slant: EP.

By Stuart Briscoe. When Paul wrote his letter to the Philippians he was a prisoner of Rome's mad Emperor Nero. He may have been confined in Ephesus or Caesarea or locked in the recesses of Rome's infamous Mamertine prison. Yet his letter--containing the thoughts of a man incarcerated--speaks only of joy and rejoicing. His confinement was in a place of damp stone, darkness and stench, and yet his letter is nothing less than a shout of victory. "We all have our prisons of one kind or another," writes Mr. Briscoe. But no matter what your own prison may be, you, like Paul, may also find a way of escape, and right in the most invidious circumstances may have a sense of triumph. This book by Stuart Briscoe is a layman's study of Paul's epistle to the Philippians, which will lift your spirits, thrill your heart, challenge your will, excite your mind and enrich your experience. 192 pages. Number S291126. Paperback. **$2.95.** Bible Commentary for Laymen Series. Bookstores or from **Regal Books, Division of GL Publications, 2300 Knoll Drive, Ventura, CA 93003.**

BROADMAN BIBLE COMMENTARY (Broadman Press) For: L,C,S. Slant: MP.

Comprehensive in scope, the commentary has the text of the Revised Standard Version in full, outlines each Bible book, and gives a paragraph-by-paragraph interpretation. Introductory material to each Bible book deals with questions of purpose, date, authorship, and setting. General articles summarize interpretative materials about the Bible and its major themes. Volumes contain 384 to 512 pages and are handsomely bound in maroon linen cloth. Twelve volumes. **Vol. 1:** Revised: **Genesis**, Francisco; **Exodus**, Honeycutt 4211-25. **Vol. 2: Leviticus**, Clements; **Numbers**, Owens; **Deuteronomy**, Watts; **Joshua**, Morton; **Judges**, Dalglish; **Ruth**, Kennedy 4211-02. **Vol. 3: 1 & 2 Samuel**, Philbeck; **1 Kings**, Matheney; **2 Kings**, Honeycutt; **1 & 2 Chronicles**, Francisco; **Ezra & Nehemiah**, Hamrick 4211-03. **Vol. 4: Esther**, Bjornard; **Job**, Owens, Tate, Watts; **Psalms**, Durham 4211-04. **Vol. 5: Proverbs**, Tate; **Ecclesiastes**,

144

COMMENTARIES ON NEW TESTAMENT BOOKS

Peterson; **Song of Solomon**, Bunn; **Isaiah**, Kelley 4211-05. **Vol. 6: Jeremiah**, Green; **Lamentations**, Laurin; **Ezekiel**, Bunn; **Daniel**, Owens 4211-06. **Vol. 7: Hosea**, Honeycutt; **Joel**, Kennedy; **Amos**, R. Smith; **Obadiah**, Creson; **Jonah**, Glaze; **Micah**, Scoggin; **Nahum**, Bunn & Dalglish; **Habakkuk**, Garland; **Zephaniah**, Eakin; **Haggai**, D. Smith; **Zechariah**, Watts; **Malachi**, Bennett 4211-07. **Vol. 8: Matthew**, Stagg; **Mark**, Turlington 4211-08. **Vol. 9: Luke**, Tolbert; **John**, Hull 4211-09. **Vol. 10: Acts**, T. Smith; **Romans**, Moody; **1 Corinthians**, Brown 4211-10. **Vol. 11: 2 Corinthians**, Beasley-Murray; **Galatians**, MacGorman; **Ephesians**, Martin; **Philippians**, Stagg; **Colossians**, White; **1 & 2 Thessalonians**, Hobbs; **1 & 2 Timothy**, Hinson; **Titus**, Hinson; **Philemon**, Robbins 4211-11. **Vol. 12: Hebrews**, Trentham; **James**, Songer; **1 & 2 Peter**, Summers; **1, 2, & 3 John**, McDowell; **Jude**, Summers; **Revelation**, Ashcraft 4211-12. Twelve-volume set. **$175.00**. Individual volumes. **$14.95**. Bookstores or from **Lifeway Home Shopping Service, Nashville, TN 37234**.

THE CHRISTIAN SOLDIER (Baker Book House) For: C,S. Slant: C, EP.

By Martyn Lloyd Jones. An exposition of Ephesians 6:10-20. The latest volume in Dr. Lloyd Jones series on Ephesians. He explores the general principles of spiritual warfare, and then examines the "whole armour of God," discussing in detail each piece of armour mentioned by the apostle. **$10.95** Bookstores or from **Baker Book House, P.O. Box 6287, Grand Rapids, MI 49506**.

CHRISTIAN UNITY (Baker Book House) For: C,S. Slant: C,EP.

By D. Martyn Lloyd Jones. An exposition of Ephesians 4:1-16. Excellent exposition on this passage concerning diversity of spiritual gifts and the unity of all believers in Christ. **$10.95**. Bookstores or from **Baker Book House, P.O. Box 6287, Grand Rapids, MI 49506**.

THE CHRISTIAN WARFARE (Baker Book House) For: C,S. Slant: C,EP.

By D. Martyn Lloyd Jones. An exposition of Ephesians 6:10-13. The author deals with the character and strategy of the devil in general terms, but he also demonstrates how discouragement, anxiety, false zeal, lack of assurance, and worldliness come under the heading "the wiles of the devil." **$10.95**. Bookstores or from **Baker Book House, P.O. Box 6287, Grand Rapids, MI 49506**.

COLLEGEVILLE BIBLE COMMENTARY (The Liturgical Press) For: L,C,S. Slant: RC, P.

A series of study guides using the New American Bible translation that provides the latest scholarship in biblical study in language directed to non-technical readers. There are eleven books in the New Testment series; a series on the Old Testament is now in preparation and will be released starting in the fall of 1984. Each book in the New Testament series contains from 64 to 128 pages and contains both the text of the book or books commented on and the commentary on the same or facing page. **$2.50** per booklet. **$25.00** for the eleven-booklet set. Bookstores or from **The Liturgical Press, Collegeville, MN 56321**.

COLOSSIANS (Baker Book House) For: L,S. Slant: EP.

By Charles Pickell. A manual for individual group study of Colossians. **$1.00**. Bookstores or from **Baker Book House, P.O. Box 6287, Grand Rapids, MI 49506**.

COLOSSIANS (Presbyterian and Reformed Publishing Co.) For: L,C,S. Slant: C, F, P, I.

By Gordon H. Clark. This concise, verse-by-verse commentary will give the reader a thorough understanding of Paul's Epistle to the Colossians. Concentrating on the message itself, Gordon H. Clark explains the meaning of the original Greek text and provides insight into the process of translation. Throughout he stresses the applicability of the message to our times. Mr. Clark is a well-known author of several works on religion and philosophy. 136 pages. **$3.95**. Bookstores or from **Presbyterian and Reformed Publishing Co., P.O. Box 817, Phillipsburg, NJ 08865**.

COLOSSIANS AND PHILEMON: BIBLE STUDY COMMENTARY (Zondervan Publishing House) For: L,C,S. Slant: EP.

By Curtis Vaughan. A lay-oriented commentary, with no Greek used within its text. The commentary deals with each biblical book section-by-section, with discussion questions at the end of each chapter. Brief bibliography. **$4.95**. Bookstores or from **Zondervan Retail Marketing Service, 1420 Robinson Road, SE, Grand Rapids, MI 49506**.

COLOSSIANS AND PHILEMON: THE WORD BIBLICAL COMMENTARY (Word Books) For: C,S. Slant: EP.

By Peter T. O'Brien. Peter O'Brien's scholarship and his experience in missions in India contribute to this volume in the World Bible Commentary. The author shows how the Colossians faced mystical and ascetic tendencies not unlike those he faced from modern Eastern thought. This book therefore gives the modern student practical and immediate access to Paul's argument. Dr. O'Brien maintains that all counsels to self-denial are inadequate if they hint that "Christ's sufferings were insufficient to redeem." The author's careful consideration of these letters and their interpreters' arguments brings him to defend their Pauline authorship, and their place in the church's canon. Hardcover. Catalog Number 0243-6. **$18.95**. Bookstores.

COMMENTARY ON THE NEW TESTAMENT (Baker Book House) For: C. Slant: EP.

By John Trapp. Trapp comments on

COMMENTARIES ON NEW TESTAMENT BOOKS

every New Testament book verse-by-verse adding to his own remarks appropriate statements from other theologians. **$24.95.** Bookstores or from **Baker Book House, P.O. Box 6287, Grand Rapids, MI 49506.**

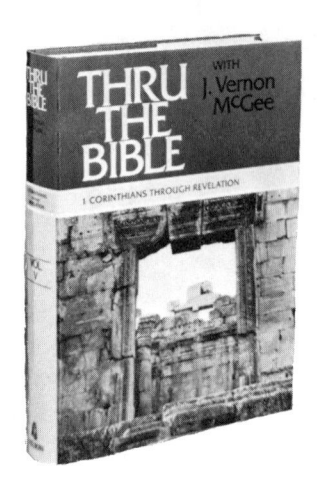

I CORINTHIANS THROUGH REVELATION: THRU THE BIBLE—VOLUME V (Thomas Nelson Publishers) For: L,C. Slant: F,EP,P,S,DI.

By J. Vernon McGee. As is true with the previous four books, Volume 5, follows J. Vernon McGee's radio messages through the Bible as preached over the radio on the **Thru the Bible** radio program. Popular and devotional in flavor, these messages provide basic information on the Bible and assistance in understanding it and applying it to life. Volume 5 will provide expository material on the New Testament books from First Corinthians through Revelation. It will complete the series. Hardcover. **$19.95.** Bookstores.

DARKNESS AND LIGHT (Baker Book House) For: C,S. Slant: C, EP.

By D. Martyn Lloyd Jones. An exposition of Ephesians 4:17-5:17. This is the final volume to appear in this eight-volume series of theological expositions of Ephesians. **$10.95.** Bookstores or from **Baker Book House, P.O. Box 6287, Grand Rapids, MI 49506.**

DAYS OF GLORY: THE PASSION, DEATH, AND RESURRECTION OF JESUS CHRIST (Servant Publications) For: L. Slant: S.

By Richard T.A. Murphy, O.P. One of America's foremost Scripture scholars brings a lifetime of prayer and study to this examination of the passion narratives. Offers a wealth of cultural, political, and religious background to help the reader enter more fully into the final days of Jesus' earthly life. Number 0824. **$4.95.** Bookstores.

DIVINE ORDER IN THE CHURCH (Baker Book House) For: L,C,S. Slant: AW.

By French Arrington. This study of 1 Corinthians presents powerful scriptural solutions to the problems of today's churches. **$4.95.** Bookstores or from **Baker Book House, P.O. Box 6287, Grand Rapids, MI 49506.**

DON'T LET GO! AN EXPOSITION OF HEBREWS (Presbyterian and Reformed Publishing Co.) For: L,C,S. Slant: C,F,P,I.

By George M. Bowman. A flood of false teaching assails the church today, just as it did the first readers of the Epistle to the Hebrews. In one way or another, counterfeit faiths draw attention away from the preeminence of Christ. **Don't Let Go!** was written to ward believers to resist all such forms of apostasy in our day. A clear and readable exposition of Hebrews, it urges professing Christians to hold fast to the finished work and Word of Jesus, and to persevere in faithful service to him. George M. Bowman has been a Bible expositor for more than thirty years. A writer and editor, he has published numerous books and articles on Christian living and stewardship. 170 pages. **$4.95.** Bookstores or from **Presbyterian and Reformed Publishing Co., P.O. Box 817, Phillipsburg, NJ 08865.**

EPHESIANS: BIBLE STUDY COMMENTARY (Zondervan Publishing House) For: L,C,S. Slant: EP.

By Curtis Vaughan. A lay-oriented commentary, with no Greek used within its text. The commentary deals with each biblical book section-by-section, with discussion questions at the end of each chapter. Brief bibliography. **$4.95.** Bookstores or from **Zondervan Retail Marketing Service, 1420 Robinson Road, SE, Grand Rapids, MI 49506.**

EPHESIANS THROUGH PHILEMON: THE EXPOSITOR'S BIBLE COMMENTARY (Zondervan Publishing House) For: L,C.S. Slant: EP.

By Frank E. Gaebelein, Editor. Commentary on Ephesians by A. Skevington Wood; Philippians by Homer A. Kent, Jr.; Colossians by Curtis Vaughan; 1 and 2 Thessalonians by Robert L. Thomas; 1 and 2 Timothy by Ralph Earle; Titus by D. Edmond Hiebert; and Philemon by Arthur A. Rupprecht. The commentary uses the New International Version. Each book has an exposition, an introduction, an outline, and bibliography. Notes and textual questions are correlated with expository units. Transliteration and translation of Semitic and Greek words are provided. Commentators seek to deal fairly with opposing views. **$17.95.** Bookstores or from **Zondervan Retail Marketing Service, 1420 Robinson Road, SE, Grand Rapids, MI 49506.**

EPISTLE OF JAMES (Moody Press) For: L,C,S. Slant: EP,S,I,M.

By D. Edmond Hiebert. Careful exposi-

COMMENTARIES ON NEW TESTAMENT BOOKS

tion of the Book of James that challenges believers to test the validity of their faith, to consistently practice what they believe. **$13.95.** Bookstores or from **Moody Bookworld, 2101 W. Howard, Chicago, IL 60645.**

THE EPISTLE TO THE GALATIANS (Baker Book House) For: L,C,S. Slant: EP.

By F.E. Hamilton. A study manual and commentary. **$1.50.** Bookstores or from **Baker Book House, P.O. Box 6287, Grand Rapids, MI 49506.**

THE EPISTLES OF JOHN (Thomas Nelson Publishers) For: L,C. Slant: EP, MP, P.

By Dr. Herschel Hobbs. First-century Gnostics taught salvation through knowledge rather than faith and regarded Jesus Christ as less than God. With such beliefs they undermined the nature and reliability of the Gospel, especially the words of John. By analyzing the epistles of John, Herschel Hobbs shows how the apostle combated the teachings of the Gnostics. In fact, Dr. Hobbs believes "the principal purpose in the writing of 1 John was to refute the false teachings of the Gnostics and to comfort and encourage those in danger of being deluded by such." Dr. Hobbs throws light on John's message by examining key Greek words, especially verb tenses. Because much of the teaching of the ancient Gnostics is in vogue today, Herschel Hobb's interpretation of John's words is as important to modern readers as John's message was to readers of the first century. Hardcover. **$9.95.** Bookstores.

AN EVERLASTING LOVE (Multnomah Press) For: L. Slant: EP, D.

By John G. Mitchell. A devotional study of the gospel of John. The apostle John gave us an intimate look into the heart of the Savior. He forever captured the individuals touched by Christ's message, His power and His grace. Now **An Everlasting Love** takes you on a journey through John's Gospel; a journey to belief and love for the Son of God. Hardback. **$13.95.** Bookstores or from **Multnomah Press, 10209 S.E. Division St., Portland, OR 97266.**

EXPOSITION OF THE SERMON ON THE MOUNT (Baker Book House) For: C,S. slant: EP.

By A. W. Pink. This sixty-four chapter book is a verse-by-verse and almost word-for-word exposition of Matthew 5 through 7. **$9.95.** Bookstores or from **Baker Book House, P.O. Box 6287, Grand Rapids, MI 49506.**

EXPOSITORY THOUGHTS ON THE GOSPELS (Baker Book House) For: C,S. Slant: EP.

By J.C. Ryle. A full and complete commentary on every verse in the Gospels, this classic set represents one of the most significant contributions to evangelical thought. Four volume set. **$45.00.** Bookstores or from **Baker Book House, P.O. Box 6287, Grand Rapids, MI 49506.**

FAITH-LOVE-HOPE (AMG Publishers) For: L,C,S,Y. Slant: C, F, EP, MP, D, P.

By Dr. Spiros Zodhiates. An exegetical exposition on the book of James. This three volume set, **The Work of Faith, The Labor of Love,** and **The Patience of Hope** is a reprint in paperback of **The Behavior of Belief,** long recognized as the most comprehensive volume available on James. The indicies of subjects, English and Greek words, and illustrations used throughout still are included. This work is intended not as "once only" reading material, but as study helps of value to the lay Christian, Sunday school teacher, preacher, and even the seminary professor. The primary object has been to make the Epistle of James live, to present vividly before the reader the claims of God through the Apostle James. This set is a must for the library of any serious student of the Bible. Dr. Zodhiates is a Greek scholar and an Editor of **Pulpit Helps** magazine. Three volume set in handsome slipcover. **$14.85.** Add **$2.00** for postage. From **Christian Media Supply, 524 Sycamore Circle, Ridgeland, MS 39157.**

FAREWELL DISCOURSE AND FINAL PRAYER OF JESUS (Baker Book House) For: C,S. Slant: EP.

By D. A. Carson. An evangelical exposition of John 14-17. Based on scholarly research and detailed exegesis of the Greek text, this exposition centers on the theology of the cross. **$9.95.** Bookstores or from **Baker Book House, P.O. Box 6287, Grand Rapids, MI 49506.**

FELLOWSHIP (Multnomah Press) For: L. Slant: EP,D.

By John G. Mitchell. Three letters from John. Knowing God and enjoying fellowship with Him are the primary thematic emphases of this exposition of John's epistles. Paperback. **$4.95.** Bookstores or from **Multnomah Press, 10209 S.E. Division St., Portland, OR 97266.**

FILIPENSES, LA EPISTOLA DEL GOZO (PHILIPPIANS) (Vida Publishers) Slant: EP.

By William Menzies. A very readable and illuminating commentary on the book of Philippians. Mr. Menzies is a noted evangelical scholar and educator. **$2.75.** Bookstores.

COMMENTARIES ON NEW TESTAMENT BOOKS

FIVE GOSPELS: AN ACCOUNT OF HOW THE GOOD NEWS CAME TO BE (Winston Press) For: L,C,S. Slant: RC, MP, S.

By John C. Meagher. A fascinating, undoubtedly controversial reconstruction of the origins and early development of Christian gospeling. This book argues that the Christian good news as we know it was formed in five successive stages; in the gospel of John the Baptist, of Jesus himself, of the Apostles, of Demetrios (an obscure figure who may be the person behind the Third Epistle of John), and the "gospel of the Ultimate" which sprang from a movement associated with the gospel of John. An excellent, stimulating resource for serious students of the Bible and for Bible scholars. Hardcover. **$17.50.** Paperback. **$9.95.** Bookstores or from **Winston Press, 430 Oak Grove, Minneapolis, MN 55403.**

FLESH AND SPIRIT (Baker Book House) For: C,S. Slant: EP.

By William Barclay. An examination of Galatians 5:19-23. Thoroughly examines Paul's idea of the warfare that takes place between body and spirit. **$2.95.** Bookstores or from **Baker Book House, P.O. Box 6287, Grand Rapids, MI 49506.**

FROM TRIALS TO TRIUMPHS (Regal Books) For: L,C,S,Y. Slant: EP.

By Derek Prime. The message of **From Trials to Triumphs** underscores the essential message of James' letter—real faith in the Lord Jesus shows itself in good deeds, in the work of faith. Genuine faith perseveres in doing good whatever the circumstances. Derek Prime effectively employs a topical approach, includes practical applications for daily living, provides helpful cross references to other portions of Scripture for illustration and clarification. **From Trials to Triumphs** will prove to be a real source of encouragement to Christians who are undergoing trials or ministering to others in such circumstances. Basic subjects such as trials and temptations, listening and doing, faith and works, and the two kinds of wisdom that influence human behavior are dealt with in depth. In a day of "instant solutions" here is a guide for Christians seeking more than pat answers to life's questions. Mass market paper. 160 pages. Number S363104. **$2.95.** Bookstores or from **Regal Books, Division of GL Publications, 2300 Knoll Drive, Ventura, CA 93003.**

GALATIANS: BIBLE STUDY COMMENTARY (Zondervan Publishing House) For: L,C,S. Slant: EP.

By Curtis Vaughan. A lay-oriented commentary, with no Greek used within its text. The commentary deals with each biblical book section-by-section, with discussion questions at the end of each chapter. Brief bibliography. **$4.95.** Bookstores or from **Zondervan Retail Marketing Service, 1420 Robinson Road, SE, Grand Rapids, MI 49506.**

GALATIANS: INTERPRETATION A Bible Commentary for Teaching and Preaching (John Knox Press) For: L,C,S. Slant: C, RC, EP, MP, LP, D, P, S, BC.

By Charles Cousar. The **Interpretation** series is a pioneering concept in Bible commentaries. It combines both the qualities of scholarly and critical commentaries with those which are devotional and personal. Written specifically for the teaching and preaching tasks of the church, it draws out and describes the significance of the biblical text for Christian life and faith. Designed for use by both clergy and laity, the language has been kept clear and nontechnical. Cloth. **$13.95.** Please add 10% for shipping. Georgia and Virginia, please add appropriate sales tax. Bookstores or from **John Knox Press, 341 Ponce de Leon Ave., Atlanta, GA 30365.**

GLIMPSES FROM THE BOOK OF REVELATION (The Brethren Press) For: L,C,S. Slant: EP, PM.

By Harold S. Martin. This is a concise commentary on the Book of Revelation from the premillennial point of view. It divides Revelation into three parts: things past, things present, and things future. The writer attempts to speak everyday language and make the message clear without using technical terms. He explores the meanings of the trumpets, the vials, and the beasts of the Book of Revelation, and then proclaims God's message of hope for the last days. Number 8-3169. **$4.95.** From **The Brethren Press, 1451 Dundee Ave., Elgin, IL 60120.**

GOD'S ULTIMATE PURPOSE (Baker Book House) For: C,S. Slant: C, EP.

By D. Martyn Lloyd Jones. An exposition of Ephesians I. The author asserts that the teaching of Ephesians can be understood only in the light of the great doctrine found in the first chapter. It is in Ephesians that God's glorious plan and destiny for the Christian church is set forth. **$10.95.** Bookstores or from **Baker Book House, P.O. Box 6287, Grand Rapids, MI 49506.**

GOD'S WAY OF RECONCILIATION (Baker Book House) For: C,S. Slant: C, EP.

By D. Martyn Lloyd Jones. Studies in Ephesians 2. These masterful expositions on the second chapter of the Book of Ephesians reach the heart of the human problem—man's estrangement from God. **$10.95.** Bookstores or from **Baker Book House, P.O. Box 6287, Grand Rapids, MI 49506.**

COMMENTARIES ON NEW TESTAMENT BOOKS

GOOD NEWS ACCORDING TO MARK (John Knox Press) For: C,S. Slant: C, RC, EP, MP, LP, S, BC.

By **Eduard Schweizer**. For the serious reader, this commentary on Mark is written by a foremost biblical scholar, Eduard Schweizer. **$16.95.** Please add 10% for shipping. Georgia and Virginia, please add appropriate sales tax. Bookstores or from **John Knox Press, 341 Ponce de Leon Ave., Atlanta, GA 30365.**

GOOD NEWS ACCORDING TO MATTHEW (John Knox Press) For: C,S. Slant: C, RC, EP, MP, LP, S, BC.

By **Eduard Schweizer**. Mr. Schweizer isolates Matthew's distinctive view of Christ by comparing Matthew's message with his sources and with parallel literature. A brilliant passage-by-passage investigation of the longest gospel. Impeccable historical research and strong critical awareness lend themselves to this enlightening study centered on Matthew's unqualified and earthshaking command to love. Cloth. **$17.95.** Please add 10% for shipping. Georgia and Virginia, please add appropriate sales tax. Bookstores or from **John Knox Press, 341 Ponce de Leon Ave., Atlanta, GA 30365.**

GOSPEL OF MARK (Baker Book House) For: L. Slant: EP.

By **Herschel Hobbs**. A study manual. This commentary explains every passage in Mark. The author provides necessary background information, relates the Gospel of Mark to the other three Gospels, and applies the text to life today. **$1.95.** Bookstores or from **Baker Book House, P.O. Box 6287, Grand Rapids, MI 49506.**

GOSPELS IN CURRENT STUDY (Baker Book House) For: C. Slant: EP.

By **Simon Kistemaker**. Second edition. An invaluable overview of Gospel studies. This second edition adds a new chapter on interpretation of the Gospels. **$6.95.** Bookstores or from **Baker Book House, P.O. Box 6287, Grand Rapids, MI 49506.**

GRACE AND TRUTH (Harvest House Publishers) For: L,C,S. Slant: C, EP, P, I, M.

This in-depth yet concise study of the Gospel of John emphasizes throughout each chapter the striking contrast between law and grace, and between faith and works. "New and precious truths have come to me from careful reading of the volume."—Dr. Lewis Sperry Chafer. Paper. Number 2616. **$3.95. Harvest House Publishers, 1075 Arrowsmith, Eugene, OR 97402.**

THE GREATEST LIFE EVER LIVED (Tyndale House Publishers) For: L,S,Y. Slant: C, F, EP, MP, D.

Events of Christ's life. Illustrated. Vest pocket paper. Packs of 25 only. **$13.75.** Bookstores.

GROWTH OF THE BODY (Vision House, Inc.) For: L,C,S,Y. Slant: EP.

By **Ray Stedman**. The second volume in the Acts trilogy depicts the Holy Spirit's operation in the early church and how the surrounding community was turned upside down within a short period of time. Covers Acts 13-20. Quality paper. 208 pages. Number A424505. **$4.95.** Packaged set also available, **The Acts of Trilogy**. Bookstores or from **Vision House, Division of GL Publications, 2300 Knoll Drive, Ventura, CA 93003.**

HARMONY OF THE LIFE OF ST. PAUL (Baker Book House) For: L,C,S. Slant: EP.

By **F.J. Goodwin**. Designed as a handbook of a continuous account of the life of the great apostle. **$8.95.** Bookstores or from **Baker Book House, P.O. Box 6287, Grand Rapids, MI 49506.**

THE HEART OF THE NEW TESTAMENT (Broadman Press) For: L,S. Slant: MP.

By **H.I. Hester**. A clear, concise guide for New Testament study written in a narrative form. This book places the New Testament in chronological order so that students may get an intelligent view of the origin and development of Christianity. See companion book, **The Heart of Hebrew History**. **$10.95.** Bookstores.

HEART OPENED WIDE (Baker Book House) For: C,S. Slant: EP.

By **Homer Kent, Jr.** Studies in 2 Corinthians. A scholarly, well-balanced commentary, enriched by the author's broad knowledge of the ancient Near East including the geography, literature and archaeology. **$4.95.** Bookstores or from **Baker Book House, P.O. Box 6287, Grand Rapids, MI 49506.**

HEBREWS (Baker Book House) For: C,S. Slant: EP.

By **A.W. Pink**. Perhaps the most

COMMENTARIES ON NEW TESTAMENT BOOKS

complete and vigorous exposition of Hebrews produced in this century for preacher, teacher, and Bible student. Now in one volume. **$24.95.** Bookstores or from **Baker Book House, P.O. Box 6287, Grand Rapids, MI 49506.**

HEBREWS—A GOOD NEWS COMMENTARY (Harper & Row, Publishers, Inc.) For: L,C. Slant: EP.

By Donald Alfred Hagner. This exemplary commentary sheds new light on the major ideas of this crucial book and shows its relevance both for the church and the individual Christian. **The Good News Commentary Series** is the first major series to use the popular English Text of the Good News Bible, which has sold in the millions. Each volume is informed by solid scholarship and the most up-to-date research, yet each is biblically faithful and readily understandable to the general reader. Features include: introductory material highlighting authorship, dating, background information, and thematic emphases—plus a map; full text of each Good News Bible book with running commentary; special end notes which give references for key words and concepts, and provide suggestions for further reading; full indexes for Scriptures, subjects, persons, and places. 288 pages. Kivar cover. Number RD 425. **$9.95.** Bookstores or from **Harper & Row, Publishers, Inc., Mail Order Department, 2350 Virginia Avenue, Hagerstown, MD 21740.**

HEBREWS: BIBLE STUDY COMMENTARY (Zondervan Publishing House) For: L,C,S. Slant: EP.

By Leon Morris. A lay-oriented commentary. Good for group or individual Bible studies. Helpful treatment of the meaning of atonement in Christ as seen against the backdrop of the Old Testament. Discussion questions. Brief bibliography. **$5.95.** Bookstores or from **Zondervan Retail Marketing Service, 1420 Robinson Road, SE, Grand Rapids, MI 49506.**

HEBREWS/THE JOHN MacARTHUR NEW TESTAMENT (Moody Press) For: L,C. Slant: EP, P, S, I, M.

By John MacArthur, Jr. First volume to be released in the new MacArthur New Testament Commentary series. A commentary designed for pastors and laymen who want to understand the message of Hebrews as well as live it and expound it effectively. Very practical, full of rich illustrations, and Old Testament background necessary to an understanding of the book of Hebrews. **$11.95.** Bookstores or from **Moody Bookworld, 2101 W. Howard, Chicago, IL 60645.**

HEBREWS THROUGH REVELATION: THE EXPOSITOR'S BIBLE COMMENTARY (Zondervan Publishing House) For; L,C,S. Slant: EP.

By Frank E. Gaebelein, Editor. Contains commentary on Hebrews by Leon Morris; James by Donald W. Burdick; 1 and 2 Peter by Edwin A. Blum; 1,2 and 3 John by Glen W. Barker; Jude by Edwin A. Blum; and Revelation by Alan F. Johnson. The commentary uses the New International Version. Each book has an exposition, an introduction, an outline and a bibliography. Notes and textual questions are correlated with expository units. Transliteration and translation of Semitic and Greek words are provided. Commentators seek to deal fairly with opposing views. **$19.95.** Bookstores or from **Zondervan Retail Marketing Service, 1420 Robinson Road, SE, Grand Rapids, MI 49506.**

HEBREWS VERSE-BY-VERSE (Moody Press) For: L,C,S. Slant: EP, S, I, M.

By William R. Newell. A verse-by-verse commentary on the challenging epistle to the Hebrews—deeply practical insights into a difficult book. **$17.95.** Bookstores or from **Moody Bookworld, 2101 W. Howard, Chicago, IL 60645.**

HERE COMES JESUS (Regal Books) For: L,S,Y. Slant: EP.

By Ed Stewart. This quick-paced commentary on Mark catapults youth into the heart of Jesus' life and ministry and helps them discover that what Jesus did and said still speaks to issues today. 160 pages. Number S101157. Paperback. **$2.25.** Teaching materials available. Bookstores or from **Regal Books, Division of GL Publications, 2300 Knoll Drive, Ventura, CA 93003.**

HOW TO BE A CHRISTIAN WITHOUT BEING RELIGIOUS (Regal Books) For: L,C,S,Y. Slant: EP.

By Fritz Ridenour. Shows why "religion" has failed and points to true Christianity and a faith that is more than "fire insurance." A study of Romans. 176 pages. Number S121158. Paperback. **$2.25.** Bookstores or from **Regal Books, Division of GL Publications, 2300 Knoll Drive, Ventura, CA 93003.**

HOW TO BE HAPPY NO MATTER WHAT (Regal Books) For: L,C,S,Y. Slant: EP.

By Tom Watson, Jr.. How can anyone be happy <u>no matter what?</u> Is it possible <u>even</u> when things go sour...friends are fickle...life has no purpose? It sounds hopeless. But it is possible to be happy no matter what, and Tom Watson, Jr. communicates this message in a readable study of Philippians. Philippians was written by Paul, the Apostle who faced more than his share of hardships, suffering and frustration. He wrote his letter to the Philippian Christians from the bleakness of a Roman prison. But Paul had the secret to being happy--knowing and living with Jesus Christ. That's why he shares such good advice on: how to find true peace, the key to making real friends, trusting God for all your needs, and more. **How to be Happy No Matter What** features true life examples of teen-agers, popular athletes, and well-known personalities who have also found the secret of being happy no matter what. Each chapter concludes with challenging, "put it to work" application questions. 160 pages. Number S103125. Paperback. **$2.25.** Teaching materials available. Bookstores or from **Regal Books, Division GL Publications, 2300 Knoll Drive, Ventura, CA 93003.**

HOW TO READ AND PRAY ST. PAUL (Liguori Publications) For: L. Slant: RC, D, P.

Brings the letters of St. Paul to life,

COMMENTARIES ON NEW TESTAMENT BOOKS

as actual letters written to real people who were searching for answers just as we are today. Includes a brief sketch of Paul's life and covers the chief themes and passages of his major letters. **$1.50.** Quantity discounts available. Bookstores or from **Liguori Publications, One Liguori Drive, Liguori, MO 63057.**

HOW TO READ AND PRAY THE GOSPELS (SPANISH EDITION ALSO AVAILABLE) (Liguori Publications) For: L. Slant: RC, D, P.

This book will help the average person read and understand the Bible. It offers prayer suggestions, ideas for family use, and questions for discussion. **$1.50** (Spanish edition, **$1.50**). Quantity discount available. Bookstores or from **Liguori Publications, One Liguori Drive, Liguori, MO 63057.**

IN QUEST OF JESUS: A GUIDEBOOK (John Knox Press) For: L,C,S. Slant: C, RC, EP, MP, LP, S, BC.

By W. Barnes Tatum. An introduction to serious study of the Gospels with an intensive historical investigation of the life of Jesus. This consideration of the historical Jesus as portrayed in the Gospels provides a basis for understanding our biblically-based faith. Paperback. **$9.50.** Please add **$1.00** for shipping. Georgia and Virginia, please add appropriate sales tax. Bookstores or from **John Knox Press, 341 Ponce de Leon Ave., Atlanta, GA 30365.**

JAMES: BIBLE STUDY COMMENTARY (Zondervan Publishing House) For: L,C,S. Slant: EP.

By Curtis Vaughan. A lay-oriented commentary, with no Greek used within its text. The commentary deals with each biblical book section-by-section, with discussion questions at the end of each chapter. Brief bibliography. **$4.95.** Bookstores or from **Zondervan Retail Marketing Service, 1420 Robinson Road, SE, Grand Rapids, MI 49506.**

JESUS AND THE FOUR GOSPELS (Harper & Row, Publishers, Inc.) For: L,C,S. Slant: EP.

By John Drane. The illustrated documentary examines the life, teachings, and times of Jesus from both historical and theological perspectives. Reflecting the best conservative Christian scholarship, Drane's approach remains faithful to the New Testament and fully aware of modern research. This book is thorough and well-informed, but never over-technical. Subjects of a more specialized interest are presented in articles separate from the main text. Photographs, line drawings, maps, and diagrams throughout enrich the presentation. John Drane does not simply retell the familiar story. He asks searching questions. How does Jesus fit into the time in which he lived? Did he really make great claims for himself or did the church later make them for him? Why did he teach in parables? What was the point of his miracles? And who recorded all the events of his life? Are those records accurate or embellished with legend? And why did he die? The fresh approach here makes the book suitable for both general reader and scholar. 192 pages. Illustrated, bibliography, and index. Number RD 264. Paperback. **$9.95.** Quantity discounts available. Bookstores or from **Harper & Row, Publishers, Inc., Mail Order Department, 2350 Virginia Avenue, Hagerstown, MD 21740.**

JESUS CHRIST TODAY (Baker Book House) For: L,C,S. Slant: EP.

By Neil R. Lightfoot. A commentary on the Book of Hebrews. A contemporary exhortation. The author rightfully asserts that "the author of Hebrews especially connects 'today' with Jesus." Although Hebrews is viewed by some as archaic, it is nonetheless a modern book with a modern message. A superior textbook for the classroom and a true guide for the pastor. **$8.95.** Bookstores or from **Baker Book House, P.O. Box 6287, Grand Rapids, MI 49506.**

JESUS' PATTERN FOR A HAPPY LIFE: THE BEATITUDES (Liguori Publications) For: L. Slant: RC, D, P.

This book invites you to dismiss the idea that the Beatitudes are a set of rules only a saint could follow, and consider the Beatitudes as a pattern for peace — a plan that can be followed in today's world. It advised us to be quiet and listen to what Jesus said in the Sermon on the Mount. Jesus gave us a pattern for daily life in His Kingdom, a way to face troubles and problems and still find peace, hope, and joy. **$2.95.** Bookstores or from **Liguori Publications, One Liguori Drive, Liguori, MO 63057.**

JOHN: BIBLE STUDY COMMENTARY (Zondervan Publishing House) For: L,C,S. Slant: EP.

By Herschel H. Hobbs. A lay-oriented commentary with no Greek used in its text. Deals with each biblical book section-by-section with discussion questions at the end of each chapter. Occasional reference to other works occurs in the text. **$4.95.** Bookstores or from **Zondervan Retail Marketing Service, 1420 Robinson Road, SE, Grand Rapids, MI 49506.**

JOHN: A NEW LOOK AT THE FOURTH GOSPEL (Tyndale House Publishers) For: L,S. Slant: AW, C, RC, F, EP, MP, LP, P, CP.

By Lloyd M. Perry and Norman R. Ericson. Two distinguished Bible scholars combine their skills to produce an excellent commentary and devotional guide to John, demonstrating some of the study methods they use as they prepare to minister to others. Trade paper. **$5.95.** Bookstores.

COMMENTARIES ON NEW TESTAMENT BOOKS

1 JOHN: A COMMENTARY (Presbyterian and Reformed Publishing Co.) For: L,C,S. Slant: C, F, P, I.

By Gordon H. Clark. In this commentary on the First Epistle of John, Dr. Clark continues his program of explaining the text of the Scriptures for the layman. Dr. Clark explains his purpose when he said, "Have there not been devout saints in every age, numerous enough to carry on a revival? Twelve such persons are plenty. What distinguishes the arid age from the period of the Reformation, when nations were moved as they had not been since Paul preached in Ephesus, Corinth, and Rome, is the latter's fullness of knowledge of God's Word. To echo an early Reformation thought, when the ploughman and the garage attendant know the Bible as well as the theologian does, and know it better than some contemporary theologians, then the desired awakening shall have already occurred." First John will go a long way toward ensuring that the farmer and the garage attendant know the Bible as well as the theologian, and far better than some contemporary theologians. 168 pages. **$4.75.** Bookstores or from **Presbyterian and Reformed Publishing Co., P.O. Box 817, Phillipsburg, NJ 08865.**

1,2,3 JOHN: BIBLE STUDY COMMENTARY (Zondervan Publishing House) For: L,C,S. Slant: EP.

By Curtis Vaughan. A lay-oriented commentary, with no Greek used within its text. The commentary deals with each biblical book section-by-section, with discussion questions at the end of each chapter. Brief bibliography. **$4.95.** Bookstores or from **Zondervan Retail Marketing Service, 1420 Robinson Road, SE, Grand Rapids, MI 49506.**

1,2,3 JOHN AND REVELATION: THE COMMUNICATOR'S COMMENTARY (Word Books) For: L,C,S. Slant: EP.

By Earl Palmer. When it comes to the Epistles of John, very few Bible students ever grasp what Earl Palmer calls "the fire and the joy" to be found there. And as for the Book of Revelation, most of us will agree with Palmer's depiction of it as "a hard book to understand, and a hard book to put down." This volume in the **Communicator's Commentary 1,2,3 John and Revelation** is written in a way that helps people feel as they read. Earl Palmer is fully aware that in John's Epistles, "there is an explosive quality that breaks out suddenly and without warning." Rather than smother the explosions in a blanket of technical detail, Palmer lets the message accelerate into the life of the modern reader. That, he feels is the main task of an expositor. And he does it supremely well. Palmer's approach to the Book of Revelation is equally fresh. Unlike some who major in this book's peripheral issues, and unlike those who have been frightened away from it altogether, Palmer shows that its central theme is "the victory of the Word of God in the very face of terror and evil." Hardcover. Catalog Number 0165-0. **$14.95.** Bookstores.

THE JOY OF FELLOWSHIP: A STUDY OF 1 JOHN (Zondervan Publishing House) For: L,C,S. Slant: EP.

By J. Dwight Pentecost. This study is a treasure for those who strive to integrate the major themes of Scripture into their lives. Each chapter concludes with questions that will assist those seeking a greater fellowship with God and their fellow man. **$4.95.** Bookstores or from **Zondervan Retail Marketing Service, 1420 Robinson Road, SE, Grand Rapids, MI 49506.**

THE JOY OF LIVING (Zondervan Publishing House) For: L,C,S. Slant: EP.

By J. Dwight Pentecost. In outline style, the author provides a clear and enjoyable commentary that makes both Paul and his words come to life. **$5.95.** Bookstores or from **Zondervan Retail Marketing Service, 1420 Robinson Road, SE, Grand Rapids, MI 49506.**

JUDE THROUGH 2 PETER: THE WORD BIBLICAL COMMENTARY (Word Books) For: C,S. Slant: EP.

For many years, these two little books of the New Testament, 2 Peter and Jude, received little attention by scholars or study by Christians generally. Not very inspirational, said the general reader. Too late and too thin theologically to interest us, said the world of scholarship. Now, however, Professor Bauckham of England's Manchester University makes a convincing case that these books deserve far more respect. Jude, he contends, "offers a rare glimpse into those original Palestinian Christian circles in which Jesus' own blood-relations were leaders." And 2 Peter, he adds, "documents the way in which one form of early Christianity managed the difficult transition from the apostolic to the post-apostolic generation." Scholars, of course, will give careful attention to this new work. But it should receive a welcome as well among ministers and serious lay biblical students—wherever new light from Scripture is appreciated. Hardcover. Catalog Number 0249-5. **$18.95.** Bookstores.

KEEP ON KEEPING ON! (Regal Books) For: L,C,S,Y. Slant: EP.

By Harold L. Fickett, Jr. Amplifies

COMMENTARIES ON NEW TESTAMENT BOOKS

Paul's message to today's Christian in vibrant, readable style. We need these words of reassurance and direction today in areas such as how we can please God, the second coming of Christ, and what happens when a Christian dies. This commentary is distinctive for its immensely practical emphasis. Dr. Fickett drives home the truths of 1st and 2nd Thessalonians with down-to-earth illustrations and insights that capture the heart of these epistles. This study offers helpful background information on the historical setting as well as valuable explanations of key Greek words and phrases. 160 pages. Paperback. Number S311100. **$2.50**. Bookstores or from **Regal Books, Division of GL Publications, 2300 Knoll Drive, Ventura, CA 93003**.

KINGDOM CITIZENS (Herald Press) For: L,S. Slant: EP.

By John Driver. Designed to accompany and orient direct study of the Sermon on the Mount. For those who desire a life of discipleship which corresponds more nearly to God's intention for His community of salvation. 1980. 160 pages. Number 1935-5. Paper. **$6.95**. Bookstores.

LET'S GET MOVING (Regal Books) For: L,C,S,Y. Slant: EP.

By D. Stuart Briscoe. Even though he was rotting in a Roman prison, Paul wrote to the church at Ephesus with a message that said, "Let's get moving, there are things to be done. There's a battle to fight." In this easy-to-read layman's commentary on Ephesians, author D. Stuart Briscoe helps today's Christian see where the battlegrounds are in the world, what kind of enemy he is fighting and, most important, how to win. Asks Briscoe: "What was the trust that had so gripped Paul's imagination that it gushed from his lips and spilled from his pen?" Briscoe leads the Christian to find practical help in such areas as: How to tune in to the work of spiritual joy; the secret to taking all of life one step at a time; how to be filled with the Spirit and stay normal and how to wear the whole armor of God with comfort. 160 pages. Number S322102. Paperback. **$2.50**. Bible Commentary for Laymen series. Teaching materials available. Bookstores or from **Regal Books, Division of GL Publications, 2300 Knoll Drive, Ventura, CA 93003**.

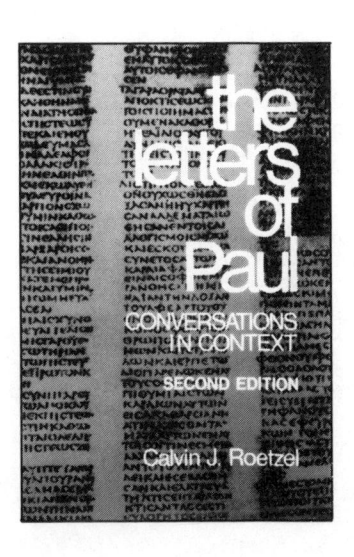

THE LETTERS OF PAUL: CONVERSATIONS IN CONTEXT (John Knox Press) For: L,C,S. Slant: C, RC, EP, MP, LP, S, BC.

By Calvin J. Roetzel. An updated, expanded edition of a classic introduction to Paul and his epistles. Roetzel gives special attention to the religious and social milieu that shaped Paul's thought. A concise treatment of each letter, emphasizing the letter form, the use of tradition, and the significant role played by adherents and opponents as Paul's partners in dialogue. Brings together material that was widely scattered and technical and presents it logically for the non-specialist. Presents the findings of the best of current Pauline scholarship in nontechnical language. Paper. **$7.95**. Please add **1.00** for shipping. Georgia and Virginia, please add appropriate sales tax. Bookstores or from **John Knox Press, 341 Ponce de Leon Ave., Atlanta, GA 30365**.

LIBERATED FOR LIFE (Regal Books) For: L,C,S,Y. Slant: EP.

By John F. MacArthur, Jr. A verse-by-verse study of Galatians. A practical look at personal and corporate Christian behavior. 144 pages. Number S301105. Paperback. **$2.50**. Bible Commentary for Laymen Series. Bookstores or from **Regal Books, Division of GL Publications, 2300 Knoll Drive, Ventura, CA 93003**.

LIBERTY BIBLE COMMENTARY ON THE NEW TESTAMENT (Thomas Nelson Publishers) For: L,C,S. Slant: F, P, S, I.

Edited by Jerry Falwell, Edward H. Hindson, and Woodrow Kroll. A verse-by-verse exposition and interpretation of the entire New Testament. Each contributor is committed to fundamental Christian doctrines. Hardcover. **$12.95**. Bookstores.

LIFE IN THE SPIRIT (Baker Book House) For: C,S. Slant: C, EP.

By D. Martyn Lloyd Jones. In marriage, home, and work, an exposition of Ephesians 5:18-6:9. An excellent guide for the solid application of the Bible to the perplexities of marriage and family living in our day; for preachers, teachers, parents, and young people. **$10.95**. Bookstores or from **Baker Book House, P.O. Box 6287, Grand Rapids, MI 49506**.

LOGOS INTERNATIONAL BIBLE COMMENTARY (Bridge Publishing, Inc.) For: L,C. Slant: EP, D, P, CP.

An easy-to-read commentary blending sound theological teaching with practi-

COMMENTARIES ON NEW TESTAMENT BOOKS

cal direction for living. A new commentary that makes systematic, meaningful Bible study available to all Christians. Employs the accurate and readable New International Version (NIV) translation. Unlike most commentaries which give notes on a verse-by-verse basis, this commentary transcends chapter and verse divisions and provides full explanations of individual units of thought. And, the **Logos International Bible Commentary** includes a complete topical index of subjects found in the Synoptic Gospels. It is a Bible dictionary, a handbook on Bible geography and culture, a complete study on the person and work of the Holy Spirit, a devotional reader and topical fact book of vital Christian truths. Volume 1 includes Matthew, Mark, and Luke in one volume. Volume 2 (in production) will include the Gospel of John and the Book of Acts. Vol. 1 (Matthew; Mark; Luke) **$16.95**. Vol. 2 in production (John, Acts). Bookstores.

LOVED AND FORGIVEN (Regal Books) For: L,C,S,Y. Slant: EP.

By Lloyd John Ogilvie. Most people will agree today that "Getting Our Heads Straight" and "Getting Our Feelings Sorted Out" are important. It was just as important 1,900 years ago when Paul wrote a book to some Christians at Colossae. Paul nailed home the profound and liberating truth that in the gospel, the greatest of human needs is met: to be loved and forgiven. Lloyd Ogilvie, in this Layman's Commentary on Colossians, gives insightful, practical interpretation of this message to our lives today, beginning with the two chapter titles above. This paragraph by paragraph study focuses on personal application: "You need to know who you are by God's Grace...What has been done for you...To Whom you belong...and That you are Loved and Forgiven." 160 pages. Number S313103. Paperback. **$2.50**. Bible Commentary for Laymen Series. Teaching materials available. Bookstores or from **Regal Books, Division of GL Publications, 2300 Knoll Drive, Ventura, CA 93003.**

LUKE: BIBLE STUDY COMMENTARY (Zondervan Publishing House) For: L,C,S. Slant: EP.

By Virtus Evans Gideon. A popular section by section commentary on Luke with study questions at the end of each chapter. **$4.95**. Bookstores or from **Zondervan Retail Marketing Service, 1420 Robinson Road, SE, Grand Rapids, MI 49506.**

MARK: BIBLE STUDY COMMENTARY (Zondervan Publishing House) For: L,C,S. Slant: EP.

By Howard F. Vos. A lay-oriented commentary with no Greek used within its text. Deals with each biblical book section-by-section, with discussion questions at the end of each chapter. Brief bibliography. **$4.95**. Bookstores or from **Zondervan Retail Marketing Service, 1420 Robinson Road, SE, Grand Rapids, MI 49506.**

MARK: THE COMMUNICATOR'S COMMENTARY (Word Books) For: L,C,S. Slant: EP.

By Dr. David McKenna. These fast-moving times are sure to heighten the demand for David McKenna's entry into Word's new person-oriented commentary. For Mark wrote to a world in dynamic flux, like ours. His message is couched in the impulsive, vivid language of the apostle Peter—action oriented terms which Dr. McKenna highlights for today's readers. As a theologian and educator also trained in psychology, Dr. McKenna is able to probe the personalities of Peter, Mark, and Jesus. He exposes Christ's inner motivations—His compassion, amazement, anger and discouragement; His quiet human hunger and fatigue, His divine love. Mark's gospel burst on a secular Roman world intent on persecuting the early Christians. His word to the suffering church was one of good news and of hope. His challenge to the persecutors still stands as a word to contemporary unbelievers: "We saw this divine man's acts of love, His mighty works, and His resurrected glory. Weigh these facts and decide!" Hardcover. **$14.95**. Bookstores.

MARK: GOOD NEWS FOR HARD TIMES (Servant Publications) For: L. Slant: P.

By George T. Montague, S.M. This new book by noted Scripture scholar George T. Montague presents the best of Scripture scholarship and interpretation in an informative, nontechnical style that will enrich study and prayer. A refreshing new commentary, written for the contemporary layman seeking the fullest appreciation, understanding, and application of the gospel's message. **Mark: Good News for Hard Times** contains the complete text of the Gospel of Mark in the Revised Standard Version, and an expertly written commentary that uncovers the richness and vast usefulness of this gospel for our lives today. Number 0964. **$5.95**. Bookstores.

MARK: THE WAY FOR ALL NATIONS (Herald Pres) For: L,C,S,Y. Slant: EP.

By Willard M. Swartley. The author guides the reader through the book with study questions, biblical references, charts diagramming Mark, and an exposition giving additional insights to the reader. There are also discussion questions to help students apply their discoveries to the contemporary dimensions of life. Revised 1981. 224 pages. Paper. Number 1977-0. **$8.95**. Bookstores.

MARK—A GOOD NEWS COMMENTARY (Harper & Row, Publishers, Inc.) For: L,C. Slant: EP.

By Larry Hurtado. The fruit of a decade of study and reflection, this

COMMENTARIES ON NEW TESTAMENT BOOKS

reliable, pastoral, and accessible commentary shows Mark's purpose at each point of his account, tells how his contemporaries understood the text, and indicates the Gospel's meaning for today. About the **Good News Commentary Series.** This is the first major series to use the popular English Text of the Good News Bible, which has sold in the millions. Each volume is informed by solid scholarship and the most up-to-date research, yet is biblically faithful and readily understandable to the general reader. Features include: introductory material highlighting authorship, dating, background information, and a thematic emphasis—plus a map; full text of each Good News Bible book with running commentary; special end notes which give references for key words and concepts, and provide suggestions for further reading; and full indexes for Scriptures, subjects, persons, and places. 288 pages. Kivar cover. Paperback. Number RD 447. **$8.95.** Bookstores or from **Harper & Row, Publishers, Inc., Mail Order Department, 2350 Virginia Avenue, Hagerstown, MD 21740.**

MARK—INTERPRETATION: A BIBLE COMMENTARY FOR TEACHING AND PREACHING (John Knox Press) For: L,C,S. Slant: C, RC, EP, MP, LP, P, S, BC.

By Lamar Williamson, Jr. Like the other volumes in this series, **Mark** is an expository commentary intended for persons responsible for the interpretation of Scripture in the community of faith. Although primarily for pastors and teachers with formal theological education, its form and content are designed so that an informed lay reader can use this resource for interpreting the Second Gospel. **Mark** is written without technical terms, biblical Hebrew or Greek. The series considers whole sections of text rather than verses. The interrelationship of biblical books is emphasized rather than focusing on selected, isolated passages. Particular attention is given to texts which appear in Year B of the three-year lectionary. Cloth. **$17.95.** Please add 10% for shipping. Georgia and Virginia, please add appropriate sales tax. Bookstores or from **John Knox Press, 341 Ponce de Leon Ave., Atlanta, GA 30365.**

MARK, MATTHEW, AND LUKE: A GUIDE TO THE GOSPEL PARALLELS (The Liturgical Press) For: L,C,S. Slant: RC,S.

By Burton H. Throckmorton, Jr. A companion text to **Gospel Parallels: A Synopsis of the First Three Gospels**, presents a unique and simple method for a comparative study of Mark, Matthew, and Luke, examining the personal characteristics of each evangelist, and giving a concise commentary on the purpose, theology, and procedure of each. 100 pages. Softbound. **$4.95.** Bookstores or from **The Liturgical Press, Collegeville, MN 56321.**

MATTHEW: BIBLE STUDY COMMENTARY (Zondervan Publishing House) For: L,C,S. Slant: EP.

By Howard F. Vos. A lay-oriented commentary with no Greek used within its text. Deals with each biblical book section-by-section, with discussion questions at the end of each chapter. Brief bibliography. **$5.95.** Bookstores or from **Zondervan Retail Marketing Service, 1420 Robinson Road, SE, Grand Rapids, MI 49506.**

MATTHEW: THE COMMUNICATOR'S COMMENTARY VOLUME I (Word Books) For: L,C,S. Slant: EP.

By Myron Augsburger. Dr. Augsburger has taken seriously his assignment to contribute to a **Communicator's New Testament Commentary.** His work on Matthew is a masterpiece of clear thinking, organization and communication. The author's biblical training and national reputation as a communicator results in a brilliant blend—a careful attention to the original message, a clear restatement for Christians today, and a call to practice and share the message. The book therefore offers teaching and preaching helps as well as inspiration and motivation to biblically principled living. Dr. Augsburger is skillful in introducing the general reader to questions of background and language. He challenges the view that Matthew wrote a Jewish book for Jewish people. Instead, he believes that the Gospel envisions an emerging people of God with their roots in the Old Covenant but their destiny extending "into all the world." Matthew's relevance for today centers in his emphasis on the church. It was not, as some thought, following a failed messianic mission. Rather, the church is a central event in the history of salvation. And the ethical demands of Matthew's Gospel are an unblinking call to purity of life in the present. Hardcover. Catalog Number 0154-5. **$14.95.** Bookstores.

MATTHEW: THY KINGDOM COME (Moody Press) For: L,C,S. Slant: EP, S, I, M.

COMMENTARIES ON NEW TESTAMENT BOOKS

By John F. Walvoord. A comprehensive interpretation of the first book of the New Testament. **$9.95.** Bookstores or from **Moody Bookworld, 2101 W. Howard, Chicago, IL 60645.**

MATTHEW—HIS MIND AND HIS MESSAGE (The Liturgical Press) For: L,C. Slant: RC, S.

An exhaustive story of the First Gospel, detailing the method of the "rabbinic" Matthew, the "meticulous" Matthew, and the "theological" Matthew. This composition criticism also contains three appendices that deal with the historicity of the Gospels, the making of a Gospel, and the Synoptic Question. Softbound. 192 pages. **$5.95.** Bookstores or from **The Liturgical Press, Collegeville, MN 56321.**

MATTHEW THROUGH ROMANS: THRU THE BIBLE—VOLUME IV (Thomas Nelson Publishers) For: L,C. Slant: F,EP,P,S,DI.

By J. Vernon McGee. A study of Matthew through Romans, the first six books of the New Testament, is included in Volume IV of this five-part series. Dr. McGee's enthusiasm for the Bible and its messages for today come alive through his lively comments and pointed anecdotes. His down-to-earth style speaks powerfully to laypeople—their hearts, minds, and wills. Each of the New Testament books is treated with an introduction, an outline, and verse-by-verse comments. Hardcover. **$19.95.** Bookstores.

MEASURE OF A CHRISTIAN—JAMES I (Regal Books) For: L,C,S,Y. Slant: EP.

By Gene A. Getz. The epistle of James is as fresh and relevant today as it was when first written. This study of the first chapter of that epistle includes clear exposition and helpful illustrations to make the book come alive for every reader. Everyone struggles with trials and temptations, needs heavenly wisdom and proper understanding of wealth. We all need help in avoiding deception, being a good listener, handling anger and learning how to control our tongue. The author deals openly with these areas with practical suggestions on finding God's solutions to man's dilemmas. Each chapter includes clear application for today and questions which call for personal response and action. This is another in the Biblical Renewal Series which includes the other **Measures Of...**books and the Old Testament personality books. Trade paper. 168 pages. Number 5417930. **$5.95. Publication Date: August, 1983.** Bookstores or from **Regal Books, Division of GL Publications, 2300 Knoll Drive, Ventura, CA 93003.**

MEASURE OF A CHRISTIAN—PHILIPPIANS (Regal Books) For: L,C,S,Y. Slant: EP.

By Gene A. Getz. You can be content regardless of the circumstances, is the theme that permeates the book of Philippians. But how, in the midst of trials, troubles, and the hassles of everyday living, is a Christian to be content? This practical study of Paul's teaching in Philippians will help. Each chapter includes anecdotes or illustrations to think about; applications, questions and projects that lead the readers to a personal application of the material studied. Dr. Getz has designed this book to help his readers become mature, content persons in the midst of an unpredictable world. Quality paper. 5 1/8 x 8 inches. 182 pages. Number 5417939. Bookstores or from **Regal Books, Division of GL Publications, 2300 Knoll Drive, Ventura, CA 93003.**

MEASURE OF A CHRISTIAN—TITUS (Regal Books) For: L,C,S,Y. Slant: EP.

By Gene A. Getz. In the face of dramatically changing social and moral values in America, what should Christians do? Can they make moral and ethical judgments on the basis of a relative and changing standard? To answer this crucial question, Dr. Gene Getz takes his readers on a thorough study of the book of Titus. By the time they have completed their study, they will have no doubt that God has an unalterable moral standard. In the midst of a changing world true believers must be sure they do not become a part of the world's system, even though they live in the midst of it. By asking important questions that lead his readers to personal application and life response, Getz helps Christians make the book of Titus foundational in their understanding of God's standards for their daily living. Quality paper. 5 1/8 x 8 inches. 196 pages. Number 5417935. Bookstores or from **Regal Books, Division of GL Publications, 2300 Knoll Drive, Ventura, CA 93003.**

MINISTRY OF RECONCILIATION (Baker Book House) For: L,C,S. Slant: AW.

By French Arrington. A popular exposition of 2 Corinthians that is timely, scholarly, understandable, and convincing. **$3.95.** Bookstores or from **Baker Book House, P.O. Box 6287, Grand Rapids, MI 49506.**

MORE THAN CONQUERORS (Baker Book House) For: L,C. Slant: C.

By William Hendriksen. An interpretation of the Book of Revelation. **$9.95.** Bookstores or from **Baker Book House, P.O. Box 6287, Grand Rapids, MI 49506.**

A NEW HEAVEN AND A NEW EARTH (Christ For the World Publishers) For: L,C,S. Slant: EP, MP, P.

By J.B. Lawrence. This commentary gives a contemporary interpretation of the Book of Revelation. The author does not deal intricately with interpretive positions. He does, however, deal with the spiritual meaning of Christ's ultimate triumph over the evils of the world, the flesh, and the devil. A very positive note of victory, much needed in this day. Softcover. **$2.95** plus shipping and handling. From **Ministry Service, P.O. Box 433, Redan, GA 30074.**

COMMENTARIES ON NEW TESTAMENT BOOKS

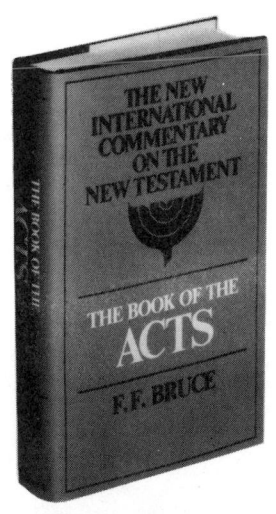

THE NEW INTERNATIONAL COMMENTARY ON THE NEW TESTAMENT (Wm. B. Eerdmans Publishing Co.) For: C,S. Slant: EP, MP, S.

By F.F. Bruce, General Editor. An authoritative and comprehensive series which is destined to give direction to conservative New Testament scholarship for years to come. Prepared under the general editorship of F.F. Bruce, NICNT is designed to provide serious students with an analysis that is abreast of modern archaeological and linguistic knowledge while remaining loyal to the Scriptures as the infallible word of God. Based on a thorough study of the Greek text, but written exclusively in English, each exposition takes into account the most important exegetical literature. More technical aspects, including grammatical, textual, and historical problems, appear in footnotes, special notes, or appendices. Indexes of Scripture references, authors, subjects, and names/places are also included. Fifteen volumes availabe. **$10.95–$19.95.** Bookstores or from **Eerdmans Publishing, 255 Jefferson Ave., SE, Grand Rapids, MI 49503.**

THE NEW INTERNATIONAL GREEK TESTAMENT COMMENTARY (Wm. B. Eerdmans Publishing Company) For: C,S. Slant: EP, MP, S.

By W. Ward Gasque and I.H. Marshall, editors. Focusing on the needs of theological students and pastors, the contributors to the **New International Greek Testament Commentary** seek to guide readers through the maze of modern biblical scholarship and to offer exegesis which is sensitive to theological themes as well as to the details of the historical, linguistic, textual, and critical context. Such thorough exegetical work lies at the heart of these commentaries, with general comments on sections being followed by a detailed verse-by-verse treatment of the text. Now available are commentaries on Luke, Galatians, and James. Three additional volumes available. **$14.95–$24.95.** Bookstores or from **Eerdmans Publishing, 255 Jefferson Ave., SE, Grand Rapids, MI 49503.**

OUR LORD'S PARABLES (Zondervan Publishing House) For: L,C,S. Slant: EP.

By R. C. McQuilkin. Examines the context and narrative of 17 of the parables of Jesus. Presents guidelines for studying parables and lists Christ's parables and parabolic scenes in four appendices. Each chapter has review questions. **$6.95.** Bookstores or from **Zondervan Retail Marketing Service, 1420 Robinson Road, SE, Grand Rapids, MI 49506.**

OUR STORY ACCORDING TO ST. MARK (Winston Press) For: L,C,S. Slant: MP.

By William H. Barnwell. An inviting exploration of Mark's Gospel. Well-researched textual comments and personal responses show readers how to relate their experiences to Mark's story. Ideal for general readers, study groups. Paperback. **$9.95.** Bookstores or from **Winston Press, 430 Oak Grove, Minneapolis, MN 55403.**

THE OVERCOMERS (Thomas Nelson Publishers) For: L,C. Slant: C, EP.

By Chuck Colclasure. A timely, important book that focuses on the spiritual principles of Revelation—what they are and how they apply to our lives today. Chuck Colclasure's refreshing approach is a return to the primary, historic view of the church and depicts Revelation as a pastoral book meant to encourage, embolden, and comfort, as well as to warn and exhort, the church of Christ. An especially helpful glossary of Revelation's figurative images is included. Summaries of

COMMENTARIES ON NEW TESTAMENT BOOKS

meanings are listed according to biblical chapter and verse and are cross-referenced to chapter numbers in **The Overcomers** for further discussion. Paperback. **$4.95**. Bookstores.

THE PARABLES OF JESUS (Baker Book House) For: C,S. Slant: EP.

By George Buttrick. An introduction to a serious study of the parables. **$5.95**. Bookstores or from **Baker Book House, P.O. Box 6287, Grand Rapids, MI 49506**.

PARABLES OF THE KINGDOM (Faith and Life Press) For: L. Slant: D.

This study guide in six lessons is based on Jesus' Parables of the Kingdom. The guide is designed to be intercultural and international. The Bible Study Notes, written by Howard Charles are intended to be as free as possible of cultural bias. Commentaries were solicited from a wide variety of persons representing diverse cultures and ethnic groups. More than 50 contributors, representing 31 nations on six continents have written for this guide. **$1.35**. From **Faith and Life Press, Box 347, Newton, KS 67114**.

PASS IT ON (Regal Books) For: L,C,S,Y. Slant: EP.

By Robert H. Mounce. A first century letter to twentieth century people! Although thousands of books of instructions have been written for churches and their leaders through the ages, none is more pertinent or viable as the two short letters written more than 1900 years ago by the Apostle Paul to Timothy. **Pass It On** is for Christians living in these end times to show the relevance of Timothy's letters today--culture, church government, etc., notwithstanding. This is a 10-chapter study of Paul's instructions regarding the development of church discipline, the elimination of false teachings, and the training of qualified church leaders. The author's thorough, readable scholarship is organized in such a relevant way that the adult reader will be able to better understand the present-day applications that can be made from Paul's communication with the early Christian church through Timothy. His treatment of 1 and 2 Timothy is characterized by balance, clarity and is written from a conservative evangelical position that incorporates trustworthy biblical scholarship. 160 pages. Number S332108. Paperback. **$2.25**. Bible Commentary for Laymen Series. Teaching materials available. Bookstores or from **Regal Books, Division of GL Publications, 2300 Knoll Drive, Ventura, CA 93003**.

THE PASTORAL EPISTLES (Moody Press) For: L,C,S. Slant: EP, P, S, I, M.

By Homer Kent, Jr. Each of the pastoral epistles is explored and explained in detail, offering a clear, concise overview. Valuable for both the student of Greek and those limited to English. **$10.95**. Bookstores or from **Moody Bookworld, 2101 W. Howard, Chicago, IL 60645**.

THE PASTORAL EPISTLES: BIBLE STUDY COMMENTARY (Zondervan Publishing House) For: L,C,S. Slant: EP.

By E.M. Blaiklock. A lay-oriented commentary with no Greek employed within its text. Deals with each biblical book section-by-section with discussion questions at the end of each chapter. Occasional reference to other works occurs in the text. **$4.95**. Bookstores or from **Zondervan Retail Marketing Service, 1420 Robinson Road, SE, Grand Rapids, MI 49506**.

PATTERNS FOR POWER (Regal Books) For: L,C,S. Slant: EP.

By D. Stuart Briscoe. A study of 12 of the parables from the book of Luke written in a Bible Commentary for Laymen. These parables deal with topics that are not just isolated Bible truths but fundamental aspects of Christian life. Each parable in **Patterns for Power** leads the reader to examine aspects of his/her relationship to God, and directs the reader toward an appropriate response. Stuart Briscoe leads the reader through the study of each parable, examining first the way to approach God's Word, then the way to hear God's Word and finally the way to respond to God's Word. The book is rich with humor, anecdotes, word studies and contemporary illustrations. These are incorporated in Pastor Briscoe's warm, yet scholarly literary style. 160 pages. Number S331101. Paperback. **$2.50**. Bible Commentary for Laymen. Teaching materials available. Bookstores or from **Regal Books, Division of GL Publications, 2300 Knoll Drive, Ventura, CA 93003**.

PAUL (Harper & Row, Publishers, Inc.) For: L,C,S. Slant: EP.

By John Drane. A visually striking documentary that follows the course of Paul's life, analyzing his letters and journeys in that framework. Both aware of current scholarship and faithful to historical detail and the New Testament text, this book is a stimulating and informative introduction to New Testament studies in general, and to the life and writings of the apostle Paul, in particular. Photographs and illustrations appear on most pages, and special sections answer common questions about Paul seldom treated in other commentaries, including why there are different accounts of his conversion in the Bible, who the Galatians were, and whether or not Paul composed the Pastoral Epistles. This skillful blend of scholarly insight and biblical faith is good news for everyone who loves the Bible. Illustrations throughout,

COMMENTARIES ON NEW TESTAMENT BOOKS

bibliography, and index. 128 pages. Number RD 208. Paperback. **$8.95.** Book stores or from **Harper & Row, Publishers, Inc., Mail Order Department, 2350 Virginia Avenue, Hagerstown, MD 21740.**

PAUL'S JOY IN CHRIST (Baker Book House) For: C,S. Slant: EP.

By A. T. Robertson. Studies in Philippians. Each chapter expounds a passage of this epistle of joy. Excellent resource for Bible studies and sermon preparation. **$4.95.** Bookstores or from **Baker Book House, P.O. Box 6287, Grand Rapids, MI 49506.**

1 AND 2 PETER (Presbyterian and Reformed Publishing Company) For: L,C,S. Slant: C, F, P, I.

By Gordon H. Clark. The epistles of Peter are messages for the twentieth century, even though the fisherman and apostle died these many centuries ago. The reason for the timeliness of the epistles lies in the fact that Peter wrote by the inspiration of the Holy Spirit. This exposition of 1 and 2 Peter takes the form of a commentary; but it is a devotional and practical rather than a technical and critical commentary. Critical commentaries have great value, but the purpose of the author is not to aid the theologian in detailed analysis of the Greek, but to lead the layman to a deeper and better understanding of the Scriptures. Gordon H. Clark is a theologian and philosopher, and the author of several well-known books. 256 pages. **$5.95.** Bookstores or from **Presbyterian and Reformed Publishing Co., P.O. Box 817, Phillipsburg, NJ 08865.**

PETER'S PRINCIPLES (Regal Books) For: L,C,S,Y. Slant: EP.

By Harold L. Fickett, Jr. Peter's first and second letters in the Bible were written to Christians living under pressure. Although some of the circumstances today are different, the pressure upon Christians is still the same. Peter's letters reflect the reality, not only of this struggle, but also of his victories. Throughout his writings he reminds the reader that this victory is available in Christ to all Christians in all circumstances through the power of the Holy Spirit. **Peter's Principles**, applied to your day-to-day struggles, will lead to encouragement, victory in Christ, personal Christian growth, and joyous discipleship. 240 pages. Number S281120. Paperback. **$3.50.** Bible Commentary for Laymen Series. Bookstores or from **Regal Books, Division of GL Publications, 2300 Knoll Drive, Ventura, CA 93003.**

PHILIPPIANS—A GOOD NEWS COMMENTARY (Harper & Row, Publishers, Inc.) For: L,C. Slant: EP.

By F.F. Bruce. An internationally respected biblical scholar here offers a pastoral inspiring appreciation of one of the most loved books of the New Testament which contains some of Paul's finest insights. About **The Good News Commentary Series**: This is the first major series to use the popular English Text of the Good News Bible, which has sold in the millions. Each volume is informed by solid scholarship and the most up-to-date research, yet each is biblically faithful and readily understandable to the general reader. Features include: Introductory material highlighting authorship, dating, background information, and thematic emphases—plus a map; full text of each Good News Bible book with running commentary; special end notes which give references for key words and concepts, and provide suggestions for further reading; full indexes for Scriptures, subjects, persons and places. 176 pages. Kivar cover. Number RD 446. Paperback. **$7.95.** Bookstores or from **Harper & Row, Publishers, Inc., Mail Order Department, 2350 Virginia Avenue, Hagerstown, MD 21740.**

PHILIPPIANS: BIBLE STUDY COMMENTARY (Zondervan Publishing House) For: L,C,S. Slant: EP.

By Howard F. Vos. A lay-oriented commentary with no Greek used within its text. Deals with each biblical book section-by-section, with discussion questions at the end of each chapter. Brief bibliography. **$2.95.** Bookstores or from **Zondervan Retail Marketing Service, 1420 Robinson Road, SE, Grand Rapids, MI 49506.**

A PILGRIM PRIESTHOOD: AN EXPOSITION OF FIRST PETER (Thomas Nelson Publishers) For: L,C. Slant: F, EP, D, P.

This scholarly, exacting examination of 1 Peter is presented in four parts: the Plan of Salvation, the Fullness of Salvation, the Testing of Salvation, and the Mystery of Salvation. Written for both pastors and lay people, this commentary is arranged in an easy-to-use format and includes a number of succinct illustrations. Chapter topics include: the proliferation of Grace; a gift with strings attached; Zion's patriots and megapolis; wars of the soul; domestic delight; to love life; the spirits in prison; preaching to the dead; fiery trials; and crowns for shepherds. Paperback. **$5.95.** Bookstores.

POWER FROM ON HIGH (Servant Publications) For: L. Slant: D, CP.

By Salvador Carrillo Alday. This meditative commentary reflects on virtually all the passages which refer to the Holy Spirit and the Spirit's role in the early church, so that modern Christians may better know and love the Spirit of God. Number 0603. **$2.95.** Bookstores.

COMMENTARIES ON NEW TESTAMENT BOOKS

PRIMERA EPÍSTOLA A LOS CORINTIOS (FIRST CORINTHIANS) (Vida Publishers) For: C,S. Slant: EP.

Are you looking for insight into Paul's writings and the early church? This is a verse-by-verse exposition in Spanish that will expand your understanding of the New Testament. The author shows how Paul's response to the problems in the Corinthian church has benefited local congregations throughout the centuries. You will find this commentary ideal for serious Bible study. **$3.00.** Bookstores.

A PROFILE OF CHRISTIAN MATURITY (Zondervan Publishing House) For: L,C,S. Slant: EP.

By Gene A. Getz. A study of Philippians with 20th-century lessons for your church. Designed to help you be a growing Christian in the midst of an unpredictable world. **$3.50.** Bookstores or from **Zondervan Retail Marketing Service, 1420 Robinson Road, SE, Grand Rapids, MI 49506.**

READING THE GOSPELS (Daughters of St. Paul) For: L,C,S. Slant: RC, P, S.

Providing a good background for understanding or explaining the Sacred text, the author takes one Gospel at a time, presenting each scriptural passage with scholarly comments and points for reflection and discussion. 311 pages. Paper. Number SC0432. **$4.00.** Cloth. **$5.00.** (Add **$.75** postage). Bookstores or from **Daughters of St. Paul, 50 St. Paul's Ave., Jamaica Plain, Boston, MA 02130.**

A PROFILE FOR A CHRISTIAN LIFE STYLE (Zondervan Publishing House) For: L,C,S. Slant: EP.

By Gene A. Getz. Each chapter begins with Scripture verses and an outline, and ends with an application, an opportunity for a "Personal Life Response," and a suggested group or individual project. **$2.95.** Bookstores or from **Zondervan Retail Marketing Service, 1420 Robinson Road, SE, Grand Rapids, MI 49506.**

REVELATION (Baker Book House) For: L,C,S. Slant: EP.

By Homer Hailey. An introduction and commentary. Firmly anchored in sound scholarship, this volume offers a complete, passage-by-passage commentary on the Book of Revelation that is both fascinating and sensible. **$12.95.** Bookstores or from **Baker Book House, P.O. Box 6287, Grand Rapids, MI 49506.**

REVELATION (C.B.C. Publications) For: L,C,S. Slant: F.

By Dr. Cecil Johnson. Mysterious is the word that most accurately describes Revelation to most individuals. Satan joys in keeping Christians in the dark concerning its message. The fact is, a blessing is promised to all who read this book (Rev. 1:3). Its message is more up-to-date than the daily newspaper. For the saints of God, Revelation is truly an intriguing and blessed book. Discover for yourself its glorious gems. **$5.95.** Bookstores or from **Christian Bible College Publications (CBC), P.O. Box 262, Enfield, NC 27823.**

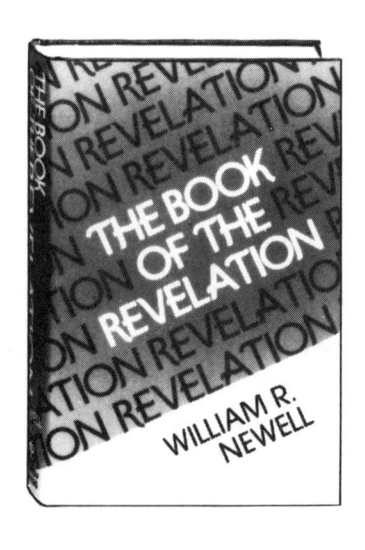

REVELATION (Moody Press) For: L,C,S. Slant: EP,S,I,M.

By William R. Newell. Clear, comprehensive outlines and exposition of the content of Revelation, including the various judgments and the "new creation." **$13.95.** Bookstores or from **Moody Bookworld, 2101 W. Howard, Chicago, IL 60645.**

REVELATION: BIBLE STUDY COMMENTARY (Zondervan Publishing House) For: L,C,S. Slant: EP.

By Alan F. Johnson. A lay-oriented commentary with no Greek used within its text. Helpful study of a fascinating and often perplexing book of the Bible. Discussion questions at the end of each chapter. Brief bibliography. **$5.95.** Bookstores or from **Zondervan Retail Marketing Service, 1420 Robinson Road, SE, Grand Rapids, MI 49506.**

COMMENTARIES ON NEW TESTAMENT BOOKS

REVELATION: DRAMA OF THE AGES (Harvest House Publishers) For: L,C,S. Slant: F, EP, P, S, I, M.

By Dr. Herbert Lockyer, Sr. With the special mastery of a great author, Dr. Lockyer paints a picture of the massive conflict between God and man during the coming days of the Great Tribulation—followed by the triumphant return of Christ to rule over the world. Trade paper. Number 2470. **$6.95.** Bookstores or from **Harvest House Publishers, 1075 Arrowsmith, Eugene, OR 97402.**

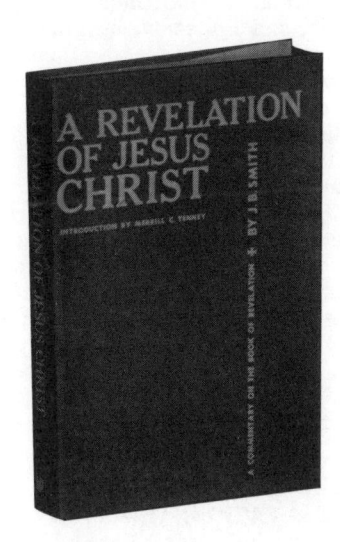

A REVELATION OF JESUS CHRIST (Herald Press) For: L,C,S. Slant: EP.

By J.B. Smith and J. Otis Yoder. The editors made an effort to avoid the language of the scholar, yet employed all the tools of Bible study. They were very conscientious in letting the Bible be its own commentary. They restricted themselves largely to those Scriptures related to Revelation by actual quotations. Dr. Merrill C. Tenney predicts, "This commentary will probably be the ministry of premillennial exposition for some years to come." 1961. 396 pages. Hardback. Number 1478-7. **$9.95.** Bookstores.

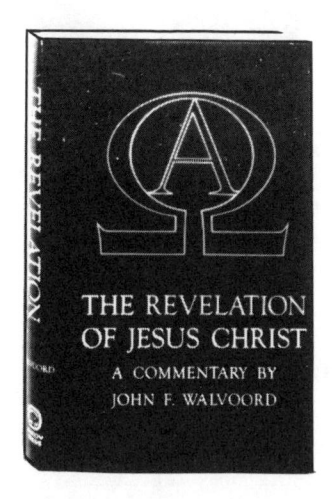

THE REVELATION OF JESUS CHRIST (Moody Press) For: L,C,S. Slant: EP, S, I, M.

By John F. Walvoord. A verse-by-verse study of the Book of Revelation. Points out the symbolic nature of the book while showing where it should be interpreted literally. **$13.95.** From **Moody Bookworld, 2101 W. Howard St., Chicago, IL 60645.**

THE REVELATION RECORD (Tyndale House Publishers) For: L,C,S. Slant: AW, C, RC, F, EP, MP, LP, S, CP.

By Henry M. Morris. Years of Bible study and research by a specialist in hydrology and geology have resulted in an excellent commentary with a scientific approach to the book of Revelation. The author believes the book of Revelation is: an actual record of the final phases of world history; a sequel to the book of Genesis; the culmination of human history which God began at creation; and deserving of scientific attention because of its many references to natural phenomena. **$16.95.** Bookstores.

REVELATION UNFOLDED (Tyndale House Publishers) For: L,C,S. Slant: AW, C, RC, F, EP, MP, LP, S, CP.

By Jack B. Scott. The author presents an understandable interpretation of the Book of Revelation. An excellent resource book for the teacher, or exciting personal reading. 123 pages. Trade paper. **$2.95.** Bookstores.

ROMANS: BIBLE STUDY COMMENTARY (Zondervan Publishing House) For: L,C,S. Slant: EP.

By Curtis Vaughan and Bruce Corley. A lay-oriented commentary with no Greek used within its text. The commentary deals with each biblical book section-by-section, with discussion questions at the end of each chapter. Brief bibliography. **$4.95.** Bookstores or from **Zondervan Retail Marketing Service, 1420 Robinson Road, SE, Grand Rapids, MI 49506.**

ROMANS: THE COMMUNICATOR'S COMMENTARY (Word Books) For: L,C,S. Slant: EP.

By D. Stuart Briscoe. The message of salvation by grace through faith, the message of Romans, stirred Augustine, Luther, Calvin and Wesley. Now, world-famous Bible teacher Stuart Briscoe relates the letter anew to our own turbulent times. With the tools of a scholar and the heart of a pastor,

COMMENTARIES ON NEW TESTAMENT BOOKS

Briscoe shows how Romans "ranges from awe-inspiring expositions of the majesty of God to deeply intimate statements concerning His compassion for sinners." The author delves into the great heart of the apostle as well as his doctrine, showing how "even Paul's formal greetings were touched with warmth," and all his teachings concerned with relating to each other in Christ-like ways. Hardcover. Catalog Number 0159-6. **$14.95.** Bookstores.

ROMANS THROUGH GALATIANS: THE EXPOSITOR'S BIBLE COMMENTARY (Zondervan Publishing House) For: L,C,S. Slant: EP.

By Frank E. Gaebelein, Editor. Contains commentary on Romans by Everett F. Harrison; 1 Corinthians by W. Harold Mare; 2 Corinthians by Murray J. Harris; and Galatians by James Montgomery Boice. The commentary uses the New International Version. Each book has an exposition, an introduction, an outline and a bibliography. Notes and textual questions are correlated with expository units. Transliteration and translation of Semitic and Greek words are provided. Commentators seek to deal fairly with opposing views. **$16.95.** Bookstores or from **Zondervan Retail Marketing Service, 1420 Robinson Road, SE, Grand Rapids, MI 49506.**

ROMANS VERSE-BY-VERSE (Moody Press) For: L,C,S. Slant: EP, S, I, M.

By William R. Newell. A major exposition of the most theologically comprehensive epistle of Paul. **$15.95.** Bookstores or from **Moody Bookworld, 2101 W. Howard, Chicago, IL 60645.**

SERMON ON THE MOUNT (Baker Book House) For: L. Slant: C.

By D.A. Carson. Shows that Christ's sermon presents inescapable demands on believers to live a pure and dedicated Christian life. More than most popular expositions, **Sermon on the Mount** is a product of thorough scholarship. **$4.95.** Bookstores or from **Baker Book House, P.O. Box 6287, Grand Rapids, MI 49506.**

SERVANT AND SON: JESUS IN PARABLE AND GOSPEL (John Knox Press) For: L, C, S. Slant: C, RC, EP, MP, LP, S, BC.

By J. Ramsey Michaels. Approaches Christianity through the personal experiences of Jesus Christ and gives new meaning to being a disciple. Michaels examines the religion of Jesus—His teachings, His parables, His visions, His self-consciousness. As the Son of God, the Son of humanity, the Harbinger of the kingdom of God, Christ lived His prophecy. Paperback. **$8.95.** Please add **$1.00** for shipping. Georgia and Virginia, please add appropriate sales tax. Bookstores or from **John Knox Press, 341 Ponce de Leon Ave., Atlanta, GA 30365.**

SEVEN CHURCHES OF ASIA (Baker Book House) For: C,S. Slant: EP,D.

By R.M. M'Cheyne. The poetic talent and expositional skills of M'Cheyne add a wealth of insight to the popular studies of the letters to the seven churches in Revelation 2 and 3. **$2.75.** Bookstores or from **Baker Book House, P.O. Box 6287, Grand Rapids, MI 49506.**

SEVEN PAULINE LETTERS (The Liturgical Press) For: L,C,S. Slant: RC,S.

With a clear and precise style, this book provides: up-to-date commentary (plus) text on 1 Thessalonians, 1 and 2 Corinthians, Philippians, Galatians, Romans, and Philemon; insights on the literary structure and theological argumentation of the letters which led to a deeper and more unified understanding of Paul's inspired message and spirituality; lengthy explanations of apocalyptic literature, eschatology, and the kenotic hymn (Phil 2:6-11); a nuanced presentation of the theological development of Paul's mind and message from his first to his last letter; a new and insightful study of Paul's magnificent theological synthesis in his profound Letter to the Romans. 296 pages. Softbound. **$8.95.** Bookstores or from **The Liturgical Press, Collegeville, MN 56321.**

SIN, SALVATION, AND THE SPIRIT (The Liturgical Press) For: L,C. Slant: RC, S.

Here are 27 essays on the theme of the parting words of Jesus as recorded in Luke. Hailed as "an important contribution to Lucan studies," the articles are authored by such top biblical scholars as Peifer, Fiorenza, Maly, Stock, Vawter, Anderson, Hellwig, Harrelson, Jensen, and Stuhlmueller, among others. 360 pages. Cloth. **$8.00.** Soft. **$6.00.** Bookstores or from **The Liturgical Press, Collegeville, MN 56321.**

COMMENTARIES ON NEW TESTAMENT BOOKS

ST. MATTHEW'S EARTHQUAKE: JUDGEMENT AND DISCIPLESHIP IN THE GOSPEL OF MATTHEW (Servant Publications) For: L. Slant: P.

By Paul Hinnebusch, O.P. A revealing gospel meditation that provides inspiring spiritual reading. Shows how the earthquake imagery in Matthew's gospel is the key to a new and deeper understanding of his message of judgment and discipleship. An interesting and insightful commentary based on sound biblical scholarship. Number 093X. **$3.95.** Bookstores.

STAND FAST IN LIBERTY (Baker Book House) For: C,S. Slant: EP.

By Robert G. Gromacki. An exposition of Galatians. The meaning of the English Text (KJV) is clarified and enriched by careful and competent explanations of key Greek words and phrases. **$5.95.** Bookstores or from **Baker Book House, P.O. Box 6287, Grand Rapids, MI 49506.**

STAND PERFECT IN WISDOM (Baker Book House) For: C,S. Slant: EP.

By Robert G. Gromacki. An exposition of Colossians and Philemon. The English Text is rich in insights from the Greek. Paul's progression of thought is carefully explained and applied. **$5.95.** Bookstores or from **Baker Book House, P.O. Box 6287, Grand Rapids, MI 49506.**

STAND TRUE TO THE CHARGE (Baker Book House) For: C,S. Slant: EP.

By Robert G. Gromacki. An exposition of 1 Timothy. Key verses in Paul's letter are expertly discussed in understandable language. Unusual words and phrases are explained and complicated passages are competently unraveled by Dr. Gromacki. **$7.95.** Bookstores or from **Baker Book House, P.O. Box 6287, Grand Rapids, MI 49506.**

STUDIES IN THE GOSPELS (Baker Book House) For: C. Slant: EP.

By R.C. Trench. These expositions on a variety of key passages from the life and teachings of Jesus Christ will enrich study or preaching from the Gospels. **$5.95.** Bookstores or from **Baker Book House, P.O. Box 6287, Grand Rapids, MI 49506.**

STUDIES IN THE LIFE OF CHRIST (Baker Book House) For: L,C,S. Slant: EP.

By R.C. Foster. An unabridged one volume edition of the four volume set. **$29.95.** Bookstores or from **Baker Book House, P.O. Box 6287, Grand Rapids, MI 49506.**

SYMBOLS OF CHRIST IN REVELATION (Bible Questions) For: L,C,S. Slant: C, F, EP, D.

A study of the various symbols used to describe Jesus Christ in the first three chapters of the book of Revelation. **$2.50.** From **Bible Questions, Box 736, Galesburg, IL 61401.**

THEMES FROM ACTS (Regal Books) For: L,C,S,Y. Slant: EP.

By Paul E. Pierson. Teaches Christians to beware of three great temptations: that of jealously clutching God's gifts to himself, not sharing what He is and does; looking upon God as inactive, one who once was great but today is powerless; and demanding that anyone who follows Christ must follow Him as we do within our culture, our denomination, our churches. The author states, "A Christian, or disciple of Jesus Christ, is one who trusts Him so much that he seeks to make God's agenda for the world the top priority in his life. That agenda is that all the ethne might hear the Good News and become followers of Christ." Paul Pierson approaches Acts from the viewpoint of the above three temptations, or barriers, that early Christians continually had to overcome. He tells how the Holy Spirit worked with them to help them become effective witnesses to the Way, and how He is still working with Christians today to continue spreading the Good News of Jesus Christ. Number S361107. Mass Paper. 176 pages. **$2.50.** Bookstores or from **Regal Books, Division of GL Publications, 2300 Knoll Drive, Ventura, CA 93003.**

THEMES FROM ROMANS (Regal Books) For: L,C,S,Y. Slant: EP.

By Robert H. Mounce. What relevance does the doctrine of the Book of Romans have to life in the twentieth century? In this Bible Commentary for Laymen, author Mounce discusses this question with a candor and knowledge that makes the study of Romans exciting, practical and provocative. The author's thorough, readable scholarship is organized in such a relevant way that the adult reader will be able to better understand the present-day applications that can be made from Paul's letter to the Romans. Dr. Mounce's treatment of Romans in this 12 chapter study is written from a conservative evangelical position that incorporates trustworthy biblical scholarship. The essential message of the book reveals what God has to say to man who constantly tries to gain righteousness by his own efforts. Chapter titles include: When Man Turns His Back on God; The Benefits of Believing; Practical Christianity; The Obligations of Love. Here is a fresh view of the Book of Romans, written from a full technical understanding of scholarly literature, but dealing with the issues important to the layman, and in language not obscured by professional jargon. Number S353102. 160 pages. Paperback. **$2.50.** Bookstores or from **Regal Books, Division of GL Publications, 2300 Knoll Drive, Ventura, CA 93003.**

THESSALONIAN EPISTLES (Moody Press) For: L,C,S. Slant: EP, P, S, I, M.

By D. Edmond Hiebert. An analysis of two strategic epistles with information on the city and culture of the Thessalonian believers. **$8.95.** Bookstores or from **Moody Bookworld, 2101 W. Howard, Chicago, IL 60645.**

1 AND 2 THESSALONIANS—A GOOD NEWS COMMENTARY (Harper & Row, Publishers, Inc.) For: L,C. Slant: EP, P.

By Earl Palmer. Invigorating and illuminating, this study brings alive the

COMMENTARIES ON NEW TESTAMENT BOOKS

world of the first century church and gives fuller meaning to Paul's letters, which deal with problems and issues that face Christians today. About **The Good News Commentary Series:** This is the first major series to use the popular English Text of the Good News Bible, which has sold in the millions. Each volume is informed by solid scholarship and the most up-to-date research, yet each is biblically faithful and readily understandable to the general reader. Features include: Introductory material highlighting authorship, dating, background information, and thematic emphases—plus a map; full text of each Good News Bible book with running commentary; special end notes which give references for key words and concepts, and provide suggestions for further reading; and full indexes for Scriptures, subjects, persons, and places. 128 pages. Kivar cover. Number RD 426. **$6.95**. Bookstores or from **Harper & Row, Publishers, Inc., Mail Order Department, 2350 Virginia Avenue, Hagerstown, MD 21740.**

1 AND 2 THESSALONIANS: THE WORD BIBLICAL COMMENTARY (Word Books) For: C,S. Slant: EP.

By F.F.Bruce. The dean of evangelical scholars, F.F. Bruce contributes here the seasoned commentary and relevant historical research his many readers have come to expect. On these pages the seeds of empire-wide persecution of Christians are germinating before our eyes. For example, Professor Bruce explains why the Christian message produced a riot at Thessalonica (Acts 17). He also traces the church's anxiety about the return of Christ, and clarifies Paul's cautious response to their overreactions. Reading the Thessalonian letters with Professor Bruce as our guide becomes a refreshing new experience for the serious Bible student. Hardcover. Catalog Number 0244-4. **$18.95**. Bookstores.

TO KNOW CHRIST JESUS (Servant Publications) For: L. Slant: RC.

By Frank Sheed. In this classic study, Frank Sheed employs wide learning, theological sophistication, spiritual insight, and a lucid style to bring the reader to a personal encounter with the living Lord. **To Know Christ Jesus** has been justly called "one of the most satisfying studies of the gospel ever made." 402 pages. 4 3/16 x 6 7/8 inches. **$3.95**. Bookstores.

TO PRAY AS JESUS (Servant Publications) For: L. Slant: D.

By George Martin. Reflects on the gospel passages to impress Christians with the deep mystery of their relationship with God. **To Pray as Jesus** is full of new insights and practical suggestions for all Christians, particularly those just beginning to appreciate the importance of prayer. 92 pages. 4 3/16 x 6 7/8 inches. **$1.95**. Bookstores.

TREASURES OF WISDOM (Baker Book House) For: L,S. Slant: EP.

By Homer Kent, Jr. A careful study of Colossians and Philemon, two New Testament books that speak to concerns of high interest in society today—the spirit world, angels, the occult, human rights, and social discrimination. **$3.95**. Bookstores or from **Baker Book House, P.O. Box 6287, Grand Rapids, MI 49506.**

TRIUMPHS OF THE BODY (Vision House, Inc.) For: L,C,S,Y. Slant: EP.

By Ray Stedman. This three-book commentary concludes by showing how the early Christians faced and conquered incredible problems—and how we can find the same triumphs today through the power of the living Lord. Covers Acts 21-28. 144 pages. Quality paper. Number A424513. **$4.25**. Packaged set also available, **The Acts Trilogy.** Bookstores or from **Vision House, Div. GL Publications, 2300 Knoll Drive, Ventura, CA 93003.**

THE TROUBLED, TRIUMPHANT CHURCH (Thomas Nelson Publishers) For: L,C. Slant: F,EP,D,P.

This is a commentary on 1 Corinthians, prepared with the January Bible Study of the Southern Baptist Convention in mind. Similar in format and approach to **A Pilgrim Priesthood.** Paperback. **$5.95**. Bookstores.

TRUST AND OBEY (Baker Book House) For: L,C. Slant: D.

By Jay Adams. A commentary on First Peter. Based on Dr. Adams' published translation, **The New Testament in Everyday English**, this commentary includes exegetical and explanatory notes together with applicatory helps for preaching, counseling, and adult Bible study. **$3.95**. Bookstores or from **Baker Book House, P.O. Box 6287, Grand Rapids, MI 49506.**

TRUST AND OBEY: A PRACTICAL COMMENTARY ON 1 PETER (Presbyterian and Reformed Publishing Co.) For: L,C,S. Slant: C,F,P.

By Jay E. Adams. This commentary sets forth the book of I Peter in the light of how it may be preached, used in daily life, and employed in counseling. Christians will find it helpful in their personal struggles with affliction. Pastors will discover valuable preaching and counseling insights on a theme close to all Christians—the reality of suffering in human life, especially in the lives of God's chosen. Expositions are followed by sermon sketches, and each section of the commentary constitutes a preaching portion. This commentary is based upon Dr. Adams' published translation, **The Christian Counselor's New Testament.** Jay E. Adams is the Director of Advanced Studies at Westminster Theological Seminary in Escondido, CA. His many works include **Competent to Counsel, The Christian Counselor's Manual,** and **Christian Living in the Home.** 162 pages. **$3.95**. Bookstores or from **Presbyterian and Reformed Publishing, P.O. Box 817, Phillipsburg, NJ 08865.**

TURNING TO GOD (Baker Book House) For: L,C,S. Slant: EP.

By William Barclay. A study of conversion in the Book of Acts and today. **$2.95**. Bookstores or from **Baker Book House, P.O. Box 6287, Grand Rapids, MI 49506.**

COMMENTARIES ON NEW TESTAMENT BOOKS

TYNDALE NEW TESTAMENT COMMENTARY (Wm. B. Eerdmans Publishing Co.) For: L,C,S. Slant: EP,P.

By R.V.G. Tasker, General Editor. This popular series aims to provide serious readers of the Bible with inexpensive tools for interpretation that are not unduly technical. "Most series are uneven; the feature of the Tyndale series is the consistent level of excellence it maintains."—William Barclay. 20-volume set. **$87.00.** Bookstores or from **Eerdmans Publishing Co., 225 Jefferson Ave., S.E., Grand Rapids, MI 49503.**

UNSEARCHABLE RICHES OF CHRIST (Baker Book House) For: C,S. Slant: C, EP.

By Lloyd Jones. An exposition of Ephesians 3. Expositions of Paul's special commission to preach the gospel to the Gentiles as fellow heirs of salvation. **$10.95.** Bookstores or from **Baker Book House, P.O. Box 6287, Grand Rapids, MI 49506.**

THE UPSIDE-DOWN KINGDOM (Herald Press) For: L,C,S,Y. Slant: EP.

By Donald B. Kraybill. Takes the reader through a careful study of the kingdom of God as found in the synoptic Gospels. Using a popular reading, interest-holding style, he provides the reader with some of the latest scholarly insights into the kingdom of God with practical suggestions and serious Bible study. He brings the words and insights of Jesus to bear upon our affluence, war-making, status-seeking, and religious exclusivism. A Christian Peace Shelf selection. Winner of the 1979 National Religious Book Award. 1978. 328 pages. Paper. 1860-X. **$6.95.** Bookstores.

WHAT MORE CAN GOD SAY? (Regal Books) For: L,C,S,Y. Slant: EP.

By Ray C. Stedman. A study of Hebrews that shows how Jesus Christ, superior to Moses and the Law, fulfills all the requirements of the Law. 256 pages. Number S283123. Paperback. **$3.50.** A Bible Commentary for Laymen Series. Teaching materials available. Bookstores or from **Regal Books, Div. of GL Publications, 2300 Knoll Drive, Ventura, CA 93003.**

WHEN THE GOING GETS TOUGH (Regal Books) For: L,C,S,Y. Slant: EP.

By D. Stuart Briscoe. It's hard to live a life of integrity in the midst of hypocrisy. It was the same for first-century Christians. And it's truly difficult to live out our faith while society pulls in the opposite direction. It was the same for first-century Christians. That's why Stuart Briscoe's commentary of 1 Peter packs such power. It speaks directly to the needs and struggles believers encounter every day. In his well-organized, thought-provoking and often humorous way, Stuart Briscoe clues his readers in on how to find joy in suffering for Jesus; discover peace in the midst of conflict and grow as Christians even when surrounded by deceit and hypocrisy. In short, he helps Christians bring glory to God by the way they live in today's world. Quality paper. 5 1/8 x 8 inches. 224 pages. Number 5417507. **$5.95.** Bookstores or from **Regal Books, Div. GL Publications, 2300 Knoll Drive, Ventura, CA 93003.**

WHERE THE ACTION IS (Regal Books) For: L,C,S,Y. Slant: EP.

By Ralph P. Martin. This commentary on Mark gives us a picture of Jesus Christ as true God and true man. 160 pages. S303108. Paperback. **$2.50.** Teaching materials available. Bible Commentary for Laymen Series. Bookstores or from **Regal Books, Div. of GL Publications, 2300 Knoll Drive, Ventura, CA 93003.**

WHICH WAY TO HAPPINESS (Regal Books) For: L,C,S,Y. Slant: EP.

By Dan Baumann. Offers new insights to the Beatitudes as he unfolds the relevance of Jesus' teaching for life in the '80s. He writes, "As we look at the Beatitudes, I want you to see that they were given to us by Jesus so that our lives would be challenged and we would change. Jesus' Sermon on the Mount, Matthew 5, 6, and 7, confronts us with a message that calls us to a distinctiveness of life, a commitment that is unique and, in the midst of the church and in the midst of the world, is a message of clarity and conviction in its distinctiveness... We as Christians are not supposed to just follow culture; we are supposed to stand up and be, in the midst of our culture, a distinctive, quality people. Throughout this book we are going to look at the Beatitudes and ask the Spirit of God to minister to us so that we become...distinctive, qualitatively unique; God's own chosen people." S351100. 144 pages. **$2.50.** Bookstores or from **Regal Books, Div. of GL Publications, 2300 Knoll Drive, Ventura, CA 93003.**

WILL THE REAL PHONY PLEASE STAND UP? (Regal Books) For: L,C,S,Y. Slant: EP.

By Ethel Barrett. A hard look at phoniness in this personalized commentary of James. 160 pages. S113104. Paperback. **$2.25.** Teaching materials available. Bookstores or from **Regal Books, Div. of GL Publications, 2300 Knoll Drive, Ventura, CA 93003.**

WINSTON COMMENTARY ON THE GOSPELS (Winston Press) For: L,C,S. Slant: S.

By Michael Fallon. A unique, popular,

COMMENTARIES ON NEW TESTAMENT BOOKS

easy-to-read, four-in-one commentary. Based on sound, ecumenical scholarship. Treats each Gospel separately, indicating comparisons between all four without blurring the identity of each. Particularly strong on the influence of Old Testament motifs. Paperback. **$12.95.** Bookstores or from **Winston Press, 430 Oak Grove, Minneapolis, MN 55403.**

On Sunday your pastor will illuminate a passage of Scripture. But who's guiding hand will be there tomorrow as you read Scripture?

Introducing the new *Concordia Self-Study Commentary,* your new personal Bible companion . . . a companion that is always ready to assist you in exploring the Word of God.

And as you explore your Bible, your new *Commentary* will assist you with special features like—

—Concise, informative introductions to each book, including authorship and historical background . . . placing the book in full historical and Scriptural context.

—Introductory outlines sketching each book in brief. Useful in sharpening perspectives of the book and pinpointing Biblical themes in study.

—Thorough Scriptural cross referencing locates other, similar passages . . . often clarifying meaning or revealing prophetic fulfillment.

—Ancient word meanings are simply described, making uncertain word usage clear and accessible for today's Bible student.

—Brief internal summaries in the *Commentary* text neatly recap major themes within a book . . . useful aid in quickly reviewing Scripture.

"Good reliable conservative commentaries on the Old and New Testaments, like this one, are hard to come by."

—Dr. Horace D. Hummel
Associate Professor
Concordia Seminary
St. Louis, Mo

Over 1,024 pages in easy-read double column format. Hardbound with jacket. Large 6¾x10 size.

------- Clip and mail today! -------

Please send me _____ copy(s) of the new *Concordia Self-Study Commentary* (15—2721) at $19.95 per copy.* If, after 30 days examination, I am not completely satisfied, I may return the book(s) and invoice and owe nothing.

Name _____

Address _____

City _____

State _____ ZIP _____

☐ I enclose $_____.
On cash orders, please add state and local taxes where applicable, and add the following for postage and handling: $15.01 and up– $2.50

☐ Bill me later.

*For FREE, instant ordering, call toll free 1-800-325-3040 during regular business hours.

CONCORDIA
PUBLISHING HOUSE
3558 SOUTH JEFFERSON AVENUE
SAINT LOUIS, MISSOURI 63118

WORD MEANINGS IN THE NEW TESTAMENT (Beacon Hill Press of Kansas City) For: L,C. Slant: AW,EP,H.

By Ralph Earle. Provides information and inspiration for the reader to deepen his or her understanding through this almost verse-by-verse study of interesting and significant words in the New Testament. An understanding of Greek is not necessary. The study follows the KJV text. Author Ralph Earle is a noted Greek scholar and member of the primary translating team responsible for the New International Version of the Bible. The six volume set includes: Vol. 1, Matthew, Mark, Luke; Vol. 2, John and Acts; Vol. 3, Romans; Vol. 4, Corinthians, Galatians, Ephesians; Vol. 5, Philippians, Colossians, Thessalonians, Timothy, Titus, and Philemon; and Vol. 6 (to be released in spring, 1984) will consist of the balance of the New Testament. Books average 300 pages. Cloth. **$9.95** each. From **Beacon Hill Press of Kansas City, Box 527, Dept. B., Kansas City, MO 64141.**

WORD PICTURES IN THE NEW TESTAMENT (Broadman Press) For: C. Slant: MP.

By A.T. Robertson. The exact meaning and every shade of meaning of every Greek word in the New Testament. Vol. 1, Matthew and Mark; Vol. 2, Luke; Vol. 3, Acts; Vol. 4, Epistles of Paul; Vol. 5, John, Hebrews; Vol. 6, The General Epistles, The Revelation of John. Six volume set. **$71.00.** Individual volumes. **$12.50.** Bookstores.

WORD STUDIES IN THE NEW TESTAMENT (Wm. B. Eerdmans Publishing Co.) For: C,S. Slant: EP,S.

By Marvin R. Vincent. Midway between the exegetical commentary and the lexicon and grammar, this four-volume set reveals the native force of individual words, in their lexical sense, etymology, history, inflection, and peculiarity of usage by the evangelists and apostles. 4-volume set. **$49.95.** Bookstores or from **Eerdmans Publishing Co., 225 Jefferson Ave., S.E., Grand Rapids, MI 49503.**

WUEST'S WORD STUDIES IN THE GREEK NEW TESTAMENT (Wm. B. Eerdmans Publishing Co.) For: C,S. Slant: EP, S.

By Kenneth S. Wuest. Simplified commentaries on the Greek Text for the Bible student who is not conversant with the Greek language. Ideal for pastors, Bible teachers, church school teachers, and all serious Bible students. Includes **The New Testament: An Expanded Translation.** 4-volume set. **$62.50.** Bookstores or from **Eerdmans Publishing Co., 225 Jefferson Ave., S.E., Grand Rapids, MI 49503.**

YOU CAN LIVE LIFE AS IT WAS MEANT TO BE (Regal Books) For: L,C,S,Y. Slant: EP.

By Lloyd John Ogilvie. This is a book about life. Life as it was meant to be. Authentic life. To help every Christian live an authentic life—a life that is original, consistent, trustworthy and true—Dr. Ogilvie has chosen one vital verse from each of the eleven chapters of 1 and 2 Thessalonians. The verses unlock the meaning of Paul's thoughts on authentic living. His thoughts together with illustrations about real people who are struggling with the same problems as the Thessalonians, make this book a Magna Charta for growing, adventuring Christians who seek for the authentic life. **You Can Live Life As It Was Meant To Be** was released in hardcover as **Life As It Was Meant To Be.** Quality Paper. 5 1/8 x 8 inches. 168 pages. Number 5417408. **$4.95.** Bookstores or from **Regal Books, Div. of GL Publications, 2300 Knoll Drive, Ventura, CA 93003.**

The COLLEGEVILLE BIBLE COMMENTARY

This entirely new series of commentaries uses the New American Bible translation and commentary directed to the non-specialist reader. The complete text of the book or books under study is included.

Single books are $2.50; the eleven-volume set is $25.00.

The Gospel According to Matthew
Daniel J. Harrington, SJ

The Gospel According to Mark
Philip A. Van Linden, CM

The Gospel According to Luke
Jerome Kodell, OSB

The Gospel According to John and the Johannine Epistles
Neal M. Flanagan, OSM

The Acts of the Apostles
William S. Kurz, SJ

Galatians and Romans
John J. Pilch

First Corinthians and Second Corinthians
Mary Ann Getty, RSM

First Thessalonians, Philippians, Philemon, Second Thessalonians, Colossians, Ephesians
Ivan Havener, OSB

First Timothy, Second Timothy, Titus, James, First Peter, Second Peter, Jude
Jerome Neyrey, SJ

The Epistle to the Hebrews
George W. MacRae, SJ

The Book of Revelation
Pheme Perkins

General editor: *Robert J. Karris, OFM*

Available at booksellers or from

THE LITURGICAL PRESS
St. John's Abbey
Collegeville, MN 56321

COMMENTARIES ON THE FULL CHRISTIAN BIBLE

Although most commentaries are on individual books of the Bible—or portions of books—a few commentaries cover the entire Christian Bible. In general, books listed as commentaries are those which contain verse-by-verse exposition of Scripture by one or more authors. This section includes works with verse-by-verse interpretation of the entire Christian Bible: Old Testament, New Testament, and, in some instances, the Apocrypha or Deuterocanonical books. Some of the works listed are single volume commentaries but many are multi-volume, multi-author works. Because commentaries are mostly one person's interpretation of Scripture, knowledge of the author's theological "slant" is more important than for other biblical reference works. In multi-volume, multi-author commentaries, the various individual volumes and authors can usually be considered to be from the same theological "school."

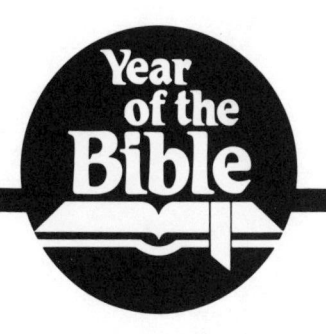

COMMENTARIES ON THE FULL CHRISTIAN BIBLE

BARNES' NOTES ON THE OLD AND NEW TESTAMENTS (Baker Book House) For: L,C. Slant: EP.

By A. Barnes. This 14-volume set is an all-purpose commentary. Verse-by-verse coverage of the scriptural text with a satisfying explanation of each verse. It is a trustworthy guide for study of the Bible. Beautiful deluxe-bound volumes. **$249.50.** Bookstores or from **Baker Book House, P.O. Box 6287, Grand Rapids, MI 49506.**

BEACON BIBLE COMMENTARY (Baker Book House) For: L,C. Slant: AW.

This 10-volume set is a comprehensive interpretation of the Scriptures based on the King James Version and written by forty able scholars. The presentation includes exposition, exegesis, homiletical suggestions and is known for its readability and excellent outline. **$104.95.** Bookstores or from **Baker Book House, P.O. Box 6287, Grand Rapids, MI 49506.**

BEACON BIBLE COMMENTARY OF THE OLD TESTAMENT AND NEW TESTAMENT (Beacon Hill Press of Kansas City) For: L,C,S. Slant: AW,EP,H.

A 10-volume set that presents a Wesleyan/Arminian commentary of the Old and New Testaments. The format is comprehensive, yet at the same time is easily used by the less-trained Bible lover. The presentation is thoroughly outlined and easy to follow. The KJV is the basic biblical text. While a product of Arminian/Wesleyan scholarship, contents reflect the middle-of-the-road conservative Protestant stance. Volumes consist of: 1, Genesis-Deuteronomy; 2, Joshua-Esther; 3, Job-Song of Solomon; 4, Isaiah-Daniel; 5, Hosea-Malachi; 6, Matthew-Luke; 7, John-Acts; 8, Romans, 1 and 2 Corinthians; 9, Galatians-Philemon; 10, Hebrews-Revelation. Average 635 pages per volume, size 6 1/2 x 9 1/2 inches. Cloth. **$9.95** per volume. **$94.95** set. From **Beacon Hill Press of Kansas City, Box 527, Dept. B, Kansas City, MO 64141**

THE BIBLE COMMENTARY (Baker Book House) For: C. Slant: EP.

By F.C. Cook. One of the few available sets offering both critical and exegetical commentary on the entire Bible. 10 volumes. **$195.00.** Bookstores or from **Baker Book House, P.O. Box 6287, Grand Rapids, MI 49506.**

THE BIBLE SPEAKS TODAY SERIES (InterVarsity Press) For: L,C,S. Slant: EP,D,P,S.

Edited by J.A. Motyer and John R.W. Stott. The Bible speaks as forcefully today as it did thousands of years ago. This is the touch stone of this contemporary series of Bible expositions. Attention is given to the accuracy of the text as well as to its contemporary application. Contributions are neither commentaries nor sermons but readable expositions of timeless messages. Nothing is more necessary for the life, growth and health of churches and individual Christians than hearing and obeying what the Spirit says to them through His ancient—yet ever modern—Word. **The Wings of Refuge: The Message of Ruth, $4.95. Songs from a Strange Land: The Message of Psalms 42-51, $3.95. A Time to Mourn, and a Time to Dance: The Message of Ecclesiastes, $4.50. The Lord is King: The Message of Daniel, $4.50. Love to the Loveless: The Message of Hosea, $4.25. The Day of the Lion: The Message of Amos, $6.95. Christian Counter-Culture: The Message of the Sermon on the Mount, $4.95. The Savior of the World: The Message of Luke's Gospel, $4.75. Only One Way: The Message of Galatians, $5.95. God's New Society: The Message of Ephesians, $5.95. Fullness and Freedom: The Message of Colossians and Philemon, $4.95. Guard the Gospel: The Message of Second Timothy, $3.50. Christ Above All: The Message of Hebrews, $6.95. I Saw Heaven Opened: The Message of Revelation, $5.25. Set of The Bible Speaks Today, (14 volumes, paper) $64.95.** Bookstores.

CALVIN'S COMMENTARIES (Baker Book House) For: C. Slant: C.

By John Calvin. A classic commentary on the Old and New Testaments, complete and unabridged. Written in a clear, lucid style, it combines a profound reverence for the Bible with a rare objectivity in its exegesis. 22 volumes. **$395.00.** Bookstores or from **Baker Book House, P.O. Box 6287, Grand Rapids, MI 49506.**

ADAM CLARKE'S COMMENTARY (Baker Book House) Slant: AW,P.

By Adam Clarke. One-volume edition, edited by Ralph Earle. A commentary on the whole Bible, abridged from the original six-volume set. **$24.95.** Bookstores or from **Baker Book House, P.O. Box 6287, Grand Rapids, MI 49506.**

COMMENTARY ON THE HOLY BIBLE (Thomas Nelson Publishers) For: L,C,S. Slant: D,P.

The merger of Matthew Henry's brilliant twelve-volume **Commentary on the Holy Bible** with Thomas Scott's detailed and practical **Holy Bible with Notes** into one three-volume set gives the most comprehensive coverage of Scripture possible in this convenient form. Explanatory, practical, and scholarly, the **Commentary on the Holy Bible** breathes with the warm devotional spirit by which both men have been known for decades. In addition to the commentaries of Henry and Scott, over 3,000 explanatory notes from more than a hundred other biblical scholars are included. Every word of Scripture (KJV) has been included along with extensive marginal notes, an introduction to each book, a full cross-reference system, a complete selection of biblical charts and tables,

COMMENTARIES ON THE FULL CHRISTIAN BIBLE

and dozens of general articles about biblical subjects. If a "perfect" commentary is possible, this is it...adequate for the most scholarly and yet understandable enough for family Bible study. Clear and concise, it retains the essence of the original twelve volumes in an easy-to-handle three volume format—truly a desk-top encyclopedia of biblical knowledge. Hardcover. **$47.95**. Bookstores.

A COMMENTARY ON THE OLD AND NEW TESTAMENTS (Wm. B. Eerdmans Publishing Co.) For: C,S. Slant: F,EP,S.

By Jamieson, Fausset, and Brown. This famous work is universally recognized as one of the finest commentaries on the entire Bible in English today. First published in Great Britain more than one hundred years ago, this "great monument of biblical learning" is clearly and competently written, easy to read and understand; it was originally intended to hold an intermediate place between a popular and purely critical exposition. Scholarly and evangelical, the three-volume series covers every chapter of every book in the Bible, thoroughly and completely, in unabridged, unabbreviated form. This American edition includes the complete text of the King James Version in large, clear type, with topical headings on each page. 3 volume set. **$65.95**. Bookstores or from **Eerdmans Publishing Company, 255 Jefferson Ave., SE, Grand Rapids, MI 49503.**

CONCORDIA SELF-STUDY COMMENTARY (Concordia Publishing House) For: L. Slant: EP.

By Walter Roehrs and Martin Franzmann. An authoritative in-home resource for students of the Bible. Easy to read and understand. Explanatory notes on virtually every verse of the Bible. Concise, informative introduction to each book of the Bible. Introductory outline sketching each book in brief. Thorough cross-referencing of similar passages in the Bible. Ancient word meanings are simply described. 950 pages. Hardcover, Item #15-2721. **$19.95**. Bookstores or from **Concordia Publishing House, 3558 South Jefferson, St. Louis, MO 63118.**

CONCORDIA SELF-STUDY COMMENTARY (Concordia Publishing House) For: L,C,S. Slant: EP, MP, LP, S.

A personal Bible companion that is always ready to assist you in exploring the Word of God. As you explore your Bible, your new commentary will assist you with special features such as concise, informative introductions to each book, including authorship and historical background placing the book in full historical and scriptural context; introductory outlines sketching each book in brief; thorough cross referencing locates other, similar passages; ancient word meanings are simply described, making uncertain word usage clear; brief internal summaries in the commentary neatly recap major themes within each book. 1,024 pages, 6 3/4 x 10 inches. Hardbound. **$19.95**. Bookstores or from **Concordia Publishing House, 3558 S. Jefferson Ave., St. Louis, MO 63118.**

DAILY DEVOTIONAL COMMENTARY (Broadman Press) For: L,C. Slant: MP.

A complete biblical commentary by authoritative biblical scholars. This four-volume set is a definitive guide for a systematic study of the entire Bible. Nontechnical, highly readable, it includes introductory articles, maps, diagrams, charts, and photographs. Volume 1, Genesis-Job. Volume 2, Psalms-Malachi. Volume 3, Matthew-Acts. Volume 4, Romans-Revelation. Four Volume Set. **$39.95**. Individual Volumes. **$10.95**. Bookstores.

ELLICOTT'S COMMENTARY ON THE WHOLE BIBLE (FOUR VOLUMES) (Zondervan Publishing House) For: L,C,S. Slant: EP.

Edited by Charles John Ellicott. The unabridged eight-volume set bound as four volumes, on which the one-volume commentary is based. A verse-by-verse explanation of the whole Bible. **$119.95**. Bookstores or from **Zondervan Retail Marketing Service, 1420 Robinson Road, SE, Grand Rapids, MI 49506.**

EVERYMAN'S BIBLE COMMENTARY SERIES (Moody Press) For: L,S. Slant: EP,P,I,M.

Designed for laymen, these commentaries deal seriously with the biblical text without being overly technical. Introductory information, doctrinal themes, problem passages, and practical applications are examined. **$4.50**. Bookstores or from **Moody Bookworld, 2101 W. Howard Street, Chicago, IL 60645.**

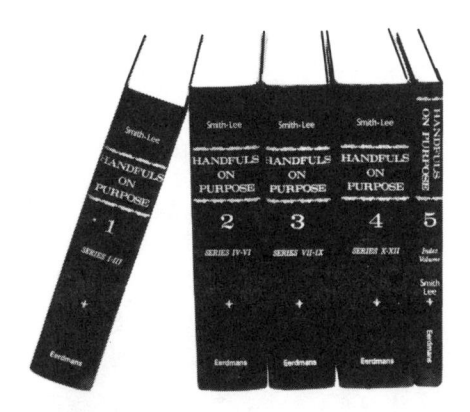

COMMENTARIES ON THE FULL CHRISTIAN BIBLE

HANDFULS ON PURPOSE (Wm. B. Eerdmans Publishing Co.) For: C,S. Slant: F,EP,D.

By James Smith and Robert Lee. A unique commentary on the whole Bible in the form of more than 2,000 deeply devotional and soundly expository outlines, suggestions for Bible reading and study, sermon outlines, Bible exposition, or devotional talks. "Here is a unique commentary on the whole Bible, not in the form of a verse-by-verse analysis but in deeply devotional and soundly orthodox outlines, readings, studies, thoughts, illustrations, and hints... The aim throughout is spiritual rather than critical or historical. The user is encouraged to dig constantly deeper into the rich veins of spiritual thought which abound beneath the surface of the Book of God." —The Ministry. Five-volume set. **$69.95.** Bookstores or from **Eerdmans Publishing Co., 225 Jefferson Ave., SE, Grand Rapids, MI 49503.**

HARPER'S BIBLE COMMENTARY (Harper & Row, Publishers, Inc.) For: L,C. Slant: MP.

By William Neil. Here is a concise, convenient, yet surprisingly thorough one-volume commentary on all the books of the Bible, from Genesis to Revelation. Neil makes full and resourceful use of a wealth of scholarship, but writes in an informal and understandable style. Stressing that the Old and New Testaments are part of one and the same revelation and cannot be understood apart from one another, the author casts a clear, bright light on what the Bible has to say about the purpose of life, about God, and about the world in which we live. "An illuminating and appetizing survey of the whole Bible." —J.B. Phillips. 544 pages. Paperback. **$6.95.** Bookstores or from **Harper & Row, Publishers, Inc., Mail Order Department, 2350 Virginia Ave., Hagerstown, MD 21740.**

MATTHEW HENRY'S COMMENTARY ON THE WHOLE BIBLE (Zondervan Publishing House) For: L,C,S. Slant: EP.

By Matthew Henry. One-volume edition. Contains all that is most valuable in the complete work in Matthew Henry's own words; nearly 2,000 pages; 3,000,000 words. A classic devotional commentary. **$27.95.** Bookstores or from **Zondervan Retail Marketing Service, 1420 Robinson Road, SE, Grand Rapids, MI 49506.**

MATTHEW HENRY: CONCISE COMMENTARY ON THE WHOLE BIBLE (Moody Press) For: L,C,S. Slant: EP,S,I,M.

A classic analysis of the whole Bible—the original commentary has been retained while spiritual applications have been updated for the modern reader. Deluxe hardback. **$22.95.** Paperback. **$11.95.** Bookstores or from **Moody Bookworld, 2101 W. Howard St., Chicago, IL 60645.**

HIGLEY SUNDAY SCHOOL COMMENTARY (Higley Publishing Corporation) For: L,C,S. Slant: MP.

The **Higley Sunday School Commentary for 1983-84** includes many helpful and time saving features to make your Bible study more meaningful and enjoyable. Based on The International Uniform Lesson Series, it offers these exciting features: Teachers' Target, Introduction, Teaching Outline, Verse by Verse Scripture Explanation, Evangelistic Emphasis, Memory Selection, Daily Bible Readings, Weekday Problems, Superintendents Sermonette, This Lesson in Your Life and Seed Thoughts. This is our 51st year of continuous publication. Kivar (paperback). **$6.95.** Cloth (hardcover). **$8.95.** (Include postage and handling **$1.50** minimum—10% of total up to $60.00; 5% of amount over $60.00). Bookstores or from **Higley Publishing Corp., P.O. Box 2470, Jacksonville, FL 32073.**

THE INTERPRETER'S CONCISE COMMENTARY (Abingdon Press) For: L,C,S. Slant: AW, EP, MP, LP, P, S, BC, H.

A new eight-volume Bible commentary for general readers. Written in an easy-to-understand style, it contains complete commentary on every book of the Bible, including the Apocrypha. It is based on the efforts of over forty widely recognized Bible scholars, offering greater perspective than single-author commentaries. And, priced at just $34.95, it's one-third the cost of most multi-volume commentaries. (Individual volumes may also be purchased for $4.95 each). The complete **Interpreter's** set includes helpful maps, diagrams, and charts, and each soft cover

COMMENTARIES ON THE FULL CHRISTIAN BIBLE

volume features a "For Further Study" section that lists additional references. The set comes in a handsome, sturdy slipcase that fits most library shelves. Vol. I, **The Pentateuch**, Genesis, Exodus, Leviticus, Numbers, Deuteronomy. Vol. II, **Old Testament History**, Joshua, Judges, Ruth, 1 and 2 Samuel, 1 and 2 Kings, 1 and 2 Chronicles, Ezra, Nehemiah, Esther. Vol. III, **Wisdom Literature and Poetry**, Job, Psalms, Proverbs, Ecclesiastes, Song of Solomon. Vol. IV, **The Major Prophets**, Isaiah, Jeremiah, Lamentations, Ezekiel, Daniel. Vol. V, **The Minor Prophets and the Apocrypha**, Hosea, Joel, Amos, Obadiah, Jonah, Micah, Nahum, Habakkuk, Zephaniah, Haggai, Zechariah, Malachi, the Old Testament and Apocrypha. Vol. VI, **The Gospels**, Matthew, Mark, Luke, John. Vol. VII, **Acts and Paul's Letters**, Acts, Romans, 1 and 2 Corinthians, Galatians, Ephesians, Philippians, Colossians, 1 and 2 Thessalonians, 1 and 2 Timothy, Titus, Philemon. Vol. VIII, **Revelation and the General Epistles**, Hebrews, James, 1 and 2 Peter, 1, 2, and 3 John, Jude, Revelation. **$4.95** each or **$34.95** per set. Bookstores or from **Abingdon Press, 201 Eighth Ave., South, Nashville, TN 37202.**

THE INTERPRETER'S ONE VOLUME COMMENTARY ON THE BIBLE (Abingdon Press) For: L,C,S. Slant: AW,EP,MP,LP,P,S,BC.

Edited by Charles M. Laymon. Seventy scholars--Protestant, Jewish, and Roman Catholic--contributed their expertise to this outstanding volume, which is aimed at a broad readership of laypersons, ministers, and students of the Bible. Based on the Revised Standard Edition of the Bible. Features include: commentary on each book of the Old and New Testaments and the Apocrypha; forty-three general articles; special reader helps on biblical chronology; measures and money; sixteen pages of Oxford maps in full-color; index of Scripture references; index of subjects; over 150 maps, photographs, and drawings; and 1,424 pages. "A good blending of the historical, critical, exegetical, and theological, producing a well-rounded interpretation of the text...The maps are superb." **Library Journal.** Regular edition. **$22.95.** Thumb indexed. **$27.95.** Bookstores or from **Abingdon Press, 201 Eighth Ave., South, Nashville, TN 37202.**

IRONSIDE COMMENTARIES (Loizeaux Brothers, Inc.) For: L,C,S. Slant: F,EP,D,P,I,M.

By H.A. Ironside. "Making the deep things of God as clear as crystal." H.A. Ironside was known and loved around the world, and has brought the truths of Scripture to thousands during his sixty years of preaching and many volumes of written ministry. His complete set of twenty-two volumes of commentaries covers 51 books of the Bible. (Available in USA only). 22 Volumes (also available in individual volumes). **$190.00.** Bookstores or from **Loizeaux Brothers, P.O. Box 277, Neptune, NJ 07753.**

JAMIESON, FAUSSET AND BROWN'S COMMENTARY ON THE WHOLE BIBLE (Zondervan Publishing House) For: L,C,S. Slant: EP.

By R. Jamieson, Fausset, and Brown. A reprint of the 1870's classic one-volume commentary. Brief verse-by-verse commentary on biblical text. **$21.95.** Bookstores or from **Zondervan Retail Marketing Service, 1420 Robinson Road, SE, Grand Rapids, MI 49506.**

LA BIBLIA A SU ALCANCE (LAYMAN'S COMMENTARY) (Vida Publishers) For: L. Slant: EP.

Layman's Commentary in Spanish. A study of the sacred Scriptures in four easy-to-handle volumes, written in simple language by eminent Bible scholars. Four volume set. **$17.00.** Bookstores.

THE LAYMAN'S BIBLE COMMENTARY (John Knox Press) For: L,C,S,Y. Slant: C,EP,MP,LP,S,BC.

For 25 years the **Layman's Bible Commentary** has provided a complete, inexpensive Bible commentary written especially for laypersons. The authors of this 25-volume set are world-renowned biblical scholars, skilled at translating their knowledge into everyday language. With the publication of this new softcover edition, there are over two million volumes in print (including a number of foreign editions). Every passage of Scripture is explained without the use of technical words and phrases in this bestselling series. **$4.25** per volume. **$96.00** twenty-five volume set. (Add 10% for postage, **$1.00** minimum; Georgia and Virginia add appropriate sales tax). Bookstores or from **John Knox Press, 341 Ponce de Leon Ave., Atlanta, GA 30365.**

THE LIBERTY BIBLE COMMENTARY (Thomas Nelson Publishers) For: L,C,S. Slant: F,P,S,I.

A one-volume, 2,700-plus page commentary on the Bible based on the

174

COMMENTARIES ON THE FULL CHRISTIAN BIBLE

fourfold editorial principle: Baptist doctrine; Fundamentalist interpretation; Historic Evangelicalism; and Premillenial, Pretribulation Eschatology. It is organized in a parallel format, with the Scriptures printed in the left-hand column and the commentary printed in the right hand column on each page. The commentary follows a verse-by-verse, paragraph-by-paragraph format; and introductions and outlines accompany each book in the Bible. A helpful book for Bible schools and colleges. Hardcover. **$29.95.** Bookstores.

FR. MCBRIDE HOMILY SERVICE (ALT Publishing Co.) For: L,C. Slant: RC, L,S.

Commentary on the Scripture readings for each Sunday's mass (Roman Catholic). Also may be used for Scripture study by groups and individuals. Subscriptions can begin with any month. **$40.00** per year. From **ALT Publishing Company, P.O. Box 400, Green Bay, WI 54305.**

F.B. MEYER BIBLE COMMENTARY (Tyndale House Publishers) For: L,C,S. Slant: AW,C,RC,F,EP,MP,LP,S,CP.

By F.B. Meyer. A commentary on the entire Bible, this monumental classic captures the excitement of Christian doctrine and of triumphant living. Meyer centers each discussion around the central meaning of each passage and its applications to daily needs. Designed for daily reading and study. Cloth. **$14.95.** Bookstores.

THE NEW BIBLE COMMENTARY (Wm. B. Eerdmans Publishing Co.) For: C,S. Slant: EP,P.

Edited by Donald Guthrie, et. als. Aiming primarily to make the meaning of the Bible plain to the average reader, this comprehensive and completely up-to-date commentary brings new richness to Bible reading. First published in 1953 as a distinctly evangelical one-volume commentary on the entire Bible, this book has come to occupy a position of prominence in the field. Accessible to scholars, pastors, teachers, and students. "...the very finest in its class."--**Christianity Today.** **$24.95.** Bookstores or from **Eerdmans Publishing Co., 255 Jefferson Ave., SE, Grand Rapids, MI 49503.**

THE NEW CENTURY BIBLE COMMENTARY (Wm. B. Eerdmans Publishing Co.) For: C,S. Slant: EP,MP,S.

Edited by Ronald E. Clements and Matthew Black. Balanced and up to date in terms of both its scholarship and its reflections of the contemporary relevance of the biblical text, this standard commentary on both the Old and New Testaments is now available in softcover. Each volume is based on the Revised Standard Version and features a comprehensive introduction, followed by a section-by-section, verse-by-verse commentary as well as a detailed bibliography. "**The New Century Bible Commentary** is a scholar's and student's commentary and will be prized by those who want exacting (and evangelical) exegetical work."--**Christianity Today.** 25 volumes available. **$5.96-$12.95.** Bookstores or from **Eerdmans Publishing Company, 255 Jefferson Ave., SE, Grand Rapids, MI 49503.**

THE NEW LAYMAN'S BIBLE COMMENTARY IN ONE VOLUME (Zondervan Publishing House) For: L,C,S. Slant: EP.

Edited by G.C.D. Howley, F.F. Bruce, and H.L. Ellison. Forty-three scholars contribute to this one volume. Includes 28 introductory articles and 29 maps. Paragraph-by-paragraph commentary provides a single up-to-date exposition of Scripture. Bibliography with each book. **$27.95.** Bookstores or from **Zondervan Retail Marketing Service, 1420 Robinson Road, SE, Grand Rapids, MI 49506.**

PEAKE'S COMMENTARY ON THE BIBLE (Thomas Nelson Publishers) For: L,C. Slant: MP,LP,S.

Edited by Matthew Black and H.H. Rowley. The latest biblical scholarship by sixty-two noted contributors from every branch of the Protestant church in Europe and America. Index, bibliographies, and full-color maps. Hardcover. **$34.95.** Bookstores.

POPULAR COMMENTARY ON THE BIBLE (Concordia Publishing House) For: L. Slant: LU.

COMMENTARIES ON THE FULL CHRISTIAN BIBLE

By Paul E. Kretzmann. A four-volume commentary on the entire Bible. Complete King James Version text included. Helpful explanations of the Bible text are provided. Two volumes contain text and explanations of the Old Testament and remaining two volumes cover the New Testament. Total pages, 2,872. Item Number 15-1201, Hardcover. **$67.50.** Bookstores or from **Concordia Publishing House, 3558 South Jefferson, St. Louis, MO 63118.**

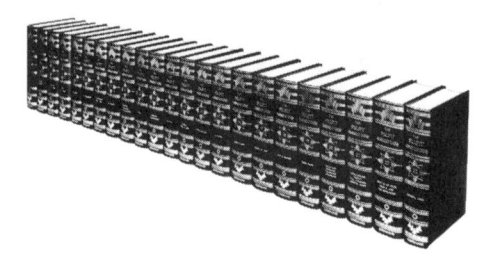

THE PULPIT COMMENTARY (Wm. B. Eerdmans Publishing Co.) For: C,S. Slant: F,EP,S.

By H. Spence and J. Exell. Vast in scope, exhaustive in content, here is undoubtedly the most valuable source of reference and sermon material available. This large-type edition is unabridged, complete with scholarly introductions, full expositions, principal and briefer homilies, an index to homiletic materials, and a complete general index. In all it contains 26,512 pages, and covers 9,500 subjects. Written by a hundred eminent contributors. 23-volume set. **$495.00.** Bookstores or from **Eerdmans Publishing Co., 255 Jefferson Ave., SE, Grand Rapids, MI 49503.**

REVIEW AND EXPOSITOR (Southern Baptist Theological Seminary) For: C. Slant: P,S.

A quarterly theological journal published by the Faculty of the Southern Baptist Theological Seminary. Each issue develops a specific theme to which outstanding scholars throughout the world contribute. One annual issue treats a specific book of the Bible. A variety of themes is reflected in titles like: Old Testament Theology, First Peter, and First Corinthians. Annual subscription. **$9.00.** Individual copies. **$3.50.** Overseas subscription. **$10.00.** Bookstores or from **Review and Expositor, 2825 Lexington Road, Louisville, KY 40280.**

THE TEACHER'S BIBLE COMMENTARY (Broadman Press) For: L. Slant: MP.

Edited by H. Franklin Paschall and Herschel H. Hobbs. This one-volume commentary offers the advantage of brief, summary writings which focus on the main idea of Scripture passages and, at the same time, difficult passages are dealt with in depth. There is an abundance of supplementary information on the geography, archaeology, and history of Bible lands. **$21.95.** Bookstores.

TO UNDERSTAND THE BIBLE-LOOK FOR JESUS (Baker Book House) For: C,S. Slant: EP.

By N.L. Geisler. The Bible student's guide to the Bible's central theme. Believing the fundamental Christian claim that the purpose of the Bible is to present the Savior, the author focuses on Christ as the unity and unfolding message of the whole of Scripture. **$3.95.** Bookstores or from **Baker Book House, P.O. Box 6287, Grand Rapids, MI 49506.**

WESLEYAN BIBLE COMMENTARY (Baker Book House) For: C. Slant: AW.

The aim of the WBC is to maintain the spiritual insight and sound Biblical scholarship of John Wesley and Adam Clarke, but to do so in the context of contemporary life and thought. It is written by a distinguished community of Wesleyan scholars representing nine evangelical denominations. **$125.00.** Bookstores or from **Baker Book House, P.O. Box 6287, Grand Rapids, MI 49506.**

WYCLIFFE BIBLE COMMENTARY (Moody Press) For: L,C,S. Slant: EP, S, I, M.

By Harrison and Pfeiffer. Along with summaries of major sections of each book, this commentary studies the entire Bible phrase-by-phrase. Hardback. **$23.95.** Paperback. **$13.95.** Bookstores or from **Moody Bookworld, 2101 W. Howard Street, Chicago, IL 60645.**

RESOURCES ON "HOW-TO-STUDY" THE BIBLE

Bible study and Bible reading can be approached many different ways from scholarly investigation of the original Greek, Hebrew, and Aramaic languages to a simple chapter-a-day reading of the text. Further, Bible reading and study has a variety of purposes ranging from devotional reading as a stimulus for prayer to scholarly investigation of biblical themes. And, each kind of Bible reading and/or study has its own peculiarities and advocates. Listed in this section are works which are designed to help readers and Bible students investigate different ways of approaching God's word. In some cases, these "how-to" materials overlap considerably with such things as Bible surveys, introductions, and handbooks and, unquestionably, many resources listed in other sections contain a certain amount of "how-to" material.

RESOURCES ON "HOW-TO-STUDY" THE BIBLE

ALLEGED DISCREPANCIES OF THE BIBLE (Baker Book House) For: L,S. Slant: EP.

By John Haley. A deathblow to the critics of the Bible. Wilbur M. Smith said, "The reading of this volume, or rather, its study, is bound to confirm one's faith in Scriptures." **$6.95.** Bookstores or from **Baker Book House, P.O. Box 6287, Grand Rapids, MI 49506.**

ANSWERS TO QUESTIONS ABOUT THE BIBLE (Baker Book House) For: L. Slant: EP.

By R.H. Mounce. With great insight and respect for the Scriptures, the author answers the questions that perplex Christians today and gives the reader valuable lessons on how to approach the Bible. **$3.45.** Bookstores or from **Baker Book House, P.O. Box 6287, Grand Rapids, MI 49506.**

THE AUTHORITY OF THE BIBLE (Baker Book House) For: L,C,S. Slant: EP.

By Jack Cottrell. A solid presentation of the case for the inerrancy of the Scripture, which is the only consistent approach to biblical authority. **$1.95.** Bookstores or from **Baker Book House, P.O. Box 6287, Grand Rapids, MI 49506.**

BEYOND BIBLICAL CRITICISM: Encountering Jesus in Scripture (John Knox Press) For: L,C,S. Slant: C,EP, MP,LP,P,S,BC.

By Arthur Wainwright. Calls us to look at the Scriptures through the teachings of Christ. Wainwright has taken biblical interpretation out of the hands of professors and scholars and has given it back to Jesus Christ. As the center of our religion, Christ taught and lived the Bible. According to Wainwright, Christ is the criterion by which we should evaluate the Scriptures. An insightful resource for grasping our faith, our God, our basis for life as Christians. Paper. **$9.95** (add **$1.00** for shipping and handling). Georgia and Virginia add appropriate sales tax. Bookstores or from **John Knox Press, 341 Ponce de Leon Avenue, Atlanta, GA 30365.**

BOOK OF EXODUS

BIBLE CROSSWORD PUZZLES (ALT Publishing Co.) For: L,C,Y,Ch. Slant: RC, MP, P.

A crossword puzzle on each book of the Bible, using terms and words from each book of the Bible, plus everyday words and terms to assist in completing the puzzles. Used by students and study groups of all ages to gain familiarity with the Bible. Complete set of puzzles. **$20.00.** (Payment grants permission for unlimited duplication in congregation). From **ALT Publishing Co., P.O. Box 400, Green Bay, WI 54305.**

BIBLE DIFFICULTIES (Concordia Publishing House) For: L. Slant: EP.

By William Arndt. In simple, clear language the author, a Bible scholar, provides answers to puzzling questions that occur to Bible readers about the accounts of Creation, the Flood, Jonah and others. Paper. 181 pages. Item No. 12-2357. **$4.25.** Bookstores or from **Concordia Publishing House, 3558 South Jefferson, St. Louis, MO 63118.**

THE BIBLE NEWSLETTER (Evangelical Ministries, Inc.) For: L,C,S. Slant: EP, P.

The Bible Newsletter is a monthly eight-page newsletter for people interested in the Bible. It offers Bible-based comments on current events; summaries of Bible-related magazine and journal articles; reviews of the latest Bible reference books, study aids, and popular expositions; modern looks at the Greek and Hebrew words of the Scripture; and a do-it-yourself guide to the study of a particular Bible passage or theme. Other features include late-breaking archaeology news; biblical advice on home management; articles on the history of Bible study and how that affects Christians today; occasional Bible-based word games and puzzles. A monthly resource packed with practical help. One-year subscription. **$15.95.** Two-year subscription. **$29.95.** From **The Bible Newsletter, 1716 Spruce Street, Philadelphia, PA 19103.**

BIBLE READING CALENDAR (The Wesleyan Church) For: L,C,S,Y,Ch.

Our daily reading guide will assist a study of the entire Bible in one year. Each day there are recommended readings from both the Old and New Testaments. Great for families, congregations, and the individual. Adapted with permission. **$2.00** per 100. From **The Wesleyan Church, Local Church Education, Box 2000, Marion, IN 46952.**

BIBLE STUDY DISCUSSION LEADERS' GUIDE (Officers' Christian Fellowship of the USA) For: L,S. Slant: EP.

An indepth guide (19 pages) for the

RESOURCES ON "HOW-TO-STUDY" THE BIBLE

Bible study discussion leader for inductive Bible studies. **$.50** per copy. From **Officers' Christian Fellowship, P.O. Box 36200, Denver, CO 80236.**

BIBLE STUDY FOR BUSY WOMEN (Moody Press) For: L,W. Slant: EP, P,I,M.

By Ethel Herr. Gives women the tools they need to begin studying the Bible and keep studying it despite the many other demands on their time. **$6.95.** Bookstores or from **Moody Bookworld, 2101 W. Howard Street, Chicago, IL 60645.**

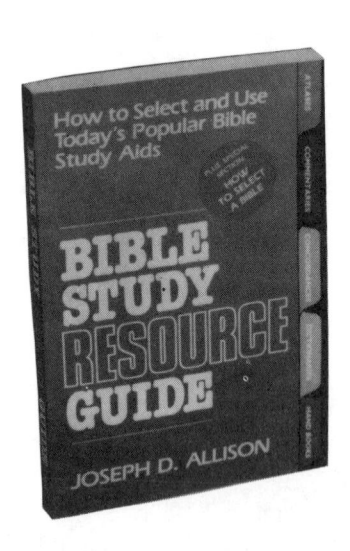

BIBLE STUDY RESOURCE GUIDE (Thomas Nelson Publishers) For: L,C,S. Slant: EP,MP.

By Joseph Allison. For those who want to study the Bible but don't know what aids are available, or for those who have heard of various Bible handbooks, dictionaries, commentaries, and concordances but don't know which are best suited to their needs. This **Bible Study Resource Guide** will answer these questions. The difference, among the various kinds of Bible study aids are clearly and simply explained, and their uses, strengths, and weaknesses are discussed. Also included is a guide to Bible translations. A special section will help readers choose the right Bible for them. Among the study aids covered in this book are: study Bibles, topical Bibles, concordances, commentaries, dictionaries, encyclopedias, handbooks, atlases, original Bible language (Greek and Hebrew) helps, Bible surveys, and harmonies. Also included are lists of Bible rebinders and out-of-print book sources. Paper. **$6.95.** Bookstores.

BIBLICAL EXEGESIS: A BEGINNER'S HANDBOOK (John Knox Press) For: C,S. Slant: C,EP,MP,LP,S,BC.

By John H. Hayes and Carl Holladay. A tool for beginning students doing Old and New Testament exegesis. Using a minimum of technical terms, introduces students to the various techniques of biblical criticism and presents exegetical theory and practice. Ideal for general Old and New Testament introductory courses, exegesis courses, homiletic and preaching courses, and courses on historical topics. Bibliography for further reading. Paperback. **$6.95** (add **$1.00** for shipping and handling). Georgia and Virginia add appropriate sales tax. Bookstores or from **John Knox Press, 341 Ponce de Leon Ave., Atlanta, GA 30365.**

THE BOOK THAT CAME THROUGH THE FIRE (Voice of Prophecy) For: L. Slant: EP.

Why does the Bible continue to be the best seller year after year? Is it a divinely inspired collection of human writings, or merely an assembly of ancient traditions? In five interesting chapters this book answers these questions. It also explains how the Bible came to be written, how it survived even when it was banned, and how it came to be translated into the English language. **$1.00.** From **Voice of Prophecy, P.O. Box 55, Dept. YOB, Los Angeles, CA 90053.**

BREAD IN A BARREN LAND (Broadman Press)

By Dr. James P. Wesberry. The author is executive director of the Lord's Day Alliance of the United States. Presents the Bible as an oasis from the ravages that surround us. It reveals the author's personal experience with the Bible for over seventy years and his personal method of studying it and shows how it became so important in his life. It shows how the Bible has been the author's survival kit in many storms and crises of life and how readers, too, can find inspiration, comfort and guidance in it. It is highly commended by Dr. Charles Allen, who has written many best sellers and by Dr. Norman Vincent Peale, who has read and found a blessing in it. **$5.95.** Bookstores or from **Dr. James P. Wesberry, 2930 Flowers Road, South, Baptist Center, Atlanta, GA 30341.**

CAN WE TRUST THE BIBLE? (Tyndale House Publishers) For: L,S. Slant: AW,C,RC,F,EP,MP,LP,P,I,CP.

Edited by Earl Radmacher. Leading theologians provide convincing arguments for clergy and laity alike, as they defend the inerrancy of the Word of God. 126 pages. Trade paper. **$4.95.** Bookstores.

CHRISTIAN HERALD MAGAZINE (Christian Herald) For: L,C. Slant: EP, D, P.

Monthly magazine with a regular feature on daily/weekly Bible study, plus frequently appearing articles on applying the Scriptures. One-year subscription. **$13.97.** Bookstores or from **Christian Herald, 40 Overlook Drive, Chappaqua, NY 10514.**

RESOURCES ON "HOW-TO-STUDY" THE BIBLE

CREATIVE BIBLE STUDY (Zondervan Publishing House) For: L,C,S. Slant: EP.

By **Lawrence O. Richards**. Attempts to deal with ideas, feelings, attitudes, or previous viewpoints that people may bring to Scripture—the matters that may cloud their understanding of the intended message of the Bible. Includes group exercises after each chapter. Indexed. **$5.95.** Bookstores or from **Zondervan Retail Marketing Service, 1420 Robinson Road, SE, Grand Rapids, MI 49506.**

CURRENT CHRISTIAN BOOKS (CBA Service Corporation) For: C. Slant: F,EP,MP.

The only complete index of Christian books and Bibles. This official publication of the Christian Booksellers Association contains alphabetical lists of over 25,000 books and Bibles as well as 11,000 authors. Each listing includes: title, author, publisher, copyright date, price, subject classification, ISBN, and binding. **Current Christian Books** is a valuable resource in your church library for: reference for church members, pastor's aid for recommending books, pastor's personal study reference, Christian Education tool for ordering books and estimating cost, catalog for ordering books from your local bookstore, librarian reference for cataloging, departmentalizing and indexing books. New 1983-84 edition. Over 600 pages (also available on microfiche). Nonmembers. **$54.95.** Members. **$44.95.** From **CBA Service Corporation, P.O. Box 200, Colorado Springs, CO 80901.**

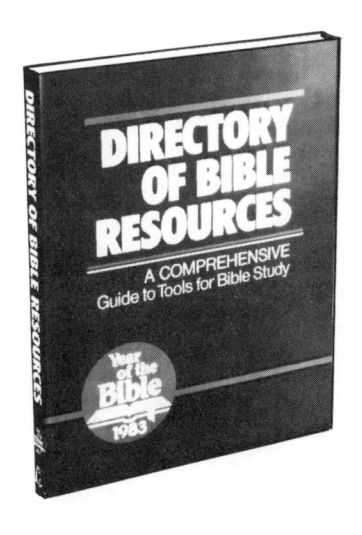

THE DIRECTORY OF BIBLE RESOURCES (Thomas Nelson Publishers) For: L,C,S. Slant: Impartial.

Prepared under the auspices of the National Committee for the Year of the Bible, this book is an attempt to list "every Bible reading and Bible study resource currently available in America: Protestant, Catholic, and Jewish." The listings are annotated, with brief descriptions of each resource provided by the publisher of the resource. Paper. **$12.95.** Bookstores or from **Year of the Bible Program and Media Office, 460 Woodycrest Ave., Nashville, TN 37210.**

DO IT YOURSELF HEBREW AND GREEK (Zondervan Publishing House) For: L,C,S. Slant: EP.

By **Edward W. Goodrick**. Introduces the alphabets and basic elements of Greek and Hebrew grammar. With this foundation, the student is encouraged to use some basic language tools, including analyticals, lexicons, interlinears, concordances, and commentaries. An introduction to biblical languages for those not interested in formal academic study. **$9.95.** Bookstores or from **Zondervan Retail Marketing Service, 1420 Robinson Road, SE, Grand Rapids, MI 49506.**

DOES INSPIRATION DEMAND INERRANCY? (Presbyterian and Reformed Publishing Co.) For: L,C,S. Slant: C,F,S,I.

By **Stewart Custer**. Christians often face the question: "Are there errors in the Bible?" The present work is an attempt to survey some of the answers to this question as the Liberals, Neo-Orthodox, Neo-Evangelicals, and strict Conservatives would give them. But the most important answer to the question is the one which Scripture itself gives. The procedure in this work is to present in Part I the teaching of Scripture on the doctrine of inspiration with special attention to its claims of inerrancy; in Part II, to present briefly the different theological opinions in inspiration; and, in Part III, to survey some of the passages often advanced as errors to see if there are reasonable explanations. Stewart Cluster is the chairman of the Department of Bible at Bob Jones University. 120 pages. **$3.50.** Bookstores or from **Presbyterian and Reformed Publishing Co., P.O. Box 817, Phillipsburg, NJ 08865.**

DOES THE BIBLE CONTRADICT ITSELF? (Concordia Publishing House) For: L. Slant: EP.

By **William Arndt**. Analyzes nearly 400 passages of the Bible containing alleged contradictions and in each case shows there is no contradiction. Book includes excellent subject index and list of Bible passages treated. Paper. 192 pages, item number 12-2623. **$4.95.** Bookstores or from **Concordia Publishing House, 3558 So., Jefferson, St. Louis, MO 63118.**

RESOURCES ON "HOW-TO-STUDY" THE BIBLE

EFFECTIVE BIBLE STUDY (Zondervan Publishing House) For: L,C,S. Slant: EP.

By **Howard F. Vos.** Explanation of sixteen different methods of Bible study. Designed to assist the reader in pursuing a specialized study and in finding a method most appropriate for his or her use. Bibliography and index. **$5.95.** Bookstores or from **Zondervan Retail Marketing Service, 1420 Robinson Road, SE, Grand Rapids, MI 49506.**

THE ENGLISH BIBLE FROM KJV TO NIV (Baker Book House) For: L,C,S. Slant: EP.

By **Jack P. Lewis.** Evaluates the strengths and weaknesses of the major translations and revisions. The most comprehensive, detailed, and scholarly book on this subject. **$16.95.** Bookstores or from **Baker Book House, P.O. Box 6287, Grand Rapids, MI 49506.**

ENJOY YOUR BIBLE (Moody Press) For: L,S. Slant: EP,P,I,M.

By **Irving Jensen.** Teaches many practical ways to approach, appreciate, absorb, and apply God's word. **$5.95.** Bookstores or from **Moody Bookworld, 2101 W. Howard Street, Chicago, IL 60643.**

EXPLORE THE WORD! (Creation-Life Publishers, Inc.) For: L,C,S. Slant: F,EP,D,P,S,I.

By **Henry M. Morris, III, D.Min.** No longer do we need to rely on "Bible Teachers" as our only source for gaining deeper meaning from God's Word. Dr. Morris bridges the gap between simple study helps and complex theoretical hermeneutics through the explanation of the use of the concordance. Laymen needn't (and indeed shouldn't) be satisfied with second-hand truth when they have the ability and equipment necessary to probe God's word for themselves. Tremendous blessings await those who care enough to **EXPLORE THE WORD!** Book number 056. **$7.95** (add **$1.00** shipping; California residents add 6% sales tax). Bookstores or from **Creation-Life Publishers, P.O. Box 15908, San Diego, CA 92115.**

GETTING INSIDE THE BIBLE (Bethany Press) For: L,C,S,Y. Slant: MP, P, BC.

By **Herbert H. Lambert.** Shows the layperson how to enter the fascinating world of Scripture. The people of the Bible come alive as we explore their struggles, their feelings, and their faith. Using examples from literature and personal experience, the writer relates the Bible to contemporary experience. No effort is made to explain all the books of the Bible, but guidance is given for further study. **$1.50.** From **Bethany Press, P.O. Box 179, St. Louis, MO 63166.**

GUIDE TO UNDERSTANDING YOUR BIBLE (Here's Life Publishers) For: L. Slant: EP,P.

By **Josh McDowell.** Learn five simple steps that will make Bible study and personal application of God's Word more exciting. These are the study techniques that have kept Josh McDowell excited about personal Bible study. They are clearly explained and fully illustrated. Includes methods for consistency, review, and handling personal crises. Product #402644. **$4.95.** Bookstores or from **Here's Life Publishers, P.O. Box 1576, San Bernardino, CA 92405.**

HANDBOOK FOR BIBLE STUDY (Baker Book House) For: L,C. Slant: EP.

By **Grant Osborne and Stephen Woodward.** The most complete guidebook for Bible study available. The first half of the book is a presentation of approaches to Bible study; the second half discusses the use of tools in Bible study. **$4.95.** Bookstores or from **Baker Book House, P.O. Box 6287, Grand Rapids, MI 49506.**

HANDBOOK OF BIBLICAL CRITICISM (John Knox Press) For: L,C,S. Slant: C, RC, EP, MP, LP, S, BC.

By **Richard N. Soulen.** Resource for ready reference to define terms in the field of biblical interpretation. Includes over 600 terms, phrases, names and notes on major methodologies, exegeses, bibliographic tools, key figures in the history of biblical research, fundamental critical problems, systems of Hebrew transliterations, common abbreviations, and different versions of the Bible. Paperback. **$9.95** (add 10%, **$1.00** minimum postage, for each

RESOURCES ON "HOW-TO-STUDY" THE BIBLE

order). Georgia and Virginia add appropriate sales tax. Bookstores or from **John Knox Press, 341 Ponce de Leon Ave., Atlanta, GA 30365.**

A HEART TO KNOW THE WORD (Roper Press) For: L,S,Y. Slant: EP, D,P.

By David Roper. A two-volume set which sets forth practical principles for how to study the Old and New Testaments. The author believes that being under the Word is no substitute for being in the Word for one's self. This two-volume guide is one more challenge to first-hand Bible study. The approach presented is uncomplicated, but its simplicity does not sacrifice accuracy in handling Biblical truth. David is a gifted teacher and expert instruction always involves the use of probing questions. Thus, these two books not only provide pointers in how to study but offer practical workbook questions and simple, but challenging, study assignments to reinforce the study technique. **How to Study the Old Testament** includes distinctive techniques for historical, narrative, hymn, wisdom and prophetic passages. **How to Study the New Testament** includes a study of Second Timothy plus suggestions for conducting group Bible studies. Old Testament. **$4.50.** New Testament. **$3.50.** From **Roper Press, 915 Dragon St., Dallas, TX 75207.**

THE HISTORICAL APPROACH TO THE BIBLE (Religion and Ethics Institute) For: L,C,S.

A concise survey of the history of the rise and development of the historical approach to the study of the Bible, and an explanation of the major methods of the approach. Introductory chapters point out unreliable methods of study, and the final chapter describes the value of the approach. 323 pages. Paperback. From **Religion and Ethics Institute, Box 664, Evanston, IL 60204.**

A HISTORY OF THE ENGLISH BIBLE (Standard Publishing) For: L,C,S. Slant: EP,I,BC.

How do we know that the Bible we have today is really THE Bible, THE Word of God as it claims to be? This book provides the assurance you need that the Bible we have today is beyond all doubt the Word of God for all ages. Code 39974. **$3.50.** Bookstores or from **Standard Publishing, 8121 Hamilton Ave., Cincinnati, OH 45231.**

HOW TO BE AN EFFECTIVE BIBLE TEACHER (Presbyterian and Reformed Publishing Co.) For: L,C,S. Slant: C, F,P,I.

By George M. Bowman. An uncompromising look at faulty methods of teaching the Bible, this book explains not only how the teaching misfits get into the church, but how the church may improve its methods for selecting, training, and appointing the effective Bible teachers. Leaders and teachers within the church, as well as the general Christian public, will gain from the readable volume a clear idea of the motives, qualities and skills that are basic to the task of teaching God's Word. Mr. Bowman has been teaching Bible for more than thirty years. A writer and editor, he has published numerous popular books and articles on Christian living and stewardship. 154 pages. **$3.95.** Bookstores or from **Presbyterian and Reformed Publishing Co., P.O. Box 817, Phillipsburg, NJ 08865.**

HOW TO GET MORE FROM YOUR BIBLE (Baker Book House) For: L,S. Slant: EP.

By Perry and Culver. Practical suggestions for studying the Bible by books, chapters, and by paragraphs. **$3.95.** Bookstores or from **Baker Book House, P.O. Box 6287, Grand Rapids, MI 49506.**

HOW TO INTERPRET THE BIBLE (Broadman Press) For: L,C. Slant: MP.

By Robert L. Cate. A step-by-step method of biblical interpretation supported by prayer and devotion. Methods for interpreting the Bible are discussed under "Approaching the Bible to Interpret It," "Preparing to Interpret the Old Testament," "Preparing to Interpret the New Testament," "Moving from Preparation to Interpretation," and "Moving from Interpretation to Presentation." Paper. **$6.95.** Bookstores.

HOW TO LEAD SMALL GROUP BIBLE STUDIES (NavPress) For: L,C,S. Slant: EP,P.

This popular handbook, originally released in 1974 as **Lead Out**, provides thorough instructions for leading a Bible study discussion group. Topics in this revised, more versatile edition include preparing lesson plans for leading the group, developing objectives for the group, preparing and asking stimulating questions, handling slow-moving groups, starting discussion, evaluating and improving leadership techniques, and training someone else to start another group. **$2.95.** Bookstores or from **NavPress, P.O. Box 6000, Colorado Springs, CO 80934.**

HOW TO READ THE BIBLE (Presbyterian and Reformed Publishing Co.) For: L,S. Slant: C, F, P, I.

By Dr. Wayne Mack. This study manual is designed to help you learn how to read the Bible with great profit. It begins with some excellent introductory reading by J.C. Ryle and Charles Haddon Spurgeon on the why and how of Bible reading. This introductory reading is followed by thought-provoking questions and case studies which will lead into a rather comprehensive and practical study that will help you to get more benefit out of your Bible study. Many of the questions asked and case studies presented will be answered by the introductory reading. However, this manual is designed to stimulate you to do some hard thinking on your own. Therefore, to answer some of the questions you will be directed to Scripture passages, which will require you to search and to think for yourself. Dr. Wayne Mack is a respected biblical counselor and speaker. He is on the staff of the Christian Counseling and Educational Foundation of Laverock, Pennsylvania. **$2.50.** Bookstores or from **Presbyterian and Reformed Publishing Co., P.O. Box 817, Phillipsburg, NJ 08865.**

RESOURCES ON "HOW-TO-STUDY" THE BIBLE

HOW TO READ THE BIBLE FOR ALL ITS WORTH (Zondervan Publishing House) For: L,C,S. Slant: EP.

By Gordon D. Fee and Douglas Stuart. Shows how to read the Bible with an appreciation for its true worth. Helps the readers to understand the distinctive occasion, purpose, and message of individual books and writings. Appendix and indexes. **$6.95.** Bookstores or from **Zondervan Retail Marketing Service, 1420 Robinson Road, SE, Grand Rapids, MI 49506.**

HOW TO START A NEIGHBORHOOD BIBLE STUDY (Tyndale House Publishers) For: L,S. Slant: AW,C,RC,F,EP, MP,LP,P,CP.

By Marilyn Kunz and Catherine Schell. A handbook for group discussions; what to do and what not to do in a discussion Bible study. A Neighborhood Bible Studies book. 24 pages. Paper. **$2.00.** Bookstores.

HOW TO STUDY THE BIBLE (Aglow Publications) For: L,W. Slant: CP.

Provides a solution to many people's need for systematic, yet easily learned ways, of studying the Scriptures. Sound dull? Not at all. As you learn the biographical and historical facts that contributed to the lives of the people of the Bible, you will find them coming as alive to you as your neighbors down the street. You'll be surprised to learn how even the geography of a given area influenced the thought and traditions of the people living there. Following the lives of Timothy and Paul throughout the New Testament, the author teaches us eight different study methods. This workbook is for everyone, student and non-student alike. As Christians we must know how to study our textbook, the Bible. **$4.95** (postage 15% of total order plus **$1.00** for handling, Washington state residents add 7.3% sales tax). Ask for free catalog. Bookstores or from **Aglow Publications, P.O. Box I, Lynnwood, WA 98036.**

HOW TO STUDY THE BIBLE (Channing L. Bete Co., Inc.) For: L,Y,Ch,W. Slant: RC,MP.

A Scriptographic Booklet designed to encourage meaningful study of the Bible. Suggests methods for Bible reading, lists study aids and much more. Tells how to apply Bible lessons in everyday life, too. Minimum order: 100 copies (titles may be mixed). Quantity discounts offered. Can be personalized on the front and back covers at the buyer's request. From **Channing L. Bete Company, Inc., 200 State Road, South Deerfield, MA 01373.**

HOW TO STUDY THE BIBLE (Multnomah Press) For: L,S. Slant: EP,P.

By James Braga. Using a single book of the Bible in each chapter, James Braga demonstrates ten different methods of Bible study. While his approach is careful and thorough, he assumes no previous background, making the book suitable for either individual study or class use. Paperback. **$6.95.** Bookstores or from **Multnomah Press, 10209 SE Division Street, Portland, OR 97266.**

HOW TO STUDY THE BIBLE (Tyndale House Publishers) For: L,S. Slant: AW, C,RC,F,EP,MP,LP,P,CP.

By Marge Fuller. This book will show you what God has to say to you through His Word. It tells you how to study a chapter, a passage, or a verse of the Bible. There is space to write down what you've learned. 59 pages. Trade paper. **$2.50.** Bookstores.

HOW TO STUDY THE BIBLE FOR YOURSELF (Harvest House Publishers) For: L,C,S. Slant: EP,P,I,M.

This best-selling book provides fascinating study helps and charts that will make personal Bible study more interesting and exciting. A three year program is outlined for a good working knowledge of the Bible. It encourages the reader to investigate the great truth of the Word for himself. No. 0214. Paper. **$4.95.** Bookstores or from **Harvest House Publishers, 1075 Arrowsmith, Eugene, OR 97402.**

HOW TO UNDERSTAND THE BIBLE (Standard Publishing) For: L. Slant: EP.

Easy-to-use Bible study tools for the layman. Step-by-step lessons, plus discussions of topics, words, customs, and contexts. For individual or class study. Code 40046. **$1.95.** Bookstores or from **Standard Publishing, 8121 Hamilton Ave., Cincinnati, OH 45231.**

HOW TO UNDERSTAND YOUR BIBLE

RESOURCES ON "HOW-TO-STUDY" THE BIBLE

(Harold Shaw Publishers) For: L,C,S,Y. Slant: EP.

By Alan Stibbs. Balanced, practical and basic guidelines for Bible interpretation and understanding. Discusses how to deal with the Bible's parables, prophecies and allegories and apply its truth to life. **$1.95.** Bookstores or from **Harold Shaw Publishers, P.O. Box 567, 388 Gundersen Drive, Wheaton, IL 60189.**

HOW TO USE THE BIBLE (Concordia Publishing House) For: L. Slant: EP.

By James and Darline Robinson. A guide to beginning students of God's Word. Clear answers to a new Bible student's most common questions, like, "Where do I start?" and "What should I look for?" With educational exercises, activities and a step-by-step format, this practical book explains the Bible's basic contents and ultimately enables readers to use the Bible on their own. Paper. 80 pages, item number 12-2808. **$2.95.** Bookstores or from **Concordia Publishing House, 3558 So. Jefferson, St. Louis, MO 63118.**

HOW TO USE YOUR BIBLE (Standard Publishing) For: L,C,S,Y. Slant: P.

A fun-to-use workbook for would-be Bible readers from age 9 through adult. Step-by-step exercises help the reader master the location skills essential to enjoyable reading and study of God's Word. Code 3200. **$2.50.** Bookstores or from **Standard Publishing, 8121 Hamilton Ave., Cincinnati, OH 45231.**

HOW WE GOT THE BIBLE (Baker Book House) For: L,C,S. Slant: EP.

By Neil R. Lightfoot. A factual account of how the Bible has been preserved and handed down to our generation. **$7.95.** Bookstores or from **Baker Book House, P.O. Box 6287, Grand Rapids, MI 49506.**

INDEPENDENT BIBLE STUDY (Moody Press) For: L,S. Slant: EP,P,I,M.

By Irving Jensen. A practical help on individual Bible study methods that will lead you to thrilling discoveries in the Word of God. **$5.95.** Bookstores or from **Moody Bookworld, 2101 W. Howard Street, Chicago, IL 60645.**

INTERPRETATION: A JOURNAL OF BIBLE AND THEOLOGY (Union Theological Seminary in Virginia) For: L,C. Slant: MP,BC.

In this issue the editors of **Interpretation** offer helps to lay and clergy interpreters of Scripture in the difficult matter of evaluating and selecting commentaries. The articles by nine skilled interpreters deal with what one may expect from a good commentary, how to evaluate both Old and New Testament commentaries, a discussion of some particularly significant commentaries and three expository articles dealing with particular texts. October, 1982, issue. **$4.00** (Make check payable to Interpretation). From **Interpretation, 3401 Brook Road, Richmond, VA 23227.**

INTERPRETING GOD'S WORD FOR TODAY: AN INQUIRY INTO HERMENEUTICS (Warner Press, Inc.) For: L,C,S. Slant: AW.

Edited by Wayne McCown and James Massey. The second book in the five-volume **Wesleyan Theological Perspectives Series** is a theological restatement of hermeneutics that covers both Old and New Testaments. It discusses the impact of modern thought on biblical interpretation as well as offers hermeneutics for contemporary preaching. This collection of essays written by nine scholars is intended to be biblical in basis, scholarly in method, and practical in emphasis. Order number D4851, Clothback, hardbound. **$14.95.** Bookstores or from **Warner Press, P.O. Box 2499, Anderson, IN 46018.**

IS THE BIBLE THE WORD OF GOD? (ACTS International) For: L. Slant: EP.

How can we motivate unchurched people to read the Bible unless they are convinced that it is indeed God's Word? To read the Bible, people need to have more than a sentimental attitude towards it. They need to grasp in their mind that it is uniquely God's message for them today! Encounter brochures provide an effective answer. They are four-page brochures, beautifully printed in full color, designed specifically for giving to church members, friends and for distributing to entire communities. The brochure, "Is the Bible the Word of God?" builds a strong case to convince readers that the Bible is uniquely God's Word. Its message is simple, short, and readable. It can be imprinted with your church's name and address and can have an Encounter letter inserted in it from you offering additional free literature or a free Bible portion from your

RESOURCES ON "HOW-TO-STUDY" THE BIBLE

church. Free samples are available on request. 100 to 400: **$15.00** per hundred; 500 to 900: **$10.50** per hundred; 1,000: **$29.50**. Imprinted with your name and address (minimum 1,000) add **$12.00** per thousand. Quantity discounts available on request. From **ACTS International, P.O. Box 157, Claremont, CA 91711.**

THE JOY OF BIBLE STUDY (Baptist Publishing House) For: L,S,Y. Slant: F,EP,MP,P.

By **Dr. Joe Pendleton.** This manual is designed to aid you in Bible study. It is written to give you a systematic, comprehensive approach to Bible study, an approach that follows methodical steps. Each session will conclude with a study of a passage of Scripture. This will enable you to put into practice the methodology of Bible study. Passages have been chosen that will provide an exposure to five basic biblical doctrines: the inspiration of the Scriptures; the eternal security of the believer; the Virgin Birth and deity of Christ; the establishment of the church; and the personal, bodily, and imminent return of Christ. Dr. Pendleton is the pastor of the First Baptist Church of Magnolia, Arkansas. He is a graduate of Jacksonville College (Texas), Texas Tech University, and Southwestern Baptist Theological Seminary. He has served as an instructor and dean of the Baptist Missionary Association Theological Seminary. He is the author of **To Be Continued: A Study in Acts. $1.95.** Teacher's Guide. **$1.50.** From **Baptist Publishing House, 712 Main, Little Rock, AR 72201.**

KEYS TO SUCCESSFUL BIBLE STUDY (Herald Press) For: L,C,Y. Slant: EP.

By **John R. Martin.** Assists the reader in understanding the unique nature of the Bible and discovering its personal message. He presents four study methods: reading, meditation, memorization, and systematic study. This easily read tool also includes a time chart of biblical history, a listing of favorite chapters, and capsule information on each book of the Bible. Also includes discussion questions. 1981. 184 pages. Paper, 1963-0. **$5.95.** Bookstores.

KEYS TO UNDERSTANDING AND TEACHING YOUR BIBLE (Thomas Nelson Publishers) For: L,S,Y. Slant: EP,D.

By **Thomas Fountain.** Hermeneutics—the study of the principles of interpreting the Bible—is usually the province of Bible colleges and seminaries. But Thomas Fountain presents these "keys" in a thoroughly understandable and interesting way. With emphasis on careful reading and right attitude, Fountain's guidebook opens up the intriguing background of the language of the Bible. He writes for both Bible teacher and student as he leads the reader through such special areas as Hebrew idioms, parables, allegories, and proverbs. Christ is clearly presented as the overriding key for interpreting any part of Scripture. Paperback. **$5.95.** Bookstores.

KING JAMES VERSION DEBATE (Baker Book House) For: L,C,S. Slant: EP.

By **D.A. Carson.** The first book-length refutation of propositions concerning the KJV such as: it is the most accurate version, it is the most durable version, it is the most reverent version, etc. **$3.95.** Bookstores or from **Baker Book House, P.O. Box 6287, Grand Rapids, MI 49506.**

A LAYMAN'S GUIDE TO INTERPRETING THE BIBLE (NavPress and Zondervan Publishing, co-publishers) For: L,C,S. Slant: EP,P.

By **Walter A. Henrichsen.** This practical manual is for those who want to learn the Bible's own guidelines for understanding the Scriptures clearly. "Biblical interpretation," says Robert Foster in his foreword, "is more than just an intellectual game that theologians play. It is the Christian life made full. Thanks to Walt Henrichsen for taking the subject out of the libraries of the seminaries...and bringing it down to where each of us is living today." This book is divided into three sections. The first examines 24 principles of interpretation. The second explains how to use the analytical, synthetic, topical, biographical, and verse analysis methods of Bible study. The last section describes the Bible student's roles as detective, decision maker, coordinator, and implementor. **$5.95.** Bookstores or from **NavPress, P.O. Box 6000, Colorado Springs, CO 80934.**

MEDITATION (NavPress) For: L,C,S. Slant: EP,P.

RESOURCES ON "HOW-TO-STUDY" THE BIBLE

By Jim Downing. God instructed Joshua to meditate on His Word day and night and to do it, and so experience success. But how does a person meditate on God's Word? In **Meditation**, Jim Downing, former Director of the Navigator ministry in Europe, the Middle East, and Africa, unfolds a step-by-step approach on how really to meditate on Scripture. He introduces biblical principles of meditation, communion and obedience—principles he has been practicing for decades. Over the years he has shared these principles with others who are convinced they work. **$2.50**. Bookstores or from **NavPress, P.O. Box 6000, Colorado Springs, CO 80934**.

MEN BEHIND THE KING JAMES VERSION (Baker Book House) For: L,C,S. Slant: EP.

By G.S. Paine. Only in this book will you make the acquaintance of all the major contributors to the KJV. Mr. Paine's book will delight any reader and draw out fresh appreciation of the KJV as a landmark in English as well as biblical literature. **$5.95**. Bookstores or from **Baker Book House, P.O. Box 6287, Grand Rapids, MI 49506**.

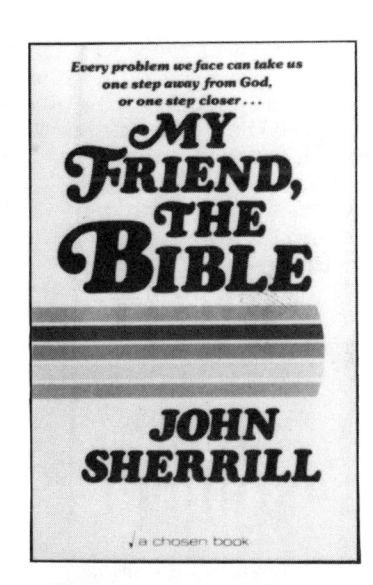

MY FRIEND, THE BIBLE (Chosen Books) For: L,C,S,Y. Slant: EP,P.

By John Sherrill. If you know the Bible can help you, and you want to unlock its treasures, **My Friend, The Bible** is the tool you need. This highly practical book offers specific material to help you reap the rewards promised you for expectant, faithful, daily Bible reading. Take advantage of "Power verses," prepare for victory with "Arsenal verses." Defend yourself against "Counterfeit Power Verses." **My Friend, The Bible** is John Sherrill's personal, searching account, written to help you find the direction you need. Sherrill learned to lean constantly on the Bible for power and hope even in the most desolate situations. This book can help you make the Bible your own. Awarded "Best Book: Personal Growth" by Campus Life. John Sherrill and his wife, Elizabeth, are well-known writers of classics like: **The Cross and The Switchblade, The Hiding Place,** and **God's Smuggler.** Paperback, catalog number 13064p. **$5.95**. Hardcover, catalog number 13064. **$7.95**. Bookstores or from **Zondervan, 1415 Lake Drive, SE, Grand Rapids, MI 49506**.

NATIONAL BIBLE WEEK (ANNUAL OBSERVANCE) (Laymen's National Bible Committee, Inc.) For: L,C,S,Y,Ch.

For forty-three years, National Bible Week has been observed as an interfaith celebration of the Bible in thousands of communities all across America. LNBC provides an assortment of biblical literature for distribution in local Bible Week observances and provides a national public service advertising campaign to unite the whole nation in a common effort to promote interest in Bible reading. It is intended that civic and religious groups of all faiths—anyone interested in the Bible—should unite in this activity. National Bible Week is always scheduled for the week in which America celebrates Thanksgiving, our only nonsectarian religious holiday. **Free.** To receive sample kit write to **Laymen's National Bible Committee, 815 Second Ave., New York, NY 10017**.

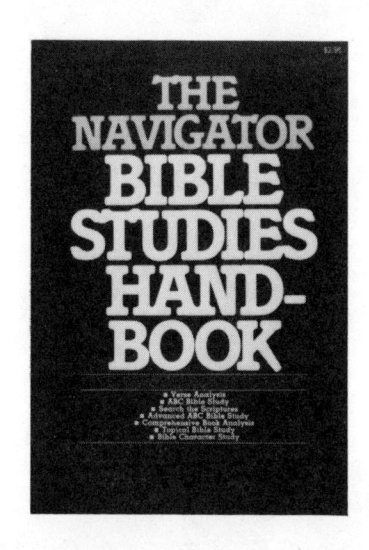

THE NAVIGATOR BIBLE STUDIES HANDBOOK (NavPress) For: L,C,S. Slant: EP,P.

Christians hungry for a deeper study of God's Word will find this handbook a treasure map to the Bible's riches. Included, with samples, are explanations of seven types of Bible study: from analyzing a verse to grasping an entire book; from studying passages to detailing specific topics or persons. An appendix contains reproducible masters of Bible study forms for the studies discussed. Also included are chapters explaining proper Bible study characteristics, fundamental beliefs about the Bible, and how to observe, interpret, and apply the truths of the Scripture. **$4.95**. Bookstores or from **NavPress, P.O. Box 6000, Colorado Springs, CO 80934**.

NEW LIFE BIBLE STUDIES IDEA BOOK (Tyndale House Publishers) For: L,S,W. Slant: AW,C,RC,F,EP,MP,LP,P,CP.

By Joyce Marie Smith. A handy resource book for women Bible study leaders, covering areas such as ministering to women's needs more effectively, setting up nursery care, developing leadership skills in your leaders, leading someone to the Lord, and developing a caring ministry among the women. 32 pages. **$2.50**. Bookstores.

PASSPORT TO THE BIBLE (Tyndale House Publishers) For: L,S. Slant: AW,C,RC,F,EP,MP,LP,D,P,CP.

By Bobi Hromas. By spending just five minutes a day studying God's Word, you'll find the Bible coming alive for you. **Passport to the Bible** is loaded with dozens of practical suggestions on how to read, understand, and apply the Bible to your everyday life. 160 pages. Trade paper. **$4.95**. Bookstores.

PERSONAL BIBLE STUDY (National Church Growth Research Center) For: L. Slant: EP,P.

A guide to learning how to study your Bible more effectively. It is written in a workbook format to encourage action as well as study. It leads the student of the Bible to learn for himself, giving him helpful experience as he goes through the book. The seven lessons may be used by an individual or in class. **$1.50** per copy. From: **National Church Growth Research Center, P.O. Box 17575, Washington, DC 20041**.

RESOURCES ON "HOW-TO-STUDY" THE BIBLE

PERSONAL BIBLE STUDY: A HOW TO (Moody Press) For: L,S,Y. Slant: EP,P,I,M.

By **Ruth Sun**. Intensely practical, this book bulges with how-to ideas for personal and group Bible study. **$4.95**. Bookstores or from **Moody Bookworld, 2101 W. Howard Street, Chicago, IL 60645**.

PREGUNTAS Y RESPUESTAS SOBRE LA BIBLIA (Liguori Publications) For: L. Slant: RC,P.

This book, written in Spanish, answers many of the most commonly asked questions about the Bible, dividing them into three themes: Old Testament, New Testament, and General. The author emphasizes the eternal value of the books inspired by God and offers a better understanding of salvation history. **$1.50** (quantity discounts available). Bookstores or from **Liguori Publications, One Liguori Drive, Liguori, MO 63057**.

READING SCRIPTURE AS THE WORD OF GOD, Second Edition (Servant Publications) For: L. Slant: P.

By **George Martin**. The original edition of this popular title sold over 100,000 copies! This second edition has been completely revised and updated by the author. In a style which is both easy to understand and interesting, George Martin offers practical help for getting started in Bible study, how to use study materials, how to keep going, and how to grow in your understanding and appreciation of God's Word. 188 pages, 5 1/4 x 8 inches. **$4.95**. Bookstores.

THE REWARDS OF BIBLE READING AND PRAYER (Scripture Union) For: L,S. Slant: EP,MP,D.

A helpful tool for beginning or improving your personal quiet time. The authors present you with a lively, easy-to-read summary of the process and benefits of daily devotions. Prayer and Bible reading are looked at closely and together, for in the Bible God speaks to you; in prayer you speak to Him. The authors demonstrate that if performed together, there are rewards for prayer and Bible reading—very real ones—including a better relationship with the heavenly Father. You are then given the opportunity to follow through on your commitment. The booklet ends with a ten-unit study through Philippians, your chance to experience the rewards of Bible reading and prayer right away. **$1.25**. From **Scripture Union, 1716 Spruce Street, Philadelphia, PA 19103**.

ROMANS: A MODEL FOR BIBLE STUDY METHODS (Moody Press) For: L,S. Slant: EP,P,S,I,M.

By **Lloyd M. Perry and Calvin B. Hanson**. A provocative, practical study guide for individuals and groups that not only is an examination of the book of Romans, but also a guide on how to study any Bible book! **$8.95**. Bookstores or from **Moody Bookworld, 2101 W. Howard Street, Chicago, IL 60645**.

SCRIPTURE-GRAM POSTCARDS (ALT Publishing Company) For: L,C,S,Y,Ch. Slant: AW,C,RC,F,EP,MP,LP,RJ,CJ,OJ,L,P.

Scripture-Gram Postcards are regulation-size postcards containing a Scripture quiz easily worked by persons of all ages on the front side. Back side is usual material found on back sides of postcards, including space for your own message and the address box. There are twelve cards per package. **$4.00**. From **ALT Publishing Co., P.O. Box 400, Green Bay, WI 54305**.

SELECTING A TRANSLATION OF THE BIBLE (Standard Publishing) For: L,C,S,Y. Slant: P.

Many Bible translations are available to today's Bible reader. Which is the best one for your personal needs? This book will help you decide based on accuracy, style, clarity, theological background and more. Contains reviews of the nine major versions currently in use including the New King James Version and the new Reader's Digest Version. The author helped translate the New International Version and the New King James Version. Code 39975. **$3.95**. Bookstores or from **Standard Publishing, 8121 Hamilton Ave., Cincinnati, OH 45231**.

SIXTY-NINE WAYS TO START A STUDY GROUP AND KEEP IT GOING (Zondervan Publishing House) For: L,C,S. Slant: EP.

RESOURCES ON "HOW-TO-STUDY" THE BIBLE

By Lawrence O. Richards. The hows, whys and wherefores of small groups is contained in this volume. **$3.95.** Bookstores or from **Zondervan Retail Marketing Service, 1420 Robinson Road, SE, Grand Rapids, MI 49506.**

SPECIAL EDUCATION SERIES (American Bible Society)

These Scripture selections are designed for persons of any age who have learning difficulties. Prepared in consultation with education specialists, these Scriptures are translated directly from New Testament Greek. Texts are in large print with simple vocabulary, easy sentence structure and phrase clusters. Two series are available: Series I with color photographs; and Series II with vivid drawings. Series I: Jesus Visits Two Friends, Order No. 06976, **$.08**; Love God, Love Others, Order No. 06977, **$.08.** Series II: The First Easter, Order No. 07066, **$.08**; The Lord My Shepherd, Order No. 07067, **$.08.** For a complete list or to order, write to **American Bible Society, Box 5656, Grand Central Station, New York, NY 10163.**

THE STUDY OF SACRED SCRIPTURE (Daughters of St. Paul) For: L,C,S. Slant: RC,P,S.

A concise study of Sacred Scripture: doctrinal aspects (Sacred Scripture, Tradition, Magisterium); present-day deviations; how Scripture should be read, studied and explained. 71 pages, number SC0446. Cloth. **$3.00.** Paper. **$2.00.** (Add **$.75** for postage). From Bookstores or **Daughters of St. Paul, 50 St. Paul's Avenue, Jamaica Plain, Boston, MA 02130.**

SUNDAY SCRIPTURE QUIZ (ALT Publishing Co.) For: L,C,Y,Ch. Slant: RC,MP,L,D,P.

A puzzle-type quiz based on each Sunday's readings at mass (Roman Catholic). Also used for Scripture study by students of all denominations. **$30.00** per year; **$60.00** for a three-year subscription covering the A,B,C cycles. From **ALT Publishing Co., P.O. Box 400, Green Bay, WI 54305.**

TAKE GOD'S WORD FOR IT (Regal Books) For: L,C,S. Slant: EP.

By John F. MacArthur, Jr. An excellent three-part exposition/study of the Bible, examining its authority, its trustworthiness, and its infallibility. It asks the following questions: Can you really take God's Word for what it says? What does God's Word do for you? How can you get the most from God's Word? While the book discusses the authority, infallibility and inerrancy of the Bible, it is not a defense of the Scriptures. Rather, it is a practical presentation of biblical truths with supporting data which a layman can understand. It helps the reader to be confident that he can take God's Word for what it says. This book focuses on changed lives as a primary evidence of its reliability. The first section looks at inspiration while examining the difference between the way God spoke through the original writers and the way He speaks and acts through individuals today. Secondly, it examines benefits of Scripture for believers. The author sees God's Word as the source of truth and freedom, as a guide to His will, a guide to growth and a means of victory over Satan. Finally, the last section is devoted to the practical application of Scripture. What does the Bible say, what does it mean, and how do I apply its truth to my daily life? The author provides readers with his own Bible study methods in the hope that they will see how careful study of Scripture will lead to a powerful, motivating faith. Includes discussion questions, key verses for each chapter. Has an appendix of useful tools for Bible study and offers Bible reading and study plans. 160 pages, no. S341107. Paperback. **$2.25.** Bookstores or from **Regal Books, Div. of GL Publications, 2300 Knoll Drive, Ventura, CA 93003.**

TEST YOUR BIBLE POWER (Ballantine Books) For: L,S,Y,Ch. Slant: F, EP, P.

Edited by Stanley Shank. Here are nearly 300 games, quiz questions, puzzles and other brain teasers. Challenges include identify famous quotes, search and find, true or false, crisscross puzzles, crossword puzzles, jumbles, multiple choice, acrostics, fill in the blank, graphs, finish the Proverb, etc. Dozens of subjects from Old and New Testaments covered. A wonderful award gift or teaching aid in Sunday School classes. Great for Bible study groups of all ages. For trivia buffs, teachers and students, and anyone who enjoys matching wits with the experts. An Epiphany Book from Ballantine. **$1.95.** Bookstores or from **Ballantine Books, 201 E. 50th Street, New York, NY 10022.**

THESE THINGS ARE WRITTEN: AN INTRODUCTION TO THE RELIGIOUS IDEAS OF THE BIBLE (John Knox Press) For: L,S. Slant: C,RC,EP, MP,LP,S,BC.

By James M. Efird. A helpful introductory examination to biblical study. Very clear and concise. Designed for the classroom and church use. Meets high standards of scholarly excellence. Paperback. **$6.95** (add **$1.00** shipping and handling, Georgia and Virginia add appropriate sales tax). Bookstores or from **John Knox Press, 341 Ponce de Leon Ave., Atlanta, GA 30365.**

THROUGH THE BIBLE IN A YEAR (American Tract Society) For: L,C, S,Y. Slant: AW,C,RC,F,EP,MP,LP,L, D,P,S,I,CP,H,M.

This tract provides a daily Bible reading schedule. Readers can read through the Bible chronologically in one year's time. The retail price varies from bookstore to bookstore, but usually is sold for **$.05** each. Bookstores or from **American Tract Society, P.O. Box 462008, Garland, TX 75046.**

RESOURCES ON "HOW-TO-STUDY" THE BIBLE

TOWARD UNDERSTANDING THE BIBLE (Faith and Life Press) For: L,C,S. Slant: P,BC.

By Perry Yoder. This study is intended as an introduction to hermeneutics (the study of the methodological principles of interpretation) for the lay person. In a chapter titled "Games People Play With The Bible," the author describes some of the approaches to the Bible that are common among lay people. He then shows how the correct meaning of the text can be found only by taking the author and his context seriously. The book treats crucial issues in biblical interpretation in a non-technical way. A good book for anyone interested in reading and understanding the Bible. **$2.45.** Bookstores or from **Faith and Life Press, Box 347, Newton, KS 67114.**

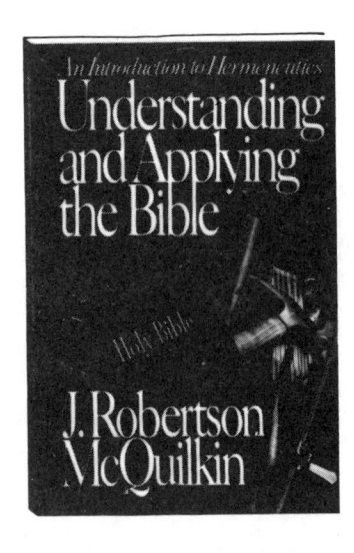

UNDERSTANDING AND APPLYING THE BIBLE (Moody Press) For: L,S. Slant: EP,P,S,I,M.

English-based textbook with guidelines to help the serious Bible student understand and apply Scripture with confidence, create their own commentaries. Teaches interpretation principles that are both simple and scholarly—and the practical skills necessary to put those principles to work. **$9.95.** Bookstores or from **Moody Bookworld, 2101 W. Howard Street, Chicago, IL 60645.**

UNDERSTANDING SCRIPTURE (Regal Books) For: L,C,S,Y. Slant: EP.

By A. Berkeley Mickelsen and Alvera M. Mickelsen. Combining their knowledge of Scripture and clear journalistic style, Alvera and Berkeley Mickelsen give every layperson an easy-to-understand handbook that will help them learn how to interpret and apply Scripture to their lives. This rewritten and enlarged edition of **Better Bible Study** includes questions and projects at the end of each chapter to help readers apply principles of biblical interpretation. The Mickelsens explore principles such as: What we can expect from Bible study; how to know what the Bible means; understanding figurative language, parables, allegories, poetry, prophecies; and building doctrine and theology. Paperback. 4 1/4 x 7 Inches. 176 pages, number 5017302. **$3.50.** Bookstores or from **Regal Books, Div. of GL Publications, 2300 Knoll Drive, Ventura, CA 93003.**

WALK THRU THE BIBLE SEMINARS (Walk Thru the Bible Ministries) For: L,C,S,Y. Slant: EP,MP,P.

Let's face it. Most Christians know many Bible stories and can name some of the people, places, events, and key spiritual truths contained in the Bible. But ask them to piece the story of the Bible together...or explain the significance of each Bible book...or apply God's Word to real-life situations, and they probably couldn't do it. Which is a pity, really, because all that can change in the space of a single day as you take a life-changing trip through the Old or New Testament with the help of a **Walk Thru the Bible Seminar.** Taught in a unique, fun, step-by-step way, a WTB Seminar moves too quickly to take notes. Yet in just one session you can remove any hesitation you've ever had about reading or studying God's Word. More than 400,000 have taken "the Walk." Isn't it about time you discovered what they are excited about? **$25.00** per individual adult; **$40.00** per married couple. Discounts apply for students, senior citizens, families, and those registering early. From **Walk Thru The Bible Ministries, Box 80587, Atlanta, GA 30366.**

WHAT THE BIBLE TEACHES ABOUT THE BIBLE (Tyndale House Publishers) For: L. Slant: AW,C,RC,F,EP,MP, LP,P,CP.

By H.D. McDonald. Who wrote the Bible? What is the meaning of inspiration and what are the facts about revelation? This is a study of the nature of the Bible itself, examining the Bible's own claims. A "Layman Series" book. 160 pages. Trade paper. **$3.95.** Bookstores.

WHAT TO DO ON THURSDAY (Presbyterian and Reformed Publishing Co.) For: L,S. Slant: C,F,P.

By Jay Adams. A layman's guide to the practical use of Scripture, here is sound advice that will help to make the Bible a practical book that can be used, not only on Sunday, but on Thursday—and every other day of the week. It will help solve in a biblical and systematic way, the problems encountered in daily life. In seeking biblical answers to the routine and not-so-routine problems of life, says Jay Adams, we must first have an awareness and a biblical understanding of every situation. Then we must be able to locate the passages from Scripture which speak to our problems, interpret them correctly, and finally, implement them in concrete situations. This practical and helpful book is actually a primer on the application of the Bible to everyday encounters. It will help you link biblical principles to practice in a systematic way. 149 pages. **$3.95.** Bookstores or from **Presbyterian and Reformed Publishing Company, P.O. Box 817, Phillipsburg, NJ 08865.**

WHO ME? LEAD A BIBLE STUDY? (Officers' Christian Fellowship of the USA) For: L,S. Slant: F.

By Joe Bayly. Five page pamphlet designed to offer basic principles of leading a group Bible study in an inductive manner. **Free.** Please send self addressed, stamped envelope to **Officers' Christian Fellowship, P.O. Box 36200, Denver, CO 80236.**

WHY AND HOW YOU SHOULD READ THE BIBLE (American Tract Society) For: L,C,S,Y. Slant: AW,C,F,EP, MP,L,D,P,S,I,CP,H,M.

This tract lists fourteen suggestions as to why and how you should read the Bible. It also includes helpful Scripture passages as a sort of "first aid to the injured." In addition, the plan of salvation is presented. The current retail price varies from bookstore to bookstore but usually is sold for **$.05** each. Bookstores or from **American Tract Society, P.O. Box 462008, Garland, TX 75046.**

THE WORD (Aglow Publications) For: L,W. Slant: CP.

The Bible has been compared to a two-edged sword, capable of dividing soul

RESOURCES ON "HOW-TO-STUDY" THE BIBLE

and spirit. It has been called a foundation, a hiding place, a fountain, a mirror and many other beautiful images. These are just a few of the discoveries for those who choose to examine the Bible in depth. This study not only encourages Christians to study the Bible, but shows us how to dig and find the rich nuggets of truth found on every page. No. 522004. **$2.95** (add 15% for postage plus **$1.00** for handling per order; Washington state residents add 7.3% sales tax). Ask for free catalog. Bookstores or from **Aglow Publications, P.O. Box I, Lynwood, WA 98036.**

THE WORD OF GOD: A GUIDE TO ENGLISH VERSIONS OF THE BIBLE (John Knox Press) For: L,C,S. Slant: C,RC,EP,MP,LP,P,S.

A guide book to ten of the most popular versions of the Bible (includes appendix devoted to the King James Version). The ten translations considered and their reviewers are: RSV (Bruce Metzger), New English (Roger Bullard), New Jewish (Keith Crim), New American Standard (Barclay Newman), Jerusalem (Bruce Vawter), Good News Bible (W.F. Stinespring), Living Bible (James Smart), New American (Walter Harrelson), New International Version (Robert B. Bratcher), King James (Roger Bullard). Six study Bibles are also compared in a special chapter. An excellent book for those asking the question, "Which Bible should I use?" Paperback. **$8.95** (add $1.00 for postage; Georgia and Virginia add sales tax). Bookstores or **John Knox Press Order Processing, 341 Ponce de Leon Ave., Atlanta, GA 30365.**

YEAR OF THE BIBLE MANUAL (Standard Publishing) For: L,C. Slant: P.

A complete manual to assist church leaders in planning Year of the Bible observances and activities. Contains introduction to the Year of the Bible, ten sermon outlines, 52 tips for promoting Bible reading and study, dramas, quotes about the Bible, clip art and more. No. 3036. **$1.95.** Bookstores or from **Standard Publishing, 8121 Hamilton Ave., Cincinnati, OH 45231.**

AUDIO-VISUAL BIBLE RESOURCES

For centuries, all of the aids to Bible reading and study were in the form of books and other written documents. However, today a growing number of resources are audio-visuals of one kind or another. This section is a "catch all" section for any Bible reading or Bible study aid that is not published and bound in some form. The section includes audio cassettes, video cassettes, films, filmstrips, slides, records, wall charts, flannelgraphs, overhead projection cells, Bible games, and computer programs. Because it is categorized by media instead of content, this section contains items which could very easily be listed in all of the other sections of this *Directory.* However, no items are cross referenced to other sections and no items are listed in more than one place. If the resource is primarily an audio-visual, it is listed in this section.

AUDIO-VISUAL BIBLE RESOURCES

ABBA EBAN READS THE PSALMS AND ECCLESIASTES (Spoken Arts, Inc.) For: L,C,S. Slant: RJ,CJ,OJ, D,P.

Ambassador Eban reads the passages in English and Hebrew. A knowledge of the latter language isn't necessary for appreciation of these portions because his voice is so lyrical that it takes the form of music. The English sections are read with rare insight. Enjoyable and inspirational for all ages. LP format only, number SA757. **$9.95.** From **Spoken Arts, Inc. 310 North Avenue, New Rochelle, NY 10801.**

ACTS OF THE APOSTLES (Christian Media) For: L,C,S. Slant: RC,P,S,CP.

By Fr. Richard Rohr, O.F.M. A continuation of Luke. The age of the church, and how Jesus' spirit-filled community first lived the good news, and brought it to the world. Ten audio lessons. **$40.00.** Nine video lessons (Beta II or VHS; U-Matic available on request). **$450.00.** Please state format. Add **$4.00** for shipping. Prepaid orders only. From **Christian Media, P.O. Box 748, Ogden, UT 84402.**

THE ACTS OF THE APOSTLES (Thomas More Cassettes) For: L,C,S. Slant: RC.

Todd Brennan reads the text and an introduction by John L. McKenzie. Professional narrator Todd Brennan's skillful reading of the complete text and an insightful introduction written by the renowned Scripture scholar John L. McKenzie make this program one of the most compelling in our biblical series. The importance of the "Acts" cannot be exaggerated. With its key themes of growth, catholicism and reconciliation, its doctrinal contributions to Salvation, Christology and the Sacraments, and its emphasis on the guiding presence of the Holy Spirit, it is not surprising that it is often called the "Gospel of the Church." TM244. Two cassettes, approximately two hours. **$17.95.** From **Thomas More Association, 225 W. Huron St., Chicago, IL 60610.**

ACTS OF THE APOSTLES—ENDUED WITH POWER (Revivaltime Media Ministries) For: L. Slant: EP,D,P.

From the **Every Day With Jesus** Bible study series, this cassette study system offers an exciting adventure into the Book of Acts (New King James Version). Revivaltime and Every Day With Jesus speaker, Dan Betzer opens a new world of practical Bible study with programmed eight-to ten-minute segments on four 90-minute tapes. Just right for "devotional breaks" at your convenience in your home, office, or car. Tapes come in a graphically designed library case. Write to producer for information and/or current price list. From **Revivaltime Media Ministries, P.O. Box 70, Springfield, MO 65801.**

AMERICAN STANDARD BIBLE ON CASSETTES (Star Bible Publications) For: L. Slant: F,EP,MP,D,P.

ASV New Testament with Psalms (read by Sexton). Sixteen tapes. Catalog Number BCL-108. **$49.50** each. Bookstores or from **Star Bible Publications, Box 181220, Ft. Worth, TX 76118.**

AMERICAN STANDARD BIBLE ON CASSETTES (Star Bible Publications) For: L. Slant: F,EP.

ASV Old Testament Complete (read by Jennings). Forty-six tapes. Catalog Number BCL-109. **$107.50.** Bookstores or from **Star Bible Publications, Box 181220, Ft. Worth, TX 76118.**

AN INTRODUCTION TO SCRIPTURE (Servant Publications) For: L. Slant: P.

By George Martin. A five cassette album companion to **Reading Scripture as the Word of God.** Combines a survey of the major books, characters, and events of the Bible with practical advice for reading and studying Scripture. Ideal for individual and group use. Contains a study guide. **$29.95.** Bookstores.

THE ART OF STORYTELLING IN THE BIBLE (CSI Publications) For: L,C. Slant: C,EP.

By Sheri Haan. Professional Advancement in Christian Education (PACE), Module #3 is for teacher inservice education (individual or small group). Detailed ways to improve story telling abilities through nine practice sessions. Includes book and two cassette tapes demonstrating effective story telling techniques. Forty-three pages. Paper. Bible module. **$4.20.** Two tapes correlated with Bible module. **$8.20.** (School discounts available). From **CSI Publications, 3350 East Paris Ave., SE, P.O. Box 8709, Grand Rapids, MI 49508.**

AS I HAVE LOVED YOU (GOSPEL OF JOHN) (Christian Media) For: L,C,S. Slant: RC,P,S,CP.

By Rev. Jim Wolff. In this series by Fr. Wolff he explores the meaning of our loving "as I have loved you"—as we are loved by the Father. Our relationship with the Father is beautifully brought out. Eight audio lessons. **$32.00.** Eight video lessons (Beta II or VHS; U-Matic available on request). **$400.00.** Please state format. Add **$4.00** for shipping. Prepaid orders only. From **Christian Media, P.O. Box 748, Ogden, UT 84402.**

AS RAIN IN THE DESERT BRINGS HOPE (The Psalms in Song) (Daughters of St. Paul) For: L,C,S,Y. Slant: RC, EP,MP,L,D.

New Psalm-songs for liturgical worship and enjoyment. While a mood of praise and prayer pervades throughout, the tempo moves from the lively refrains of "Not to Us" (Ps. 115), to the mellow harmony of "The Lord is My Joy" (Ps. 118), to the spirited finale of "As Rain in the Desert Brings Hope" (Ps. 126). Each arrangement adds a refreshing brightness to ageless biblical prayers. Length 40 minutes. Stereo-cassette, CS0865. **$6.50.** Stereo record, RE0015. **$7.50.** Songbook, MU0012. **$5.95.** Add **$1.00** for postage. Bookstores or from **Daughters of St. Paul, 50 St. Paul's Avenue, Jamaica Plain, Boston, MA 02130.**

AUDIO CASSETTE CATALOG (Bible Cassette Library, Inc.) For: L,C,S,Y, Ch. Slant: C,F,EP,MP,D,P,I,BC,M.

Bible teaching on cassette tape... A most practical way to study the Scriptures and biblical truth. This resource of indepth and conservative Bible teaching on cassettes now totals over 4,300 messages of over 100 of the best Bible teachers and expositors in America, i.e., MacArthur, Strauss, Hindson, McGee, Barnhouse, Pentecost, and others. We loan our messages to people in all walks of life. We send cassettes to prisoners across America, many of whom cannot read. We are providing new materials for Bible study

AUDIO-VISUAL BIBLE RESOURCES

groups, counselors, pastors, teachers, and families. Marriages are being saved by applying the biblical principles. The ministry is expanding as many new people each month ask for our services and products. Also, we are exploring new ways to communicate God's Word using modern technology, including video cassettes and microfilm. Church communicators across America are getting in on this new and dynamic resource. If you would like our catalog of messages or have tapes you would like us to consider for our library, write us. Request **Audio Cassette Catalog**, and include a tax deductible gift of **$2.00**. From **Bible Cassette Library, 524 Sycamore Circle, Ridgeland, MS 39157**.

BAPTISM IN THE NEW TESTAMENT (Christian Media) For: L,C,S. Slants: RC,P,S,CP.

By Rev. Joseph Lackner, S.M. Unless we be born again by water and the Spirit, our Lord tells us, we cannot enter the Kingdom. Fr. Lackner will carefully explore what the New Testament tells us concerning the first of the Christian sacraments. Five audio lessons. **$20.00**. Five video lessons (Beta II or VHS; U-Matic available on request). Please state format. **$250.00**. Add **$4.00** for shipping. Prepaid orders only. From **Christian Media, P.O. Box 748, Ogden, UT 84402**.

BEFORE YOU SAY, I DO (Training Church Leaders, Inc.) For: L,C,S,Y. Slant: EP,P.

By Dan DeHaan. A vital series packed full of positive principles for establishing lasting relationships. Scores of churches are using this study in their youth meetings and many universities are finding the study used by God to change lives. This comprehensive study covers areas from what the Bible says a guy and girl should be before marriage to creative ideas for dates. Titles of sessions are: Introduction; Guidelines for Singles; Bliss of Singleness; Love Is...; Infatuation versus Love; Love versus Sex; Symptoms of No Standards; Setting Standards; Creative Dating; and Questions and Answers. Audio cassettes. **$27.35**. Also available on video—write for rental or purchase information. From **Training Church Leaders, Inc., 6080 New Peachtree Road, Atlanta, GA 30340**.

THE BIBLE: A PROGRESS REPORT (Thomas More Cassettes) For: L,C,S. Slant: RC.

By John L. McKenzie. A report on the status of current biblical research—the area which is making new findings which shed so interesting but often troublesome light on the Scriptures as we have understood them. Has biblical scholarship gone as far as it can go? TM 136. One hour. **$9.95**. From **Thomas More Association, 225 W. Huron St., Chicago, IL 60610**.

BIBLE BACKGROUNDS FILMSTRIPS (Sixteen Sound Filmstrips) (Moody Institute of Science) For: L. Slant: EP.

Four sets of 35mm sound filmstrips: Set I, Petra, Temples, Tyre, Babylon; Set II, Byblos, Tombs, Egypt I, Rome; Set III, Baalbek I, Egypt II, Greece, Baalbek II; Set IV, Greek Gods, Palmyra, Jordan, Pompeii. Filmstrip, cassette and guide in vinyl case. Set of four filmstrips. **$53.00**. Individual titles. **$14.95**. All prices plus postage. Bookstores, film rental libraries or from **Moody Institute of Science, 12000 E. Washington Blvd., Whittier, CA 90606**.

BIBLE CITIES AND GEOGRAPHY FILMSTRIPS & SLIDES (Star Bible Publications) For: L,C,S. Slant: F, EP, P, S.

By Harvey Porter. The Harvey Porter film series on Bible Cities and Geography is the product of ten years travel and research. The pictures are the best from a collection of several thousand slides from Bible Lands. Catalog Number 974, all ten filmstrips with narration on cassettes. **$100.00**. Catalog Number 975, all ten slides sets with narration on cassettes. **$135.00**. Bookstores or from **Star Bible Publications, Box 181220, Ft. Worth, TX 76118**.

BIBLE LISTENING PROGRAM (Hosanna) For: L,C,S. Slant: F,EP,D,P,I,CP.

In 1977 Hosanna Ministries encouraged several churches to try a unique concept in Bible study, the **Bible Listening Program**. The churches involved reported dramatic results. The general spiritual level increased. Attendance went up. Pastors were counseling more people. One church reported a cash surplus for the first time in its history. The pastors gave direct credit to the **Bible Listening Program**. Simplicity is one reason for this program's effectiveness. With only 45 minutes of listening a day, you can go through the entire New Testament in one month. Time spent driving to work, cleaning the house, washing dishes, can now be Bible study time. Think what could happen if every Christian in this country went through the New Testament every month! You can purchase these high quality recordings of the New Testament for your church for only **$12.00** each plus shipping. Already several thousand churches have responded to our Bible Listening offer. We at Hosanna want to make this offer available to every church in America. Help get a **Bible Listening Program** started in your church today. Designate King James or Revised Standard Version. One, **$20.00**. Six, **$77.00**. Eighteen, **$228.00**. Twenty-five, **$312.00**. Prices include shipping. Old Testament also available. From **Hosanna, 146 Quincy, NE, Albuquerque, NM 87108**.

BIBLE MAPS AND CHARTS (Standard Publishing) For: L,C,S. Slant: P.

Colorful, attractive classroom wall maps and charts for Bible study. Convenient size, interesting illustrations, simple designs, bold lines and bright colors. Old Testament maps and charts contain 7 maps and 4 charts. New Testament maps and charts contains 8 maps and 4 charts. Old Testament (2607) or New Testament (2608) **$7.95** each. Bookstores or from **Standard Publishing, 8121 Hamilton Ave., Cincinnati, OH 45231**.

BIBLE MEMORY CARDS (Standard Publishing) For: L,Y,Ch. Slant: P.

Beatitudes, Books of the Bible, Lord's Prayer, Shepherd Psalm (23rd) and Ten Commandments. Complete texts with full-color illustration. **$.10** each; **$1.00** per dozen; **$7.50** per 100. Codes 1015—1019 respectively. Bookstores or from **Standard Publishing, 8121 Hamilton Ave., Cincinnati, OH 45231**.

BIBLE MEMORY CHARTS (Standard Publishing) For: L,Y,Ch. Slant: P.

Six colorful charts: The Complete Beatitudes, Books of the Bible, Lord's Prayer, Shepherd's Prayer, Ten Commandments, and words and music for the song, "The Twelve Apostles." 19 x 25 inches and storage envelope. Code 2614. **$4.95**. Bookstores or from **Standard Publishing, 8121 Hamilton Ave., Cincinnati, OH 45231**.

AUDIO-VISUAL BIBLE RESOURCES

BIBLE QUESTIONS ANSWERED A TO Z (Star Bible Publications) For: L. Slant: F,EP,P,S.

By James R. Jarrell. James Robert Jarrell answers questions that were actually put to him from radio audiences, correspondents, or from members of the congregations where he has been preaching for over 20 years. He does not side-step any issue that is put before him, but hits head-on hundreds of questions on Bible-related subjects, from Abortion to Zoroastrianism. 160 pages. No. 2063. **$2.95.** Bookstores or from **Star Bible Publications, Box 181220, Ft. Worth, TX 76118.**

BIBLE SEARCH COMPUTER SOFTWARE (Scripture Software) For: L,C,S,Y. Slant: AW,C,F,EP,MP,L,D,P,S,I,CP,H,M.

A program for the home computer that allows analysis of Scripture in ways never before possible, yet requires no computer background. Capabilities allow user to display or print any portion of Bible text from disk files, scan the text for topics desired, and edit and retain for future use reference lists of verses selected. Among its other features is the ability to add, delete, and flag single references as well as load the text for references in the list into the program so verses can be seen all at once. If desired, verses can then be printed (on user's line printer) with multiple copies for use in a group Bible study. Program currently requires a TRS-80 (TM of Tandy Corp.) Model I or III with 48K memory and 2 disk drives. For more information send for free flyer. Software, comprehensive instruction manual and KJV New Testament database. **$140.00.** Old Testament available separately in late 1983. From **Scripture Software, P.O. Box 6131-C, Dept. BR, Orlando, FL 32853.**

BIBLE STUDY CASSETTES (The Bible Study Hour) For: L. Slant: EP,D,P.

Over 1,500 Bible Study Cassette titles are available by Bible Study Hour founder Dr. Donald Grey Barnhouse and speaker Dr. James Montgomery Boice. Each features unique and practical Bible study material as gleaned from the Bible Study Hour radio broadcast. Studies (for individuals or groups) include: Foundations of the Christian Faith; the 270-part study on John; How the Holy Spirit relates to You; Sex, Marriage and Divorce; Romans (456 messages); Prophecy and the Bible; the Psalms; and Genesis. Each cassette features two messages and can be purchased individually or as part of an entire study series. The Bible Study Hour was founded in 1949 to help people understand God's Word better through a practical yet in-depth study of His Word. Two messages per cassette. **$4.00** each; three for **$11.00**. Write for free catalog listing 1500 titles. From **The Bible Study Hour, 1716 Spruce Street, Philadelphia, PA 19103.**

BIBLE STUDY HOUR VIDEO (The Bible Study Hour) For: L. Slant: EP,D,P.

Bible Study Hour video offers Bible Study Hour speaker James M. Boice's in-depth Bible study material for church, Sunday school, and Bible study groups. The current two offerings include the practical and evangelistic study on **John: Part I** and the Christian growth series on **Getting to Know God. John: Part I** features Dr. Boice's warm messages on telling others about Christ, as well as challenging you in knowing your faith better. **Getting to Know God** is an excellent overview of the inerrancy of Scripture, the attributes of God, and Creation. Both series are 13 parts in length. Study manuals are also available. Bible Study Hour video is a part of Bible Study Hour ministries, including Dr. Boice's weekly Bible Study Hour radio broadcast, audio cassettes, and **Bible Studies** magazine. The Bible Study Hour was founded by Dr. Donald Grey Barnhouse in 1949. Rental for 13 week-series. **$260.00.** Purchase of 13-part series. **$995.00.** Study Manuals. **$1.95** each. From **The Bible Study Hour, 1716 Spruce Street, Philadelphia, PA 19103.**

BIBLE THEMES ON CASSETTE (Baptism and Confirmation in the Light of the Bible) (Daughters of St. Paul) For: L,C,S,Y. Slant: RC,D,P.

Scripture passages and commentary which emphasize the importance of these two sacraments and the transformation they bring about in us. Length approximately thirty minutes. **$5.95** (add **$.75** for postage). Bookstores or from **Daughters of St. Paul, 50 St. Paul's Ave., Jamaica Plain, Boston, MA 02130.**

BIBLE THEMES ON CASSETTE (Charismatic Gifts) (Daughters of St. Paul) For: L,C,S,Y. Slant: RC,EP,MP,D,P.

A reflection and commentary on Chapters 12-14 of St. Paul's Letter to Corinthians, which contain his teaching on the importance, value and use of charismatic gifts. Length approximately thirty minutes. Number CS0140. **$5.95** (add **$.75** for postage). Bookstores or from **Daughters of St. Paul, 50 St. Paul's Avenue, Jamaica Plain, Boston, MA 02130.**

BIBLE THEMES ON CASSETTE (Christ is God—What Can He Do For Us?) (Daughters of St. Paul) For: L,C,S,Y. Slant: RC,D,P.

A commentary on those Scripture passages which present Jesus as true God and true Man. The question, "Who is Jesus?" is also discussed as an invitation for us to deepen our relationship with Him. Length approximately thirty minutes. Number CS0150. **$5.95** (add **$.75** for postage). Bookstores or from **Daughters of St. Paul, 50 St. Paul's Ave., Jamaica Plain, Boston, MA 02130.**

BIBLE THEMES ON CASSETTE (Christian Historic Person) (Daughters of St. Paul) For: L,C,S,Y. Slant: RC,EP,MP,D,P.

Readings from various sources (both non-Christian and Christian) which give historical proofs for Christ's existence. Length approximately thirty minutes. Number CS0160. **$5.95** (add **$.75** for postage). Bookstores or from **Daughters of St. Paul, 50 St. Paul's Ave., Jamaica Plain, Boston, MA 02130.**

BIBLE THEMES ON CASSETTE (The Eucharistic Celebration) (Daughters of St. Paul) For: L,C,S,Y. Slant: RC,D,P.

A thorough, up-to-date explanation of the Mass with Scripture quotes and commentary. Length approximately thirty minutes. Number CS0170. **$5.95** (add **$.75** for postage). Bookstores or from **Daughters of St. Paul, 50 St.

AUDIO-VISUAL BIBLE RESOURCES

Paul's Ave., Jamaica Plain, Boston, MA 02130.

BIBLE THEMES ON CASSETTE (Family, State and Church in the Light of the Bible) (Daughters of St. Paul) For: L,C,S,Y. Slant: RC,D,P.

Scripture passages and commentary on the place of the Christian in the three societies that are necessary for his well-being: the family, civic society (that is, the state) and religious society (that is, the church). Two cassettes, approximately thirty minutes each. Part I, Family and State, Number CS0180; and Part II, The Church, Number CS0190. **$5.95** each (add **$.75** for postage). Bookstores or from **Daughters of St. Paul, 50 St. Paul's Ave., Jamaica Plain, Boston, MA 02130.**

BIBLE THEMES ON CASSETTE (Jesus' Miracles) (Daughters of St. Paul) For: L,C,S,Y. Slant: RC,P.

Scripture passages and commentary on the miracles Jesus worked to cure those with physical and spiritual afflictions. Length approximately 30 minutes. Number CS0220. **$5.95** (add **$.75** for postage). Bookstores or from **Daughters of St. Paul, 50 St. Paul's Ave., Jamaica Plain, Boston, MA 02130.**

BIBLE THEMES ON CASSETTE (Mary in the Light of the Bible) (Daughters of St. Paul) For: L,C,S,Y. Slant: RC, D,P.

The admiration and praise which is due Mary as the Mother of God is presented with Scripture quotes and commentary. Length approximately thirty minutes. Number CS0230. **$5.95** (add **$.75** for postage). Bookstores or from **Daughters of St. Paul, 50 St. Paul's Ave., Jamaica Plain, Boston, MA 02130.**

BIBLE THEMES ON CASSETTE (The Mystery of Suffering and the Gift of Joy) (Daughters of St. Paul) For: L,C,S,Y. Slant: RC,D,P.

Scripture passages and commentary on how a Christian can possess joy, hope and peace, even in the midst of trial and suffering. Length approximately thirty minutes. Number CS0250. **$5.95** (add **$.75** for postage). Book-stores or from **Daughters of St. Paul, 50 St. Paul's Ave., Jamaica Plain, Boston, MA 02130.**

BIBLE THEMES ON CASSETTE (The Mystery of the Eucharist in the Light of the Bible) (Daughters of St. Paul) For: L,C,S,Y. Slant: RC,D,P.

Scripture passages and commentary on Christ's Real Presence in the Holy Eucharist. Length approximately thirty minutes. Number CS0240. **$5.95** (add **$.75** for postage). Bookstores or from **Daughters of St. Paul, 50 St. Paul's Ave., Jamaica Plain, Boston, MA 02130.**

BIBLE THEMES ON CASSETTE (Penance and Reconciliation in the Light of the Bible) (Daughters of St. Paul) For: L,C,S,Y. Slant: RC,D,P.

Scripture passages and commentaries which stress God's readiness to forgive us as a loving Father. Also stressed are the Scripture passages which declare that we have been redeemed through Jesus Christ, our intercesssor with the Father. Length approximately thirty minutes. Number CS0280. **$5.95** (add **$.75** for postage). Bookstores or from **Daughters of St. Paul, 50 St. Paul's Ave., Jamaica Plain, Boston, MA 02130.**

BIBLE THEMES ON CASSETTE (Prayer in the Light of the Bible) (Daughters of St. Paul) For: L,C,S,Y. Slant: RC, EP, MP, D, P.

The power of prayer is a theme that recurs often in the Bible. The importance of prayer and how to improve one's prayer are included in this Scriptural commentary. Length approximately thirty minutes. Number CS0290. **$5.95** (add **$.75** for postage). Bookstores or from **Daughters of St. Paul, 50 St. Paul's Ave., Jamaica Plain, Boston, MA 02130.**

BIBLE THEMES ON CASSETTE (Sermon on the Mount) (Daughters of St. Paul) For: L,C,S,Y. Slant: RC,EP, MP,D,P.

The Sermon on the Mount (Matthew: Chapters 5-7) with introduction, commentary and closing prayer. Length approximately thirty minutes. Number CS0310. **$5.95** (add **$.75** for postage). Bookstores or from **Daughters of St. Paul, 50 St. Paul's Ave., Jamaica Plain, Boston, MA 02130.**

BIBLICAL METHODOLOGY AND INTERPRETATION (Catholic Education Center) For: L,C,S. Slant: RC,BC.

By Dr. David Noel Freedman. Dr. Freedman approaches this presentation by posing three main questions: What is the nature of biblical materials and how should we treat them? What do you do with a text you can't read? What is the integrity of the text and how do we deal with it? These questions are posed as biblical scholars analyze the early tradition and historical accuracy of the Old Testament. Length is 62 minutes. Rental in Beta I and U-Matic formats. **$15.00.** Purchase in all common video formats. **$70-$100.00.** From **Catholic Education Center, Media Department, 328 W. Sixth Street, St. Paul, MN 55102.**

BIBLICAL PROVERBS (Daughters of St. Paul) For: L,C,S,Y. Slant: D,P.

These maxims on human and divine wisdom for right living are read with appropriate introduction and closing prayer. Length approximately thirty minutes. Number CS0130. **$5.95** (add **$.75** for postage). Bookstores or from **Daughters of St. Paul, 50 St. Paul's Ave., Jamaica Plain, Boston, MA 02130.**

BIBLICAL SPIRITUALITY (Dove Publications) For: L,C,S. Slant: RC,P.

This set of five cassettes helps us root our spirituality in the central insights and convictions of the Bible: freedom; personal meeting with God; reaching God through prayer and thanks; sonship and brotherhood; reconciliation with a vulnerable God. Books explored by Donald Mouton, FSC (president of the College of Santa Fe) are Exodus, Leviticus, Job, Psalms, Jonah, parables of Jesus, the death/resurrection of Jesus. **$16.00** (add **$1.30** for postage). From **Dove Publications, Pecos, NM 87552.**

THE BOOK OF JOB (Thomas More Cassettes) For: L,C,S. Slant: RC.

Narration by John McGiver. Commentary by John L. McKenzie. The distinguished actor John McGiver reads generous portions of Job—almost two hours from the splendid Jerusalem translation. Father McKenzie's commentary is designed to put the book in the broader context of the Bible but also to probe the theological implications. "Will cast exciting contemporary light upon one of the more neglected portions of the Bible."—**Today's Parish**. Three cassettes approximately two and one-half hours. TM159 and TM160. **$16.95**. From **Thomas More Association, 225 W. Huron St., Chicago, IL 60610.**

THE BOOK OF JOB, THE BOOK OF JONAH (Christian Media) For: L,C,S. Slant: RC,P,S,CP.

By Bro. Donald Mouton, F.S.C. These presentations will explore the significance of the theological message of these masterpieces of the Hebrew Scriptures for our Christian faith. The Jonah parable and the Job poem vividly portray some of the most fundamental dimensions of the biblical faith. Four audio lessons. **$16.00**. Four video lessons (Beta II or VHS; U-Matic available on request). **$210.00**. Please state format. Add **$4.00** shipping. Prepaid orders only. From **Christian Media, P.O. Box 748, Ogden, UT 84402.**

THE BOOK OF REVELATION (Christian Media) For: L,C,S. Slant: RC,P,S,CP.

By Rev. Frank Montalbano, O.M.I. An introduction to the Apocalyptic (Old and New Testament) fundamentalism and dispensationalism. It is continually emphasized "What does this book say to us today?" Ten audio lessons. **$40.00**. Ten video lessons (Beta II or VHS; U-Matic available on request). **$475.00**. Please state format. Add **$4.00** shipping. Prepaid orders only. From **Christian Media, P.O. Box 748, Ogden, UT 84402.**

THE BOOK OF REVELATION (Thomas More Cassettes) For: L,C,S. Slant: RC.

Narration by Todd Brennan. Commentary by John L. McKenzie. Professional narrator Todd Brennan presents the complete Book of Revelation on one cassette. A careful listening is rewarding in its own right but used in conjunction with **The Book of Revelation** cassette by John L. McKenzie, in which the eminent biblical scholar discusses and analyzes the same text, it can be especially illuminating. Two cassettes, approximately two hours. TM61 and TM211. **$16.95**. From **Thomas More Association, 225 W. Huron St., Chicago, IL 60610.**

THE BOOK OF SIRACH: WISDOM FROM THE OLD TESTAMENT (Christian Media) For: L,C,S. Slant: RC,P,S.

By Sr. Celia Deutsch, N.D.S. This series develops the rich theme of wisdom in the book of Sirach, and how this book reflects on wisdom and presents it in a new way. The true nature of wisdom is explored by using various texts in this book. There are different levels in wisdom which are outlined. Wisdom is shown as a gift of God available to all who will acknowledge and accept her. Pride is shown to be the great obstacle to seeking wisdom. The great wealth of wisdom is shown throughout the text. Four audio lessons. **$16.00**. Four video lessons (Beta II or VHS; U-Matic available on request). **$210.00**. Please state format. Add **$4.00** shipping. Prepaid orders only. From **Christian Media, P.O. Box 748, Ogden, UT 84402.**

THE BOOK THAT WOULD NOT BURN (International Films) For: L,S,Y. Slant: F,EP,MP,LP.

Ranivo, a teenager in a Madagascar village, sees her people's lives transformed as they read the missionaries' Bibles. Hundreds of people become Christians. The queen, however, is suspicious of this new faith. Soon Bibles are being burned and the Christians tortured and killed unless they renounce their faith. Ranivo, though fearing persecution, wants the same peace of heart shared by her Christian friends. When her turn comes to die, God intervenes—to allow this true story to be told to succeeding generations. This powerful mission emphasis film shows the importance of memorized Scripture and faithfulness despite persecution. Rental. **$30.00**. Also available in Spanish. Film rental libraries.

CAMPSITES OF VICTORY (Faith Venture Visuals, Inc.) For: L,C,S,Y,Ch. Slant: D,P.

A study on the book of Joshua which can be broken into five to thirteen lessons. The set includes 12 transparencies and 24 masters for additional transparencies, and a human interest story about the camping adventures of Uncle Chad and his twelve Sunday school boys. This expositional Bible study can be used for summer Bible school, camps, junior church, home Bible studies, church services, school assemblies and five-day clubs. **$21.50**.

AUDIO-VISUAL BIBLE RESOURCES

Bookstores or from **Faith Venture Visuals, Inc., P.O. Box 423, 510 E. Main Street, Lititz, PA 17543.**

CAMPUS CRUSADE FOR CHRIST MEDIA RESOURCE CATALOG For L,C,S,Y. Slant: EP,P.

Campus Crusade for Christ International is an interdenominational movement of Christians committed to taking the gospel to the nations. For more than 30 years, we've helped train and equip Christians to more effectively share the good news of God's love and forgiveness through Jesus Christ. To help believers from all walks of life grow in their relationship with Christ, we've developed a variety of excellent, biblically based training materials. A Media Resource Catalog—cassette tapes and albums, films and videotapes on discipleship, evangelism and the Spirit-filled life—is free on request. **Free**. Call toll free (800) 392-7542, except California (714) 886-5224, ext. 1118. Or write **Marketing Services (60-10), Campus Crusade for Christ International, Arrowhead Springs, San Bernardino, CA 92414.**

A CELEBRATION OF VISION (Catholic Education Center) For: L,C,S. Slant: RC,D,S.

By Eugene LaVerdiere, SSS. This presentation addresses primarily the relationship of vision to symbol, and the relation of symbol and vision to Scripture. Eugene LaVerdiere explains scriptural symbols that speak to him presently and that are relevant for the future. The distinction is made between the manifestation of God in the Old and New Testament. Length 33 minutes. Rental for Beta I and U-Matic formats. **$15.00**. Purchase in all common video formats. **$70-$100.00**. From **Catholic Education Center, Media Department, 328 W. Sixth Street, St. Paul, MN 55102.**

THE CHALLENGE OF THE BEATITUDES (ROA Filmstrip Co.) For: L,C,Y. Slant: RC,P.

This catechetical program presents the Beatitudes in their scriptural context as part of the teaching of Jesus on the Kingdom of God. Each filmstrip contributes to building a total Beatitude catechesis, defining both "Kingdom" and "Beatitude." The program considers the Beatitudes as Jesus' plan for realizing the Kingdom of God and

AUDIO-VISUAL BIBLE RESOURCES

discusses them as a simple, practical guide for reaching that goal. Objectives: to understand the Beatitudes as practical guides for Christian living; to create an understanding and appreciation of the meanings of Kingdom; to deepen awareness of the Beatitudes as presented in Scripture; to develop a deeper relationship with Jesus. Main audience: Grades 4 to 8. Eight filmstrips, eight cassettes or records, eight teacher's guides. **$180.00.** From **ROA Filmstrip Co., 6633 W. Howard St., Niles, IL 60648.**

CHRIST IN THE GOSPELS (Dove Publications) For: L,C,S. Slant: RC.

This set of thirteen cassettes presents the Old Testament background to the Synoptics as well as the particular background of each of the four evangelists and its influence on his writing. Jesus is revealed as Messiah, Son of Man, Prophet, and Son of God. The speaker, Fr. Albert Zsigmond, is a professor, pastor, and lecturer. **$42.00** (add **$2.52** for postage). From **Dove Publications, Pecos, NM 87552.**

CHRISTIAN VIDEO TAPES CATALOG (Christian Video Service) For: L,C,Y. Slant: EP,P.

Hundreds of video taped presentations available in either VHS or beta format. May be either purchased or rented. Variety of topics: youth, soul-winning, teacher training, inspirational, doctrinal, motivational, exegetical, women's classes, leadership training, etc. Rental rates are **$5.00** per presentation, and purchase is **$15.00** plus **$5.00** per presentation. Catalog. **$2.00** (applied to first order). From **Christian Video Service, Box 4174, Lancaster, CA 93539.**

THE CHRISTIAN WAY IN LUKE AND ACTS (Christian Media) For: L,C,S. Slant: RC,P,S,CP.

By Rev. William Kurz, S.J. The Christian way is the journey followed by Jesus in response to the will of the Father. All Christians are called to follow the same way in faith, trusting in the love of God for strength and support. The Christian is shown to be both a steward and a servant which involves considerable sacrifice of self. The way leads one to the cross, but it also leads to victory. It is the victory that was promised by Pentecost to those who would accept and persevere in a commitment to the cause of Christ. Ten audio lessons. **$40.00.** Ten video lessons (Beta II or VHS; U-Matic available on request). **$475.00.** Please state format. Add **$4.00** shipping. Prepaid orders only. From **Christian Media, P.O. Box 748, Ogden, UT 84402.**

THE CHRISTIAN'S WALK IN THE EIGHTIES (Moody Institute of Science) For: L,C. Slant: EP.

Album of four audio cassettes in vinyl cover with study guide. Speakers are Dr. John MacArthur, Jr., Dr. Earl Radmacher, and Dr. Gordon MacDonald. The Bible is specifically dealt with in "Learning from God" cassette. **$23.95.** Plus postage. Bookstores, film rental libraries, or from **Moody Institute of Science, 12000 E. Washington Blvd., Whittier, CA 90606.**

COLOSSIANS, EPHESIANS (Christian Media) For: L,C,S. Slant: RC,P,S,CP.

By Fr. Bob Sargent, S.M. The headship of Christ and God's plan of salvation in the mystery of the church, according to Paul's blueprint. Ten audio lessons. **$40.00.** Ten video lessons (Beta II or VHS; U-Matic available on request). **$475.00.** Please state format. Add **$4.00** shipping. Prepaid orders only. From **Christian Media, P.O. Box 748, Ogden, UT 84402.**

COMMUNICATING THE WORD OF GOD (Christian Media) For: L,C,S. Slant: RC,P,S,CP.

By Fr. John Bertolucci. Effective ways of listening to the word of God and of communicating that word to our contemporary world. An excellent presentation of tradition in the Catholic Church. Nine audio lessons. **$36.00.** Nine video lessons (Beta II or VHS; U-Matic available on request). **$450.00.** Please state format. Add **$4.00** shipping. Prepaid orders only. From **Christian Media, P.O. Box 748, Ogden, UT 84402.**

COMPLETE IN HIM Ministry Support Series (Visible Light, Inc.) For: L,C,S,Y. Slant: EP,MP,D,P,S,I,CP,M.

Designed to educate and entertain the believer in the foundational truths of God's word. Each lesson incorporates the technique of "memorization without realization" through repetition of the visual, spoken, and the written word, that is, through: multi-media presentation (video cassette format); interactive classroom environment; and booklet for study. This artistically produced series with music and media provides the student with the maximum potential for retention. Primary applications are: church growth classes, evangelistic follow-up programs, and Bible studies as well as for home use. This audio-visual Christian Growth series currently contains the following six Bible basic lessons: 1. The Alpha and Omega (Who is God?); 2. The Word of His Power (The Bible); 3. One Must Die For Many (Salvation); 4. Our Identity (Baptism By Water); 5. In Love For Me (Communion); and 6. A Vessel of Gold (Your Place In the Body). Certificate of Achievement available. Video Tape VL7000A (lessons 1-3). Video Tape VL7000B (lessons 4-6). Video Cassette (3 lessons). **$119.95.** Student booklets (one per lesson). **$3.00** each. Teacher's manual (one per video cassette). **Free.** Certificate of Achievement (8 x 10). **$1.00** each. From **Visible Light, Inc., P.O. Box 8605, Orlando, FL 32856.**

COMPUTER BIBLE BALL (ALT Publishing Co.) For: L,Y,Ch. Slant: RC, MP,LP,P,S.

Computer Bible Ball is a computerized Bible game based on the Bible and the game of baseball. Designed to promote biblical knowledge in students of all ages. It is adapted to the Apple computer. Several additional computer programs will follow this game which

AUDIO-VISUAL BIBLE RESOURCES

is the first in a series. First game. $39.95. Complete series of five games. $159.95. From **ALT Publishing Co., P.O. Box 400, Green Bay, WI 54305.**

CONVERSION: WHAT DOES RETURN TO THE LORD MEAN? (Catholic Education Center) For: L,C,S. Slant: RC, D.

By Nathan Mitchell, OSB. Father Mitchell's poetic and reflective style is an inspiration to adults, catechists and liturgists regarding the topics of conversion and repentance in relation to the parables. He states, "Parables do not inform us, they reform us." He develops this premise by describing the parables of Jesus, then shows how these parables open us up to the radical challenge of conversion and repentance. Finally, he explores some of the ways in which the New Testament message of these two concepts are intertwined in our life experiences. Length is 58 minutes. Rental for Beta I and U-Matic formats. **$15.00.** Purchase in all common video formats. **$70-$100.00.** From **Catholic Education Center, Media Department, 328 W. Sixth Street, St. Paul, MN 55102.**

CORINTHIANS (Christian Media) For: L,C,S. Slant: RC,P,S,CP.

By Rev. George Montague, S.M. This series portrays the problem of the community at Corinth as very much like those of our church community today. It was a community struggling to assert itself and its members in an environment of vice and violence. The charismatic gifts were readily apparent and yet there was much disunity and lack of harmony. We are shown how Paul called this community to turn from the wisdom of the world to the wisdom of God. Ten audio lessons. **$40.00.** Ten video lessons (Beta II or VHS; U-Matic available on request). **$475.00.** Please state format. Add $4.00 shipping. Prepaid orders only. From **Christian Media, P.O. Box 748, Ogden, UT 84402.**

CRISIS OF COMMITMENT (Training Church Leaders, Inc.) For: L,C,S,Y. Slant: EP,P.

By Dan DeHaan. Taken from II Timothy 2, this series is exhorting Christians today to keep pressing on in a deeper commitment with the Lord. Through Paul's illustrations of teachers, soldiers, athletes, farmers, craftsmen, vessels, and servants, the ingredients of true commitment are revealed. The Scriptures have been so watered down today that the precise meaning of words are no longer taught. There is a cry to get back to the real biblical meaning of words like "commitment." God is looking for people today who understand commitment and are willing to live it. Titles of sessions are: Look for Faith in Men; The Battle is Raging; Win the Prize and Reap the Crops; A Craftsman and a Useful Vessel; and Servanthood and Commitment. Audio cassettes. **$8.80.** From **Training Church Leaders, Inc., 6080 New Peachtree Road, Atlanta, GA 30340.**

DALLAS SEMINARY VIDEO BIBLE STUDY (Dallas Seminary) For: L,C,S,Y. Slant: F,EP,P,M.

Dallas Seminary Video Bible Studies are book and topical studies with a text and study guide optional. Each is a series of five to ten video tapes and their length is approximately thirty minutes. They are basically "lay" targeted. From **Dallas Theological Seminary, 3909 Swiss Ave., Dallas, TX 75204.**

THE DANGER OF DRIFTING (Training Church Leaders, Inc.) For: L,C,S.Y. Slant: EP,P.

Audio cassettes by Dan DeHaan. This series shows the pattern of spiritual decay that can attack and defeat the believer. It lists clearly the steps to spiritual decline, beginning with laziness as the first destructive step. It also covers the key issues in being consistent for the Lord and shows apathy to be the deadliest sin in the church. This study is a warning and gives causes and cures for spiritual drifting. Titles of sessions are: Ten Steps to Drifting; The Five Greatest Warnings in the Bible; The Five Deadliest Sins in Life; Being a Disciple Not a Drifter; The Four Imperatives for the Last Days. Audio. **$25.40.** Write for rental or purchase information on video. From **Training Church Leaders, Inc., 6080 New Peachtree Road, Atlanta, GA 30340.**

DANIEL (Jimmy Swaggart Ministries) For: L,C. Slant: CP.

This dynamic teaching series vividly unfolds the many prophecies held within this powerful Old Testament book. The many symbols, Daniel's panoramic view of coming world kingdoms, the apocalyptic implications for our own day...this teaching series details the entire Book of Daniel. This thirteen hours of teaching are contained on twelve cassettes. Product No. 04-021. **$30.00.** From **Jimmy Swaggart Ministries, P.O. Box 2550, Baton Rouge, LA 70821.**

DANIEL COMBO (Jimmy Swaggart Ministries) For: L,C. Slant: CP.

A comprehensive Bible study tool. You'll thrill to see Daniel's prophetic utterances being fulfilled in this very day! Watch God's timetable take effect in this 12 cassette/248 page series. Learn God's order of events in this world system as Daniel tells us the country the Antichrist will come

AUDIO-VISUAL BIBLE RESOURCES

from; the future of the Jews; insight into the great tribulation; activities of the Antichrist plus many more "revelations." This series will provide the most in-depth study of the Book of Daniel you could find! Product number 06-011. **$39.00**. From **Jimmy Swaggart Ministries, P.O. Box 2550, Baton Rouge, LA 70821.**

DAVID AND JONATHAN (Daughters of St. Paul) For Y,Ch. Slant: RC,P.

A filmstrip/cassette program on David, the young shepherd who rose from the fields to the royal throne. The story of his friendship with King Saul's son, Jonathan is also told. 96 color frames, fourteen minutes. Number FC0080. **$19.95** (add **$1.00** for postage). From **Daughters of St. Paul, 50 St. Paul's Ave., Jamaica Plain, Boston, MA 02130.**

DEVOTIONAL SPOTS (White Lion Pictograph) For: L,C,S. Slant: D.

A series of Scripture-based television spots designed for local church promotion and ministry. Produced by White Lion Pictograph, an award-winning Christian film producer, the spots are ideal tools for community outreach through broadcast or cable television, while at the same time establishing church awareness and identity. The **Devotional Spots** were produced on location around the world, each spot a sensitive visual and musical interpretation of Scripture. Churches place the ads on local television much like an advertiser would place ads, reaching people at times when they are most likely to be watching television. Spots are available in thirty, sixty and longer lengths with space at the end of each spot for the church sponsor's message. Lease fees vary according to use and market size. From **White Lion Pictograph, 146 Melrose Place, San Antonio, TX 78212.**

DISCERNMENT IN SCRIPTURE AND TODAY (Christian Media) For: L,C,S. Slant: RC,P,S,CP.

By **Fr. William Kurz, S.J.** This series will study examples from Scripture, supplemented by St. Ignatius and contemporary experience, on how to learn whether an inspiration, impulse or prophecy is from God or not. Topics include true and false prophecy, walking in the spirit, fruits of the Spirit, the two ways and spiritual warfare. Nine audio lessons. **$36.00**. Nine video lessons (Beta II or VHS; U-Matic available on request). **$450.00**. Please state format. Add **$4.00** shipping. Prepaid orders only. From **Christian Media, P.O. Box 748, Ogden, UT 84402.**

DO IT YOURSELF HEBREW AND GREEK (Multnomah Press) For: L,C,S. Slant: EP,P.

By **Edward W. Goodrick.** Everybody's guide to the language tools. Designed for the serious Bible student who wants to discover as accurately as possible what the Bible meant in its original languages, this manual introduces one to Greek and Hebrew and opens the door to the use of study tools based on the original languages. The optional language cassette gives pronunciation help for both Hebrew and Greek. Workbook with cassette. **$12.95**. Workbook only. **$9.95**. Bookstores or from **Multnomah Press, 10209 S.E. Division Street, Portland, OR 97266.**

ENCOUNTER IN ISRAEL (American Baptist Films) For: L,C,S,Y. Slant: EP,MP.

Persons studying at the Ecumenical Institute at Tantur, Israel, not only have access to a library of biblical resources, but they regularly visit archaeological digs and historic sites dating back to Bible times. This 80-frame color filmstrip with reading script follows students as they encounter the rich resources of the Holy Land that enable them to gain new insights into the Judeo-Christian Scriptures. **$5.50** plus postage. From **American Baptist Films, Valley Forge, PA 19482.**

EUCHARIST IN THE NEW TESTAMENT (Christian Media) For: L,C,S. Slant: RC,P,S,CP.

Rev. Joseph Lackner, S.M. These presentations will examine the Eucharist in the New Testament: the origin in Jesus; the background found in the Old Testament and Liturgical celebration in the New Testament. We are given some new and intriguing insights into the significance of the Eucharist in the life of a true Christian. It is an invitation to enter into a new life which is a foretaste of eternal life in Heaven. The Eucharist is a celebration of a life lived in faith, hope, and love by members of the community. Five audio lessons. **$20.00**. Five video lessons (Beta II or VHS; U-Matic available on request). **$250.00**. Please state format. Add **$4.00** shipping. Prepaid orders only. From **Christian Media, P.O. Box 748, Ogden, UT 84402.**

EXPOSITORS MICROFILM LIBRARY (AMG International) For: L,C,S,Y. Slant: C,F,EP,MP,D,P,S,I,BC,M.

This resource can provide you with the very best in expository books in one of the most technological and easiest forms of retrieval—microfilm. The library contains over 6000 volumes or books and over 23,000 fiche with still many more being filmed daily. College, university, and church libraries of all sizes, as well as pastors and teachers are taking advantage of this low cost method of building their biblical resources. Microfilm can be stored in only a fraction of the space regular texts require. The entire library can be stored in a table-top cabinet. Pastors, teachers, students, and laymen now have access to the best in: apologetics, Christology, commentaries, dictionaries, encyclopedias, illustrations, outlines, theology, and dozens more all at a fraction of the costs of regular books. Many volumes available that are out of print today! Write for full information. **$1.25** per fiche. Special prices on sets and quantities. From **Christian Media Supply, 524 Sycamore Circle, Ridgeland, MS 39157.**

FAITH, COVENANT AND COMMUNITY IN EXODUS AND DEUTERONOMY (Christian Media) For: L,C,S. Slant: RC,P,S,CP.

By **Fr. Richard Rohr, O.F.M.** This series will prayerfully explore some of the great themes of salvation history as God has revealed them in the pages of the books of Exodus and Deuteronomy, themes that speak of the faith of the people of Israel, their covenant relationship with God, and their sense of community. Ten audio lessons. **$40.00**. Ten video lessons (Beta II or VHS; U-Matic available on request). **$475.00**. Please state format. Add **$4.00** shipping. Prepaid orders only. From **Christian Media, P.O. Box 748, Ogden, UT 84402.**

AUDIO-VISUAL BIBLE RESOURCES

THE FAITH OF JESUS (Christian Media) For: L,C,S. Slant: RC,P,S,CP.

By Bro. Donald Mouton, F.S.C. This is a very challenging series that gives many new and intriguing insights into the faith of Jesus and how we are called to live in that same faith. It was the faith of Jesus that made it possible for him to preach the Kingdom of God despite much opposition and misunderstanding. He not only preached it, but also lived out the reality of it in his daily life, even though it led to his death. The series also develops an excellent appreciation of the inner meaning of the parables and the death and resurrection of Christ. Nine audio lessons. **$36.00**. Nine video lessons (Beta II or VHS; U-Matic available on request). **$450.00**. Please state format. Add **$4.00** shipping. Prepaid orders only. From **Christian Media, P.O. Box 748, Ogden, UT 84402**.

FAMILY BIBLE FUN (Home Computer Software) For: L,C,S,Y,Ch.

These are the first commercially available computer Bible games for home computers. They operate on the Atari 400/800 and Apple II, II+ and IIe with 48K memory and disk drive capability. Subjects covered are as follows: Know Your Bible I and II; Life of Christ I and II; Life of David; Prophets; Patriarchs; Book of Acts; Great Men and Women of the Bible. Family Bible fun is suited to the home, church and school environment. It can be used by preschool children through adults. It was specifically designed to bring the family together for a time of enjoyment and education. First set of Bible Games including master disk. **$49.95**. All subsequent programs. **$29.95**. Bookstores or from **Train Depot, 982 El Monte Ave., Mt. View, CA 94040**.

FILM AND VIDEO CASSETTE CATALOG (Christian Film and Video Center) For: L,C,S,Y,Ch. Slant: AW,C,RC, F,EP,MP,LP,L,D,P,S,I,H,M.

Non-denominational distributor of Christian Audio-Visuals, particularly films and video cassettes. From **Christian Film & Video Center, 1726-B 19th Street, Lubbock, TX 79401**.

THE FIRST EPISTLE OF JOHN (Daughters of St. Paul), For: L,C,S,Y. Slant: D,P.

The epistle of John (which speaks of Christ's humanity and divinity) is read with appropriate introduction and closing prayer. Length approximately thirty minutes. Number CS0200. **$5.95** (add **$.75** for postage). Bookstores or from **Daughters of St. Paul, 50 St. Paul's Ave., Jamaica Plain, Boston, MA 02130**.

THE FIRST LETTER OF JOHN (Christian Media) For: L,C,S. Slant: RC,P, S,CP.

By Rev. Jerry Bevilacqua, O.S.A. This series has a particular quality that is almost explosive in its provocative insights on what it means to be a Christian and live and function in a Christian community. Each disciple is called to live the life that Jesus lived with all the tensions and stress of a life lived in the light of truth and justice. Five audio lessons. **$20.00**. Five video lessons (Beta II or VHS; U-Matic available on request). **$250.00**. Please state format. Add **$4.00** shipping. Prepaid orders only. From **Christian Media, P.O. Box 748, Ogden, UT 84402**.

THE FIRST LETTER OF PETER (Christian Media) For: L,C,S. Slant: RC,P,S,CP.

By Fr. Joseph Lackner, S.M. The riches of this early letter, largely a homily preached on the meaning and implications of Christian initiation, will be explored for their relevance to our lives today. Four audio lessons. **$16.00**. Four video lessons (Beta II or VHS; U-Matic available on request). **$210.00**. Please state format. Add **$4.00** shipping. Prepaid orders only. From **Christian Media, P.O. Box 748, Ogden, UT 84402**.

THE FULFILLMENT THEME IN MATTHEW'S GOSPEL (Christian Media) For: L,C,S. Slant: RC,P,S,CP.

By Rev. Paul Hinnebusch, O.P. Matthew interprets the life and words of Jesus in the light of Old Testament themes. This series examines many of these themes in their full Old Testament context, and presents Matthew's portrait of Jesus against this background. We are also provided some excellent insights into the true nature of the ministry of healing. Ten audio lessons. **$40.00**. Nine video lessons (Beta II or VHS; U-Matic available on request). **$450.00**. Please state format. Add **$4.00** for shipping. Prepaid orders only. From **Christian Media, P.O. Box 748, Ogden, UT 84402**.

GENESIS, EXODUS (Christian Media) For: L,C,S. Slant: RC,P,S,CP.

By Fr. Frank Montalbano, O.M.I. Beginning in faith and covenant and the relevance of these great themes for Christian living today. Ten audio lessons. **$40.00**. Ten video lessons (Beta II or VHS; U-Matic available on request). **$475.00**. Please state format. Add **$4.00** shipping. Prepaid orders only. From **Christian Media, P.O. Box 748, Ogden, UT 84402**.

GOD: I WANT TO KNOW YOU! (Training Church Leaders, Inc.) For: L,C,S,Y. Slant: EP,P.

Audio cassettes by **Dan DeHaan**. What is God like? Many people have a very incomplete view of God. Our view of God determines our motivation for Him. This study provides a close-up look into His character and how it relates to our everyday lives; therefore, producing security and meaning to the whole Christian life. This series brings His infinite personality into perspective for our own growth (Jeremiah 23:9). Principles are also given for working with agnostics. Titles of session are: The Glory of God—What Is God Like? His Unchangeableness, Omnipresence, Omnipotence, Omniscience, Wisdom, Goodness, Sovereignty and Holiness—Ezekiel's Penetrating Vision of God—God the Father—The Character of God in the Book of Exodus—The Anger of God Displayed to Moses—Introduction to the Ten Commandments—The Ten Commandments—How to Worship God. **$38.20**. From **Training Church Leaders, Inc. 6080 New Peachtree Road, Atlanta, GA 30340**.

THE GOD OF SPACE (Faith Venture Visuals) For: L,C,S,Y,Ch. Slant: D,P.

AUDIO-VISUAL BIBLE RESOURCES

Sailing On Life's Sea uses a nautical theme to present five expositional Bible lessons. The set contains four background transparencies, 50 paper masters, a 39-page leader's guide, the words to 13 songs and choruses, and suggestions for handcrafts and patterns. **$12.95.** Bookstores or from **Faith Venture Visuals, Inc., P.O. Box 423, 510 E. Main Street, Lititz, PA 17543.**

GOD THE SON (Argus Communications) For: L,C,S,Y. Slant: RC,EP,MP,LP, L,D,P.

By Donald Senior. This filmstrip series is about building a closer relationship with Jesus. By becoming more aware of the milieu in which Jesus lived, His mission, His crucifixion and resurrection, and His call for discipleship, we come to see more clearly and believe more deeply that Jesus in His person and work, is our salvation. Set of four filmstrips. **$79.95.** From **Argus Communications, Department 50, One DLM Park, Allen, TX 75002.**

GOD THE SPIRIT (Argus Communications) For: L,C,S,Y. Slant: RC,EP, MP,LP,L,D,P.

By Donald Senior. The gift of the Spirit is Jesus' legacy to all of us. This filmstrip series explores what the Bible has to say about the Spirit and gives us contemporary examples of people who lead Spirit-filled lives. Set of three filmstrips. **$59.95.** From **Argus Communications, Department 50, One DLM Park, Allen, TX 75002.**

GOSPEL ACCORDING TO MATTHEW SERIES (Catholic Education Center) For: L,C,S. Slant: RC,P.

By Robert Burke and Loretta Girzaitis. The purpose of this series is to prepare facilitators to lead the study of the Gospel of St. Matthew. The presentations appear on eleven separate video programs, each running between thirty and forty minutes. Programs can be used separately or used in pairs (one and two; three and four). The first program in the pair deals with biblical exegesis and the second with contemporary interpretation. Rental in Beta I and U-Matic formats. **$15.00.** Purchase in all common video formats. **$70-$100.00.** From **Catholic Education Center, Media Department, 328 W. Sixth Street, St. Paul, MN 55102.**

THE GOSPEL ACCORDING TO ST. JOHN (Thomas More Cassettes) For: L,C,S. Slant: RC.

Todd Brennan reads the text and introduction by John L. McKenzie. Professional narrator Todd Brennan's reading of the complete text of John, following Father McKenzie's brilliant introduction, brings out new meaning and dimension. In his introduction (read by Mr. Brennan), biblical expert John McKenzie says that "it is probably no exaggeration to say that Jesus, known only through the fourth Gospel, would appear to be a visitor from another world." There are enormous differences, omissions and additions in John as compared with the Synoptic Gospels. "In modern times the principles of history and of criticism do not permit students of the New Testament to ignore the differences nor to recoil from their implications." Certainly, Father McKenzie does not recoil from a close look at the differences—rather, he illuminates them with meaningful new insights. TM228. 3 cassettes, 2 hours 24 minutes. **$24.95.** From **Thomas More Association, 225 W. Huron St., Chicago, IL 60610.**

THE GOSPEL ACCORDING TO ST. LUKE (Thomas More Cassettes) For: L,C,S. Slant: RC.

Todd Brennan reads the text and an introduction by John L. McKenzie. Todd Brennan narrates the entire Gospel of Luke as well as an introduction written by the eminent biblical scholar, John L. McKenzie. Luke's key theme is the spreading of the Good News to the disciples and, as a result, displays the most universal outlook of all the evangelists. In addition, he is a strong stylist who uses novelistic techniques to tell such memorable stories as The Good Samaritan, Dives and Lazarus, Zacchaeus and The Prodigal Son. Above all, Luke's gospel is infused with joy and hope as Luke continually emphasizes Jesus the Messiah. As Fr. McKenzie summarizes, "If there is one title more than another which distinguishes Jesus as he appears in Luke, it is Savior: savior from disease, savior from sin, savior from the sorrow of the world. The Gospel of Luke is the Gospel of hope." TM263. 3 cassettes, approximately 3 1/4 hours. **$24.95.** From **Thomas More Association, 225 W. Huron St., Chicago, IL 60610.**

THE GOSPEL ACCORDING TO ST. MARK (Thomas More Cassettes) For: L,C,S. Slant: RC.

Todd Brennan reads the text and an introduction by John L. McKenzie. In his introduction (read by Mr. Brennan) biblical expert John McKenzie says that in spite of the fact that Mark is placed second in the New Testament's ordering of the Gospels, "Mark is regarded by scholars as the earliest Gospel and the first written account of any kind which we have about Jesus." While this does not mean that there were not earlier sources, Mark is the earliest one we have and, thus deserves our very special and close attention. There is a unique reward in listening to, rather than simply reading, the Gospels—for that is, after all, the way the vast majority of Christians have encountered them down through the centuries. Professional narrator Brennan's reading of the complete text of Mark, following Father McKenzie's illuminating and detailed introduction, brings out new meaning and dimension. TM220. 2 cassettes, approximately 2 hours. **$17.95.** From **Thomas More Association, 225 W. Huron St., Chicago, IL 60610.**

THE GOSPEL ACCORDING TO ST. MATTHEW (Thomas More Cassettes) For: L,C,S. Slant: RC.

Todd Brennan reads the text and an introduction by John L. McKenzie. Gifted narrator Todd Brennan reads the beautiful and authoritative Jerusalem Bible translation of St. Matthew's Gospel and an introduction by Scripture scholar John L. McKenzie. Matthew, the most quoted and probably the most popular Gospel, offers a very clear picture of the development of Jesus' public life and gives us perhaps the most detailed account of the words of Jesus. According to Fr. McKenzie: "Matthew composed the sayings of Jesus carefully, and gave them that lapidary form which makes them memorable and quotable." A spiritually rewarding experience. TM247, 3 cassettes, approximately 2 1/2 hours. **$24.95.** From **Thomas More Association, 225 W. Huron St., Chicago, IL 60610.**

THE GOSPEL OF JOHN (Christian Media) For: L,C,S. Slant: RC,P,S,CP.

By Fr. George Montague, S.M. Jesus as seen through the eyes of the fourth

AUDIO-VISUAL BIBLE RESOURCES

evangelist: the revealer of the Father and the Giver of the Spirit. Ten audio lessons. $40.00. Ten video lessons (Beta II or VHS; U-Matic available on request). $475.00. Please state format. Add $4.00 shipping. Prepaid orders only. From **Christian Media, P.O. Box 748, Ogden, UT 84402.**

THE GOSPEL OF LUKE-ACTS OF THE APOSTLE (Christian Media) For: L,C,S. Slant: RC,P,S,CP.

By **Daniel Giordano.** In order to understand the pastoral concerns in Luke-Acts, selected Lucan texts are examined for their meaning. An excellent comparative study is done with these Scripture texts. Ten audio lessons. $40.00. Ten video lessons (Beta II or VHS; U-Matic available on request). $475.00. Please state format. Add $4.00 shipping. Prepaid orders only. From **Christian Media, P.O. Box 748, Ogden, UT 84402.**

THE GOSPEL OF LUKE—A PHYSICIAN'S VIEW OF CHRIST (Revivaltime Media Ministries) For: L. Slant: EP, D,P.

From the **Every Day With Jesus** Bible study series, this cassette study system offers an exciting adventure into the Gospel of Luke (New King James Version). Revivaltime and Every Day With Jesus speaker, Dan Betzer, opens a new world of practical Bible study with programmed 8-to 10-minute segments on four 90-minute tapes. Just right for "devotional breaks" at your convenience in your home, office, or car. Tapes come in a graphically designed library case. From **Revivaltime Media Ministries, P.O. Box 70, Springfield, MO 65801.**

THE GOSPEL OF MARK (Christian Media) For: L,C,S. Slant: RC,P,S,CP.

By **Fr. George Montague, S.M.** The exciting good news by the first evangelist. Mark shows us Jesus as preacher, healer, son of man and son of God. Calling his disciples to follow him to the cross. Ten audio lessons. $40.00. Ten video lessons (Beta II or VHS; U-Matic available on request). $475.00. Please state format. Add $4.00 shipping. Prepaid orders only. From **Christian Media, P.O. Box 748, Ogden, UT 84402.**

THE GOSPEL OF MATTHEW (Christian Media) For: L,C,S. Slant: RC,P,S,CP.

By **Rev. Richard Rohr, O.F.M.** In this commentary, we are invited to experience the struggles of community and to be a church of the poor. We are led to understand what the Lord is asking of us as Christians. He describes his experience in light of the gospel message. Ten audio lessons. $40.00. Add $4.00 for shipping. Prepaid orders only. From **Christian Media, P.O. Box 748, Ogden, UT 84402.**

THE GREAT LEADERS (San Paolo Films) For: L,C,S,Y. Slant: RC,EP, MP,D,P.

The story of two Old Testament heroes, Gideon and Samson. Gideon, the simple farmer who, armed with God's wisdom outwits a mighty army. Samson, the man blessed by God with an extraordinary strength, yet who falls victim to Delilah, the ambitious woman who betrays him. 110 minutes, color, 16 mm. $50.00 rental. Film rental libraries or from **Daughters of St. Paul, 50 St. Paul's Ave., Jamaica Plain, Boston, MA 02130.**

HEBREWS AND JUDE (Christian Media) For: L,C,S. Slant: RC,P,S,CP.

By **Fr. Frank Montalbano, O.M.I.** "God, who spoke in times past through the prophets, has in these final days in which we live, spoken to us through his son." Jesus comes alive against the rich backdrop of the Old Testament liturgy. Ten audio lessons. $40.00. Ten video lessons (Beta II or VHS; U-Matic available on request). $475.00. Please state format. Add $4.00 for shipping. Prepaid orders only. From **Christian Media, P.O. Box 748, Ogden, UT 84402.**

HOME LIFE SERIES (Training Church Leaders, Inc.) For: L,C,S,Y. Slant: EP, P.

Audio cassettes by Dan DeHaan. Satan is not blind to how God uses a family. If your family is having difficulties, these tapes may be used to correct those problems and make your family what God intended it to be. Satan would have you believe that the conditions around you create how you should react. These tapes refute that philosophy from biblical principles. Titles of the sessions are: Results of Losing Your First Love; Character Creates Conditions; The Discipline of Children; How to Motivate Children; and How To Twist Your Parents Around Your Finger. $20.30. From **Training Church Leaders, Inc., 6080 New Peachtree Road, Atlanta, GA 30340.**

HOW RELEVANT IS THE BIBLE? (Thomas More Cassettes) For: L,C,S. Slant: RC.

By **John L. McKenzie.** Father McKenzie makes it clear that much of our confusion at not finding specific answers in the Bible stems from the fact that our modern method of solving human problems begins with institutional reform, whereas the biblical approach is directed toward the redemption of the individual. Challenging, direct and thought-provoking—for all who seek a deeper understanding of the Bible. TM268. 32 minutes. $8.95. From **Thomas More Association, 225 W. Huron St., Chicago, IL 60610.**

HOW TO ORGANIZE A BIBLE STUDY GROUP (Catholic Education Center) For: L,C,S. Slant: RC,P.

By **Ann Tadvick.** Explanation of the steps involved in setting up a full scale, intensive Bible study that includes prayer, study, discussion, and fellowship. She shares the experience of a regional group of 180 women who meet for 24 weeks annually. Length 32 minutes. Rental in Beta I and U-Matic formats. $15.00. Purchase in all common video formats. $70-$100.00. From **Catholic Education Center, Media Department, 328 W. Sixth Street, St. Paul, MN 55102.**

HOW TO START A NEIGHBORHOOD BIBLE STUDY (Tyndale House Publishers) For: L,S. Slant: AW,C,RC,F, EP,MP,LP,P,CP.

By **Marilyn Kunz and Catherine Schell.** A cassette with a handbook for group discussions; what to do and what not to do in a discussion Bible study. A Neighborhood Bible Studies book. 24 pages. $8.95. Bookstores.

HOW TO STUDY THE BIBLE (The Liturgical Press) For: L,C,S,Y. Slant: RC,P,S.

A series of five cassette tapes presenting the rules and tools needed for Bible study with practical suggestions and comments on how to apply the rules and tools. Five

AUDIO-VISUAL BIBLE RESOURCES

cassettes with study guide. **$37.50**. Bookstores or from **The Liturgical Press, Collegeville, MN 56321**.

HOW TO TEACH THE BIBLE SERIES (Broadman Films) For: L,C.

By Lucien E. Coleman, Jr. A series of four 28-minute videocassettes on formats of 3/4 inch U-Matic and 1/2 inch Beta, and 1/2 inch VHS. Individual titles in the series are: How to Study a Lesson; How to Select Goals for Teaching; How to Develop a Teaching Plan; and How to Use Teaching Methods. The same series is available on motion picture film. 3/4 inch U-Matic format. **$330.00** (entire series) **$90.00** (individual titles). 1/2 inch Beta and VHS formats. **$300.00** (entire series) **$80.00** (individual titles). Rental: **$90.00** (all formats, entire series) **$25.00** (individual titles). From film rental libraries.

I, PAUL (Gateway Films, Inc.) For: L,C,S. Slant: EP,MP,D,P.

Moving, dramatic presentation of Paul writing his second epistle to Timothy. Set as a one-man play, Paul writes—and speaks—from the confines of chains, a prisoner for the Lord. In **I, Paul**, the only script is the classic majesty of the King James translation of II Timothy. Brings new life and insight to a familiar Scripture. Use **I, Paul** as part of a sermon or for a prayer meeting message. Dramatic, 25 minutes, color. Rental. **$33.00**. Film rental libraries or from **Gateway Films, Box A, Lansdale, PA 19446**.

I WILL AWAKE THE DAWN—THE PSALMS IN SONG (Daughters of St. Paul) For: L,C,S,Y. Slant: RC,EP, MP,L,D.

Set to contemporary yet reverent tunes, these psalm-songs capture the biblical spirit of adoration and praise, of trust and hope, of love and generosity. These songs reflect the many situations and circumstances of each of our lives. But through all these events, there remains God—the One who will never abandon us, the One whose praises will never be exhausted. Length 33 minutes. Stereo cassette Number CS0857. **$6.50**. Stereo record Number RE0105. **$7.50**. Songbook, Number MU0055. **$5.95**. (add **$1.00** for postage). Bookstores or from **Daughters of St. Paul, 50 St. Paul's Ave., Jamaica Plain, Boston, MA 02130**.

THE IMAGE OF JESUS IN THE NEW TESTAMENT (Christian Media) For: L,C,S. Slant: RC,P,S,CP.

By Rev. Joseph Lackner, S.M. "Who do you say I am?" This was the question Jesus asked of his disciples. Fr. Lackner will try to answer that question in the light of the New Testament witness. Five audio lessons. **$20.00**. Five video lessons (Beta II or VHS; U-Matic available on request). **$250.00**. Please state format. Add **$4.00** for shipping. Prepaid orders only. From **Christian Media, P.O. Box 748, Ogden, UT 84402**.

IN THE LAND OF JESUS (Arena Lettres) For: L,C,S,Y,Ch. Slant: RC, EP,MP,LP,L,P,S.

Four full-color filmstrips, cassettes and study guide in a bound storage case. These filmstrips are authentic photographs of the land where Jesus lived, walked, preached and died for our salvation. Beautifully photographed in exquisite detail, they trace the Gospel story and capture the flavor of the land that Jesus made Holy by His presence. Excellent for retreats, Bible study-sharing groups and classroom use. **$99.95**. From **The Word of God Institute, 487 Michigan Avenue, NE, Washington, DC 20017**.

ISAIAH (Thomas More Cassettes) For: L,C,S. Slant: RC.

Selections From by John McGiver; Reflections On by John L. McKenzie. On two separate cassettes, the distinguished actor, John McGiver, who has captivated audiences in everything from **Tartuffe** to the movie **Midnight Cowboy**, brings his great narrative skills to bear on reading chapters 40-55 of Second Isaiah. On the second cassette the eminent Scripture scholar and author of **The Dictionary of the Bible** and the forthcoming **Light on the Epistles**, Father John L. McKenzie, reflects on these same chapters. TM199 and TM200. 2 cassettes, 1 hour 41 minutes. **$14.95**. From **Thomas More Association, 225 W. Huron St., Chicago, IL 60610**.

ISAIAH OF JERUSALEM-PROPHET OF FAITH: ISAIAH OF BABYLON-PROPHET OF HOPE (Christian Media) For: L,C,S. Slant: RC,P,S,CP.

By Rev. Frank Montalbano, O.M.I. An exploration in-depth of Isaiah as the prophet of faith, prophet of hope, the man, and the tradition. Includes the historical background of the prophets of Israel. Ten audio lessons. **$40.00**. Ten video lessons (Beta II or VHS; U-Matic available on request). **$475.00**. Please state format. Add **$4.00** for shipping. Prepaid orders only. From **Christian Media, P.O. Box 748, Ogden, UT 84402**.

JACOB—THE MAN WHO FOUGHT WITH GOD (San Paolo Films) For: L,C,S,Y. Slant: RC,EP,MP,D,P.

The great figures of the Book of Genesis, Adam and Eve, Cain and Abel, Noah, Abraham and Isaac, Esau and Jacob, are dramatically portrayed in this moving biblical masterpiece. Length 120 minutes, color, 16 mm. **$50.00** rental. Film rental libraries or from **Daughters of St. Paul, 50 St. Paul's Ave., Jamaica Plain, Boston, MA 02130**.

JENSEN'S BIBLE STUDY CHARTS (Moody Press) For: L,C,S. Slant: EP,P,I,M.

By Irving Jensen. Sixteen transparencies and 153 transparency masters make the facts of the Bible easy to understand. **$19.95**. Bookstores or from **Moody Bookworld, 2101 W. Howard, Chicago, IL 60645**.

JESUS' FAREWELL DISCOURSE (Daughters of St. Paul) For: L,C,S,Y. Slant: D,P.

Chapters 13-17 of John's Gospel—Jesus' Farewell Discourse—are read. Length approximately thirty minutes. Number CS0210. **$5.95** (add .75 for

AUDIO-VISUAL BIBLE RESOURCES

postage). Bookstores or from **Daughters of St. Paul, 50 St. Paul's Ave., Jamaica Plain, Boston, MA 02130.**

JOB AND THE MYSTERY OF SUFFERING (Christian Media) For: L,C,S. Slant: RC,P,S,CP.

By Rev. Richard Rohr, O.F.M. "In the land of Uz, there was a blameless and upright man named Job, who feared God and avoided evil." So begins the Book of Job. Yet, despite his innocence, Job suffers and his fidelity is tested. Fr. Rohr will prayerfully explore the message of this great wisdom book of the Old Testament and seek its applications for our lives and times. Ten audio lessons. **$40.00.** Ten video lessons (Beta II or VHS; U-Matic available on request). **$475.00.** Please state format. Add **$4.00** for shipping. Prepaid orders only. From **Christian Media, P.O. Box 748, Ogden, UT 84402.**

JOURNEY THRU GENESIS (The Liturgical Press) For: L,C,S. Slant: RC, P.

An exciting epic and serious saga that reveals God's loving ways with his frequently weak, sometimes wicked, and always wondering/wandering people. This five-cassette series begins "in the beginning" and covers the avalanche of alienation which takes God's chosen people from bad to worst. We are introduced to the pioneer patriarchs, Abraham and Isaac, and the "dynamic duo," Jacob and Esau. Set of five cassettes with study guide. **$37.50.** Bookstores or from **The Liturgical Press, Collegeville, MN 56321.**

KJV NEW TESTAMENT ON CASSETTES (Impact Books, Inc.) For: L,C,S,Y,Ch.

Complete KJV New Testament on 16 cassettes. Comes packaged in an attractive vinyl album. **$39.95.** Bookstores or from **Impact Books, Inc., 137 W. Jefferson, Kirkwood, MO 63122.**

KING JAMES VERSION COMPLETE BIBLE ON CASSETTE TAPE (International Cassette Corporation) For: L,C,S,Y.

Narrated by Steven B. Stevens. The complete Bible consists of 48 cassette tapes and is packaged in one leatherette album with a large velcro closure and sturdy handle. The King James Version may also be purchased separately as a New Testament or as an Old Testament. Complete Bible. **$159.98.** Old Testament. **$119.98.** New Testament. **$39.98.** Bookstores, film rental libraries, or from **International Cassette Corporation, P.O. Box 1928, Greenville, TX 75401.**

THE KING JAMES VERSION NEW TESTAMENT ON CASSETTE (Singspiration) For: L,S,Y. Slant: EP.

Set includes 14 cassettes for 14 listening hours. Also sold in a set of the Gospels only. New Testament. **$49.95.** Gospels. **$29.95.** Bookstores or from **Zondervan Retail Marketing Association, 1420 Robinson Road, SE, Grand Rapids, MI 49506.**

KINGS OF ISRAEL AND JUDAH CHART (Star Bible Publications) For: L,C,S. Slant: F,EP,P,S.

By Shawn Tyler. A beautiful new six-color wall chart size 23"x 29". Gives a graphic chronology with dates of the reign of all the kings and shows who their contemporaries were. Nothing like it. Catalog Number 2010. **$5.00** each. Bookstores or from **Star Bible Publications, Box 181220, Ft. Worth, TX 76118.**

LEARNING FROM GOD (Moody Institute of Science) For: L,C. Slant: EP.

One of four 16mm films in the series, "The Christian's Walk in The Eighties" with Dr. Earl Radmacher, Dr. Gordon MacDonald, and Dr. John MacArthur, Jr. Each film is forty minutes in length. "Learning from God" specifically deals with the Bible and its interpretation. **$50.00** (**$62.50** in Canada). Rental of the whole series, **$180.00** plus local charges. Film rental libraries.

LETTER TO THE PHILIPPIANS (Christian Media) For: L,C,S. Slant: RC,P, S,CP.

By Rev. Ralph Weishaar, O.F.M. This epistle reveals the heart of Paul's spirituality and mission. It combines sublime teaching on the Lordship of Jesus with practical norms for the Christian life. This series stresses how all are called to holiness, and how it is the Holy Spirit at work, in self and in all situations that seeks to make perfect all those who respond with a whole heart to the spirit of love. Five audio lessons. **$20.00.** Five video lessons (Beta II or VHS; U-Matic available on request). **$250.00.** Please state format. Add **$4.00** for shipping. Prepaid orders only. From **Christian Media, P.O. Box 748, Ogden, UT 84402.**

LIFE OF CHRIST COMBO (Jimmy Swaggart Ministries) For: L,C. Slant: CP.

A panoramic view of our Lord's life is found in this unique combo. The in-depth teaching on the 16 cassette tapes, coupled with the enclosed Life of Christ study guide, provides any Bible student with the equivalent of a seminary class on the life of our Lord. This series reveals the personality of Christ: His conduct, attitude, actions; and themes of salvation and forgiveness as Christ first related them. Come walk the same roads Jesus walked, see through His eyes the ancient world, meet the men and women He knew, experience His miracles and sit with Jesus on the hillside as He

AUDIO-VISUAL BIBLE RESOURCES

multiplies the loaves and the fishes. Product Number 06-007. **$39.00**. From **Jimmy Swaggart Ministries, P.O. Box 2550, Baton Rouge, LA 70821.**

LISTENING TO THE BIBLE—THE ENTIRE NEW TESTAMENT ON CASSETTE (Daughters of St. Paul) For: L,C,S. Slant: RC,EP,MP,D.

The New Testament (New American Bible translation) reverently proclaimed by Rev. Frederick Ryan, M.Div. 16 cassettes. 90 minutes each. CS0740. **$44.95**. Please include **$1.00** postage. From **Daughters of St. Paul, 50 St. Paul's Ave., Jamaica Plain, Boston, MA 02130.**

LISTENING TO THE BIBLE—THE ENTIRE PENTATEUCH ON CASSETTE (Daughters of St. Paul) For: L,C,S. Slant: RC,EP,MP,RJ,D.

The books of Genesis, Exodus, Leviticus, Numbers, and Deuteronomy (New American Bible translation) are reverently proclaimed by Professor Robert Baram. 16 cassettes. 60 minutes each. Number CS0744. **$38.95**. Please include **$1.00** postage. From **Daughters of St. Paul, 50 St. Paul's Ave., Jamaica Plain, Boston, MA 02130.**

LISTENING TO THE BIBLE—THE ENTIRE PROPHETIC BOOKS ON CASSETTE (Daughters of St. Paul) For: L,C,S. Slant: RC,EP,MP,RJ,D.

The Prophetic Books of the Bible (New American Bible translation) reverently proclaimed by Rev. Frederick Ryan, M. Div. 16 cassettes. 60-90 minutes each. CS0743. **$39.95**. Please include **$1.00** postage. From **Daughters of St. Paul, 50 St. Paul's Ave., Jamaica Plain, Boston, MA 02130.**

LISTENING TO THE BIBLE—THE ENTIRE WISDOM BOOKS ON CASSETTE (Daughters of St. Paul) For: L,C,S. Slant: RC,EP,MP,RJ,D.

The books of Job, Psalms, Proverbs, Ecclesiastes, Song of Songs, Wisdom, Sirah (Ecclesiasticus), New American Bible translation, are reverently proclaimed by Rev. Frederick Ryan, M. Div. 12 cassettes. 90 minutes each.

CS0741. **$34.95**. Please include **$1.00** postage. From **Daughters of St. Paul, 50 St. Paul's Ave., Jamaica Plain, Boston, MA 02130.**

THE LIVING BIBLE: INDIVIDUAL CASSETTES (Tyndale House Publishers) For: L,S,Y. Slant: AW,C,RC,F,EP,MP,LP,P,CP.

(Mark, Luke, John, Acts, 2 Corinthians thru Colossians, and 1 Thessalonians thru James). Individual stereo cassettes that provide inspirational listening. Background sound and music are combined with individual voices to produce the individual books of the **Living New Testament in Living Sound**. **$11.95** per cassette. Bookstores.

THE LIVING BIBLE IN LIVING SOUND: GENESIS (Tyndale House Publishers) For: L,S,Y. Slant: AW,C,RC,F,EP,MP,LP,RJ,CJ,OJ,D.

The book of "beginnings" from **The Living Bible**...on cassette tape, supported by background sound and music in stereo. Set of three cassettes. **$18.95**. Bookstores.

THE LIVING NEW TESTAMENT GIFT PACKAGE (Tyndale House Publishers) For: L,S,Y. Slant: AW,C,RC,F,EP,MP,LP,D,CP.

Fourteen stereo cassettes contains more than twenty hours of inspirational listening. Background sound and music are combined with individual voices to produce the complete **Living New Testament in Living Sound**. Includes gift case. **$69.95**. Bookstores.

THE LIVING OLD TESTAMENT (Tyndale House Publishers) For: L,S,Y. Slant: C,F,EP,MP,D.

More than seventy hours of inspirational listening for people who need or prefer to listen to the Bible rather than read it. Forty stereo tapes are packaged in three compact bookshelf binders. **$179.95**. Bookstores.

LIVING PSALMS AND PROVERBS IN LIVING SOUND (Tyndale House Publishers) For: L,S,Y. Slant: AW,C,RC,F,EP,MP,LP,RJ,CJ,OJ,P,CP.

These Bible books dramatically unfold in a stereo cassette presentation. Narration, sound, and music help today's listener experience the ancient writers' fears and sorrows, joys and worship. Five cassettes in gift package. **$34.95**. Bookstores.

A LOOK AT LUKE (Catholic Education Center) For: L,C. Slant: RC,P,S.

By Daniel Durken, OSB. Part I, Preaching the Gospel of Luke (47 minutes). In clear, comprehensible journalistic fashion, Daniel Durken illuminates the who, what, where, when, and why of Luke's Gospel, in Cycle C of the 1983 Lectionary, particularly in light of preaching. Part II, Luke's Theology and Themes (38 minutes). Explanations are provided as to where Luke acquires his material, along with highlights of his theology of preaching, of geography, and the historical perspective of the periods of salvation history. Part III, Luke and the Lectionary: Selected Sections (36 minutes). Examining the key sentences in each pericope, the journey motif of Jesus is explained as the Gospel in perpetual motion. Part IV, Luke as

AUDIO-VISUAL BIBLE RESOURCES

Presider, Preacher and Pastor (25 minutes). By looking into the manner in which the disciples contacted Jesus, we are provided with a model for contemporary ministry. Rental in Beta I and U-Matic formats. **$15.00**. Purchase in all common video formats. **$70-$100.00**. From **Catholic Education Center, Media Department, 328 W. Sixth Street, St. Paul, MN 55102**.

A LOOK AT LUKE (The Liturgical Press) For: L,C,S. Slant: RC,P.

The Gospel of St. Luke is designated the Gospel for 1983, and this five-cassette program provides a helpful study of the theology of Luke, with a commentary on key passages and reflections on such Lucan themes as banquet, poverty, prayer, the Holy Spirit and joy. Set of five cassettes and study guide. **$37.50**. Bookstores or from **The Liturgical Press, Collegeville, MN 56321**.

LUKE (Christian Media) For: L,C,S. Slant: RC,P,S,CP.

By Fr. Richard Rohr, O.F.M. The series describes faith as revelation and responded to in love. Jesus, in faith, was the revelation of the fullness of God in love, mercy, and compassion. Life is portrayed as a process that takes place on a journey of faith. Ten audio lessons. **$40.00**. Ten video lessons (Beta II or VHS; U-Matic available on request). **$475.00**. Please state format. Add **$4.00** for shipping. Prepaid orders only. From **Christian Media, P.O. Box 748, Ogden, UT 84402**.

MAN FROM TARSUS (Harvest Productions) For: L. Slant: F,EP,MP,P.

A dramatic 16mm color motion picture on the early life of the Apostle Paul. Some knew him as Saul...some as Paul. Yet all knew him as a potential world leader. Who was this **Man From Tarsus**? Was he for real? He was, in fact, a well-trained student of the Law under the renowned Gamaliel. Persuasive in speech, he evidenced that courage and genius to be a person who could change the world. He was a person, not too different from you. He had problems finding life's meaning. He also wanted answers. **Man From Tarsus** is that dramatic biography about his early life, filmed in the Middle East with that essential touch of biblical realism. This **Man From Tarsus** found the answer to Life's meaning, and leads others on the same highway. Rental. **$48.00**. Purchase. **$595.00**. Film rental libraries or from **Harvest Productions, Box 2225, Kokomo, IN 46902**.

MARCHING THRU EXODUS (The Liturgical Press) For: L,C,S. Slant: RC,P.

In this set of cassettes we hear what God is doing and saying in the story of Moses. We meet the people of Exodus in a new way and discover the people and places that praise God for the promises He made to His people. Moses' mission from plagues to Passover is covered as well as the trek through sand and sea to Sinai. We hear how the covenant was proclaimed and put into practice and also the echoes of the Exodus in Israel, Jesus, and us. Set of six cassettes with study guide. **$45.95**. Bookstores or from **The Liturgical Press, Collegeville, MN 56321**.

MARK'S MESSAGE (The Liturgical Press) For: L,C,S. Slant: RC,P.

A clear and concise introduction to the Gospel of Mark, providing the basic pattern of Jesus' works and offering an understanding of Jesus Christ, the Son of God. The growth of the Good News is traced through Mark's writings. Set of five cassettes with study guide. **$37.50**. Bookstores or from **The Liturgical Press, Collegeville, MN 56321**.

MARY IN THE NEW TESTAMENT (Christian Media) For: L,C,S. Slant: RC,P,S,CP.

By Rev. Pat Gaffney, S.M.M. Christians of our day are re-examining the role of Mary, the mother of Jesus, in God's plan. Fr. Gaffney will search diligently the Scriptures to indicate what God has revealed concerning this promised woman. Nine audio lessons. **$36.00**. Nine video lessons (Beta II or VHS; U-Matic available on request). **$450.00**. Please state format. Add **$4.00** for shipping. Prepaid orders only. From **Christian Media, P.O. Box 748, Ogden, UT 84402**.

MATTHEW (Christian Media) For: L,C,S. Slant: RC,P,S,CP.

By Fr. George Montague, S.M. Some excellent insights into the appreciation of the community of Matthew, as to whom Jesus was, what he taught, and how he lived out what he taught. Jesus is seen by this community as a manifestation of the love of the Father, and a model for the relationship the Father desired with each and every member of the community. Nine audio lessons. **$36.00**. Nine video lessons (Beta II or VHS; U-Matic available on request). **$450.00**. Please state format. Add **$4.00** for shipping. Prepaid orders only. From **Christian Media, P.O. Box 748, Ogden, UT 84402**.

MINISTRY AND AUTHORITY IN THE NEW TESTAMENT (Christian Media) For: L,C,S. Slant: RC,P,S,CP.

By Fr. Richard Rohr, O.F.M. The charisms lead to ministry. How authority is itself a gift and necessary to the charismatic community. How to exercise ministry and authority according to the New Testament pattern. Ten audio lessons. **$40.00**. Ten video lessons (Beta II or VHS; U-Matic available on request). **$475.00**. Please state format. Add **$4.00** for shipping. Prepaid orders only. From **Christian Media, P.O. Box 748, Ogden, UT 84402**.

MYTHS IN THE BIBLE (Thomas More Cassettes) For: L,C,S. Slant: RC.

Father McKenzie examines some of the apparent historical contradictions of the Bible such as the Genesis myths and those surrounding the accounts of the birth of Christ—in fact, for instance, there is no historical evidence of a census being taken in the way depicted in the Gospels. TM72. 42 minutes. **$9.95**. From **Thomas More Association, 225 W. Huron St., Chicago, IL 60610**.

NRB CASSETTE CATALOG (National Religious Broadcasters) For: L,C,S. Slant: C, RC, F, EP, MP, D, P, I, CP.

One of the most popular services of National Religious Broadcasters is the audio cassette tape library. World renowned religious leaders such as Billy Graham, Malcolm Muggeridge, Francis Schaeffer, Carl Henry and many other notable people have been recorded so that your library can contain their biblical teachings and opinions. Workshops offer practical "how to" instruction in all phases of broadcasting. Plenary sessions, workshops,

AUDIO-VISUAL BIBLE RESOURCES

and special events of national and regional conventions, summer institutes, and other activities are recorded and reproduced on site for instruction and use in radio and TV stations, churches, ministries, and individual homes. Not only can participants of these programs have a permanent record of these events, but can share them with others. Catalog. **Free.** From **National Religious Broadcasting, CN 1926, Morristown, NJ 07960.**

NEW INTERNATIONAL VERSION- COMPLETE BIBLE ON CASSETTE TAPE (International Cassette Corporation) For: L,C,S,Y.

Narrated by Steven B. Stevens. The complete Bible, consisting of 48 cassette tapes, is packaged in one leatherette album with a large velcro closure and sturdy handle. The New International Version may also be purchased separately as a New Testament or as an Old Testament. Complete Bible. **$239.98.** Old Testament. **$179.98.** New Testament. **$59.98.** Bookstores, film rental libraries, or from **International Cassette Corp., P.O. Box 1928, Greenville, TX 75401.**

THE NEW INTERNATIONAL VERSION BIBLE ON CASSETTE (Singspiration) For L,S. Slant: EP.

The NIV Bible on cassette, fully dramatized. Sixty-eight cassettes in the entire set with sixty-eight listening hours. Sold in four volumes—3 volumes of the Old Testament and 1 volume of the New Testament. **$59.95** each volume. Bookstores or from **Zondervan Retail Marketing Association, 1420 Robinson Road, SE, Grand Rapids, MI 49506.**

NEW KING JAMES BIBLE ON CASSETTE (New Testament) (Revivaltime Media Ministries) For: L. Slant: D,P.

Narrated by Dan Betzer. A 16-cassette package providing 24 hours of recorded Scripture. The New Testament comes alive as Revivaltime Evangelist Dan Betzer (a former newscaster) narrates the exciting New King James Version. Ideal for family devotions, Scripture memorization, ministry to shut-ins, etc. Easy to hear and understand. These broadcast quality tapes come in a library style vinyl case. Current price list from **Revivaltime Media Ministries, P.O. Box 70, Springfield, MO 65801.**

NEW TESTAMENT IN ARABIC (Christian Duplications International, Inc.) For: L,C,S,Y,Ch. Slant: All Christians.

An attractive, well-produced package of sixteen audio cassettes in vinyl album. **$69.50.** From **Audio-Forum, A Division of Jeffrey Norton Publishers, Inc., On-The-Green, Guilford, CT 06437.**

NEW TESTAMENT IN FRENCH: SEGOND VERSION (Christian Duplications International, Inc.) For: L,C,S,Y,Ch. Slant: All Christians.

Narrated by Charles Guillot. An attractive, well-produced package of sixteen audio cassettes in vinyl album. **$69.50.** From **Audio-Forum, A Division of Jeffrey Norton Publishers, Inc., On-The-Green, Guilford, CT 06437.**

NEW TESTAMENT IN GERMAN LUTHER EDITION (Christian Duplications International, Inc.) For: L,C,S,Y,Ch. Slant: All Christians.

Narrated by Edwin Auchenbach. An attractive, well-produced package of twenty-four cassettes in two vinyl albums. **$84.50.** From **Audio-Forum, A Division of Jeffrey Norton Publishers, Inc., On-The-Green, Guilford, CT 06437.**

NEW TESTAMENT IN ITALIAN RIVEDUTA VERSION (Christian Duplications International, Inc.) For: L,C,S,Y,Ch. Slant: All Christians.

Narrated by Elio Milazzo. An attractive, well-produced package of sixteen audio cassettes in vinyl album. **$69.50.** From **Audio-Forum, A Division of Jeffrey Norton Publishers, Inc., On-The-Green, Guilford, CT 06437.**

NEW TESTAMENT IN KOREAN (Christian Duplications International, Inc.) For: L,C,S,Y,Ch. Slant: All Christians.

Narrated by Dr. Billy Kim. An attractive, well-produced package of twenty-four cassettes in vinyl album. **$84.50.** From **Audio-Forum, A Division of Jeffrey Norton Publishers, Inc., On-The-Green, Guilford, CT 06437.**

NEW TESTAMENT IN PORTUGUESE ALMEIDA VERSION UPDATED (Christian Duplications International, Inc.) For: L,C,S,Y,Ch. Slant: All Christians.

Narrated by David Nunes. An attractive, well-produced package of sixteen audio cassettes in vinyl album. **$69.50.** From **Audio-Forum, A Division of Jeffrey Norton Publishers, Inc., On-The-Green, Guilford, CT 06437.**

NEW TESTAMENT IN SPANISH (1960 Revised Version, Reina-Valera) (Christian Duplications International, Inc.) For: L,C,S,Y,Ch. Slant: All Christians.

Narrated by Samuel H. Montoya. An attractive, well-produced package of sixteen audio cassettes in vinyl album. **$69.50.** From **Audio-Forum, A Division of Jeffrey Norton Publishers, Inc., On-The-Green, Guilford, CT 06437.**

NEW TESTAMENT ON CASSETTES (Trinity Tapes, Inc.) For: L,C,S,Y,Ch.

Read by Efrem Zimbalist, Jr. Scofield's King James Version. 16 tapes in a vinyl cassette holder. Distributed exclusively by Trinity Tapes, Inc. **$59.95.** Add **$1.50** for UPS delivery (no extra charge for parcel post). California residents add tax **$3.90.** Bookstores or from **Trinity Tapes, Inc., 16604 Arminta St., Van Nuys, CA 91406.**

THE NOW MEANING OF SCRIPTURE (Christian Media) For: L,C,S. Slant: RC,P,S,CP.

By Dr. George Martin. An examination of selected biblical passages in an effort to bridge the gap between what they meant and what they mean today for those of us trying to live a Christian life. Nine audio lessons. **$36.00.** Nine video lessons (Beta II or VHS; U-Matic available on request). **$450.00.** Please state format. Add **$4.00** for shipping. Prepaid orders only. From **Christian Media, P.O. Box 748, Ogden, UT 84402.**

AUDIO-VISUAL BIBLE RESOURCES

OLD TESTAMENT TAPES OF THE LIVING BIBLE, VOL. I (Genesis – 2 Samuel 16) (Tyndale House Publishers) For: L,S,Y. Slant: AW,C,RC,F,EP,MP,LP,RJ,CJ,OJ,D,CP.

Covers Genesis through 2 Samuel 16. Inspirational listening for people who need or prefer to listen to the Bible rather than read it. Thirteen stereo tapes are packaged in a compact bookshelf binder. **$65.95.** Bookstores.

OLD TESTAMENT TAPES OF THE LIVING BIBLE, VOL. 2 (2 Samuel 17 – Psalms) (Tyndale House Publishers) For: L,S,Y. Slant: AW,C,RC,F,EP,MP,LP,RJ,CJ,OJ,D,CP.

Covers 2 Samuel 17 through Psalms. Inspirational listening for people who need or prefer to listen to the Bible rather than read it. Fourteen stereo tapes are packaged in a compact bookshelf binder. **$65.95.** Bookstores.

OLD TESTAMENT TAPES OF THE LIVING BIBLE, VOL. 3 (Proverbs – Malachi) (Tyndale House Publishers) For: L,S,Y. Slant: AW,C,RC,F,EP,MP,LP,RJ,CJ,OJ,D.

Covers Proverbs through Malachi. Inspirational listening for people who need or prefer to listen to the Bible rather than read it. Thirteen tapes are packaged in a compact bookshelf binder. **$65.95.** Bookstores.

THE ORIGINAL CHRISTMAS STORIES (The Liturgical Press) For: L,C,S. Slant: RC,P.

These three cassettes provide a closer examination of the genuine and original Christmas stories, stripping away the tinsel and tonic, the frenzy and frolic of today's usual celebration. This series outlines the theological meaning and message of the birth and early years of Jesus as described by Matthew and Luke in their gospels. Set of three cassettes with study guide. **$22.50.** Bookstores or from **The Liturgical Press, Collegeville, MN 56321.**

PAINTED VISIONS OF REVELATION (Star Bible Publications) For: L. Slant: F,EP.

By Alyce Hart. Sixty, 35mm slides of paintings by Alyce Hart in full color. Ministers acclaim this series as "the most accurate and best teaching aid on the Book of Revelation ever produced. Over five years in production. Catalog Number 1517. **$19.95** each. Bookstores or from **Star Bible Publications, Box 181220, Ft. Worth, TX 76118.**

PARABLES OF JESUS (Catholic Education Center) For: L,C,S. Slant: RC,BC.

By Frank McCool, SJ. A professor at Pontifical Biblical Institute, Rome, deals with the parables of Jesus according to modern exegesis. Throughout this four-tape series, Fr. McCool presents principles for interpreting parables, shows the process of embellishment from the early oral tradition through the work of the Synoptics and points out implications of the parables for Christians. Father McCool's contagious excitement coupled with his expert scholarship make these programs beneficial to pastors and professional religious educators. Length 225 minutes. Rental in Beta I or U-Matic formats. **$15.00.** Purchase in all common video formats. **$70–$100.00.** From **Catholic Education Center, Media Department, 328 W. Sixth Street, St. Paul, MN 55102.**

THE PARABLES OF JESUS (Thomas More Cassettes) For: L,C,S. Slant: RC.

The parables of Jesus, says biblical expert John L. McKenzie, are popular wisdom at its finest. Even the most critical modern scholars think that we are closer to the actual words spoken by Jesus in the parables than in other New Testament passages. Following an illuminating introduction, Father McKenzie comments on a key parable which is then read by professional narrator Todd Brennan. Parables and commentaries presented are: The Sower, The Laborers in the Vineyard, The Great Banquet, The Dishonest Steward, The Good Samaritan, The Prodigal Son, The Rich Man and Lazarus, The Talents, and The Pharisee and The Tax Collector. A rewarding and fascinating cassette rich in sermon and discussion possibilities. TM 216. Approximately 50 minutes. **$9.95.** From **Thomas More Association, 225 W. Huron St., Chicago, IL 60610.**

THE PASSION AND RESURRECTION OF OUR LORD (Daughters of St. Paul) For: L,C,S,Y. Slant: D,P.

Chapters 14, 15, and 16 of Mark's Gospel are read with appropriate introduction and conclusion. Approximately thirty minutes. Number CS0260. **$5.95** (add .75 for postage). Bookstores or from **Daughters of St. Paul, 50 St. Paul's Ave., Jamaica Plain, Boston, MA 02130.**

PAUL IN HIS EARLY LETTERS: THESSALONIANS, PHILIPPIANS, GALATIANS (Christian Media) For: L,C,S. Slant: RC,P,S,CP.

By Rev. George Montague, S.M. An exploration of the earliest New Testament writings, the picture they present of fervent Christian communities and the challenge Paul's message continues to offer us. The Lord is coming (Thessalonians), He is present now in our sufferings (Philippians), and it is His grace rather than the law which saves us (Galatians). Ten audio lessons. **$40.00.** Ten video lessons (Beta II or VHS; U-Matic available on request). **$475.00.** Please state format. Add **$4.00** for shipping. Prepaid orders only. From **Christian Media, P.O. Box 748, Ogden, UT 84402.**

PAUL TO THE EPHESIANS (Daughters of St. Paul) For: L,C,S,Y. Slant: D,P.

Paul's Letter to the Ephesians (which speaks of Christian Truths and Christian Love) is read with appropriate introduction and music. Approximately thirty minutes. **$5.95** (add .75 for postage). Bookstores or from **Daughters of St. Paul, 50 St. Paul's Ave., Jamaica Plain, Boston, MA 02130.**

PAUL'S LETTERS TO THE CORINTHIANS (Christian Media) For: L,C,S. Slant: RC,P,S,CP.

By Rev. Richard Rohr, O.F.M. We are presented with a study of the person and mission of Paul as a church-builder and reconciler. The texts will be used to illustrate how Scripture may be used and interpreted for today's needs. Ten audio lessons. **$40.00.** Ten video lessons (Beta II or VHS; U-Matic available on request). **$475.00.** Please state format. Add **$4.00** for shipping. Prepaid orders only. From **Christian Media, P.O. Box 748, Ogden, UT 84402.**

AUDIO-VISUAL BIBLE RESOURCES

PAUL'S MASTERPIECE OF CHRIST (Training Church Leaders, Inc.) For: L,C,S,Y. Slant: EP,P.

Audio cassettes by Dan DeHaan. A study in the book of Colossians. An expository verse-by-verse study of Paul's greatest book on exhalting Christ. There is hardly a stone unturned in Colossians through this study. If you desire to teach or study Colossians, this study is for you! **$83.20.** From **Training Church Leaders, Inc., 6080 New Peachtree Road, Atlanta, GA 30340.**

1 PETER: GETTING READY FOR THE END (Training Church Leaders, Inc.) For: L,C,S,Y. Slant: EP,P.

Audio cassettes by Dan DeHaan. 1 Peter is a book for testing how real your Christian life is. After listening to this series you will know whether your walk is genuine Christianity or counterfeit. Will your life stand true if God chooses to place you in times of persecution? What does pressure produce in your life? This study will give you the opportunity to answer these questions and others based on biblical principles. This is an expository verse-by-verse study of I Peter. **$83.20.** From **Training Church Leaders, Inc., 6080 New Peachtree Road, Atlanta, GA 30340.**

PLEASE DON'T READ THE BIBLE UNLESS... (Catholic Education Center) For: L,C,S. Slant: RC,P.

By Daniel Durken, OSB. In his scholarly, yet humor-filled fashion, Father Durken suggests that the "surgeon general warns, 'Reading the Bible can be hazardous to your health.'" This well-known Scripture scholar explains at length that reading is an art to be developed, and that art applies to Scripture as well. He continues to offer practical means of developing the art, and its application to Bible reading. Dangers and pitfalls are noted, but the program ends optimistically, encouraging the Scripture reader to have a sense of humor, as we are created from earth...humus...humor! Length 60 minutes. Rental in Beta I or U-Matic formats. **$15.00.** Purchase in all common video formats. **$70-$100.00.** From **Catholic Education Center, Media Department, 328 W. Sixth Street, St. Paul, MN 55102.**

THE POLKA DOT PEOPLE AND THE LIGHT (Kerr Associates) For: L,C,S,Y,Ch. Slant: AW,C,RC,EP,MP,LP,P.

Written and illustrated by Ronn Kerr. A graphic and symbolic telling of the great theme of the Bible: God's constant love and continuous reaching out to His people. In cartoon style, God is symbolized as the bright, shining and unturnoffable Light. Human kind is depicted in a non-ethnic, non-racial style in blues, greens, and purples, polka dots, stripes and checks. Throughout the filmstrip, the Light keeps shining through the creation but the people turn away into darkness. Then God sends the patriarchs, but the people again turn to the darkness. Finally, God comes Himself as the God-Man from Nazareth to show the people what God is like and what they can become. But the people kill the God-Man and return to the darkness. And, this time it seems as if the darkness will be permanent. But, the God-Man comes back to life! Then, a few people begin to understand and follow. Then, a few more, and more. **The Polka Dot People and the Light** is primarily for adults and youth, but can be used for children. One 90-frame full-color filmstrip and one 14-minute sound and music cassette. Number K 345. **$29.95.** From **Kerr Associates, 460 Woodycrest Avenue, Nashville, TN 37210.**

PRAYER IN THE NEW TESTAMENT (Christian Media) For: L,C,S. Slant: RC,P,S,CP.

By Rev. Ralph Weishaar, O.F.M. Models and teaching on prayer from Matthew and Revelations are examined, focusing on the meaning and the various kinds of prayer and their significance for Christians today. Five audio lessons. **$20.00.** Five video lessons (Beta II or VHS; U-Matic available on request). **$250.00.** Please state format. Add **$4.00** for shipping. Prepaid orders only. From **Christian Media, P.O. Box 748, Ogden, UT 84402.**

PROJECTABLE BIBLE ATLAS (Faith Venture Visuals, Inc.) For: L, C, S, Y, Ch. Slant: D,P.

The FVV **Projectable Bible Atlas** is the only available projectable atlas which offers 100% coverage of Bible geography: five base maps, 19 overlays, 48 masters for additional transparencies; overlays for each of the base maps show contemporary names—an invaluable aid to studying Bible geography and current events; includes alternate names, variant spellings, and Scripture references; print big enough to be read by large audiences; comes in a sturdy, attractive, two-part vinyl covered box. **$49.95.** Bookstores or from **Faith Venture Visuals, Inc., P.O. Box 423, 510 E. Main Street, Lititz, PA 17543.**

PRONUNCIATION OF BIBLE NAMES (Broadman Films) For: L,C,S,Y.

A series of two audio cassettes with a 32-page manual. Thirty-six hundred proper names of the Bible are pronounced on these two cassettes. The manual provides a respelling of each word for clarification. Example Aaronite is respelled AIR'n night. Tapes and manual come in bookstyle album. Two audio cassettes. **$12.50.** Bookstores.

THE PROPHETS (Christian Media) For: L,C,S. Slant: RC,P,S,CP.

By Fr. Richard Rohr, O.F.M. The

212

AUDIO-VISUAL BIBLE RESOURCES

voice of the prophets still rings loud and clear in our day, calling us to authentic discipleship and showing us how to live a prophetic life. Nine audio lessons. **$36.00**. Nine video lessons (Beta II or VHS; U-Matic available on request). **$450.00**. Please state format. Add **$4.00** shipping. Prepaid orders only. From **Christian Media, P.O. Box 748, Ogden, UT 84402.**

PROVERBS OF SOLOMON (Revivaltime Media Ministries) For: L. Slant: EP,D,P.

Narrated by Dan Betzer. From Revivaltime's "Selected Scripture Series," **Proverbs of Solomon** will fill your home or car with a whole new dimension of scriptural blessing. This 4-tape set is narrated from the King James Version. Tapes come in an attractively designed library case. Write for current price list. From **Revivaltime Media Ministries, P.O. Box 70, Springfield, MO 65801.**

PSALMS (Christian Media) For: L,C,S. Slant: RC,P,S,CP.

By Fr. George Montague, S.M. A prayerful presentation on how the Spirit-inspired songs of Israel are inspired prayers for us today. Ten audio lessons. **$40.00**. Ten video lessons (Beta II or VHS; U-Matic available on request). **$475.00**. Please state format. Add **$4.00** for shipping. Prepaid orders only. From **Christian Media, P.O. Box 748, Ogden, UT 84402.**

THE PSALMS (Thomas More Cassettes) For: L,C,S. Slant: RC.

Selections by Todd Brennan; Reflections by John L. McKenzie. Professional narrator Todd Brennan reads selections from the Psalms which are interspersed with the illuminating and expert commentary of biblical scholar John L. McKenzie. Brennan's articulate and nuanced reading combined with Father McKenzie's detailed commentary, based on the latest biblical research combine to reveal not only the beauty of these most lyrical of all scriptures, but a fuller appreciation and understanding. TM197. 2 cassettes, approximately 1 3/4 hours. **$14.95**. From **Thomas More Association, 225 W. Huron Street, Chicago, IL 60610.**

PSALMS—OF ADORATION, THANKSGIVING, SUPPLICATION, CONFIDENCE, AND PENANCE (Daughters of St. Paul) For: L,C,S,Y. Slant: D,P.

Psalms 96, 111, 23, 142, 32, 51, 6, 38, 102, 130, 143 are read with appropriate introductions and music. Approximately thirty minutes. Number CS0300. **$5.95** (add .75 for postage). Bookstores or from **Daughters of St. Paul, 50 St. Paul's Ave., Jamaica Plain, Boston, MA 02130.**

THE PSALMS: GLAD, SAD, AND MAD (The Liturgical Press) For: L,C,S. Slant: RC,P.

The Psalms are the Roman Catholic Church's official prayer, and in these four cassettes they are explored in context and content. The Psalms are first treated generally, and then specific basic forms are covered: the Glad Psalms of praise and thanks; the Sad Psalms of lament or complaint; and the Mad Psalms of anger and frustration. Set of four cassettes with study guide. **$30.95**. Bookstores or from **The Liturgical Press, Collegeville, MN 56321.**

PSALMS AND PROVERBS ON CASSETTES (Trinity Tapes, Inc.) For: L,C,S.

Read by Efrem Zimbalist, Jr. Scofield's King James Version. 6 tapes in a vinyl cassette holder. Distributed exclusively by Trinity Tapes, Inc. **$29.95**. Add **$1.50** for United Parcel Service delivery (no extra charge for parcel post). California residents add **$1.95** tax. Bookstores or from **Trinity Tapes, Inc., 16604 Arminta St., Van Nuys, CA 91406.**

PSALMS AND PROVERBS ON CASSETTES (Trinity Tapes, Inc.) For: L,C,S,Y.

Read by Alexander Scourby. King James Version. 6 tapes in a vinyl cassette holder. **$16.95**. Add **$1.50** for United Parcel Service delivery (no extra charge for parcel post). California residents add **$1.11** tax. Bookstores or from **Trinity Tapes, Inc., 16604 Arminta St., Van Nuys, CA 91406.**

THE PSALMS IN HEBREW AND ENGLISH (Spoken Arts, Inc.) For: L,C,S,Y. Slant: RJ,CJ,OJ,D,P.

These psalms are among the immortal poems of the world's literature, poems that express the faith by which these ancient poets lived. Read by Morris Carnovsky whose performances at Stratford's Shakespeare Festival have been outstanding highlights, the album is a moving experience for every poetry lover. Available in LP format only, product number SA 776. **$9.95**. From **Spoken Arts, Inc., 310 North Avenue, New Rochelle, NY 10801.**

THE REAL JESUS (Thomas More Cassettes) For: L,C,S. Slant: RC.

By John L. McKenzie. One of the keys to tracing the "real" Jesus, Father McKenzie suggests, is to understand the nature of the written materials in which Jesus is represented. Historical accuracy was not of primary importance to the New Testament authors because they were more concerned with presenting Jesus as he was believed rather than as he was remembered. Drawing on his many years of prominent research and scholarship, the renowned biblical scholar expertly separates historical fact from myth and provides a fascinating study of the real Jesus. TM261. Approximately 34 minutes. **$9.95**. From **Thomas More Association, 225 W. Huron Street, Chicago, IL 60610.**

THE REAL MARY (Thomas More Cassettes) For: L,C,S. Slant: RC.

By John L. McKenzie. The real Mary, as Fr. McKenzie readily admits, is difficult to know. We know nothing of her physical appearance and few of her words are recorded directly so she is a perfect subject for myth-making. Fr. McKenzie differentiates the Mary of popular imagination and the Mary of historical record. A reverent, honest look at Mary, with fresh perspectives and striking insights. TM265. 40 minutes. **$9.95**. From **Thomas More Association, 225 W. Huron Street, Chicago, IL 60610.**

REVELATION (Dove Publications) For: L,C,S. Slant: RC,P.

AUDIO-VISUAL BIBLE RESOURCES

Six cassettes of reflections on the main sections and unifying themes of the Book of Revelation. Fr. Jim Wolff, retreat master and counselor, stresses the positive, hopeful and pastoral dimensions of John's victory message. **$19.50** (add **$1.30** for postage). From **Dove Publications, Pecos, NM 87552.**

REVELATION (Revivaltime Media Ministries) For: L. Slant: EP,D,P.

Narrated by Dan Betzer. Dynamically narrated from the King James Version by evangelist Dan Betzer. This 4-cassette album takes the listener on an exciting journey through one of the Bible's most intriguing books. From Revivaltime's "Selected Scripture Series." Write for information and price list. From **Revivaltime Media Ministries, P.O. Box 70, Springfield, MO 65801.**

REVELATION (Jimmy Swaggart Ministries) For: L,C. Slant: CP.

By Jimmy Swaggart. Many Christians have commented on the difficulty of understanding the Book of Revelation. Verse-by-verse and chapter-by-chapter. Brother Jimmy Swaggart explores and makes clear the symbols and the applications they have for our lives today. These twelve cassettes contain twenty hours of teaching. Product Number 04-019. **$30.00.** From **Jimmy Swaggart Ministries, P.O. Box 2550, Baton Rouge, LA 70821.**

THE REVELATION CASSETTE SERIES (Jimmy Swaggart Ministries) For: L,C. Slant: CP.

By Jimmy Swaggart. Bound in a handsome vinyl case, these 24 tapes examine, verse-by-verse, the vastness and complexity of the Book of Revelation. All of your questions concerning these momentous coming events will be answered in this long awaited series. All the symbols veiled for so long are now uncovered and explained thoroughly and insightfully. Jimmy Swaggart teaches Revelation on tape as he taught it on television to bring you into the fullness of end-time prophecy. In this momentous day and age, what more important study could there be! Product Number 04-031. **$40.00.** From **Jimmy Swaggart Ministries, P.O. 2550, Baton Rouge, LA 70821.**

REVELATION REVEALED CASSETTE LIBRARY (Jack Van Impe Ministries) For: L,C,S,Y. Slant: F.

An expositional walk through the Book of Revelation, verse by verse. Includes the seven churches of Asia, the Rapture, the 21 Tribulation judgements, the rise of Antichrist, Russia's invasion of Israel, the Battle of Armageddon, Christ's return and a preview of new Jerusalem. Eight cassettes per library, attractively packaged in a handsome vinyl carrying/storage case. **$50.00** gift. From **Jack Van Impe Ministries, P.O. Box J, Royal Oak, MI 48068.**

REVELATIONS (Christian Media) For: L,C,S. Slant: RC,P,S,CP.

By Rev. George Montague, S.M. This series helps to clarify many of the questions about the book of Revelation, such as: Is it a book of prophecy? What about the Rapture? What about the Millenium? What about the Antichrist? The book is portrayed as a book of hope particularly for those who are called to persevere under prolonged persecution. The book is explained as prophetic of the past, present, and future, but is presented more as a vision rather than a carefully concealed calendar of events that outline a countdown to catastrophe. Ten audio lessons. **$40.00.** Ten video lessons (Beta II or VHS; U-Matic available on request). **$475.00.** Please state format. Add **$4.00** for shipping. Prepaid orders only. From **Christian Media, P.O. Box 748, Ogden, UT 84402.**

REVISED STANDARD VERSION COMPLETE BIBLE ON CASSETTE TAPE (International Cassette Corporation) For: L,C,S,Y.

Narrated by Alexander Scourby. The complete Bible consists of 48 cassette tapes and is packaged in one leatherette album with a large velcro closure and sturdy handle. The Revised Standard Version may also be purchased separately as a New Testament or an Old Testament. Complete Bible. **$159.98.** Old Testament. **$119.98.** New Testament. **$39.98.** Bookstores, film rental libraries, or from **International Cassette Corp., P.O. Box 1928, Greenville, TX 75401.**

ROMANS (Christian Media) For: L,C,S. Slant: RC,P,S,CP.

By Fr. George Montague, S.M. This series develops Paul's insights on the

AUDIO-VISUAL BIBLE RESOURCES

way to salvation and of living a life strengthened and supported by the Holy Spirit. It portrays the people as "the beloved of God" who are called to holiness and who are justified by their decision to follow Christ on their journey of faith through the world. Salvation is a gift of God. The Christian is called to accept this gift and live out a life in the truth of salvation. Ten audio lessons. **$40.00**. Ten video lessons (Beta II or VHS; U-Matic available on request). **$475.00**. Please state format. Add **$4.00** for shipping. Prepaid orders only. From **Christian Media, P.O. Box 748, Ogden, UT 84402**.

ROOTS OF OUR BIBLE (It Is Written Telecast) For: L,S. Slant: MP,D,P,I,BC.

Six, one-half inch, VHS cassettes presenting a faith-building series on "The Roots of Our Bible." George Vandeman takes you on an exciting journey to Egypt to learn how the Royal Papyrus was made for the preservation of the Scripture. You will visit Qumran near the Dead Sea, where devoted Essene scribes meticulously copied the sacred manuscripts and then hid them in caves to protect them from destruction. The development of God's Holy Bible is traced as you stand in the famous Bodleian Library in Oxford, England and are caught up in the evangelistic fervor of John Wycliffe and the Lollards as they went out to proclaim the message of the Book. Your faith in the certainty of God's Word will be confirmed through "Dead Men Do Tell Tales," "Drama At the Dead Sea," "The Bible in Olde England," "With and Without the Bible," "Polling the Evidence," and "The Wounded Healer." **$30.00** per tape. From **It Is Written, Box O, Thousand Oaks, CA 91360**.

SALVATION IN THE NEW TESTAMENT (Christian Media) For: L,C,S. Slant: RC,P,S,CP.

By Fr. Richard Rohr, O.F.M. This series gives a well-developed outline of the foundation for faith in salvation in both the Old Testament and New Testament. Salvation is portrayed not as something to be gained, but as a life to be lived. Life is a journey through the world in the light of faith, hope, and love. Ten audio lessons. **$40.00**. Ten video lessons (Beta II or VHS; U-Matic available on request). **$475.00**. Please state format. Add **$4.00** for shipping. Prepaid orders only.

From **Christian Media, P.O. Box 748, Ogden, UT 84402**.

SAUL AND DAVID (Daughters of St. Paul) For: L,C,S,Y. Slant: RC,EP,MP,D,P.

The action-packed story of Saul, a brave but jealous king; David, a daring and loyal youth; and the people who loved them both and had to choose which one to follow. 110 minutes, color, 16 mm. **$50.00** rental. Film libraries or from **Daughters of St. Paul, 50 St. Paul's Ave., Jamaica Plain, Boston, MA 02130**.

SCIENCE AND NATURE—TWO VOTES FOR GOD (Star Bible Publications) For: L,C,S,Y. Slant: F,EP,S,BC.

By Bert Thompson and Wayne Jackson. In a time of increasing atheism, agnosticism, liberalism, etc., the faith of young and old alike is being challenged almost daily. Most people are ill-prepared to meet these challenges. Accordingly, Bert Thompson and Wayne Jackson have prepared a series of tapes to answer the crucial issues which confront Christians in modern society, and to help non Christians examine the evidences upon which historical Christianity is based. Sixteen cassettes in vinyl album. Catalog Number BCL-590. **$45.00**. Bookstores or from **Star Bible Publications, Box 181220, Ft. Worth, TX 76118**.

SCRIPTURE FILMS AND FILM STRIPS (American Bible Society) For: L.

The following films are among the many available from ABS on a free-will offering basis: **A Journey of Hope.** Millions of people throughout the world are just learning to read. Shot on location in Africa, this new and important film describes how the Bible Society, through their exciting Good News for New Readers Program, is providing special Scriptures to meet their needs. From the market ladies in provincial towns to the nomads of Illenyamu, see how new readers are discovering for themselves the strength and hope found in reading His Word. Color, 22 minutes. Order Number LH-240. **Light Upon the Earth.** The compelling story of how the Word of God can change lives when it is read and understood. Moving stories of people who unexpectedly found new life in the pages of the Book they had long ignored. Your faith in the power of God's Word will increase as you see this soul-stirring film. Color, 22 minutes. Order Number LH-160. For a complete listing of films and filmstrips, write for the **ABS Catalog of Scripture Resources.** When ordering films, indicate title, order number and show date. From **American Bible Society/Film Rentals, 1865 Broadway, New York, NY 10023**.

SCRIPTURE FILMSTRIP SERIES (Thomas S. Klise Company) For: L,Y,Ch. Slant: RC,MP,LP,P.

Five colorful filmstrips on key figures and themes of the Old Testament. The series combines the most recent biblical scholarship with marvelously vivid sketches to create for your students a convincing set of images for major biblical themes. Each unit begins with a vignette from American history; a two-minute mood setter, which suggests or discloses the religious values dealt with in the scriptural part of the filmstrip. **Homeward to the Future:** The Story of Abraham; **Free At Last!:** Moses and the Exodus; **A More Perfect Union:** Moses and the Sinai Covenant; **The Man Who Had Everything:** David and the Kingdom; **In Dreams Begin Fidelities:** The Prophets of Israel. Units average about 70 frames each, 12 minutes running time. Each comes with a rich teacher guide, keyed to leading texts. Five filmstrips, 5 records or cassettes, and printed guide. **$110.00**. Single unit price 1 filmstrip, 1 record or cassette, and 1 printed guide. **$25.00**. From **Thomas S. Klise Company, P.O. Box 3418, Peoria, IL 61614**.

THE SCRIPTURES AND THE MODERN WORLD (Catholic Education Center) For: L,C,S. Slant: RC,D,P.

By Dr. James Limburg. Every age grapples with the basic themes in the Bible attempting to relate these themes to its own times. The questions and issues these themes present to us today are raised in this presentation. Dr. Limburg answers this pressing question for religion teachers, catechists and adults, "How can we make Scripture come alive for students, children, and ourselves?" He does so by focusing on the interpretation of a variety of our scriptural passages and exploring scriptural passages relating to the four key words of "Wonder," "Providence," "Mission," and "Grace." Dr. Limburg's refreshing style brings together Scripture and the world in which we live. Length is 62 minutes.

AUDIO-VISUAL BIBLE RESOURCES

Rental in Beta I or U-Matic formats. **$15.00**. Purchase in all common video formats. **$70-$100.00**. From **Catholic Education Center, Media Department, 328 W. Sixth Street, St. Paul, MN 55102**.

SCRIPTURES IN BRAILLE (American Bible Society) For: L,C,S,Y,Ch.

Since 1911, ABS has provided Braille Scriptures for the blind. These are offered at a price that represents less than the full cost of production and handling. For a complete list of ABS Braille Scriptures, write for our free catalog, **Scriptures for the Visually Impaired**. Grade 2 Braille. New Testament: Today's English Version. 5 volumes. Order No. 10397. **$65.50**. King James Version. 4 volumes. Order No. 09981. **$52.40**. Psalms: Today's English Version. Order No. 10414. **$13.10**. King James Version. Order No. 09890. **$13.10**. From **American Bible Society, 1865 Broadway, New York, NY 10023**.

SCRIPTURES ON CASSETTES AND RECORDS (American Bible Society)

For those who need or prefer the spoken word, Scriptures are available on records and cassettes from ABS. Each cassette and record has both printed and braille identification. (Not for commercial resale.) For a complete list of ABS recorded Scriptures, write for our free catalog, **Scriptures for the Visually Impaired**. New Testament. Today's English Version. 15 cassettes in a vinyl album. Order No. 11809. **$35.50**. New Testament and Psalms. King James Version. 18 cassettes. Order No. 16009. **$15.00**. New Testament. King James Version. 18 records (33 1/3 RPM). Order No. 16000. **$15.00**. From **American Bible Society, Box 5656, Grand Central Station, New York, NY 10163**.

SELECTED FAVORITE PSALMS (Revivaltime Media Ministries) For: L. Slant: EP,D,P.

Narrated by Dan Betzer. From Revivaltime's "Selected Scripture Series" comes this 4-cassette package of beautifully recorded Scripture from the King James Version. Narrated in the mellow baritone voice of Revivaltime evangelist Dan Betzer, these Psalm selections are set against the restful background strings of the harp. Tapes come in an attractively designed library case. Write for current price list. From **Revivaltime Media Ministries, P.O. Box 70, Springfield, MO 65801**.

SERMON ON THE AMOUNT (Training Church Leaders, Inc.) For: L,C,S,Y. Slant: EP,P.

Audio cassettes by Dan DeHaan. Madison Avenue techniques have been used to get young Christians manipulated. Slick campaigning to get Christians to loosen up their money is standard procedure today. The methods of the world are used to get the message of heaven across. If God has a heavenly message, would He not also have a heavenly method to accomplish it? An in-depth look at "tithing" from the Old and New Testaments is taken to find God's plan of giving and receiving. Titles of sessions are: Earning-Spending-Giving; Hindrances in Saving; Is There a Difference Between Old and New Testament Giving?; Malachi 3:10; Matthew 17 and 23; Investing with God; Percentage Giving: Right or Wrong?; and God's View of Receiving. **$17.60**. From **Training Church Leaders, Inc., 6080 New Peachtree Road, Atlanta, GA 30340**.

SIMPLE ENGLISH NEW TESTAMENT ON CASSETTE TAPE WITH FOLLOW ALONG BIBLE (International Cassette Corporation) For: L,C,S,Y.

Narrated by Steven B. Stevens. Using only simple sentences and a 3,000 word vocabulary, the Simple English Bible can be comprehended by the entire family. The accompanying New Testament has large, stylish typefaces and frequent headings to allow youngsters to follow along. The Bible and 12 cassette tapes packaged in a leatherette album are shrink-wrapped together to be purchased as one unit. **$49.98** (includes follow-along Bible). Bookstores, film rental libraries, or from **International Cassette Corp., P.O. Box 1928, Greenville, TX 75401**.

SON BEAMS DIAL (Voice of Prophecy) For: L. Slant: EP.

Dozens of Bible references to the life and ministry of Christ. With a spin of the dial, Bible references for any one of 10 subjects appear in the information window. Learning is interesting, sharing is easy, and the dial is a convenient size for pocket, purse, or right in the front of your Bible. Single copy **Free**. From **Voice of Prophecy, P.O. Box 55, Dept. YOB, Los Angeles, CA 90053**.

THE SONG OF SONGS (Spoken Arts, Inc.) For: L,C,S,Y. Slant: RJ, CJ, OJ, D, P.

Read in English by Carol Veazie. Read in Hebrew by Morris Carnovsky. The beauty and dignity of pure love and fidelity in the **Song of Songs** is admirably expressed in the image, diction, and tone of this recording. English reading is from the traditional King James. Available in LP format only, number SA777. **$9.95**. From **Spoken Arts, Inc., 310 North Avenue, New Rochelle, NY 10801**.

SPIRITUALITY OF JOHN'S GOSPEL (Christian Media) For: L,C,S. Slant: RC,P,S,CP.

By Rev. Jim Wolff. By focusing on the spirituality of John's Gospel, we are shown how each person today can find her or his spiritual identity in this gospel. Nine audio lessons. **$36.00**. Nine video lessons (Beta II or VHS; U-Matic available on request). **$450.00**. Please state format. Add **$4.00** for shipping. Prepaid orders only. From **Christian Media, P.O. Box 748, Ogden, UT 84402**.

STORIES THAT LIVE (International Cassette Corporation) For: L,C,S Y,Ch.

The greatest stories in the world on six exciting twenty-minute cassette tapes. Included on these cassettes are stories such as Adam and Eve, Joseph the Dreamer, David and Goliath, Happy Birthday, Stories of Jesus and He's Coming Back. Each is narrated by various voices with careful enunciation to allow easy follow-along reading in accompanying full-color Bible storybooks. This series is even more enjoyable with each 8 1/2 x 11 inch, full-size companion coloring book covering each of the stories in the cassette/book pack. Displays are available. Cassette/Book Pack. **$4.98**. Coloring Book **$.88**. Bookstores, film rental libraries or from **International Cassette Corp. P.O. Box 1928, Greenville, TX 75401**.

A SURE FOUNDATION (Family Life Distributors) For: L. Slant: I.

AUDIO-VISUAL BIBLE RESOURCES

A young pastor, Gary Brooks is confronted by his board chairman, Will Marlowe, about his stand on biblical inerrancy. Mr. Marlowe wants to maintain peace in the church, while Pastor Brooks wants to proclaim the truth. Conflict is inevitable. While trying to cut costs in his construction business, Mr. Marlowe nearly kills one of his workers in an accident. In addition he is faced with his daughter's announcement that she plans to move in with her boyfriend. Shocked by his daughter's weak moral stand, he recognizes he is responsible. Mr. Marlowe finally realizes that without an inerrant Bible, man, not God, becomes the final authority. This film is packed with excitement, humor and biblical truth. Length 55 minutes. **$66.00** per showing plus shipping and insurance. Film rental libraries or from **Fellowship Films, P.O. Box 2330, Springfield, IL 62705**.

TEACHER TRAINING (Training Church Leaders, Inc.) For: L,C,S,Y. Slant: EP,P.

By Dan DeHaan. A three-tape audio cassette series that gives helpful information on being a teacher of the Word. If you find yourself involved in teaching, but find you need help with preparation, speaking, application, etc., these tapes will give you guidelines to benefit your teaching opportunities. Titles of sessions are: Priorities of a Teacher and How to Teach the Word of God. **$8.70**. From **Training Church Leaders, Inc., 6080 New Peachtree Road, Atlanta, GA 30340**.

TEACHING VISUALS FROM WILLMINGTON'S GUIDE TO THE BIBLE (Tyndale House Publishers) For: L,C. Slant: AW,C,RC,F,EP,MP,LP,P,CP.

By H. L. Wilmington. A set of 250 professionally prepared charts, lists, diagrams, maps, and illustrations from **Willmington's Guide to the Bible.** Can be viewed directly by small groups or used to make overhead visuals for large groups. Punched for three ring notebook. Perfect bound 8 1/2 x 11". **$14.95**. Bookstores.

TOPICAL PRESENTATIONS (International Cassette Corporation) For: L,C,S,Y.

Narrated by Steven B. Stevens. Produced by ICC, these special presentations contain Scripture only, obtained from numerous translations and versions - no commentary or opinion. These series are available on subjects such as Healing, the Godhead, and Freedom. All may be purchased as a set with each consisting of four cassette tapes in a leatherette album or to be purchased individually in a single leatherette album or poly box. Each series (set of four). **$16.98**. Individual cassette: Album **$5.98**; Poly Box **$3.98**. Bookstores, film rental libraries, or from **International Cassette Corp., P.O. Box 1928, Greenville, TX 75401**.

THE TRUE SHEPHERD AND HIS FLOCK (Faith Venture Visuals, Inc.) For: L,C,S,Y,Ch. Slant: D,P.

An inspirational study of Psalm 23 and related Scriptures on the Shepherd theme. Each lesson has six to eight activities for adults and children. The transparencies depict 12 different experiences common to the eastern shepherd. This expositional Bible study can be used for any age, race or language, in Sunday school, weekend retreats, home Bible studies, worship services, camp, youth rallies, and vacation Bible school. **$15.95**. Bookstores or from **Faith Venture Visuals, Inc., P.O. Box 423, 510 E. Main Street, Lititz, PA 17543**.

UNDERSTANDING SCRIPTURE (The Liturgical Press) For: L,C,S. Slant: RC,P.

This single cassette will provide a general background against which all scripture study can be viewed. The Bible is explored both as literature and as history to complete the presentation and both the Old and the New Testament are bridged. Single cassette. **$5.95**. Bookstores or from **The Liturgical Press, Collegeville, MN 56321**.

UNDERSTANDING SCRIPTURE (ROA Filmstrip Company) For: L,C,S,Y. Slant: RC,MP,P.

More than just a series of filmstrips on Scripture, this program not only conveys information, but also creates a desire to independently read and learn more about the sacred writings. **Understanding Scripture** can stand alone as a thorough presentation on the Bible, beginning with the origins of the Bible, tracing its heritage and development, and examining its structure and literary forms and devices. To understand Scripture, it is necessary to understand not only its message, but also its form. Therefore, the first seven filmstrips in the program highlight key literary forms found in the Bible. The important distinction is also made between history as event (something happened) and history as record (an interpretation of what happened)--the Bible is presented as history as record. Includes ten filmstrips; ten cassettes or five records; and ten teacher's guides. From **ROA Filmstrip Co., 6633 W. Howard Street, Niles, IL 60648**.

VIDEO CASSETTE CATALOG (Video Bible Library, Inc.) For: L,C,S,Y,Ch. Slant: EP,D,P,S.

Bible-centered video programs for all ages, covering a wide range of subjects, from children's stories to a complete college course in New Testament Greek, from counseling to church leadership. Most programs include printed study guides. Excellent for personal study, church and Sunday school, home fellowship groups or classroom instruction. Sampler tape available. Catalog free. Bookstores or from **Video Bible Library, Inc., P.O. Box 17515, Portland, OR 97217**.

VIDEO CASSETTE CATALOG (Video Library) For: L,C,S,Y. Slant: C,F,EP, MP,D,P,I,BC,M.

Eternal Biblical truth applied to today's needs through tomorrow's technology. We can assist your church through a strong and helpful library of video tapes that communicate biblical truth, answers to problems, and encouragement to all. Never before have there been more people without Christ, nor have there been more Christians who need to grow spiritually. Now God has allowed us to have the technology that can greatly enhance the ministry of the local church. The video tapes are available in VHS,

BETA, and 3/4 inch formats. Excellent resource for several uses including: training Sunday school teachers, special elective courses for Sunday school, small groups, midweek prayer meetings, retreats, church training classes, and others. Excellent teachers like: MacArthur, Briscoe, Brandt, Toussaint, Dehann, Havner, Narramore, Stanley, and others. Men you may never have any other way, are yours on our convenient video cassettes. Request Video Cassette Catalog. **$1.00.** From **Bible Video Library,** 524 Sycamore Circle, Ridgeland, MS 39157.

WAR AND PEACE IN THE NEW TESTAMENT (Thomas More Cassettes) For: L,C,S. Slant: RC.

By John L. McKenzie. Father McKenzie speaks with his customary uncompromising directness and authority on a subject that is of vital importance to the Church's credibility with contemporary youth. TM4. 30 minutes. **$8.95.** From **Thomas More Association, 225 W. Huron St., Chicago, IL 60610.**

THE WAY OF JOY (PHILIPPIANS) (Ambassadors For Christ (USA), Inc.) For: L,C,S. Slant: EP,P.

Audio cassette by Ian North. Written from prison by a brilliant and energetic man confined for his bold testimony, the letter to the Philippians holds the secret of joy and contentment under the most depressing circumstances. This series highlights the main concerns in Paul's letter to the Philippians and contains the secret of joyful inward detachment from circumstances because of undivided attachment to Jesus Christ Himself. Titles of sessions are: Progress Through Persecution; Pattern for Prayer; Poise Through Praise; Promising Prospects; Productive Partnership; Pioneering Personalities; Profit Through Parting; Possessed to Possess; Painful Prognosis; and Panoply of Pearls. **$28.20.** From **Training Church Leaders, Inc., 6080 New Peachtree Road, Atlanta, GA 30340.**

WHAT IS THE DIFFERENCE BETWEEN BIBLE STUDY AND BIBLE SHARING? (Catholic Education Center) For: L,C,S. Slant: RC,P.

By Loretta Girzaitis. Ms. Girzaitis outlines the ingredients that are important for groups that are focusing primarily on Bible sharing and prayer. She also draws the parallels and differences between Bible sharing and Bible study and facilitates the process in a Bible sharing activity. Length is 32 minutes. Rental in Beta I and U-Matic formats. **$15.00.** Purchase in all common video formats. **$70–$100.00.** From **Catholic Education Center, Media Department, 328 W. Sixth Street, St. Paul, MN 55102.**

WHAT'S THIS WORLD COMING TO? (The Liturgical Press) For: L,C,S. Slant: RC,P.

In the Book of Revelation, John of Patmos writes a loud, clear call for "the endurance and faith of the saints." Father Daniel Durken, OSB, leads the listener through rich symbolism John uses to give his co-sufferers new hope. The seven letters, seals, trumpets, signs, bowls, and other symbolism are defined. Set of four cassettes with study guide. **$30.95.** Bookstores or from **The Liturgical Press, Collegeville, MN 56321.**

GIVE YOUR FAMILY THE COMPUTER ADVANTAGE WITH Family Bible Fun

NEW EDUCATIONAL SOFTWARE FOR YOUR ATARI* OR APPLE**

Each Family Bible Fun Disc contains hours of family activity that test and teach—Discs that feature The Prophets, Life of David, The Patriarchs, Life of Christ, The Book of Acts, Great Men of the Bible, Great Women of the Bible plus two that explore through General Bible quizzes.

"I personally feel that FAMILY BIBLE FUN programs will renew your interest in the values of Christian living and your appreciation of the greatest book on earth. The Bible."
Art Linkletter

See them all now at The Sparrow Software Center in your local bookstore.

or write Sparrow
Canoga Park, CA 91304
for your free brochure.

*Atari 400
Atari 800
Atari 1200
**Apple II
Apple II+
Apple IIE

© 1983 Sparrow
HomeComputer Software
SPARROW

WHERE YOUR TREASURE IS—SONGS OF FAITH (Daughters of St. Paul) For: L,C,S,Y. Slant: RC,EP,MP,L,D.

Inspired by sacred Scripture, these songs convey the message of God's ever-present love and care for each of us. Selections range from the confident invitation of "Cast Your Cares," to the moving ballad of the prodigal son; "Come Back Home," to the powerful refrains of "Who Will Separate Me?" Although the message is a familiar one, the originality of the music and arrangements adds a new zest, a new reason for praising the Lord God who is ever abundant with His gifts. Forty minutes. Stereo cassette, number CS0854. **$6.50.** Stereo record, number RE0200. **$7.50.** Songbook, number MU0100. **$5.95.** (add **$1.00** for postage). Bookstores or from **Daughters of St. Paul, 50 St. Paul's Ave., Jamaica Plain, Boston, MA 02130.**

WISDOM FOR LIVING IN THE SPIRIT (Christian Media) For: L,C,S. Slant: RC,P,S,CP.

By Fr. John Randall, O.P. The way of wisdom in the Old and the New Testaments is studied with emphasis on living with, and praying for, wisdom in our everyday Christian living. Ten audio lessons. **$40.00.** Ten video lessons (Beta II or VHS; U-Matic available on request). **$475.00.** Please state format. Add **$4.00** for shipping. Prepaid orders only. From **Christian Media, P.O. Box 748, Ogden, UT 84402.**

WORD OF FIRE (International Films) For: L,S,Y. Slant: F,EP,MP,LP.

Throughout the ages it has always been Satan's purpose to destroy the Bible—through Roman Caesars, through Korean rulers, through African queens, through Communist governments. But God has been faithful to keep the Bible alive through His people. This film will inspire today's Christians to appreciate their Bibles as they learn the terrible price others have paid so that we and our children can have God's revealed Word. (Also available in Spanish). Rental price: **$30.00.** Film rental libraries.

Campus Crusade for Christ International.
We're not just on campuses.

We're more than a ministry. We're a movement. An interdenominational movement of Christians committed to helping people reach people worldwide with the good news of Jesus Christ.

For more than 30 years we've provided other believers with training, resources and strategies to help them reach their world for Christ—students, executives, internationals and laymen.

To help you reach others for Christ, we've developed a Media Resource Catalog of cassette tapes, films and videotapes on discipleship, evangelism and the Spirit-filled life.

Send for your free copy today.

Write to: Marketing Services (60-10), Campus Crusade for Christ International, Arrowhead Springs (YOB), San Bernardino, CA 92414. Or **call toll free, (800) 392-7542,** in Calif. (714) 886-9711, ext. 1118.

Now use your home computer for IN-DEPTH BIBLE STUDY

Fast! Thorough! For serious students of the Bible, an exciting new tool for analysis of Scripture is available through the use of computer technology. BIBLE SEARCH Version 1.3* allows you to display or print any portion of New Testament text from disk files, scan the text for topics you specify, and edit and retain reference lists of selected verses for future use.

Software, comprehensive instruction manual, and King James Version New Testament database_____$140

When ordering, please specify disk format and DOS.

Old Testament available soon at an additional cost (less than $100).

Send check or money order to:

Scripture Software
P.O. Box 6131-C, Dept. BR
Orlando, FL 32853 (305) 896-4264

*Bible Search currently requires a TRS-80 (TM of Tandy Corp.) Model I or III with 48K memory and two disk drives. Inquire about its availability on other computers.

AUDIO-VISUAL BIBLE RESOURCES

THE WORD PROCESSOR (Bible Research Systems) For: L,C,S,Y. Slant: P.

The entire text of the King James Version of the Bible stored on floppy disks. Accessible by a personal computer with programs that search the Bible for any word or phrase, sentence, prefix, suffix or paragraph. Any portion of the Bible text can be displayed on the computer screen or printer. Cross-referenced indexes can be built on any subject, sermon, lesson or personal study that is meaningful to the user. All verses cross-referenced to a common topic can be printed together. Every Bible study you do can be stored on the computer disks for future reference. An ideal tool for effective use of time spent on personal Bible study and direct access to any Bible content. User must already own a personal computer. **$199.95**, plus **$3.00** for postage and handling. Bookstores or from **Bible Research Systems, 9415 Burnet Road, #208, Austin, TX 78758**.

A WORD STUDY IN PHILIPPIANS (Jimmy Swaggart Ministries) For: L,C. Slant: CP.

A powerful study of the Apostle Paul's epistle to the church at Philippi. This complete study taken from the Greek examines verse by verse the many truths and personal applications within this letter. One of the most interesting studies ever conducted into the workings of the life of the Apostle Paul. Some terrific insights into parts of his life reveal things such as his parents were probably very wealthy, he was raised in an atmosphere where very little manual labor was carried out, and his imprisonment sparked revival in Rome. This tremendous eight hours of teachings on six cassettes are a must for any student of the Bible. Product No. 04-026. **$20.00**. From **Jimmy Swaggart Ministries, P.O. Box 2550, Baton Rouge, LA 70821**.

For Those Who Seek.

Bible study aids from Bible Research Systems include the complete KJV Bible text on disks. THE WORD processor can search the Scriptures for any word or phrase. Any portion of the Bible can be printed or displayed. Create your own library of research materials or use ours, called TOPICS. TOPICS contains cross-reference indexes on over 200 of the primary subjects discussed in Scripture.

Bible Research Systems applies computer technology to personal study of the Scriptures.

TOPICS
$49.95

Bible Research Systems
9415 Burnet, Suite 208 • Austin, TX 78758
(512) 835-7981

THE WORD
processor
$199.95
Plus $3 postage/handling

Requires APPLE II+, IBM-PC, TRS80-III or CP/M 8" (Trademarks of APPLE, IBM, Tandy, Digital Research Corporations)

BIBLE RESOURCES FOR CHILDREN

This is an unusual section. All of the other sections in this *Directory* are organized around specific types of Bible resources such as commentaries, audio-visuals, or group study guides. However, this section is organized around Bible resources for a specific audience—children. Therefore, this section on *Bible Resources for Children* is, in effect, a miniature *Directory* with items similar to those in all other sections. Here, you will find Bibles, concordances, dictionaries, commentaries, and audio-visuals—all produced especially for children and teachers of children. None of the items listed in this section are listed or cross referenced to the adult sections. However, a few items which can be used with children but are primarily for youth and/or adults are listed in the other sections under their appropriate headings.

BIBLE RESOURCES FOR CHILDREN

ABRAHAM: GOD'S FAITHFUL PILGRIM (Regal Books) For: Y,Ch. Slant: EP.

By Ethel Barrett. God speaks often to Abraham, His friend. And Abraham speaks back to God. With warmth, humor and realism, the great Abraham is depicted as an earnest family man who struggles to understand God and His will. Through his marriage to Sarah, a long journey to Canaan, his fatherly concern for Lot, and the births of Ishmael and Isaac, Abraham witnesses the miracles of God. The older Abraham gets, the more he loves and trusts God. Ethel Barrett is one of North America's favorite writers and Bible storytellers. Her **Stories to Grow On** series was nominated for a Gold Medallion Award in 1979. Young readers Grades three through six will know Abraham - and God - much better after reading this enjoyable book. They will see how they can relate to God with honesty and intimacy. 4¼ x 7 inches. 128 pages. Paperback. Number 5810906. **$2.50.** Bookstores or from **Regal Books, Div. of GL Publications, 2300 Knoll Drive, Ventura, CA 93003.**

ADVENTURES FROM GOD'S WORD —GRADE 3 (Standard Publishing Co.) For: Ch. Slant: D,P.

Twenty-four Old and New Testament stories are divided into units of reader interest: Moving to a New Home, Special Days, Sea Stories, Meeting New Friends, and Choices. Part of Standard Basic Bible Readers; fourth revision of this popular series. Each book contains a word list that gives special attention to the new Bible words and names. Library binding. Number 2953. **$7.95.** (Pre-pub price **$6.95.**) Bookstores or from **Standard Publishing, 8121 Hamilton Ave., Cincinnati, OH 45231.**

THE APOSTLES (Daughters of St. Paul) For: Y,Ch. Slant: RC,P.

A filmstrip/cassette program on the first twelve men to follow Christ. Although the filmstrip concentrates primarily on the Acts of the Apostles, a brief account of each of the apostles of the Lord is also given. 42 color frames, 30-minute cassette. Number FC0180. **$14.95** (add **$1.00** for postage). From **Daughters of St. Paul, 50 St. Paul's Ave., Jamaica Plain, Boston, MA 02130.**

ETHEL BARRETT TELLS BIBLE STORIES TO CHILDREN VOLUME I (Regal Books) For: Y,Ch. Slant: EP.

By Ethel Barrett. "Did you ever watch your mother bake a cake?" What a marvelously understandable way to introduce God's plan of creation to children! "Did you ever have to obey when it didn't make any SENSE?" What a captivating introduction to "The Strangest Boat Ride in the World." And how interesting for children to listen to and enchanting for adults to read. It's even more exciting when a child reads for himself. But then, how else would Ethel Barrett write? This new kind of read-aloud book is for families who recognize the value of reading and talking together. It's just what families with young readers and little listeners have wanted. Volume I contains "Stories of the Beginnings" and "Stories of Joseph" while Volume II continues with "Stories of Moses" and "Stories of Jesus." Each story catches the child's interest at the outset with a real life illustration even the younger children will understand. This leads right into a Bible story, followed by ideas to think and talk about, a Bible verse, thoughts to express in prayer, and the Scripture reference for the story. Illustrated. 128 pages. Quality paper. Number 5602904. **$3.25.** Bookstores or from **Regal Books, Div. of GL Publications, 2300 Knoll Drive, Ventura, CA 93003.**

ETHEL BARRETT TELLS BIBLE STORIES TO CHILDREN VOLUME II (Regal Books) For: Y,Ch. Slant: EP.

By Ethel Barrett. Because Ethel Barrett leaves children asking for more—here are Bible stories about Moses and Jesus. Also includes ideas to talk, think and pray about plus Bible verses to know. Illustrated. Quality Paper. 144 pages. Number 5603005. **$3.25.** Bookstores or from **Regal Books, Div. of GL Publications, 2300 Knoll Drive, Ventura, CA 93003.**

ETHEL BARRETT TELLS FAVORITE BIBLE STORIES (Regal Books) For: Y,Ch. Slant: EP.

By Ethel Barrett. When God made the world, there was no litter! How many stars did He create? Impossibadrillions! Exciting? Of course, because you'll find this in **Ethel Barrett Tells Favorite Bible Stories** by this extraordinary storyteller who makes the Bible come alive for youngsters, oldsters and all those in between. Ethel Barrett's Bible characters - from the Old and New Testament - are portrayed so vividly that they can be identified with people today...such as your postman, your preacher, or the very old lady next door who always has cookies and milk ready for hungry children. Illustrated. Quality Paper. 128 pages. Number 5605806. **$3.25.** Bookstores or from **Regal Books, Div. of GL Publications, 2300 Knoll Drive, Ventura, CA 93003.**

ETHEL BARRETT TELLS FAVORITE STORIES: OLD AND NEW TESTAMENTS (Vision House, Inc.) For: Y,Ch. Slant: EP.

By Ethel Barrett. A fresh look at the Old and New Testaments. Bible stories come alive on cassettes with fun sound effects, voice characters and real-life examples that children can understand and apply. "What was the first Easter like?" and "What should a best friend be like?" are two of twelve entertaining episodes which help children think about their lives at home, at school, with friends, and enjoy Bible stories at the same time. Guitar background adds emphasis to Ethel Barrett's enthusiastic narration. Expanded book versions are available. **Ethel Barrett Tells Favorite Old Testament Stories.** Numbesr A127087. **$5.98. Ethel Barrett Tells Favorite New Testament Stories.** Number A127072. **$5.98.** Bookstores or from **Vision House, Div. of GL Publications, 2300 Knoll Drive, Ventura, Ca 93003.**

BIBLE CURRICULUM GUIDE, K-3 (CSI Publications) For: Ch. Slant: C,EP,P.

By John Brondsema. This detailed guide of 218 lesson plans and enrichment ideas for primary students gives memory work, songs, poems, finger plays, filmstrips, movies, arts and crafts projects. Includes correlation with Grades 4-9 of the CSI Historical Study curriculum. 1969. 241 pages. Paper. **$12.50.** School discounts available. From **CSI Publications, 3350 East Paris Ave., P.O. Box 8709, Grand Rapids, MI 49508.**

BIBLE RESOURCES FOR CHILDREN

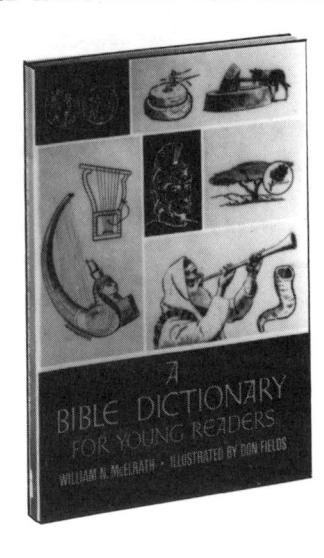

A BIBLE DICTIONARY FOR YOUNG READERS (Broadman Press) For: Ch. Slant: MP.

By **William McElrath.** Eunuch, sojourn, tares, tetarach, and other hard to understand words are defined to make Bible reading more interesting. Facts about people, customs, history, and geography of Bible times are also included. Illustrated. Grades 4-6. **$8.95.** Bookstores.

THE BIBLE FOR CHILDREN (Daughters of St. Paul) For: Ch. Slant: RC,P.

Covering the Old and New Testament, the most important happenings in the history of salvation are presented in the light of recent biblical studies. Biblical maps and colorful illustrations add to this volume. 182 pages. Item No. CH0070. Cloth. **$6.00.** Paper. **$5.00** (Add **$.75** for postage.) Bookstores or from **Daughters of St. Paul, 50 St. Paul's Ave., Jamaica Plain, Boston, MA 02130.**

THE BIBLE FOR YOUNG PEOPLE (Daughters of St. Paul) For: Ch. Slant: RC,P.

Rich in biblical language, these stories from the New Testament come alive in word and picture. Biblical maps highlight events in Christ's life and the missionary journeys of St. Paul. Ages 9-13. 142 pages. Number CH0080. Cloth. **$6.00.** Paper. **$5.00.** Add **$.75** for postage. Bookstores or from **Daughters of St. Paul, 50 St. Paul's Avenue, Jamaica Plain, Boston, MA 02130.**

THE BIBLE FOR YOUNG READERS (Daughters of St. Paul) For: Ch. Slant: RC,P.

God's plan of salvation in language children understand. A book which awakens their desire to know more about their heavenly Father and about the Son whom He sent to save us. Large print; two and four-color pictures. 102 pages. Ages 4-8. Item Number CH0090. Cloth. **$5.00.** Paper. **$3.00.** (Add **$.75** for postage.) Bookstores or from **Daughters of St. Paul, 50 St. Paul's Ave., Jamaica Plain, Boston, MA 02130.**

BIBLE GUIDE A: CREATION—SAUL (CSI Publications) For: Ch. Slant: EP, P.

By **Martha and Jessie Mae Bruinooge.** A workbook with six units and review chapters for Grades 4-6. Covers history from Creation to Saul. Has vocabulary helps, memory texts, blanks to fill in, and extra activities. Teacher's Manual features lesson helps. Part of the CSI K-9 Historical Studies Series. 1960. 157, 150 pages. Paperback. Bible Guide A. **$5.00.** Teacher's Manual. **$12.00.** School discounts available. From **CSI Publications, 3350 East Paris Ave., P.O. Box 8709, Grand Rapids, MI 49508.**

BIBLE GUIDE B: DAVID—MALACHI (CSI Publications) For: Ch. Slant: C,EP,P.

By **Martha and Jessie Mae Bruinooge.** Workbook with six units and review chapters for Grades 4-6. Includes biblical accounts from David to the end of the Old Testament. Teacher's Manual contains lesson guides and answer keys. Part of the CSI K-9 Historical Studies Series. 1961, 1963. 144, 176 pages. Paper. Bible Guide B. **$5.00.** Teacher's Manual. **$12.00.** School discounts available. From **CSI Publications, 3350 East Paris Ave., P.O. Box 8709, Grand Rapids, MI 49508.**

BIBLE GUIDE C: GOSPELS—ACTS (CSI Publications) For: Ch. Slant: C,EP,P.

By **Martha and Jessie Mae Bruinooge.** Workbook with nine units and review chapters for Grades 4-6. Studies the Gospels and Acts. Teacher's Manual contains worthwhile aids. Part of the CSI K-9 Historical Studies Series. 176-192 pages. 1962, 1963. Paper. Bible Guide C. **$5.00.** Teacher's Manual. **$12.00.** School discounts available. From **CSI Publications, 3350 East Paris Ave., P.O. Box 8709, Grand Rapids, MI 49508.**

BIBLE GUIDEBOOK (Broadman Press) For: Ch. Slant: MP.

By **William McElrath.** Designed to help children become better acquainted with the Bible. Topics include: what the Bible is, how to read the Bible, how to use Bible helps, when the Bible events happened, what the Bible books are, where to find interesting parts of the Bible and how the Bible came to us. Grades 3-6. From **Broadman Press, Nashville, TN 37234.**

THE BIBLE IN PICTURES FOR LITTLE EYES (Moody Press) For: Ch. Slant: EP.

By **Ken Taylor.** Classic Bible story book that covers the Bible from Genesis to Acts in bright pictures and simple text. **$10.95.** Bookstores or from **Moody Bookworld, 2101 W. Howard, Chicago, IL 60645.**

BIBLE PEOPLE (Standard Publishing) For: Ch. Slant: P.

Simplified definitions of a select list of Bible people. Part of the Basic Bible Dictionary series. A useful reading aid for children, youth, and adults, these dictionaries include many words from the King James Version which now have different meanings. Illustrated. Code 2781. **$1.95.** Bookstores or from **Standard Publishing, 8121 Hamilton Ave., Cincinnati, OH 45231.**

BIBLE PLACES (Standard Publishing) For: Ch. Slant: P.

Simplified definitions of a select list of Bible places. Part of the Basic Bible Dictionary series. A useful read-

BIBLE RESOURCES FOR CHILDREN

ing aid for children, youth, and adults, these dictionaries include many words from the King James Version which now have different meanings. Illustrated. Code 2782. **$1.95.** Bookstores or from **Standard Publishing, 8121 Hamilton Ave., Cincinnati, OH 45231.**

BIBLE STORIES TO LIVE BY (Here's Life Publishers) For: Ch. Slant: EP.

An exciting retelling of 90 Bible stories for children. Each story highlights one of more than 45 character values and provides parents with thought questions and application suggestions. Product Number 950501. **$10.95.** Bookstores or from **Here's Life Publishers, P.O. Box 1576, San Bernardino, CA 92402.**

BIBLEARN SERIES (Broadman Press) For: Ch. Slant: MP.

Twenty-four beautifully illustrated volumes telling the highlights of the lives of Bible personalities. Each chapter contains a brief section entitled "Thinkback" that offers questions, activities, or other activities which encourage the child to retain the content. Suggested for Grades 1-6. Can be read by the individual children or used as a teaching tool in a Sunday school class. 24 volume set. **$129.95.** Individual volumes. **$5.95.** Bookstores or from **Lifeway Home Shopping Service, Nashville, TN 37234.**

CAMP BIBLE STUDY CURRICULUM (Camp Cherith) For: Y,Ch. Slant: EP, P.

Three-year Bible study curriculum designed for use in youth camps; available for four age-groups (ages 7-9, 9-12, 12-15, 15-18); daily Bible study material includes complete lesson plans and teaching hints; daily memory verse relating to Bible study; common scriptural theme for all age groups; studies geared to outdoor setting. Leader/Counselor Manuals. **$2.25** each. Camper morning devotional booklets. **$.50** each. From **Camp Cherith, Box 788, Wheaton, IL 60189.**

THE CHILDREN'S ILLUSTRATED BIBLE DICTIONARY (Thomas Nelson Publishers) For: Ch. Slant: D.

The Children's Illustrated Bible Dictionary is one of the most colorful, interesting reference books available for the young reader. It features 1,214 entries of words, terms, and proper names in the Bible. Every entry is accompanied by a full-color illustration by Alvaro Mairani. Scripture references which direct the reader to relate subject matter in the Bible are included at the end of each entry. A Scripture index at the back of the book lists every reference found in the text. Parents and children will enjoy using this colorful volume as a starting point for Bible stories and discussions. **The Children's Illustrated Bible Dictionary** will instill an enjoyable association with Bible study that will continue into the child's adult years. Paperback. **$6.95.** Bookstores.

A CHILD'S FIRST BOOK OF BIBLE STORIES (Standard Publishing) For: Ch.

A "read to me" edition of 50 Bible stories--the first book in a young child's library. Stories are from both Testaments, beginning with the creation in Genesis and ending with John's view of Heaven in Revelation. The simple texts are illustrated with large, beautiful paintings which are biblically accurate and help the child understand the meaning of the stories. Recommended to introduce new readers to Standard Basic Bible Reader series. Library Binding. Number 2949. **$7.95.** Bookstores or from **Standard Publishing, 8121 Hamilton Ave., Cincinnati, OH 45231.**

CLOTH STORY BOOK PATTERNS (Honeybee Books) For: Ch. Slant: EP.

Cloth storybook patterns with instructions for making three 12 page cloth storybooks on the following subjects: The Christmas Story ("Baby Jesus"), The Flood (Noah) and Creation ("Who Made the Honeybee, God Did!"). Completed books contain action pictures for small children ages 18 months to 2 years to be used in conjunction with a teaching program and include a printed story line to aid adults in teaching young babies to sound words and impart simple Bible truths. Patterns. **$4.00** each; or 3 for **$12.00.** From **Honeybee Book Patterns, P.O. Box 6339-R, Rockford, IL 61125.**

CREATION (Daughters of St. Paul), For: Y,Ch. Slant: RC,P.

A filmstrip/cassette program on the magnificent account of God's creation and the first chapters of salvation history from our first parents to the Tower of Babel. 25 color frames, six-minute cassette. Number FC0010. **$9.95** (add **$1.00** for postage). From **Daughters of St. Paul, 50 St. Paul's Ave., Jamaica Plain, Boston, MA 02130.**

DAILY BREAD (CEF Press) For: Ch. Slant: EP,D.

Boxed set of **Daily Bread** devotional guides. Light up children's lives. Give them daily devotionals for gifts and awards. Theme related booklets for one year, non-dated; can begin any month. Scripture readings with applications, hide and seek words, plus illustrations. 3 1/2 x 5 1/2 inches. 12 booklets per set. Two sets available. **$5.49** per set. Bookstores or from **CEF Press, Warrenton, MO 63383.**

BIBLE RESOURCES FOR CHILDREN

FOR SUCH IS THE KINGDOM OF HEAVEN (Visible Light, Inc) For: Ch. Slant: RC,EP,MP,P,I,CP,M.

The purpose of this series is to poetically and musically teach children the parables of the Lord Jesus Christ. Repetition with audio-visual aids is the best proven method of teaching. This learning process we call, "Memorization Without Realization." Children, and adults alike, learn and memorize without study just by repetitiously listening while reading, coloring, and singing along with the audio cassette. Learning the Bible can be fun and easy! **For Such Is the Kingdom of Heaven** is available in the following six audio cassettes with accompanying coloring/story books: The Wedding Feast; The Ten Virgins; The Talents; The Tares and The Wheat; The Prodigal Son; The Husbandmen. Order by individual title, audio cassette and accompanying story book. **$4.98.** Individual coloring/story book. **$2.00.** Set of six audio cassettes and six books. **$24.98.** All six audio cassettes. **$14.95.** All six coloring/story books. **$9.98.** From **Visible Light, Inc.**, P.O. Box 8605, Orlando, FL 32856.

GOD GIVES THE LAND (Herald Press) For: Ch. Slant; EP.

This is volume three in the Story Bible Series. The content covers Joshua, Judges, and Ruth. 1983. 176 pages. Paper. Number 3332-3: **$5.95.** Bookstores.

GOD, HAVE YOU GOT IT ALL TOGETHER? (Regal Books) For: Y,Ch. Slant: EP.

By Ethel Barrett. The author takes young readers on an overview trip of the Bible, pointing out how God's plan of redemption has been carried out despite the efforts of Satan. Quality paper. Illustrated. 160 pages. Number S064154. **$1.95.** Bookstores or from **Regal Books, Div. of GL Publications**, 2300 Knoll Drive, Ventura, CA 93003.

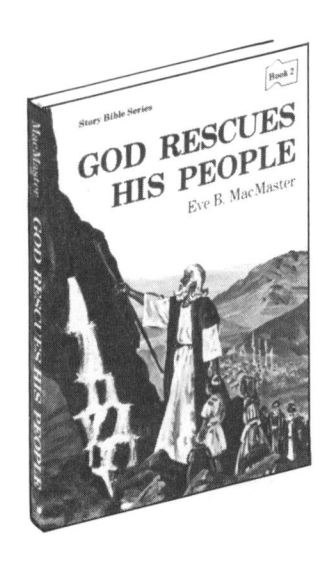

GOD RESCUES HIS PEOPLE (Herald Press) For: Ch. Slant: EP.

By Eve MacMaster. Second book in the Herald Story Bible Series retells the stories from Exodus, Leviticus, Numbers, and Deuteronomy. Tells how God's family becomes the nation of Israel, and Moses, servant of God, leads God's people out of slavery, teaches them God's law, and brings them through the great and terrible wilderness to the very edge of the Promised Land. 1982. 176 pages. Paper. Number 1994-0. **$5.95.** Bookstores.

GOD'S CHOSEN KING (Herald Press) For: Ch. Slant: EP.

By Eve MacMaster. This is volume four in the Story Bible Series written for the fifth and sixth grade reader. The content covers I and II Samuel, I Chronicles, and the Psalms. Contains the stories of Hannah's request for Samuel, the people's request for a king, the story of Saul, and the story of David. 1983. 176 pages. Paper. Number 3344-4. **$5.95.** Bookstores.

GOD'S FAMILY (Herald Press) For: Ch. Slant: EP.

By Eve MacMaster. The first book in the Herald Story Bible series, stories of God and his people. **God's Family** retells Genesis, the story of how God made everything and what happened next, how he chose one family to bring all the people of the world back to him. Appealing to everyone from 8 to 80, this is a unique story Bible; complete and true to the original, and fun to read. This version does not moralize or theologize, but simply lets the stories speak for themselves. 1981. 152 pages. Paper. Number 1964-9. **$5.95.** Bookstores.

GOD'S STORY - Bible Film Series (Oliver Hunkin for Yorkshire Television) For: Ch. Slant: RC,EP,MP,LP,D,P.

A new series of ten, fourteen minute, 16mm color films designed to teach Bible stories to children of all ages. Titles in the series: Jesus the Child; Jesus the Leader; Jesus the Storyteller; Jesus the Friend; Jesus in Danger; The Easter Story; Peter; Paul Meets Jesus; Paul the Traveler; and Paul the Prisoner. This versatile teaching resource presents the Bible stories in accurate, simple, clear language that makes the stories understandable, while vivid details make them interesting to today's children. The Bible stories are illustrated by noted British painter Alan Parry in dynamic images and brilliant colors. British film and television actor Paul Copley narrates the stories in a lively and expressive style. The choristers of Leeds Parish Church provide the music for the series. **God's Story** is recommended for children of all ages in Church School, Vacation Church School, Story Hour, Children's Homily, religion classes, summer camps or family night programs. Rental, each film. **$25.00.** Rental any five films. **$20.00** each. Purchase. **$250.00** each. Brochure available on request. From **Mass Media Ministries, 2116 North Charles Street, Baltimore, MD 21218.**

THE GOOD BOOK-NEW TESTAMENT FOR CHILDREN (Tyndale House Publishers) For: Ch. Slant: C,F,EP,MP,D.

Young readers will love this giant print (16 point type), easy-reading Living New Testament with Psalms and Proverbs. Illustrated by Richard and Frances Hook. Cloth. **$11.95.** Bookstores.

GROWING IN WISDOM, MATURITY AND FAVOR (ROA Filmstrip Co.) For: Y,Ch. Slant: RC,P.

This filmstrip program utilizes a new approach in religious education that is particularly appropriate for the preteen student. The material teaches about life in terms of Scripture and teaches Scripture in terms of the student's life experiences. Each filmstrip uses Luke's Gospel as the focal point for Jesus' teachings and parables. The overall aim of this program is to draw helpful insights from Jesus and his teachings for students as they grow and seek maturity. Viewers share personal feelings and experiences as a response to the Scripture stories and are helped to resolve problems specific to this age group. Main audience: Grades 4-8. Materials: 10 filmstrips, 10 cassettes or records; and 10 resource guides. **$220.00.** From **ROA Filmstrip Co., 6633 W. Howard Street, Niles, IL 60648.**

GROWING WITH BIBLE HEROES, GRADE 4 (Standard Publishing) For: Ch. Slant: D,P.

Seven units of reader interest present Bible heroes the reader can admire and identify with: Pioneers, Kings, People Who Wouldn't Give Up, Jesus the Messiah, Jesus the Teacher, Jesus the Savior, and Preachers. The 35 stories are from both Old and New Testaments. Part of Standard Basic Bible Readers; fourth revision of this popular series. Each book contains a word list that gives special attention to the new Bible words and names. Library binding. Number 2954. **$7.95.** (**$6.95** pre-pub price.) Bookstores or from **Standard Publishing, 8121 Hamilton Ave., Cincinnati, OH 45231.**

HAPPYFACE LANGUAGE ARTS CURRICULUM (Redemptive Publications) For: Ch. Slant: C,RC,EP,MP,P,S, I,CP,M.

Based on a two fold promise dear to every Christian educator: It is important that specific basic skills be mastered as the child enters the world of reading and writing; and it is important that a child learn these basic skills in the context of the Christian faith. Children acquire a view of life by the context of their lessons. If a child learns his first lessons (pre-school or kindergarten) in a secular context, he is well on his way to an unscriptural

BIBLE RESOURCES FOR CHILDREN

(by definition, anti-scriptural) view of life. Slowly and surely he learns to draw a line between spiritual things and school things. That line is hard to erase at any later date. Thus, the HappyFace Curriculum for little children was formed. Each of the six workbooks are academically sound and biblically oriented. Application: Christian pre-school. 148 words. **$5.00** per workbook; order in sequence, books 1-6. Bookstores or from **National Organization for Christian Child Care, 933 Andrews Road, West Palm Beach, FL 33405.**

I LEARN TO READ ABOUT JESUS PRIMER (Standard Publishing) For: Ch. Slant: D,P.

Beginning readers will enjoy these seven stories about Jesus including the Baby Jesus, Jesus and the Boy Who Shared His Lunch, and The Little Lost Lamb. A Child's Prayer and two beloved poems about Jesus provide a reverent change of pace. Part of Standard Basic Bible Readers; fourth revision of this popular series. Each book contains a word list that gives special attention to the new Bible words and names. Library binding. Number 2950. **$7.95** (pre-pub price **$6.95**). Bookstores or from **Standard Publishing, 8121 Hamilton Ave., Cincinnati, OH 45231.**

I READ ABOUT GOD'S CARE, GRADE 2 (Standard Publishing) For: Ch. Slant: D,P.

Sixteen New Testament stories (A Special Baby, Jesus and John, The Man in the Tree, and 13 others), nine Old Testament stories (God Made the World, David and the Giant, and seven more), The Coming of the King (a story of today), plus poems and prayers to learn, puzzles to do, and Bible verses that offer direction for a child's life. Part of Standard Basic Bible Readers; fourth revision of this popular series. Each book contains a word list that gives special attention to the new Bible words and names. Library binding. Number 2952. **$7.95** (pre-pub price **$6.95**). Bookstores or from **Standard Publishing, 8121 Hamilton Ave., Cincinnati, OH 45231.**

I READ ABOUT GOD'S LOVE, GRADE 1 (Standard Publishing) For: Ch. Slant: D,P.

In Bethlehem, Jesus in the Temple, Noah's Boat, and A Little Basket Boat

BIBLE RESOURCES FOR CHILDREN

are among the 17 stories. In addition, Reader 1 includes poems and prayers to learn and puzzles to do. God's Promises and Songs of David are among the six Bible verses to read. Part of Standard Basic Bible Readers; fourth revision of this popular series. Each book contains a word list that gives special attention to the new Bible words and names. Library binding. Number 2951. **$7.95** (pre-pub price **$6.95**). Bookstores or from **Standard Publishing, 8121 Hamilton Ave., Cincinnati, OH 45231.**

I'M NO HERO (Regal Books) For: Y,Ch. Slant: EP.

By Ethel Barrett. The exciting accounts of how some very ordinary Old Testament people became God's heroes. Quality paper. Illustrated. 160 pages. Number 5406803. **$1.95.** Bookstores or from **Regal Books, Div. of GL Publications, 2300 Knoll Drive, Ventura, CA 93003.**

JESUS IN THE GOSPEL (Daughters of St. Paul) For: Ch. Slant: P.

This book will help children learn more about Jesus and how he proved his love for each of us. The life, teaching, death and resurrection of Jesus are presented all in the words of the Gospel. 135 full color pictures. 304 pages. Cloth. Number CH0288. **$12.00.** Add **$1.00** for postage. Bookstores or from **Daughters of St. Paul, 50 St. Paul's Ave., Jamaica Plain, Boston, MA 02130.**

JET CADETS (Christian Ed. Publishers) For: Ch. Slant: EP.

A club program that will bring lively inquisitive juniors (Grades 4, 5, and 6) to an understanding of the Scriptures and the Christian way of life. **Jet Cadets** promotes spiritual growth by involving juniors in challenging achievement projects and activities to bring about understanding of the Scriptures and the Christian way of life. The award program as well as the program material itself are all Bible based and Christ honoring. This program has weekly lessons, activities and projects for each child. Annual subscription. **$88.00.** From **Christian Ed. Publishers, 7348 Trade Street, San Diego, CA 92121.**

JOB (Daughters of St. Paul) For: Y,Ch. Slant: RC,P.

A filmstrip/cassette program on God's faithful servant, Job. 20 color frames, eight-minute cassette. Number FC0020. **$9.95** (add **$1.00** for postage). From **Daughters of St. Paul, 50 St. Paul's Ave., Jamaica Plain, Boston, MA 02130.**

JOSEPH (Daughters of St. Paul) For: Y,Ch. Slant: RC,P.

A filmstrip/cassette program on Jacob's son, Joseph, which shows the power of God's providence. 27 color frames, eleven-minute cassette. Number FC0040. **$9.95** (add **$1.00** for postage.) From **Daughters of St. Paul, 50 St. Paul's Ave., Jamaica Plain, Boston, MA 02130.**

JOSEPH (Regal Books) For: Y,Ch. Slant: EP.

By Ethel Barrett. The long ago story becomes a "here and now" drama of Joseph's life as a son, slave, prince and forgiving brother. Illustrated. 128 pages. Paperback. Number 5607701. **$1.95.** Bookstores or from **Regal Books, Div. of GL Publications, 2300 Knoll Drive, Ventura, CA 93003.**

JOSHUA (Regal Books) for: Y,Ch. Slant: EP.

By Ethel Barrett. The slave, the spy, the leader, the hero will captivate every reader in this hair-raising, true adventure story. Illustrated. 128 pages. Paperback. Number 5607000. **$1.95.** Bookstores or from **Regal Books, Div. of GL Publications, 2300 Knoll Drive, Ventura, CA 93003.**

JOSHUA-THE JUDGES-RUTH (Daughters of St. Paul) For: Y,Ch. Slant: RC,P.

A filmstrip/cassette program on the story of God's chosen people under the leadership of Joshua and the Judges. Ruth is included in the ancestry of the Savior. 51 color frames, seventeen-minute cassette. Number FC0060. **$14.95** (add **$1.00** for postage.) From **Daughters of St. Paul, 50 St. Paul's Ave., Jamaica Plain, Boston, MA 02130.**

JUDITH AND ESTHER (Daughters of St. Paul) For: Y,Ch. Slant: RC,P.

A filmstrip/cassette program on two of the Old Testament's most valiant women. 27 color frames, eleven-minute cassette. Number FC0140. **$9.95** (add **$1.00** for postage). From **Daughters of St. Paul, 50 St. Paul's Ave., Jamaica Plain, Boston, MA 02130.**

KING DAVID (Daughters of St. Paul) For: Y,Ch. Slant: RC,P.

A filmstrip/cassette program on King David's reign. Under his leadership, God's chosen people prosper. 39 color frames, eight-minute cassette. Number FC0090. **$11.95** (add **$1.00** for postage). From **Daughters of St. Paul, 50 St. Paul's Ave., Jamaica Plain, Boston, MA 02130.**

KING SAUL (Daughters of St. Paul) For: Y,Ch. Slant: RC,P.

A filmstrip/cassette program which follows Saul's rule from its glorious and triumphant beginning to its sad and tragic end. 45 color frames, eighteen-minute cassette. Number FC 0070. **$14.95** (add **$1.00** for postage). From **Daughters of St. Paul, 50 St. Paul's Ave., Jamaica Plain, Boston, MA 02130.**

THE KING WHO LIVES FOREVER (Regal Books) For: Y,Ch. Slant: EP.

By Alice Schrage. Written for children ages 8 through 12, this is the second of two books about the life and ministry of Jesus. This book, like the first one by author Schrage, is a fitting companion to the "Great Heroes of the Bible Series" by Ethel Barrett. **The King Who Lives Forever** is a book of twelve action-packed stories about Jesus during the last part of his life on earth. Young readers will meet Jesus' personal friends; they will learn some of the important stories Jesus told and what he taught about prayer; they will discover that Jesus was criticized, even when he was friendly and helped others. Children will sense the great excitement when Jesus was proclaimed King...be amazed when he was falsely accused and beaten...feel sadness when he was crucified and buried...and then will clap their hands with joy when he rises from the dead to live forever...King of Kings and Lord of Lords! Illustrations contribute to reader interest, along with a map and a Bible dictionary section to clarify words for young readers. 128 pages. Illustrated. Paperback. Number 5810604. **$1.95.** Teaching materials available. Bookstores or from **Regal Books, Div. of GL Publications, 2300 Knoll Drive, Ventura, CA 93003.**

BIBLE RESOURCES FOR CHILDREN

KJV LOLLIPOP CHILDREN'S TEXT BIBLES (Zondervan Bible Publishers) For: L,C,S,Ch. Slant: EP.

A superior line of children's text Bibles. Ideal for presenting as a gift or as a "very first" Bible. Features: presentation page and family record; 18 full color illustrations by Frances and Richard Hook; table of daily Bible readings; 128 page concordance; full color maps; 18 pages of Bible study helps; illustrated Bible dictionary; words of Christ printed in red; and more. Durable imitation leather limp binding. Licorice Black, Snow White, Blueberry Blue, Strawberry Red, Chocolate Brown. **$12.95.** Licorice Black or Snow White zippered. **$16.95.** Bookstores or from **Zondervan Retail Marketing Service, 1420 Robinson Road, SE, Grand Rapids, MI 49506.**

LEADING LITTLE ONES TO GOD (Wm. B. Eerdmans Publishing Co.) For: Ch. Slant: C,EP,D.

By Marian Schoolland. Now regarded as a classic, **Leading Little Ones to God** has, since its publication almost 20 years ago, been widely used by both teachers and parents who are concerned to develop in very young Christians a personal relationship with God. In simple, conversational language, the book discusses such important matters as the nature of God, of sin, and of salvation; the Christian life, the church prayer—even the Second Coming. This devotional for small children is now available in an attractive new format, with original illustrations by artist Paul Stoub and larger pages and type to encourage beginners to read it for themselves. **$12.95.** Bookstores or from **Eerdmans Publishing Co, 255 Jefferson Ave., SE, Grand Rapids, MI 49503.**

LEARNING ABOUT JESUS (Daughters of St. Paul) For: Ch. Slant: RC,P.

Beginning with God's wonderful promise of a Savior, each main event of Jesus' life is imaginatively portrayed. The film is done in full-color limited animation. Age level: pre-primary to primary. Twenty minutes. Purchase. **$250.00.** Rental. **$20.00.** Film rental libraries or from **Daughters of St. Paul, 50 St. Paul's Ave., Jamaica Plain, Boston, MA 02130.**

LEARNING TO FOLLOW GOD (Faith and Fellowship Press) For: Ch. Slant: LU.

By David Rinden. A thirteen-lesson study on the Ten Commandments for children in Grades 4, 5, and 6. Stories from the Old and New Testament are used to illustrate the teaching of each commandment. New International Version is used. Illustrated. **$2.95.** Postage paid on cash orders. From **Faith & Fellowship Press, Box 655, Fergus Falls, MN 56537.**

LIFE OF CHRIST (Flannelgraph Lessons) (Christian Publications, Inc.) For: Ch. Slant: EP,MP,P.

These flannelgraph sets of ten complete lessons are prepared in the file folder size for handy filing and are printed on the "hold-tite" flocking stock. Number 1, Earlier Events in Jesus' Life; and Number 2, Later Events in Jesus' Life. **$6.95** each plus postage and handling. From **Ministry Services, P.O. Box 433, Redan, GA 30074.**

THE LIFE OF CHRIST (Daughters of St. Paul) For: Y,Ch. Slant: RC,P.

A filmstrip/cassette program on Christ, the Lord of history who inserted himself into the framework of human time some two thousand years ago. That brief lifetime has become the pivotal point of all time. This filmstrip explores the teachings, example and the events surrounding the life of the God-Man, our Way, Truth and Life. 156 color frames, 46 minutes (3 filmstrips and 3 cassettes). Number FC0160. **$24.95** (add **$1.00** for postage). From **Daughters of St. Paul, 50 St. Paul's Ave., Jamaica Plain, Boston, MA 02130.**

LISTEN! THEMES FROM THE BIBLE RETOLD FOR CHILDREN (Servant Publications) For: Ch. Slant: RC.

Instructs children about the major events and characters of the Bible in words and pictures they can understand. Number 1065. **$7.95.** Bookstores.

LITTLE PEOPLE'S SCRIPTURE STORIES (ROA Filmstrip Co.) For: Y. Slant: RC,MP,P.

Based on the "Little People's Paperbacks," this series of filmstrips leads the young child to an appreciation of the Bible message and builds a familiarity with well-known parables and psalms. The interest of the child is sustained through frequently changing visuals and the simple, childlike art provides a framework for the beauty of the Scripture message. There is a minimum of narration, and the vocabulary is maintained at a child's level while still retaining the essence of the Bible stories. Objectives: to introduce young children to the Bible consistent with their age and experience; to add dimension to children's encounters with Bible stories at home or in church; to highlight God's love as expressed in the gift of His Son, Jesus; and to guide children in prayerful response to God's love. Main audience: Grades K-3. 20 filmstrips; 20 cassettes or 10 records; 20 teachers guides; and 20 sharepapers. **$325.00.** From **ROA Filmstrip Co., 6633 W. Howard Street, Niles, IL 60648.**

LITTLE STORIES ABOUT GOD (Daughters of St. Paul) For: Ch. Slant: RC,P.

The whole biblical story delightfully

BIBLE RESOURCES FOR CHILDREN

retold in a child's language by a mother of five children. This Bible for little ones (ages 3-6) is illustrated with full-color pictures on almost every page. 134 pages. Item Number CH0330. Cloth. **$5.50.** Paper. **$4.50.** (Add **$.75** for postage.) Bookstores or from **Daughters of St. Paul, 50 St. Paul's Ave., Jamaica Plain, Boston, MA 02130.**

THE MACCABEES (Daughters of St. Paul) For: Y,Ch. Slant: RC,P.

A filmstrip/cassette program on Judas Maccabeus and his followers who banded together against the pagan kings who would not let them practice the Mosaic law. Stories of wars and persecutions, victories and defeats are the resulting events that make up the major part of the two books of Maccabees. 33 full-color frames, nine minute cassette. Number FC0150. **$9.95** (add **$1.00** for postage). From **Daughters of St. Paul, 50 St. Paul's Ave., Jamaica Plain, Boston, MA 02130.**

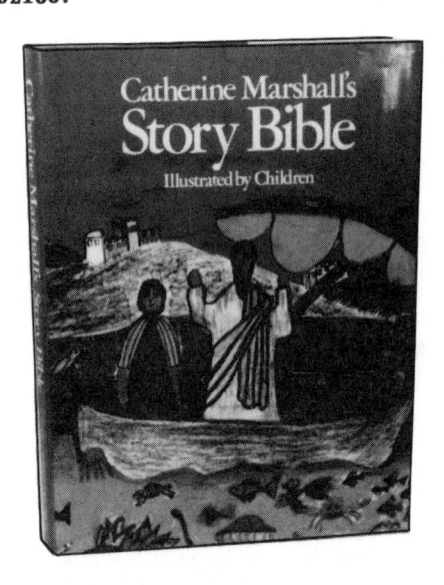

CATHERINE MARSHALL'S STORY BIBLE (Chosen Books and The Crossroad Continuum) For: Ch. Slant: EP.

By **Catherine Marshall.** Catherine Marshall, one of America's most beloved inspirational authors, retells the Bible's timeless narratives in this special volume for children. Seventy-seven beautifully creative, full-color paintings by children from countries around the world enhance the text. The vibrant, memorable paintings were collected over a period of twelve years. Story Bible was specially printed and bound in Europe. The large format volume measures 9 1/2 x 12 1/2 inches. Certainly, this will be a cherished gift for children, parents, and grandparents alike. Awarded a Citation of Appreciation by the Laymen's National Bible Committee. Hardcover (Cat. No. 13002). **$17.50.** Bookstores or from **Zondervan, 1415 Lake Drive, SE, Grand Rapids, MI 49506.**

MEET JESUS: GOD'S FRIENDS (Scripture Union) For: Ch. Slant: EP,MP,P.

Meet Jesus and **God's Friends** are "Pointing Out" books to help 3-9 year olds explore the Bible. Five Bible stories per book are taught to children by a threefold method: listen, look and do--each stage providing lots of fun and learning. Your child will enjoy listening to stories about Joseph, Moses, Naaman and others and will become enthralled with each two-page, color picture spread which details the stories. These highly detailed pictures present a realistic background for the story to add depth to the child's understanding. Each story and picture is then reinforced with suggestions on activity pages which will turn the child back to the stories and pictures again and again. Both pre-school and elementary school ages will enjoy the various projects, and the message of God's Word will come across to them in terms which are relevant to their ages and experience. **$5.95.** From **Scripture Union, 1716 Spruce, Philadelphia, PA 19103.**

THE MIRACLES AND PARABLES OF JESUS FOR CHILDREN (Thomas More Cassettes) For: Ch. Slant: RC.

By **Todd Brennan.** Stories from the Taize Picture Bible engagingly read, including the grateful leper, the Good Samaritan, Martha and Mary, the widow's mite, etc. Number TM272. Approximately 40 minutes. **$6.95.** From **Thomas More Association, 225 W. Huron St., Chicago, IL 60610.**

MOSES (Daughters of St. Paul) For: Y,Ch. Slant: RC,P.

A filmstrip/cassette program on Moses, the leader of the Chosen People. Through Moses, God leads the people from slavery to the Promised Land where He reveals His law to Israel. 45 color frames, nineteen minute cassette. Number FC0050. **$14.95** (add **$1.00** for postage). From **Daughters of St. Paul, 50 St. Paul's Ave., Jamaica Plain, Boston, MA 02130.**

MOSES: FROM DARKNESS TO LIGHT (Daughters of St. Paul) For: Y,Ch. Slant: P.

The powerful drama of the first covenant comes to life before young viewers. Watch God's mysterious plan unwind - the call of Moses, the burning bush, the plagues, the escape, the desert wanderings, the trials,...and finally, the land of promise. Excellent introduction to the study of the Ten Commandments. 77 color slides, twenty minute cassette, and leader's guide. Number SL0060. **$19.95** (add **$1.00** for postage). From **Daughters of St. Paul, 50 St. Paul's Ave., Jamaica Plain, Boston, MA 02130.**

MOSES: MISSION IMPOSSIBLE! (Regal Books) For: Y,Ch. Slant: EP.

By **Ethel Barrett.** A superb Bible storyteller. Ethel Barrett introduces her young readers to a Moses who is real and alive with the same emotions they feel. He is angry, afraid, weary and confused. He faces many difficult situations—there isn't enough water or food for the Israelites; strong and frightening enemies attack; the people rebel against him; they prolong their desert wanderings by forty years because they disobeyed God. Yet—Moses leads on. He is faithful to God. As children see Moses as a real man with real problems and real faith, they will learn that they, too, can trust God to keep his promises. Paperback. 4 1/4 x 7 inches. 128 pages. Number 5811201. **$2.50.** Bookstores or from **Regal Books, Div. of GL Publications, 2300 Knoll Drive, Ventura, CA 93003.**

BIBLE RESOURCES FOR CHILDREN

MY BIBLE DICTIONARY (Standard Publishing) For: Ch. Slant: P.

Simple definitions of 400-plus words. Forty-eight illustrated pages. Excellent study help for children. Code 3040. **$1.95.** Bookstores or from **Standard Publishing, 8121 Hamilton Ave., Cincinnati, OH 45231.**

MY BIBLE STORY ACTIVITY COLORING BOOKS: OLD TESTAMENT PEOPLE (Regal Books) For: Ch. Slant: EP.

Most children like to color. Now they can learn more about Old Testament people and events as they are involved in an activity they enjoy. For ages 4-8. Manual/illustrated. 28 pages. Number 5603218. **$1.25.** Bookstores or from **Regal Books, Div. of GL Publications, 2300 Knoll Drive, Ventura, CA 93003.**

MY BIBLE STORY ACTIVITY COLORING BOOKS: PICTURES ABOUT JESUS (Regal Books) For: Ch. Slant: EP.

Children 4 to 8 will enjoy learning more about Jesus as they color in this book. Manual/illustrated. 28 pages. Number 5603307. **$1.50.** Bookstores or from **Regal Books, Div. of GL Publications, 2300 Knoll Drive, Ventura, CA 93003.**

MY BIBLE STORY ACTIVITY COLORING BOOK: PICTURES ABOUT PEOPLE JESUS HELPED (Regal Books) For: Ch. Slant: EP.

Children, ages 4 to 8, will learn more about Jesus' love and care as they color scenes of Jesus helping others. Manual/illustrated. 32 pages. Number 5603404. **$1.25.** Bookstores or from **Regal Books, Div. of GL Publications, 2300 Knoll Drive, Ventura, CA 93003.**

MY BIBLE STORY READERS (Moody Press) For: Ch. Slant: EP.

By M. Palmer. Exciting Bible stories that children can read all by themselves by the time they reach second grade. Available for the story of David and the story of Noah. **$1.95.** Bookstores or from **Moody Bookworld, 2101 W. Howard, Chicago, IL 60645.**

MY FRIEND JESUS (Daughters of St. Paul) For: Ch. Slant: RC,P.

A filmstrip/cassette program on the life of Jesus simply told for young children (pre-primary to primary age level). 63 color frames, fifteen minute cassette and leader's guide. Also available in a slide/sound format. Filmstrip/cassette, Number FC0260 **$12.00** (add **$1.00** for postage). Slide/Sound presentation, Number SL0070 **$24.95** (add **$1.00** for postage). From **Daughters of St. Paul, 50 St. Paul's Ave., Jamaica Plain, Boston, MA 02130.**

MY FRIEND JESUS (Standard Publishing) For: Ch.

A wipe-clean story book that emphasizes Jesus' love for children. Special paper wipes clean with a damp cloth. Number 2699. **$.98.** Bookstores or from **Standard Publishing, 8121 Hamilton Ave., Cincinnati, OH 45231.**

NIV CHILDREN'S BIBLE (Zondervan Bible Publishers) For: L,C,S,Ch. Slant: EP.

Sure to interest children and hold their attention. Filled with full color illustrations of the major Bible stories. For children ages 6-10. Has full color illustrated cover; full-color illustrated presentation page; church and family record pages; 36 exclusive full color illustrations; 4 page illustrated Bible time lines; 8 pages of exclusive full color Zondervan maps; double column format. Cloth edition. **$13.95.** Bookstores or from **Zondervan Retail Marketing Service, 1420 Robinson Road, SE, Grand Rapids, MI 49506.**

OLD TESTAMENT STORIES (Flannelgraph Lessons) (Christian Publications, Inc.) For: Ch. Slant: EP,MP,P.

Prepared in the file folder style for handy filing and printed on the "hold-tite" flocking stock. Each set has ten complete lessons and applications. Number 1, Creation to Jacob; Number 2, Jacob to Elijah; Number 3, Story of Elisha and Elijah, Jonah, etc. **$6.95** each, plus postage and handling. From **Ministry Services, P.O. Box 433, Redan, GA 30074.**

THE PATRIARCHS (Daughters of St. Paul) For: Y,Ch. Slant: RC,P.

A filmstrip/cassette program on the ancient bearers of the promise, Abraham, Isaac, and Jacob. 29 color frames, thirteen-minute cassette. Number FC0030. **$9.95** (add **$1.00** for postage). From **Daughters of St. Paul, 50 St. Paul's Ave., Jamaica Plain, Boston, MA 02130.**

PAUL (Regal Books) For: Y,Ch. Slant: EP.

By Ethel Barrett. The author takes children on an incredible journey as she reveals to them the troubles and triumphs of the Apostle Paul. Paperback. Illustrated. 128 pages. Number 5810701. **$1.95.** Teaching materials available. Bookstores or from **Regal Books, Div. of GL Publications, 2300 Knoll Drive, Ventura, CA 93003.**

THE PEOPLE WHO COULDN'T BE STOPPED (Regal Books) For: Y,Ch. Slant: EP.

By Ethel Barrett. An exciting history of the growth and vibrance of the New Testament church. Illustrated. Quality paper. 144 pages. Number S063107. **$1.95.** Bookstores or from **Regal Books, Div. of GL Publications, 2300 Knoll Drive, Ventura, CA 93003.**

PETER (Regal Books) For: Y,Ch. Slant: EP.

By Ethel Barrett. Peter--the fiery fisherman. Peter--the great and fearless apostle. Ethel Barrett introduces children to Peter in the way no one else can. Paperback. Illustrated. 128 pages. Number 5810809. **$1.95.** Teaching materials available. Bookstores or from **Regal Books, Div. of GL Publications, 2300 Knoll Drive, Ventura, CA 93003.**

PICTURE STORIES FROM THE BIBLE

BIBLE RESOURCES FOR CHILDREN

(Jimmy Swaggart Ministries) For: Ch. Slant: CP.

From the Garden of Eden to the exciting events of the New Testament, your child will spend hours with his own fully illustrated, colorful **Picture Stories from the Bible.** Over 350 pages of vivid illustrations and a solid biblical story line will enable your child to learn about the Bible in his own way at his own level. A marvelous Bible story book for children! This Bible is totally original, wonderfully unique with New and Old Testaments. All the Bible stories will give your child many happy hours of reading pleasure. Product Number 32-007. **$12.00.** From **Jimmy Swaggart Ministries, P.O. Box 2550, Baton Rouge, LA 70821.**

PICTURE STORIES FROM THE BIBLE: THE NEW TESTAMENT IN FULL COLOR COMIC STRIP FORM (Scarf Press) For: Y,Ch. Slant: RC,F,EP, MP,LP,P.

The Life of Jesus and the story of the formation of the early Christian Church in the full-color comic-strip format that children love and read. "...a superb teaching aid of Bible truths."—Dr. Norman Vincent Peale. Words of Christ printed in red. 144 pages. Hardcover. Entire book in full color. **$7.95.** Bookstores or from **Scarf Press, 58 E. 83rd Street, New York, NY 10028.**

PICTURE STORIES FROM THE BIBLE: THE OLD TESTAMENT IN FULL COLOR COMIC STRIP FORM (Scarf Press) For: Y,Ch. Slant: RC,F,EP, MP,LP,RJ,CJ,P.

The fascinating Old Testament stories, from Adam and Eve to Jonah and the Whale, in the full color comic strip format that children love and read. Winner of special award from sponsors of National Bible Week. 224 pages. Hardcover. Entire book in full color. **$9.95** Bookstores or from **Scarf Press, 58 E. 83rd Street, New York, NY 10028.**

THE PLAN OF SALVATION - BIBLICAL POSTERS (Daughters of St. Paul) For: Ch. Slant: RC, EP, MP, P.

Twenty full-color posters which illustrate the main events of Jesus' life and ministry. The captions on the front of each poster are in six languages: English, Spanish, French, Portuguese, Polish, and Vietnamese. Appropriate biblical citations and commentaries are on the reverse side of each poster. Number PB0131. **$20.00** (add **$1.00** for postage). Bookstores or from **Daughters of St. Paul, 50 St. Paul's Ave., Jamaica Plain, Boston, MA 02130.**

PRAISE! SONGS AND POEMS FROM THE BIBLE RETOLD FOR CHILDREN (Servant Publications) For: Ch. Slant: RC.

Helps children begin to turn to God in prayer, teaches them how to offer him thanks and praise and to petition him for their needs. Number 1073. **$5.95.** Bookstores.

THE PROPHETS (Daughters of St. Paul) For: Y,Ch. Slant: RC,P.

A filmstrip/cassette program on the great prophets of the Old Testament: Elijah, Jeremiah, Ezekiel, Isaiah, etc. Called and sent by God, they never tired of reminding the people that only the true God of Israel was to be worshiped and that His commandments were to be obeyed. 69 color frames, 29-minute cassette. Number FC0120. **$17.95** (add **$1.00** for postage). From **Daughters of St. Paul, 50 St. Paul's Ave., Jamaica Plain, Boston, MA 02130.**

QUEST (Scripture Union) For: Ch. Slant: EP,MP,D.

A Bible reading guide designed specifically to communicate God's Word to today's 7-10 year olds. Each day the child is directed to read a short biblical passage and is then offered a lively, understandable explanation. The main points are re-emphasized through the child's involvement with such animated activity mateial as fill-ins, dot-to-dots, puzzles, and memory games. Children will also learn through the illustrations and will enjoy coloring on their own. **Quest** is a remarkable and unique study guide which will not only teach important scriptural truths, but will begin a child on a lifetime adventure with God's Word. This is a perfect gift for the child you love. 12-month membership contribution. **$6.00.** From **Scripture Union, 1716 Spruce St., Philadelphia, PA 19103.**

READ-ALOUD BIBLE STORIES (Moody Press) For: Ch. Slant: EP,I,M.

By Ella Lindvall. A Bible story book for children with brightly colored pictures and a simple text to read aloud. **$15.95.** Bookstores or from **Moody Bookworld, 2101 W. Howard, Chicago, IL 60645.**

REVELATION-RESPONSE (CSI Publications) For: Ch. Slant: C,EP,P.

Coordinated by Sheri Haan and Arnold Snoeyink. This K-9 curriculum recognizes the Bible as God's authoritative and trustworthy revelation to which students respond intellectually, decisionally, and creatively. The **Revelation-Response** goal is to elicit response which results in informed, obedient, creative service to God and others. Incorporating Old and New Testament material at every grade level, **Revelation-Response** presents the history, poetry, and prophecy of the Old Testament as well as the Gospels and letters of the New Testament. Throughout the curriculum, which can also be used out of grade level or by combined grade levels, the concept levels are appropriate to the phases of student development. Student books K-9 are organized around twelve key concepts, such as God's Great Love, Salvation and Service, etc. One concept is primary in each book. Teacher guides, test items with objectives, and in-service instruction materials in teaching **Revelation-Response** are part of the curriculum. Student books. **$2.00 to $7.50.** Teacher guides/editions. **$12.50 to $15.00.** School discounts available. From **CSI Publications, 3350 East Paris Ave., P.O. Box 8709, Grand Rapids, MI 49508.**

RULES—WHO NEEDS THEM? (Regal Books) For: Y,Ch. Slant: EP.

By Ethel Barrett. Some Old Testament people didn't like rules, so they broke them. Others learned to live with rules and enjoyed life. Quality paper. Illustrated. 160 pages. Number 5407001. **$1.95.** Bookstores or from **Regal Books, Div. of GL Publications, 2300 Knoll Drive, Ventura, CA 93003.**

RUTH (Regal Books) For: Y,Ch. Slant: EP.

By Ethel Barrett. The suspenseful story of a beautiful young woman who left her family and her country because she loved God. Exciting things happened to her in the new land and God made her famous. Paperback. Illustrated. 128 pages. Number 5810418. **$1.95.** Bookstores or from **Regal Books, Div. of GL Publications, 2300 Knoll Drive, Ventura, CA 93003.**

SCRIPTURE ACTIVITY BOOKS (American Bible Society) For: Y,Ch.

This exciting series of Scripture activity books dramatically introduces best-loved heroes of the Bible. Puzzles, word games, drawing and coloring activities make learning fun and easy; at the same time, students will reinforce important cognitive skills. Designed for ages 8-12. Text from the Good News Bible in Today's English Version. Each book measures 8 x 11 inches. **The Story of Noah.** TEV Order Number 08006. **$.25. The Story of Joseph.** TEV Order Number 08007. **$.25. Moses: Journey to Freedom.** TEV Order Number 08008. **$.25. Moses: Journey to a New Land.** TEV Order Number 08009. **$.25. The Story of Ruth.** TEV Order Number 08010. **$.25. The Young David.** TEV Order Number 08011. **$.25.** From **American Bible Society, Box 5656 Grand Central Station, New York NY 10163.**

SCRIPTURES FOR NEW READERS (American Bible Society) For: Y,Ch.

New readers from children to adults will enjoy learning about the life and teachings of Jesus in this graded series of stories from the New Testament. The booklets in each series are written in a special ABS translation and are designed for a particular level of reading ability. For a complete listing, write for the **ABS Catalog of Scripture Resources.** Series A: **The Poor Woman's Offering.** Order Number 06889. **$.05. Jesus Blesses Little Children.** Order Number 06890. **$.05.** Series B: **The Boy Jesus in the Temple.** Order Number 06896. **$.05. The Story About Seeds.** Order Number 06900. **$.05.** Series C: **The Birth of Jesus.** Order Number 06931. **$.05. Wise Men from the East.** Order Number 06882. **$.05.** Series D: **Bound Complete.** Order Number 06282. **$.55.** From **American Bible Society, Box 5656, Grand Central Station, New York, NY 10163.**

SOLOMON (Daughters of St. Paul) For: Y,Ch. Slant: RC,P.

A filmstrip/cassette program on King Solomon—wisest of men and builder of the Lord's Temple. 27 color frames, eleven-minute cassette. Number FC0100. **$9.95** (add **$1.00** for postage). From **Daughters of St. Paul, 50 St. Paul's Ave., Jamaica Plain, Boston, MA 02130.**

SPACE CUBS (Christian Ed. Publishers) For: Ch. Slant: EP.

Space Cubs is a club program for children ages 4-5. Its purpose is to prepare pre-schoolers to grow up in the love of Christ. The **Space Cubs** program is built around an exciting award program that will help prepare pre-schoolers for a life of service and commitment to Jesus Christ. The program contains an award program, weekly lessons, and take home papers, all of which are Bible based and Christ honoring. Annual subscription. **$88.00.** From **Christian Ed. Publishers, 7348 Trade Street, San Diego, CA 92121.**

ST. PAUL (Daughters of St. Paul) For: Y,Ch. Slant: RC,P.

A filmstrip/cassette program on the great missionary apostle, Paul. Once persecutor, now persecuted for the Word, he faces every danger to spread the Gospel to the farthest boundaries of the world. Ideal background study of the Pauline Epistles and early church history. 177 color frames, 42 minutes, two cassettes. Number FC0170. **$24.95** (add **$1.00** for postage). From **Daughters of St. Paul, 50 St. Paul's Ave., Jamaica Plain, Boston, MA 02130.**

THE STORY OF JOSEPH FOR CHILDREN (Thomas More Cassettes) For: Ch. Slant: RC.

Narration by Todd Brennan. The spellbinding story of Joseph, his jealous brothers who sold him into slavery, his amazing intepretation of the Pharaoh's dreams of seven rich and seven lean years which made him the Pharoah's favorite and his eventual confrontation and reunion with his brothers and father—all artfully read from the pages of the popular **Taize Picture Bible** by Todd Brennan. Number TM 269. 40 minutes. **$6.95.** From **Thomas More Association, 225 W. Huron St., Chicago, IL 60610.**

THE STRANGEST THING HAPPENED (Regal Books) For: Y,Ch. Slant: EP.

By Ethel Barrett. The strangest things began to happen when God stepped into the lives of Old Testament people.

BIBLE RESOURCES FOR CHILDREN

Quality paper. Illustrated. 144 pages. Number S061104. **$1.95.** Bookstores or from **Regal Books, Div. of GL Publications, 2300 Knoll Drive, Ventura, CA 93003.**

THE VISUALIZED BIBLE SERIES (Bible Visuals, Inc.) For: Y,Ch. Slant: F,EP.

A series of illustrated lessons which teach Bible doctrine. Each volume presents one specific doctrine. Bible narratives illuminate the truths of the doctrine. In addition to the main teaching text, outlines clarify main points of the lesson. Each volume contains: four lessons, sixteen colored illustrations (10" x 14"), and one map (where useful). Each volume is complete in itself, ready to use and easy to file! 46 volumes cover New Testament books of Matthew through Revelation. 19 volumes are now available in the Old Testament for Genesis through Ruth. **$3.95** per volume. Bookstores or from **Bible Visuals, Inc., Box 4842, Lancaster, PA 17604.**

WHICH WAY TO NINEVEH? (Regal Publications) For: Y,Ch. Slant: EP.

Ethel Barrett. Old Testament people plotted their own stories by the choices they made when God called. Quality paper. Illustrated. 144 pages. Number S062100. **$1.95.** Bookstores or from **Regal Books, Div. of GL Publications, 2300 Knoll Drive, Ventura, CA 93003.**

WHIRLYBIRDS (Christian Ed. Publishers) For: Ch. Slant: EP.

A club program that will help children in first through third grades discover the riches of the Christian faith. This program is built around an exciting achievement plan that enables boys and girls to grow spiritually while having fun earning attractive awards. The program material and the achievement plan are all Bible based and Christ honoring. There are weekly lessons, projects, and activities for each child. Annual subscription. **$88.00.** From **Christian Ed. Publishers, 7348 Trade Street, San Diego, CA 92121.**

THE WORLD INTO WHICH JESUS CAME (Standard Publishing) For: Ch. Slant: P.

This new encyclopedia for children in grades 4 through 8 explains Jewish history, laws, daily life, customs, places and events in comprehensive, yet readable text and handsome color illustrations. Following a brief overview of Jewish history, the book looks at the customs and activities of daily life through the fictional characters of Michael and his family and friends. Throughout the book, sidebars relate the customs, places and events to Jesus' life on earth. Library binding. Code 4951. **$12.95.** Bookstores or from **Standard Publishing, 8121 Hamilton Ave., Cincinnati, OH 45231.**

TAYLOR'S BIBLE STORY BOOK (Tyndale House Publishers) For: Ch. Slant: A,W,C,RC,F,EP,MP,LP,P,CP.

By Kenneth N. Taylor. Over 200,000 sold! A treasury of 193 Bible stories for children. Revised and improved, with over 130 full-color illustrations by Richard and Frances Hook. 432 pages of inspiring stories that communicate Bible events and truths. Simple, thought-provoking questions at the end of each story. Cloth. **$15.95.** Bookstores.

KENNETH TAYLOR'S BIBLE STORY BOOK (Cassette Album) (Vision House) For: L,C,S,Y,Ch. Slant: EP.

By Kenneth Taylor. A heart-warming series of New Testament stories spoken directly to children in language they can understand. Narrated by TV's "Tony the Tiger" - Thurl Ravenscroft. Cassette Album (6 tapes). Number A286307. **$34.98.** Bookstores or from **Vision House, Div. of GL Publications, 2300 Knoll Drive, Ventura, CA 93003.**

TOBIT (Daughters of St. Paul) For: Y, Ch. Slant: RC,P.

A filmstrip/cassette program on the Book of Tobit. It is a story that illustrates God's presence and intercession in the lives of those who remain faithful to Him. 27 color frames, ten-minute cassette. Number FC0130. **$9.95** (add **$1.00** for postage). From **Daughters of St. Paul, 50 St. Paul's Ave., Jamaica Plain, Boston, MA 02130.**

THE TWO KINGDOMS (Daughters of St. Paul) For: Y,Ch. Slant: RC,P.

A filmstrip/cassette program on the two kingdoms which resulted from the division of the tribes of Israel after King Solomon's death. Both kingdoms have one ruler after another who lead the people away from their covenant with Yahweh. Without the blessings of the Lord, the Israelites fall easy prey to enemy nations. They become an exiled people for many years until they are finally able to return to their homeland. Number FC0110. **$19.95** (add **$1.00** for postage). From **Daughters of St. Paul, 50 St. Paul's Ave., Jamaica Plain, Boston, MA 02130.**

THE VERY BEST BOOK OF ALL (Standard Publishing) For: Ch. Slant: D.

Full color photographs present the Bible as the greatest book ever written. Part of the Happy Day Book series. For ages four to eight. Hardcover, Code 3591. **$1.29.** Bookstores or from **Standard Publishing, 8121 Hamilton Ave., Cincinnati, OH 45231.**

LIST OF CONTRIBUTORS

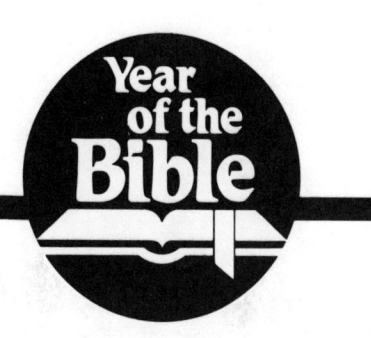

LIST OF CONTRIBUTORS

Abingdon Press
201 Eighth Avenue, South
Nashville, TN 37202

ACTS International
Box 157, 101 S. Spring Street
Claremont, CA 91711

Aglow Publications
Box 1
Lynwood, WA 98036

Alba House
2187 Victory Boulevard
Staten Island, NY 10314

Aletheia Community Church
1432 E. Elizabeth St.
Pasadena, CA 91104

ALT Publishing Company
Box 400
Green Bay, WI 54305

Ambassadors For Christ (USA), Inc.
6080 New Peachtree Road
Atlanta, GA 30340

American Baptist Films
Valley Forge, PA 19482

American Bible Society
1865 Broadway
New York, NY 10023

American Tract Society
Box 462008
Garland, TX 75046

AMG Publishers
Box 22000
Chattanooga, TN 37422

Arena Lettres
8 Lincoln Place
Waldwick, NJ 07463

Argus Communications
Department 50, One DLM Park
Allen, TX 75002

Audio-Forum
Jeffrey Norton Publishers, Inc.
On-The-Green
Guilford, CT 06437

Ave Maria Press
Notre Dame, IN 46556

Baker Book House
Box 6287
Grand Rapids, MI 49506

Ballantine Books
201 E. 50th Street
New York, NY 10022

Baptist Publishing House
712 Main
Little Rock, AR 72201

Beacon Hill Press of Kansas City
Box 527
Kansas City, MO 64141

Channing L. Bete Company, Inc.
200 State Road
South Deerfield, MA 01373

Bethany Press
Box 179
St. Louis, MO 63166

Bible Cassette Library, Inc.
524 Sycamore Circle
Ridgeland, MS 39157

Bible Newsletter
1716 Spruce Street
Philadelphia, PA 19103

Bible Pathway Ministries
Box 1515
Murfreesboro, TN 37133

The Bible Study Hour
1716 Spruce St.
Philadelphia, PA 19103

Bible Questions
Box 736
Galesburg, IL 61401

Bible Reading Fellowship
Box M
Winter Park, FL 32790

Bible Research Systems
9415 Burnet Road
Austin, TX 78758

Bible Video Library
524 Sycamore Circle
Ridgeland, MS 39157

Bible Visuals, Inc.
Box 4842
Lancaster, PA 17604

Biblical Andragogy Clinic
1243 Woodland Ave.
Mississauga, Ontario, Canada

The Brethren Press
1451 Dundee Ave.
Elgin, IL 60120

Bridge Publishing, Inc.
2500 Hamilton Blvd.
South Plainfield, NJ 07080

Broadman Press
127 Ninth Ave., North
Nashville, TN 37234

Wm. C. Brown Company Publishers
Religious Education Division
2460 Kerper Blvd.
Dubuque, IA 52001

Camp Cherith
Box 788
Wheaton, IL 60189

Catholic Education Center
Media Dept.
328 W. Sixth Street
St. Paul, MN 55102

CBA Service Corporation
Box 200
Colorado Springs, CO 80901

CEF Press
Warrenton, MO 63383

Central Christian Church
First & Central, Box 876
Arkansas City, KS 67005

Chief, Inc.
Box 37000
Phoenix, AZ 85069

Chosen Books
Lincoln, VA 22078

Christ For The World Publishers
Box 3428
Orlando, FL 32802

Christian Bible College Publications
Box 262
Enfield, NC 27823

Christian Book Service
336 Gundersen Drive
Carol Stream, IL 60187

Christian Business Men's Committee of USA
1800 McCallie Avenue
Chattanooga, TN 37404

Christian Duplications International, Inc.
1710 Lee Road
Orlando, FL 32810

Christian Education Publishers
7348 Trade Street
San Diego, CA 92121

Christian Film and Video Center
1726-B 19th Street
Lubbock, TX 79401

Christian Herald
40 Overlook Drive
Chappaqua, NY 10514

Christian History Institute
Box 540
Worcester, PA 19490

Christian Life Missions
396 E. St. Charles Road
Wheaton, IL 60188

LIST OF CONTRIBUTORS

Christian Literature International
Box 777
Canby, OR 97013

Christian Media
Box 748
Ogden, UT 84402

Christian Media Supply
524 Sycamore Circle
Ridgeland, MS 39157

Christian Outreach
200 Asbury Drive
Wilmore, KY 40390

Christian Publications, Inc.
3825 Hartzdale Dr.
Camp Hill, PA 17011

Christian Video Service
Box 4174
Lancaster, CA 93539

Church Bible Studies
191 Mayhew Way
Walnut Creek, CA 94596

Concordia Publishing House
3558 S. Jefferson Ave.
St. Louis, MO 63118

Creation House
396 St. Charles Road
Carol Stream, IL 60187

Creation-Life Publishers, Inc.
Box 15666
San Diego, CA 92115

The Crossroad/Continuum
575 Lexington Ave.
New York, NY 10022

CSI Publications
3350 East Paris Ave., Box 8709
Grand Rapids, MI 49508

Dallas Theological Seminary
3909 Swiss Ave.
Dallas, TX 75204

Daughters of St. Paul
50 St. Paul Ave.
Jamaica Plain, Boston, MA 02130

Dove Publications
Pecos, NM 87552

William B. Eerdmans Publishing Co.
225 Jefferson Ave., S.E.
Grand Rapids, MI 49503

Evangelical Ministries, Inc.
1716 Spruce Street
Philadelphia, PA 19103

Faith and Fellowship Press
Box 655
Fergus Falls, MN 56537

Faith and Life Press
Box 347
Newton, KS 67114

Faith For Today
Box 1000
Thousand Oaks, CA 91359

Faith Venture Visuals, Inc.
Box 423, 510 E. Main St.
Lititz, PA 17543

Family Life Distributors
Box 20059
El Cajon, CA 92021

Fellowship Films
Box 2330
Springfield, IL 62705

Franciscan Herald Press
1434 West 51st Street
Chicago, IL 60609

Gateway Films, Inc.
Box A
Lansdale, PA 19446

Michael Glazier, Inc.
1732 Delaware Ave.
Wilmington, DE 19806

God's Word Today
Box 7705
Ann Arbor, MI 48107

Gospel Light Publications
2300 Knoll Drive
Ventura, CA 93003

Gospel Publishing House
1445 Boonville Ave.
Springfield, MO 65802

Grace Outreach Ministries
Box 2158
Maryland Heights, MO 63043

Grace World Outreach Center
2695 Creve Coeur Road
Maryland Heights, MO 63043

Greek Orthodox Archdiocese
Department of Education
50 Goddard Aven
Brookline, MA 02146

Group Books
Box 481
Loveland, CO 80539

Kenneth Hagin Ministries
Box 50126
Tulsa, OK 74150

Harper and Row,
Mail Order Department
2350 Virginia Avenue
Hagerstown, MD 21740

Harper and Row, Publishers, Inc.
1700 Montgomery St.
San Francisco, CA 94111

Harvest House Publishers
1075 Arrowsmith
Eugene, OR 97402

Harvest Productions
Box 2225
Kokomo, IN 46902

Virgil W. Hensley, Inc., Publisher
6116 E. 32nd Street
Tulsa, OK 74135

Herald Press
616 Walnut Ave.
Scottdale, PA 15683

Here's Life Publishers
Box 1576
San Bernardino, CA 92402

Higley Publishing Corp.
Box 2470
Jacksonville, FL 32203

Holman Bible Publishers
127 Ninth Ave., North
Nashville, TN 37234

Home Computer Software
1307 South Mary #209
Sunnyvale, CA 94087

Honeybee Book Patterns
Box 6339-B
Rockford, IL 61125

Hosanna
146 Quincy N.E.
Albuquerque, NM 87108

IDE House, Inc.
4631 Harvey Drive
Mesquite, TX 75150

Impact Books, Inc.
137 W. Jefferson
Kirkwood, MO 63122

Institute For Biblical Literacy, Inc.
337 S. Milledge Ave.
Athens, GA 30605

Institute For Christian Renewal
26 Washington St.
Malden, MA 02148

International Cassette Corp.
Box 1928
Greenville, TX 75401

International Films
1530 E. Elizabeth St.
Pasadena, CA 91104

LIST OF CONTRIBUTORS

International School of Theology
Box 50045
San Bernardino, CA 92412

Interpretation
3401 Broad Road
Richmond, VA 23227

InterVarsity Press
Box F
Downers Grove, IL 60515

It Is Written Telecast
Box 0
Thousand Oaks, CA 91360

Jewish Publication Society of America
1930 Chestnut St., 21st Floor
Philadelphia, PA 19103

Johnson Publishing
Box 100704
Nashville, TN 32710

The Kerygma Program
300 Mt. Lebanon Blvd., Suite 2217
Pittsburgh, PA 15234

Kerr Associates
460 Woodycrest Ave.
Nashville, TN 37210

Thomas S. Klise Co.
Box 3418
Peoria, IL 61614

John Knox Press
341 Ponce De Leon Ave., N.E.
Atlanta, GA 30308

Kregal Publications
Box 2607
Grand Rapids, MI 49501

Laymen's National Bible
Committee, Inc.
815 Second Ave.
New York, NY 10017

Lifeway Home Shopping Service
Nashville, TN 37234

Light and Life Press
999 College Ave.
Winona Lake, IN 46590

Liguori Publications
One Liguori Drive
Liguori, MO 63057

The Liturgical Press
St. John's Abbey
Collegeville, MN 56321

Loizeaux Brothers, Inc.
Box 277
Neptune, NJ 07753

Maranatha Publications
Box 1799
Gainesville, FL 32602

Mass Media Ministries
2116 North Charles St.
Baltimore, MD 21218

Ministry Services
Box 433
Redan, GA 30074

Moody Institute of Science
12000 E. Washington Blvd.
Whittier, CA 90606

Moody Press
2101 W. Howard Street
Chicago, IL 60645

Thomas More Press
225 W. Huron Street
Chicago, IL 60610

Mott Media
1000 E. Huron St.
Milford, MI 48042

Multnomah Press
10209 S.E. Division St.
Portland, OR 97266

National Church Growth
Research Center
Box 17575
Washington, DC 20041

National Organization for
Christian Child Care
933 Andrews Road
West Palm Beach, FL 33405

National Religious Broadcasters
CN 1926
Morristown, NJ 07960

NavPress
Box 6000
Colorado Springs, Co 80934

Thomas Nelson Publishers
Nelson Place at Elm Hill Pike
Nashville, TN 37214

Northwestern Publishing House
3624 W. North Avenue
Milwaukee, WI 53208

Officers' Christian Fellowship
of the USA
Box 36200
Denver, CO 80236

Oxford University Press
200 Madison Ave.
New York, NY 10016

Pacific Press Publishing Association
1350 Villa Street
Mountain View, CA 94042

Pathway Press
1080 Montgomery Ave.
Cleveland, TN 37311

The Paulist Press
545 Island Road
Ramsey, NJ 07446

Paulist National Catholic
Evangelization Assoc.
3031 Fourth St., N.E.
Washington, DC 20017

Pelican Publishing Company
1101 Monroe Street
Gretna, LA 70053

Presbyterian and Reformed
Publishing Co.
Box 817
Phillipsburg, NJ 08865

Redemptive Publications
933 Andrews Road
West Palm Beach, FL 33405

Regal Books
2300 Knoll Drive
Ventura, CA 93003

Religion and Ethics Institute
Box 664
Evanston, IL 60204

The Restitution Herald
Box 100
Oregon, IL 61061

Revivaltime Media Ministries
1445 Boonville Rd.
Springfield, MO 65802

ROA Filmstrip Company
6633 W. Howard St.
Niles, IL 60648

Roper Press
915 Dragon St.
Dallas, TX 75207

The Salvation Army
1424 N.E. Expressway
Atlanta, GA 30329

Scarf Press
58 E. 83rd Street
New York, NY 10028

Schocken Books, Inc.
200 Madison Ave.
New York, NY 10016

Scripture Press
1825 College Ave.
Wheaton, IL 60187

Scripture Software
Box 6131-C, Dept. BR
Orlando, FL 32853

LIST OF CONTRIBUTORS

Scripture Union
1716 Spruce Street
Philadelphia, PA 19103

Sedbury Service Center
Somers, CT 06071

The Seabury Press
815 Second Avenue
New York, NY 10017

Servant Publications
Box 8617
Ann Arbor, MI 48107

Harold Shaw Publishers
Box 567
Wheaton, IL 60189

Singspiration
1415 Lake Drive S.E.
Grand Rapids, MI 49506

Southern Baptist Theological Seminary
2825 Lexington Road
Louisville, KY 40206

Spoken Arts, Inc.
310 North Avenue
New Rochelle, NY 10801

St. Croix, Inc.
14918 E. Dunton Drive
Whittier, CA 90604

Standard Publishing
8121 Hamilton Ave.
Cincinnati, OH 45231

Star Bible Publications
Box 181220
Ft. Worth, TX 76118

Jimmy Swaggart Ministries
Box 2550
Baton Rouge, LA 70821

Train Depot
982 El Monte Ave.
Mt. View, CA 94040

Training Church Leaders, Inc.
6080 New Peachtree Road
Atlanta, GA 30340

Trinity Bible Studies
Box 25101
Dallas, TX 75225

Trinity Tapes, Inc.
16604 Arminta St.
Van Nuys, CA 91406

Tyndale House Publishers, Inc.
336 Gundersen Drive
Wheaton, IL 60187

Union of American Hebrew Congregations
838 Fifth Ave.
New York, NY 10021

Union Theological Seminary in Virginia
3401 Brook Road
Richmond, VA 23227

Jack Van Impe Ministries
Box J
Royal Oak, MI 48068

Victor Books
1825 College Ave.
Wheaton, IL 60187

Vida Publishers
3360 N.W. 110th St.
Miami, FL 33167

Video Bible Library, Inc.
Box 17515
Portland, OR 97217

Visible Light, Inc.
Box 8605
Orlando, FL 32856

Vision House, Inc.
2300 Knoll Drive
Ventura, CA 93003

Voice of Prophecy
Box 55
Los Angeles, CA 90053

Walk Thru the Bible Ministries
61 Perimeter Park, N.E.
Atlanta, GA 30366

Warner Press, Inc.
Box 2499
Anderson, IN 46011

Washington Bible College
Lanham, MD 20706

Dr. James P. Wesberry Baptist Center
2930 Flowers Road, South
Atlanta, GA 30341

The Wesleyan Church
Dept. of Local Church Education
Box 2000
Marion, IN 46952

White Lion Pictograph
146 Melrose Place
San Antonio, TX 78212

Winston Press
430 Oak Grove
Minneapolis, MN 55403

Wisconsin Evangelical Lutheran Synod Board for Parish Education
3614 West North Avenue
Milwaukee, WI 53208

Word, Inc.
4800 W. Waco Drive
Waco, TX 76710

The Word Of God Institute
487 Michigan Ave., NE
Washington, DC 20017

Word of Grace
Box 7
San Antonio, TX 78291

Year of the Bible
Program and Media Office
460 Woodycrest Ave.
Nashville, TN 37210

Zondervan Publishing House
1415 Lake Drive, S.E.
Grand Rapids, MI 49506

Zondervan Retail Marketing Service
1420 Robinson Road S.E.
Grand Rapids, MI 49506